University, Court, and Slave

University, Court, and Slave

Pro-slavery Thought in Southern Colleges and Courts and the Coming of Civil War

ALFRED L. BROPHY

OXFORD
UNIVERSITY PRESS

OXFORD
UNIVERSITY PRESS

Oxford University Press is a department of the University of Oxford. It furthers
the University's objective of excellence in research, scholarship, and education
by publishing worldwide. Oxford is a registered trade mark of Oxford University
Press in the UK and certain other countries.

Published in the United States of America by Oxford University Press
198 Madison Avenue, New York, NY 10016, United States of America.

Library of Congress Cataloging-in-Publication Data
Names: Brophy, Alfred L., author.
Title: University, court, and slave : pro-slavery thought and southern
colleges and the coming of Civil War / Alfred L. Brophy.
Description: New York, NY : Oxford University Press, 2016.
Identifiers: LCCN 2016009495 (print) | LCCN 2016011052 (ebook) |
ISBN 9780199964239 (hardcover : alk. paper) | ISBN 9780199964246 (E-book) |
ISBN 9780190263614 (E-book) | ISBN 9780190625931 (Online Component)
Subjects: LCSH: Slavery—Law and legislation—United States—History—
19th century. | Jurisprudence—Southern States—History—19th century. |
Southern States—Intellectual life—19th century.
Classification: LCC KF4545.S5 B76 2016 (print) | LCC KF4545.S5 (ebook) |
DDC 342.7308/7—dc23
LC record available at http://lccn.loc.gov/2016009495

3 5 7 9 8 6 4 2

Printed by Sheridan Books, Inc., United States of America

For Barbara F. Thompson, my favorite librarian

CONTENTS

PART III   THE CORE OF SOUTHERN LEGAL THOUGHT

TIMELINE

1776 Declaration of Independence

1790 Thomas Ruffin born

1795 Dred Scott born in Southampton, Virginia

1800 Nat Turner born in Southampton, Virginia

1804 Haitian revolution ends and Haiti becomes a separate country

1808 Congress outlaws importation of enslaved people into United States

1817 American Colonization Society founded

1820 Missouri Compromise

1825 John Robinson leaves seventy-three people and his plantation to Washington College

1827 Francis Wayland becomes president of Brown University

1829 David Walker's *Appeal* published

1830 North Carolina Justice Thomas Ruffin delivers *State v. Mann* opinion

1831 Nat Turner Rebellion

1832 Debate in Virginia legislature over slavery
      William Gaston opposes slavery in speech at University of North Carolina
      Professor Thomas R. Dew publishes pro-slavery *Review of the Debate in the Legislature*
      Jesse Harrison publishes response to Dew

1834 Nathaniel Beverley Tucker becomes law professor at William and Mary
      Slavery abolished in British West Indies
      North Carolina Justice William Gaston delivers *State v. Will* opinion

1835 Brown President Francis Wayland publishes *Elements of Moral Science*
      American Anti-Slavery Society begins widespread distribution of literature in the South through the U.S. mail

1836 Centre College president John Young opposes slavery in address at Miami University of Ohio

1837   Basil Manly becomes president of University of Alabama
        Ralph Waldo Emerson delivers *American Scholar* address at Harvard
1838   James McDowell delivers anti-abolition address at Princeton
        Virginia Military Institute founded
1843   Miami University of Ohio President George Junkin opposes abolitionists
1845   Francis Wayland and South Carolina Minister Richard Fuller debate
        slavery
        First edition of *Narrative of the Life of Frederick Douglass* appears
1847   Washington College President Henry Ruffner opposes slavery in debate
    in Lexington, Virginia
        Emory College President Augustus Longstreet publishes *A Voice from
            the South*
1848   Henry Ruffner resigns as president at Washington College
        George Junkin becomes president of Washington College
1850   Compromise of 1850 enacted, including Fugitive Slave Act of 1850
1851   Phi Beta Kappa orators at Brown and Yale urge support for Fugitive
        Slave Act
        U.S. Representative David Kaufman delivers pro-slavery speech at
            Princeton
        Frederick Douglas advances antislavery interpretation of the
            Constitution
1852   Ralph Waldo Emerson delivers antislavery speech in Concord
        U.S. Representative Abraham Venable delivers pro-slavery speech at
            Princeton
        Harriet Beecher Stowe publishes *Uncle Tom's Cabin*
1853   William Goodell publishes *American Slave Code in Theory and Practice*
        Harriet Beecher Stowe publishes *A Key to Uncle Tom's Cabin*
1856   University of Virginia professor Albert Taylor Bledsoe publishes *Liberty
            and Slavery*
        Harriet Beecher Stowe publishes *Dred: A Tale of the Great Dismal Swamp*
1857   *Dred Scott* decided by U.S. Supreme Court
1858   Thomas R. R. Cobb publishes *An Inquiry into the Law of Negro Slavery*
        James Henry Hammond delivers "mud sill" speech in U.S. Senate
        University of Virginia law professor James Holcombe argues natural law
            supports slavery
        U.S. Supreme Court Justice John A. Campbell warns of secession in
            speech at University of Alabama
        Georgia Supreme Court delivers *American Colonization Society v. Gartrell*
            opinion
1859   Mississippi Supreme Court delivers *Mitchell v. Wells* opinion

1860   Board of Trustees of University of Mississippi try Chancellor Frederick
Barnard for taking testimony from a slave against a student
Georgia Justice Ebenezer Starnes publishes pro-slavery novel *Slaveholder
Abroad*
Abraham Lincoln elected president
Thomas R. R. Cobb supports secession in Georgia
South Carolina secedes

1861   University of Virginia Professor James Holcombe supports secession in
Virginia legislature
James Henley Thornwell publishes pamphlet in support of secession
Civil War begins

PREFACE

The Setting and the Themes

Our country entered the American Revolution with the high goal of the liberation of our people from monarchy. The "Influence of America on the Mind," as one early American wrote, was toward freedom, toward the Enlightenment truths that all people are created equal, and that the people should govern through law rather than their arbitrary dictates of hereditary monarchs and their agents. Those aspirations were lofty. They emerged from reading books like Montesquieu's *Spirit of the Laws*, Locke's *Two Treatises of Government*, and from religious writing as well, which taught the dignity of human beings. Such ideas were promulgated though the press, which made Thomas Paine's *Common Sense* widely available. They were also taught in schools and disseminated in the courthouses, churches, and taverns that populated the landscape. A new world seemed possible as the rebel forces and their ideas, joined by European powers that sought to humble Great Britain for their own purposes, swept the field.

Putting those grand Enlightenment ideas into practice . . . that proved much more difficult. Our Constitution protected property in humans. The Fugitive Slave Clause required the return of runaway slaves, and the Constitution ensured that slaves would count as three-fifths of a person for apportioning representation in Congress, thus adding political strength to the states with large slave populations. The Constitution ensured that slaves could be imported until the early nineteenth century, for Article I, Section 9 prohibited Congress from outlawing the importation of slaves until 1808. Later in our nation's struggle with slavery that fact became important when leading antislavery advocates like the former slave Frederick Douglass pointed to it to show that the Constitution contemplated the limitation of slavery.

Even more important than the Constitution's protection for slavery was the reality that Americans relied on slave labor. The U.S. Census counted 697,897

slaves in 1790, 1,538,038 in 1820, and 3,953,760 in 1860. Legislatures and
courts increasingly sought to protect property rights in humans. The Virginia
legislature made it more difficult to emancipate the enslaved in 1806. After
that, newly freed people had to leave the state in twelve months or face re-en-
slavement. The Republic was becoming a place of increased slavery. The loss of
the idea of freedom was apparent when that icon of the American Revolution
General LaFayette returned from France to the United States in 1824 to
say goodbye to ancient friends and to see what had become of the nation
he helped bring into existence. LaFayette's visit carried him throughout the
nation, and he was surprised and disappointed by slavery. Like many others
he despaired of a solution. Where Thomas Paine had written in *Common Sense*
that in America law is king, in the nineteenth century in America slavery was
becoming king.

Elsewhere in the western hemisphere, slaves were rising up. The revolution in Haiti, inspired by the revolution in France, began in 1791. Meanwhile,
many white people fleeing the bloodshed in Haiti washed ashore in the United
States—often in Charleston, but in Philadelphia, and Louisiana, too. And in the
United States there were continuing efforts to end slavery in the southern states.
The American Colonization Society, founded in 1817, had fanciful and impractical schemes to emancipate enslaved people and send them to Africa. Others
offered more direct suggestions. In 1829 David Walker's *Appeal to the Coloured
Citizens of the World* harkened back to the Enlightenment idea of a natural right
to freedom. The ideas in Walker's *Appeal* threatened to open the world to something very dangerous: rebellion.

That is precisely what happened in August 1831 in Southampton County,
Virginia. The rebellion, led by Nat Turner, did not get far. It was put down with
extraordinary brutality. The rebellion also pushed Virginians to talk about the
future of slavery. In January 1832 Virginia's House of Delegates debated what
to do next. A few from counties with small enslaved populations advocated a
gradual abolition plan. Even a few legislators from the counties with large populations of enslaved humans had the courage to call for planning to end slavery,
but the House of Delegates concluded that further action against slavery was not
expedient. Property rights and slavery were reasserting themselves; in March the
legislature approved an overhaul of the criminal code regarding slaves and free
African Americans, which tightened restrictions on their freedom. From the
debate emerged a young man, a professor of history at the College of William
and Mary, Thomas Roderick Dew. Dew crystallized the arguments against
emancipation; after him, throughout the South, the idea of emancipation was
largely, though not always, a joke.

Academics throughout the South taught their students about the centrality of
slavery to American life. It was good for masters because it made them prosperous

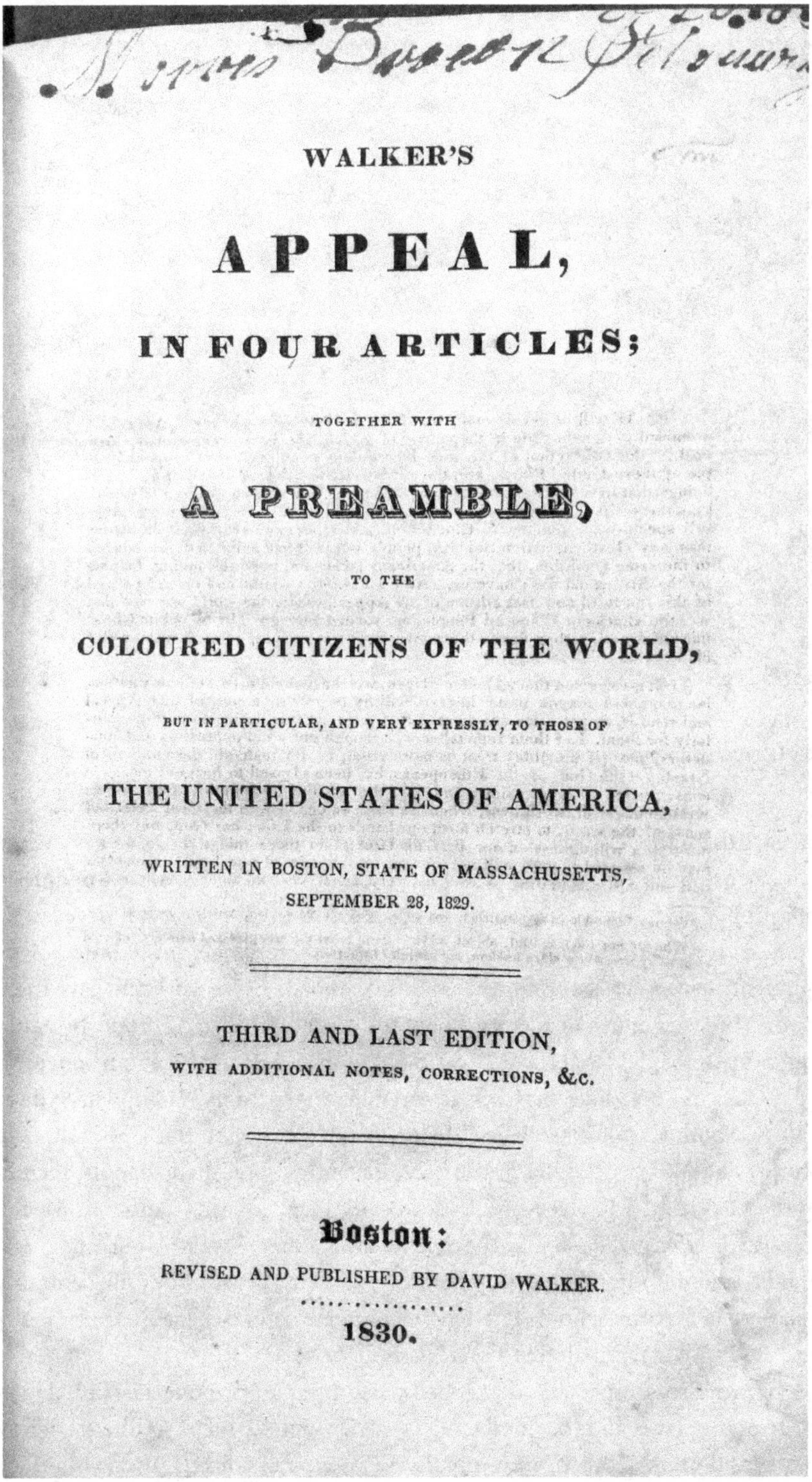

WALKER'S

APPEAL,

IN FOUR ARTICLES;

TOGETHER WITH

A PREAMBLE,

TO THE

COLOURED CITIZENS OF THE WORLD,

BUT IN PARTICULAR, AND VERY EXPRESSLY, TO THOSE OF

THE UNITED STATES OF AMERICA,

WRITTEN IN BOSTON, STATE OF MASSACHUSETTS,
SEPTEMBER 28, 1829.

———————————

THIRD AND LAST EDITION,

WITH ADDITIONAL NOTES, CORRECTIONS, &c.

———————————

Boston:

REVISED AND PUBLISHED BY DAVID WALKER.
....
1830.

Illustration 0.1 Title page of David Walker's *Appeal to the Coloured Citizens of the World.* (University of North Carolina Wilson Library)

Illustration 0.2 The Wren Building at the College of William and Mary, where Thomas Dew taught. (photography by author)

and gave them the leisure time to pursue the life of the mind; it also gave white men a sense of rough equality and placed the inferior and enslaved people in their proper place. But as abolitionists appealed to the humanity of slaves as an argument for their freedom, pro-slavery writers increasingly turned to another argument: slavery was good for the enslaved; it made them work and gave them a home. The well-educated faculty taught the students drawn disproportionately from the planter class that slavery was right, indeed, a necessity. From venerable and ancient schools like the College of William and Mary, Hampden-Sydney College, South Carolina College, Washington College, and the Universities of Georgia and North Carolina to the more recently established schools, including the Citadel, the College of Charleston, Emory College, Randolph Macon College, Southern University, the Universities of Alabama, Mississippi, and Virginia, and the Virginia Military Institute, students heard about the centrality of slavery. In fact, the schools often justified their existence because their faculty generated and disseminated pro-slavery thought.

Law professors, especially, developed those arguments about the natural inferiority of the slaves and the good that slavery brought to all of southern society. They rested on the "practical in morals," what we call considerations of utility. They argued that slavery was economically necessary. As academics developed

AN

ESSAY

ON

SLAVERY,

BY THOMAS R. DEW,

LATE PRESIDENT OF WILLIAM AND MARY COLLEGE,

WILLIAMSBURG, VA.

C

SECOND EDITION.

90872

Richmond, Va.:

J. W. RANDOLPH, 121 MAIN STREET.

Also for sale by Franck Taylor, Washington; Cushing & Brother, Baltimor
W. B. Zieber, Philadelphia—H. Long & Brother, New-York,
and by Booksellers generally.

1849.

Illustration 0.3 Title page of William and Mary Professor Thomas Dew's *An Essay on Slavery* (Richmond, J.W. Randolph, 1849), which reprinted Dew's *Review of the Debates in the Virginia Legislature of 1831 and 1832* (Richmond, T.W. White, 1832). Professor Dew's essay remainded a popular pro-slavery text for decades and was reprinted frequently. (Washington and Lee University Library)

these ideas in conjunction with lawyers, politicians, religious leaders, physicians, newspaper editors, and planters, the intellectual power of southern society was brought to bear to justify the present system. Their books and articles told of the research they had done on history and on contemporary society, too. They sought to prove with scientific precision that slavery was nearly ubiquitous in history and that there could be no end to slavery in the near future. Often the justification was made in terms of what slavery did for the owners, though as abolitionists gained strength, the terms shifted to the supposed benefits of slavery for the enslaved. Pro-slavery writers compared the conditions of slaves with those of white workers in the North and in Great Britain and told themselves that the slaves led better lives than the free workers. Slavery was the system that best promoted the slaves' welfare, many slave owners told themselves.

Northerners often saw the world in terms sympathetic to southern slave owners. During debate over the Fugitive Slave Act of 1850, as Southerners demanded additional protections for their slave property in the form of expanded rights to reclaim fugitive slaves, Massachusetts Senator Daniel Webster pled for those rights for the South. Webster attacked abolitionists who emphasized humanity for the individual slave over the calculus of what was best for the Union. Yet some antislavery activists thought the world should be ordered differently. Harriet Beecher Stowe, Henry David Thoreau, and Frederick Douglass advanced an alternative jurisprudence based on sentimental concerns for the enslaved. Sometimes antislavery writers took on the pro-slavery writers' empirical defense of slavery. Abolitionists sought to show that slavery came with many costs, to the enslaved and to the Republic, too. Stowe and William Goodell argued that in practice slavery corrupted the morals of the owners, created despots, and degraded enslaved humans. They presented the case that slavery was not, in fact, good for the enslaved. Yet, the antislavery position was only slowly gaining ground. Stowe asked why the arguments about utility and against slavery were so powerful in her obscure 1856 novel *Dred: A Tale of the Great Dismal Swamp*. She created a character, a judge, who was antislavery in private but who acted in keeping with the pro-slavery expectations of his society.

Stowe was a perceptive interpreter of the southern judiciary. For most judges were bound by the constraints of the pro-slavery law, which drew on the empiricism of pro-slavery thinkers. They wrote about the historical evidence that demonstrated slavery could not be ended and about the contemporary evidence that showed slavery would end in violence and poverty for the slave owners. They also employed cold legal logic, which supported the owners' rights in their enslaved human property. Thomas Ruffin wrote in these terms in his 1830 decision in *State v. Mann*, which freed a man who had abused a female slave in his custody from criminal liability for the abuse. There were some moderating voices among the southern judiciary, but the central tendency was toward support for slavery by making emancipation difficult, by releasing owners from liability for abuse of their slaves, and by rules that facilitated commercial transactions in slaves. In short, judges did what they could to make slavery commercially viable. One law professor in Athens, Georgia, Thomas R. R. Cobb, wrote a comprehensive treatise that surveyed slavery's history from ancient Egypt through the emancipations in Haiti and the West Indies. He used that history to understand the law. It was a capstone of decades of southern thinking on slavery that pulled together from religion, history, and economics, to law. Cobb used what he saw as empirical evidence to justify slavery.

Judges were mostly dependent variables in this story; they implemented the pro-slavery ideas circulating in southern culture. But judges also helped establish that culture. They were proponents of the market and the ideas of slavery in circulation around them. They turned to evidence from history and their own observations about economics to make the case for slavery. The wealthy and well educated created a culture that supported their world.

This book is about the pro-slavery ideas in circulation in southern society from 1831 to the Civil War. It looks to those ideas in the academy, where they were explored in depth, then it turns to the ideas in the judiciary, where they were implemented. It, thus, deals with how southern judges worked in conjunction with their surroundings to put pro-slavery ideas into operation. As judges struggled to keep the enslaved in slavery and counter antislavery writers, a jurisprudence based on economics, religious teachings, and empirical observation about slavery emerged.

That jurisprudence that promoted slavery spanned every area of law that touched the institution, from criminal law and evidence to tort and property law. The criminal law, for instance, largely freed owners from liability for abusing their human property. Tort law limited owners' liability for actions of their slaves. Commercial law provided a well-functioning market so that slaves could be sold and buyers could hold sellers to warranties for the slaves. Moreover, property law made it possible to have mortgages on slaves, which facilitated the financing of slavery. Judges and legislators limited the emancipation of slaves; they told themselves that freed slaves would destabilize the institution. Freed people made those remaining in slavery more restless, and they might facilitate rebellion. Property in slaves was protected vigilantly, but not the right of individual owners to free their slaves. Judges limited the ability of freed slaves to stay in southern states. The southern world was to be one of white freedom and black slavery, of hierarchy, and often brutality.

The end of this story is the movement for secession, where Southerners— often judges and lawyers—used the ideas about the centrality of slavery and property as they decided to leave the Union. In the secession debates academics like Thomas Cobb and University of Virginia professor James Holcombe demonstrated the relevance of pro-slavery ideas to the creation of a Confederate nation. The ideas of the Constitution's protection of slavery and its place at the center of the southern economy and society so carefully and extensively developed by judges and lawyers before the war were central to secession. The judges and lawyers had legitimized a world view that said threats to slaves as property was unconstitutional and justified war.

ACKNOWLEDGMENTS

As with my other projects, I have been the beneficiary of a terrific circle of friends and teachers. I continue to benefit from my graduate school teachers, particularly Morton Horwitz, who supervised my dissertation. Alan Heimert was there when I started working on law in the old South, and he influenced me significantly, as did my other dissertation committee members, Charles Donahue and Bernard Bailyn. This also benefits from Walter Licht's instruction in quantitative methods.

In Tuscaloosa, where this project took shape, I owe a huge debt to my friends at the law school, William S. Brewbaker, Bryan Fair, Daniel M. Filler, Kenneth Rosen, Norman Stein, and Wythe Holt, and my dean Ken Randall, as well as the history and political science professors Lawrence Kohl, Lisa Lindquist Dorr, Gregory Dorr, Josuah Rothman, Utz McKnight, and Ted Miller. I owe a special debt to Robert Moore and Patricia Bauch and to President Robert Witt. For part of this project grows out of the spring 2004 campaign for the University of Alabama to talk about its connections to slavery.

I finished this project in Chapel Hill. In the triangle, Anthony Baker, Sandy Darrity, Laura Edwards, Sally Greene, Mitu Gulati, Eric Muller, John Orth, Roman Hoyos, Gregg Polsky, Dana Remus, Robert J. Smith, Harry Watson, and John Wertheimer all helped, as did James T. Campbell and his terrific Steering Committee on Slavery and Justice at Brown University, particularly Michael Vorenberg, Seth Rockman, and Neta Crawford. Mark Auslander, Sven Beckert, Chandos M. Brown, Spencer Crew, Kelley Deetz, Ariela Gross, Sally Hadden, Leslie Harris, Martha S. Jones, Alfred Konefsky, Rebecca McIntyre, Terry Meyers, William Novak, Dylan Penningroth, Marc Roark, Elizabeth Schwenger, David Tanenhaus, and Chris Tolmins have loaned me their expertise. Sam Thomas at the T.R.R. Cobb House has hosted me several times and taught me a lot about Cobb. I am especially grateful to Jeannine DeLombard, Fred Konefsky, and Leslie Harris and the anonymous referees for their close reading of the entire manuscript. My friends Mary Sarah Bilder, Mark Brandon, Christina Forth, Sally Greene, Daniel Hulsebosch, Daniel Hamilton, Arthur LeFrancois, and Sarah Nelson Roth contributed in many ways to the ideas and to working out a lot of these themes. And I am immensely grateful for the help of David McBride, my editor at Oxford, who stayed with this for a very long time and helped make this a heck of a lot better, and Stacey Victor, Leslie Johnson, and India Gray who supervised the production.

I have benefited from workshops at Duke, Harvard, the Universities of Alabama, Georgia, Iowa, Maryland, Michigan, North Carolina, South Carolina, and Virginia, Washington and Lee, and William and Mary, the audiences at the Hutchins Lecture at UNC, the Hendricks Lecture at Washington and Lee, and the University of Florida's Center for the Study of Race and Race Relations annual lecture, as well as the American Bar Foundation, the American Society for Legal History, and the Southern Intellectual History Circle. And I've ben-efited from many student papers over the years and from some really stellar re-search assistants. They are Rebecca Schwartz and Clay Taylor at Alabama and Freddie Akrouche, Elizabeth Carroll, Chris Dwight, Marc Kornegay, Anna Elizabeth Lineberger, Susannah Loumiet, Jennifer Richelson, Catherine Smith, Anna Tison, and Thomas Thurman, at North Carolina. The students whose papers have most informed this project are Amy Jo Pierce, Stephanie Litteral, Grant Lucky, Gina Blackwell, Scott Mitchell, Judson Crump, Kelly Taylor, Heidi Rickes, Jessica Thompson, Benjamin K. Kleinman, and Chris Dwight.

I am grateful for the hospitality and expertise of the librarians at the University of Alabama, Columbia Theological Seminary, Davidson College, Duke University, Harvard University, the Library of Virginia, the University of North Carolina, the North Carolina State Archives, the University of Virginia, Wake Forest University, Washington and Lee University, and the College of William and Mary. Among the many librarians who've spent considerable time, I would especially like to thank Bob Anthony and Donna Nixon of UNC, Tom Crew of the Virginia State Library, Lisa McCown and Thomas Camden of Washington and Lee, and Jessica Lacher-Felman of the University of Alabama (now LSU).

This book draws upon work that I have published over many years. Sometimes I use substantial sections of previously published work; in other cases I use only selected paragraphs, or just data. I thank the journals who have allowed me to use work that appeared first in their pages. Chapter 1 draws upon "The Nat Turner Trials," 91 *North Carolina Law Review* 1817–80 (2013) and "Considering William and Mary's History with Slavery: The Case of President Thomas Roderick Dew," 16 *William and Mary Bill of Rights Journal* 1091–1139 (2008). Chapter 3 draws on " 'The Law of the Descent of Thought': Law, History, and Civilization in Antebellum Literary Addresses," 20 *Law and Literature* 343–402 (2008) and "The Republics of Liberty and Letters: Progress, Union, and

Constitutionalism in Graduation Addresses at the Antebellum University of North Carolina," 89 *North Carolina Law Review* 1879–1964 (2011); Chapter 6 was first published as "Utility, History, and the Rule of Law: The Fugitive Slave Act of 1850 in Antebellum Jurisprudence," in *Transformations in American Legal History: Essays in Honor of Morton J. Horwitz* 109–28 (Daniel W. Hamilton & Alfred L. Brophy eds., 2009); Chapter 7 is drawn from "Humanity, Utility, and Logic in Southern Legal Thought: Harriet Beecher Stowe's Vision in *Dred: A Tale of the Great Dismal Swamp*," 78 *Boston University Law Review* 1113–61 (1998); and Chapter 8 draws upon "Thomas Ruffin: Of Moral Philosophy and Monuments," 87 *North Carolina Law Review* 799–854 (2009).

ILLUSTRATIONS

Tables

University, Court, and Slave

Introduction

Nathaniel Beverley Tucker returned home to the College of William and Mary in 1834. After graduating in 1801, Beverley studied law and practiced in Virginia. Times were tough in Virginia in the early years of the nineteenth century, so he went to Missouri in 1815 to seek his fortune as a land speculator and lawyer and later as a judge. Missouri did not quite work out either, so he went back to Virginia in 1832, in part to participate in the nascent nullification movement. Tucker saw the prospect of a southern nation in South Carolina's protests against the federal tariff that burdened the products of slave labor. The movement proved less robust than Tucker had hoped. Yet, in 1834, Tucker was offered a teaching job at the school where he had been educated and where his father, St. George Tucker, had also been a professor. Beverley Tucker went home to Williamsburg to reclaim his position in Virginia society and to defend the institution of slavery.[1]

Much of Tucker's teaching at William and Mary was about tradition—traditions within law and a defense of the ancient institution of slavery. Yet, he also departed from tradition. The first two law professors at William and Mary were opponents of slavery. And therein lies a story, for occupants of William and Mary's chair in law parallel the South's changing attitudes toward slavery. As the South became more committed to slavery, so did the southern academy and the judiciary.

The origins of Thomas Jefferson's ideas for the Declaration of Independence lie in Virginia—in Albemarle County, where he grew up, and in Williamsburg, where he attended William and Mary and absorbed the Enlightenment ideas that drove our country's Revolution.[2] After studying at William and Mary from 1760 to 1762, Jefferson studied law with George Wythe, a lawyer who offered instruction in Williamsburg. Wythe and Jefferson together joined the Revolutionary cause, and in 1779 Wythe became the first professor of law in America when he filled at William and Mary the newly created chair of law and police.[3] Wythe taught there for a decade, until 1789, when he became a judge. Some hints of Wythe's antislavery ideas survive in opinions he wrote for Virginia's chancery court between 1789 and his death in 1806. For instance, in the 1806 case *Hudgins v. Wright* Chancellor Wythe faced the question whether two black people, descendants of a free Indian woman, could be held as slaves. Wythe held that they could not. According to the scant surviving report, Wythe used the Virginia Constitution's Bill of Rights to conclude that "freedom is the birthright of every human being."[4]

Most telling of Wythe's attitudes toward slavery, however, were his actions in his personal life. Wythe freed two of his slaves, Lydia Broadnax and her son Michael Brown (who may also have been his son). Then an amendment to his will placed his lands around Richmond in trust for the benefit of Michael Brown. Wythe left the remainder of his estate to his grandnephew, George Wythe Swinney. Swinney, however, enraged at losing part of Wythe's estate, laced the coffee of Brown and Chancellor Wythe with arsenic; both died within hours. Swinney escaped punishment because under Virginia law Lydia Broadnax, the one surviving witness to the events, could not testify against white people.[5] We will see again this theme of the legal process attempting to silence enslaved people.

The symbolic divide between the Enlightenment and nineteenth-century America widened further a few months after Wythe's death when *Hudgins* was appealed. Judge St. George Tucker upheld the result—that the alleged slaves were free—but on different grounds from Wythe. Tucker thought that the law prohibited Wythe's broad dictum. "I do not concur with the Chancellor in his reasoning on the operation of the first clause of the Bill of Rights, which was notoriously framed with a cautious eye to this subject, and was meant to embrace the case of free citizens . . . and not by a side wind to overturn the rights of property," Tucker wrote.[6]

Though the transition away from the Enlightenment was underway, St. George Tucker was still on the side of termination of slavery. He had taken over Wythe's chair at William and Mary in 1789 and taught there until 1804. During that time he published an essay urging the gradual abolition of slavery. The essay on "Slavery in Virginia," first published in 1796 and later included in Tucker's 1803 edition of *Blackstone's Commentaries*, demonstrated the role of history and reasoning in understanding both what the law was and what it ought to be. Since ancient times, slavery had been almost universal in human society; desire for profit by both northern merchants involved in the slave trade and southern planters accounted for the introduction of slavery to America. That legacy of servitude in America, stretching back to 1619 when a Dutch merchant vessel first delivered twenty black people to the Virginia colony did not, however, justify slavery.[7] "If ever there was a cause, if ever an occasion, in which all hearts should be united, every nerve strained, and every power exerted, surely the restoration of human nature to its unalienable right, is such."[8] After surveying the criminal and civil law regulating slaves, Tucker concluded that Virginia's slave law, based as it was on the need to control slaves, was the product of injustice. He was struck by "how frequently the laws of nature have been set aside in favour of institutions, the pure result of prejudice, usurpation, and tyranny."[9]

History also taught, however, that there were no alternatives available. Once the English government had introduced slavery, it was too lucrative to English merchants for them to abolish. Tucker's analysis of the hazards of immediate emancipation on the one hand and continued slavery on the other led him to advocate gradual abolition. The lessons of the French West Indies showed that immediate emancipation might lead to bloodshed. Plus, there were also legal obstacles to emancipation, primarily the prohibition on government taking property without paying compensation.[10] Tucker's struggle with the appropriate legal response to slavery appeared in his observation that the "claims of nature, it will be said, are stronger than those which arise from social institutions only." He appeared to recognize slaves' claims to justice and thus to immediate emancipation. But, Tucker responded to himself, "nature also dictates to us to provide for our *own* safety, and authorizes all *necessary* measures for that purpose."[11] Tucker wove together arguments, based on Virginia's security and constitutional law, to propose a gradual abolition plan that would retain in bondage all the slaves living at the time of the adoption of his plan, but free the children of female slaves born after the plan was adopted, when they reached age twenty-eight.[12]

While St. George Tucker's plan appears incomplete and slow, it was an attempt to end slavery. Yet, the optimism of the Enlightenment at William and Mary was disappearing. Three more people followed Tucker in the chair in law from 1804 to 1833, though none left much evidence of their ideas about slavery.[13] Events large and small solidified southern attitudes in favor of slavery as our country moved away from beliefs in universal truths and began to laugh at concepts like Thomas Jefferson's statement in the Declaration of Independence that "all men are created equal." The causes were partly economic. Slaves were a source of wealth for the southern economy. In 1860, more than 30% of the people in the southern states were enslaved; more than 45% of the people in Deep South states were enslaved.[14] The causes were also partly cultural. Increasingly, Southerners spoke of the centrality of slavery to their society. There was a defensive mentality, as Southerners realized that Northerners opposed the extension of slavery for their own economic and cultural reasons. Moreover, the pro-slavery attitudes were a response to events like the revolution in Haiti from 1791 to 1804, during which the enslaved freed themselves—and killed many of their former owners.

As is discussed in depth in the next chapter, a key turning point was Nat Turner's rebellion in August 1831. The rebellion itself was short-lived, although Turner evaded capture for several months. Shortly after Turner's execution in November 1831, the Virginia legislature convened a discussion of what should be done about slavery in Virginia. It was one of the rare instances in our history when violence begat a serious discussion. William and Mary Professor Thomas Roderick Dew cataloged the debate and told his readers that emancipation would be "utterly subversive of the interest, security, and happiness of both blacks and whites, and consequently, hostile to every principle of expediency, morality, and religion." He grimly remarked emancipation was "totally impractical."[15] Professor Dew's often-reprinted essay marked the end of serious discussion of emancipation; from 1832 when it was published until the Civil War, few in Virginia advocated even gradual emancipation.[16] Shortly thereafter Beverley Tucker joined Dew; together they contributed to the pro-slavery academic literature. Politicians and judges employed similar arguments; together, they spoke a common language of pro-slavery thought.

Beverley Tucker's inaugural lecture to law students at William and Mary reworked William Blackstone's philosophy, which celebrated the freedom found in a state of nature.[17] Tucker instead drew upon his experience, a central teacher for antebellum Southerners, to locate truths about human behavior and government. Tucker opposed the common belief that freedom was greatest in a state of nature. He pointed to the political organization of Native Americans. Where Blackstone had reverence for natives, Tucker depicted such "primitive" societies as places of violence.[18]

Such experiences led in turn to Tucker's belief in the evolution of societies. In different stages, societies had different needs.[19] Like Hegel, Tucker rejected universal Enlightenment truths in favor of a contextual analysis. "There is no best in government. That which is best for one people, is not best for another," Tucker told his students. Moreover, people needed to be ready for freedom.

> [I]t is not the office of free government to qualify a people for it. It must find them already so qualified. It can never make them so. The capacity for freedom is a capacity for self-government; and, wanting that, a people restored to freedom will but use it to seek a master. The rigid mould of despotism may act upon the subject mass, and shape it to its purpose; but, in all other cases, the reverse of this takes place.[20]

Such focus on context and on history was a key point of departure from the Revolutionary era's focus on abstract and universal truths. Tucker agreed that theories could be useful sometimes, for "[s]ound theory is never falsified by results."[21] Yet, he found error "in confiding too much in untried theories." Instead, Tucker suggested a scientific method: "We reason from cause to effect, and where history affords examples where the effect we would produce has resulted from the causes we are about to put in action, we may confide in conclusions thus verified by experience."[22] While Tucker's method derived from the Enlightenment idea that government should be based on observation of the surrounding world, the observations were notoriously incomplete in many instances.[23]

Tucker explained to his law students how societies began with aristocracies and evolved, through protection of private property, into republics—how nobles purchased their liberties and how the rule of law emerged.[24] Thus, property was central to Tucker's world; slaves as property were at the very center.

In another one of his lectures, Tucker examined William Blackstone's discussion of slavery. Noting Blackstone's reverence for English institutions, Tucker asked for the same indulgence of such "sentiment so essential to the preservation of every thing that is valuable" in defense of slavery.[25] Tucker then told his students that slavery made freedom possible for whites. It kept the laboring class laboring. Tucker began with a bold statement about the utility of slavery:

> [I]t has done more to elevate a degraded race in the scale of humanity; to tame the savage; to civilize the barbarous; to soften the ferocious; to enlighten the ignorant; and to spread the blessing of Christianity among the heathen, than all the missionaries that philanthropy and religion have ever sent forth.[26]

Tucker then turned to the right to enslave people who are captured during war. However, he thought slavery's origins unimportant, since slavery was ubiquitous. The question of the legitimacy of slavery was of increasing importance, however, given the northern attacks on it. For now a conviction that slavery was proper "may be necessary to man our hearts and brace our nerves for the impending struggle."[27]

Two key pro-slavery arguments appeared in Tucker's lecture. First, slaves were taken care of by their owners, while employers of free workers did not care for them. Thus, slavery was good for the slaves. "To those who know him best," Tucker said of the slave, "he certainly seems a stranger to despair." Second, slavery preserved freedom for white people. While we might think that linking freedom to slavery is paradoxical, there was a long lineage to the belief that they went hand-in-hand. And therein lies an unusual story.[28]

Tucker traced the lineage of slavery's "contribution" to the idea of freedom to Edmund Burke, who was a member of Parliament during the American Revolution. Burke's "Speech Conciliation with the American Colonies," which he delivered in March 1775—just before the outbreak of war in April 1775—summarized the reasons why the American colonies were so attached to the idea of liberty. Some of the reasons had to do with Americans' heritage of liberty, with religious attitudes in the North, and with respect for Anglo-American law. Burke also credited the institution of slavery as another cause of Americans' respect for liberty. Slavery in Virginia and the Carolinas led the masters there to have respect for freedom because of the benefits that slavery conferred on them.

[I]n any part of the world, those who are free are by far the most proud and jealous of their freedom. Freedom is to them not only an enjoyment, but a kind of rank and privilege. Not seeing there, that freedom, as in countries where it is a common blessing and as broad and general as the air, may be united with much abject toil, with great misery, with all the exterior of servitude; liberty looks, amongst them, like something that is more noble and liberal.

Burke credited slavery—as Tucker and many pro-slavery thinkers did in later years—with freeing the master class from toil and giving them a new respect for freedom. Burke found sentiments of freedom in "the nature of man." Thus, he concluded that in the southern colonies, the people "are much more strongly, and with an higher and more stubborn spirit, attached to liberty than those to the northward. Such were all the ancient commonwealths; such were our Gothic ancestors; such in our days were the Poles; and such will be all masters of slaves, who are not slaves themselves. In such a people the haughtiness of domination combines with the spirit of freedom, fortifies it, and renders it invincible."[29]

Tucker concluded that slavery was good for the owners and all white people. He thought this for two reasons. First, it taught owners the value of freedom. Second, it gave owners the ability to devote time to politics and to study. Tucker stated simply what others elaborated in the years leading to the Civil War:

Slave labor pre-occupies and fills the low and degrading stations in society. Menial offices are altogether discharged by it; and all the tasks of mere brute strength are left to it. To the freeman belong those services which imply trust and confidence or require skill, which therefore command higher wages than mere animal labor, and give a sense of respectability and a feeling of self-respect.[30]

Moreover, he took the world as it was. Tucker warned against too harsh a judgment on the past (which was an allusion to the framing of the Constitution and its protection of slavery). While some in the North might attack that compromise with slavery, he urged Southerners to have a different attitude.[31]

While Tucker made slavery seem natural, indeed desirable, others in Virginia struggled with those ideas.[32] In February 1835 the *Southern Literary Messenger* printed an extended, anonymous article that questioned Tucker's argument that slavery was correct and natural.[33] There was a struggle over how to think about

slavery, but Tucker's side was winning and would continue to win in the southern academy and in southern minds for years.

Tucker produced another public statement on slavery in April 1836 with a
review of two pro-slavery books: James Kirke Paulding's *Slavery in the United
States* and Henry Drayton's *The South Vindicated from the Treason and Fanaticism
of the Northern Abolitionists*. Paulding was a New Yorker and a former secretary
of the Navy. Drayton, a South Carolinian, had relocated to Philadelphia in 1833
in the wake of South Carolina's nullification crisis. At the end of the decade, he
became president of the Second Bank of the United States. Both Paulding and
Drayton were trying to calm antislavery agitation and plead the case of the South.

In the review, Tucker expanded the arguments of his October 1834 lecture
on slavery and his critique of Blackstone's *Commentaries* opposition to slavery.
He argued that slavery was legal and, on balance, beneficial.[34] Recalling that the
French Revolution's attack on property began with an attack on property in the
form of slavery, Tucker predicted that once property in humans was attacked,
other attacks on property would likely follow. Abolitionists were the vanguard
of an attack on all property.[35]

Tucker's mind and that of many of his contemporaries orbited around the
institution of slavery, so much that he not only found it central to the economy
of the United States, but he also found it central to our country's liberty as well.
Tucker's work contains an insight into southern thought: it was, indeed, not
democratic. Moreover, slavery lent a character of conservatism to southern politics and culture.

Tucker's most expansive work on slavery came in the form of two articles,
which he had originally written for delivery at the convention of the National
Institute for the Promotion of Science in Baltimore in 1844. The essay proved
too controversial, and it appeared, instead, in the *Southern Literary Messenger*.[36]
Tucker began with the proposition that ideas flowed like water from high points
to low; that is, from the worthy to the rest of society.[37] It was the model of intellectual influence that he pursued with his students and that formed a cornerstone of southern society. The better ruled everyone else, and Tucker was one
of the better, who taught his students and a larger southern audience about the
positive effects of slavery.

Tucker understood that he had to offer a defense of slavery. The "spirit of
our institutions and the spirit of the age alike demand an account of everything
which seems like a disturbance of the natural equality or an invasion of the natural rights of man."[38] The defense came in crediting slavery with helping the steady
progress of both blacks *and* whites. Of course slavery had its origins in the sordid
and inappropriate motive for profit, Tucker acknowledged, but now, on balance,
slavery was beneficial.[39] Judging utility from the present state, slavery offered
the least evil alternative. "It is not for us to do evil that good may come, for it

may never come, or it might be divinely accomplished at no expense of evil. But when it is accomplished, shall we reject it? When the price has been paid and cannot be recalled, when God has been pleased to overrule the evil to his own good purposes, shall we cast away the benefit?"[40] For slavery was the "condition most favorable to virtuous contentment, a state of steadily progressive advancement in the comforts of civilization, and in the moral and intellectual improvement that civilization imparts."[41] How did slavery lead to improvement? For this, he turned to Proverbs 15:17: "wisdom cometh by the opportunity of leisure," which led to his conclusion that "the curse that dooms the mass of mankind to toil, dooms them also to ignorance."[42] Where the Smithsonian Institution was designed to facilitate the promulgation of knowledge, to democratize it, and to make it more accessible, Tucker's speech was focused on the ways that education was the province of the privileged. The centerpiece of the defense of slavery was that it made some wealthy and thus gave them the opportunity for education and that it joined the interests of white men of all classes against the slaves and thus contributed both financially and intellectually to the spirit of republicanism.[43]

Beverley Tucker taught at William and Mary from 1834 to his death in 1851, shortly before his sixty-first birthday.[44] William and Mary's trajectory followed the progression of southern thought from the Revolution through the Civil War.

After the mid-1830s, southern universities justified themselves as places where students learned to defend southern values. In the early days of the Civil War, an orator at Southern University in Greensboro, Alabama, now Birmingham Southern College, called for support for southern schools because they would support southern literature. Those schools held great sway in the public mind:

> The fetters of bondage to an alien intellectual dynasty are to be broken for a people only by the ministry of their own common schools, academies, colleges, and universities. These alone can unclose the bars of their mental prison and bring deliverance to their captive minds. Hence the literary and intellectual emancipation of the South demands, as the condition of its achievement, the establishment and support, within her own limits, of literary institutions of every grade, but especially the university, which wields so despotic an influence in the realm of letters and mind.[45]

That orator, Joseph Taylor, a lawyer and newspaper editor, had spoken in similar terms at the University of Alabama more than a dozen years before in 1847. He focused particular attention on the utility of the University to Alabama in defending southern values. Taylor saw southern colleges, the southern pulpit, and the southern press as the defenders of slavery:

> The sons of the South are its legitimate, its reliable, and its appointed defenders; and, in the Universities of the South, they must be imbued

Illustration I.1 Southern University, Greensboro, Alabama. Library of Congress, Prints &
Photographs Division, HABS, Reproduction number HABS ALA,33-GREBO,11.

with the skill and force in the use of the weapons of reason necessary
to the high encounter to which they are called. If they be educated
elsewhere, may they not imbibe the doctrines of our assailants, and
thus, returning to us in the guise of friends, help to drag over the walls
and into the very citadel of our domestic Troy, some fatal horse pregnant with the impediments of fanatic propagandists and unreformed
reformers?[46]

While some asked scholars to bring hope, the dominant mode of thinking at
colleges was support for slavery. There were, as Ralph Waldo Emerson told
an audience at Concord, Massachusetts, in 1851, many forces aligned in favor
of slavery. "The learning of the Universities, the culture of the eloquent society, the acumen of lawyers, the majesty of the Bench, the eloquence of the
Christian pulpit, the stoutness of Democracy, the respectability of the Whig
party are all combined" in the pro-slavery mission of kidnapping a fugitive
slave, Emerson said.[47]

Not only did schools support slavery, however. Slavery also supported
schools. This happened while Southerners justified slavery in part because it afforded them leisure and money to obtain an education. Much of this came to
fruition in Senator James Henry Hammond's "mud-sill" theory of slavery, which
taught that there must be a class of people who did the work to make it possible

for others to do the thinking. It has particular relevance when speaking of universities' connections to slavery:

> In all social systems there must be a class to do the menial duties, to perform the drudgery of life. That is, a class requiring but a low order of intellect and but little skill. Its requisites are vigor, docility, fidelity. Such a class you must have, or you would not have that other class which leads progress, civilization, and refinement. It constitutes the very mud-sill of society and of political government; and you might as well attempt to build a house in the air, as to build either the one or the other, except on this mud-sill. Fortunately for the South, she found a race adapted to that purpose to her hand. A race inferior to her own, but eminently qualified in temper, in vigor, in docility, in capacity to stand the climate, to answer all her purposes. We use them for our purpose, and call them slaves.[48]

Although Hammond spoke in general terms, this sentiment gained particular force in intellectual and literary contexts, where the South was seen, ideally, as better positioned than the North to contribute to Western civilization because its thinking members—white men *and* women—were released from menial labor and freed to pursue higher intellectual callings. As antebellum Southerners argued, the intellectual and cultural pursuits that define universities were underwritten, indeed made possible, by slave labor.[49] In fact, slavey labor was explicitly used to finance education.[50]

University, Court, and Slave recovers Beverley Tucker's world, of lawyers, judges, politicians, and academics who moved our country from the world of the Enlightenment, which aspired to universal freedom, toward the Romantic era's focus on context and empirical and economic analysis of slavery. It is about how the pro-slavery ideas, taught in southern universities to the next generation of leaders, illuminate the intellectual world of southern politicians and judges. It uses academics' writings to create a picture of the world of moral philosophy that politicians and judges employed. That world saw hierarchy rather than equality, required some to labor for the benefit of others, and judged morality often by utility. Southern politicians and judges told themselves that slavery was justified by the past, was economically necessary, and was moral.

University, Court, and Slave seeks to refine our understanding of how legal thought relates to its surrounding culture through the laboratory of the old South. To recover that world, it turns to the writings of professors at southern institutions who defended slavery. The writings of teachers like Thomas Dew and Beverley Tucker of William and Mary; William A. Smith of Randolph Macon; Albert Taylor Bledsoe, George Frederick Holmes, and James Philemon Holcombe of the University of Virginia; R. H. Rivers of Alabama Wesleyan College; and Thomas R. R. Cobb of the Lumpkin Law School held a constellation of ideas. They used history and economics in their calculations of utility and also looked to the Bible's seeming endorsement of slavery. Together that led them to argue that slavery was preferable to freedom for both the enslaved and the slaveowners. Many employed a political theory that concluded that slavery enhanced the freedom of whites, though by the 1850s the more common argument was that slavery benefited the enslaved rather than that it benefited the enslavers. There is a story of progression (or maybe it is better phrased as retrogression), where southern thinkers moved from a world that thought slavery should be limited, even eliminated if possible, perhaps through colonization. That world acknowledged that slavery was sometimes good for the white people. Later, perhaps in response to antislavery advocacy and also as part of the defense of slavery, Southerners began to emphasize the ways that slavery supposedly benefited enslaved people. All the while, the judicial opinions drew from the common well of cultural ideas about slavery's history and its utility.

The first part of *University, Court, and Slave* is the story of those academics who were closely aligned politically and economically with the slaveholding class and politicians. The first chapter is set in motion by Nat Turner's rebellion, which set off a debate among Virginia's leaders about the future of slavery. That led William and Mary professor Thomas R. Dew to publish in 1832 his *Review of the Debates in the Virginia Legislature*. Across several hundred pages, Dew crystalized many of the key pro-slavery arguments—that slavery was more humane than the alternative (execution of the enslaved) and that it was common, indeed nearly ubiquitous, in human society; that slaves were not fit for freedom but needed to be compelled to work, for their own good and that of their owners; that slavery was preferable to emancipation at this point in the South (with particular contrast to the aftermath of slavery in Haiti); and that slavery made equality among white people possible. Virginia lawyer Jesse Harrison responded with an article supporting the feasibility of gradual emancipation, but Dew's argument stood.

The second chapter extends to Dew's successors at institutions throughout the South in the 1840s and 1850s. It looks from Washington College in the Shenandoah Valley, to Transylvania University in Lexington, Kentucky, the University of Virginia and Randolph Macon College in eastern Virginia, and then to schools in the deeper South like Emory College in Oxford, Georgia, and the Greensboro, Alabama Female Seminary. Faculty publications show a remarkable diversity of opinion, including occasionally antislavery writings. But mostly what students heard in their moral philosophy classes and what the public heard from academics were a variety of pro-slavery arguments. Often academics emphasized the role of the educated in governing the rest of society and the virtues of slavery by making it possible for some to have a life of leisure and study and the importance of schools in teaching pro-slavery thought.

The third chapter turns to other ideas on the campuses. Its major sources are the literary and graduation addresses given by politicians, writers, and judges. The chapter focuses particular attention on the University of Alabama, with looks at other schools around the South. For example, Senator Jefferson Davis of Mississippi brought his pro-slavery ideas to the University of Mississippi in 1852. The addresses, given by leading politicians, lawyers, and judges, reveal the interaction of schools with other parts of southern elite culture.

To better understand the boundaries of pro-slavery thought, it must be viewed alongside antislavery thought. The fourth chapter moves to a debate undertaken in a series of letters between Brown University President Francis Wayland, one of the leading antislavery moralists, and South Carolina Baptist Minister Richard Fuller, a leading pro-slavery thinker. Their letters show the conflicts between pro- and antislavery moral philosophy as they brushed up against each other. The concluding chapter of the first part turns to the trial the University of Mississippi's Board of Trustees conducted of Chancellor F. A. P. Barnard. He was charged with taking the testimony of a slave over a student. In addition to highlighting the interaction of students, slaves, and faculty, the trial illustrates how legal concepts structured the academy's dealings with slavery.

The second part of the book turns to the ideas of politicians and lawyers who established and worked within a pro-slavery legal system and the antislavery critquers of that system. It shifts focus from academic thought to the ideas of people in Congress and lawyers elsewhere in the country. The academics were using similar terms for discussion of slavery as other southern leaders. There are two chapters in Part II. The first of those, Chapter 6, begins with an examination of the Senate's debate over the Fugitive Slave Act of 1850. The debate crystalized the reasons Southerners favored slavery. It illustrates the considerations of history, political experience, natural law, and utility that led many to say that slavery was superior to even gradual abolition. That public debate pulls together the ideas of moral philosophy, history, and contemporary politics that academics discussed. This is a story not just of dreamers who inhabited an ivory tower in a land so distant in time and mores from us that it appears foreign. It is, instead, a story of pro-slavery ideas and rhetoric put into action. That chapter then turns to the public's response to the Fugitive Slave Act, and particularly the response of Harriet Beecher Stowe, to see southern law from the vantage of its opponents.

The precision of those antislavery minds allowed them to understand and detail how southern judges reasoned. There are two key pieces of the antislavery critique of southern law. First, there was a jurisprudence of sentiment that Stowe and other abolitionists, like Frederick Douglass, developed. It was based on considerations of the individual slaves rather than considerations of southern society.

In addition to Stowe's shrewd observations about the constraints on southern jurists, another abolitionist legal thinker, William Goodell, provided an extended critique of southern legal thought. In two books, *The American Slave Code in Theory and Practice* and *Views of American Constitutional Law*, Goodell provided a sober, pragmatic assessment of the legal system's support of slavery. Moreover, William Goodell's *American Slave Code in Theory and Practice* developed an empirically based critique of slavery. Goodell used statutes and reports of appellate cases, as well as newspaper accounts, to detail the brutality of slavery. He employed appeals to natural justice and also sentimental feelings on behalf of enslaved humans to critique the law of slavery and make immediate reform appear necessary. And Goodell engaged Southerners on some of their own territory—the empirical assessment of slavery and the question of whether considerations of utility supported slavery or its termination.

Chapter 7 turns to Harriet Beecher Stowe's *Dred: A Tale of the Great Dismal Swamp*, which provides a perceptive critique of how southern judges reasoned. In *Dred*, Stowe explained why people who felt the inhumanity of slavery nevertheless supported it. She explored this question through the character of Judge Clayton who was antislavery in private but issued a pro-slavery decision. In fact, that fictional judge was based on an actual jurist, North Carolina Supreme Court Justice Thomas Ruffin.[51] His 1830 opinion in *State v. Mann* freed a man who had abused a slave in his custody from criminal liability. Stowe detected in the opinion "the conflict between the feelings of the humane judge and the logical necessity of a strict interpreter of slave-law."[52] She concluded that Ruffin could not oppose slavery because he was confined by a set of ideas about law that emphasized the greatest good of the greatest number and because he could not break free from precedent. That philosophy tells us of the workings of the minds of those southern jurists who constructed and supported the legal system around which slavery grew—and that structured how politicians and voters in the states of the South viewed the threat to slavery and guided their steps toward disunion.

Part III of *University, Court, and Slave* turns to the judiciary and the author of a legal treatise to illustrate how the ideas about utility, history, economics, and precedent combined to make pro-slavery law. Chapter 8 focuses on Thomas Ruffin's opinions beyond *State v. Mann* to give a fuller picture of the operation of his mind and the considerations that Stowe identified in him. To help see what is special about Ruffin and what is more deeply embedded in southern law, that chapter compares him to another more moderate member of the North Carolina Supreme Court, William Gaston, who advocated termination of slavery and worked as a lawyer to help his Quaker clients allow their slaves to live in virtual freedom.

Chapters 9 and 10 turn southward, to Georgia. Chapter 9, like Chapter 8, focuses on jurists—Joseph Henry Lumpkin, the Chief Justice of the Georgia Supreme Court, and Georgia Justices Ebenezer Starnes and Henry L. Benning— to further fill out the picture of how southern judges blended pro-slavery ideas, moral philosophy, and ideas about economics in their opinions and their non-judicial writings. It reveals a consistent emphasis on considerations of economy and protection of slavery in their writings.

Chapter 10 turns from judges to a treatise writer. It uses Thomas R. R. Cobb's 1858 treatise *An Inquiry into the Law of Negro Slavery in the United States of America* to explore southern thinking on the relationship of history and economics to slave law. Cobb was a lawyer and legal educator (he cofounded the Lumpkin Law School in Athens, Georgia, which later became the University of Georgia law school). He was also a general in the Confederate army, and he died, fighting for the cause, on the battlefield at Fredericksburg in December 1862. His work bridges academics' writings and the legal world. In particular, Cobb's treatise links the parts of pro-slavery thought that are put to use in the legal system. Cobb focused on the benefits of slavery to the slave over the free worker and on how throughout human history there has been slavery. Cobb presented a detailed empirical argument about slavery in history and in contemporary society to support his natural law interpretation—some people are suited to slavery and others to freedom. This evidence supported a pro-slavery law by demonstrating the universal nature of slavery.

Chapter 11 turns to two ways that slaves sought freedom to gauge jurists' support for slavery. It looks to grants of emancipation in their owners' wills and by travel to free states. Over the course of the nineteenth century, legislatures and courts restricted the ability of slave owners to free their slaves. This was particularly noticeable when owners tried to free slaves at their death. Where once states permitted testators to free their human property at death, legislatures and judges increasingly refused to give effect to wills emancipating slaves. They were skeptical, too, of wills that allowed slaves to choose between leaving the state and being free or remaining in the state in slavery. Such wills give too much autonomy to slaves to decide their fate and seemed to recognize too much humanity within the enslaved people themselves. By the 1850s, judges often could abide this.

Slaves also often claimed freedom when they had been taken to a free state. But as with the emancipation by will cases, southern courts were increasingly skeptical of such claims. Finally in 1857 in *Dred Scott v. Sandford* the U.S. Supreme Court denied Dred Scott the right to sue in federal court for his freedom because, as they said, he was not a citizen. The Court made southern beliefs in the Constitution's protection of property in humans the center of its constitutional law. What had been political and academic dogma became "law."

The southern constitutional vision, legitimized in *Dred Scott* and in class-rooms, courts, and legislative halls throughout the South, helped shape the responses of southern voters and politicians in the wake of the election of Abraham Lincoln. The final chapter briefly takes up the role that academics and their arguments played in the discussion of secession. The ideas so extensively developed in and promulgated by the southern academy illustrate how deeply and passionately white Southerners clung to slavery and how they were willing to bring destruction on themselves to preserve their property in humans.

The goal in those chapters is to detail the ways that judges employed consid-erations of precedent, utility, and their understanding of natural law and history to decide concrete cases. Ruffin and Lumpkin illustrate those considerations in a wide variety of cases from tort and contract to criminal law; the emancipation chapter provides an in-depth look at one area of the law to understand the matrix of ideas motivating judges and how that world fits together. The ideas of empiri-cism and evolution, as well as natural law, that were so powerful for the judges circulated widely in southern thought. Though we often think of American juris-prudence as beginning in the 1870s with Oliver Wendell Holmes, the antebel-lum thinkers—academics, members of Congress, jurists, and even antislavery novel writers—cared deeply about law. They engaged with each other on im-portant issues of the role of sentiment and utility, how to deal with change over time, and where property rights fit. These ideas were the matrix within which judges operated. The origins of important parts of American jurisprudence, such as the postwar focus on empiricism, utility, obedience to law, and the compet-ing obligations to morality over law all appear in the antebellum debate about slave law.[53]

Finally, and perhaps most speculatively, we can use pro-slavery legal thought to make some further assessments about the secession movement. What re-mains a constant puzzle is why the southern states, which had for so long re-ceived protection for slavery, sought to exit the United States. Given the central-ity of lawyers to the movement and the centrality of legal thinking, this study can help us focus on how legal thinking supported a sense that secession was right and necessary, how the modes of thought so dominant among southern elites channeled their beliefs that slavery was indispensable to southern society, and how the destruction of property and slavery would destroy the natural order and their society. Secession was a movement driven by economic reality and by ideas; and at the core of the ideas were the concepts of utility, property, and history, which demonstrated the ubiquity of slavery and the economic disaster that followed emancipation in the West Indies. This work is, thus, a part of the new constitutional history that places Supreme Court doctrine in its intellec-tual context and demonstrates how constitutional law in the Supreme Court and in the minds of politicians and voters is supported by—and sometimes in turn legitimates—ideas in the larger culture.

By looking at the pro-slavery academic literature and its relationship to legal literature, I hope to repackage and expand on a series of data sets that have been examined before in other ways to see relationships and trend lines that have previously been invisible. The constellation of ideas about the market, history, political theory, and experience came together to craft a legal culture of respect for property and for slavery. And in that we see the development of sophisticated ideas about law and the law's dependence on its surrounding society that were in circulation in antebellum America.

This book is about the ideas of the slave-owning class and their educators, politicians, lawyers, and judges. The people who brought down this system were enslaved people, formerly enslaved people, and their allies, people who for economic or religious or cultural motives opposed slavery. The antislavery actors on the battlefield of the Civil War and the political and economic arenas ended slavery and are critical to the story of freedom in our country. The antebellum United States was shaped by reaction to enslaved people and to abolitionists, so sometimes the enslaved appear in these pages. But right now I focus on the ideas of the pro-slavery majority in the South, who defended slavery and whose ideas led the way to secession and the war that rather abruptly ended slavery.

This project, then, reconstructs the architecture of conservative thought and respects its power and its appeal. Once the Civil War began to turn against the fortunes of the South, these ideas cascaded downward with astonishing speed. The corollary to the aphorism that "there is nothing so powerful as an idea whose time has come" is "there is nothing so powerless as an idea whose time has past." The day of reckoning for the institution of slavery was coming and at a speed few appreciated. But in their time, these ideas were triumphant. For a period these ideas, so carefully worked out in the academy and the judiciary, held sway. And in their making and in the response to them, we can see the central themes of American law.

I hope this book speaks to several key themes in the history of slavery and law. First, I hope to contribute to the rapidly growing literature on universities and slavery. From the 2001 report by Yale graduate students, *Yale, Slavery, and Abolition*, to Brown University's 2006 report *Slavery and Justice* written by James T. Campbell, Sven Beckert's and Katherine Stevens' work on Harvard, and Craig Wilder's *Ebony and Ivy*, the literature has largely dealt with northern schools, where there are connections to antislavery and pro-slavery thought.[54] I join scholars such as Peter Carmichael and Michael Sugrue who have looked at the pre–Civil War southern academy.[55] By focusing on the South, my data reveals a more ardently pro-slavery story in many cases than we have seen by looking at northern schools. I am more focused on the ideology of slavery in the college classroom and in the minds of college faculty than much of the previous work. And part of my theme is the way that self-interest bent the scholarship that faculty produced. That is, that "truth" as southern professors understood it was influenced by the economic and social interests of their culture.

Second, and closely related to the first goal, I hope this contributes to our understanding of the growing strength of pro-slavery thought and to how it drew upon history, economics, philosophy, and law. That is, this is part of the literature on the intellectual history of the old South.[56] In particular Sarah Nelson Roth has portrayed the shifting focus from the benefits of slavery for white people to the supposed benefits for the enslaved, as pro-slavery writers responded to the abolitionists' critique of slavery. Moreover, the actors here reveal that the pro-slavery arguments were wielded by people at the center of southern society, such as judges, not just intellectuals at the margins.[57]

Third, this speaks to the literature on the relationship between capitalism and slavery. A vibrant debate among historians asks about the nature of the relationship between antislavery and the market. Many point out that the market (capitalism) grew in conjunction with antislavery sentiments.[58] There is much to be said for this, as Ralph Waldo Emerson recognized in his "Young American Address." "The philosopher and lover of man have much harm to say of trade," Emerson acknowledged, "but the historian will see that trade was the principle of Liberty; that trade planted America and destroyed Feudalism; that it makes peace and keeps peace, and it will abolish slavery."[59] While historians have written about how capitalism led to antislavery sentiments, they have devoted less attention to how it led to the growth of pro-slavery sentiments in the South. For the market also correlated in the South with pro-slavery values. Property and slavery were closely allied in southern legal thought, and southern lawyers mobilized to protect each. Where historians like Elizabeth Fox-Genovese and Eugene Genovese have depicted slavery as in some ways anticapitalist or anti-market, the subjects here reveal pro-slavery thinkers to be engaged in important ways in the market and as people looking to promote economic growth.[60] This interpretation fits well with the recent literature on modernity and economy in the old South.[61]

Fourth, I hope it will contribute to work on legal history by providing a detailed examination of the role of economic and empirical thought in the judiciary in the old South and also by exploring how judges drew upon and then contributed to pro-slavery arguments. For several decades, since the publication of Morton Horwitz's *Transformation of American Law, 1780–1860* in 1977, legal historians have seen law as an instrument of economic development. This study draws upon Horwitz and the many articles and books focused on the South since his publication to further depict the role of economic thought in the southern judiciary.[62] There was a struggle over the meaning of the rule of law and the place of violence among southern judges. Judges who allowed slave owners to use extraordinary violence clashed with those who wanted the legal system to impose restrictions on the violence. There were also conflicts over the role of sympathy for the enslaved and the cold calculations of economics and legal precedent.[63] Thus, I hope this will help us better understand the nature of jurisprudence in the old South and perhaps even the origins of the late nineteenth-century turn to history and empiricism. I also hope it will show how the cultural ideas about slavery supported southern constitutional arguments. That is, the social movement supporting slavery bolstered southern constitutional interpretations. The book suggests that the judges' concern with utility and history further supported the steps taken by other Southerners that defended slavery. As academics and judges justified slavery, they supported a system of property, bondage, and violence. I hope this book will help us understand better how such ideas functioned and how they contributed to the enslavement of millions and then impelled slave owners toward the war that led to freedom.

PART I

THE CONTOURS OF ACADEMIC
PRO-SLAVERY THOUGHT

The violence of Nat Turner's rebellion in late August 1831 in Southampton County, Virginia, set in motion serious discussion in the Virginia legislature about the evils and benefits of slavery. One prominent response was a pro-slavery pamphlet by Professor Thomas R. Dew from William and Mary. It argued that slavery was nearly ubiquitous in human history, that it was central to Virginia's economy, and that emancipation was impractical.

The academics who expanded on those arguments appear in chapter 2. At the University of Virginia, for instance, Professor James Holcombe thought because slavery and hierarchy were so pervasive in human history that natural law supported slavery. While some continued to argue that slavery made republican government possible by making white people independent and equal, academics in the 1840s and 1850s more often turned to the supposed benefits of slavery to the enslaved. The enslaved were only fit for slavery, and slaves were treated no worse than many free people, so the arguments went. Considerations of economic necessity, history, and property rights combined to support slavery.

Colleges justified themselves in part because they provided support for slavery. They did this not just in the classroom; students rehearsed the moral and economic arguments supporting slavery in their literary societies. Visiting dignitaries who spoke on campus, who were often judges, lawyers, or politicians, made similar and sometimes more extreme claims. They often had a political theory of hierarchy, which countered Jefferson's

Declaration of Independence and concluded that people were not equal and that some should labor for others.

But in some places, such as Brown University, a few academics challenged slavery and told individuals that they had to abide their conscience rather than just saying that economy or law supported slavery. At the University of Mississippi, a northern-educated academic, F. A. P. Barnard, expelled a student who abused one of his slaves and then stood up to charges that he had offended southern morals by taking the testimony of a slave against a white person.

Pro-slavery academics put considerations of economy and utility at the center of their arguments. They advanced a natural law argument and a political theory supporting slavery. Their abstract theories rarely looked at the inhumanity of slavery. These ideas, so difficult for us to understand because they are so wildly different from our world, reveal the intellectual world of the old South.

1

The Rebel and the Professor

Nat Turner, Thomas Roderick Dew, and the Utility of Slavery

Before the rebellion, there was a law. It was designed to stop black people from learning about the ideas of freedom. And before that law, there was a book. David Walker's *Appeal to the Colored People of the World,* published in 1829, set the stage for revolution. The Virginia legislature, fearing the ideas of revolution loosed by antislavery books like Walker's, made it a crime in April 1831 for free black people to teach other free black people to read.[1] But by 1831 the ideas of freedom were already too powerful to be constrained much longer. The progressive spirit of the age, the Declaration of Independence, Walker's *Appeal,* and other antislavery writings, such as Robert Alexander Young's *Ethiopian Manifesto,* invited an inquiry into slavery. Events such as the revolution in Haiti that ended slavery there served as tangible lessons in the possibilities of freedom. Perhaps, too, some basic principle, like the innate desire of humans for freedom, motivated Nat Turner's rebellion in August 1831. Whatever its origins, what followed the rebellion was a discussion in the Virginia legislature about what to do, followed by a renewed defense of slavery, formulated by a man who used his pulpit at one of the great Virginia colleges to develop a sustained defense of slavery.

Of the 16,000 people who lived in Southampton County in 1830, nearly 8,000 were enslaved.[2] Turner, a preacher and a worker on a plantation, was one of them. He had been planning rebellion for some time, perhaps years.[3] His plans first came to light at the end of August after he and six other men gathered at a millpond near Turner's home on the evening of Sunday, August 21.[4] The rebels began by killing the family that owned Turner: James Travis, and Travis' wife and three children, including Putnam Moore, in the early morning of August 22, 1831. They ransacked the house, took weapons, gun power, ammunition, and horses. Then they moved on to the homes of Salathiel Francis, where they killed him, and Piety Reese, where they killed her, her son, and an overseer. The rebels picked up a few supporters and coerced a few others to join them as they moved through the night. They reached Elizabeth Turner's house around dawn, where they killed Turner, her sister, and the overseer Hartwell Peebles.[5]

By around nine in the morning, the alarm was already spreading, though the killing continued. They went to other farms, including to Levi Waller's estate, where they killed Mrs. Waller and eleven or so children. Close to noontime they reached Rebecca Vaughn's house, where they killed her, her niece, and her son. That was the rebels' last killing.[6] The remaining killings were of rebels and those suspected of cooperating with them.

Turner's initial plan seems to have been to travel a few miles east from Travis' house to the town of Jerusalem. Moving from Vaughn's house east toward Jerusalem, they met a band of mounted militia; there was an exchange of gunfire near the property of James W. Parker, who served as a judge at the trials of some of the rebels. Some rebels were killed there and nearby.[7] The rebellion was losing steam, and rebels were deserting the cause.[8]

Turner and his army could not go directly to Jerusalem, for the road to it was heavily fortified by this point. So the rebels then headed a bit south, toward a cypress bridge that crossed the Meharrin River. The bridge offered another way to town. But that, too, was guarded. Turner's band moved on . . . to find more deserted farmhouses. Turner turned back in the direction of the Travis farm where the rebellion had started less than twenty-four hours before. His group had made something of a circle. The rebels spent the night near the slave quarters of Major Thomas Ridley, who owned around eighty people. Perhaps the rebels hoped to recruit from Ridley's slaves. Instead, throughout the night more supporters deserted the cause.[9]

Meanwhile, militia companies poured in from the surrounding counties. A company of dragoons rode the sixty miles from Richmond. Dispatched on Monday evening, they arrived late Monday night. The options for Turner's army were thinning, as the militia companies pursued them. They met in brief battle on Tuesday morning, not far from where the rebellion began, at the estate of Dr. Blount, where Blount and his son (who later received an appointment to the Naval Academy for his actions), assisted by several slaves, fought back. Semicredible estimates put their size at around twenty by the time of this final battle. Several were seriously wounded and captured.[10] The rebels were dispersed; throughout the day others were captured or killed, though Turner escaped with a few loyal followers. Turner gave orders to them to go out, raise what forces they could, and reconvene at the millpond where the rebellion began less than two days before. None ever showed up.[11] The rebellion was over. The torture and killing of enslaved people was just beginning. As militia companies poured into Southampton from neighboring counties, they rounded up enslaved people and tortured them. The head of one was stuck on a poll, left as a grim reminder of the fate of the rebellion and the swiftness and the power of the state to respond.[12]

There is still a road in Southampton County called "Blackhead Signpost Road" as enduring evidence of the aftermath of the rebellion.

The rebellion was bloody, to be sure. About sixty white people were killed. So was its aftermath. Perhaps a dozen slaves and free blacks were killed during the rebellion and its immediate aftermath. Others stood trial before a court called just for the purpose of hearing their cases in Southampton County where the rebellion took place. The Southampton court heard about fifty cases from September through November. Thirty-one slaves were convicted and sentenced to death; ten of those had their sentences commuted to transportation out of the state. Nearly a dozen were tried in neighboring Sussex County, and a few others were tried in other counties in Virginia.[13]

The trials reveal disputes within the white community about how many people were culpable, whom to blame, and the amount of violence necessary to restore the pro-slavery order. A few were acquitted, and a few others had their cases dismissed before trial. The trial records are sparse, though the proceedings must have been brief, because frequently several people were tried each day.[14]

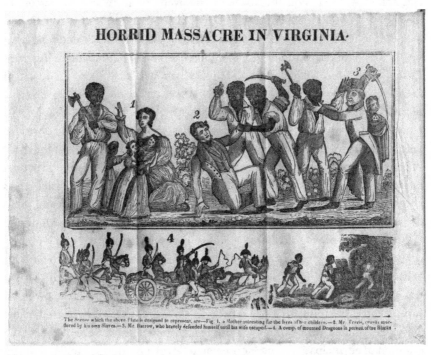

Illustration 1.1 "Horrid Massacre in Virginia." Samuel Warner's *Authentic and Impartial Narrative of the Tragical Scene which was Witnessed in Southampton County (Virginia) on Monday the 22d of August last, when fifty-five of its Inhabitants (Mostly Women and Children) were Inhumanely Massacred* by *the Blacks!* (New York, Warner & West 1831) (UNC Library). Warner's *Narrative* was one of the first pamphlets about the rebellion.

Meanwhile, Turner eluded capture until October, when he, too, was caught and tried by the special court assembled to hear the cases of the rebels. Before his trial he gave a statement to a local attorney, Thomas R. Gray, who had defended some of the other slaves. Turner was convicted and sentenced to death on November 3 and executed on November 11, 1831. Shortly afterward, Gray published the statement in a short pamphlet called the *Confessions of Nat Turner*.[15]

Turner's rebellion led to much violence and sparked something more unusual: a serious discussion in Virginia about the institution of slavery. Virginians petitioned the legislature to do something. Some used Revolutionary era rhetoric about natural liberty to advocate freedom; others urged colonization of free blacks; yet others urged more control of slaves.[16] By early December, at the opening of the legislature's session, Governor Floyd pressed further action. The legislature's House of Delegates appointed a Select Committee to investigate appropriate responses, which ranged from stricter regulation of slaves, to increased military preparations to deter and put down future rebellions, to removal and colonization of free blacks. But it soon appeared that some wanted the legislature to go further.

Just how far those proposals might go became apparent on Wednesday, December 14, 1831. William Roane of Hanover County, where 57 percent of the county's 16,000 inhabitants were slaves in 1830, introduced two petitions, including one from a meeting of Friends (Quakers). The Friends' petition sought a plan for the "ultimate manumission of the slave population of Virginia." Roane came from a distinguished Virginia family. He was the grandson of Patrick Henry and the son of jurist William Spencer Roane, a leading advocate of states rights. He was no abolitionist. Shortly Roane would tell the Virginia House of Delegates how important slavery was; in fact, in January he observed that "history, experience, observation, and reason have taught me, that the torch of liberty has ever burnt brightest when surrounded by the dark and filthy, yet nutritious atmosphere of slavery."[17] But at this stage, he told the delegates it was necessary to listen to debate, so that legislators might "catch the ideas and views of the citizens of the various parts of the state."[18] This brought an objection from William Goode of Mecklenburg, a county near Southampton. Nearly 60 percent of Mecklenburg County's 20,000 residents were slaves in 1830, so Goode's constituents had much at stake in these debates. Goode, who was born in 1798, was an 1819 graduate of William and Mary and also a lawyer and the owner of seven people. He thought that the petition should not even be referred to the Select Committee, for he thought that the Committee should not deal with the question of emancipation. The House voted down a motion, 27 to 93, to reject the Friends' petition.[19] The debate was coming. Sandwiched between the reading of the Friends' petition in December and the final votes in March on a bill restricting the rights of Virginia's African Americans, both free and enslaved, was a remarkable debate.

The Virginia Legislature's Slavery Debate, January to March 1832

The public debate began, perhaps somewhat perversely, with someone who wanted it not to begin at all. William Goode rose and asked that the House of Delegates instruct the Select Committee to hear no more petitions. Although he had already lost a December motion to deny the Quaker petition, on January 11 Goode proposed to end the Select Committee's consideration of petitions regarding emancipation. In essence, Goode's motion would have ended discussion of emancipation.

The legislature's response was mixed. In the case of Goode's motion, like much of the rest of the debate, the responses of legislators divided, more or less, along the geographic lines of the state. There were four key areas of Virginia.[20] The rich agricultural land of the coast, called the Tidewater area because it was below the fall line of Virginia's many rivers, had many of the slaveowners and the slaves, too, of course. Next further inland is the Piedmont, also an area with many slaves; then the Blue Ridge Mountains and the adjacent Shenandoah Valley. Beyond the Valley was the Trans-Allegheny region. Slaves were much rarer in the Valley and the Trans-Allegheny, for reasons of culture and economy, than in the Piedmont and Tidewater. Thus, during the Civil War the western part of the state split off and stayed with the Union; that region is now the state of West Virginia. In the Tidewater and Piedmont, slaveowners and their interests largely predominated. In the Valley and Trans-Allegheny, antislavery interests predominated. It was mostly from the Valley and portions of the Piedmont that the moderate, swing delegates came. Goode represented the Tidewater, and he behaved as one would predict.

The antislavery advocates took Goode's resolution trying to cut off further debate as the opening for their response. Samuel McDowell Moore of Rockbridge County, across the Blue Ridge Mountains, a county where fewer than one in four of their 12,000 residents were slaves, was the first to speak in response. Moore had been born in Philadelphia, Pennsylvania, in 1796, then grew up in the Shenandoah Valley; he attended Washington College in Lexington, Virginia, a school that benefited from slavery but also maintained an antislavery bent into the 1840s.[21]

Moore was well schooled in a common argument against slavery: it corrupted slaves because to maintain obedience, masters had to promote slaves' ignorance. While he acknowledged that there might be a justification for slavery and that some slaves might have better lives than free workers, Moore called upon the rhetoric of natural rights: "That all men are by nature free and equal." And he concluded that "slavery is at best but an intolerable evil, and can never be submitted to, except from stern necessity." He resisted the calculations of utility of slavery so effectively employed by the pro-slavery forces. "Liberty is too dear to the heart of man, ever to be given up for any earthly consideration."[22]

That set the stage for the most promising actions of the antislavery forces. Thomas Jefferson Randolph, grandson of Thomas Jefferson, sought to encourage more debate and, perhaps, even some concrete action. Randolph, who was born in 1796, and was educated at the University of Pennsylvania and in Richmond, was more than just Jefferson's grandson; he was the executor of Jefferson's estate and protector of Jefferson's memory. Randolph published a collection of Jefferson's writings in 1830, four years after Jefferson's death. Randolph represented Jefferson's home county of Albemarle, where slightly over half the residents in 1830 were enslaved.

Jefferson's antislavery reputation has been tarnished in the early years of the twenty-first century, in part because of the children he almost certainly had with Sally Hemmings (though the exact nature of his relationship with Sally Hemmings is open to interpretation),[23] and because he failed to be aggressive in freeing slaves using money left by the Revolutionary War hero and Polish patriot Tadeusz Kosciuszko.[24] However, in the 1830s, Jefferson's legacy was more antislavery than those of many others in Virginia. On Wednesday, January 11, in place of Goode's resolution to cut off debate, Thomas Jefferson Randolph advance a counterproposal.[25] He proposed that children born on or after July 4, 1840, be freed upon reaching the age of majority and then transported to Africa, unless their owner had sold them to another state before then. Hope, however feeble, was on the way.[26]

The pro-slavery position was defended the next day by James Gholson of Brunswick County, near Southampton County. More than 60 percent of Brunswick County residents in 1830 were enslaved. Gholson was born in Brunswick County in 1798 and graduated from Princeton in 1820. Gholson responded to Moore's invocation of natural rights with legal doctrine and political philosophy. While reformers spoke about natural rights, Gholson thought those natural rights were insufficient to settle the right of slaves to freedom. While Samuel Moore believed "new lights"—Enlightenment ideas—should guide the state, Gholson mocked such ideas of new lights: "I have heard of these lights before, but I have looked for them in vain—I have never seen them. The wretched and misguided fanatic, who excited the horrors of the late Southampton massacre, thought he saw them. It proved, however, an elusive meteor." New lights led to the revolution in France and the revolution in Haiti.[27] In the United States, moreover, the "Northern lights" were abolitionist pamphlets. Yet, those abolitionist ideas were breaking apart government. If the legislature followed Moore's lead, Gholson ominously concluded, "the bands which bind society together would at once dissolve—the relations of husband and wife, parent and child, master and apprentice, and even our present deliberations would be 'most strange and unnatural.' "[28]

Gholson thought that it better to go by long-standing principles and look to what was practical. Property rights were central to his argument. Indeed, he thought the owners' rights absolutely dispositive. He dismissed appeals to policy. People "in pursuit of their favorite theory, have adventured on the boundless ocean of *policy*, expediency, and even *speculation* and as they have taken along with them on board, my rights and my property, I hope I shall be excused if I pursue them, though the sea is rough and the voyage dangerous." For Gholson believed that property rights were a key foundation of society. "This sacred principle of meum and tuem does not derive its sanctions from conventional charters–it has its foundations laid deep in principles of justice—it is the very ligament which binds society together. . . . Without this principle, there is no civilization—no government."[29] Yet, the legislature threatened the sacred and long-standing rights of property on the basis of claims of necessity. Gholson found such justifications hollow:

> Gentlemen, in the heat of their own intemperance, and by the aid of their own disturbed and distempered fancies, raise spirits and spectres at pleasure—gaze at them with horror, and then set about to show their skill in exorcism. These spirits and spectres they call "necessity," "self-preservation," "public safety." The exorcism is the simple process of taking eighty or one-hundred millions of private property for public use, without compensation.[30]

But there was not such necessity. Slavery did not threaten the safety of Virginians.[31] Gholson drew on long-standing and widely dispersed arguments in favor of slavery as a stabilizer of society. The argument looked to history and contemporary society to see the dangers of reform. History and property held sway.

Though some, like Samuel Moore, attacked the evils of slavery "and the abstract questions of piety, justice, and morality," Gholson saw little purpose in debating abstract issues of natural rights or the justification of slavery in the abstract. "It is as unkind as it is unjust to reproach a generation for misfortunes transmitted to her by generations before her and from which no exertion of hers could relieve her."[32] Instead, he thought that slaves were treated well, certainly better than the serfs of Europe and Northern workers. He also questioned the argument that slavery injured slave owners' morality.[33] Gholson's defense of slavery was based on practicality, and he thought further discussion was counterproductive. In short, "with the indiscretion of children, we are playing with torches and fire-brands, either regardless or forgetful that magazines are under and around us."[34] From the speeches in the legislature and from the writings of academics and later judges, we learn they believed that they could not escape their world as it was ordered nor would many want to even if they could. Some saw the difficulty of escaping from the world of slavery. Yet other legislators abandoned talk of the evils of slavery in favor of a view that slavery was, indeed, best.

One individual who feared the effects of reform was Thomas Marshall of Fauquier County, born in 1801. Marshall was a graduate of Princeton, a lawyer, and the son of the Chief Justice of the United States, John Marshall. The 31-year-old Marshall represented a northern Virginia county, nearly half of whose population of 26,000 people (48%) was enslaved. He was one of the moderate antislavery advocates; moderate in that he voted against Goode's proposal to discharge the petitions.[35] Yet he saw problems with emancipation. Compensation would be due to slaveowners for anyone emancipated, even those not yet born. By way of analogy, Marshall asked whether the legislature could take a farmer's interest in crops not yet planted. Could the legislature decree that the grain of next year's harvest be seized by the state without compensation? No, was the conclusion. The only grounds for seizure was stern public necessity. "Whenever the tranquility and security of society shall imperiously demand this sacrifice, the rights of property must yield to the preservation of happiness and life; but still it is a sacrifice, and one for which compensation should be made."[36] Marshall devoted most of his speech to arguing that colonization was practical.

As the positions for and against slavery were developed, the proposals in the legislature multiplied. On January 16, Henry Brodnax, the chair of the Select Committee, reported its resolution that it was "inexpedient for the present to make any legislative enactments for the abolition of slavery." Brodnax's resolution brought a counterproposal from William Preston of Montgomery in the Trans-Allegheny (in current day West Virginia), where about 16 percent of the 1830 population was enslaved. He was an 1824 graduate of Hampden-Sydney College and a lawyer, trained at the University of Virginia. Preston moved that the Committee's report be changed to read that it was expedient to consider legislative action on emancipation. There were a lot of proposals in front of the legislature. To help keep them straight, Table 1.1 summarizes them and provides information on their ultimate disposition in the House of Delegates. The members of the House of Delegates discussed their views of slavery and the merits of a gradual abolition plan, and their debates, published in the pages of Richmond's newspapers, provided the spectrum of ideas on the morality and utility of slavery.

Thomas Jefferson Randolph rose to defend the proposal of gradual emancipation and also Thomas Jefferson's image as an antislavery advocate on January 20. Where some had interpreted Jefferson as recognizing and thus protecting slave property, or realized that the practical part of Jefferson ended up supporting slavery, Randolph wanted, then, to preserve the antislavery legacy of his grandfather. Randolph read much of Jefferson's 1814 letter to Edward Coles

Table 1.1 **Proposals Regarding Slaves and Free Black People in the Virginia House of Delegates, 1831–1833**

Date	Proponent and Proposal	Outcome, Citation
12/14/31	Goode's motion to table Charles City Quaker petition	Defeated 27–93, JHD 29
1/25/32	Witcher's motion to indefinitely postpone	Defeated 60–71, JHD 109
1/25/32	Preston's motion that emancipation action is expedient	Defeated 58–73, JHD 109
1/25/32	Bryce's motion to append acknowledge evil of slavery to Select Committee report	Passed 67–60, JHD 110
1/25/32	Select Committee report that emancipation action is inexpedient, including Bryce addition	Passed 65–58, JHD 110
2/6/32	Morris' motion to postpone Bryce's amendment for the deportation of people emancipated after 1806	Defeated 28–94, JHD 134-35
2/7/32	Bryce's proposal requiring deportation of persons "who may become free" and those already free	Defeated 49–77, JHD 136[136]
2/7/32	Campbell's motion to fund only voluntary colonization	Passed 71–54, JHD 136-37
2/15/32	Brown's proposal to limit funding for colonization to people already free	Defeated 41–60, JHD 157[137]
2/16/32	Funding for voluntary colonization of "free persons of colour" and newly manumitted slaves	Passed 79–41, JHD 158
2/27/32	Increased restrictions on slaves and free black people (final Senate approval of House's amendments on 3/15/32, JHD 235)	Passed 79–36, JHD 187-88
2/28/32	Funding Northampton County up to $15,000 for the removal of "free coloureds"	Passed with no roll call, JHD 189
2/27/33	1833 Funding for transportation of qualifying "freed coloureds" (1832–1833 JHD at 227–28).	Passed 68–51

Note: JDH is the Journal of the House of Delegates

that warned, among other things, of the potential for slave rebellion. The letter, though, was more optimistic. It played little on fear and much on emotion. One of the last lines was "[i]t is an encouraging observation that no good measure was ever proposed, which, if duly pursued, failed to prevail in the end."[37]

During the debates, the status of humans as property took center stage. Slave owners spoke of their rights to their human property. Where Thomas Jefferson Randolph had argued for emancipation of slaves born after July 4, 1840, James Bruce of Halifax thought the legislature had no right to take away enslaved property, whether born already or years in the future. Bruce, who graduated from the University of North Carolina in 1822, was later one of the wealthiest people in Virginia. He built the extraordinary Greek-Revival plantation home of Berry Hill in Halifax and spoke widely on the cause of reform. Bruce was a staunch defender of property rights. As property was being unsettled, Virginians' society was threatened, too.[38]

Many reformers responded to the argument that the state could not interfere with property in slaves. They believed that property in humans was not entitled to protection. Charles Faulkner, a lawyer from Martinsberg in Berkeley County (in what is now West Virginia), where fewer than one in five of the 10,000 residents were enslaved in 1830, advanced one of the strongest critiques of the slaves-as-property theme. Faulkner posited that "property is the creature of civil society"; thus property rights were dependent on their surrounding community. Slave owners "hold their slaves—not by any law of nature—not by any patent from God . . .—but solely by the acquiescence and consent of the society in which they live. . . . Private rights and individual claims must yield to the over-ruling and paramount interests of the common weal." This was radical doctrine, which denied the natural rights of property and instead placed them in the context in which they arose. It contained the seeds of a radical critique of property and threatened to displace owners' rights to their human property. The next step was to investigate whether the Virginia community should continue to recognize those rights in human property. Faulkner employed an analogy to nuisance law to make his case that slavery could be eliminated without compensation.[39]

Resolving the Issues

The extensive debate came to a focal point on January 25, 1832. There were votes on four key issues that day (see Table 1.1). The day began when William Preston proposed a direct alternative to the Select Committee's report, which stated "it is inexpedient, for the present, to make any legislative enactment for the abolition of slavery." Preston's proposal was that "it is expedient to adopt some legislative enactments for the abolition of slavery." The introduction of Preston's antislavery alternative led Vincent Witcher of Pittsylvania County to move that the legislature postpone all further action on the Select Committee's report. Witcher's proposal was defeated by 60 to 71. Debate could go forward, but it would not go far.[40]

Following the defeat of Witcher's motion to postpone, the House of Delegates voted on Preston's motion that it would be expedient to take further action on emancipation. That proposal was also defeated, 58 to 73. This illustrated the de-cided opinion of the legislators that they were against emancipation legislation now. That was the most radical antislavery proposition that was voted on, for Randolph's gradual abolition plan never came to a vote. The vote on Preston's motion reveals that a significant minority of legislators were in favor of further emancipation talk.

Then followed a third vote, a resolution by Archibald Bryce to append to the Select Committee's report a statement that recognized the great evils of slavery, but said that there should be no immediate action. Bryce's proposal read:

> Profoundly sensible of the great evils arising from the condition of the coloured population of this commonwealth; induced by humanity, as well as policy, to an immediate effort for the removal in the first place, as well of those who are now free, as of such as may hereafter become free; believing that this effort, while it is in just accordance with the sentiment of the community on the subject, will absorb all our present means; and that a further action for the removal of the slaves should await a more definite development of public opinion.[41]

Bryce's proposed amendment passed, 67 to 60. This was moderately antislav-ery in that it recognized the evils of slavery; however, it delayed action and so might be opposed by those who wanted something more immediate. Bryce's amendment, thus, pointed in two directions, as did much of southern thought on slavery at the time—both toward an awareness of the evils of the institution and an awareness of the difficulty, perhaps even impossibility, of doing anything significant about it at the moment.

The fourth and final vote, which also pointed in two directions, on January 25, was on the adoption of the Select Committee's report. Voting in favor of the report signaled that slavery was evil; yet, at the same time, the report concluded that any action to curb or end it was currently inexpedient. It is difficult to in-terpret because, like much legislation, it was a compromise. It passed, 65 to 58. Some solidly pro-slavery representatives voted against the bill. It is likely they found the idea of moral condemnation difficult.[42]

Though dealt some setbacks, for sure, the antislavery side was optimistic. Reformers usually are. Thomas Jefferson Randolph wrote to his wife claiming the movement had gone forward and would not go back.[43] Yet, despite Randolph's optimism, January 25, 1832, was the high watermark of the antislavery move-ment in that session of the legislature. In fact, it was the high watermark in the Virginia legislature for decades.

It was not, however, the end of the legislature's debate for the year. Having decided to not act on emancipation, there were still some plans to consider

regarding colonization and other measures to prevent more outbreaks of violence. William Henry Brodnax proposed compulsory colonization of Virginia's
free black population. Brodnax thought that free people would not leave the state
voluntarily, so they ought to be forced to do so. He referred to a Baltimore meeting in 1831 of free blacks who opposed emigration and asked others to not go,
which testifies to how white Southerners paid attention to the writings of black
people about slavery and freedom.[44] Thomas Marshall, as mentioned, the son of
the U.S. Supreme Court Chief Justice, spoke against Brodnax's plan; he thought
it would inhumanely separate Virginia's black population from their homes.[45]

On February 6, Isaac Morris of Wood County in the Trans-Alleghany, where
less than 15 percent of the nearly 7,000 residents were slaves, proposed to indefinitely postpone further discussion on the colonization proposal. Morris' motion
failed by a vote of 27 to 94.[46] That led to a vote the next day on a bill by Archibald
Bryce. Bryce's proposal was to deport even people who were already free, as well
as those who were freed in the future. A more moderate proposal came from
John C. Campbell of the Trans-Alleghany Brooke County, where only 3 percent
of the nearly 7,000 residents were enslaved. Campbell softened Bryce's proposal
to allow those who had been freed—even if they had been freed after 1806 and
thus were in Virginia illegally—to choose whether they wanted to emigrate. It
passed 71 to 54.[47]

By the end of the February, then, what had begun in the legislature as a discussion
of gradual emancipation became a plan for deportation of free African Americans.
Yet, that resolution was indefinitely postponed in the Senate. The colonization bill
never became law. There were, however, two final proposals, which became law. The
first, identified in Table 1.1 as the "compromise bill," restricted the rights of both free
blacks and slaves. The Act, which passed the House 79 to 36 on February 27,[48] prohibited slaves and free black people from preaching, restricted the publication and
circulation of antislavery literature, disallowed free blacks from owning or possessing
firearms, prohibited free blacks from purchasing slaves (other than family members),
and moved criminal cases involving free blacks from the county courts to special
courts, known as oyer and terminer, just like the ones that tried the slaves following
the Nat Turner rebellion. But the Act was careful to protect the rights of slave owners
to give religious instruction to their slaves and to bring their slaves to religious worship. The boundaries between religious instruction and insurrection were hazy, and
likely to shift over time. A second act provided $15,000 to remove free black people
from Northampton County, on Virginia's eastern shore, which passed on March 5.[49]
What had begun as a discussion of emancipation ended with the shackles fastened
harder on slaves.

The legislators' votes reveal a close—even if unsurprising—connection between the presence of slaves in a legislator's county and his voting. Generally,
legislators from the more heavily enslaved counties were more likely to vote in

a pro-slavery direction than those from counties with fewer slaves. They voted to end debate, that taking action was inexpedient, that free blacks should be coerced to leave the state, and that restrictions on free African Americans and slaves should be increased. This appears in Table 1.2, which reports the correlations between percentage enslaved population in delegates' home counties, the number of slaves that delegates owned, and the percentage of the free African American

Table 1.2 **Point-biserial Correlations of Delegates Votes with Percent Enslaved Population in Delegates' Home County, Delegates' Slaves, and Percent Free Black People in Delegates' Home County**

Vote	Enslaved Population		Delegates' Slaves			% Free Black People		
	r	N	r	N	P	r	N	P
Quaker petition	.37	117	.22	110	.02	−.05	117	.58
Indefinitely postpone (Witcher)	.69	127	.39	123	.00	.30	127	.001
Preston amendment (immediate action)	−.78	127	−.43	123	.00	−.39	127	.0000
Bryce preamble ("great evils," of slavery, but no immediate action)	−.69	124	−.43	120	.00	−.25	124	.01
Overall report	−.67	120	−.37	116	.00	−.24	120	.01
Campbell colonization amendment	−.43	121	−.21	116	.03	−.21	121	.0002
Colonization final bill	.38	116	.19	111	.04	.41	116	.0000
Consolidated restrictions	.65	112	.34	108	.00	.34	112	.0002

The 1830 Census surveyed the 108 counties (five were "cities") in the Commonwealth at that time. Twenty-eight counties were each represented by two delegates, and Frederick and Loudoun Counties were each represented by three delegates. Seventy-one counties had only one delegate. This analysis excluded four cases because population data were not available for a delegate's county (or for one of his counties when he represented more than one). The excluded cases were Jacob Helms of Floyd County, where there was no county data; William M. Robertson of Page County, where there was no county data; Nehemiah Smith of Mason and Jackson Counties, where there was no data for Jackson County; and John Stephenson, of Nicholas and Fayette Counties, where there was no data for Fayette County.

There are five cases in which a delegate represented two counties. For those counties, I used a weighted average of the slave and free populations to construct a measure of the percentage enslaved in the delegate's home counties. The delegates are James D. Halyburton of Charles City and New Kent; Alexander Jones of Elizabeth City and Warwick; Houlder Hudgins of Mathews and Middlesex; Robert W. Carter of Lancaster and Richmond; and Robert Shield of York and James City. (Williamsburg was enumerated with James City in the 1830 Census.)

population in the delegates' home counties, and their votes on several key measures. They generally reveal a significant correlation between votes and the presence of slaves in a delegate's home county and the delegate's personal ownership of slaves. Yet, the correlations between percent enslaved population and voting is not perfect. Therein lies a very important lesson about interests and ideology. That lesson is critical to legal history, where judges filter the values of the surrounding culture through the prism of legal doctrine and where they often arrive at results that are at odds with what a bare analysis of interests would dictate.

The stark reality of economic interest and support for slavery explains a great deal about the ideology of slavery in the years leading to Civil War. And it is that ideology and the way that ideology appeared in the judiciary that is the subject of much of the rest of this book. We return often to this question of how ideology (and later in this book, legal doctrine) and economic interest interact. It is the story of law often bent in a pro-slavery direction.

Interpreting the Debate

The legislative debates were over, but the debate was still going on for several months in the Virginia newspapers. Benjamin Watkins Leigh, who was not in the legislature, contributed two letters about the debate to the *Richmond Enquirer*. Leigh, who published his letters using the pseudonym Appomattox, graduated from William and Mary in 1802 and then studied law in Petersburg and practiced there.[50] He defended property in slaves. Leigh's argument was at once a statement about the importance of property and a statement that those who did not own slaves should not be passing laws for those who owned slaves. And in response to assertions that slavery should be terminated, Leigh thought that there were a few other things that should be done instead. First, maintain adequate slave patrols; second, go to the polls and vote for people who will stop talk of gradual emancipation; third, exercise coercion to stop talk of emancipation in the press and in public.[51] Later in life, while serving as a Whig in the U.S. Senate, Benjamin Watkins Leigh strenuously opposed further discussion of the abolition of slavery.[52]

Reformers were optimistic and held out hope for next year. Some correspondents in the Virginia newspapers supported their cause and responded to Leigh. For instance, one person under the pseudonym "Locke" argued in a series of letters that slavery could, legally, be ended by the legislature without compensation.[53] But the status quo rarely gives up on an idea until time has thoroughly passed it by. And in 1832 slavery was still a viable idea among many white southerners—and northerners, for that matter. It was not long before the conservative response took hold. In the spring 1832 elections, Henry Bolling, who had the temerity to vote in favor of Preston's resolution declaring that emancipation legislation was expedient, was not returned to the House of Delegates. The voters of Bolling's county of Buckingham disapproved; 60 percent of their population of 18,300 was enslaved.[54] The great hope that 1833 would bring more antislavery action was not to be, either. By the spring of 1833, the nation was consumed with debates about South Carolina's plans for nullification—a refusal to follow the federal tariffs on South Carolina's agricultural products. Slavery lay close to the heart of that debate.

William and Mary Professor Thomas Dew Evaluates the Debate

Perhaps even more important than what the House voted on was the nature of the debate: What should be done about slavery? William and Mary Professor Thomas Dew responded to the debates with a book opposing abolition: *Review of the Debate in the Virginia Legislature of 1831 and 1832*.[55] Dew was born in 1802 in King and Queen County, Virginia, then educated at William and Mary beginning in 1818. Following his graduation with a master's degree, he spent several years studying in Europe. He returned home in 1826 and was appointed a professor at William and Mary, where he taught history and political economy.[56]

Dew's *Review* was an attack on the idea of abolition.[57] It was a book-length treatment of the history of slavery and a defense of its place in Virginia society. Dew helped end serious consideration of the viability and efficacy of termination of slavery. The *Review* was one of the leading pro-slavery works in the forty years leading into Civil War. The *Review* (also known as Dew's *Essay on Slavery*) was reprinted numerous times, including in 1849 as a freestanding pamphlet and again in the 1852 volume *The Pro-Slavery Argument*. But Dew did not live to see this success. He ascended to the presidency of William and Mary in 1836 and died, prematurely, while visiting France in 1846 on his honeymoon. Several years after his death, his lectures to his students at William and Mary were published under the title *A Digest of the Laws, Customs, Manners, and Institutions of the Ancient and Modern Nations*.[58] It stands as one of the most comprehensive interpretations of history in the entire nineteenth century.[59]

Dew's *Review of the Debates* gives us a window into Dew's mind and a sense of the pro-slavery ideas in circulation at William and Mary. William and Mary law professor Nathaniel Beverley Tucker told students that "[i]n this reading age . . . he who writes a people's books, need not care who makes their laws."[60] And in the years leading to the Civil War, Southerners frequently spoke of the need for southern literature, particularly in southern colleges. In 1850, John Thompson, editor of the *Southern Literary Messenger*, for instance, asked the literary societies of Washington College in Lexington, Virginia, for a southern literature "of our own, informed with the conservative spirit, the love of order and justice, that constitutes the most striking characteristic of the Southern mind."[61] Dew is proof of the utility of such literature and of the phenomenon that Tucker described.

Dew's essay harnessed fear of change, indeed the impracticality of change, along with a narrative of the benefits of slavery for the slave owners, non-slave-owners, and the slaves, too. We learn that slavery is central to America in the very first line: "In looking to the texture of the population of our country, there is nothing so well calculated to arrest the attention of the observer, as the existence of negro slavery throughout a large portion of the confederacy."[62]

Dew began his task by legitimizing slavery. He found the origins of slavery in response to war-conquered people who were enslaved rather than killed. And he even, surprisingly, invoked Voltaire. Though where Voltaire said "slavery is as ancient as war, and war as human nature," Dew thought Voltaire did not do slavery justice, "for many wars have been too cruel to admit of slavery."[63] In that way, slavery joined self-interest to help conquer the spirit of revenge. Thus, Dew found that slavery, even at its origins, was about civilization. "Slavery was established and sanctioned by divine authority," and its near universal nature are signs of its growth in conjunction with civilization.[64]

Dew began with an emphasis on "reason" (however much we may now see things differently). He tried to slow emancipation talk and action by simply noting that ending slavery would require enormous—and likely insurmount-able—effort. "The evil of yesterday's growth may be extirpated *today*, and the vigor of society may heal the wound; but that which is the growth of *ages*, may require *ages* to remove."[65] One only needed to look to the emancipation in Haiti to see the destruction that would come to the white community. Yet, he urged calm in response to Nat Turner's rebellion.[66] He asked for the return of the "empire of reason" to govern subsequent policy. Dew wrote of reason and math-ematical proofs. He concluded that emancipation was "*totally* impractical."[67] Impracticality ended debate and might have masked Dew's ideas about slavery.

But he thought emancipation plans would increase problems. "[T]he great question of abolition," Dew wrote, would come down to emancipation and whether, then, to allow newly freed people to stay in Virginia. "We think," he con-cluded, such a plan "can easily be shown to be utterly subversive of the interests, security and happiness of both the blacks and whites, and consequently, hostile to every principle of expediency, morality, and religion."[68] Because he thought that even discussion of such a plan was improvident, he avoided it "in conse-quence of the injurious effects which might be produced on the slave popula-tion." That is, Dew and others understood that the mere discussion of freedom might open the minds of enslaved people to the idea of freedom. And they could not run the risk of such possibilities. Yet, in the wake of the Virginia legislature's discussion, Dew turned to the question of abolition. He pushed aside prudential concerns against discussion of emancipation.[69] Dew invoked common phrases used against antislavery advocates. He spoke of their "misguided philanthropy" and then spoke of his own to look to calculations of "truth, justice and expediency." The rest of the essay was organized around three themes:

1. "The Origins of Slavery and Its Effects on Civilization"—by which Dew meant the multiple ways in which slavery was recognized throughout human history, how slavery was recognized by the Bible, and how slavery contributed to the growth of civilization.
2. "Plans for the Abolition of Negro Slavery," which was directed at demonstrating the impossibility of colonizing freed slaves.
3. "Injustice and Evils of Slavery," which Dew discussed in order to minimize them.[70]

Those components of the *Review* reveal Dew's mindset and the contributions he made to the cause of support for slavery—the origins of slavery and its effect on civilization, the impracticality of plans for abolition, and a critique of arguments on the evils and injustice of slavery.

1. Origins of Slavery and Its Effects on Civilization

Dew depicted slavery as a humane alternative to war and, indeed, as a civilizer itself. Slavery was, Dew declared, "the principal means for impelling forward the civilization of mankind."[71] Dew went on to establish the virtues of slavery in bringing about civilization. It led people to go from a state of hunter-gathers to farmers, for slavery

> necessarily leads on to the taming and rearing of numerous flocks, and to the cultivation of the soil. Hunting can never support slavery. Agriculture first suggests the notion of servitude, and, as often happens in the politico-economical world, the effect becomes, in turn, a powerfully operating cause. Slavery gradually fells the forest, and thereby destroys the haunts of the wild beasts; it gives rise to agricultural production, and thereby renders mankind less dependent on the precarious and diminishing production . . . it converts the idler and the wanderer into the man of business and the agriculturist.[72]

Thus, in his mind slavery brought about civilization. Dew even saw this among the Native Americans who adopted slavery. "What are the causes of this dawn of civilization among the Cherokees," he asked? The adoption of slavery, of course, which allowed the tribes to indulge what Dew thought was their natural laziness. It was an extraordinary acknowledgment of the benefits that slavery conferred on a people—the ability to have someone else labor for them. But here, as elsewhere, Dew cautioned against abstract theories of right or justice such as "all men are born equal," "slavery in the abstract is wrong," and "the slave has a natural right to regain his liberty." "No set of legislators ever have," he asserted, "or ever can, legislate upon purely abstract principles, entirely independent of circumstances, without the ruin of the body politic."[73] Such concern for the specific rather than the abstract was a hallmark of pro-slavery thought.

2. Plans for Abolition of Negro Slavery

Having spent much time discussing the benefits of slavery, Dew then turned to the impracticality of abolition. The property value amassed in human beings would not allow it. Virginia's 470,000 enslaved people were worth approximately $100,000,000 in 1832 dollars, which represented about one-third the state's wealth. Slavery was simply too important economically to contemplate its end. Some had proposed elaborate colonization schemes, but they were doomed to failure.[74] And if slaves were emancipated and sent away, there would be no one left to do the work of the laboring class.[75] Dew grimly concluded, after more pages of argument, "Virginia will be a desert."[76]

At this point, having established the practical reasons for the impossibility of abolition, Dew turned to the "most dangerous of all the wild doctrines advanced by abolitionists in the Virginia legislature": "*that property is the creature of civil society, and is subject to its action even to destruction.*"[77] By singling out the attack on property as the "most dangerous" of the abolitionists' arguments, Dew connected political theory regarding property in a concrete way to pro-slavery thought.

Dew was responding to antislavery delegates, such as James McDowell and Charles Faulkner, who argued that slavery was not constitutionally protected private property—the state could regulate or even abolish property rights regarding slaves.[78] The argument was a restatement of the common law doctrine that the state may regulate dangerous property, like gunpowder.[79] In this case, the analogy was that property in humans was dangerous to society and thus subject to extensive regulation.

Dew did not treat property rights so lightly. "The doctrine of these gentlemen," Dew thought, "so far from being true in its application, is not true in theory."[80] Property is the foundation of government, and the object of government is the protection of property.[81] Contemporaneous history supported Dew's argument. "There is not a government at this moment in Christendom, whose peculiar practical character is not the result of the state of property."[82] In Dew's view, it was property that preceded and created government, not the other way around.

"The great difficulty in forming the government of any country arises almost universally from the state of property, and the necessity of making it conform to that state."[83] As the recent state constitutional convention demonstrated, Virginia's government was constituted and affected by slavery.

Certainly, eminent domain might be used to take property for the "general weal." But that required, at least, just compensation, which the abolitionists in the Virginia legislature did not appear willing to pay. They reasoned that slave property was a nuisance, which should be abated without compensation. The common law reasoning of the abolitionists, Dew thought, was flawed. Despite their argument that a state could abate a nuisance, slaves were not nuisances, as their value in the marketplace was testified.[84] Dew concluded that the interests of all white Virginians were related to slave property. "All the great interests of society, are really interwoven with one another—they form an indissoluble chain; a blow at any part quickly vibrates through the whole length—the destruction of one interest involves another. Destroy agriculture, destroy tillage, and the ruin of the framer will draw down ruin upon the mechanic, the merchant, the sailor, and the manufacturer—they must all escape together from the land of desolation."[85]

Moreover, slaves were unfit for freedom, economically and morally.[86] Dew looked to other countries and times and determined that emancipation led to the degradation of blacks and whites. "It is easier to descend than ascend and nothing will prevent the *facilis descensus* but slavery."[87] And even the discussion of abolition would lead to further revolts. Dew did not believe they would be successful— "power can never be dislodged from the hands of the intelligent, the wealthy, and the courageous, by any plans that can be formed by the poor, the ignorant, and the habitually subservient; history scarce furnishes any example"—but revolts would lead to much bloodshed.[88] When Dew looked to the West Indies, he found that "the slave cannot be converted into free labor without imminent danger to the prosperity and wealth of the country where the changes take place."[89] And that in the aftermath of the French Revolution, as slavery was reasserted in some of the West Indies, "generally the re-establishment of slavery was attended with the most happy consequences, and even courted by the negroes themselves, who became heartily tired of their short-lived liberty."[90] While modern readers may see the linking of technological and economic progress with the institution of slavery as contradictory, it made sense to Dew. He linked progress, the market, and slavery because he thought that progress was made possible through respect for property.[91]

3. Evils and Injustice of Slavery

The final major section of Dew's *Review* returned to the topic of the supposed evils of slavery. Dew brought the argument back home, with the suggestion that slavery was not so bad. It was an attempt to minimize the problem. He looked to, for instance, Haiti where slaves had freed themselves in the 1790s, and he found the horrible destruction of slaveowners; but he also believed that freedom had not benefited the formerly enslaved: "The negroes have gained nothing by their bloody revolution."[92]

Thus, Dew formulated an important statement on the virtues of slavery. It was a bold account of the positive goods that sprung from slavery—there were benefits for the enslaved and the slaveowner, and he happily concluded that "we have no doubt but that [slaves] form the happiest portion of our society. A merrier being does not exist on the face of the globe, than the negro slave of the U. States."[93] This is likely a subtle response to a book that Dew dared not name: David Walker's *Appeal*. Walker wrote that there "are not a more wretched, ignorant, miserable, and abject set of beings in all the world, than the blacks in the Southern and Western sections of this country, under tyrants and devils."[94] Dew's language suggests that he was familiar with Walker's charge, and he turned it upside down. Up to the time of the Civil War, southern academics told themselves and their audiences that enslaved people were happy and that they should accept their lot— even as jurists like Thomas Ruffin of the North Carolina Supreme Court realized that few would accept their fate as slaves unless forced to.[95]

Why should there be this abolitionist agitation—this false philanthropy? Dew asked why abolitionists sought to disturb slavery.

> Why, then, since the slave is happy, and happiness is the great object of all animated creation, should we endeavor to disturb his contentment by infusing into his mind a vain and indefinite desire for liberty—a something which he cannot comprehend, and which must inevitably dry up the very sources of his happiness.[96]

More talk of abolition would just court further insurrections.[97] And that led Dew to state that he believed he had proven his case "almost as conclusive as the demonstrations of the mathematician . . . that the time for emancipation has not yet arrived, and perhaps it never will."[98] His final words in the *Review* were those of opposition to change: "Let us . . . learn wisdom from experience; and know that the relations of society, generated by the *lapse of ages*, cannot be altered in a *day*."[99]

The Origins of Dew's Thought

Dew was writing in the wake of generations of pro-slavery thought, and among many in the South the amplitude of the pro-slavery argument was increasing. He drew on contemporary pro-slavery arguments, including, it seems likely, South

Carolina chancellor William Harper's 1828 essay in the *Southern Review*.[100]
Sometimes, as with Harper's essay, the influence is deduced from circumstantial
evidence, in that Dew employs similar arguments. There are several other important pamphlets that seem likely to have influenced him or at least influenced
the culture he worked in. The immediate precursors were the writings of the
1820s, including Whitemarsh Benjamin Seabrook's *Concise View of the Critical
Situation, and Future Prospects of the Slave-holding States, in Relation to their
Coloured Population*.[101] Seabrook, a young lawyer who graduated from Princeton
in 1812, was destined to become governor of South Carolina. His key points
were that slavery was necessary to South Carolina's prosperity and that there
were no other practical alternatives to slavery. Such pro-slavery arguments were
increasingly heard in legislatures and newspapers, particularly after the Missouri
Compromise in 1820.[102] Dew helped bring order and rigor to the pro-slavery
argument.

Dew also drew on a wider context of pro-slavery writing, including Richard
Nisbet's 1779 pamphlet *Slavery Not Forbidden by Scripture, Or, A Defence of
the West-India Planters*, which responded to the charges against slavery by
Philadelphia physician Benjamin Rush. We know about many of Dew's sources
because he cites them; many are contemporary histories. They included Robert
Wallace's *A Dissertation on the Numbers of Mankind, In Ancient and Modern
Times*, Henry Hallam's *Middle Ages*, Bryant Edwards' *West Indies*, William
Mitford's *History of Greece*, Mungo Parke's *Travels into the Interior of Africa*, John
Marshall's *Life of Washington*, Hugh Henry Broughman's *Colonial Policy*, Joel
Roberts Poinsett's *Notes on Mexico*, even the American Colonization Society's
Fifteenth Annual Report. Dew also used more common texts in political and
economic thought, including Voltaire, Thomas Jefferson's *Notes on the State of
Virginia*, St. George Tucker's edition of *Blackstone*, Edward Filmer, John Locke,
Adam Smith's *Wealth of Nations*, Thomas Cooper's *Political Economy*, Aristotle's
Ethics, Plutarch's *Lives*, Thomas Malthus, and David Hume.[103] Dew borrowed
from and contributed to the utilitarian ideas supporting slavery, advanced by
South Carolina writers Thomas Cooper and William Harper.[104]

But those books by themselves did not make up Dew's argument. His was
more than an encyclopedia entry on thoughts about slavery.[105] Dew's contribution was that he systematized the pro-slavery argument. He brought together diverse strands, linking ancient and recent history, even contemporary politics and
economics with political philosophy. Dew pulled those diverse sources together
and assembled a comprehensive argument. Then he popularized the idea that
slavery not just a necessary evil; it was, in fact, good. Good for the slave owners
(this had been heard in many ways before) and also good for the enslaved. Once
those intellectual justifications were harnessed to the economic reality that slavery was helpful to the development of the South, the antislavery crowd had a

very, very difficult task ahead of them. To develop ways to end slavery peacefully and from within would be hard—quite probably impossible.

Consequentialist reasoning was central to Dew's advocacy of slavery.[106] Dew, like many others in his day, would not condone an act if it led to greater harm. Dew invoked his contemporary, British utilitarian philosopher John Stuart Mill, though they disagreed on the issue of slavery.[107] Later Dew wrote that "any question must be determined by its circumstances, and if, as really is the case, we cannot get rid of slavery without producing a greater injury to both the masters and slaves, there is no rule of conscience or revealed law of God which *can* condemn us."[108] However, the ways that considerations of utility worked differed greatly according to who was doing the computing. Pieces of his argument went well beyond the argument against gradual abolition to conclude that slavery was a sign of civilization and that it was the best state of society possible for the enslaved. While others were arguing for gradual abolition through, for instance, colonization, Dew was using his intellectual might to argue against any change in the institution of slavery.

Responding to Dew

To gauge how Dew fit on the intellectual landscape, it is helpful to see how his contemporaries responded to him.[109] Jesse Harrison published a response to Dew in the December 1832 *American Quarterly Review*, the same journal where Dew published the first version of his *Review*. Harrison was, like Dew, a young man. He was twenty-seven in 1832 and had been educated at Hampton Sydney College, then Harvard Law School. His essay was ostensibly a review of the moderately antislavery speech by Thomas Marshall of Farquier County. Marshall had voted against William Preston's resolution that immediate action was expedient and Vincent Witcher's resolution to table all further discussion. Marshall opposed the most extreme positions on both the antislavery and pro-slavery sides, and Marshall was, thus, an ideal person for Harrison to put at the center of his essay. But Harrison's article was more about the evils of slavery to the white community than Marshall's moderate speech.[110]

The intellectual roots of Harrison's article lie in Thomas Jefferson's *Notes on the State of Virginia*, which detailed the harm to the white community of slavery. Like Jefferson, Harrison believed in the elimination of slavery and also in the virtues of and need for colonization. It was antislavery mixed with Enlightenment ideas, from fear of race wars to racial hierarchy to republicanism mixed with racism. Harrison identified a number of harmful consequences of slavery felt in Virginia. Prime among them was the injury slavery did to citizens' "public spirit." Slavery led to an "inertness of most of the springs of prosperity." This happened in several ways. There was little incentive to invest in manufacturing; slavery discouraged manual labor among white workers; and it encouraged over-use of the soil. Overseers, who were commonly paid in crops, employed a pro-cedure to maximize crops in a single year without considering a long-term agri-cultural plan. Harrison came back to his initial point and concluded that slavery destroys "all those springs of prosperity which depend on economy, frugality, and enterprise."[111] There was no property that led to more inequality than prop-erty in humans; Harrison provided a classic attack on slavery for what it did to equality and the economy in the white community. Calculations of harm to the slave played no part in his defense.

But he defended the idea of philanthropy—in what might be called the "excuse rationale." Harrison explained that people would manufacture reasons to support what they thought was a moral action. While statements of philan-thropy generally did not fair well in the debates, Harrison proceeded under the guise of philanthropy. A few years before, in debates over the constitutional con-vention of 1829–1830, the extent of Virginia's drift away from Enlightenment ideas was captured by Phillip Dodderidge, one of the boldest defenders of Revolutionary principles:

> In the whole progress of this debate, the name of Thomas Jefferson, the great apostle of liberty, has never once been invoked, nor has one appeal been made to the author of the Rights of Man, whose immortal work, in the darkest days of our revolution, served as a political deca-logue and operated as a talisman to lead our armies to victory. Then, the authority of the sage of Monticello would have stood against the world; now, there are "none so poor as to do him reverence." Then, was Burke regarded as the enemy of human rights and the firmest defender of ar-istocracy and monarchy—but now Burke, Filmer, and Hobbes, judging from their arguments, have become the textbooks of our statesmen.[112]

In response to conservatives' charges that reform was unnecessary, Lucas Thompson asked, "When were men in power ready for reform?"[113]

Thompson and other reformers vainly struggled for Enlightenment principles over the calls for expediency made by conservatives. "Does" the right of suffrage "not command the assent of every unprejudiced and unsophisticated mind as almost a self-evident truth? Is it not the affirmation of a principle written by the pen of nature upon the heart of every human being, whose spirit is not bowed down by oppression and political degradation," he asked. The people, "in whom the right of sovereignty resides, whose polar star is right, and not expediency" concur, Thompson believed, in supporting general suffrage.[114] Conservatives' arguments in opposition to innovation might have been advanced against other successful reforms, such as the statute docking entails, the abolition of primo-geniture, and the act of religious toleration.

Harrison characterized the debate as one about fundamental questions of slavery and policy. "Everything tells of a spirit that is busy inspecting the very foundations of society in Virginia—a spirit new, suddenly created, and vaster in its grasp than any hitherto called forth in her history." The debate became a question of gradual emancipation and then expulsion of the newly freed people from the state.[115]

Jesse Harrison's response to Dew in the *American Quarterly Review* alluded to how far Dew had migrated from the usual position of Virginians. While most Virginia owners believed slaves should be emancipated if it could be done "to the advantage of the slave and without greater injury to the master than is implied in the continuance of the bondage,"[116] Dew held another, more positive and dangerous view of slavery. Harrison urged the rejection of Dew's views and noted how extreme they were:

> If an anti-abolitionist who regards domestic slavery as the optimum among good institutions, while asserting the benign and sacred character of the relation of master and slave as observed in Virginia, should boast that Virginia is "in fact a *negro raising* State for other States," and that "she produced enough for her own supply and six thousand for sale," we must say that this is a material subtraction from the truth of his picture of the sanctity of the relation. It would be well to recall it and thrust it from view.[117]

Harrison's view was not successful; in part it may have rested too much on a will-o'-the-wisp: the hope that enslaved people be deported. It was never practical—too costly in money for freedom and then transportation, to say nothing of the cost in lost labor. And too costly in human emotions; many people did not want to leave their home in the United States. Emancipation was up against some mighty powerful forces.

Dew's Followers

Even though some like Jesse Harrison opposed Dew, many others followed him. Particularly after abolitionists employed the U.S. mail to distribute literature throughout the South in 1835, Southerners no longer abided much public abolition talk. Instead, the debate was about property and slavery and the practical realities instead of theoretical rights. Dew's prose crept into other works. William Drayton's 1836 book, *The South Vindicated from the Treason and Fanaticism of the Northern Abolitionists*, relied in important ways on the structure and arguments of Dew's *Review*. Drayton, who was born in 1776, had served in Congress as a representative South Carolina from 1825 to 1833. During the nullification crisis in South Carolina, he supported the Union and he moved in 1833 to Philadelphia. He served as president of the Second Bank of the United States in 1840 and 1841. Drayton was obviously both sympathetic toward slavery and knowledgeable about the arguments regarding it.[118]

Drayton's book, like Dew's before him, covered the spectrum of pro-slavery arguments. Drayton began with the ubiquity of slavery, emphasized its human-ity (because it was less harsh than killing captives taken in war), then attributed its presence in the South to northern and European merchants. It pointed to Jefferson's statement in the Declaration of Independence that the slave trade was one cause of the Revolution.[119] And Drayton believed that Great Britain stopped the slave trade only when the trade was no longer expedient.[120]

Slavery had been entailed upon Southerners (that is, it was an inheritance they were stuck with). Yet, slavery was responsible for the South's affluence. In short, slavery aided the advance of civilization.[121] Of course, as some Southerners pointed out, the belief that slavery facilitated equality among nonslaves was an an-cient argument. Not only did people in the 1830s make it, and not only had Burke made it in the 1770s, but Aristotle made it as well.[122] Slaves, like their owners, were beneficiaries of the institution. Slaves had a better life than free workers.[123]

> "[T]he negro never suffers from the thirst for knowledge. Voluptuous and indolent, he knows few but animal pleasures; is incapable of appre-ciating the pride and pleasure of conscious intellectual refinement; and passes through existence, perhaps with few of the white man's mental enjoyments, but certainly with still fewer of his harassing cares and anxieties. The dance beneath the shade surpasses, for him, the groves of the academy; and the simple tones of the banjo have charms which even the lyre of Phoebus could not rival.[124]

Like Dew, Drayton emphasized the difficulty of ending slavery. There was no practical solution—colonization was too difficult and the enslaved people could not be freed and kept in the community, either. Again, like Dew, Drayton wrote of the slaughter that attended the end of slavery in Haiti at the beginning of the nineteenth century.[125] Drayton added commentary on the decline that some identified in the economy in the British West Indies, where slavery ended in 1833 and thus was new since Dew wrote his *Review*.

In one important way Drayton moved well beyond Dew: he charged that abolitionists were treasonous. Drayton was writing in response not just to Southerners' debate about the future of slavery; he was also responding to the growth of radical northern abolitionists—people who argued in favor of im-mediate emancipation, perhaps through violence. The impetus to Drayton's book was the 1835 campaign to send abolitionist literature to Southerners. The American Anti-Slavery Society, based in New York City, used the U.S. mail to send such literature to Southerners.[126] That crisis led to varied responses in the South, from a burning at the Charleston, South Carolina, post office at the end of July 1835 to an indictment of New York abolitionist Robert Williams, publisher of the *Emancipator*, by the Tuscaloosa County grand jury on September 26, 1835. Though Williams had never visited Alabama, the grand jury indicted him for inciting conspiracy, insurrection, and rebellion by sending the *Emancipator* to Tuscaloosa. The grand jury singled out one statement in particular: "God commands, and all nature cries out, that man should not be held as property. The system of making men properly, has plunged 2,250,000 of our fellow countrymen into the deepest physical and moral degradation, and they are every moment sinking deeper."[127]

Drayton's book sought to expose the abolitionists' designs and charge them with treason. To that end, part of his book quoted the abolitionist press to show how they supported armed and immediate rebellion. For example, he quoted extensively from abolitionist tracts such as the periodical *Human Rights*. One, for instance, proclaimed, "Suppose the intelligence should reach this city today, that the slaves had risen in insurrection, and were scattering dismay and death through the South, would not the veriest child know the cause? 'They Are Fighting for their Freedom,' would be the universal cry."[128]

Again drawing on Dew's lead, Drayton predicted dire scenes in the South— bloody wars and vicious reprisals, if a slave insurrection ever appeared:

> Two millions and a half of negroes, hardy, robust, ferocious, ignorant and brutal, let loose upon our brethren of the South—chartered to rob, burn, violate, and murder—to sweep the fair South like a pestilence—and leave it an added monument of the horrors of fanaticism. History has no page which can afford a picture so fearful, so revolting, so full of dread.[129]

In short, abolitionists threatened the South's garden:

> Let the wily philanthropist but come and whisper into the ear of such a slave that his situation is degrading and his lot a miserable one—let him but light up the dungeon in which he persuades the slave that he is caged—and that moment, like the serpent that entered the garden of Eden, he destroys his happiness and his usefulness.[130]

In fact, it was slavery that made the Garden of Eden in the minds of many Southerners: slavery made it possible to wrest from wild nature the swampland of the South and turn it into a pastoral, middle-class world.[131]

As Drayton showed, the status quo was not going to give up easily. And though the day of reckoning was approaching with a speed few expected, the side of slavery and slave owners was still becoming more powerful. This was especially true after 1835, when abolitionists became more strident and so did pro-slavery advocates.[132]

Dew's contemporaries frequently praised his contribution to the debate—as the person whose work stopped the movement for emancipation with colonization and the idea of colonization entirely. "After President Dew," South Carolina Chancellor James Harper said, "it is unnecessary to say a single word on the practicability of colonizing our slaves."[133] Dew's work came to stand for the proposition that slavery contributed much to Virginia. "President Dew," Chancellor Harper wrote, "has shown that the institution of Slavery is a principal cause of civilization." Harper's next sentence then extended Dew's viewpoint: "Perhaps nothing can be more evident than that it is the sole cause."[134]

Another way to judge influence is to search beyond explicit references to the impact of ideas. These kinds of questions of influence, however, pose some of the greatest problems in the historical method. How do we know that a person's ideas mattered? Even sketching answers to those kinds of questions is enormously difficult. What may be particularly important here is that Dew's ideas helped stop talk of gradual abolition; that is difficult to gauge, for sure. We know that after March 1832, the subject was not again so seriously and openly discussed again in the legislatures of the major slaveholding states of the old South.

Dew was a very smart and well-educated man, telling other well-educated people that what they were doing was right. In this he seemed to have convinced a lot of people or at least confirmed their preexisting dispositions. Dew is representative of William and Mary's intellectual leaders who generated the arguments to support slavery. William and Mary law professor Beverley Tucker told graduating students in 1847, William and Mary "is what Virginia made her. Virginia continues what she is in part because the spirit of her ancient chivalry continues to act on her through William and Mary. Each is at once cause and effect, and each is necessary to the other."[135]

Pro-slavery Academic Thought in the 1840s and 1850s

In 1825 the elderly John Robinson wrote his will leaving his entire estate, including seventy-three slaves and his Harts Bottom plantation along the James River in the Shenandoah Valley, to Washington College. Robinson, who professed admiration for the principles of the American Revolution,[1] expected the College to advance the cause of the Revolution. Robinson's will further instructed that neither the plantation nor the slaves be sold for fifty years.[2] Robinson did say that troublesome slaves could be sold. But he clearly wanted the slaves and their children to stay together on the land where they had lived when he was alive. Such restrictions on the sale of humans were somewhat common in Rockbridge County and elsewhere around the South,[3] though those restraints were typically on the sale of one or a few people, rather than the entire population of a major plantation.[4] Perhaps Robinson thought that within fifty years slavery would have ended, and he wanted to keep his enslaved humans together.

Washington College in Lexington, Virginia, proceeded to hire an overseer to manage Harts Bottom,[5] and it also rented out a number of its enslaved humans. An 1826 broadside advertised that the College planned to rent about twenty people at the end of the year.[6] (Illustration 2.1) They owned so many people that they had form contracts printed with Washington College's name as the owner to facilitate the rental of their humans.[7] (Illustration 2.2). That worked for a few years, but soon the College found that it would prefer to sell the plantation and their slaves. An 1829 opinion from Harrisonburg lawyer Chapman Johnson told the trustees that they might sell Harts Bottom, despite the clear instructions that the property was not to be sold. Johnson's opinion stated starkly that the common law repudiated restraints on alienation.[8]

Though Johnson's opinion related exclusively to Robinson's Harts Bottom estate, its reasoning applied as well to the restraint against the sale of the College's humans. In January 1836 the College sold many of the slaves they received from Robinson to Hugh Garland of Lynchburg, for use on his plantation in Hinds

Illustration 2.1 Advertisement for rental of slaves owned by Washington College, 1826. (Washington and Lee University Leyburn Library, Special Collections.)

County, Mississippi. A few other people were sold locally.[9] The College continued to own some people who were acquired from Robinson's estate. In the early 1840s, the college paid $300 a year to provide care for six elderly slaves whom they owned, at least four of whom came from the Robinson bequest.[10]

The money made from the sale of those slaves was used to build Robinson Hall, which still stands on the campus of Washington and Lee University. Thus, Washington College significantly benefited from the labor of enslaved people. Yet, its faculty and students engaged in a vigorous debate about slavery in the 1830s and 1840s. Many other slave owners and educational institutions in the old South felt no such qualms. While some faculty openly questioned slavery, many more embraced it and developed extensive economic, moral, and religious justifications for slavery.

This chapter examines the ideas about slavery developed by college faculty. It ranges from schools in border areas like Washington College in Lexington, Virginia, in the Shenandoah Valley and Transylvania in Lexington, Kentucky, to those in places where slavery was more central to the economy, such as the University of Virginia, Randolph Macon College, Emory College in Georgia, and even the female seminaries in Tuscaloosa and in Greensboro, Alabama. This

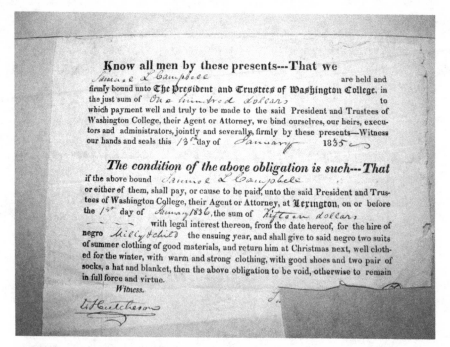

Illustration 2.2 Contract for rental of slaves owned by Washington College, 1835.
(Washington and Lee University Leyburn Library, Special Collections.)

chapter tells the story of ideas of faculty at a number of schools because those stories are individually important, and collectively these stories reveal the variety of arguments for and sometimes against slavery in circulation in the old South. They reveal that some faculty at a few colleges were antislavery, and they spoke out against slavery on economic and, sometimes even, moral grounds. But those faculty were shrinking in number, especially by the 1840s. The central tendency of faculty in this era was to follow the lead of professors like Thomas Dew and Nathanial Beverley Tucker of William and Mary. They wrote, often in depth, about the virtues of slavery for the southern economy; they defended slavery for its place in bringing stability to southern states, and they challenged religious critiques of slavery. They advanced a sophisticated political theory that looked at inequality in nature and in human history to argue that some were fit to rule and others fit to be ruled. Their broad based support for slavery, from economics and history to political theory and religion, led the way for students and alumni to defend slavery on their campuses, too. The story of southern faculty is that they supported slavery with their scholarship and in their teaching. Later chapters will link this scholarship to what students heard at graduations and at their literary societies and then how these ideas correlate with what judges were doing as they heard cases involving slaves and, finally, how these ideas appeared in debates over secession.

Washington College

At the center of the debate over slavery at Washington College was Henry Ruffner, whose family's salt business benefited from enslaved labor.[11] Yet Ruffner, who had been on the faculty since 1819 and became president in 1837, spoke against slavery. Thus Ruffner like his school, illustrates the contradictions that caught many people who gained from slavery even as they opposed it. While Ruffner was benefitting from the institution of slavery, he was also deeply concerned about it.[12] Sometimes Ruffner's public opposition to slavery came in oblique ways. One piece of evidence of Ruffner's discomfort with slavery comes from an undated story that he wrote sometime near the end of his tenure at Washington College about a slave, Jack Neal. Neal had been promised freedom in Maryland by his owner's will, but before the will was probated and Neal freed, he was kidnapped and put on a boat down the Ohio River toward Louisiana. Somewhere near Ruffner's home in Kanawha County, Virginia, Neal killed one of his captors and then was sentenced to death. Many people in Richmond, where Neal's appeal was heard, thought his case warranted further investigation, and so he received a new trial. However, at that trial Neal was again sentenced to death. Just a day before the scheduled execution, he escaped. Neal was recaptured, then granted another reprieve and, eventually, freed.[13] Ruffner's story recalls a meeting with Neal while he was in jail. While the story contains an attack on the abolitionists and some disparaging remarks about slaves in general (Neal was "free from the vices common to slave"), it suggests that Ruffner thought that Neal, though not justified in killing his kidnapper, should not be punished with death.[14] Ruffner was also consistently in favor of transporting slaves outside the state after emancipation. He was a leading figure in the Rockbridge Colonization Society, the local branch of the American Colonization Society.[15] These seem to have been popular ideas in Lexington, because Washington College classics professor George Dabney was also a member of the Society. In fact, Dabney freed several of his slaves. Some years later they went to Liberia.[16]

Ruffner also spoke against slavery. In June 1843 he delivered a major speech to the Rockbridge Colonization Society,[17] and in August 1847 Ruffner took the bold step of criticizing slavery in a debate at the Franklin Society in Lexington.[18] Shortly afterward Ruffner published a pamphlet summarizing his Franklin Society debate. The key part of Ruffner's argument was that slavery was economically inefficient. Here Ruffner followed James Bruce, one of the wealthiest people in Virginia at the time and a slave owner, who also worried about the economic effects of slavery. Bruce stated in a now-lost July 4 oration in 1846 to the agricultural societies of Mecklenburg, Virginia, and neighboring Granville, North Carolina, that "the slave adds nothing to the moral and physical strength of the country, and if his labor be profitless, of course he is a nuisance, and the sooner we rid ourselves of him the better."[19] Ruffner suggested that slave labor was unproductive and thus injured agriculture; that because so much money was invested in slaves, Virginians neglected manufacturing and transportation; and that because the white population was widely dispersed, public education was difficult. All this led Ruffner to the conclusion that "slavery is pernicious to the welfare of states."[20] He resurrected the idea of emancipation of children of slaves born sometime after the passage of an emancipation act.[21] Such an act would allow the slaveowners to amortize their investment. Ruffner's emancipation proposal, thus, tapped into a discussion that was several decades old. Like Jesse Harrison's response to Thomas Dew,[22] Ruffner argued only slavery's adverse economic effects, not the immorality of slavery. Given the difficulties of colonization, Ruffner seemed oddly unconcerned with its practicalities.

Ruffner's economic attack on slavery focused on the effects slavery had on white people. The discussion of the efficiency of slave versus free labor correlates with twentieth-century historians' arguments about the profitability of slavery and the material lives of slaves. Historians often believe the arguments of anti-slavery Southerners that slavery was unprofitable—arguments designed to show that slavery should end and thus were advocacy oriented.[23]

Ruffner was opposed in the debate at the Franklin Society by John White Brockenbrough, a federal judge based in Lexington who also taught at the Lexington Law School.[24] We have no record of Brockenbrough's arguments, so it is necessary to draw inferences from common pro-slavery arguments made by lawyers in the 1840s. It is likely he employed many of the stock arguments in circulation regarding utility: emancipation is impractical; and historical and demographic data suggest that emancipation would be a disaster for Virginia and for the enslaved as well, as William and Mary professor Thomas R. Dew's argued.[25] Perhaps he took on Ruffner's argument about the economic costs of slavery.

Another participant in the Franklin Society debate was Francis Henney Smith, a professor at the Virginia Military Institute, a state military college in Lexington, next door to Washington College. Smith's views on slavery appear in an 1857 report to the Virginia legislature. Smith justified the Institute because it supported slavery. He found that the "military discipline of the institution gives protection and efficiency to the peculiar institutions of the state and of the south." In a moment of particular clarity, Smith explained the Institute's role in the defense of slavery:

> Slavery is a material element of southern power and southern polity; and to rightly defend and direct it, constitutes an important duty on the part of those who form the mind and habits of our southern youth. There is no labor so profitable, none so free from pernicious influences to society, as slave labor. Military institutions, by the order and system

and responsibility which their discipline encourages, discharge a most important function in these respects. And in the enumeration of these benefits, none are more decided or more worthy of consideration than those which result from the discipline of these schools in promoting the material comfort and well being of the slave himself.[26]

Smith represented both the role of educational institutions, particularly military academies, in protecting slavery and the argument that slavery was good for the enslaved. Where in the 1830s people like Beverley Tucker had promoted slavery because it made white people equal, now the popular southern arguments were that slavery was an economic necessity and that slavery benefited the enslaved.

While Ruffner and George Dabney were taking action to end slavery, others on the Washington College faculty supported it. George Armstrong, who taught at Washington College from 1838 to 1851 and then served as a Presbyterian minister in Norfolk, published in 1857 the pro-slavery pamphlet *The Christian Doctrine of Slavery*. It defended slavery as consistent with the Bible and also urged obedience to the law, even if individuals found the law distasteful.[27] Armstrong was surprisingly silent about owners' duties to treat their slaves in a Christian manner, which was a common part of southern works on Christianity and slavery in the 1840s and 1850s.[28]

The Franklin Society debate exacerbated already existing conflicts Ruffner had with the trustees and the community, which led ultimately to his resigning in June 1848.[29] Though Ruffner's letter of resignation stated that family health reasons were his motivation,[30] and the trustees emphasized in their letter the excellent service that Ruffner had performed for the College,[31] there seem to have been other factors at play. Rumors circulated that some of the Board of Trustees wished all the faculty to resign, so that the Board could recompose the faculty.[32]

Ruffner left Lexington shortly after his resignation, but that was not the end of his antislavery advocacy. He is credited with publishing a response to Ellwood Fisher's *Lecture on the North and the South*.[33] Ruffner,[34] writing under the pseudonym "Justice"—took on Fisher's argument that slavery was economically beneficial to the South, as had several other pamphlets.[35] Ruffner wrote proudly to his former colleague George Dabney with details about his response to Fisher, "It is rather longer than my Address to West Virginia, and dissects Friend Fisher's Calhoun Nullifying, Pro-slavery Statistical Fallacies and Absurdities, completely, and I trust effectually too." Ruffner had reason to be proud of the work and be optimistic about the cause of freedom. "Fisher's production is said to be the strongest publication[;] yet it[']s weak on the pro-slavery side. Miserably weak is the cause that cannot be better defended."[36] Ruffner's opposition was phrased in economic terms, but that may have been a mask for moral grounds, because at the time, the only grounds on which there could be opposition to slavery was economic, not humanity for the enslaved.[37]

About the same time that Ruffner was speaking about the evils of slavery, Miami University president George Junkin was in Ohio arguing against abolitionists. In an 1843 lecture on the "Union versus abolitionists," Junkin took on antislavery religious and moral arguments.[38] It was an examination of the biblical support for slavery.[39] However, in two places—in the introduction and at the end of the nearly eighty-page pamphlet that emerged from his lecture—Junkin turned to the implications of the Bible's recognition of slavery for American religion and politics. He thought it improper to criticize masters or deny them communion in church for owning people.[40] In fact, Junkin thought those who criticized slave owners or denied them communion were despotic people who had substituted their judgement for that of God.[41] The abolitionists' argument, Junkin posited, was that "slavery as it exists and is practiced in the United States involves many great and crying moral evils" and it should, therefore, be abolished. Yet Junkin limited the critique of slavery by arguing that although slavery was sometimes inhumane, inhumanity was not inherent to slavery. In fact, many institutions allowed inhumane things to happen, but they were not abolished. Inhumane conduct existed in some marriages, for instance, yet no one suggested marriage should be abolished.[42]

Yet, even if abolitionists could show that slavery necessarily involved evil, Junkin denied that would make the case for immediate abolition. He set the abolitionists to a high standard, based on a utilitarian calculation of costs and benefits of abolition. Abolition was only justified when "abolition would remove the remaining evils and not introduce greater."[43] And Junkin thought that immediate abolition would be of no benefit to the enslaved people and thus would be a violation of the Golden Rule.[44] From that he went on to conclude that if abolitionists refused communion to Southerners "and denounce[d] them as guilty of damning sin, as kidnappers and menstealers, as worthy of the penitentiary" there would be "a dissolution of the Union—a civil, and perhaps a servile war."[45] The Union would end in a war of "uncompromising extermination, that will lay waste this vast territory, and leave the despotic powers of Europe exalting over the fall of the Republic."[46] This expanded on his introduction in which he labeled abolition "a treasonable movement against the Constitution" and hypothesized that abolitionists were working with the British government "in an extended scheme to divide and destroy the republic, whenever a war with England occurs, by means of black troops from the West Indies and Canada, co-operating with a slave insurrection."[47]

Junkin's primary argument was that slaveholding was not immoral, and therefore slaveowners should not be censured. He translated that into a constitutional argument: antislavery advocates threatened the Union by their censure of slavery. This joined the argument that slavery was constitutional with an argument about expediency. Junkin then employed a macrolevel utilitarian argument that abolitionists threatened the Union. This was a religious version of the argument heard frequently in politics—and also in judicial decisions—that the Union was more important than the values of antislavery.

Junkin's argument was a popular one in the 1840s in some circles, for it was similar to that of Daniel Webster's March 7, 1850, speech in favor of the Fugitive Slave Act. Webster argued for tolerance of slaveowners in order to preserve the Union.[48] Where Junkin had been concerned pretty much exclusively with a religious defense of slavery, Webster advanced a legal argument, that Southerners were entitled to respect for their property. Both Junkin and Webster were joined in the constitutional argument that Union required forbearance against criticism of slaveowners.[49]

Junkin presented a religious analog to arguments circulating in the judiciary, in which even antislavery judges urged support for the constitutional rights of slaveowners because the preservation of the Union was at stake.[50] Some who made that argument may have been antislavery in private, yet they believed that the Constitution's injunction to tolerate southern states' institutions—or the value of Union—commanded a pro-slavery result. However, Junkin was not antislavery in private. He, in fact, believed that the Bible supported slavery, and he spoke repeatedly in favor of slavery. Junkin spoke of the harm that abolitionists caused the Constitution, as well as the biblical support for slavery. The value of Union trumped other considerations. It was part of the way that Whigs in particular appealed to national unity. At one point they argued for the enduring value of the Union—about how it was impossible to calculate its value. Junkin was in a middle position in pro-slavery advocacy, for an important part of the generation of southern nationalism went even further. Ministers frequently moved from the Bible's support of slavery to the position that Southerners were entitled to secede.[51] For later Southerners began to calculate the value of Union and found it costing them more than it provided them.

George Junkin's argument was popular with some but not at Miami University of Ohio. The pamphlet seems to have cost him his job at Miami, and he returned to LaFayette College in Easton in 1844. Then in 1848 when Washington College was looking for a new president, the trustees turned to Junkin.[52]

Junkin's July 1, 1856, address to the Rutgers literary societies offered his most extensive discussion of political theory. It presents a complete vision of a Christian union, a commercial republic based on Protestant ideas that focuses on the individual and links agriculture, manufacturing, and commerce. Junkin began with an attack on Materialism (the idea that we are determined more by our surroundings than religious beliefs) and Transcendentalism.[53] He posited, in explicit contrast to French historian François Guizot, that the Bible was a central factor in the development of Western civilization.[54] Building from that basis, he asserted that Protestant thought contributed to American development— Junkin says of the early settlers of America that the Bible "became their chart across the Atlantic, and faith stood at the helm and guided every vessel to these wilderness shores. . . . Here they find their simple democratic religion . . . the very element of their political freedom."[55] He found in America the working out of God's plan: "government, too, is an ordinance of God, not a device of human ingenuity. . . . The great principles of law, and the necessity of their application, and the power of government—all are of God."[56]

At the conclusion of his address, Junkin turned to the threat to Union, what he called that "grand providential problem in the nineteenth century"—slavery.[57] Here his belief that the hand of God lay behind America posed something of a problem. How to explain slavery? For Junkin it was another part of God's design to Christianize the enslaved. Junkin was blunt: "He has civilized as well as chris- tianized in two hundred and thirty-six years, a larger portion of human beings, than have been civilized and christianized by the agencies of all churches in all the world for the last thousand years."[58]

Junkin thought that God's plan was to return enslaved people to Africa. "He will take them back to the place of their fathers' sepulchers in sufficient num- bers to use them for the civilization and christianization of a mighty continent." This, despite that for two decades few people had thought that colonization had much future.[59] Junkin's admonition was "let the human master exercise all his legal rights, but whenever God shall put it into his heart to send his servant home to his fatherland, let us furnish the means."[60] He did not, however, offer much in way of a plan or even hope. His suggested a constitutional amendment that would permit Congress to appropriate up to five million dollars a year for colonization.[61]

Some sense of Junkin—and of his similarities as well as differences with Ruffner—appears in an address that Ruffner gave on July 4, 1856, just three days after Junkin's Rutgers speech, at Kanawha Salines, near Morganton, Virginia (now West Virginia), where his family had a lucrative salt business.[62] It was Ruffner's last public address. Ruffner's July Fourth oration took, also, the theme of Union. And he appealed to sentiments of Union, but mostly to the economic benefits of the Union—the ways that it facilitated the growth of cities, manu- facturing, and agriculture. The speech looked to the commercial benefits of Union and speculated that seventy years hence the United States would be a vast republic. That address emphasized the value of Union through a character- istic, for Ruffner: economic analysis. Like Junkin, Ruffner appealed to romantic images of prosperity in the landscape: "Now over what a vast expanse do we see fields teeming with the fruits of agriculture! Southern industry produces bales of cotton by the million, and hogsheads of sugar by the hundred thousand. Further north, a million of barns are yearly filled with plenty."[63] Commerce had grown and steam and electricity made it possible to cover huge distances in little time. "Mountains have ceased to be an obstruction to trade and travel. Currents are a very slight impediment to navigation. Distance is of little importance, when men and things can be whirled over five or six hundred miles in a day and a night, and the telegraph can shoot a dispatch over one thousand miles in a minute."[64] Ruffner credited religion and Union rather than race for much of the progress. Ruffner did not suggest as Junkin had, that slavery might be a benefit to the enslaved, though he did add that Africans "must remain ever distinct" and thus, one presumes, incapable of sharing in the United States' bounties.[65]

Ruffner, as had Junkin, suggested the dire consequences of disunion—war, economic ruin, and the end of liberty. He placed blame on both abolitionists and extreme pro-slavery advocates, and warned that separation "if it come at all, must come with blood and slaughter." He thought there might be other places that the abolitionists and pro-slavery forces might wage their conflict: "If the restless spirits of the country are so eager for war, let them go abroad and filibuster; let the fiery abolitionists and their disunionist adversaries in the South, go to Cuba, and try the experiment of a slavery and anti-slavery war in that island of slaves, before they destroy the peace and prosperity of their own great and happy country. The result may teach them a useful lesson, and so cool their blood, as to make the survivors willing to let the Union abide in peace."[66] But the prescription for how to deal with the threat of disunion was different; where Junkin proposed a fanciful plan of colonization and a constitutional amendment to fund it, Ruffner wanted something more moderate, the election of "only sober-minded conservative men, who will behave themselves like Christian gentlemen."[67]

Another pro-slavery faculty member was D. H. Hill—later a famous Confederate general—who taught mathematics at Washington College from 1849 to 1854 before moving to Davidson College in North Carolina. While at Davidson, Hill published a mathematics text that used some word problems to depict Yankees and abolitionists in an unflattering light. For instance, one difficult problem dealt with emancipation and the generosity of the North and South:

> A gentleman in Richmond expressed a willingness to liberate his slave, valued at $1000, upon the receipt of that sum from charitable persons. He received contributions from 24 persons; and of these there were 14/19ths fewer from the North than from the South, and the average donation of the former was 4/5ths smaller than that of the latter. What was the entire amount given by the latter?[68]

The appeal to moderation was losing ground on both sides, particularly on the southern side. Southerners expanded their constitutional theory of the equal

dignity of states to have their property and institutions recognized in the territories, and their ideas that the Constitution required Northerners to take lengthy
measures to protect slavery. By the time of secession, they had constructed an
argument that the election of Lincoln was itself a violation of the Constitution
because he would not sufficiently protect property in humans. To understand
how different the ideas in circulation at Washington College were from those
elsewhere in the South, it is necessary to turn to the context in Lexington, elsewhere in Virginia, and in South Carolina.

Transylvania University

The fluctuation in ideas about slavery at Washington College was repeated else-
where in the border South states. President John C. Young of Centre College in
Danville, Kentucky, promoted the cause of colonization in 1832, later freed the
slaves he owned, and wrote an antislavery pamphlet in 1836.[69] Two years later
Young delivered a speech at Miami University of Ohio supporting abolition and
Native American property rights.[70] Young was popular and retained his job at
Centre College until his death in 1857. Other proponents of antislavery ideas
were not so fortunate. Howard Malcolm, president of Georgetown College in
Kentucky, resigned in 1849 because his antislavery views were unwelcome.[71]

At Transylvania University in Lexington, Kentucky, the faculty fluctuated in
their attitudes toward slavery and Union. Transylvania's law faculty, including
George Robertson and sometimes Henry Clay, emphasized respect for Union,
the dignity of the legal profession, and the stability borne of the rule of law.
George Robertson, who was born in 1790, educated at Transylvania, and served
in Congress from 1817 to 1822 and on the Kentucky Court of Appeals from
1829 to 1843, joined the faculty in 1833 and taught until 1857. He spoke eloquently about the goals of the Declaration of Independence, in a way seldom
heard in the 1830s, as people in the South moved away from Jefferson's grand,
optimistic, Enlightenment thinking. "Universal liberty and universal light are inseparable,"[72] he said in a July 4, 1833, speech at Centre College. Robertson spoke
eloquently about the evils of the institution of slavery and his expectation that
slavery would soon end:

> The philanthropist has still to lament, that a curse imposed on our an-
> cestors when in colonial subjection, still lingers among us. Domestic
> slavery cannot be suddenly abolished in all the States, consistently
> with the welfare of either the black man or the white. A premature
> effort of inconsiderate humanity, might be disastrous, and would cer-
> tainly tend to defeat or retard the ultimate object of every good and

wise man—universal emancipation. But we feel that public sentiment, public policy, and individual interest, are all conspiring to extirpate the great household evil, and will, in convenient time, and in some just and eligible mode, satisfactory to all, banish it forever from our land.[73]

That condemnation was becoming rare in the South of the 1830s. Less than two years after Turner's rebellion, Robertson was crafting a middle ground in the discussion of slavery. Yet, Robertson also minimized the problems of slavery. "[T]hese are slight blemishes at which we have just glanced—what are *they* in the sublime prospect which this day opens to our view? They are but the spots on the sun; and though the microscopic vision of misanthropy may magnify them, they are lost in the great panorama which our country presents in the eye of an instructed and comprehensive patriotism."[74]

Three lines of Robertson's thinking are important in understanding his teachings regarding slavery. First, he minimized its harms. Second, he employed a utilitarian calculus, common to politicians in the antebellum era. He told the entering students in 1835 that "the greatest attainable good of the greatest number is the ultimate object of political association."[75] Thus, Robertson's framework for understanding slavery was confined by a belief that no one should abolish slavery as long as it was more beneficial to the slave owner than it was harmful. His thinking did not lend itself to considering the slaves' interests. That utilitarian calculus was central to arguments in favor of slavery and against its abolition throughout the antebellum era. Finally, Robertson had great faith in and fidelity to the rule of law. The rule of law and disdain for those who might try to substitute their own sense of morality for the community's sentiments, as expressed in statutes and judicial decisions, was one of his constant themes. Together, those principles led Robertson to a relatively pro-slavery result.

Thus, in places when it really mattered (such as the Kentucky legislature's debate over a bill to restrict the importation of slaves into Kentucky), Robertson failed to act to restrict slavery. He argued in favor of continued importation of slaves into Kentucky in 1833, for instance. He wondered whether slavery was "finally productive of more aggregate good than evil in human destiny."[76] Robertson's argument fit with the growing paternalist argument made by academics like Thomas R. Dew that slavery was good for the slaves. However, Robertson clung to the possibility of colonization, even as people, such as Dew, predicted its impracticality.

Robertson's lecturing on slavery spanned much of the antebellum period, from the early 1830s until the early 1850s. It thus covers the period from when a major question was colonization to the time when there were increasing threats to the United States itself. In the early 1850s, Robertson used his intellectual muscle to urge support for the Union and to warn those who might secede that they did not have the right to do so. Much of an address he delivered on the anniversary of Washington's birthday in 1852 was aimed at reminding listeners of the value of Union and the ways the Constitution bound the country together. Part of it, however, was also aimed at abolitionists who might place their ideas above the Constitution as well.[77] Robertson supported law over individual conscience, a topic taken up in-depth in Chapter 6 on the Fugitive Slave Act of 1850.

As national and local attitudes toward slavery shifted, so did those at Transylvania. Where in the early part of the nineteenth century, Transylvania was a beacon of the Enlightenment, by 1856 when Lewis Green gave his inaugural address as the new president of Transylvania, he was more ardently pro-slavery than Professor Robertson had been in 1834. President Green warned of the dangers of abolitionists' appeal to the "Higher Law"—their appeals to a conscience-inspired law of God against slavery. He invoked imagery of the French Revolution and the despotism that followed it and then the fear of the loss of law:

> The interests here involved rise, infinitely, above all considerations of section, or of party. . . . It is our hearths and our firesides—our alters and our homes—our property and our lives—not here or there, but every where, and all alike, imperilled. For let it be remembered, and deliberately pondered, that every element of evil, now arrayed in the crusade against our property and lives, is of equally explosive and destructive power against themselves. That Higher Law, to which they now appeal, as superseding all human legislation, cannot be found in the word of God. They must seek it, high; in the perverted reason, the diseased conscience, or the mad passions of men. Amidst the wild uproar of these tumultuous and insurgent passions, all human laws, all written constitutions, will be as paper bulwarks before the sweep of a hurricane.[78]

Green saw abolition as encouraging dangerous sentiments about equality; it would lead, in his mind (as in that of other pro-slavery writers) to leveling, then violence, then destruction of society:

> That mad equality of which they speak, is really an equality, *in all things and for all men—of every country, as well as every color*—in property, as well as power; an equality of idleness and industry, of vice and virtue—of the reckless spendthrift and in the industrous frugal man of business; an equality at war with the everlasting laws of God, and nature; which can never be realized, except amidst the total subversion of human society; when industry would cease to labor, because she could

not enjoy the fruits of her toil; and rapine would cease to plunder, only because, *amidst the universal desolation, there was nothing left to rich or poor–nothing for violence to seize, or cupidity and lust to crave.*[79]

Such was the story of southern institutions on the borderlands of the South. Often the faculties were mild opponents of slavery in the 1830s and sometimes in the 1840s, but by the 1850s faculties increasingly supported slavery. There is another story of institutions closer to the center of the South, which is illustrated by institutions like the University of Virginia. There the story is much more often of faculty who developed and disseminated robust defenses of slavery.

The University of Virginia

"The power of the pen now exceeds that of the purse, the sword, and the tongue," thirty-three-year-old University of Virginia law professor James P. Holcombe told his school's alumni in 1853. This was a central tenet of belief for a law professor, and Holcombe embraced his position of authority to argue the cause of slavery. But he arrived at that position by a circuitous route, for Holcombe had been born in Lynchburg, Virginia, in 1813 to parents who ultimately freed their fifteen slaves and left the state for Indiana. Once in that free state, Holcombe's father, a Methodist minister, preached colonization. The younger Holcombe took a different route. Following education at Yale College, he entered the University of Virginia law school, where he graduated in 1841. After practicing in Cincinnati, Holcombe returned as a professor to the University. In Charlottesville he took up the defense of slavery.[80]

Holcombe turned to the French Revolution to argue for the value of conservative literature. Edmund Burke's writings provided the "moral break-water" that saved England from the radical ideas of the French Revolution.[81] That example of learning and of writing for conservative purposes justified the University. Southern universities offered the hope of a new literature supporting slavery. Up to this point, Northerners had taken the lead in presenting the evils of slavery. Their antislavery arguments were winning converts. "We can no longer cover the salient points of our institutions through the halls of Congress," Holcombe worried. "The voice of the statesman the orator can not reach the masses, with whom lie the issues life and death. Literature alone can dispossess the demon of fanaticism by its 'sweet compulsion.'"[82]

Only Southerners could properly interpret slavery for the rest of the world. Until "a class of native authors, Southern born and Southern bred," arrived to explain slavery, "the rest of the world" would never understand slavery.[83] Harriet Beecher Stowe's *Uncle Tom's Cabin* had been out for only a short while when

Holcombe addressed the alumni, but already it disclosed "the most formidable danger which crosses our line of future march."[84] Southern literature offered the best hope of repudiating the abolitionists. Holcombe spoke in apocalyptic terms. "We shall divide the public opinion of the world, break the force of its sympathy, and by pouring through the bosoms of our people the living tide of hope, strengthen their hearts for the day of trial, and cover our land and its institutions with a shield of fire."[85]

Over the next few years, the faculty of the University of Virginia produced some of that southern literature that Holcombe hoped for. Holcombe's colleague Albert Taylor Bledsoe made a detailed case for the consistency of slavery with moral philosophy. Bledsoe's major work was his treatise *Liberty and Slavery*, published in 1856 by the leading Philadelphia house of J. B. Lippincott. *Liberty and Slavery*, the most extensive philosophical treatment of slavery ever produced by a southern academic, was reprinted frequently in the years before the Civil War.[86] It sought to vindicate positive law from the charge that it was a restriction on liberty. For, in opposition to generations of political philosophers, from Locke to Blackstone, Bledsoe saw laws that restricted action not as restraints on natural liberty but as ensurers of liberty. From that position, Bledsoe developed the argument that laws allowing slavery were, in fact, not deprivations of liberty but ensurers of the proper social order.

Bledsoe came to this topic with a background in law and religion and a passion for order. Bledsoe was born in Frankfort, Kentucky, in 1809, grew up in Ohio, graduated from West Point in 1830, and, after several years' military service, returned to Ohio to become a lawyer. He practiced in Ohio and Illinois (where he knew Abraham Lincoln), taught mathematics at Kenyon College and Miami University from 1833 to 1836 and then at the University of Mississippi from 1848 to 1854 and finally at the University of Virginia from 1854 to 1879.[87]

Bledsoe looked to history, for it was a stable guide to what was feasible. History was a form of guidance and a standard to judge what might be done. He turned to it early in *Liberty and Slavery* to rein in the claims of the antislavery religious zealots. "Even here, in this glorious land of ours, how often do the *too-religious* Americans seem to become deaf to the most appalling lessons of the past, while engaged in the frantic worship of their tutelary deity!"[88]

Though history could tell what was possible, there was a separate question of the content of liberty. Here Bledsoe drew a distinction between natural liberty and civil liberty. Liberty was frequently invoked and often misused as a standard. "O Liberty," Bledsoe claimed, "what crimes are perpetrated in thy name!"[89] The former was the focus of many in the era of Enlightenment, but the latter was the standard for the modern era. Locke defined natural liberty as the power of acting as one thinks fit, within the limits prescribed by the law of nature. But that definition gave too much authority to liberty. "As no man possess a natural right to do mischief, so the law which forbids it does not diminish the natural liberty of mankind. The law which forbids mischief is a restraint not upon the *natural liberty*, but upon the *natural tyranny*, of man."[90] The key to Bledsoe's counter to Locke was that restrictions were necessary to maintain order and that they were not necessarily restraints on liberty.

> As government implies restraint, it is evident that something is restrained when we enter into it; but it does not follow that tins something must be our natural liberty. The law which forbids the perpetration of mischief, or any other wrong, is a restriction, not upon the liberty, but upon the tyranny, of the human will. It sets a bound and limit, not to any right conferred on us by the Author of nature, but upon the evil thoughts and deeds of which we are the sole and exclusive originators. Such a law, indeed, so far from restraining the natural liberty of man, recognizes his natural rights, and secures his freedom, by protecting the weak against the injustice and oppression of the strong.

From there he optimistically concluded that "no good law ever limits or abridges the natural liberty of mankind."[91] There was, thus, a distinction between rights and liberties—in which there are natural rights and those rights are secured through civil society, which protects us from others.[92]

> It is a frightful error to regard the civil state of government as antagonistic to the natural liberty of mankind; for this is, indeed, the author of the very liberty we enjoy. Good government it is that restrains the elements of tyranny and oppression, and introduces liberty into the world. Good government it is that shuts out the reign of anarchy, and secures the dominion of equity and goodness. He who would spurn the restraints of law, then, by which pride, and envy, and hatred, and malice, ambition, and revenge are kept within the sacred bounds of eternal justice,–he, we say, is not the friend of human liberty. He would open the flood-gates of tyrant and oppression; he would mar the harmony and extinguish the light of the world.[93]

The question is "how a real public order, whose claims are identical with those of private liberty, may be introduced and maintained." How, indeed? This is where Bledsoe mixed his understanding of history with his theory about the proper restraints on natural liberty. His understanding of slavery—like that of many other

Southerners—was that there could be no emancipation. As had been argued for decades, since Thomas Dew's *Reviews of the Debates in the Virginia Legislature*, slavery was necessary:

> The practical solution of this problem, for the heterogeneous popula-
> tion of the South imperatively demands, as we shall endeavor to show,
> the institution of slavery; and that without such an institution it would
> be impossible to maintain either a sound public order or a decent pri-
> vate liberty. We shall endeavor to show, that the very laws or institution
> which is supposed by fanatical declaimers to shut out liberty from the
> Negro race among us, really shuts out the most frightful license and
> disorder from society. In one word, we shall endeavor to show that in
> preaching up liberty to and for the slaves of the South, the abolition-
> ist is "casting pearls before swine," that can neither comprehend the
> nature, nor enjoy the blessings, of the freedom which is so officiously
> thrust upon them. And if the Negro race should be moved by their fiery
> appeals, it would only be to rend and tear in pieces the fair fabric of
> American liberty, which, with all its shortcomings and defects, is by far
> the most beautiful ever yet conceived or constructed by the genius of
> man.[94]

The impracticality of emancipation might be one of the things that supported Bledsoe's belief that freedom from slavery was not an "inalienable right." At any rate, discussion of such rights was dangerous. "Such abstractions are edge-tools of political science, with which it is dangerous for either men or children to play. They may leave deep wounds on the cause of humanity; they can throw no light on the problem of slavery." The retreat from the Enlightenment had reached its high point here. The mere discussion of Enlightenment abstractions might cause irreparable injury to humanity.[95]

In the second chapter of *Liberty and Slavery*, Bledsoe engaged the argu-ments of leading abolitionists Francis Wayland, Charles Sumner,[96] William Ellery Channing,[97] and Henry Charles Carey[98] in a series of seventeen sections on "fallacies of the abolitionists." The key stalking horse was Brown University president Francis Wayland and his debate with South Carolina Baptist minister Richard Fuller. Bledsoe argued that slavery was not as bad for the enslaved as abolitionists charged and that owners did not have moral culpability for slavery because they had not enslaved their human property but were born into a system where slavery already existed. The third chapter turned to a defense of slavery in the Bible. And the final chapter provided a defense of slavery from the view-point of the "public good"—a classic defense of slavery based on the benefits to the enslaved (it forced them to work and thus maintain an adequate standard of living) and to society more generally.

Bledsoe's vision was that slaves were naturally lazy; they would not work unless compelled to. There was ample evidence of what would happen when slavery ended in the Western world. He turned to the "experiment" of Britain's emancipation in 1833 for evidence.[99] Bledsoe saw Jamaica retreating from industry and lamented that "there will be none left to represent the wealth, intelligence, and hospitality for which the Jamaica planter was once distinguished."[100] In Bledsoe's world, slavery was justified because it improved the slaves' industry and that of the surrounding country. He took the view that law was consistent with natural liberty and that there was no right to chaos and to do whatever one would like; thus he found liberty greatest under a system of law.[101]

Bledsoe linked political theory with his understanding of facts—of history, of contemporary society, of economics, of human nature.

> Facts can no more be overlooked by the political architect, than magnitude can be disregarded by the mathematician. The man, the political dreamer, who pays no attention to them, may be fit, for aught we know, to frame a government out of moonshine for the inhabitants of Utopia: but, if we might choose our own teachers in political wisdom, we should decidedly prefer those who have an eye for facts as well as for abstractions.[102]

He also sought the restraint of passions—of humans—through law. He turned to the favorite examples of the French Revolution and the revolution in Haiti to conjure up images of unrestrained passion. Then he projected that "the passions of men will burst into anarchy, the most frightful of all the forms of tyranny." Such a scene could not be called liberty.

> Shall we seek the secure enjoyment of natural rights in a wild reign of lawless terror? As well might we seek the pure light of heaven in the bottomless pit. It is, indeed, a most horrible desecration of the sacred name of liberty, to apply it either to the butcheries and brutalities of the French Revolution, or to the more diabolical massacres of St. Domingo.[103]

The treatise, thus, restated and expanded a series of pro-slavery arguments about the need for hierarchy and order, and the decline in the economy of the West Indies that had attended the end of slavery there in 1833. That led to his argument that slavery was essential to the maintenance of social and economic order.

Others understood those key aspects of *Liberty and Slavery*. One volume responded with the revealing title "*Is Slavery a Blessing?*" It was published in Boston in 1857 by J. P. Jewett, the house that published Harriet Beecher Stowe's *Uncle Tom's Cabin*. Although it was published anonymously, it is commonly attributed to Virginian Charles B. Shaw, who taught engineering at the University of Virginia on an adjunct basis in 1854 and 1855.[104] Shaw's critique engages with what he called the "Paixhan gun" of the pro-slavery battery—Bledsoe—whom Shaw disingenuously called "this oracular professor, this honest and energetic seeker after truth."[105] Shaw thought that Bledsoe's assertion that slavery was a blessing was ethical heresy. Slavery was not, in Shaw's mind, fit for the progressive era of the 1850s.

Where Bledsoe thought that nature was wild and needed to be restrained by law, Shaw thought that wild things (like human nature) might be improved. And Shaw countered Bledsoe's argument that enslaved people were not ready for freedom could not be the basis for continuing slavery until the slaveowners had attempted to educate their slaves. It was also an argument that appealed to what might be, rather than what was.[106] There was evidence from southern states of enslaved people who learned trades. There were owners who wrote wills to free all of their slaves, liberating entire plantations. Such examples were proof that slavery could be ended.[107]

And Shaw believed—along with those whom Bledsoe had attacked, like John Locke—that there was a tension between liberty and order. Shaw countered Bledsoe's reliance on order as a securer of liberty, for Shaw thought that as the government imposed more restrictions on humans it infringed their liberty. Slavery was one such case; and Shaw, unlike Bledsoe, saw little reason for imposing slavery. Though he did not phrase it in utilitarian terms, one might imagine Shaw saying that the enormous cost of slavery was not worth the benefits to order.

Shaw recalled the efforts of William Rives in the debates after Nat Turner's rebellion to suggest that slavery was evil, even if there was little that Rives' generation could do to combat it. Although Rives' argument had been received well, time had made even his moderate position unsustainable. "Gradually a funeral pall has been drawn over any rational discussion of the slavery question. . . . No person now can safely reside in the South who is suspected of liberal views on the subject of slavery."[108] As further evidence of this, Shaw included a lengthy appendix imploring Northerners to abstain from interfering with slavery and suggesting that slavery would end more easily through forbearance than agitation.[109] Shaw's sober conclusion was that "fanaticism at the North first begot the sophistry which defended slavery. The growth of that false logic is fostered by persistent abuse of that institution, until it begins to assume, in the minds of the uninquiring, a character . . . of religious truth. The South have been urged to the brink of a precipice from which they may wildly leap if urged too far."[110] Shaw was prescient, though he was by no means alone in perceiving the dire threat to the United States that was looming.

Shaw demonstrates the diversity of ideas in circulation at the University of Virginia in the 1850s, but the center of balance among faculty was in favor of slavery. George Frederick Holmes, another professor at the University of Virginia, was an important pro-slavery author. Born in Georgetown in British Guiana in 1820 and educated in Great Britain, Holmes taught at Richmond College from 1845 to 1847, then at William and Mary from 1847 to 1848, when he became the first president of the University of Mississippi. Holmes' inaugural address at the opening exercises of the University in November 1848 presented an attack on the "revolutionary spirit of the day."[111] Holmes thought that in the North "we have among ourselves Socialism, Mormonism, Fanny Wrightism, and we are rapidly naturalizing St. Simonism, Fourierism, and the other diversified forms of Agrarianism."[112] Holmes recognized that utilitarianism, of people like Bentham, was tending toward antislavery, for that version took into consideration the slaves. But Holmes thought the values antislavery thinkers used in their calculations imperfect. "This Utilitarianism has forced its way into our statesmanship and politics, but it leaves the most abstruse problems of government without anything better than a temporary and provisional solution, because it leaves wholly beyond its range those higher principles of practical policy, from which alone a satisfactory solution could be deduced."[113] In Holmes' mind, a true calculation of the costs and benefits of slavery yielded a result which concluded slavery should be promoted. Holmes did not stay in Oxford, Mississippi, long; by 1849 he had resigned and moved back to Virginia and worked for a period as an independent scholar. In 1850, Holmes published an extensive article on natural law and slavery contained in Aristotle's politics.[114] And shortly afterward he published a critique of *Uncle Tom's Cabin*, which focused on how Stowe's emphasis on humane sentiments for the slave rather than cold logical reasoning "strikes at the very essence and existence of all community among men, it lays bare and roots up all the foundations of law, order, and government." Holmes thought that "pandemonium itself would be a paradise compared with what all society would become, if . . . action were accordingly regulated by it."[115]

The most active and important supporter of slavery was law professor James Holcombe, whose pro-slavery work was mostly in the form of public addresses. His best-known address was given at the Virginia State Agricultural Society in 1858. It asked, "Is Slavery Consistent with Natural Law?"[116] Holcombe probably aspired in the address to contribute to the southern literature that would form a moral break-water akin to Burke's *Reflections on the Revolution in France*. In a little more than twenty pages, Holcombe produced the state-of-the-art pro-slavery legal argument.

Holcombe took the Virginia legislature's debate in the wake of Nat Turner's rebellion as a key point in the move from Jefferson's definition of natural law toward an embrace of the hierarchy inherent in nature. The South had moved from Jefferson's declaration "that he knew no attribute of the Almighty which would take of the side of the master in a contest with his slave." Among the educated classes in the South, "the justice, the humanity" of slavery "has become the prevailing conviction."[117]

The path to the predetermined answer, "yes, slavery is consistent with natural law" owed much to Aristotle and little to Jefferson. Holcombe defined natural law as the "ethical rules . . . which, upon the grounds of their own fitness and propriety, and irrespective of the sanction of Divine authority, commend themselves to the most cultivated human reason." In other words, natural law was the law that humans might develop based on the surrounding circumstances, not some Jeffersonian notion of rights existing in a state of nature. This was an important shift that allowed Holcombe to position slavery as consistent with the law as it had been constructed. He did not need to face arguments about rights in nature or grand Enlightenment pronouncements that all people were created equal. By defining natural law as the dictates of "cultivated human reason," Holcombe opened up the possibilities that natural law was dependent on human understanding of history and that rights might vary depending on the stage of development of enslaved people. Such a definition owed much to the particular surroundings; it maintained that natural law for some people was different from that for others. That might not be what most people would think was the "natural law," but it was consistent with the ways that southern thinkers were rewriting the definitions of freedom and natural right.

Holcombe posited that slavery was consistent with natural law because if the community were starting over, it would institute slavery. "It would be our right and duty to reduce the negro to subjection," he boldly stated. Virginians would reinstitute slavery because it was necessary to the well-being of their state. In fact, the claim of the state was a bedrock principle in setting the law. Because humans seemed to live in society—rather than a state of individualism—humans had to give up some of their rights. Humans' rights had to be balanced against others in society. That trimmed the rights of humans. Quite simply, the "horizon of unbounded liberty of nature" was limited "under those complex and refined forms which have been developed by Christian civilization."[118]

Those limitations on rights were, in turn, based on the capacities of those who were governed.[119] "Owing likewise to this variety of condition, and of moral and intellectual endowment, it is impossible to prescribe any stereotype forms admitting of universal application, under which the restraining discipline of law should be exercised."[120] In successive stages of government, the restrictions on the individual would change. "The ends of social union remain the same through all ages, but the means of realizing those ends must be adapted to successive stages of advancement, and change with the varying intelligence and virtue of individuals, and classes, and races, and the local circumstances of different countries."[121]

Holcombe rejected reasoning from a state of nature; instead, he reasoned from the understanding that humans are naturally social creatures and that humans exist in society, so he asked what kind of social organization made sense. Here he spoke of the supposed benefits of slavery to the enslaved, of the inability to have anyone else do the work of the slaves, and of the social chaos that would ensue if the slaves were freed. Where some pro-slavery writers justified slavery simply because it existed, Holcombe went further and said that it would be proper to institute slavery even if did not exist.

> The State in every age must provide a constitution and laws, if it does not find them in existence, adapted to its special wants and circumstances. African Slavery in the United States is consistent with Natural Law, because if all the bound s of public authority were suddenly dissolved, and the community called up onto reconstruct its social and political system, the relations of the two races remaining in other respects unaltered, it would be out right and duty to reduce the negro to subjection.[122]

Holcombe's vision gave the state substantial authority. Though he protested that the state's control was limited and that he was not advocating "social absolutism," in fact Holcombe required humans to give up "any claim inconsistent with [the state's] existence, or its value as an agency of civilization."[123] This theory was focused on the good of the state, as judged by history and economy and by Holcombe's ideas about the incapacity of the enslaved.[124] Those things that benefited the state—like slavery—were consistent with natural law. It was a theory of natural law that rested on the good of the state, on a biased sense of history and economy, and on racial subordination. Gone were Enlightenment ideas of universal truths; in their place was a specific law based on context.

Holcombe abandoned talk of what slavery did for the equality of white people. Here we had an exploration of the benefits to slaves and to society. It was a utilitarian, nonreligious defense. Slavery was, quite simply, the bedrock of southern society:

> The main-wheel and spring of your material propriety, interwoven with the entire texture of your social life, underlying the very foundations of the public strength and renown, to lay upon it any rash hand would put in peril whatever you value; the security of your property,

the well-being–if not the existence of that dependent race which Providence has committed to your guardianship–the stability of your government, the preservation in your midst of union, liberty, and civilization.[125]

In contrast to defenses of slavery from the 1830s and early 1840s made by people like Beverley Tucker at William and Mary, Holcombe said nothing about the way that slavery supported republicanism or brought political equality to white people.

Such principles were supported by "inductive reasoning" and by observation.[126] Holcombe looked far, as well as near, for his observations. The British colonization of India provided an apt comparison. "It was a despotism no doubt, but it was a mild and paternal one; and no form of restraint less stringent could be substituted with equal advantage to those upon whom it was to operate." The circumstances on the ground showed that colonization was appropriate, indeed, beneficial. "Any is right in the concrete, when necessary to the welfare of the community in which it exists, or beneficial to the subject upon whom it is imposed."[127]

> The people of the United States accepting without much reflection, those expositions of human rights embodied in the infidel philosophy of France, and glowing with that generous enthusiasm to communicate the blessings of liberty which is always inspired by its possession, have been disposed to look with common aversion upon all forms of un-equal restraint. . . . Forgetting the ages through whose long night their fathers wrestled for this blessing, they have regarded an equal liberty, as the universal birth-right of humanity. . . . But alas! the crimes which have been committed in the name of liberty, the social disorder and political convulsion which have attended its progress, if they have not broken the power of spells over the heart, have dispersed the illusions of our understanding.[128]

The revolutions in France, Italy, Greece, Mexico, and Latin America provided evidence that not all people were suited for freedom. Some were "swallowed up in the gulfs of anarchy and despotism—the rest still float above the wave, but with rudder and anchor gone, stripped of every bellying sail and steadying spar, they only serve 'Like ocean wreaks, to illuminate the storm.'"[129] The evidence he amassed to show the futility of emancipation and transportation out of the state and that slaves were—by and large—treated well demonstrated that slavery needed to continue. "Arithmetic is the enemy of rhetoric" was his solemn conclusion.

The picture was of the utter destruction that would attend the end of slavery. Much of Holcombe's story, though, was of the supposed benefit to slaves.

> African slavery is no relic of barbarism to which we cling from the ascendency of semi-civilized tastes, habits, and principles; but an adjustment of the social and political relations of the races, consistent with the purest justice, commended by the highest expediency, and sanctioned by a comprehensive and enlightened humanity.
>
> Its history when fairly written, will be its ample vindication. It has weaned a race of savages from superstition and idolatry, imparted to them a general knowledge of the precepts of the true religion, implanted in their bosoms sentiments of humanity and principles of virtue, developed a taste for the arts and enjoyments of civilized life, given an unknown dignity and elevation to their type of physical, moral and intellectual man, and for the two centuries during which this humanizing process has taken place, made for their subsistence and comfort, a more bountiful provision, than was ever before enjoyed in any age or country of the world by a labouring class. If tried by the test which we apply to other institutions, the whole sum of its results, there is no agency of civilization which has accomplished so much in the same time, for the happiness and advancement of our race.[130]

This was Holcombe's vision of the centrality of slavery and its benefits to enslaved and enslavers. Holcombe, Bledsoe, and Holmes thus appear as people who advanced a doctrine of pro-slavery political and legal theory that upended the Enlightenment idea that all people were created equal. They advanced a political theory of hierarchy and then a natural law theory to go along with it, which joined that political theory with observations about history to argue that slavery was consistent with natural law. This theory was wielded by lawyers and judges in the 1850s as well (as we will see when we discuss Thomas Cobb's *An Inquiry into the Law of Negro Slavery* in Chapter 8). Professor Holcombe appears again at the end of this book, as he urges Virginia to secede.[131]

Randolph Macon College

In Charlottesville, in the foothills of the Alleghenies, the professors worked out fine-spun theories of political and moral philosophy to support slavery. Closer to the coast, at Randolph Macon College, the writings in support of slavery were more direct. Twenty-first-century readers know Randolph Macon College as an elite college in Ashland, Virginia, on the interstate highway between Richmond and Washington. It relocated there after the Civil War. Until the war, the school, which was founded in 1830, was in Boydton, the seat of Mecklenburg County. Mecklenburg, which had produced some of the strongest advocates for slavery in the wake of the Nat Turner rebellion, had 12,000 slaves in 1850. Sixty percent of the county's 20,000 residents were enslaved. The curriculum at the Methodist institution fit the interests of slaveowners.

As with many schools, in the early 1830s, the school was moderate, perhaps even somewhat antislavery. Stephen Olin, the school's first permanent president, who arrived in 1834, was believed to have been at most moderately pro-slavery—and he was a Northerner.[132] But Olin, who later became president at Wesleyan in Connecticut, left in 1837. After that, as happened at so many schools in the South—and with so many individuals—the support of slavery became more pronounced. Landon Cabel Garland, a literature professor, then served as president until 1846 when he moved to the University of Alabama.

William A. Smith, who became president of the college in 1846, developed a set of lectures, over many years, which he published in 1857 with the revealing title, *Lectures on the Philosophy and Practice of Slavery*.[133] William Smith's lectures covered the theological analogs to the legal issues discussed by James Holcombe who said natural law supported slavery. Smith began by asking, "Is the institution of domestic slavery sinful?" He added a practical concern to the question of sinfulness of slavery by also asking how the belief that it was sinful affected the safety of the entire republic.[134] "The foundations of public thought have to a greater extent been poisoned."[135] Even well-meaning politicians, like Phillip Doddridge, William C. Rives, Henry Clay, and Daniel Webster, who defended slavery often did so following an attack on slavery in the abstract.[136]

Smith's lectures, which were delivered to seniors at Randolph Macon, were well-received in southern legal circles. Alexander Hamilton Sands' *Recreations of a Southern Barrister*, published in 1859, provided an extensive and positive joint review of Smith and Bledsoe.[137] There was a similarly positive review in the *Southern Literary Messenger* in 1856, entitled, "The Duty of Southern Authors." The author of that review, perhaps William R. Aylett, who was a graduate of the University of Virginia, used Smith's book to write of the need for a history of southern slavery that proved it was necessary to the conservation of society.[138] Smith's publisher advertised the book as "An Offset to Helper's Book!"—a reference to Hinton Helper's book that criticized slavery on economic grounds.[139] Yet, some in the North had a different attitude. "We pray that this gentlemen may live long enough to be ashamed of his book, as we are of him," said the *Methodist Quarterly Review*.[140] As with Albert Bledsoe's essay, there was a book-length response to Smith's lectures.[141]

By the time he published his defense of slavery, William Smith had already been a central figure in pro-slavery thought for several decades. He had published a series of letters promoting pro-slavery thought in response to Rev. Norval Wilson of Fredericksburg.[142] And then in 1850, he spoke in Loudoun County, in northern Virginia along the Maryland border, apparently for nearly five hours. That elicited a written response from a Quaker living there, Samuel M. Janney. The Loudoun County grand jury indicted Janney for publishing an article that might incite slaves to insurrection; then, following the dismissal of charges, Janney published a pamphlet defending freedom of speech.[143] Smith's pro-slavery work also touched off a lawsuit regarding title to property of the Methodist church following the split between northern and southern Methodist congregations. The suit went all the way to the Supreme Court.[144] He was, to be sure, a steadfast defender of slavery.

Smith's lectures were based on his belief that despite the abolitionist offensive against slavery, based on the abstract doctrine of Jefferson's Declaration of Independence,[145] slavery continued to deliver practical results of stability. Slavery, Smith thought, fended off the "disturbing and ruinous influence of insurrection movements against the social order and even the safety of governments."[146] Two centuries of slavery's existence in America testified that the system "is *underlaid* somewhere by a *vast mine of principles—pure essential truths*—which are firmly rooted in the belief of all civilized and honest men, and which, all along, have imparted a spontaneous being and activity to the system, and will continue to do so perhaps as long as any considerable portion of the race shall remain in the country."[147]

Smith began his exploration with an inquiry into whether slavery is *in the abstract* a sinful institution. It comes as no surprise that the answer was no. He developed a theoretical defense of slavery based on his understanding of government's role in regulating society. Neither unrestrained freedom nor its correlative, the complete subjection of self, were practicable in government. Too much freedom leads to anarchy; too much restraint tends toward despotism. "A good government is such a harmonious union."[148] When those principles are appropriately balanced, there is a democratic republic. Slavery was defended broadly, as part of the fact of social organization that requires one to be a subordinate of another. "To secure the highest amount of happiness," government must balance the "antagonistic elements of *liberty and slavery*."[149] The appropriate form of government was determined by the conditions and state of society and those being governed. Given the ubiquity of slavery, Smith concluded that "no man in his sense will gravely affirm of an essential principle of government that it is wrong!"[150] Smith described in particularly direct detail the utility of slavery to political stability. When whites held menial jobs, which in southern states were fulfilled by slaves, they felt jealousy. That jealousy tempted them to "unsettle the foundations of society" by the use of leveling legislation.[151]

In response to the argument that slavery abridges natural rights, Smith advanced an argument similar to that made by many pro-slavery academics, that "the natural state of man is the state for which he was made—the state to which his entire nature is adapted—there can be no dispute, the *social* state is the *natural* state of man."[152] Thus, Smith rested upon an understanding that humans were, inherently, a part of society, and, therefore, that there never was a state of nature in which men were free. Smith named both Jefferson and Locke as the propagators of the myth of equality, which he termed socialism.[153] Pro-slavery writers in attacking Jefferson might attribute the Declaration of Independence to excited passions. As William Smith wrote, "our excellent forefathers, when they pronounced this truth to be self-evident, were not in the best mood to become philosophers, however well calculated to approve themselves the best of patriots."[154] Those theoretical political philosophers had incorrectly perceived human nature and natural law. The natural state of man "is a state of slavery in combination with liberty, *which is the complex idea of government.*"[155]

The legitimate object of government is to secure for the people the highest amount of freedom which their moral condition and relative circumstances will admit. Freedom was characterized by securing to each person the enjoyment of natural rights.[156] It was not freedom when the government secured rights for citizens that they were not prepared to handle. Having defined natural rights as "the highest amount of freedom of which their condition would admit" then made easy Smith's task of demonstrating that slavery did not violate slaves' natural rights.[157] He went on at length about the ways that slaves were not suited to independence. From that, he concluded that "duty to ourselves and humanity to [slaves] alike forbid that civil liberty be conferred on them."[158]

Smith's argument was similar to Bledsoe's, but it was more practical and it was more focused on the individual relationships of slaveowners to their enslaved human property. Where Bledsoe was theoretical, Smith was pragmatic. He spoke in direct terms, as one might expect of a book that originated as college lectures. The lectures emphasized the impossibility of emancipation and concluded with some suggestions that owners try to improve the lot of their slaves through education. Such was Smith's vision of a patriarchal slavery.

There is less direct evidence of the beliefs of other Randolph Macon faculty. For instance, Albert Barnes' antislavery book, *An Inquiry into the Scriptural Views of Slavery*, quoted Randolph Macon professor Edward Dungoold Sims as saying "extracts from holy writ unequivocally assert the right of property in slaves, together with the usual incidents of that right, such as the power of acquisition and disposition in various ways, according to municipal regulations. . . . Thus we see, that the slavery which exists in America was founded in right."[159]

The stories of the literature produced by University of Virginia and Randolph Macon College faculty members illustrate the place that southern faculty found for their ideas. Perhaps, as some have suggested, these ideas were part of making the faculty relevant. Maybe it was a way for outsiders to justify their institution. And in some ways one might find these figures tragic—people who ended up bending their ideas and positions to conform to what was profitable for them and their institutions. Partly this was because of the precarious nature of faculty employment. Tenure is a development of the twentieth century. Faculty members in the antebellum period were routinely fired for political reasons.[160]

It was the academies that rewarded those who fit with already-existing prejudices. And these stories of pro-slavery faculty can be retold across the South, from Emory College to the universities of Georgia, Alabama, and Mississippi—and at women's colleges as well. The remainder of this chapter will briefly sample some of the literature produced by faculty at southern schools.

William and Mary: Beyond Beverley Tucker and Thomas R. Dew

Thomas Roderick Dew died prematurely in 1846. But his dream lived on. William and Mary faculty continued to contribute to the pro-slavery cause and conservative political theory. The political theory moved from a defense of slavery as supporting republican principles for white men toward an increased focus on the fitness of people for freedom. That theory calibrated how much liberty people should have to their history and their supposed current conditions. It told of the aristocratic origins of Virginia's love of liberty, an origin located as far back as the barons' wresting the Magna Carta from King John, and it drew examples from across time and across the planet. That theory was told by Nathaniel Beverley Tucker's son-in-law Henry Augustine Washington, who carried the argument in complex (and at times, paradoxically, mildly antislavery) ways until nearly the Civil War. Following an education at Georgetown College and Princeton University and law training in Richmond, he joined the faculty in 1849. Washington took over Dew's position as professor of history and political economy. He was not yet thirty years old. Washington taught there for the nine years, until his death in 1858.[161]

Much of Washington's time was spent editing other people's work. He produced eight volumes of Thomas Jefferson's correspondence and collected Thomas Dew's lecture notes into a book *A Digest of the Laws, Customs, Manners, and Institutions of Ancient and Modern Nations*. Washington's thought appears in two key places—an essay the "Social System of Virginia," published in 1848 in the *Southern Literary Messenger*, and in an address on the Virginia constitution of 1776, delivered before the Virginia Historical Society in 1852.[162]

The "Social System of Virginia" purports to be a review of Robert Reid Howison's *History of Virginia* (and to a lesser extent Charles Campbell's *History of the Colony and the Ancient Dominion of Virginia*).[163] But it is more a key to two parts of Washington's thought. First, the purposes of writing history and what we might hope to learn from it; second, a defense of the aristocratic origins and nature of Virginia's history. Pieces of his essay suggest problems that slavery poses for the development of Virginia society, though at no point does that lead to a suggestion that slavery should be ended. It is more resignation regarding the problems of social and economic progress that slavery entailed upon Virginia society.

Washington began with a call, inspired by European historians, for a more scientific study of history. Washington identified a shift from theory to fact, from speculation to observation in history. In place of studies of history concerned with "courts, camps, and battle-fields," Washington proposed a study of the places where "the life of the people is spent"—"in the field, the work-shop, and the factory." He revealingly quoted Thomas Carlyle about the need to study the lives of people who made the discoveries that improved humanity's lot in life rather than study dry laws.

> Laws themselves, political constitutions, are not our life, but only the *house wherein our life is led*; nay, they are but the bare walls of the house; all whose essential furniture, the inventions, and traditions and daily habits that regulate and support our existence, are the works, not of Dracos and Hampdens, but of Phoenician mariners, of Italian masons, and Saxon metallurgists, of philosophers, alchemists, prophets and all the long train of artists and artisans; who, from the first, have been jointly teaching us how to think and how to act, how to rule our spiritual and our physical nature.[164]

Washington wanted to write "a history of the PEOPLE."[165] By which he meant "what they did, thought and felt, and how they spent their daily being."[166] Washington urged attention to data, as opposed to theory. Such attention to data would show how society progressed, presumably, as many others argued, because of slavery. However, Washington recognized a role for theory to help order facts and vice versa.[167] Washington concluded that the purpose of history was "to elucidate those great moral principles which connect themselves with the social progress of every people." To do this, he envisioned joining the facts of history with the principles of philosophy.

Washington addressed a central paradox in Virginia's history: How could society produce so many great statesmen, how could it so develop individual character, while not progressing economically as much as the North? His answer turned on Virginia's culture of "landed aristocracy," in which the master class obtained complete domination over the class of slaves.[168] Washington found three traits dominant in the social system of Virginia: the master-slave relationship, the predominance of the landed aristocracy, and isolated life in the country.[169] Together, those encouraged the development of a culture of individual liberty (as opposed to New England's tradition of civil liberty) and provided little impetus for economic and technological progress in society. "Where individualism reigns absolute and each man insists upon all his natural rights, it is manifest that there can be no society."[170] For slaves would likely see little benefit, Washington realized, to themselves. "The great law of human progress is not for him. As he is born, so must he die." And that question led in turn to an understanding that slaves might not work hard for their owners, since there was little for them.[171] That led to a modest indictment of slavery: "Is it not obvious that a system, which thus takes from labor its legitimate rewards and relieves idleness from its proper penalties, is fatal to exertion, and, consequently, to production." Washington did not support abolition of slavery; he was only advancing the idea that Virginia was burdened by slavery. "It is political economy and not humanity which raises its voice against" slavery, he concluded.[172] And having identified the burden, he hoped and expected that Virginia would move to correct it at some point, not perhaps through emancipation but through a shift in the practice of slavery.

Centenary College

Thomas Thornton, who served as president of Centenary College in Brandon Springs, Mississippi, from 1841 to 1844, published in 1841 a lengthy, though rarely discussed, pro-slavery treatise, *An Inquiry into the History of Slavery*.[173] Thornton was born in 1794 in Dumfrees, Virginia, and became a Methodist minister at age nineteen. After his presidency at Centenary, he helped form a school that lasted a few years in Jackson, Mississippi, known as the "College of Jackson." It provided both secondary and college education. Among the other instructors was Daniel Mayes, who had previously taught law at Transylvania. The College of Jackson soon closed, or maybe it is more proper to think of the school as transforming into another school in Brandon. In 1851 that school became known as Madison College. Thornton served Madison College until his death in March 1860.[174]

Thornton's treatise, written while he was a resident of Washington, DC, and published after he was appointed president at Centenary, began in a common way, with a statement about slavery's ubiquity and its origins in history before recorded time. The treatise was certainly pro-slavery, yet, Thornton occupied a more moderate position than Thomas Dew's text nearly a decade earlier.

Thornton pushed the cause of colonization; he argued against emancipation unless the newly freed people were removed from the southern states.[175]

Thornton blamed slavery in the South on England and on northern merchants and then talked about the impossibility of termination, but he represented something of a more moderate (or least less zealously pro-slavery) stance than many of his contemporaries. He refused to defend slavery in the abstract. "We do not believe that any benefit could justify the outrage committed by European tyranny and cruelty on oppressed Africa." But, as others said, "God has already brought . . . good out of this enormous evil."[176]

Thornton accepted that slavery in the abstract was wrong—a revealing and soon to be rare concession—but he thought that in context slavery was not a "moral evil." He thought the attacks of abolitionists like William Ellery Channing unfair to Southerners because they charged all slaveowners with the heinous acts carried out by a few.[177] Moreover, slavery was necessary to bring the uncultivated African race into contact with civilized whites.[178] Many of the elements of later works are here—but not well-developed, including that slaves are treated better than free workers in the United Kingdom and freed slaves become criminals.[179] The larger argument was that immediate emancipation would subvert southern safety and was a bad idea for the enslaved, too. It made ominous predictions about a servile insurrection and the bloodshed of white people along the lines of the revolution in St. Domingue (Haiti) and also predicted that if there ever were a servile insurrection, slaves would be slaughtered wholesale.[180] Yet, it also supported the American Colonization Society and the Virginia Colonization Society. A concluding chapter turned to a recent case in the U.S. Supreme Court, *Groves v. Slaughter,* which raised the question whether Mississippi could exclude slaves from being sold into the state.[181] The Supreme Court cautiously and disingenuously maneuvered around the question of whether slaves were articles of commerce. The Court interpreted the Mississippi constitution as not actually prohibiting the introduction of slaves and thus avoiding the issue of whether a state could not exclude them or whether the Interstate Commerce Clause prohibited Mississippi's regulation. But Thornton quoted extensively from the arguments of Mississippi senator Albert Berrian to show that there were important interests at stake that permitted the state to regulate slavery and to act to protect itself. Those arguments gained force, as well shall see in the last chapter, in the years immediately before the war. Thornton, even though moderate in many ways in comparison with other college professors, was part of the radicalization of southern ideas, which appeared in stark form in the southern secession debates.

Thornton resigned from Centenary in 1844, and several years later, in 1848, Augustus Longstreet arrived at Centenary College—by then relocated to Louisiana—from a decade of service as president of Emory College in Georgia. And therein lies a story of a forceful and important pro-slavery thinker.

Emory College

August Baldwin Longstreet is best remembered as a humorist, the author of *Georgia Scenes,* and sometimes considered a predecessor to Mark Twain. That does not, however, do justice to his lengthy career. Born in 1790 in Georgia, he graduated from Yale in 1813 and was educated for a year at Tapping Reeve's law school in Litchfield, Connecticut. He was admitted to the bar in 1815. Longstreet's career after that involved practicing law, serving briefly in the Georgia legislature beginning in 1821, and then as a superior court judge from 1823 to 1825. For more than dozen years after that, his career was practicing law and farming; in 1838 he became a Methodist minister, and in 1840 he became president of Emory College. For eight years he was president of Emory, during which time he wrote two pro-slavery pamphlets, the obscure *Letters on the Epistle of Paul to Philemon* published in 1845, and a series of letters *A Voice from the South: Letters from Georgia to Massachusetts* published in 1847.[182] Longstreet was, with William A. Smith, of Randolph Macon College, central to the split of the Methodist Episcopal Church, which occurred because of the slavery controversy.[183]

Longstreet's first set of letters, on Paul's letter to Philemon, was designed to show that slaveholding is not sinful and there is no moral evil in slavery.[184] But at the time he wrote it, Longstreet already realized that the gap between Northerners and Southerners was enormous. Southerners thought of Northerners as "a tribe of self-infuriated mad-men, rushing through the country with the Bible in one hand and a torch in the other—preaching peace, arousing to butchery—lauding liberty, and firing liberty's last temple."[185] That work was aimed at other Southerners. His more widely read work, *Voice from the South,* was written in the form of letters from the state of Georgia to her "sister," the state of Massachusetts. The nine letters review common tropes about slavery— that it was imposed on the South by northern merchants, that the South supported the North during the Revolution (and was owed support in return now), that emancipation was impractical, that the North would not even support the American Colonization Society, and that abolitionists violated the Constitution and incited slaves to rebellion.[186] Longstreet predicted that abolitionists would lead to the destruction of the Union.[187] He was already in 1847 boasting about how secession would be successful, in part because of the economic importance of cotton.[188] Central among Longstreet's complaints was the Wilmot Proviso, which would have barred slavery from territory acquired from Mexico during the Mexican-American War. He thought—in common with many at the time— that the Wilmot Proviso was unconstitutional and, further, that abolitionists, even though they admitted the Constitution was pro-slavery, attacked it by urging people to break their oaths to the Constitution, by trying to limit slavery in the territories, and by proposing that free states leave the Union and thus separate themselves from the South.[189] Longstreet's book demanded the South's rights and supported secession. While he conceded that some slave owners abused slaves, Longstreet thought that abolitionists exaggerated the harms.[190] Longstreet threatened disunion. Three other letters, styled letters from Georgia to her "sister" states of the South, appeared at the end of the book. Those letters focused on the Constitution—and the violations of the Fugitive Slave Clause and the Wilmot Proviso—and urged military preparation for war with the North.

In 1848, Longstreet left Emory College for a brief term as president of Centenary College—which had moved from Mississippi to Jackson, Louisiana, after Thomas Thornton's presidency. But Longstreet was there only briefly. In the fall of 1849 he became chancellor (president) of the University of Mississippi, where he stayed until 1856. In 1857, Longstreet became president of the South Carolina College (now the University of South Carolina), which he served until the war began in 1861. His 1859 graduation address at South Carolina College illustrates his pro-slavery and prosecession sentiments and his misplaced optimism about the prospects of a southern nation. For even as Longstreet urged preparation for war, he predicted secession could happen without war.[191]

Mississippi Planters' College

Among the more obscure academics who defended slavery is Ebenezer Newton Elliott. He was born in 1805 in Kentucky and educated at Miami University in Ohio, where he graduated in 1830. He taught mathematics at Indiana University from 1832 to 1836, when he became president of Mississippi College. After that he was president of Oakland Scientific School and then Planters' College in Port Gibson, Mississippi (it was later known as Ghent College and Washington Scientific School). Very little is known about either Elliott or the Planters' College. In fact, it may have been more of a high school than a college. But Elliott is remembered now as the editor of *Cotton Is King, and Pro-Slavery Arguments: Comprising the Writings of Hammond, Harper, Christy, Stringfellow, Hodge, Bledsoe, and Cartwright, on this Important Subject.* Elliott provided a brief but illuminating essay "Slavery in the Light of International Law" in *Cotton Is King.*[192]

That brief essay is helpful because it so boldly presents the culmination of southern thought. It is less about international law than about the pro-slavery perception of the world. It used John Quincy Adams' 1841 speech on trade with China to develop the principle that international law is dependent in large part on the conditions of countries involved in the law. Elliott drew an inference about trade with European and other nations, which taught in essence that the law among "civilized" countries is different from that among barbarous ones. Elliott then suggested the principles that European nations were justified, for instance, in taking land from Native Americans and labor from inferior races. The principle that the law differed according to the conditions of the country or people, framed the evidence that slavery was beneficial to slaves and helpful to enslavers; therefore, it should continue. Elliott's brief essay is particularly useful because it is unvarnished in its approach. Elliot asserted that slaves came from an inferior race. God had placed them there. "[T]heir own happiness and well-being, their duties to the human race, the claims of civilization, the progress of society, the law of nations, and the ordinance of God, require that they should be placed in a subordinate position to a superior race."[193] Even if one pointed to slaves' progress in the United States as evidence of their fitness for freedom, Elliott thought continued slavery was indispensable. "Like the electro-magnet, whose power is lost the moment it is insulated from the vivifying power of electricity, so the servile race loses its power when removed from the control of a superior intellect."[194] Elliott's system contemplated, it seemed, only continued slavery. It was not a particularly trenchant essay, but it contained the basic ingredients of the pro-slavery mind just before the Civil War. History, religion, and contemporary economics all pointed toward the justness of holding other people in slavery, for the good of everyone. That position contained the core of jurisprudence: a sense that law varied according to its context and an attention to what that context was. It was not deep, but it was revealing.

The Greensboro Female Academy and the Tuscaloosa Female Seminary

Another important site of education in the old South were the female seminaries. The secondary literature on southern female institutes has focused on divisions between male and female, in particular on the social meaning of female education in southern society. The literature usually explores how female institutes prepared women for their place in southern society. So we know a fair amount, but perhaps not as much as we might, about who the students and faculty were. We also know some tantalizing pieces of the curriculum, which included scientific subjects like anatomy, chemistry, and botany, as well as domestic topics.[195] Moreover, we know of some of the books that students were expected to read at the South Carolina Female Collegiate Institute in 1836. Those books included classics of college literature like Henry Hallam's *History of the Middle Ages* and Francis Wayland's *Moral Philosophy*.[196] William Gilmore Simms spoke of education as the primary duty of humanity in his inaugural address at the Spartanburg, South Carolina, Female College in 1855. Simms also spoke of the women's spheres and so helped confirm and police the boundaries between the subjects of male and female education.[197]

There are some tantalizing possibilities of what was discussed in the female institutes, seminaries, and colleges in the old South. One comes from the Greensboro Female Academy located in Greensboro, Alabama, one of the seats of wealth in Alabama's rich cotton country of Greene County. Greene County itself had a diversity of ideas. It was home to several proponents of the American Colonization Society. For instance, when Presbyterian minister John Witherspoon died in 1835 he left nearly thirty human beings in trust to Henry Clay, as president of the American Colonization Society. Another Greene County resident experimented with slaves running a plantation by themselves, in anticipation of moving them to Liberia. This is a version of what came to be known as holding people in a state of quasi-freedom. The owner, John Cocke, oversaw the plantation from afar; he lived in Virginia, and the experiment proved a failure. Despite those small examples, the vast majority of the thousands of people held in bondage in Greene County labored under harsh conditions.[198] For instance, important evidence of the lives of enslaved people comes from a lawsuit over George Hays' slaves. Hays' children challenged his widow's operation of the plantation with a brutal overseer.[199] Meanwhile, a local newspaper, the *Alabama Pilot*, reprinted excerpts from *A Defense of Slavery*, a book published in 1852 by Columbus, Mississippi, physician Matthew Estes. It discussed the history of slavery in Western civilization, as well as the benefits to both the enslaved and the slave owners.[200]

About the Greensboro Seminary, we know relatively little. It seems to have been started in the 1830s.[201] Nor do we know much about the school's principal, Baptist minister C. F. Sturgis. But we know something of Reverend Sturgis' writings. He wrote an essay on the duties of Christian masters, in the form of a dialogue between two brothers: the older is a politician and a lawyer named Joseph Melville; the younger is a man of Christian sentiments, William Melville. Sturgis called them the "Melville Letters." Perhaps we can reconstruct something of the culture of the school from Sturgis' essay; at the very least we can see how an important educator thought about "Christian slavery." The set of letters was one of three award-winning essays on the duties of Christian masters published by the Alabama Baptist Association in 1851.[202]

The Melville letters began with a question from the younger brother, William, to his brother, George, about masters' duties to their slaves. William phrased the questions as involving three linked issues: how a master might act for the benefit of the servant, the master, and for the country. George warned that he did not want William to become "righteous over-much," for even the discussion of masters' duties raised the potential for agitation that resulted in harsher conditions for the slaves.[203] Sturgis' formulation of "Christian duties" seemed to include little, if anything, that was inconsistent with the owners' best economic interest. What Sturgis urged as the best practices for treating enslaved humans were also—probably not coincidentally—practices that would allow owners to govern the enslaved people with the least resistance. How much, if any, of this was taught or discussed at the Greensboro Female Institute is unknown. At the very least, the young women at the Institute were in contact with a man who thought and wrote about slavery and did what he could to make it a "Christian" institution.

The most exciting possibility on what was taught and spoken in female seminaries comes from Caroline Hentz. Hentz, a native of Massachusetts, married in 1823 in Northampton, Massachusetts, where her husband, Nicholas Hentz, ran a school. In 1826, he began teaching French at the University of North Carolina. While in Chapel Hill, Caroline Hentz worked with George Moses Horton, a slave in nearby Chatham County, to help him publish some of his poetry. In 1833, shortly after leaving Chapel Hill, she published a novel, *Lovell's Folly*, which had a subplot of several slaves owned by a university president, modeled, it seems likely, on the University of North Carolina's president Joseph Caldwell.[204] Beginning in 1830, the couple operated a series of female seminaries—first, in Covington, Kentucky, then two years later, in Cincinnati, then again after two years, in 1834 they moved to Florence, Alabama, where they ran the Locust Dell Academy. The nine years spent in Florence turned out to be the longest time the couple spent anywhere. In 1843 they moved to the university town of Tuscaloosa, where they operated the Tuscaloosa female academy for two years. In 1845 they moved to Tuskegee, Alabama, and then in 1848 to Columbus, Mississippi, where they stayed until 1852. They retired together in 1852 to Florida, where both Nicholas and Caroline died in 1856.[205]

Over that time, Hentz wrote a series of important novels and short stories. The one for which she is best known is her 1854 book *The Planter's Northern Bride*. That was a topic on which she could speak perhaps somewhat autobiographically for she was a transplanted Northerner. But that book was also more clearly and unambiguously pro-slavery than much of her other work. With *The Planter's Northern Bride*, Hentz emerged as a vigorous defender of the South. The novel, a response to *Uncle Tom's Cabin*, recounts the conversion that the northern bride Eulalia underwent, from antislavery to pro-slavery, after she married a southern planter and learned of the virtues of slavery and, perhaps more importantly, the evils of abolitionism.

Another pro-slavery, and ambitious in some ways, short story by Hentz was about a college president. Set in an unnamed college town, which may have been Chapel Hill or perhaps Tuscaloosa, "The Stolen Boy," recounts the kidnapping of a free black child by a slave trader. The boy's mother, a free woman, seeks the assistance of the college president for whom she works. The president mortgages his home to buy back the child. The story is designed, as Hentz tells us, "as one of many instances of Southern kindness and humanity to a lowly race—whose feelings the Southron is too often accused of disregarding and trampling under foot." If a white employer could take so much interest in the child of a black employee, in whom he had no property interest, that would illustrate—as did Hentz's other fiction—the moonlight and magnolia world of Southerners' concern for their slaves. However transparently false that might be to readers, Hentz designed it to show that slavery was humane.[206] It illustrates the type of sentimental literature that Southerners produced in an effort to rebut the harshness of slavery and the persuasive antislavery literature like *Uncle Tom's Cabin*.[207]

Other Schools

These stories might easily be multiplied across many other schools. Some other scholars have dealt in fine detail with the pro-slavery ideas and actions at southern schools. For instance, Michael Sugrue makes a compelling case that South Carolina College (now the University of South Carolina) was the single most important school for pro-slavery politicians and thinkers.[208] Well before other schools began the move toward aggressive promotion of slavery, South Carolina College faculty were promoting slavery. For instance, in 1826, South Carolina College President Thomas Cooper published a defense of slavery.[209]

The best-known slavery advocate at South Carolina College was its president James Henley Thornwell. Born in South Carolina in 1812, he graduated from South Carolina College in 1831, then taught for a short while in Sumterville, South Carolina, studied briefly at Andover Seminary and Harvard Divinity School in 1834, and returned to Columbia, South Carolina, to study at the Presbyterian seminary there. He returned in 1838 to teach at South Carolina College, became the school's chaplain in 1841, and its president from 1851 to 1855, when he began teaching at the Columbia Divinity School. Over that time, he wrote extensively about Presbyterian doctrine and became one of the leading theologians in the United States.[210] Thornwell's work often promoted slavery.[211] Like many other southern educators, he justified expenditures on education in part as a way of defending southern values.[212] In addition to its pro-slavery faculty, orators at the school delivered influential lectures on the importance of slavery, and its alumni influenced thought and debate throughout the South, indeed, throughout the nation.[213]

Sometimes we have extensive knowledge of the nature of thought on colleges. We know a great deal about the University of Virginia, South Carolina College, and William and Mary. At other times, there is less to work with. Sometimes what remains are the writings of a single professor, which offer only a brief suggestion of what happened on college campuses far away from the centers of knowledge and away from the places where faculty could easily publish their work. We know relatively little about schools like LaGrange College in Florence, Alabama, and Oakland College in Louisiana. But what we know suggests an active and important circulation of ideas about slavery, its utility, and its future.

For instance, President Richard H. Rivers of Wesleyan University in Alabama (also known as LaGrange College), produced a textbook on moral philosophy for southern students.[214] LaGrange College had been founded in northwest Alabama by Methodists in 1830. The school splintered in the mid-1850s, when much of the school moved to nearby Florence. At that time it had about 250 students. Richard H. Rivers, who was born in Tennessee and had graduated in LaGrange's first class in 1835, began teaching ancient languages there in 1836. In 1843 Rivers left to become president of the Female Institute in Athens, Alabama (now Athens State University), and then he moved to Centenary College in Summerfield, Alabama, near Selma, where he served as president. There were a number of institutions that called themselves colleges which were more like high schools. Alabama's Centenary College, which was also some-times known as the Summerfield College and the Centenary Institute, was one such institution. Its impressive building, shown in Illustration 2.3, testifies to the wealth of Dallas County, Alabama, planters, but perhaps it is better thought of as a high school.[215]

Illustration 2.3 Centenary College, Dallas County, Alabama. (Library of Congress, Prints & Photographs Division, HABS, Reproduction number HABS ALA,24-SUM,2A—1.)

Rivers left Centenary College and went home to La Grange as its president in 1854. Rivers published several books after becoming president of LaGrange, including one on moral philosophy. In his discussion of "Practical Ethics," Rivers justified slavery in part because "slavery has been, and still is, a blessing to the negro."[216] Rivers drew heavily upon the lectures of William Smith at Randolph Macon, particularly his utilitarian defense of slavery, and invited readers to refer to them.[217] One of Rivers' colleagues at LaGrange, Edward Goodwin, published a novel, *Lily White*, in 1858, which described in idyllic terms the life of an owner and his slaves in Mississippi.[218]

Another college president who wrote a moral philosophy text for students is John L. Dagg, who was born in Virginia in 1794. Though he had little formal schooling, he served as a Baptist minister in Philadelphia from 1824 to 1834, served for two years as the president of the Haddington Literary and Theological Institute in Pennsylvania, and then moved to Alabama to teach at the Alabama Female Athenaeum in Tuscaloosa. Dagg taught there from 1836 until 1844 and then was president at Mercer University from 1844 to 1856. He published a textbook on moral philosophy, *Elements of Moral Science*, in 1859, whose two concluding chapters dealt with the need for slavery and the evils of abolition.[219]

Dagg believed that the tendency of the present age was against slavery. But Dagg wondered whether the move toward liberty—which appeared in France and in the British West Indies—was wise.[220] And Dagg thought that the limited efforts at emancipation in the United States suggested that emancipation was not a good idea. Dagg thought that slaves had adapted to the condition of slavery well and that slavery in the United States made them better off. "The Africans have multiplied in their slavery; have been better provided for than they would have been in the land of their forefathers; have been protected from the tyranny of oppressive kings, and the miseries of desolating wars; and, above all, have been brought under the influence of the gospel, in circumstances far more favorable to their civilization and evangelization than heathen nations generally enjoy."[221]

Dagg rehearsed a series of pro-slavery religious arguments. He began with the prevalence of slavery in the Old and New Testaments, as well as Roman law. He pointed to the episode in Corinthians where Paul sent Onesimus, who had run away, back to his owner.[222] Dagg admitted that slavery contained abuses, but thought that it was still necessary.[223] Its end would not come through the means that abolitionists advocated. Instead, the end had to come gradually.[224] The abolitionists' proposed reform shook "the foundations of the republic" and threatened harm. Dagg's grim conclusion to his book was a prayer that "if abolitionism is fanaticism," which he clearly believed it was, "undermining government, and opposing the will of Heaven, may God, in his mercy, deliver us from its power."[225]

At other schools the connections to slavery appeared less in the form of faculty's publications and more in terms of what happened on campus. Oakland

Illustration 2.4 Belles Lettres Literary Society, Oakland College, Mississippi.
(Library of Congress, Prints & Photographs Division, HABS, Reproduction number HABS
MISS,11-ALCO.V,1—2.)

College in Mississippi saw violence around slavery. Its president Jeremiah
Chamberlain, who was a member of the American Colonization Society, was
stabbed to death in September 1851 by George Briscoe, a local man angered in a
dispute over the faculty's supposed teaching of pro-Union doctrine.[226] A picture
of the Belles Lettres Literary Society's building on Oakland's campus (now part
of Alcorn State University) is Illustration 2.4.

The tables in this chapter convey a sense of the scope of southern collegiate
education in the years leading to the Civil War. Table 2.1 lists southern colleges and universities in operation in the 1840s and 1850s, Table 2.2 provides
the number of students enrolled in colleges in the southern states in 1850, and
Table 2.3 gives that same data for 1860. Finally, Table 2.4 presents a similar set of
data: the size of college libraries for those schools that had 1,000 or more books
in the late 1850s. Books are crucial for transmitting ideas. They have been the
focus of much of this work so far—and as the first chapter tried to convey, books
were key places that pro-slavery thinkers turned to help understand the world.
William and Mary professor Thomas Dew constructed his argument not just
out of the world he observed around him; he also relied on books to build his
argument. He looked to works by authors in ancient Greece, from eighteenth-
century England, and from contemporary England and the United States.
Often Dew read and critiqued antislavery work, but he also—obviously—used

Table 2.1 **Southern Colleges and Universities in Operation in 1840s and 1850s**

Alabama
  Centenary Institute
  East Alabama Female College
  East Alabama Men's College (now Auburn)
  Howard College
  Judson Female Institute
  La Grange College
  Southern University
  Spring Hill College
  University of Alabama

District of Columbia
  Georgetown
  George Washington

Georgia
  Legrange Female College
  Mercer
  Oglethorpe
  Oxford College (now Emory University)
  University of Georgia
  Wesleyan Female College

Kentucky
  Bacon (after the Civil War, University of Kentucky)
  Bethel
  Centre
  Georgetown
  Kentucky Military Institute
  Paducah
  St. Joseph's College
  Transylvania
  University of Louisville

Louisiana
  Centenary College
  Jefferson College
  Louisiana State University
  Mt. Lebanon College
  Tulane

Maryland
  Loyola
  Mount St. Mary's
  St. Johns
  University of Maryland
  Washington College

(continued)

Table 2.1 **Continued**

Mississippi

   College of St. Andrews, Jackson

   Jackson College

   Jefferson College

   Planters' College (originally Southern Scientific Institute)

   Mississippi College

   Madison

   Oakland

   Semple-Broaddus

   University of Mississippi

Missouri

   Central

   Culver-Stockton

   Lindenwood Female College

   St. Louis University

   University of Missouri

   Washington University

   Westminster

   William Jewell

North Carolina

   Catawba

   Chowan Female Collegiate Institute

   Davidson

   Greensboro

   Trinity

   University of North Carolina

   Wake Forrest

South Carolina

   The Citadel

   College of Charleston

   Columbia College

   Erskine

   Furman

   Newburg

   South Carolina College

   Wofford

Tennessee

   Bethel

   Carson Newman

   Cumberland

   Madison Female College

(continued)

Table 2.1 **Continued**

Maryville
Tusculum
Union
University of Nashville
Texas
Austin College
Baylor College
Virginia
Emory and Henry
Hampden-Sydney
Randolph Macon
Richmond College
Roanoke College
University of Virginia
Union Theological Seminary
Washington College
William and Mary

I have listed schools in existence in the 1840s and/or the 1850s; this list tends toward over-inclusion and a generous definition of "college." For some, such as the Planters' College of Mississippi, little is known. In fact, Colin B. Burke, perhaps the leading historian of antebellum colleges, speculates that it may have been more of an academy than a college.

Sources: JOHN MCCARDELL, IDEA OF A SOUTHERN NATION AT 348–49 (1981); COLIN B. BURKE, AMERICAN COLLEGIATE POPULATIONS (1982); DONALD G. TEWKESBURY, THE FOUNDING OF AMERICAN COLLEGES AND UNIVERSITIES 211–20 (1932); AMERICAN EDUCATIONAL YEAR-BOOK (BOSTON, JAMES ROBINSON AND COMPANY 1858); WILLIAM HENNINGTON WEATHERSBY, A HISTORY OF EDUCATIONAL LEGISLATION IN MISSISSIPPI FROM 1798 TO 1860 (1921); TWENTY-FOURTH ANNUAL REPORT OF THE DIRECTORS OF THE AMERICAN EDUCATION SOCIETY 107 (1840) (lists schools and number of faculty and students at each school, as of 1840).

pro-slavery works to show the centrality of slavery. Chapter 10 turns again to an intensive study of books, this time ones that Thomas Cobb relied on to construct his pro-slavery legal treatise.[227]

While twenty-first-century readers are likely accustomed to hearing about liberal faculty who take up causes of social justice, the southern academy in the years leading to the Civil War was quite different. By looking at the writing of faculty at southern schools from the 1830s to the Civil War, it becomes apparent that they were writing and teaching about the importance of slavery; less often they challenged it. The faculty defended slavery in a variety of ways. Often the defense was based on empirical grounds of history and economics. That is, the centuries-long embrace of slavery by other cultures and the apparent economic need for enslaved labor were bedrock principles in the defense of slavery. The

Table 2.2 **Number of Colleges, Faculty, and Students, 1850**

State	Number of Colleges	Number of Teachers	Number of Students
Alabama	5	55	567
Arkansas	3	14	150
Georgia	13	34	1,535
Kentucky	15	100	1,873
Louisiana	6	41	469
Maryland	13	98	1,127
Mississippi	11	45	308
Missouri	9	65	1,009
North Carolina	5	29	513
South Carolina	8	43	720
Tennessee	18	83	1,605
Texas	2	7	165
Virginia	12	73	1,343

Sources: J. D. B. DeBow, Statistical view of the United States . . . Being a Compendium of the Seventh Census 141 (Washington, Beverley Tucker 1854). The Census acknowledges the problems with its estimate, because census marshals sometimes misclassified academies as colleges. A note that precedes the aggregate data on Education observes that female colleges, law institutions, etc., had been sometimes classed improperly with academies. *Id.* at 141. Some sense of the problems with the table is gained by comparison with another at page 145 of the same census, which purports to tabulate colleges, theological, medical, and law schools. That table, which one might think would be more comprehensive than the one reproduced in part here, lists different (and often significantly lower) numbers of schools, faculty, and students for each state.

The Census data was, in turn, used in the *Southern Literary Messenger* to show that southern states had a larger percentage of their white males in college than did northern schools. (The key component was that the article excluded black men from the calculation.) See *Progress of Education in Virginia; The University and The Colleges*, 24 S. Lit. Messenger 161 (March 1857).

self-serving economic arguments reveal where the slave-owning class stood. These ran alongside extensive defenses of slavery on religious grounds, which is largely outside the scope of this volume.[228]

The empirical arguments often supported the political theory of slavery and hierarchy. Sometimes faculty argued that slavery provided the basis for republican government by making white men independent and equal. That was an argument that seemed to have more favor in the 1830s than later. By the 1850s the political theory in favor among many southern academics was that enslaved people were unfit for freedom, which was bolstered by arguments about the

Table 2.3 **Number of Colleges, Faculty, and Students, 1860**

State	Number of Colleges	Number of Teachers	Number of Students
Alabama	17	116	2120
Arkansas	4	9	225
Georgia	32	181	3302
Kentucky	20	110	2485
Louisiana	15	86	1530
Maryland	9	82	628
Mississippi	13	50	856
Missouri	36	211	4291
North Carolina	16	94	1540
South Carolina	14	90	1384
Tennessee	35	149	2932
Texas	25	107	2416
Virginia	23	163	2824

Source: STATISTICS OF THE UNITED STATES ... IN 1860 ... OF THE EIGHTH CENSUS 502-10 (Washington, 1866). Similar statistics are available in HISTORICAL STATISTICS, MILLENNIAL EDITION, Table Bg194-206 (liberal arts college enrollment rates and private liberal arts colleges, by state and region: 1800–1860, which is based on COLIN B. BURKE, AMERICAN COLLEGIATE POPULATIONS: A TEST OF THE TRADITIONAL VIEW Table 1.2, Tables 2.1–2.25, Appendix A, and passim (1982)), and Table Bg166-175 (private and nonprofit elementary, secondary, and higher education schools, enrollment, and personal consumption expenditures: 1800–1999).

Table 2.4 **Southern Colleges with 1,000 or More Library Volumes, Late 1850s**

State	Institution	Volumes
Alabama		
	Howard College	2,200
	Howard Theological Institute	1,000
	La Grange	5,529
	Spring Hill	8,000
	University of Alabama	11,500*
	Wesleyan College	2,000

(continued)

Table 2.4 **Continued**

State	Institution	Volumes
Georgia		
	Emory	6,685*
	Medical College of Georgia	3,500
	Mercer	5,500
	Oglethorpe	6,500
	University of Georgia	18,000*
	Wesleyan Female College	1,500
Kentucky		
	Augusta	3,000
	Bethel	3,000
	Centre	7,100*
	Cumberland	1,210
	Georgetown	8,000*
	Kentucky Military Institute	10,000
	St. Joseph's	6,685
	Shelby	4,000
	Transylvania	22,000*
Louisiana		
	Baton Rouge	1,000
	Centenary	6,200*
	Jefferson	6,000
	Jesuits	2,000
	Louisiana	3,000
	St. Charles	6,000
	Washington	1,800
Maryland		
	Baltimore Female College	3,000
	Calvert College	2,000
	College of St. James	8,970*
	Mt. St. Mary's	4,000
	St. John's	3,292

(continued)

Table 2.4 **Continued**

State	Institution	Volumes
	St. Mary's	13,000
	U.S. Naval Academy	7,500
	Washington	2,000
Mississippi		
	Mississippi College	1,600
	Oakland College	4,640*
	University of Mississippi	9,000*
North Carolina		
	Davidson	8,000
	University of North Carolina	9,501*
	Wake Forest	7,400*
South Carolina		
	College of Charleston	7,000
	Furman	1,500
	South Carolina College	25,000
	Wofford	1,000
Tennessee		
	Columbia Female College	3,500
	Cumberland University	12,000
	East Tennessee University	5,200
	Franklin College	20,500*
	Greenville College	3,300
	Hiawassee College	1,100
	Jackson College	4,000*
	Southwest Theological Seminary	4,275
	Tusculum College	1,000
	Union University	2,500
	University of Nashville	18,159
	Washington College	1,800
Texas		
	Baylor	1,000

(continued)

Table 2.4 **Continued**

State	Institution	Volumes
Virginia		
	Bethany College	2,577
	Chesapeake Female College	3,000
	College of William and Mary	9,000
	Emory & Henry College	16,507
	Hampden-Sydney	8,612*
	Randolph Macon College	6,300*
	Rector College	2,500
	Richmond College	1,500
	Roanoke College	2,500
	University of Virginia	16,982
	Virginia Military Institute	4,872*
	Washington College	2,500

* Includes college literary society libraries' collections, which are listed separately in Rhees.

Sources: WILLIAM J. RHEES, MANUAL OF PUBLIC LIBRARIES, INSTITUTIONS, AND SOCIETIES, UNITED STATES, BRITISH PROVINCES OF NORTH AMERICA 585–650 (Philadelphia, J. B. Lippincott, 1859). Many of the libraries reported their holdings as of 1857, but some used earlier years. *See also* ISAAC W. STEWART, ON THE CLASSICAL TONGUES AND THE ADVANTAGES OF THEIR STUDY . . . SOUTH CAROLINA COLLEGE . . . DECEMBER 12, 1835 (A. S. Johnston, Columbia, SC, 1835) (listing libraries in North Carolina).

economic disaster that would follow emancipation. Where in the 1830s Thomas Dew argued in favor of slavery because it made white people prosperous and improved in some ways the conditions of the enslaved, by the 1850s pro-slavery academics pointed to the benefits to the slaves of slavery as well as to the need for hierarchy.[229] There was no longer talk of the natural law that all people are created equal. The optimism of Thomas Jefferson and the Enlightenment was replaced with the natural law of Aristotle as promulgated by University of Virginia law professor James Holcombe. Others, like University of Virginia professor Albert Taylor Bledsoe, had a parallel political theory that justified freedom for some and slavery for others. Bledsoe thought that society should be ordered so that some ruled over others.

Thus, the nature of the pro-slavery argument shifted over time. Perhaps this was partly due to the shifting nature of the antislavery argument. As antislavery advocates shifted their vision of enslaved people as beasts who should be feared to virtuous citizens who were wrongfully enslaved, pro-slavery writers responded. They had spoken of the virtues of slavery for white people—and continued to do so. But they also increasingly emphasized why the enslaved were not suited for freedom. A corollary to that argument was that slavery was supposed to be good for the enslaved, because it compelled them to work and because they were best suited to being governed by others. These were bitter doctrines, designed to tell the wealthy and well educated that what they were doing was natural, necessary, and even moral. Such ideas were not just promulgated by the faculty in the classroom and in their writings. The students also heard them from visiting dignitaries who spoke to literary societies and at graduations. The students themselves debated these ideas in their literary societies. The next chapter turns to ideas about slavery in circulation on campus outside the classroom. It finds again a broad defense of slavery, from economy to political theory; it also finds direct engagement with the Constitution and ideas of Union and later secession. The students, like the faculty and the rest of southern culture, defended slavery with increasing vigor. The ideas of slavery were on the march in many places.

3

The Southern Scholar

In 1837 Ralph Waldo Emerson delivered the American Scholar Address to the Harvard Phi Beta Kappa Society.[1] Emerson assigned scholars, by which he mostly meant students, the task of looking through to the truth. The scholar, Emerson thought, "is the world's heart. . . . [W]hatsoever new verdict Reason from her inviolable seat pronounces on the passing men and events of to-day,— this he shall hear and promulgate."[2] Emerson expressed the optimism of the era when he told students there are new thoughts to be explored. "There are new lands, new men, new thoughts." It was natural, then, for Americans to "demand our own works and laws and worship."[3] Such searching questions led Emerson and many other transcendentalists to oppose slavery. Emerson's ideas reflected the radical potential of schools.

Some in the South in Emerson's time saw a special role for scholars. In 1846 a young orator at Wake Forest College praised the Declaration of Independence as the principle Francis Bacon applied to politics. That was a reference to the seventeenth-century English scientist, who is credited with developing the scientific method.[4] The Declaration was feared by many because it pointed the way to freedom. But it also suggested that irrational hierarchy would be pushed down. No longer would people rule by divine right, but voters would take control for themselves.

Youth tends to bring out optimism. Henry Tutwiler, then only two years out of the University of Virginia, arrived in Tuscaloosa, Alabama, in 1831 as one of the first faculty for the University of Alabama. He brought with him some of the vestiges of the Enlightenment, including a commitment to the gradual termination of slavery. Tutwiler wrote of slavery in 1832 that "almost all moral and political evil in this state may be traced to this fruitful source—it exhausts our soil, corrupts our morals, and is the chief cause of that diversity of interest which is fast tending to rend asunder our political fabric."[5] Tutwiler joined those already in Tuscaloosa who were working against slavery. In 1831 leading citizens of Tuscaloosa founded the Alabama Colonization Society, a branch of the American Colonization Society. Four years before that, in 1827, several Tuscaloosans had worked to free a young African American boy who had been kidnapped in Philadelphia and then sold into slavery to a local tin smith. Through extraordinary efforts by local Methodist ministers and the mayor of Philadelphia, a Tuscaloosa County jury set young Cornelius Sinclair free. Then the minsters put him on his way back to Philadelphia.[6] Similarly, at the University of North Carolina's graduation ceremonies in 1832, William Gaston, soon to be a member of the North Carolina Supreme Court, expressed the hope that slavery would be ended, as had a graduation speaker there in 1829. (Gaston's speech is discussed at the end of Chapter 8.)[7] Yet, the arc of thought shifted toward the defense of slavery over time at the University, as it did throughout the South. This meant Tutwiler and James Birney, one of the trustees of the University of Alabama and an advocate of colonization—and later a candidate for president on the Liberty Party ticket—were on the losing side in Tuscaloosa.

In 1834, Tutwiler gave a graduation address to students at the University with an optimistic assessment of the ability to make moral progress. Humans have the desire for progress in knowledge and take pleasure in it, Tutwiler told the students. The address represents the Enlightenment thought that was still dominant in parts of Virginia in the 1810s and 1820s of Tutwiler's youth. Tutwiler, then still in his twenties (he was born in 1807), spoke to Alabama's Erosophic and Philomathic literary societies of the duties of students and teachers to think for themselves. The dark ages had been the result of unquestioned authority. "What," he asked, "but the disposition to receive at second hand the opinions of others without examination, shed such disastrous twilight, for so many centuries, over the human intellect—when it was a sufficient reason for theories the most absurd and repugnant to common sense to say the master hath said it? when Aristotle was every thing and reason nothing." Liberation came when students questioned those ideas and they fell away.[8] Tutwiler urged a similar kind of activity for his audience. "We must think for ourselves, and not be the mere passive receptacles of the thoughts of others."[9] Students particularly needed to be skeptical of the ideas in books.[10] Tutwiler was suspicious of books, with good reason. As have already seen and as we shall see again, many books frequently taught a doctrine of obedience to the existing order. Yet, Tutwiler's was an optimistic address, concluding with a celebration of moral progress.

Tutwiler represented a final glimmer of the Enlightenment in antebellum Tuscaloosa, where the University of Alabama was located. Tutwiler's address represents the idea that the search for truth sets scholars on lonely paths, which may lead them to ask unsettling questions about the world around them. The early optimism and antislavery advocacy at Alabama ended in 1837. That was the year that Baptist minister Basil Manly came from his pulpit in Charleston, South Carolina, to Tuscaloosa to serve as president. Shortly after Manly's arrival, Tutwiler left the University. The center point of thought was shifting in Tuscaloosa, as elsewhere in the South, toward slavery.[11] Manly was an important

disseminator of pro-slavery rhetoric. He became a frequent target of abolitionists for his statement that he supported the right of Southerners to sell slaves at
will—and that "however great the trial to my feelings in other respects, I have
none as to the rights of property."[12]

Some scholars, then, were part of Emerson's call for the scholar to be the
"bringer of hope." Some, but not a lot. This chapter examines the addresses
given at southern schools to literary societies and at graduations. Where the
last chapter focused on the writing of faculty, this chapter focuses on the visiting dignitaries—often lawyers, judges, and politicians—and also the ideas
of students on those campuses. Thus, this chapter brings the leaders of the
southern community and the students into focus. It suggests the close relationship between slave-owning southern society and the schools. This chapter follows up on the survey of pro-slavery academic thought in the last chapter with a sample of the hundreds of addresses given at southern schools. The
literary addresses provide a gauge of the ideas that were valued, the direction
of thought at the institution, and the ways that the political and intellectual
leaders raised the next generation of leaders. Selections from the universities
of Alabama and Virginia, and several schools in Mississippi, may illustrate the
main currents of southern thought. The addresses point to common elements
of moral philosophy, of support for established order, and of the invocation
of history.[13]

Literary Addresses as Sites of Pro-slavery Thought

William Gilmore Simms, one of the leading novelists of the old South and editor
of the important literary journal the *Southern Quarterly Review*, wrote about the
importance of literary addresses in a review of several orations in 1851. Printed
addresses were evidence of the southern intellect. They were key vehicles for the
propagation of ideas and key markers of southern ideas:

> Lectures, orations and addresses, in the South, are required to assert a
> higher rank than they are apt to do in other regions. They, in fact, con-
> stitute a great portion of the literature proper of our section, and we
> should be doing the greatest possible wrong to the native intellect, were
> we to pass it by as a thing simply of occasion and without permanent
> claims to our recognition and regards. In these performances lie the
> most ample proofs, of our giving, of our intellectual activity. Here must
> we look for the evidence of our politics and philosophy, our fancy and
> imagination. This is the only open medium by which the leading minds
> of the South may approach their people.[14]

While literary addresses certainly had their share of what one reviewer in the *Southern Quarterly Review* (perhaps William and Mary professor Beverley Tucker) termed "vapid common places, and stereotyped pedantry," many of the addresses invite serious scrutiny for evidence of the place of oratory in southern thought and others for the content of southern ideas, particularly about constitutionalism.[15] In 1854, the *Southern Quarterly Review* expressed optimism about the prospects for southern literature produced by southern scholars. Libraries, schools, and books were three key pieces of evidence of the growth in southern thought and evidence, too, that the "Southern people are at last awakening to a true sense of what they owe to themselves." And there was a growing public demand for the "Southern scholar" to "address the reading public."[16]

The shift from the 1830s to the 1850s provides a gauge of southern thought. At northern and southern colleges, addresses commonly celebrated order and moderate progress. Sometimes Southerners traveled north of the Mason-Dixon line to deliver addresses. In 1838, for instance, James McDowell, who was a leader of the antislavery delegates in the Virginia legislature in 1832, spoke at Princeton. Given his advocacy in 1832, one might have thought that he would argue against slavery. But things had changed in the six years since the debates in the wake of the Nat Turner rebellion. McDowell did not hazard antislavery sentiments in the Princeton address.[17] Instead his address was an eloquent appeal to Union and to the virtues of democracy. Despite the common Whig argument that democracy would lead to licentiousness, McDowell argued that political legitimacy grew out of "popular sovereignty."[18] He urged the Princeton audience to cast aside "every prejudiced conception of the popular capacity."[19] McDowell took a moderate Democrat stance and minimized the party conflicts. "The party excesses which now and then have distinguished our political contests, have thus far broken and exploded upon our system, only as the meteoric lights which glade and terrify for a moment, and then break and explode upon the earth, without jostling or impeding in the least its onward and its massive movement."[20] McDowell spoke of the empire of democracy that was part of an ancient tradition of self-government. The United States was "a sort of providential decree, universal, enduring, baffling all efforts of man to check or limit its control." And only in the United States had those principles and that hope reached their "full development." McDowell predicated that the United States' democracy would spread around the world. "The spirit of our laws, let superstition and ignorance and power do what they like to destroy it, will abide upon the earth as the redeeming spirit of after times, and shall pass from hand to hand, like the inextinguishable fire of the Grecian temples, till all the nations be filled with its brightness."[21]

McDowell was also wary of abolition "fanatics." And thus while his talk appealed to democracy, it warned of the conflicts that might arise from excessive party politics and a failure to compromise. McDowell pled the case of Union in the face of what he saw as fanaticism. This was part of McDowell's drift away from antislavery principles and toward an embrace of slavery, which gained momentum after he entered the U.S. House of Representatives. In September 1850 during debate over the Wilmot Proviso, which would have excluded slavery from territory acquired from Mexico during the Mexican-American War, McDowell returned to the theme of his Princeton address, about the way that the United States provided hope to the rest of the world and how disunion would be the end of that hope. He thought that the maintenance of southern rights regarding slavery was critical to the Union. "Ours . . . is the high duty of replacing and maintaining the Union in which that country, as a whole, consists, not upon the hesitating consent—not upon the broken confidence—not upon the discounted but quelled spirit, and not upon the surrendered safety of any of its parts, but upon the honorable conciliation, the responding forth, and the cordial agreement of them all."[22] McDowell feared that the abolitionists had unleashed a subject—"with a wild and explosive energy"—that would call into question "the very body and being of the state."[23] The abolitionists, in short, threatened the "happy and united country" with disunion and war.[24] That was in a transitional period, when many Southerners were trying to take a moderate stance between the zealously pro-slavery views that appeared in the 1840s and 1850s and the emerging immediate abolitionist views. People with McDowell's moderation were on the wane. Two other Southerners spoke at Princeton in favor of slavery in the 1850s. They appear at the beginning of the next chapter.

Colleges were places where students were disciplined to follow and accept traditional values such as patience, and obedience to established thought and hierarchy, as well as universal values like hard work and patriotism. In the 1830s, addresses frequently focused on individual duties of patriotism and hard work. Orators began shifting their focus to more explicitly political and pro-slavery purposes in the 1840s, and by the 1850s the addresses were often stridently pro-slavery and prosouthern. In the 1840s and 1850s the addresses often focused on a set of ideas, the role of the educated in supporting the values of society, and the role of schools in promoting the values of slavery, property, and law.

This chapter discusses some of the key addresses from schools around the South, with specific arguments shifting over time and in different settings. A set of key principles emerged from the addresses. First, they often justified schools as places of promulgation of southern values (that is, support of slavery) and as places where students could learn to defend slavery. For instance, the editor of Richmond's periodical the *Southern Literary Messenger*, John Reuben Thompson, delivered an address at Washington College's 1850 graduation. Thompson was a leading figure in the literary movement of the South and a leading proponent of southern literary nationalism and of pro-slavery thought. He took over the editorship of the *Southern Literary Messenger* in 1847 when he was only twenty-four and he continued until 1860.

Thompson's address, on the "present condition of education and literature in Virginia,"[25] was an explanation of the role that literature played in Virginia society. Thompson called for broad general education, which he supported with the argument that people were only entitled to self-government if they were fit for it. This was the political theory that was becoming so popular in southern literary addresses: enslaved people were not fit for self-government.[26] In this way, hierarchy was used to advocate education. Moreover, in contrast to many speakers (often Democrats) who emphasized the positive nature of widely distributed literature, Thompson saw much contemporary literature as subversive—either because it lacked morals or because it was antislavery.[27] "Fanaticism in . . . that fell shape of modern abolition, which, with impious tread, has dared to confront the presence of the Divine Majesty itself and mock at its revelation, stalks abroad through the land."[28] Thompson had a particular cure for this, which may be seen as somewhat self-serving given his occupation as editor of a literary journal. "There is but one way to counteract this influence," Thompson said, "and this is by a literature of our own, informed with the conservative spirit, the love of order and justice, that constitutes the most striking characteristic of the Southern mind."[29]

While many of the addresses, such as Thompson's, aimed at justifying southern schools because they produced southern scholars who defended southern institutions, other addresses directly defended slavery and the political theory underlying it. Especially in the early 1850s, some of the addresses tell the story of political theory, of hierarchy, and the suitability of some people to slavery. For instance, Robert Toombs, who served as a U.S. Senator from Georgia from 1853 to 1861 (and then as a general in the Confederacy) defended slavery in an address given to the Few and Phi Gamma Literary Societies at Emory College in Oxford, Georgia, in 1853. (Illustration 3.1 is of the Few Literary Society building on the Emory Campus). He found that slavery gave stability to the South. "In glancing over the civilized world, the eye rests upon not a single spot where all classes of society are so well content with their social system, or have greater reason to be so, than in the slaveholding states of the American Union." Slavery was responsible for the world of order. As Toombs phrased it, "Stability, progress, order, peace, content and prosperity reign throughout our borders."[30] Nevertheless, he understood that many disagreed with his assessment. So his purpose was to "vindicate the wisdom, humanity, and justice of the system, to show that the position of the African race in it, is consistent with its principles [and] advantageous to that race and society."[31] Then followed an investigation of history, ranging from the American colonies, where slavery was commonplace, back to ancient Egypt, where the ancient monuments "furnish evidence both of [the Africans'] national identity and his social degradation before history began." Toombs depicted Africans as suited only to slavery. "We find him then without government, or laws, or protection, without letters,

Illustration 3.1 Few Literary Society Hall, Emory College, Georgia,. (Library of Congress, Prints & Photographs Division, HABS, Reproduction number HABS GA,109-OXFO,2B—2.)

or arts, or industry, without religion, or even the aspirations which would raise him to the rank of an idolator."[32] Toombs pointed to Haiti, the British West Indies, and Jamacia and claimed that experiments in freedom in those places similarly showed the incapacity of enslaved Africans for freedom. Yet, when he turned to the American South he found that the slave population was increasing, a sign of the success of the institution. Toombs presented both a concise and broad defense of slavery. His simple conclusion was that "the adoption of no other system under our circumstances would have exhibited the individual man (bond or free) in a higher development, or a society in a happier civilization."[33]

While Toombs looked across a series of arguments, other speakers concentrated their attention. In 1852 mathematics professor William Porcher Miles of the College of Charleston spoke about a controversial topic, which illustrated how far South Carolinians were from the idea of universal equal rights. The title of his address was also its thesis: "Republican Government not everywhere and always the best; and Liberty not the Birth-right of Mankind." It was an address about the power of public opinion. At some points in history, people followed what they were told—they accepted aristocracy for example. Yet at other times, they rejected it. Miles put public opinion, then, in context. Some nations at some points were well suited to freedom, and at other times they were not suited to it. He mocked what he labeled Thomas Jefferson's "monstrous and dangerous fallacy" in the Declaration of Independence that all people are created equal. His conclusion was that liberty "must be rooted in the nature, manners and habits, no less than the thoughts and affections, of a People. You cannot force or rear it under the bell-glass of a mere Written Constitution."[34] This was an indictment of universal freedom and an endorsement of slavery. Miles was an academic when he gave that 1852 address at the College of Charleston, but soon afterward, in 1855, he was elected mayor of Charleston and then the next year he was elected to Congress, where he became a leading voice in favor of secession.[35]

Perhaps the most strident literary address of the antebellum era was William Stiles' "Southern Education for Southern Youth," delivered in 1858 at Georgia's Cherokee Baptist College. Stiles was in some ways an unlikely author of that address, for he had given several other literary addresses on more traditional topics, such as the relationship between eloquence and liberty, which he delivered at the University of Georgia in 1852.[36] But by 1858, the fifty-year-old Stiles had served in Congress and as the speaker of the Georgia House of Representatives, and he was ready to declare in favor of the *Educational Independence of the South*." This was an issue of even more importance than commercial, financial, and literary independence.[37] Stiles feared that northern education made Southerners unfit "for their native institutions." Worse still, though, it "implant[ed] in them a deadly hostility to" slavery, "which nothing but its destruction could possibly appease."[38]

Stiles thought abolitionists tried to disseminate their ideas.[39] He focused attention on Harvard and Yale in particular. Where they had once been "looked to as the great conservators of the peace and harmony of this confederacy," in recent years they were no longer beacons to guide supporters of the Constitution. Now they are "fired by fanaticism," which "shed their light, and heat, and baneful influence over the mind and literature of the entire North."[40] Stiles pointed out that Harvard Law School had recently "deposed their best law professor," Judge Edward P. Loring, who had returned Anthony Burns to slavery in 1854.[41] Stiles described the general antislavery tenor of Boston, which sent Anson Burlingame to Congress to proclaim that "we need an anti-slavery Constitution, an antislavery Bible, and an anti-slavery God."[42]

In such an environment, Stiles wondered about the future of southern scholars:

> But the evil is not confined to the influence of abolitionist instructors.
> Their collegiate course embraces a series of abolition textbooks all
> breathing the most violent hostility to our institutions and conveying

the most unjust and invidious comparisons against the South, . . . up to the higher law reasoning of "Wayland's Moral Science" is a constant effort to impress the mind with the sinfulness and degrading tendency of slavery, and the responsibility of all citizens, whether at the North or the South in its existence. . . . The whole moral atmosphere in the vicinity of those Northern institutions is so highly impregnated as to render it impossible for a student to breathe it without inhaling abolition at every breath.[43]

The address proceeded to offer a southern education on the importance of slavery, indeed, on its centrality to civilization.[44] Stiles sought to "gather the wisdom from the teachings of the past" as he covered well-known ground about the ubiquity of slavery, the revolution in Haiti, and economic problems following emancipation in the West Indies. He conclusion was that wherever slavery existed, "it was accompanied by the highest civilization and greatest prosperity."[45] The final words of his speech were ones of defiance. "Our motto *shall* be '*Independence now, Independence forever*.'"[46]

In 1854 John Randolph Tucker spoke before the William and Mary literary societies about the political theory of republicanism. He offered a defense of republicanism for the checks it offered to democratic impulse.[47] Tucker's abstract address first turned to the republican idea in the United States, which combined democratic and representative principles, and balanced the power of the people with the liberty of individuals. In fact, liberty, which involved protection of individual rights, was central to Tucker's world. He thought that humans are entitled to the utmost civil liberty that can exist while still maintaining society. Tucker's world, like that of other Southerners, was one of ordered liberty, in which democratic majorities were restrained from infringing the property and personal rights of individuals. Tucker drew the distinction between equality of rights and equality of condition. Everyone, he thought, had equal rights to civil liberty; however, the limiting principle here was that they had only rights to so much liberty as their condition permitted. Thus, the amount of rights that individuals were entitled to varied according to their station in society. This was part of Tucker's attack on agrarianism, an English movement that sought the redistribution of wealth.[48] "The true corollary is, that as each has separate gifts from his Creator, and comes into the social compact to preserve them, equality of right demands that each be left to work out his own destiny, freely and manfully—to accomplish all which by nature he is fitted to accomplish, without hindrance from his fellows, and without help or interference form this government."[49] Tucker had a pithy phrase to encapsulate his theory: "The world the arena, men the athlete, government the mere police, God the arbiter, and the reward the laurel he can gather, and the crown he can win."[50]

Tucker's theory calibrated rights to social position; it was a long way from the Enlightenment idea that all people are created equal—and have equal rights, for instance, to be free from slavery. Instead, the theory was that rights and constitutions should be made to fit the condition of the people being governed.

> The man who writes constitutions by the dozen, and keeps them on hand for use or distribution, without a careful investigation of the social capacities of the people for whom they are designed—he who *guesses* that our institutions would be admirably suited for China or Japan, or that our federative system of republics would work with facility and success under a President Roberts upon the coast of Africa, is a dangerous empiric–a mere pretender, whose reward should be fixed in perpetual banishment from the counsel of a wise people. And in the solitude of an asylum for political lunatics.[51]

Tucker spoke about the reality of life in the South, about the place of enslaved people and about history. He asked whether "any man" could deny "the most favorable condition for the African is slavery, and the only condition for the Saxon, consistent with his progress or even existence, is that of being director of the physical and moral energies" of the enslaved people.[52] "Republicanism," Tucker tersely concluded, "demands the maintenance of" slavery.[53] And, as others were also saying at this time, the mere promises of the Constitution were not enough to maintain southern rights. Tucker reached beyond the paper document; he understood the importance of a constitutional culture that supported slavery. This is further evidence of why ultimately secession was seen as so necessary—because political reality suggested that the North would at some point end slavery. The testimony of people who lived through the era, like Tucker, remind us of the salience of cultural ideas to Union, whether those ideas were like Henry Ruffner's in favor of Union and against slavery, or in favor of Union and in favor of slavery like Junkin's, or against Union and in favor of slavery, like many other Southerners by the time of secession.

The addresses supported a political theory of slavery and at times took on antislavery literature or addressed specific issues related to slavery, such as the benefits to the white community and the supposed benefits of slavery over freedom for the enslaved. Often in the 1850s the addresses dealt with the question of Union and the cost of secession, too. To see how these operated over time, this chapter now examines the addresses at schools in several sections of the south—in Alabama, Mississippi, and Virginia.

University of Alabama

By the late 1830s, orators at the University of Alabama fairly consistently defended the values of order, hierarchy, and slavery. They drew on various arguments, often emphasizing the importance of southern educational institutions for providing an education in pro-slavery principles. Those principles frequently included racial hierarchy, and sometimes the students assembled in the University's rotunda (Illustration 3.2) to hear the addresses. The July 4, 1841, oration of Alabama legislator Alexander Gates to the Alabama literary societies expressed fear for the future. He recognized that societies had differing needs based on their systems of government.[54] For example, the United States was well suited to democracy. Other governments were not.

Illustration 3.2 University of Alabama, 1859 (W.S. Hoole Special Collections Library, The University of Alabama)

The photograph of the Alabama campus, with the Rotunda housing the library and the literary societies at center, was taken in 1859. Addresses to the literary societies were delivered in that building. Dormitories are visible on both the extreme left and right of the photograph.

Gates represented the common belief of southern political philosophers that not all people were meant for freedom. This was part of a belief that people and nations were different in character. All people were not equal and one needed to accept the world as it was and work for the best government given the constraints of surrounding realities. The American system of democracy was, however, well suited to us as a people. There was a question of republicanism constraining the excesses of democracy. As Gates said,

> Notwithstanding this goodly prospect—this golden sunshine, a dark and tempestuous cloud might then have been seen peering above the horizon, which was destined to exert its blighting influence on all that was grand–on all that was beautiful. "The fell-destroyer came;" the King was dethroned, and his family driven into exile. An unprejudiced observer might have predicted, from the spirit manifested on this occasion, the ultimate result of the French Revolution. But alas for humanity! It must ever stand, in the world's history, an illustrious example of the fact, that "goodly virtues" do, at times, "bloom upon the poisonous branches of ambition." The spirit of Liberty, as is always the case, where the great body of the people are not virtuous and intelligent, sunk into the most loathsome depths of anarchy and licentiousness.[55]

And while Gates celebrated the virtues of equality in the American system, he also feared the future. For equality led to radicalism.

> The spirit of revolution is abroad in the land; and in what it shall result can be known only to posterity. In our own country, we are rather apprehensive, that it will engender the lawless spirit of Agrarianism; already are its seed sown: that fanatical spirit, which has so plainly manifested itself in some parts of our country, both in religion and in politics, can forebode no possible good. It is but the smoke of a dreadful volcano, which lies concealed under the surface, and will ere long, unless the corrective is applied, and that speedily, break forth in all its ghastly splendor.[56]

The addresses increasingly reflect the shifting attitudes toward pro-slavery thought, as well as toward hierarchy and order.[57] They also reflect a shift toward a belief that the University is a place of education for very special people—men who were separate from the rest of Alabama's society. Joseph Wright Taylor's 1847 address "A Plea for the University," takes up that theme.[58] Taylor was born in 1820 in Burkesville, Kentucky, and graduated from Cumberland College in 1838. He served in the Alabama legislature from 1845 to 1849 and also worked as editor of the *Eutaw Whig*, a newspaper in neighboring Greene County, and in the 1850s he was a trustee of Southern University in Greensboro, Alabama.[59] Taylor offered a series of justifications for the University. He saw the University as training the intellectual leaders of the state. Those leaders would help spread learning throughout the state.

> High seminaries of learning do more for a nation than to develop its gifted intellects; they elevate the great mass of its mind and give it new impulses and nobler aspirations. . . . Is one great mind developed and sent forth from the University? It becomes a sun in the intellectual firmament, illuminating the valleys as well as the mountain tops of society. Thousands of inferior minds rejoice in its brightness and are led by its guidance. . . . In this way all who may not be able to visit the fountain source, may yet drink of its cooling waters percolating through channels which pour the refreshing tide through all the ramifications of the social edifice. . . . This diffusible equality of knowledge constitutes the agrarian law of the kingdom of mind, by which its riches are distributed, in due proportion, among all the inheritors of reason.[60]

Taylor employed many analogies to the physical world in discussing the contributions of the University of Alabama to the public mind. For instance, he likened the University to "electric bars" that when "passed over metallic particles [students] attract them to their surface, when, in due time, they fall off to be succeeded by other particles, until the whole mass is brought under electric influence." The students then returned to their home communities and, like the particles that fell off the electric bars, "help to electrify" the masses "by imparting portions of their own supply."[61] He saw the University as educating teachers for the common schools, which would then bring the University's light and morals to the rest of the state. The University, moreover, prepares people for participation in the "well-regulated popular sovereignty."[62]

Prime among the justifications for studying at the University was its support for slavery. As Taylor said, "The University is useful in enabling the State to protect the peculiar rights and institutions which belong to it, as one of the Plantation States of the South."[63] Taylor professed love for the Union and hope that a destructive conflict would never occur. "Never may [the Union's] proud banner flutter out, with diminished stars and stripes, beneath skies blushing red with the hue of blood shed in the fratricidal conflicts of the warring fragments of a once united and powerful confederacy!"[64] The institution of slavery was essential to southern wealth, constitutionally protected, and morally right. Slaves "have grown up with us, and have become an element of our social life, which cannot be, harmlessly, removed. We believe them to be lawful, judged either by the laws of reason or by the canons of Revelation."[65] But the South was under attack by those who held a "misguided philanthropy": "The pulpit and its instrumentalities, the press and its agencies, are the weapons they yield. The world is the field of battle; mankind the spectators; institutions, vital to the South, the guerdon of the victor; God and the right the arbiters of the final issue."[66]

Taylor alluded to Cassius M. Clay who left Kentucky for an education in New England and returned to his home state as an abolitionist. Clay was unsuccessful in the abolitionist mission, but the cause of slavery was still injured. "[A]s when Lucifer fell from the bright sphere of heaven, there is one less in the ranks of the champions of God and the right, and one fallen spirit more to tempt others to . . . revolt against institutions and the rights of the South."[67] Taylor was happy that Clay had been ineffectual, but he worried that others who received an education in the North would return with similar abolitionist views. "Suppose one hundred or five hundred such erring minds were to turn loose their energies in the mad work of fanaticism in the State, how long would it be before Kentucky would see her blooming fields redden with blood shed in a servile war?" Here we see Taylor's principle of the educated spreading their influence again (though obviously for ill in his mind).[68] Should Alabamians send their children, Taylor asked rhetorically, "to be educated in the colleges of other States, that they may return with dangerous heresies coiled, like serpents, in their hearts, which will leap forth some day, instinct with a powerful vitality, to destroy the peace and to endanger the institutions of the State?"[69] Just as Southerners thought they needed to maintain separate schools to protect their children from the influences of abolitionist sentiments, they urged one another not to even vacation in the North. In the early 1850s they worried that Southerners vacationing in Saratoga, New York, had to face socialists who wanted to redistribute property and lure away their slaves.[70] The attack on things northern cut across a number of areas—from education to religion, even to tourism.

George Shortridge, who delivered an address to alumni in 1850, similarly argued that southern schools should defend slavery. Shortridge was born in 1814 in Mt. Sterling, Kentucky, and graduated from the University of Alabama in 1833. He became a lawyer in 1835 and later ran for governor on the Know-Nothing ticket. In 1850 he was a judge in Tuscaloosa County, where the University is located.[71] Like Taylor, he was educationally zenophobic. "The formation of a distinct, independent State character, is absolutely conditioned upon the education of our youth upon their native soil, in our own social atmosphere, amidst our own political institutions, under our own southern sky."[72] Shortridge justified and celebrated the role of the University's education for Southerners. "Our social institutions, our social and political sympathies are intensely *southern*," he said. Then he wondered the effect of sending "your sons to New England, to Virginia and to the Carolinas, to have their sympathies and opinions molded under influences, which may prepare them for other circumstances, but not for ours."[73] It is remarkable that Shortridge found education in Virginia and the Carolinas potentially alien to the interests of Alabama.

The University of Virginia

The University of Virginia's faculty were authors of leading pro-slavery works, as was discussed in the last chapter. The addresses given by alumni and visiting speakers at the University of Virginia, as well as the students, fill out the picture of ideas about jurisprudence and constitutionalism that were in circulation there. By looking at the literary addresses, which were given by political and social leaders at key points in the academic year—often at graduation, but sometimes at the beginning of the year—we can see the ideas in circulation on the campuses. The ideas shifted rather dramatically from the 1830s, when, for instance, Robert M. T. Hunter delivered a Fourth of July address at the University of Virginia that emphasized the virtues of democracy, through the 1850s, when the addresses in Charlottesville explicitly engaged the need to adhere (or not) to Union. Some calculated the value of Union, as they discussed how the Constitution protected slavery and might allow disunion.

The year 1850 marked a turning point at the University of Virginia. From 1850 onward, there were increasing discussions at southern schools (and in southern politics) about the costs of the Union and constitutional rights to slavery. In 1850, Muscoe R. H. Garnett delivered an extended address—something of a coming-out address, for he was not quite thirty. Garnett had been born in 1821 in Essex County, Virginia, then studied at his father's school and later graduated from the University of Virginia and its law school in 1842.

Garnett's address was ostensibly about the ways that intellectuals affected—one might even say controlled—the world. He found that literature was closely related to the form of government; that in governments that provided for humans' wants, there was insufficient incentive for people to struggle. Those governments, which Garnett labeled socialist, did not produce great literature.[74] In places where individuals had to depend on themselves, however, literature developed. But the address was more than about literature; it was about how socialist governments caused people to depend too much on a central government. He thought that federal governments, which dispersed power between sovereigns, would slow the evils of centralization, but even in a federal system, laborers were left vulnerable to employers. And thus appeared the argument, advanced in greater amplitude in the 1850s, that slavery protected laborers as much as any system could. Slavery, Garnett asserted, gave owners an incentive to make sure that labor was treated well.[75] This was an argument that others, like George Fitzhugh, developed more fully later in the decade—they suggested that slavery was an antidote to the excesses of capitalism. While the market certainly left many free workers in dire straits, it was a hard case to make—and one that few people found convincing—that slavery protected slaves more than the market protected free workers.

Much of Garnett's address then was about the relationship between types of government and freedom. This was the philosophical framing for the argument that slavery was necessary for the maintenance of democracy of white people. Slavery best allowed the preservation of decentralized, republican government, and, relatedly, it nullified conflicts between labor and capital. Southern schools occupied a particularly important place in this defense of slavery, for they permitted such truths to be told in the face of antislavery domination of the northern schools. Garnett recalled that "the few who received education at Northern colleges brought back second hand history and shallow philosophy." That led Southerners to think that slavery might, indeed, be evil.[76]

Because of institutions like the University of Virginia, Southerners learned a different story. "We read history, and we see that slavery is coeval with society, and almost co-existent with the human race; that it was *commanded* in God's chosen theocracy, and *sanctioned* by his Apostles in the Christian Church; that where ever it has been abolished, its substitute has been found in an aristocratic distinction of castes, or in poor laws, and a war, ever increasing in bitterness, between the owners of food and property, and the poor."[77] Southern institutions taught the correctness of slavery—in fact, that slavery was indispensable to democratic government. Garnett was speaking several years before James Henry Hammond's 1858 speech in the U.S. Senate that popularized the "mud sill" theory; that is, slaves provided the mud sill on which white democracy was built. Yet, Garnett was talking about those same ideas and emphasized, indeed justified, the University's role in defending slavery. Lessons learned at southern schools led, in Garnett's mind, to a further embrace of slavery. "The more we reflect upon our situation, the better we shall be contented, the more will we determine to devote ourselves to developing its rich resources, instead of sentimental whinings over what we neither can, nor ought to change."[78]

In the same year as Garnett's University of Virginia alumni address he also published, anonymously, a pamphlet, *The Union, Past and Future*, also designed to support southern constitutional rights.[79] That pamphlet addressed in economic and political terms what Garnett's alumni address dealt with in literary and philosophic terms: the need for the defense of slavery and a decentralized government based on the principles of slavery. *The Union* examined the history of the Constitution to show the importance of slavery and the South's early domination of the nation's economy, then moved forward to a narrative of how northern antislavery activists were systematically working to take away enslaved property and to restrict the South's economic development. It was a call for southern economic development through manufacturing, as well as a call for a robust defense of the South's constitutional rights. For instance, Garnett emphasized the growing theory about the equality of the states, which held that the federal government could do nothing that would injure the rights of slaveholding states. Under that theory, the federal government could not tax disproportionately the products of slave labor, nor could it exclude slavery in the territories or take similar action against slavery, such as abolishing slavery in the District of Columbia. Garnett at this point aspired to a career as a politician and an intellectual, similar to his uncle Robert M. T. Hunter. In part through *The Union* pamphlet, Garnett achieved that career—first at the 1850 state constitutional convention, then later in the U.S. House of Representatives from 1856 to 1861, and finally in the Confederate Congress.

The year after Garnett's address, in 1851, the students, through the vehicle of the UVA Southern Rights Association, became increasingly active. Their resolutions asserted that they were advocating southern rights "under the banner of 'Justice and the Constitution.' "[80] That same year, John Randolph Tucker, the son of University of Virginia law professor Henry St. George Tucker and the grandson of St. George Tucker, addressed the University of Virginia alumni. Tucker was less than thirty years old (he was born in 1823), but he showed already a mastery of southern constitutional ideas. Tucker's extensive address surveyed constitutional history, particularly during the founding period, to argue that states could judge for themselves violations of the Constitution and choose to secede if they wished. This argument was aimed at opposing "consolidation." While he argued for the right of secession, he claimed at the end of his speech that if southern states asserted their rights to set their own policy against the consolidation of the federal government that this would preserve the Union, presumably because there would be no need to secede.[81]

In the years just before the war, orators at the University of Virginia urged adherence to Union even as they spoke of the South's rights to slavery and to autonomy. For instance, Joseph Hodgson, a Fluvanna merchant, spoke in 1857 about the permanence of the Union: "Our constitution is not an experiment, but the very climacteric of experience, an everlasting Truth deduced from the errors of past ages. It cannot fall, or history is mere tradition, and humanity false."[82] Hodgson worried about the invocation of higher law by abolitionists, people who dared to identify a law "higher than any your fathers laid down in the constitution, higher than philanthropy, higher than expediency, higher than necessity, higher than the will of God."[83] Yet, despite the charges that "our fathers and we are tyrannical monsters," Hodgson believed that the Union would endure.[84]

In an address on July 4, 1860 at the University of Virginia, the U.S. attorney for Indiana Daniel Voorhees presented pro-slavery sentiments in greater amplitude than Hodgson and joined them with pro-slavery constitutional arguments. But he ended with a call for Union.[85] Voorhees, for instance, spoke about the "entire

supremacy of the Anglo-Saxon race in all useful achievements," and he argued
that "the best and brightest eras of civilization" all relied on slavery. Quite simply,
Voorhees believed, history supported slavery. "[T]he philosophy and teaching of
all ages, as well as the wisdom of God himself, sanction and justify the existence of a
dependent and vassal condition on the part of an inferior toward a superior race."[86]
Voorhees worried that if the Union were destroyed "through fanaticism and sectional hate" that would be the end of liberty.[87] Yet, there was no need for disunion,
because the Constitution was founded on the idea "that each member was its own
domestic ruler."[88] Voorhees appealed for Union: "We can appeal to the American
citizen to allow the house which his fathers built to stand forever—that though divided it may be in its domestic economy, yet it is not divided unto its fall."[89]

Howard College

Further south, the speakers often did not have the resources to match the intellectual output of the speakers at the University of Virginia. And the schools often
published fewer addresses. But in the pieces that remain, we can see their core
ideas. Take, for instance, Marion, Alabama, the seat of Perry County. Marion is
remembered, if at all, as one of the places where the modern civil rights movement picked up steam. Near the Perry County Courthouse, a civil rights protes-
tor, Jimmy Lee Jackson, was shot on February 18, 1965, after a struggle with
a law enforcement officer. He died a few days later in a Selma hospital, apparently the victim of poor medical treatment. A state prosecutor in Montgomery
reopened the case, and in 2010 a retired state trooper, who had told local media
in 2005 that he had shot Jackson, pled guilty to misdemeanor manslaughter. He
was sentenced to six months in jail.[90] In 1965, the shooting was an important
impetus to the first Selma to Montgomery march, which was turned back on the
Edmund Pettus Bridge not far from where the march began.[91] Obscure Marion,
thus, helped spur the modern civil rights movement—a sign that inspiration is
often found in the most unlikely of places.

In the antebellum era, Marion was home to both Judson Female College and
Howard College, a Baptist college for men. Very limited information is available about the culture at Howard College, but some sense of the environment
appears in the few literary addresses that have survived. In 1850, T. G. Keen,
then a minister in Mobile, told Howard College graduates that southern colleges
thwarted radicalism. "Where are we to look for the spirit and power of conservatism which shall regulate the storm," Keen asked. He answered "to our young
men and emphatically to our colleges."[92]

There was a tragic fire on October 15, 1854, that took the life of a student, a tutor, and a slave named Harry, owned by Howard's president Henry
Talbird. In 1857, the school erected a monument to Harry, of whom it was

Illustration 3.3 Monument to Harry in Marion, Alabama cemetery.
Harry was an enslaved man owned by the Howard College president, who died helping
students escape from a fire at Howard College. Source: Photo by the author.

said acted selflessly to save students from the fire. (Illustration 3.3) He died
as a result of jumping from the fourth floor during the fire. The inscription on
the monument reads:

> A consistent member of the Baptist Church, he illustrated the character
> of a Christian servant—"faithful unto death."
>
> As a grateful tribute to his fidelity, and to commemorate a noble act,
> this Monument has been reared by the Students of Howard College
> and the Alabama Baptist Convention.

He was employed as a waiter in the College, and when alarmed by the flames at midnight, and warned to escape for his life, replied: "I must wake the boys first;" and thus saved their lives at the cost of his own.[93]

The story of Harry was powerful, for it suggested, as an article in the *Marion American* newspaper attested when the monument was erected, "his self-sacrificing devotion and fidelity mark in letters of living light the reciprocal affection between the master and the servant, as grand as any in the great annals of history."[94] The faithful slave was someone to be celebrated, for his devotion up to the point where he gave his life provided evidence to the Marion, Alabama, community that the enslaved really did love their owners and, thus, confirmed (they told themselves) the soundness of slavery. (Later we shall encounter a book written by a Georgia jurist that was dedicated to a slave owner who sacrificed his life for his slave—the mirror image of the faithful slave was the faithful owner.) The story of Harry is different from the suspicions that followed a series of fires set at Jefferson College in Washington, Mississippi, in 1836. (Illustration 3.4). The suspicion was that a slave had done it, and several were arrested and examined, but the identity of the arsonist was never proven.[95]

Illustration 3.4 Jefferson College, Washington, Mississippi. (Library of Congress, Prints & Photographs Division, HABS, Reproduction number HABS MISS,1-WASH,2—5.)

Mississippi Schools

Further south, at the University of Mississippi, George Frederick Holmes, the first president of the university, included in his inaugural address at the opening of the University in November 1848 an attack on the "revolutionary spirit of the day."[96] Holmes' lecture was an attack on abolitionists, a topic he continued to advance throughout his career. We met Holmes, who later taught at the University of Virginia and was a fierce critic of Harriet Beecher Stowe's *Uncle Tom's Cabin*, in the last chapter. [97] Though he did not stay in Mississippi long, Holmes' early leadership of the University of Mississippi set it on the path to supporting pro-slavery ideas.

Senator Jefferson Davis delivered an address to the literary societies at the University of Mississippi in 1852. He spoke of an "unholy crusade against the domestic institutions of the south." Davis pointed to the failure of abolitionists to abide the Constitution. "In vain have appeals been made, to the requirements of the Constitution, and the duties of the states. All obligations, social and political, their self-canonized saints proclaim to be annulled by the higher law revealed to them, and which was theirs to execute, though ruin should be brought upon a section, and misery be the future lot of both the happy races now inhabiting it." Davis concluded with a recommendation of John Fletcher's *Studies on Slavery*.[98] Illustration 3.5 is the University of Mississippi's Lyceum, the main building on the campus in the early 1850s.

U.S. senator from Mississippi Albert Gallatin Brown delivered an address in 1859 at Madison College in Sharon, Mississippi, on "southern education." It was an attack on the practice of sending students north for education and a defense of slavery. By this point, the arguments against slavery were not much discussed; Brown took it as an article of faith that slavery was necessary, though like Jefferson Davis earlier in the decade, he referred readers to John Fletcher's *Studies on Slavery*.[99] Senator Brown warned against sending children north for an education, for such children "will take on the constitutional habitudes of that climate, and become as much an alien to the South as one born in the latitude of Cambridge or New Haven."[100] In the North "the school-room has become little better than an anti-slavery lecture room."[101] Even the textbooks of the North— like Brown University president's Francis Wayland's text on moral philosophy— were antislavery. "I hold in my hand," the Senator said, " 'The Elements of Moral Science.'" Then he pointed out places where Wayland criticized slavery as a violation of "the personal liberty of man as a *physical, intellectual, and moral being.*" After quoting a number of other passages about the ways that slavery injured both morals and the economy, Brown concluded with Wayland's sensational account of the effect of slavery on the sexual morality of slave owners and slaves,

Illustration 3.5 University of Mississippi Lyceum. (Library of Congress, Prints & Photographs Division, HABS, Reproduction number HABS MISS,36-OXFO,14—2.)

too. For slavery presented "objects on whom passion may be satiated without resistance and without redress," and thus "tends to cultivate in the master *pride, anger, cruelty, selfishness*, and LICENTIOUSNESS." Brown wondered if the audience wanted their children hearing such reports about them as slave owners.[102] To Brown's anger, he found that Wayland's book was used in a female seminary in Mississippi. He was told, though, that the school had sealed the twenty pages on slavery and sexual morality to prevent the students from reading it. "As if there had ever been a daughter born into the world since Eve sinned in Paradise who would not break the seals just that she might taste the forbidden fruit."[103]

The Virginia Military Institute in the 1850s

Just next door to Washington College in Lexington, Virginia, was the Virginia Military Institute (VMI). Francis Henney Smith, the Institute's superintendent, justified the institution to the Virginia legislature in 1857 in part based on the support it gave to slavery:

> The military discipline of the institution gives protection and efficiency to the peculiar institutions of the state and of the south. Slavery is a material element of southern power and southern polity; and to rightly defend and direct it, constitutes an important duty on the part of those who form the mind and habits of our southern youth. There is no labor so profitable, none so free from pernicious influences to society, as slave labor. Military institutions, by the order and system and responsibility which their discipline encourages, discharge a most important function in these respects. And in the enumeration of these benefits, none are more decided or more worthy of consideration than those which result from the discipline of these schools in promoting the material comfort and well being of the slave himself.[104]

The Virginia Military Institute was located adjacent to Washington College in Lexington, Virginia, but it was a different place ideologically. In contrast to Washington College's focus on classical education and on Whig ideas, VMI was a place of Democrat ideas, with a practical curriculum based on engineering and mathematics.[105] This represented a shift in higher education, from a classical curriculum to a practical one. It correlated with practical ideas about economy and utility in law as well.[106] And we can see through graduation addresses given at VMI over the course of the 1850s the unfolding of attitudes toward Union and ultimately secession.

On July 4, 1850, John White Brockenbrough delivered an address to com-memorate the laying of a cornerstone of VMI's new barracks. Brockenbrough, who was a federal trial judge and also professor at the Lexington Law School, dealt with VMI's role in Virginia government and the values of the Union VMI could promote. "The Union is dear to the hearts of our people, not only be-cause of the historic glories that cluster around it," Brockenbrough said, "but because it is identified in their convictions and judgment with their freedom and happiness." These were cultural values that worked in conjunction with the economic prosperity made possible by Union and in this regard it is similar to the Washington College addresses on the value of Union. But a subtle shift was taking place on that campus. Brockenbrough thought that the people only loved the Union "which the Constitution gave us." This was an idea that became cen-tral to the secession debates: that the South should be loyal to the Constitution as they interpreted it. It was a contingent affinity for Union. And when the North interpreted the Constitution differently—or violated it, depending on one's perspective—then the South was not bound by that interpretation.

Brockenbrough thought that a "fanatical majority in Congress may effectively subvert the Constitution while its forms may be studiously preserved. Its potency for good will then be destroyed, its efficacy for evil only will survive."[107] In this address we see how the cultural values supporting Union were shifting; and how a southern interpretation of the Constitution—that its form might be followed while still violating its spirit—was emerging as well. This is a transition point from Union to secession. "Suppose . . . that the madmen who make war upon the essential principles of the Constitution shall accomplish their fell purpose, can any doubt that the clustering stars and stripes of the Union will go down in blood?"[108] Though he hoped it would not come to that, Brockenbrough said that if war broke out, VMI alumni would be central to the defense of Virginia.[109]

B. J. Barbour of Orange County delivered a wide-ranging address on July 4, 1854, that covered topics such as the wasteful state spending for internal im-provements (spending for improvements such as turnpikes and railroads), the virtues of individualism and limited government, and the Bible as literature and as a source of insight. Barbour also made passing reference to the problems of antislavery advocacy, what he called that "morbid philanthropy and calculat-ing humanity, which takes a fugitive slave for its hero, drapes a city in mourn-ing when the constitution is obeyed, appeals to a higher law for revenge, . . . and comes, with blood on its hands and scripture on its lips, to lift the assas-sin's knife and light the incendiary's torch, in the name of a meek and lowly Savior."[110] Barbour was referring to Harriet Beecher Stowe's *Uncle Tom's Cabin* and to Massachusetts Judge Edward Loring's decision that returned Anthony Burns to slavery in Virginia. Loring's decision to return Burns to slavery led to a sermon by Thomas Wentworth Higginson challenging the Fugitive Slave Act of 1850.[111] Yet, Barbour was somewhat more optimistic about the future than

Brockenbrough had been three years earlier. He hoped that there would remain "a Union of free and equal states." For that to happen, Virginians had to protect "the right of each community to manage its own affairs."

The Turn Away from Union

By 1857 southern schools had been promulgating the pro-slavery message for decades. On the morning of July 3, 1857, James W. Massie, an 1849 graduate of VMI and a graduate of the Lexington Law School, who was then a professor of mathematics at VMI, delivered an address that stoked division between North and South through a historical account of the differences between North and South. He premised his lecture on the idea that North and South had separate civilizations—a theme that was popular in the South in the 1850s. This stands in stark contrast with the Washington College addresses that referenced the Puritans and the unified culture of North and South. His major premise was that Massachusetts and Virginia had substantially different cultures. Massie used those states as stand-ins for the North and South generally.[112] While Massie said little directly about law, he laid out the cultural differences that supported a different interpretation of the Constitution.

He returned to the founding of Massachusetts and Virginia and explained Massachusetts as a radical colony, founded by religious fanatics. Such an interpretation actually had strong purchase in historical circles through the middle of the twentieth century, and it is interesting to contemplate how the ideas borne of sectional division may have influenced historical interpretation for decades afterward until Perry Miller appeared and revived the Puritan intellectuals as a subject of serious inquiry. By contrast, Massie found the Virginia founders to be pragmatists, interested in transplanting British law and thought to the Americas. This explained the differing policies on slavery, more than climate. Among the charges Massie brought against the Puritans was they were not interested in rational liberty. Their opposition to slavery was another sign of this; they supported abolition even when it was inappropriate and the slaves incapable of handling freedom.[113] What was a little ambiguous was how the American Revolution emerged in Virginia; Massie explained it—as did other leading Southerners—as a conservative revolt against monarchy.

Meanwhile, the Massachusetts philanthropists had become fanatics. Massie warned against the reform spirit of the age, which seemed so popular in the North:

> It is a mistake to suppose that progress, necessarily involves cardinal change. Change is the child of error, like Death or Sin; progress is development, enlargement, growth. When society is progressing most

rapidly, it is either limiting the operation of well-established principles, or extending those principles to new and before untried emergencies.[114]

However, in the South, slavery helped protect against irrational and inappropriate change. "The Southern mind is fully alive to [slavery's] incalculable benefits, and even the North are beginning to feel its want as a conservative element."[115] Massie spoke as well of individualism, as did others like Senator Hunter, of conservative principles such as opposition to political change, and of white equality. It was a stark address; there should be no surprise that Massie would later support secession.

For VMI orators, the deliberations were about the constitutional rights of the South and biblical and utilitarian arguments about slavery. They were less about the preservation of the Union and more about preservation of southern rights. By 1858, there was no longer a perceived need to even talk about the virtues of slavery. At that time Willoughby Newton, a former member of the U.S. House of Representatives from the Virginia Piedmont, was able to say that slavery was unquestionably proven to be good. "The day" for an argument about slavery "is past. Such a flood of light has been shed upon it during the last few years, in all its aspects, moral, social, religious, and politico-economical, that nothing more remains to be said."[116]

Newton acknowledged that there may have been differences of opinion on this in the South as recently as twenty-five years before, but he believed that "all thoughtful and practical men are now agreed as to its necessity." He continued with extreme praise of the origins of slavery

> The landing in Virginia from a Dutch ship in the month of August, 1620, of twenty African slaves, has been in its results, one of the most remarkable events in the history of mankind. Inconsiderable in itself, revolting as it may be to natural feeling, no calm observer of the progress of human affairs can fail to perceive in it the beginning of a mighty agency for the advancement of the wealth, happiness, civilization, and refinement of the world.[117]

While Newton made the concession—more perhaps characteristic of the 1820s than the 1850s—that natural feeling revolted at the idea that slavery was so beneficial, his extraordinary praise of the institution continued. "No event in the history of modern times, save the discovery of America itself, is of equal importance." It was of such grand importance because it

> cleared the forests, and opened the rich lands of Virginia to cultivation; it produced in such abundance corn and tobacco, as soon to diffuse

through the Colony, a feeling of security and content. It raised up a class of independent and intelligent landed proprietors, who became the law-givers of the Colony, and the guardians of the liberties of the people. It inspired the white race with an intenser love of freedom, and a more watchful jealousy of encroachments upon their rights. And had no little influence in forming that race of great men, who, in the Colonial Assembly, laid broad and deep the foundations of public liberty . . . and carried through with success, in the council and the field, the great work of the Revolution.[118]

What was particularly important about Newton's address is that after he established the economic and political predicate for slavery, he then turned to the ways that the North was undermining slavery. Newton put this into a constitutional framework, not just saying that the North was undermining the foundational piece of the southern economy and political culture, but that the North was violating the South's constitutional rights as well. "The power of the Government has passed to the North, and all the checks of the Constitution are broken down. In the House of Representatives, in the Senate, and in the Electoral Colleges, the South finds no safety and is subject to the will of an unchecked majority, whose power will soon be as overwhelming as it is despotic."[119] While John C. Calhoun had proposed giving the South a veto power, Newton thought that would not be enough to save the South.[120] The grim truth was that "[d]isguise it as we may, the time is fast approaching when there will be no alternative but separation from the North, or tame submission to uncontrolled despotism."[121] Newton envisioned a separate southern nation and began to hypothesize how it might be funded and what it might accomplish in terms of internal improvements.[122] The stage was being set by people like Newton to condition the public mind for secession; a theory of how the North violated the constitutional rights of the South was well developed; a distinctly southern history and a southern interpretation of slavery, economy, and religion supported disunion. The pieces were being put in place for a southern nation, indeed, perhaps even a southern empire, that might in the words of Newton "give new development to the capacity and progressive power of the Anglo-Saxon race, and to bring within the range of free government and regulated liberty, the semi-barbarous hordes that now encumber the Southern portion of this continent."[123]

Literary Society Debates and Literary Magazines

While politicians sometimes moderated their opinions when speaking to college audiences or shifted from purely political topics to ones better suited to students, graduation and literary addresses at colleges are reasonable gauges of the southern mind. In addition to addresses by visiting dignitaries and faculty writing, the students and their families provided another injection of pro-slavery ideas on campus. It was for the students, after all, that the schools existed. They catered to the pro-slavery ideas of the students and helped reinforce them. Students were—completely unsurprisingly—drawn from the slave-owning class.[124] Students heard pro-slavery ideas in the classroom and in turn debated slavery in their literary societies, in their literary magazines, and sometimes spoke about it at graduation. There are extensive records of the topics that students themselves chose and then debated at their literary societies. While the speeches the students gave are rarely available, at schools from Washington College, University of Virginia, and William and Mary in Virginia, to Davidson College, the University of North Carolina, and Wake Forest in North Carolina, to the Emory College, University of Georgia, and Mercer in Georgia, and a few other schools, such as South Carolina College, the topics students debated and sometimes the votes on them have survived.[125]

The literary societies often provided the most stimulating intellectual experiences of the students' careers. Students turned to literary societies, which had extensive libraries, to talk and read about important issues of politics and morality. Professor Edward Joynes delivered an address at the opening of the rebuilt hall for the Phoenix Literary Society at William and Mary in 1860. They had lost their library and their records when the main hall at William and Mary was gutted by fire in 1859. Joynes, however, celebrated the place literary societies served for students. He thought literary societies provided "the freest arena of college life" and that they controlled "the public opinion of the students." The literary society was "the arena of independent thought, and of personal action, which tests the manhood as well as the memory." It provided those "moral and intellectual powers . . . which make the strong man and ensure success in every sphere of action."[126] By turning to the records of literary society debates we can begin to gauge the opinions of the students.

Literary societies generally met several times a month during the academic year. It seems that most societies chose a topic and several speakers, then gave the debaters several weeks to prepare their remarks. The speakers delivered brief prepared remarks, then other members joined in, and ultimately the students voted to affirm or to reject a resolution. The topics ranged widely—historical, moral, and religious questions were raised, such as whether Queen Elizabeth was justified in executing Mary Queen of Scots,[127] whether a monarchical or republican form of government was best suited to the promotion of literature,[128] whether the crusades injured Europe,[129] whether literature exercised a bad influence over government,[130] and whether "the Roman Catholic religion or slavery [was] the greatest evil to our country."[131] They also debated topics of more immediate political concern, such as whether there should be internal improvements, whether the death penalty should be abolished in favor of incarceration, whether immigration should be restricted, whether Texas should be annexed to the United States,[132] and whether "nullification in South Carolina [was] justifiable."[133] And sometimes they discussed more abstract issues of political theory. For instance, Emory's Phi Gamma Society debated "Are all men equal by nature?" in 1850. They concluded in the negative, which reflects that students were thinking along similar lines to faculty like Albert Taylor Bledsoe of the University of Virginia and visiting speakers like John Randolph Tucker, whose address at William and Mary was premised on the idea that hierarchy is inherent in nature and that political rights should be calibrated to reflect that inequality.[134]

As with the writings of academics and the addresses to literary societies by visiting dignitaries, the student debate topics reflect a broad set of questions regarding slavery. Explicit issues of race and slavery arose frequently. As mentioned above, some dealt with abstract issues of political theory, such as are all people created equal. Questions at such a high level of generality reflect a central theme in southern thought, that is, the importance of hierarchy. Many debates operated at a more specific level, for example, the morality of slavery. In 1844 students at Mercer in Georgia debated, "Is slavery a moral evil?" They concluded that slavery was not evil.[135] That same year the students of Emory's Phi Gamma Society debated the same question and came to the same conclusion.[136] Students at Wake Forest's Euzelian Society had debated that same topic twice in 1843 and divided—once they concluded yes, and another time no.[137] In 1859 they debated "Is slavery an evil offense?" and found it was not.[138] In 1847, 1849, and again in 1850 Wake Forest's students concluded that slavery should be tolerated.[139] In 1855 students at Washington College's Graham Literary Society also debated "Is slavery in itself an evil?" and decided no, it was not.[140] That same year the students debated "Is slavery in accordance with the dictates of Humanity?" and concluded that it was.[141] As late as 1859 students at Washington College were debating "Is slavery a moral and political evil?" and concluded that it was not.[142]

The topics illustrate that slavery was a question of much interest to the students, and the votes on some of the debates suggest that for some there was unease about slavery, even as the majority found it moral and acceptable. The Wake Forest Euzelian Society debated "Has the institution of African slavery been beneficial to the United States?" in 1858 and 1859 and answered in the affirmative both times.[143] Not only was the institution moral, but it was also likely to continue. In 1858 the students of Mercer's Ciceronian Society debated whether "African slavery [would] be perpetual in the US?" Those students concluded yes, which might have been a reasonable assumption at the time, even though events would shortly prove them very wrong.[144] The institution would continue, and some even thought it should expand. On the eve of the Civil War, as southern attitudes were becoming even more pro-slavery, the students at Washington College took a radical step. They debated not whether steps should be taken to limit slavery, but whether it should be expanded. In 1859, they asked "Should the African Slave trade be reopened?" and concluded yes.[145]

Yet, even as they accepted slavery as a moral institution, students sometimes thought it should be softened. In 1845 Mercer's Phi Delta Society debated a somewhat less controversial question, whether slaves should be educated and concluded they should.[146] Although in 1857 Washington College students supported the prohibition of teaching slaves to read.[147] And at other times students debated other "reforms," such as colonization. At Washington College the students debated such questions as "Ought the Congress of the United States to provide a means for the exportation of the Blacks to Africa?" and concluded that it should.[148]

Often the debates about morality and race were linked as well to Native Americans. Students at many colleges debated other issues of racial justice, such as "were the Europeans justifiable in taking possession of America against the will of the Aborigenes?" They answered yes by a vote of thirteen to two.[149] Students at William and Mary's Licivyronean Society debated the same topic in 1845 and came to the same conclusion.[150] And at other times the students addressed some of the more esoteric issues related to race. One of the questions that southern scientists and divines were debating was whether Europeans and Africans had separate origins—known as polygenesis.[151] Partly this pitted belief in the Old Testament against the pseudo-science of race, although some "scientists" of race lined up on the side of religion that all humans had common ancestors. This debate appeared in Georgia when the students of Mercer's Phi Delta Society decided in the affirmative that "the unity of our species [can] be proved independent of revelation."[152]

Another way of approaching the literary society debates is to look at the changes over time at a single institution as a gauge of how attitudes change. Because the University of North Carolina records of debate topics are remarkably complete, it is possible to detect something of a shift in attitudes toward slavery from the 1830s until the Civil War.[153] In the 1830s students at the Dialectic Society, which drew its students from the western part of the state where slavery was less prominent than in the eastern part, debated whether North Carolinians should be allowed to educate slaves.

They concluded yes. Yet the Dialectic Society students also realized the South's economic dependence on slavery when they voted that the United States would not flourish more if slaves were emancipated and that Southerners should not abolish slavery.[154] In the late 1840s, when many Southerners held the view that slavery in the territories was protected against restriction by

Congress, the students of the Dialectic Society twice concluded that the Congress had the power to abolish slavery in the territories.[155] That is, they took a broad vision of the federal Constitution and perhaps by implication the value of Union. Yet, at the same time, they also thought it was impolitic for Congress to agitate on slavery.[156] And they were taking a stronger stand in favor of slavery. In 1849 they concluded "slavery is of divine origin"[157] and that slavery is not justly reproached.[158]

In addition to the literary society debate topics, we can also sometimes discern ideas from the occasional speech to a literary society that is preserved and also from graduation speeches given by students.[159] As with the debate topics, often all we know are the titles of the addresses, but they are suggestive of a growing pro-slavery and anti-Union sentiment.[160]

In addition to their debates, a few schools, mostly in Virginia, also produced literary magazines. Articles in those magazines reflect in compact space many of the same arguments that faculty advanced in their writing and one presumes in the classroom, too. Some of the articles address broad topics that have no immediate relation to slavery. For instance, some articles were on feudalism, others on the Crusades.[161] While seemingly distant from contemporary concerns, those articles often defended property rights or made the point that the much-maligned feudal era produced positive benefits for society. It would not take much abstraction to see an analogy between feudalism and slavery. Like feudalism, slavery was heavily criticized, but it also produced (in the minds of the students) benefits. At other times their turn to history demonstrated respect for property rights.[162] Another theme in the literary magazines was that steady economic and moral progress was more important than passions, which was an implicit critique of antislavery writers who were often charged with stirring passions without regard to consequences.[163] Other essays addressed the lessons of history, which so frequently were seen as teaching that moral processes took a long time and that not all cultures were ready for freedom.[164] They also established a political theory that was useful for the defense of slavery. In "Government A Divine Institution," the *Virginia University Magazine* developed the notion that government was inherent to human society and thus divinely instituted. It was, therefore, the duty of all citizens to follow the law and they should do nothing to undermine it. And when they undermined law, results like those in the French Revolution were likely to follow. Those who upended society were often the victims of the revolution they set in motion.[165] Another article, nominally about the University of Virginia's ordinances regulating student conduct, argued that laws could work effectively only if they have the support of the governed. As with the articles about history, this one had implications for the critique of antislavery activists who wanted to free slaves. Southerners frequently argued that enslaved people were not fit for freedom, so a law granting freedom would not be effective—nor would white Southerners support it. Moreover, reform of culture could only proceed gradually, not via legal reform mandated from above.[166]

Sometimes the literary magazines engaged slavery directly. In 1859 an article entitled "Southern Education for Southern Youth,"—which had the same title and theme as William Stiles' address at Cherokee Baptist College the year before—was published in the *Hampden Sydney Magazine*. The grim conclusion of that article was that southern students should not be educated in the North. A northern education implanted in southerners "a deadly hostility to the institutions which nothing but its destruction could appease."[167] At the University of Virginia, where students had the chance to learn from such important pro-slavery writers as Albert Taylor Bledsoe, James Holcombe, and George Frederick Holmes, students also produced some of the most sophisticated discussions of slavery among any of the literary magazines. One article in 1856 argued, contrary to the opinions of many in the South, that the discussion of slavery in public was positive because it led to several important insights. Most of the insights were taken pretty directly from Albert Taylor Bledsoe's *Liberty and Slavery*: humans are inherently social and that human society is inherently hierarchical. Thus, society's function is to protect individuals and in protecting individuals it gives only so much liberty as "is consistent with . . . happiness and prosperity."[168] The article explicitly disavowed Jefferson's formulation of equality in the Declaration of Independence and supported instead a state that calibrated rights according to an individual's place in society. The enslaved were not, in this author's mind, entitled to as much freedom as others. This remade political theory to justify slavery. Another article turned to George Fitzhugh's 1857 book *Cannibals All, Or Slaves Without Masters*.[169] It endorsed several key elements of Fitzhugh's volume, including that free workers often had hard, indeed terrible, lives and that their employers paid them poorly; that slaves were treated better than free workers; and that emancipation would be worse for slaves than continued slavery. Those hotly contested propositions were fast becoming staple "truths" to many Southerners as they sought to make slavery look better than it was and to argue their case against the increasingly powerful and vocal antislavery and free labor North.

And sometimes there were very specific arguments regarding slavery, such as an article in the *Erskine Collegiate Recorder* regarding support for slavery in international law.[170] Moreover, like the literary society debates, the literary journals discussed Native Americans, too. In 1859 the *Erskine Collegiate Recorder* published a justification of taking Native Americans' land called "The Expulsion of the Indians."[171] On the other hand, the *Virginia University Magazine* published a gothic and macabre short story, "The Scalp Tree," that portrayed somewhat sympathetically the plight of a young Cherokee chief whose village was wiped out by European settlers. The chief then hunted the settlors for decades, collected their scalps, and hung them on a tree near his hut in a remote, primeval forest. Eventually the chief died, and some years later white hunters came across his skeleton and the scalps. Yet, the scalp tree remained a haunted place that hunters and settlers always sought to avoid.[172]

After they left college some students continued to expand on the pro-slavery ideas taught in school. For instance, Henry Hughes, who graduated from Oakland College in 1847, wrote a *Treatise on Sociology: Theoretical and Practical*. Hughes used the common critique of free labor—that it left free workers worse off than slaves—to defend slavery. In his two books, *Treatise on Sociology* and then *Sociology for the South*, he built a positive defense of slavery from what had been only an attempt to make slavery look less harmful. Hughes tried to make slavery look like a solution to a critique of capitalism advanced by people like Thomas Carlyle. But Hughes was running far ahead of many other Southerners, for he urged the conversion of slavery from a system of private ownership into a system where the government controlled labor. Hughes called this warrenteeism.[173] Such ideas were later developed further by the self-educated Virginian George Fitzhugh in his book *Cannibals All*.

Other people, like Hughes not immediately connected with universities but the products of them, also contributed to the pro-slavery literature. For instance, Vidalia, Louisiana, lawyer George S. Sawyer's *Southern Institutes* was the product of his extensive learning about the Roman and common law of slavery. Though he wrote this while practicing law, rather than while serving as an academic, it was his training that gave him the tools for making the extended and learned pro-slavery argument. Samuel Cartwright, a leading advocate of the theory of polygenesis—that the races had separate origins—published his work in 1847 in Vidalia, Sawyer's hometown, which is along the Mississippi river, opposite Cartwright's home of Natchez, Mississippi. John Fletcher, another independent scholar, seems to have lived nearby and wrote the lengthy *Studies in Slavery*, published in Natchez in 1852. It was pitched at a precollege student audience.[174]

The speeches given at colleges by both the invited speakers and students operated at a high level of generality, as they linked constitutional culture to the conflicts of party ideology—democracy and republicanism—to the issues of moral and economic progress, and slavery. These addresses, along with other public discussions of slavery and jurisprudence, operated at a general (or maybe abstract is a better word) level. They were also less expansive than were the academics' writings. That is, the addresses to student literary societies and graduations made their case for the importance of slavery in a short space. They linked the economic importance of slavery to a political theory of hierarchy that justified unequal treatment of slaves and free people. Speakers often linked antislavery advocates to other reformers as they made the case for conservative values that supported slavery and property against reformers who would redistribute wealth. Antebellum Southerners understood, as did Americans more generally, that efforts to abolish slavery tended to undermine the rights of property. They agreed with Emerson's observation that "[s]lavery and anti-slavery is the question of property and no property . . . and anti-slavery dare not yet say that every man must do his own work. . . . Yet that is at last the upshot."[175] It was a political theory of hierarchy that, in the 1850s, tended toward a belief that property, not equality, was the central feature of successful republics. The speakers employed economic and historical data to justify their world of slavery, and they saw southern schools as a central part of creating and sustaining that world.

Southern scholars learned the lessons of slavery and then were expected to put them into practice. They learned the lessons of empiricism and the rejection of Enlightenment generalities in favor of laws and policies that were calibrated to the world as it was. They began to match their understanding of economics, history, and political theory to the Constitution and law. As we try to understand the role of constitutional ideas and ideas related to constitutionalism, such as concepts of patriotism and Union, in shaping (and explaining) the coming Civil War, it is good to remember that the Constitution operated as a set of words and also as a set of ideas. College literary addresses, as well as speeches in Congress and on the hustings, worked at accessible and general levels in their discussion of the Constitution and Union as a set of concrete legal rules and as a set of grand ideas.

4

Brown University's President
Confronts Slavery

Despite the refrain of many Southerners that northern schools were insufficiently pro-slavery, many schools in the North supported slavery. In the early
1850s, when many antislavery Northerners were taking a stand against what they
saw as the inhumane return of fugitive slaves to slavery, speakers to the Phi Beta
Kappa societies at Harvard, Yale, and Brown all urged support for the rule of
law.[1] At Harvard, Professor Timothy Walker of the Cincinnati Law School (now
the University of Cincinnati Law School), told his audience that abolitionists
and other reformers were fanatics who sought to tear up civilization. "Reform,
then, is the watchword of the hour. . . . But it does not necessarily signify to improve, to make better, to exalt . . . [A] reformer, however benevolent his designs,
is not necessarily a benefactor, but may, by possibility, be the greatest of malefac-
tors." Walker continued with an assessment—and an indictment—of the 1850s
as the "age of reform." He mocked those who wanted to remake society; instead,
he wanted a return to stable and well-worn forms of thought:

> The shout that goes up from myriad voices, all over the globe, is,—Let
> old things be done away, and all things become new; let the old land-
> marks be obliterated. We will no longer walk in the ancient paths; no
> longer work with the ancient tools; no longer think in the ancient for-
> mulas; no longer believe the ancient creeds. . . . . [W]e pronounce an-
> tiquity a humbug, precedent a sham, prescription a lie, and reverence
> folly. We have been priest-ridden, and king-ridden, and judge-ridden,
> and school-ridden, and wealth-ridden, long enough. And now the time
> is come to declare our independence in all these respects. We cannot,
> indeed, change the past,—that is for ever immutably fixed; but we can
> repudiate it, and we do. . . . We renounce all fealty to their antiquated
> notions. Henceforth to be old is to be questionable. We will hold noth-
> ing sacred which has long been worshiped, and nothing venerable

which has long been venerated. These are the glad tidings which we the reformers of the age, are commissioned to announce.[2]

Orators, similarly, feared that the advancements of the age were leading to too high expectations. The people might be led to think only about Revolution, it seemed. New York lawyer Daniel Lord told the Yale Phi Beta Kappa Society in 1851 that the expectation of scientific improvements should not be translated into changes in jurisprudence:

> The great advances of the present age in the physical sciences and in their applications to the arts of life, the inventions of the electrical tele-graph and daguerrotype, the new developments of steam navigation, the discoveries in geology, the disinterment of long buried cities, the interpretation of languages for centuries unknown, have produced a deep effect, in stimulating the expectations of men as to further attain-ments: they have filled all minds with new and restless activity. Man has thus been led to think that his present condition is in every way an infancy, and that to his coming manhood nothing will be impossible. He is tempted presumptuously to deem every existing thing worn out and unsuitable.[3]

But Lord did not think there should be reform of jurisprudence. His address was about the ways that lawyers and ministers acted as stabilizers in society.

Two literary addresses given at Princeton in 1850 and 1851 illustrate the sup-port for slavery that often appeared on college campuses, even in the North. On July 24, 1850, David S. Kaufman, who then represented Texas in the U.S. House of Representatives, delivered an address to the joint Whig and Cliosophic liter-ary societies. Kaufman, an 1833 graduate of Princeton, spoke about the virtues of slavery. "Who does not see in the transplanting of the Africans to America, the means of restoring to the degraded descendants of Ham the benefits of civi-lization and Christianity," Kaufman asked toward the end of his speech. "In no country on earth is the African as happy, as useful to himself or to the country he inhabits, as the southern slave. Our inestimable slavery does not fail even when it is subjected to the scrutinizing gaze of the inquirer. It confers unnum-bered blessings upon the black man as well as the white."[4] Kaufman recognized, in language similar to Timothy Walker's at Harvard less than two weeks earlier, that reform threatened institutions other than slavery. "The Bible is to be pro-nounced a Cheat, Christ to be proclaimed an imposter, . . . marriage is to be de-spised, the present framework of society will be totally disorganized, property declared theft, and Agrarianism, Communism, Fourierism, and Socialism will supplant the present order of things; anarchy, and bloodshed close the horrific picture!"[5]

The next year, Abraham Watkins Venable, who served in the U.S. House of Representatives as a Democrat from eastern North Carolina from 1847 to 1853, spoke again in favor of slavery to the two Princeton literary societies. Venable was born in 1799 in Springfield, Virginia, and studied at Hampden-Sydney College. He later graduated from Princeton in 1819. Venable's address, like many to college literary societies, was about the "claims of the world on a citizen-scholar."[6] Though many spoke of progress, Venable warned that there could be backward as well as forward progress. That led him to warn of fanaticism, which threatened to eliminate slavery. "There is no evil," Venable thought, "under which the country suffers that is productive of greater practical mischief."[7]

William Greene spoke at Brown with a theoretical discussion of the need for upholding the law. Greene was concerned about the political upheaval wrought by reformers.[8] One group of reformers attracted his attention in particular. It was abolitionists (although he referred to them obliquely) who sought to undue law by making it bow to immediate public sentiment. And yet public sentiment measured any way other than at the ballot was improper. More evils flowed from law bowing to sentiment than were corrected by it, for when law was overridden by sentiment, there was a lack of control:

> Public sentiment, however overwhelming, cannot enact law. It can, at the most, only express the tone with which the powers of government should be administered; in the opinion of those by whom that sentiment is entertained. Whether or not it be entitled to authoritative influence in the administration of the government, the ministers of power for the time being, must, upon their proper responsibility, be the sole judges. If, perchance, the law making power enact a law in opposition to the public sentiment, there are two ways of meeting the difficulty: first, by direct resistance to the law; and, second, by patiently awaiting its repeal, by the election to power of a new and more faithful set of men. The first is rebellion; which in resisting one law, violates all; and thus breaks up the government. The second, in due time, breaks up the law and maintains the government. The first, in correcting one evil, perpetrates a thousand others. The second, by correcting an evil, does a good and nothing more. The first, is anarchy, with a liability to all the desolating mischiefs that pertain to it. The individual second, is the every day experience of the best systems of government, and nobody is disturbed. The government itself, remains sacred as it was.[9]

Greene urged, in keeping with the majority of jurists at the time, a reliance on the political process to change the Fugitive Slave Law. He also criticized abolitionists for their impatience with the world. Instead of accepting the world, idealists—like abolitionists—focused disproportionately on the evils of the world. Idealists' "error . . . consist, generally, . . . in attempting to do, not what *should* not, but what *cannot*, be done; and thus in *wasting* power, with undiscriminating judgment, rather than *abusing* it, with an unworthy purpose."[10] The reformers lived in a parallel universe; their world was one of fiction, not fact. And, on balance, they did more harm than good, for "they make ends of what should perhaps be only means; and are apt to lose sight of a general purpose, however important, in their exclusive devotion to what should be regarded only as a particular step in the attainment of it."[11] Greene's argument rested on considerations of utility. What behavior, his political calculus asked, would result in the most good, on balance. "Carried out," the proposition that individuals should disobey a law was "full of uncalculated and uncalculable mischief. It would destroy government, by the very means it proposes to sustain it. It suggests anarchy as a cure for bad legislation—a wisdom of the sort of that which would kill off the whole human race to get rid of sin."[12]

But at Brown . . . the President had different goals.

In 1827, thirty-one-year-old Francis Wayland became president of Brown University. (University Hall, the central building on Brown's campus at the time, built in part through slave labor, appears in Illustration 4.1.)[13] At times in his early career, he seems to have taken a relatively modest stance against slavery; in one early writing, he even suggested that there was no duty to free slaves.[14] But his textbook, *Elements of Moral Science*, which was the most popular college moral philosophy textbook of the era from 1835 through the Civil War, was antislavery. The book actually had widespread adoption in the South. It was used, for instance, at the University of Alabama, Howard College, and Washington College throughout much of the antebellum era. But in the 1850s southern schools began to abandon the textbook.[15]

Wayland wrote that slavery "violates the personal liberty of man as a physical, intellectual, and social being."[16] Slavery was, in Wayland's mind, inconsistent with the Golden Rule. We are required "to cherish as tender and delicate a respect for the right which the meanest individual possesses over the means of happiness bestowed upon him by God, as we cherish for our own right over our own means of happiness, or as we desire any other individual to cherish for it."[17] Slavery, in any form, is inconsistent with such a charge. Though he believed slavery inconsistent with the Bible, Wayland thought that the evil should be removed immediately, but assumed—for the sake of argument—that immediate emancipation would do more harm than good.[18] Under those circumstances (about which Wayland expressed some skepticism), it was the duty of the master

Illustration 4.1 University Hall, Brown University, (Library of Congress, Prints & Photographs Division, HABS, Reproduction number HABS RI, 4-PROV, 81A—1.)

to keep the slave not "on the ground of right over him, but of obligation to him, and of obligation to him for the purpose of accomplishing a particular and speci-fied good. And, of course, he who holds him for any other purpose, holds him wrongfully, and is guilty of the sin of slavery."[19] Wayland gave slave owners the benefit of the doubt that perhaps slavery was still necessary because slaves were unfit to govern themselves, but he still charged slave owners with the sin of slav-ery and also charged them with the duty of elevating slaves to the status where they could be free.[20]

A number of southern scholars responded to the moderate antislavery aspects of *Elements of Moral Science*. One of the first was George Baxter of Hampden-Sydney, who in 1836 published an attack on abolitionists. Baxter had recently relocated to Prince Edward County from Washington College, where he was president. Baxter first served as a professor at the Union Theological Seminary, which was adjacent to Hampden-Sydney College, and in 1835 was interim presi-dent of Hampden-Sydney. That school had, like William and Mary, undergone a shift from a place where Enlightenment ideas held sway to a place of pro-slavery thought. For Hampden-Sydney was founded in the eighteenth century and named for the seventeenth-century theorists of representative government John Hampden and Algernon Sydney. And some indicators are that it nurtured antislavery ideas in the early nineteenth century. Jesse Harrison, the person who challenged Thomas R. Dew's pro-slavery ideas in the wake of the Virginia legislature's 1832 debate, was a graduate of Hampden-Sydney.[21]

But by the middle of the 1830s George Baxter's pamphlet *An Essay on the Abolition of Slavery* presented a wide-ranging attack on abolition. Baxter, like many people of his era, turned to considerations of utility to judge slavery. Then Wayland's concession that *perhaps* slaves were not yet ready for freedom became a centerpiece of Baxter's argument that freedom would lead to more harm than good. Baxter turned to the English historian Henry Hallam for evidence of the near ubiquity of slavery in human history, which helped normalize slavery and make the point that they were unfit for freedom.[22] Baxter jealously guarded the idea of freedom; he concluded, "there is no greater evil than to give the multitude a degree of liberty, which they are unprepared to enjoy." Emancipation was the worst evil Baxter could imagine. He believed that if a legislator "were authorized to pass over Africa, Asia, and a large part of Europe, and to abolish slavery as he went . . . he would carry heavier judgments in his course than the destroying angel of Egypt."[23] All of this was a prelude to Baxter's critique of Wayland's conclusion that slave owning was a sin. Baxter countered that slavery was legal and moral while slaves were unfit for freedom.[24]

University of North Carolina science professor Elisha Mitchell likewise attacked Wayland's position that slave owning was sinful in his 1848 pamphlet *The Other Leaf of Nature*.[25] Mitchell focused on one point, that slavery was no more sinful than any other form of property ownership. Mitchell explored in depth the unequal distribution of property throughout the United States and Europe and the misery that poverty created. Mitchell's argument might have been the basis for holding more property in common ownership, rather than as private property. Or it might have been the basis for redistributing property to those who had little. But for Mitchell it served a more mundane purpose: to point out the hypocrisy of abolitionists. This indicted Wayland and other antislavery thinkers by showing that the sins of slavery were the same as the sins of unequal ownership of property and that Wayland and others did not care about those problems.[26]

Although Wayland's *Moral Science* accepted that perhaps slavery had to continue for the present, his critique of the sinfulness of slavery continued to draw the attention of southern intellectuals and readers in the North and South. In 1845, Wayland elaborated on these themes in an important and public debate with the Reverend Richard Fuller of South Carolina, published in inexpensive, pamphlet form, designed to reach the masses. The debate was called *Domestic Slavery Considered as a Scriptural Institution*.[27] Wayland's attack on slavery began with simple, common-sense reasoning: he feels he is a human, who has natural rights, so others must feel the same way; it is a violation of God's law to interfere with those rights.[28] The nature of slavery was inherently a deprivation of rights; no matter how humanely masters might treat slaves, there was still deprivation.

In the face of the Old Testament's seeming recognition of slavery, Wayland argued that standards of morality were evolving. In his third letter, Wayland confronted the claim that the Bible sanctioned slavery. Wayland thought the Bible sanctioned slavery only in a limited place and during an ancient time. "We cannot plead in this case . . . that what was permitted without rebuke in a darker age is permitted to us to whom greater light has been given." He looked to the context of slavery in the Old Testament and thought that evidence demonstrated that slavery, like other relics of ancient times, was now prohibited:

> Take for instance the whole Mosaic code of civil law, its severe enactments, its very frequent capital punishments, its cities of refuge, its tenures of real estate. Could any legislator at present day enact similar laws, and justly plead as a sufficient reason that God had sanctioned, nay enacted, such laws for the Jews? Would this be a sufficient reason for abolishing the trial by jury in a case of accidental homicide, (as for instance when the head of an axe slipped from the helve and wounded a man to death,) and enacting that the next a kin might slay an innocent person if he overtook him before he arrived at a city of refuge? I think every one must immediately perceive that this law was a humane limitation to the spirit of Oriental vindictiveness, but that it would be very wrong to put it in practice at the present day.[29]

Wayland saw the New Testament as incorporating an expanding—indeed progressing—code of morality. He even linked those moral standards to the Declaration of Independence. He wrote that the New Testament

> inculcates those truths concerning the characters, rights, responsibilities, and obligations of man, which have been ever since working out the freedom of the human race; and which have received, as I believe, their fullest development in the principles of the American Declaration of Independence. Indeed, in no other manner could the New Testament have become a system of religion for the whole human race, adapted to meet the varying aspects of human depravity.[30]

Wayland's interpretation of the Bible's adaptability to changing conditions illustrates how liberal northern divines could be so in love with the idea of progress; it was part of working out Christianity's promise. Southerners had a more difficult time with these ideas; they did not see the same change in moral standards.[31] Perhaps part of the difference was attributable to the ways that slavery bent the understanding of southern (and many northern) religious thinkers. Those differences appear in a series of attacks that southern academics advanced against

Wayland. University of North Carolina professor Elisha Mitchell, for instance, prepared an attack on Wayland and several other antislavery writers.[32] Richard Fuller, Wayland's opponent in the 1845 debate, argued in favor of slavery because it was supported by the Bible and it was, in practice, better for slaves than freedom.

Fuller, whose pulpit was the First Baptist Church of Beaufort, South Carolina (Illustration 4.2), had several points.[33] First, he denied the idea of evolution

Illustration 4.2 First Baptist Church, Beaufort, South Carolina (Library of Congress, Prints & Photographs Division, HABS, Reproduction number HABS SC,7-BEAUF, 3—6.)

in Christianity; what the Bible permitted would be permitted always. He approached this by questioning how modern day thinkers could possibly know more than those in the era of the Bible. "Is it true," Fuller asked, "that a Christian at the South possesses greater advantages than a Christian in apostolic times, for ascertaining his duty? If he does, whence does he derive them?"[34] That revelation would not come from natural religion. Fuller refused Wayland's model of evolution of morality.

> I protest, then, against any permission given to men, to tamper with the word of God on the pleas that the times are changed. And I deny, too, that my means of deciding on the moral character of slavery are superior to those which Timothy and Philemon enjoyed—the latter of whom was a slave-holder, and confirmed in slaveholding by Paul—and the former was enjoined, as an evangelist, to inculcate precepts, and pursue a line of conduct, utterly at variance with the doctrine that slave-holding is itself, and always, a heinous crime.[35]

Moreover, slavery, in practice, was not so bad. In fact, for slaves, it was better than freedom.

> With reference to my own servants, their condition is as good as I can make it. They are placed under a contract, which no instrument of writing could make more sacred. By this contract they, on their part, perform not one half the work done by free laborers; and I, on my part, am bound to employ a missionary to teach and catechize them and their children; to provide them a home, and clothes, and provisions, and fuel, and land to plant for themselves; to pay all medical bills; to guaranty to them all the profits of their skill and labor, in their own time; to protect them as a guardian; and to administer to the wants of the children, and of those that are sick, and infirm, and aged. Such is their state, nor have I any idea that they would consent to be removed. But will my brother, or any man at the North, undertake to remove them, and give me bond and security that their condition shall be improved? If so, let him speak; and I will then make a proposition which shall, at once, and by a test more sure than all the writing in the world, determine who is the friend of the slave, and who is willing to make sacrifices for his good, and how many abolition Acaciuses and Paulinuses are ready to be forthcoming with church plate for the crucible, and even a moiety of their estates "for the redemption of the captives."[36]

The humanity of the slave system was a common point in pro-slavery writing. That argument sought to make the present system appear more palatable. When Wayland's third letter admitted that slavery might be humane, Fuller presented that as the common nature of slavery. "Now, here is slavery. Here is no painting of fancy; no impracticable, Utopian abstraction; but slavery as you have known it, and as others know it to exist."[37] But slavery was not just humane; it was the only practicable course. "Suppose ... this government, using the lights of wisdom and experience, is convinced that the black population cannot be admitted to the privileges of free citizens, but that the good of the whole community, the safety and existence of the republic, and the negroes' own best interests, require that their personal liberty be restrained. Will it be pretended that such conduct would be criminal?"[38] Moreover, abolition would work a great harm:

> [S]lavery was everywhere a part of the social organization of the earth; and slaves their masters were members together of the churches; and minute instructions are given to each as to their duties, without even an insinuation that it was the duty of masters to emancipate. . . . What, then, are we to think of those who revile us as pirates and thieves, and fulminate anathemas and excommunications against every Christian at the South, no matter what his conduct or character, simply because he will not submit to the arrogant behests of mortals who are, like himself, loaded with imperfections; and because he esteems the Bible a safer directory than the dogmas of men, most of whom are everyday proving themselves destitute of the sound mind and charity of the gospel—of people who are essentially monomaniacs—who cannot live without running into some insanity—who, if slavery were abolished, would be just as mad upon amalgamation, or masonry, or Millerism, or some other matter–and with whom, in fine, whatever your course may be as to us, neither you, nor anybody at the North who loves Christ and the gospel better than self, and strife, and fanatical intolerance, will long be able to harmonize?[39]

Much of Wayland's evidence (as with other antislavery advocates) for slavery's harshness came from southern statutes. But Fuller, like other pro-slavery writers, emphasized sentiment, rather than law. It was masters' kind sentiments— not the harsh slave code—that characterized slavery in the South. "Your entire argument—though put abstractly against slavery—was really framed against the slave laws, and applied only to them," Fuller wrote.[40] That critique of law, which appeared in Harriet Beecher Stowe's *Uncle Tom's Cabin,* is part of an antebellum debate over jurisprudence. Should we measure society by the laws on the books or by how people behave? And even if we measure by the latter, do people behave more humane than their laws? Or, as William Goodell wrote in *The American Slave Code in Theory and Practice,* "men may be better than their laws, but seldom are."[41]

Wayland defended his reliance on statutes as a gauge of slavery. "If the public opinion had decided that slaves had rights, which it was the duty of society to protect, I cannot but believe that a great and radical change would long since have been effected in the statute-books of our Southern States."[42] For Wayland, the harshness of slavery was found in southern statute books, much as seeds of the nineteenth century's antislavery morality were found in the New Testament. "The reason of the duty to abolish slavery is found in the moral relations and responsibilities of a human being. But these moral relations and responsibilities were at this time wholly unknown. . . . It was certainly reasonable to postpone the inculcation of the *duty* until the *truths* were promulgated on which this duty *was founded.*"[43]

Wayland saw guilt as dependent on an individual's relationship to the society and to revealed morality.[44] Not only had standards of morality changed since the time of Christ, they also continued to evolve even in the last few decades. He used the example of Yale's president, Ezra Stiles, who had owned a slave and then recognized the inhumanity of ownership. When Stiles owned a slave in the late eighteenth century, that was acceptable; but just a few decades later, it was unthinkable in Connecticut.

> I have been told that the Rev. Dr. Stiles, afterwards president of Yale College, during his residence in Newport, R.I., being in want of a do-mestic, sent by the captain of a slave ship, a barrel of rum to the coast of Africa, to be exchanged for a slave. The venture was successful and in due time, a negro was brought back. It chanced that sometimes af-terwards, in passing by his kitchen, he observed the boy in tears. He asked him the reason of his sorrow, and the poor fellow answered that he was thinking of his parents, and his brothers and sisters, whom he should never see again. In an instant, the whole truth flashed upon the master's mind and he saw the evil he had done. He could not return the boy to Africa, but he made every reparation in his power. He provided every means for his improvement, was the means of his conversion, and treated his afterwards not as a servant, but as a brother beloved. Newport, for that was his name, survived Dr. Stiles by several years, and he was, until the end of his life, supported by a legacy, which his former master left for him.[45]

From that story, which has occupied an important part of recent debate over slavery at Yale,[46] Wayland illustrated the changing nature of guilt. "Dr. Stiles sending a barrel of rum to Africa for a person is of close to unparalleled evil today; sixty or seventy years ago it was not so bad."[47] Even over the past few years, there was great moral progress. "It is much more difficult for a man at the present time to hold his fellow-man in bondage, and be guiltless, through ignorance, than it was twenty years since. The whole civilized world has been agitated upon this question."[48]

But there is yet another lesson buried in Wayland's wisdom about changing morality. It is a caution to us about moral judgments that we make about the past. And perhaps a caution that we need to look to the context of the actors: How did Brown University look in comparison with other schools at the time? While we look back we can gain an appreciation of the difficult struggles over morality of the antebellum period. Of course, as Wayland well understood, subsequent generations would judge Brown University and others. He said in his funeral oration for Nicholas Brown in 1841, "We can associate our names with succeeding ages, only by deeds or by thoughts which they will not willingly forget."[49]

Wayland's celebration of Nicholas Brown's contribution may be of some help in thinking about Brown University's culpability as well. Nicholas Brown's contribution to the Providence Athenaeum's library placed "the means of rich and varied intellectual and moral cultivation . . . within the reach of every individual among us."[50] And of Brown University itself, Wayland thought:

> An institution has been here founded, which we hope will continue to all future time to scatter abroad "the benefits of service and the blessings of religion." Its cheering influences have been already observed in the courts of justice and in the halls of legislation. Already has it swayed the senate with its eloquence, and illuminated the bench with by its wisdom. . . . All this will, we hope, go on increasing to unnumbered generations.[51]

Wayland understood that subsequent generations would likely apply a different— and higher—standard when judging the actions of his generation. The knowledge that people will apply different standards in the future might cause actors to contemplate reform. Already we could see in his time the changing standards of morality; progress was a large part of antebellum thought. Wayland contributed to the change in standards of behavior, in part by reminding readers that in the United States they had the power to change law. Those progressing standards of morality—and the fact that people lived in a community—made them responsible for the wrongs of the community:

> Before the formulation of this compact, the individual was responsible only for his own wrong; now he is responsible both for his own, and

also, since he is a member of the society, for all the wrong which the society binds itself to uphold and render perpetual.[52]

Wayland asserted that those who failed to take action against slavery were culpable for their inaction. He saw the power of people to change the law as implicating them if they failed to do so:

> If the laws are wrong, he, as a member of society, is bound to exert his full constitutional power to effect their abolition. If the moral sentiment of the state is wicked, he is bound to labor with his whole power to correct it. If his fellow citizens oppress him, he is called upon with every sentiment of manliness, constitutionally, to resist this oppression. If they oppress his fellow men, he is bound by every sentiment of philanthropy to defend the oppressed and raise up the down-trodden. Unless he do this, he cannot, as a member of the society, be free from the guilt or the wrong which the society perpetrates.[53]

Wayland suggested that masters stop benefiting from their slaves' labor. Even if they had to continue to own humans, the master should hold slaves for their benefit not his own, a reprisal of a point made in his *Elements of Moral Science*.[54] Wayland relied on the United States' democracy to suggest the culpability that attends the failure to change the law of slavery:

> Slavery is established and maintained by the power of society, and it can be universally abolished only by legislation. The case was the same in the early ages of Christianity. There is, however, this one remarkable difference. Then, the laws were nothing but the published will of a despot. The subject had no power to make or unmake them. It is by no means the same with us. *We make our own laws*. Every citizen who exercises the right of suffrage, is himself responsible for every law that is made, unless he has put forth his full constitutional power to prevent it.[55]

He used an extended analogy to illustrate the culpability. It was an analogy to misappropriated property. While one may have acquired the property improperly, to continue to hold it compounds the harm. The owner must cease the retention of a wrongfully obtained benefit. Wayland thought the owner must give up that benefit.[56] And, as Wayland spoke to the need to free slaves (or at the very least hold them for their own benefit and not the owners'), he spoke of the need to give them adequate compensation for the work they performed.[57]

The focus on the duty of the individual appeared in other work, too. In a series of sermons on *The Duty of Obedience to the Civil Magistrate* delivered at Brown's chapel around the time of the Mexican-American War, Wayland began with the proposition that individuals must obey the law. But in keeping with Wayland's focus on individual morality, he also enjoined individuals to follow their understanding of morality. Just because a magistrate commanded something did not absolve an individual of moral responsibility for following that act. Wayland's counsel was that people "must obey God rather than man."[58] This was a midway point between those who argued that all properly passed laws had to be obeyed and those who in the wake of the Fugitive Slave Act of 1850 urged widespread disobedience. Wayland, thus, urged individuals to take action to remake the law. He presented a morality based on individual conscience and sought to make changes from the individual outward toward society, by charging individuals to make the right decisions and then expecting that collectively the state would make the right decisions, too. Wayland's model of an evolving standard of morality stood in contrast to the position of many Southerners that took the world as it was. The actual was put in opposition to the ideal. This was a conflict that played out in many places in the debates over slavery, from discussions of religious leaders to legal and political thinkers. The Wayland-Fuller debate is just one of the points of conflict between antislavery thinkers who appealed to universal ideas of freedom and looked forward to the days of liberation and those who urged that reform was not possible or desirable now, that the Bible and history supported slavery, and that slavery was beneficial for the enslaved. The stage was being set in many colleges and other parts of American culture for an epic clash of visions of morality, economy, and slavery.

Wayland stood firmly with the antislavery side at Brown, though many other orators at Brown spoke of ending slavery as well. On the eve of the Civil War, Unitarian minister Andrew Peabody's Phi Beta Kappa lecture was radically opposed to slavery.[59] Peabody spoke of the immutable truth—revealed religion's instructions to humans. "The Bible," he said, "is the geometry, the mechanics, the astronomy, of the spiritual universe."[60] That immutable truth, God's law, was higher and more compelling than human law, which is so frequently based on considerations of expediency rather than morality. He criticized those, like Senator Daniel Webster, who rejected higher law in favor of the Fugitive Slave Act:

> In the whole political history of our own country, there has been no sin so atrocious as the repudiation of a higher than human law. It is stark atheism; for, with the law, this position virtually denies also the providence of God, and makes men and nations sole arbiters of their own fortunes.

Slavery appears by name only once in Peabody's oration, but there are allusions to it on virtually all pages. It was imperative to end slavery, Peabody thought.

> The nations that have passed away, the decaying nations, the convulsed thrones, the smouldering rebellion-fires, of the Old World, reveal the elements of national decline and ruin, and hold out baleful signals over the career on which our republic is hurrying; assuring us, by the experience of all climes and ages, that slavery, the unprincipled lust of power and territory, official corruption and venality, aggressive war, partisan legislation, are but "sowing the wind to reap the whirlwind."[61]

The Chancellor, the Slave,
and the Student

During the Civil War and in the years following it, Frederick A. P. Barnard served as president of Columbia University, where he set the foundation for the world-class institution that Columbia is today. Among the reforms Barnard sought was education of women at the University. So when Columbia University established a separate women's college in 1889, around the time of his death, it was named after him.[1] Barnard was chosen as president of Columbia in the midst of the Civil War. All of that seemed rather improbable just a few years before. For at the outbreak of the war, he had been in Mississippi, where he served as chancellor of the University of Mississippi. Jefferson Davis offered him a position in the Confederacy, supervising sulphur mining in Tennessee, which Barnard turned down. Then he went to Norfolk, Virginia, and stayed along the coast. When U.S. troops liberated that part of Virginia in May 1862, he was again back in the United States and offered a position the U.S. War Department (working on producing maps of the coast for the war effort).[2] Barnard published a pro-Union tract in 1863.[3] Among the things that Barnard—a longtime supporter of the cause of Union—wrote about in that tract were the evils of slavery. He described it as "that relic of primeval barbarism, that loathsome monument of the brutalities of the ages of darkness, that monster injustice—cursed of Christian men and hated of God."[4] In 1864 Barnard was offered the presidency of Columbia.

The Chancellor and Slavery

Before the war began, Barnard had long-standing connections to the South. He worked at two southern institutions for twenty-two years before the Civil War. He taught first at the University of Alabama from 1838 to 1854 and then served as professor at the University of Mississippi, beginning in 1854. Shortly after his arrival in Oxford, a financial scandal brought down Mississippi's president,

Augustus Baldwin Longstreet, and Barnard was promoted to the position (subsequently called chancellor), which he held until 1861. He helped raise the quality of education and constructed an observatory on the campus, which still stands. Barnard, everyone agrees, was a colorful character. He was born in 1809 into a family of conservatives (his father had been a pro-British sympathizer during the War of 1812) in western Massachusetts. He was educated at Yale University, where he graduated in 1828; he then taught in New York and made his way south in 1838, to the University of Alabama.[5]

Barnard's energy and enthusiasm put him at the center of the University and the Tuscaloosa community. A student who had known him in the 1830s recalled, "He has never been idle, and seldom out of a place of prominent usefulness." He edited a newspaper for a time (the *Tuskaloosa Monitor*, a Whig paper), set up a photographic studio, and wrote poetry, in addition to teaching. In short, "he was ever keenly in pursuit of knowledge of every kind—the first edge of an eclipse or the last faint ray of a departing comet was alike inviting to his eager curiosity and commanded his closest scrutiny."[6] Barnard also started a Phi Beta Kappa chapter on the University of Alabama's campus. His 1854 Phi Beta Kappa address, "Art Culture: Its Relation to National Refinement and National Morality," pointed out the refinement of manner and morals that comes from the cultivation of art. It was an attempt to ground the study of art in utility, a classic issue for Barnard, who urged education for practical purposes.[7] And it was also a part of the Whig belief in the contributions that beauty made to civilization—a theme that appeared in the Whig emphasis on fine art and the cultivation of gardens, even rural cemeteries.

It was partly that advocacy of the practicality of education that brought Barnard into conflict with the University's president, Basil Manly. Barnard published extensively on the need for a practical, as opposed to a classical, curriculum, which brought him into conflict with the editor of the *Mobile Register* and the University's administration. Perhaps, then, the allegations that Barnard was antislavery were just easy cover for an attack on Barnard's attitudes toward education. For there was some conflict, especially in the early 1850s, about the standards and whether students should be permitted to take elective courses or must follow a prescribed curriculum.[8] Some of Barnard's other controversies on campus were more mundane. He drank more alcohol than some thought appropriate and perhaps spent more time around students than he should have.[9]

Some of the disputes that swirled around Barnard were political. He was a member of the Masons, which carried with it substantial controversy in that era when Democrats were skeptical of secret societies. Barnard gave an address in 1841, "Claims of Masonry upon the Respect and Veneration of Mankind," which was a defense of tradition. At the moment transcendentalists were arguing against venerable institutions and suggesting that one should reject old modes of thought, Barnard used longevity as evidence of truth. He thought institutions that have stood for ages had time itself to testify to their merits.[10]

Then there were the whispers that Barnard did not have sufficient Southern sympathies, that is, he was insufficiently committed to the cause of slavery.[11] He gave a pro-Union oration in Tuscaloosa on July 4, 1851.[12] In it, he sought first to calm fears about the Constitution's support for slavery. He recalled that abolitionists had made little headway in politics and that, in fact, through the Fugitive Slave Act of 1850, the Union was helping reclaim fugitives.[13] Then he turned to what the South might do to promote manufacturing and education. He sought to calm fears and inspire Southerners to make more effort to promote their own economic well-being. It was a classic conservative oration, designed to point out both how (relatively) good life is and the dangers of political upheaval.[14]

Barnard supported pro-slavery faculty at the University,[15] and he was a more direct participant in the institution of slavery. Barnard used a slave named Sam as a laboratory assistant. What duties Sam performed are unknown.[16] The University's president, Basil Manly, recorded in his diaries frequent conflicts with a Sam. Once, Sam "behaved very insolently to Thos. G. Grace, and refused to measure or receive a load of coal which Grace had brought." Manly then recorded Sam's punishment and his refusal to be humbled. "By order of the Faculty, he was chastised, in my room, in their presence. Not seemingly humbled, I whipped him a second time, very severely."[17] In fact, all the "disciplining" of the University's slaves had to take place under the supervision of the faculty. This was a reform that the faculty instituted, apparently to help establish order on the campus and to keep students from beating slaves on campus[18] (see Illustration 5.1).

One of the first acts of the University, three years before it opened to students in 1831, was to purchase a slave named Ben. Thus, though we may think of the University of Alabama as a place reserved for white people until it was integrated in 1963, in fact African Americans were present at the school even before there were students there. The faculty owned a number of slaves, and the University owned and rented slaves, too.[19] In 1831, a court in Huntsville ordered Isaac Winston to sell a slave to satisfy the University's claim against him.[20] Another person, Thomas Aldredge, conveyed slaves in trust for the benefit of the University; the trustee, one Tarver, then billed the University $102.50 for administering the trust.[21] When slaves died, they were occasionally buried on campus.[22]

Barnard also owned several people while he taught at the University of Alabama. There is slim evidence of their lives, but what little there is, is shocking. President Manly complained to his diary in 1851 that one of Barnard's male slaves, Morgan, acted "as a pimp to get out Barnard's women—especially the younger Luna, whom they use in great numbers, nightly." Nothing else is known

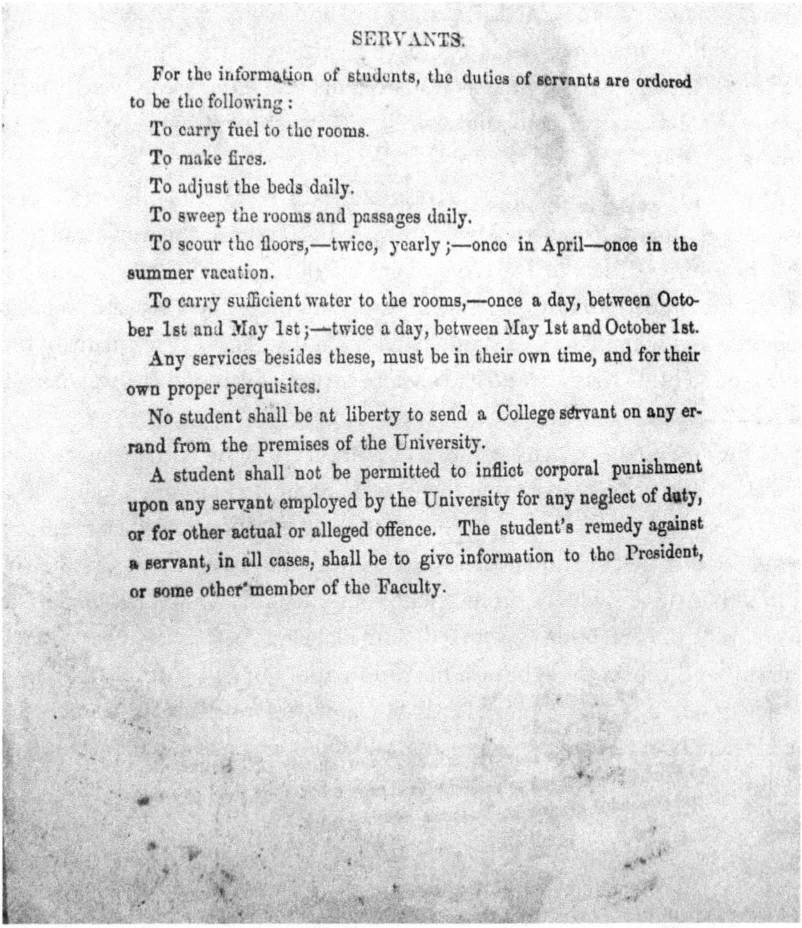

SERVANTS.

For the information of students, the duties of servants are ordered to be the following :

To carry fuel to the rooms.

To make fires.

To adjust the beds daily.

To sweep the rooms and passages daily.

To scour the floors,—twice, yearly ;—once in April—once in the summer vacation.

To carry sufficient water to the rooms,—once a day, between October 1st and May 1st ;—twice a day, between May 1st and October 1st.

Any services besides these, must be in their own time, and for their own proper perquisites.

No student shall be at liberty to send a College servant on any errand from the premises of the University.

A student shall not be permitted to inflict corporal punishment upon any servant employed by the University for any neglect of duty, or for other actual or alleged offence. The student's remedy against a servant, in all cases, shall be to give information to the President, or some other member of the Faculty.

Illustration 5.1 University of Alabama regulations. The *By-Laws of the University of Alabama* (Tuscaloosa, M. D. J. Shade 1854) prohibited students from beating the University's slaves. (Duke University Library)

about this, and it is important to be cautious in interpreting this sketchy evidence, for it comes from Barnard's primary detractor on campus.[23] However, that episode hints at life lurking beneath the surface of the University of Alabama.[24]

President Manly, who owned thirty-eight slaves according to the 1855 state census,[25] recorded in his diary a number of episodes of violence by students against slaves on the campus.[26] Perhaps because of violence by students against slaves, as well as the desire to maintain more control over the University, in 1845 the University's trustees acted to put the slaves "owned or employed by the University ... under the protection, as well as control, of the Faculty." Consequently, the trustees forbade students "to strike or chastise" slaves. The students, instead, were supposed to report problems to the President. When, if "chastisement shall be judged necessary by the Faculty . . . such chastisement shall be inflicted in presence of one of the Faculty."[27] The 1854 regulations of the University of Alabama detailed for students the duties slaves were expected to perform on campus and the restrictions on students beating slaves (see Illustration 5.1).

Abuse continued, even after the resolution. In 1850, students who thought that Moses, one of President Manly's slaves, had accused them of stealing turkeys, beat him.[28] Then, in 1851, Sam beat "an old man named Tom in the service of Professor Barnard on some altercation connected with the well." The students then whipped Sam. Manly recorded in his diary: "Very many of them were around him—some 5 or 6 had switches and Lee was one that was using the switch."[29]

At the University of Mississippi in 1858, Chancellor Barnard again found himself in controversy regarding slavery. He addressed an "open letter" to the trustees of the University, urging the creation of a "Universitas Scientarium," a university that taught students and was dedicated to research, across the spectrum of human knowledge, from science and literature to agriculture, law, and medicine.[30] The reception was mixed. Some labeled the University a "citadel of atheism" and others thought it "a hotbed of abolitionism." Moreover, Barnard found continuing conflict with friends and family members of his predecessor at the University of Mississippi, Augustus Baldwin Longstreet, an important writer of southern fictional literature, particularly humor.[31]

The Slaves, the Students, and the Chancellor

On the evening of May 11, 1859, two students, J. P. Furnis and Samuel Humphreys went to the home of the Barnards. The Barnards were not there; they were in Vicksburg, attending the Southern Commercial Convention, a meeting promoting southern manufactures. Only Barnard's slaves were at home. (According to the 1860 federal census, the Barnards owned two women, aged thirty and thirty-five.)[32] Humphreys sexually assaulted and beat one of Barnard's slaves, Jane. The next night Professor E. C. Boynton heard an argument and looked over the brick fence separating his yard and the Barnards' yard. He saw two people, whom he later learned were Furnis and Humphreys.[33]

Chancellor Barnard arrived home on the evening of May 17. The next morning, he heard that story, first (apparently) from his wife Margaret, then from Professor Boynton.[34] Shortly thereafter, Barnard confronted Humphreys and demanded that he leave school. Humphreys consented, but then did not leave, so the faculty commenced to try him at a faculty meeting on May 23, 1859. There were two charges:

1st. Visiting the dwelling of the President in his absence, and while it was occupied by defenceless female servants, with shameful designs upon one of the said servants;

2d. Committing a violent assault and battery upon the servant afore-said, and inflicting severe personal injury, whereby the said servant was for some days incapacitated for labor, and of which the marks are still, after the lapse of many days, plainly visible.[35]

The trial revealed divisions within the faculty. They were not completely convinced of Humphrey's guilt. The faculty rejected (by a 3 to 5 vote) a res-olution to suspend Humphreys from the University.[36] There was some sug-gestion that Jane's identification was faulty, because she said she had been attacked by a student who was missing a front tooth. Humphreys was not.[37] Moreover, some thought that three students provided a sufficient alibi for Humphreys.[38] Still, the faculty was pretty convinced that Humphreys was guilty. After the first resolution failed, they voted on another, more mild reso-lution, stating that they believed Humphreys guilty, but that they wanted to distinguish between their moral conviction that the student was guilty and evidence sufficient for legal conviction.[39] The division was not so much over whether they believed Humphreys was guilty but whether there was legally sufficient evidence that he was guilty—that is, whether there was evidence that would be admitted in a legal trial. This is yet another instance in which the standards established by law affect other parts of society, including in this case the trial of a student. Some of the faculty were bothered that the origin of Barnard's knowledge derived from testimony given to his wife by one of their slaves.[40]

Barnard subsequently requested Humphrey's guardian to withdraw him from school, which happened. Humphreys was out of school, but the controversy continued to fester, for Professor Carter spoke to people outside the faculty about the trial.[41]

The Trial of the Chancellor

I am as "sound on the slavery question" as Dr. Branham, or any member of this Board.

—F. A. P. Barnard[42]

The conflict appeared again, in stark relief, in early 1860, when Chancellor Barnard was accused by Henry R. Branham, a physician in Oxford, of being insuf-ficiently pro-slavery; in fact, of taking the testimony of a slave against a student. Branham had reason to dislike Barnard; his father-in-law was A. P. Longstreet, recently ousted president of the university. Branham was also brother-in-law to L. Q. C. Lamar, who was then serving in the U.S. Congress (and would later serve as an associate justice on the U.S. Supreme Court). Barnard reported that Branham had made a series of charges, including:

> That he (Barnard) was unsound upon the slavery question. . . .
>
> That he was in favor of, and did advocate, the taking of negro testimony against a student. . . .
>
> That H. (a student) was arraigned and tried upon negro testimony. . . .
>
> That upon the question of the expulsion of H., the vote was sectionally divided—Barnard, Boynton and Moore voting in the affirmative, and the Southern men voting in the negative. . . .
>
> That, pending the discussion upon the case of H., Barnard asked [Professor W. G.] Richardson if he would not believe his negro man, Henry, against a student, and when Richard said he would not, Barnard said *he would*. . . .
>
> That all the information in the H. case was furnished by a negro woman; and that it was proposed by the other members of the Faculty, that, if Barnard and Boynton had other sources of information and would assert positively that they knew H. was guilty, they (the other members) would vote accordingly. . . .
>
> That Barnard stated that Jane (the negro woman) afterwards recognized H., and pointed him out as the man who had assailed her. . . .
>
> That notwithstanding the vote of expulsion failed, Barnard wrote to the guardian of the student to take him away, which he did. . . .
>
> That if the Board of Trustees persisted in their refusal to arraign and try Barnard for taking negro testimony against a student, he (Barnard) would publish the whole thing, in the *Mississippian*, to the people of the State, over his own signature.[43]

Those charges led Barnard to ask in early February 1860 for a trial before the University of Mississippi trustees, which took place on March 1 and March 2, 1860.[44] Barnard wanted, in essence, to clear his name and resolve some of the conflict. He succeeded and then the record of the trial was printed—in Jackson, Mississippi.[45]

The trial opens a window into the world of the antebellum southern university and especially into the points of conflict between students, faculty, and slaves. The trial allows speculation on three key issues: first, Barnard's own attitudes toward slavery; second, slavery on the campus of the University of Mississippi; and, finally, the meaning of slave testimony.

Branham tried to define the issues narrowly:

> 1st. That Dr. Barnard offered the statement of a negro as evidence
> against a student of the University of Mississippi. . . .
>
>   2nd. That after the Faculty refused to sustain the charge upon the
> testimony adduced, Dr. Barnard without the authority of the Faculty,
> wrote to his guardian a letter which resulted in the withdrawal of Mr.
> H[umphrey] from the University.
>
>   3rd. That Dr. Barnard interposed and objected to Mr. H[umphrey]'s
> re-admission into the University at the opening of the following ses-
> sion, and thus prevented his return.[46]

Barnard wanted a broader inquiry, which established that Barnard was convinced of Humphrey's guilt independent of Jane's testimony, that the faculty was
morally convinced of Humphrey's guilt, and that it was appropriate to encourage
his guardian to remove him from school and to further refuse his readmission.[47]

The trial proceeded to take testimony from all the faculty and Branham.
Branham's testimony gives some insight into what Barnard had done to offend
his faculty. Barnard was seen as insufficiently supportive of slavery, as a "free-
soiler," a reference to those who believed that the territories should be free territory.[48] When asked why he thought that Barnard was a free-soiler, Branham had
three reasons: Barnard used the testimony of a slave against a student; he wanted
Van Norden, a New York printer, to print the university's catalog because southern printers were not as good; and because he considered a position at Yale.[49]

Much of the trial revolved around the extent to which Barnard relied upon
Jane's testimony (which he presumably heard about through his wife, Margaret)
and what that might say about Barnard's antislavery sentiments. There were
several elements of the "taking the testimony of a slave against a student." First,
whether—as Barnard suggested—his wife's retelling of a conversation with Jane
was actually the slave's testimony or something else, like merely corroborating
evidence (what one person called historical evidence rather than testimony).[50]
Along those lines, there was a confrontation between Barnard and Professor
Wilson G. Richardson over the extent to which owners should believe their
slaves. The exchange went something like this: Barnard asked Richardson, "If
your servant Henry should tell you that a student had taken your horse or saddle
from the stable, would you believe him?" Richardson replied, "I would not, if
his statement conflicted with the statement of a student, and especially if his
method of identifying the party should prove false or defective."[51] (Barnard later
countered with a somewhat different hypothetical question: "Suppose that your
servant, Henry, should tell you that your saddle is missing from your stable;

would you not believe him without going to see for yourself?" That question did not juxtapose a student against a slave.[52]) While some, like Richardson, thought that Barnard had no testimony other than that derived from his slave Jane,[53] Professor Boynton testified that he had also heard that Humphreys had attacked Jane and that the source of that information was not a slave.[54] The confrontation between Richardson and Barnard is particularly surprising, because Richardson, a professor of Latin, had been Barnard's student at the University of Alabama, and he had helped recruit Barnard to the University of Mississippi.[55] Others thought there was sufficient evidence against Humphreys. Law Professor William F. Stearns,[56] who like Barnard was born in Massachusetts, thought that there was enough evidence to find Humphreys guilty and that he "underst[ood] that the statement was offered only as a corroborating circumstance."[57]

From the trial record, we hear only one word from Jane. And that word is reported through Barnard. After Humphreys' trial, Barnard told the trustees, that Humphreys stopped by the Barnards' house and Jane opened the door. After Humphreys left, Barnard asked Jane "Is that the man you call H[umphrey]?"[58] Barnard said, "She replied—'yes.'" So "yes" is the only word we ever hear Jane speak–and we hear that only second-hand. Barnard further explained to the trustees that he had never had another conversation with Jane about Humphreys; he distinguished between Jane's identification and her testimony about the identity of her attacker—a distinction that seemed to matter to Barnard but which seemed not to matter to the others. "I never said anything at all to her about the *fact*. The injury to my servant was very severe. The traces of it lasted till after commencement—two months."

Barnard thought the issue more a question of "social and political economics" than law. He also told the trustees that he was sound on the issue of slavery: Barnard sought to be accepted in the South as pro-slavery: "I was born at the North. That I cannot help. I was not consulted in the matter. I am a slaveholder, and, if I know myself, I am 'sound on the slavery question.'" And he had been sound his whole life: "As to my sentiments on the subject of slavery, my record is clear for my whole life."[59] At the conclusion of the testimony, Judge Jacob Thompson, a member of the Board of Trustees, came to Barnard's defense. Judge Thompson found no problem with Barnard listening to his slave's complaint that she had been attacked. Instead, Thompson thought that Barnard ought to listen to this servant:

> Your fault is that you received information, from your servant girl, which implicated a student, and you acted on that information to reach the truth; and this is set down as showing your free-soil proclivities. If this be so, I am the worst free soiler in the State: I am a downright abolitionist. No man strikes my negro that I do not hear his story. I will listen to my negro's grievances. Before God and man I believe this to be

my duty. No man has a right to touch him or her without my consent, and he who would not do the same would be despised by every man in Oxford.[60]

The trustees unanimously supported Barnard and ordered that the trial be published, presumably to help silence Barnard's critics. The final word on the trial was an appendix, in form of a letter written by a student, Kinloch Falconer, which reported that Humphreys admitted his guilt to Falconer. The letter was not introduced at the trustees' trial, but perhaps Barnard thought it necessary to squash lingering doubt about what the University had done. He seems to have been effective in satisfying the trustees and two of his most vocal critics on the faculty, who left shortly afterward. Carter left for another institution and Richardson resigned as well; although he then attempted unsuccessfully to retract his resignation. He subsequently taught at Davidson College, the University of North Carolina, Central University in Kentucky, and Austin College.[61]

Barnard was a pragmatic man, it seems—and so perhaps the comments of his late nineteenth-century biographer (written at a time when abolitionists had a reputation not much better than secessionists) may be taken as an accurate rendering of his opinion on slavery: it was an unwelcome fact of life and nothing could (or ought) to be done about it:

There is nothing to show that he ever entertained any strong feelings on that subject. He was not a man whose feelings governed his convictions. Born at the North and under the influence of antislavery agitation, he was brought up to regard slavery as an evil in itself and as a misfortune to the country. Yet even in his youth, he perceived the full force of the argument that property in slaves was recognized in the Constitution of the United States, and held that the Federal Government was bound by the Constitution to protect slave property according to the terms of that instrument. Hence Barnard was never an abolitionist; as long as the Whig party continued to exist he was a resolute and ardent adherent of that party. Before he went to the South he was inclined to favor the African colonization scheme which contemplated the voluntary emancipation of the slaves by their masters, and their deportation to the west coast of Africa. When he had lived for a time at the South, he saw that the colonization scheme was visionary. Compulsory emancipation was out of the question. There seemed to be no way to the abandonment of slavery without some bloody revolution which it would be wickedness to precipitate. He was not a man to waste his time or his energies on the solution of insoluble problems, and there is no evidence that he gave any large amount of thought to the slavery question. He accepted slavery as an unwelcome fact; he acquiesced in it as an established fact; he defended it as a fact that could not, in his opinion, be annulled or eliminated from the social state of the South; and, finally, he participated in it by becoming, of his own will, a slaveholder.[62]

Or maybe Barnard's experience with slavery reveals something more: while he probably understood the inhumanity in the system, he participated in it. Self-interest bent his attitude, as it did for so many people in the years before Civil War. This may help us understand how the system of slavery and its advocates bought supporters among the white voters of the South, and how it also bought supporters among the academy. Self-interest is a powerful force. Some academics, like Francis Wayland of Brown University and Henry Ruffner of Washington College, stood against slavery; others, like Frederick Barnard, did not strongly stand against it and even participated in some ways. Others like Thomas Dew and Beverley Tucker of William and Mary, Albert Taylor Bledsoe, James Holcombe, and Geroge Frederick Holmes of the University of Virginia, Basil Manly of the University of Alabama, and William Smith of Randolph Macon College stood resolutely in defense of slavery.

In some places in the southern academy there was a vigorous debate about slavery, although the southern academy was generally a staunch pillar of intellectual support for the slavery. Southern universities from Virginia to Mississippi educated slave-owning students and those who aspired to own slaves and told them, mostly, that slavery was natural and right. Those ideas so carefully developed in the academy correlated with the ideas in circulation in southern politics and law. That is not surprising given that the academy was closely connected to the leaders of the southern states. The rich and powerful and well educated all traveled in the same circles. Yet, the in-depth writings of academics and the debates on the campuses of southern schools help us understand the terms of the debate over slavery in political and legal circles. The next two parts of this book turn to those areas to see how the arguments about economy and morality influenced the contours of Southerners' defense of slavery as our nation headed toward Civil War.

CONNECTING MORAL PHILOSOPHY
AND LEGAL THOUGHT

Southern academics developed extensive arguments about the centrality of slavery to their society and economy. These arguments fit well with
what southern politicians were saying as well. Part II of this book looks
at how the ideas of history, economy, morality, and law that academics
wrote about operated in legal and political settings. It reveals that politicians and academics spoke in similar terms. For instance, in the debates
over the Fugitive Slave Act of 1850, pro-slavery politicians turned to the
same kinds of arguments that southern academics advanced. Antislavery
advocates sometimes rejected the terms of debate; for instance, Harriet
Beecher Stowe rejected appeals to utility over humanity. However, abolitionists also sometimes argued that slavery caused more harm than the
good it produced.

The next two chapters correlate the modes of thought of academics
discussed in the first part to the modes of thought of politicians and lawyers. Chapter 6 unpacks the arguments of southern politicians about why
the Fugitive Slave Act was necessary because it fit with the need for order.
Chapter 7 looks from the vantage of an antislavery writer, Harriet Beecher
Stowe, who critiqued the calculations of utility so central to southern
legal thought in her 1856 novel *Dred: A Tale of the Great Dismal Swamp*.
These chapters set the stage for the final part of this book, which looks at
how judges drew upon considerations of utility, history, economics, legal
logic, and precedent to create and sustain pro-slavery law.

6

The Fugitive Slave Act of 1850

The Grammar of Pro-slavery Thought

By 1850 southern frustration with attacks on slavery led to serious discussion about the prospects for disunion. The Wilmost Proviso, which would have barred slavery from territory acquired from Mexico; northern speeches about slavery's evil; and efforts to bar slavery from the District of Columbia were often cited as evidence of the failure of Northerners to respect Southerners' rights. So too was the refusal of northern states to cooperate in returning fugitive slaves to their owners in southern states. That led, in turn, to efforts by some moderates in the North, like Daniel Webster, to pass what was known as the Compromise of 1850.

The five parts of the Compromise settled, usually on terms favorable to the south, constitutional and political issues related to slavery and the federal government. The first two parts organized the territories of New Mexico and Utah under a plan of settler sovereignty, which allowed settlers there to determine if they would have slavery when their states were admitted to the Union; the third part admitted California as a free state (although slavery existed there at the time and continued afterward); the fourth part provided a strengthened Fugitive Slave Law; and the final part banned the slave trade in the District of Columbia, though slavery continued through part of the Civil War. Through examination of the debate over the Fugitive Slave Act and the responses to it, we can see the importance of the ideas of moral philosophy and jurisprudence developed in the first part of this book. The Fugitive Slave Act crystalized issues in jurisprudence and allows us see how those sometimes ambiguous ideas about slavery's history and morality worked.

The Fugitive Slave Act of 1850 had several key provisions. It established Federal Commissioners who had the authority to require private citizens to pursue fugitives. They also had jurisdiction to issue certificates of removal for fugitive slaves. The Commissioners took testimony from the slave owner in person and from affidavits; the alleged slaves were not permitted to testify. Then, the

Commissioners issued the certificates of removal once they established the identification of the slave as the person claimed to be a fugitive. There was no jury trial and no defenses were permitted. Thus, the Commissioners' function was limited to determining the identity of the person being returned, not whether the person actually *was* a fugitive. Commissioners received more compensation ($10) if they ordered the slave returned than if they found the alleged fugitive was not the person claimed by the slave owner ($5). The Act preempted the personal liberty laws of several northern states, which prohibited state officers from cooperating in the return of fugitive slaves. Those who interfered with the return of fugitives were subject to a $1,000 fine and six months imprisonment.[1] The Act, thus, limited the rights of accused fugitives and pressed private citizens into the service of the pro-slavery state. Such provisions led Henry David Thoreau to say on July 4, 1854, that "there are perhaps a million slaves in Massachusetts."[2]

Even before the Act, debate about the rendition of fugitive slaves centered on the admiration for utility that was so central to academics' pro-slavery thought. Henry David Thoreau's "Resistance to Civil Government" (popularly known, though not in Thoreau's time, as "Civil Disobedience"), delivered in 1849, illustrates the considerations of utility at the base of the rendition of fugitive slaves. Drawing on a passage in William Paley's *Moral Philosophy*, which was a guiding text in moral philosophy for antebellum Americans, Thoreau spoke of Americans' respect for utility (which Thoreau refers to as expediency):

> Paley resolves all civil obligation into expediency; and he proceeds to say that "so long as the interest of the whole society requires it, that is, so long as the established government cannot be resisted or changed without public inconvenience, it is the will of God . . . that the established government be obeyed–and no longer."[3]

Thoreau, however, thought there were places where "the rule of expediency" was not the guide, "in which a people, as well and an individual, must do justice, cost what it may." He concluded that "this people must cease to hold slaves, and to make war on Mexico, though it cost them their existence as a people." Thus, Thoreau reached the central point of the debate: should the United States do justice to individual slaves or do what maximized the utility of the actor (in this case the nation). Many abolitionists, obviously, thought that justice to the individual *also* maximized the utility of the nation, but that was not what most Americans thought. Thoreau's transcendental project was to replace the collective law with an individual conscience. He asked,

> Is it not possible to take a step further towards recognizing and organizing the rights of man? There will never be a really free and enlightened

State until the State comes to recognize the individual as a higher and independent power, from which all its own power and authority are derived, and treats him accordingly.[4]

The Fugitive Slave Act of 1850 occupies an important place in thinking about the coming of the Civil War and antebellum jurisprudence.[5] The majority of jurisprudential writing about the Act has focused on those opposed to it and why people comply with unjust laws. For example, Robert Cover focused on the variety of antislavery responses to the Act in his 1975 book *Justice Accused*.[6] Cover sought to understand not the antislavery forces that were motivated by conscience to violate the law, but the judges who followed the law, no matter the dictates of their internal moral compass. He emphasized the importance of studying those people, for they were among the leaders at the time. And while they may have been antislavery in private, many worked in the pro-slavery legal system.[7] Henry David Thoreau recognized as much the year before the Act was passed, as Americans debated the return of fugitive slaves. Thoreau criticized those who refused to take action against slavery:

> There are thousands who are in opinion opposed to slavery and war, who yet in effect do nothing to put an end to them; who, esteeming themselves children of Washington and Franklin, sit down with their hands in their pockets, and say that they know not what to do, and do nothing; ... What is the price-current of an honest man and patriot today? They hesitate, and they regret, and sometimes they petition; but they do nothing in earnest and with effect.[8]

Cover addressed the problem of complicity in evil, so prevalent in the era of slavery. There are important issues about how the law constrained and channeled those who were antislavery in private. Left out of Cover's examination are the ways that Americans discussed law outside the judiciary and the ideas of those who *supported* slavery. Judges rarely employed the sentiment urged by Thoreau, for law was a stable field of thought concerned with preservation of vested rights, with expansion of the economy, and with the rule of law.[9]

This chapter turns to the debates in Congress and the early responses to the Fugitive Slave Act with the goal of reading them for insight into the nature of legal thought. It turns mostly to the ideas of obedience to law that were triumphant, those of the defenders of slavery. But in addition to the legislators, lawyers, and ministers, who supported the Act, this chapter also examines a famous antislavery novelist, Harriet Beecher Stowe, with the goal of understanding the ideas supporting the Act, the rule of law more generally, and those attacking the law.

The debates illuminate a rich understanding of the intersection of constitu-tionalism, law, and slavery in American thought. Together, the debates and the response to the Act illustrate key points of contention in antebellum thought: the roles of practical, utilitarian considerations, based on a reading of history and a society's current mores and the opposition; a religiously inspired search for moral perfection and individual humanity. Several key points of conflict emerge. First, a conflict between the considerations of utility to society and humanity to individuals. This is part of a calculation of the entire effects, a cost-benefit analysis. Second, and closely related, is the centrality of utilitarian calculations in legislation, particularly in legislation supporting slavery and considerations in the abstract of rights. Finally, in determining the values to plug into the util-ity calculus, historical evidence was central to the supposed necessity of slavery. The historical ubiquity of slavery was one important way that pro-slavery writers opposed morality-based critiques of slavery.

The most famous speech related to the Fugitive Slave Act was Daniel Webster's March 7 speech, which supported a moderate position. It stepped back from the brink of disunion by recognizing that southern states had a legitimate complaint about the loss of their slaves and noting that well-intentioned abolitionists were, nevertheless, harming the slaves.[10] One might recall that Henry David Thoreau referred to the Act as "Webster's Fugitive-Slave Bill."[11]

Webster first exculpated the pro-slavery ministers of the South: thousands believed slaveholding was not sinful and thousands more—maybe even more numerous—found "slavery to be an established relation of the society in which they live, can see no way in which . . . the present generation [can] relieve them-selves from this relation."[12] Thus, a central element is the practical in politics and law: take the world as it is rather than as it ought to be.[13]

Webster juxtaposed such practical reason with abolitionist extremism. For abolitionists saw the right clearly; they thought others ought to see it also, and they were disposed to establish a broad line of distinction between what is right and what is wrong. Webster said starkly: "I think their operations for the last twenty years have produced nothing good or valuable."

Webster surveyed Virginia legislature's 1832 debate in the wake of Nat Turner's rebellion as evidence that the South was moving toward the termina-tion of slavery. He urged his audience

> to recur to the debates in the Virginia House of Delegates in 1832, and . . . see with what freedom a proposition made by Mr. Jefferson Randolph for the gradual abolition of slavery was discussed in that body. Every one spoke of slavery as he thought; very ignominious and disparaging names and epithets were applied to it. The debates in the

House of Delegates on that occasion, I believe, were all published. They were read by every colored man who could read, and to those who could not read, those debates were read by others. At that time Virginia was not unwilling or unafraid to discuss this question, and to let that part of her population know as much of discussion as they could learn. That was in 1832.[14]

Then the abolition societies began in 1835 to send literature to southern states. The South retreated from discussion of termination in response to abolition societies. That led to harsher attitudes toward slavery.

> The bonds of the slave were bound more firmly than before, their rivets were more strongly fastened. Public opinion, which in Virginia had begun to be exhibited against slavery, and was opening out for the discussion of the question, drew back and shut itself up in its castle. . . . [E]very thing that these agitating [abolitionists] have done has been, . . . to bind faster the slave population of the South.[15]

Webster found that their fanaticism led them to see moral absolutes in stark and distinct terms: "They are not seldom willing to establish that line upon their own convictions of truth or justice; and are ready to mark and guard it by placing along it a series of dogmas, as lines of boundary on the earth's surface are marked by posts and stones."[16] Those lines—boundaries—between right and wrong are central to abolitionist thinking and to the evangelical mind more generally. Abolitionists' single-minded pursuit of a goal led to larger harm. For they "do not see how too eager a pursuit of one duty may involve them in the violation of others, or how too warm an embracement of one truth may lead to a disregard of other truths equally important." That was a crucial distinction for antebellum Americans: should they do justice in individual cases or look at the world as a whole? Many politicians spoke about this calculus: their vision of morals is such that they should do justice on the whole. That utilitarian calculus appeared in moral philosophy texts.[17] Abolitionists thought that such questions could be answered with a mathematical certainty.[18] And that narrow, mathematical reasoning admitted few opportunities for compromise.

> They are apt, too, to think that nothing is good but what is perfect, and that there are no compromises or modifications to be made in consideration of difference of opinion or in deference to other men's judgment. If their perspicacious vision enables them to detect a spot on the face of the sun, they think that a good reason why the sun should be struck down from heaven. They prefer the chance of running into

utter darkness to living in heavenly light, if that heavenly light be not absolutely without any imperfection. There are impatient men; too impatient always to give heed to the admonition of St. Paul, that we are not to "do evil that good may come"; too impatient to wait for the slow progress of moral causes in the improvement of mankind.[19]

So there is practicality, a consideration of the complete picture rather than issues by themselves, and then there is one other key legal element in the speech: the duty that the Constitution imposes on Congress and on individual citizens.

That world of law included an analysis of history. The practical view looked at the world as it was, and history was an important teacher.[20] The lessons were conservative—slavery was ubiquitous and could not be ended. Tennessee senator John Bell reasoned from his understanding of history to argue that slavery was both morally just and practically necessary. While Bell conceded that slavery was "sometimes abused and perverted, as all human institutions" are, he thought that it was "still contributing to advance the cause of civilization."[21] The conclusion that slavery was immoral, Bell thought, could not be proven.[22] And like Webster, Bell also focused on the fanaticism among the abolitionists: "There is a fanaticism of liberty as well as a fanaticism of religion and philanthropy—a fanaticism exhibiting itself in theories which admit no distinction of races and claims for all a perfect equality, social and political; theories which reject all practical or useful schemes of government which have ever existed, or can be devised."[23]

Instead of abolitionists' moral absolutes, supporters of the Fugitive Slave Act saw slavery as conferring more benefits than harms. Senator Jacob Miller of New Jersey focused on the benefits of the rule of law's protection of property rights. His focus was on the rights of slaveholders.

> Twenty millions of freeman are living under the best system of laws ever devised by man; their daily avocations un-oppressed by any tyrannical laws, undistributed by any high-handed aggression upon their rights, and sending up no complaints against arbitrary government. From the extreme North, where the Yankee whaler strikes the monster of the deep, to the South, where the slave labors contentedly in the cotton-fields for his master—everywhere throughout this mighty empire, the rights of property and the rights of the citizens are protected and defended by the Constitution and the laws of slavery.[24]

There might come a time when social and moral progress might allow the termination of slavery, but the time had not yet arrived.[25] The attack on abolitionist fanatics was in part an attack on sentimental novelists. Bell linked sentimental

writers, readers of sentimental literature, and abolitionists. He criticized sentimental literature for contributing to the agitation against slavery, indeed, against
life as it was more generally.[26]

Indeed, abolitionists had developed a sophisticated and powerful critique of
slavery—and of pro-slavery law in particular. At the time that Senator Bell was
speaking, there was already an extensive antislavery literature that played on the
sentimental emotions of readers to create sympathy for slaves.[27] The nonfiction
antislavery literature often drew upon reports of law cases to detail the torture
that slaves suffered. Theodore Weld's *One Thousand Lashes for Freedom* relied on
cases to illustrate the brutality at the base of slavery. Soon that literature would
grow much larger and more powerful.

Supporters of the Act spoke of what was possible, what was practical, and also
the history of slavery and its current practice, which put slavery and abolition
into a context for understanding how moral or immoral it was. They looked to
examples of history and what had happened and was happening. Senator John
Bell of Tennessee read "the law of nature" by the "lights" and necessity of history. He analogized the dispossession of Natives from their land and found that
acceptable with the law of nature.

> As to the lawfulness or sinfulness of the institution of slavery–whatever
> . . . the disciples of a transcendental creed of any kind may hold or teach
> . . . I must claim the privilege of interpreting the law of nature by what
> I see revealed in the history of mankind from the earlier period of re-
> corded time, uncontradicted by Divine authority. But above all I have
> seen here, on this continent, and in these United States, the original
> lords of the soil subdued . . . and the remnant still held in subordina-
> tion; and all this under an interpretation of the law of nature which
> holds good at this day among our northern brethren.

Senator Bell then looked to the institution of slavery and found it necessary.

> There are three millions of the African race, whose labor is subject to the
> will of masters, under such circumstances that their condition cannot
> be changed, though their masters should will it, without destruction
> alike to the interests and welfare of both master and slave. These are the
> lights by which I read and understand the law of nature.[28]

This vision of utility was intertwined with a theological strand of belief in divine
benevolence. Huntsville, Alabama, Presbyterian minister Frederick A. Ross'
Slavery Ordained of God told of the good that slavery brought to masters and
slaves, and he predicted it would continue until it passed away in the "fulness of

Providence."[29] Senator Bell concluded with a plea to put slavery in context and understand the practicalities:

> These examples show that there are certain abstract truths and principles which, however incontrovertible in themselves, like every other good thing, may be and often are misconceived and abused in their application. It is the business of statesmen to apply them with safety and to give them the utmost practical influence of effect consistent with the existing state of society.[30]

So the debates on the Act contain much about the connections of morality and legislation. They also contain the grammar of Constitutional interpretation. The Constitution enjoins a duty upon states and state legislators, also. Southerners did not believe that Northerners had a right to interfere with southern constitutional and property rights.[31]

In the debates we also learn about the rule of law: why should people abide by a law if they disagree with it. Some of the reasons for abiding are religious: it is the duty, as many interpreted Paul's second letter to the Corinthians, to abide by the commands of human governments. As Senator Joseph Underwood of Kentucky said, "it is generally combined arrogance and folly for a minority to denounce the legislation of the majority, and to threaten resistance and defiance in consequence of an alleged conflict with the law of God."[32] He concluded, "government is ordained of God; . . . it is a duty to submit to the powers that be, and to render unto Caesar the things which are Caesar's."[33] There is a proper and constitutional mode by which bad laws "may be assailed and repealed; but until repealed, they must be obeyed, or it is the end of government."[34] Moreover, following the law holds the government together. Many recognized the close connection between morals and legislation and worried that because the Act would not have the support of the community, it would be ineffective.[35]

After enactment, the Fugitive Slave Act of 1850 became a centerpiece of discussion about the rule of law. The debate focused under what, if any, circumstances could one violate the rule of law. A vibrant antislavery jurisprudence emerged around the Act, which emphasized the right to violate the law and demonstrated both the truth of legislators' predictions that the law would be a nullity and the limits of the power of law. Antislavery ministers discussed the ways that human-created laws were limited and subordinate to one's conscience.[36] Some, like Samuel Spear, saw a middle path between abiding all laws and violating them: he suggested that judges who opposed the Act should resign.[37]

Much of the debate appeared in pulpits. John Lord of Buffalo's First Presbyterian Church delivered a widely distributed sermon, "The Higher Law, in Its Application to the Fugitive Slave Bill," in 1851.[38] Lord's sermon proceeded from the fear that following a "higher law" would result in an "open and forc-ible resistance by arms."[39] He believed, based on his reading of Matthew, that "obedience to governments, in the exercise of their legitimate powers, is a reli-gious duty, positively enjoined by God himself."[40] Much of Lord's reasoning was based on his interpretation of the Bible, which held that government is divinely constituted, that government has jurisdiction over contemporary affairs, and the decisions of governments within their jurisdiction are absolute. But Lord also reasoned that the higher law doctrine was unworkable, for it would abrogate all law. "Freedom of opinion by no means involves the right *to refuse obedience to law*; for, if this were so, the power to declare war and make peace; to regulate and levy taxes; in short, to perform the most essential acts of government, would be a mere nullity."[41] The state may enact laws regarding slavery and one had to abide those laws. Anything else would "contradict the decision of the Apostle—[and] subject every established principle, whether human or divine, on which rests the authority of civil government." Lord looked to the United States' history, such as the ubiquity of slavery during the colonial period, to conclude that slavery did not violate any "higher law." He also looked to other countries, such as China, to conclude that slavery, at least in some circumstances, was permissible.[42]

Ichabod Spencer explained in even more detail the purposes and functions of law (and why it must be obeyed) in his November 1850 sermon in the Second Presbyterian Church in Brooklyn.[43] Laws are necessary to restrain those who do evil. Therefore, "[l]aw is a friend of the human race. It is the protector of the good man; and it punishes the bad man, only for the purposes of securing rights,—property, liberty, life. And even the bad would be worse off a thousand fold than they are, if there were no efficient Law to restrain them by its authority and sanctions."[44] Spencer embraced law as what facilitates and creates happiness and property. Though he acknowledged that in some instances one might violate an unjust law, those situations were few and far between. "Law is too important and delicate a thing to have its majesty trifled with by the wicked nonsense of a half-obedience."[45] He urged against rebellion, for that would lead to even worse harm. Revolutions "bring horrid evils along with them." Spencer engaged in the balance of harm and benefit at the center of utilitarian reasoning. "It would be better to bear the injury for a while, than to involve the nation in confusion and blood."[46] And when he looked around, he thought the law, on balance, brought substantially more benefit than harm. "[G]overnment with all its unavoidable imperfection and errors, on the whole is beneficial—indispensable—we could not do without it. And rarely, very rarely indeed, is there a single instance of an individual man . . . whom Law has injured *more* than it has benefitted."[47]

Nevertheless, law was losing some of its majesty.[48] Ralph Waldo Emerson was one of many people who advanced an alternative interpretation of law, which might admit of some antislavery sentiments. In an 1851 address at Concord,

Emerson urged that the higher law, then so commonly invoked in antislavery circles, was part of the common law. Contrary to what many lawyers said, Emerson
reported that his research showed support for the higher law. "A few months
ago, in my dismay at hearing that the Higher Law was reckoned a good joke in
the courts, I took pains to look into a few law books." He looked for signs that
"immoral laws are void" and found that "the great jurists, Cicero, Grotius, Coke,
Blackstone, Burlamaqui, Montesquieu, Vattel, Burke, Mackintosh, Jefferson, do
all affirm this." Yet, Emerson did not cite those passages in defense of his argument. For "no reasonable person needs a quotation from Blackstone to convince
him that white cannot be legislated to be black."[49] Soon there would be a novel
affirming Emerson's belief.

As cases of fugitive slaves began to appear in courts, the debates increasingly
took on the question about whether individuals should actively stop rendition
of fugitive slaves. The most famous case arose in Boston in 1854 when Anthony
Burns was arrested as a fugitive slave and, after Judge Edward Loring ordered
him returned, abolitionists set to free him.[50] President Franklin Pierce employed
federal troops to make sure that Burns was put on a ship to return to Virginia.[51]
Burns' trial brought home to many the obligations that law imposed, and many
believed those obligations were odious. While some courts found creative ways
to avoid the law, most commonly and most importantly, they followed it.[52]
Thoreau was led to ask in the wake of Anthony Burns' trial, "does anyone think
that justice or God wait on Mr. Loring' decision?"[53] As those courts upheld law,
its credibility declined.

Subsequent events vindicated the moral perspective of abolitionists, but from
the perspective of the early 1850s, the crisis over fugitive slaves touched on central issues of moral philosophy. Abolitionists were pessimistic. The language of
moral philosophy and those modes of thinking were employed from the university lecture hall, to the pulpit, to the halls of Congress, and the courtrooms
throughout the nation. For a time those pro-slavery ideas triumphed. They emphasized a version of history that taught the ubiquity and, therefore, inevitabil-
ity, indeed necessity, of slavery. They then tied that pro-slavery vision of history
together with a moral philosophy that emphasized considerations of utility and
rested on a belief in the need to abide the rule of law.

Though, despite the efforts to justify slavery and make it look acceptable,
commonplace, and legal, others saw through this. Massachusetts Senator
Charles Sumner spoke about the violence inherent in the institution. "Slavery
is a[n] institution of force and not of right, as our law books teach—the private
force of the master being made efficient and sufficient by the public force of the
state."[54] It was the triumph of the antislavery position that it was able to make
people see the force and brutality that pro-slavery law politicians, judges, and
intellectuals tried to explain away. It is to the antislavery critique of pro-slavery

in Harriet Beecher Stowe's novel *Uncle Tom's Cabin* that we now turn in order to view southern legal thought as others saw it.

Harriet Beecher Stowe's Critique of Slave Law

By early 1851 Stowe was frustrated with the "exceedingly cool" arguments justifying cooperation in the return of slaves. She asked her husband in February, "Must we forever keep calm and smile and smile when every sentiment of manliness and humanity is kicked and rolled in the dust and lies trampled and bleeding?"[55] Stowe set out to write several sketches "to hold up in the most lifelike manner possible Slavery."[56] Before she was done, the few sketches had grown to a novel of more than thirty chapters.

Like much abolitionist writing, especially that published after 1840, *Uncle Tom's Cabin* attacks the law.[57] First, she portrays the harshness of the law itself, not just the practice of slavery. She attributes the harshness of slavery to bad laws, rather than to only to bad people. Second, in a few places she advocates (or at least depicts as noble) breaking the law in favor of some higher justice. Stowe links slavery with law right from the beginning of the novel. In the preface she predicts that "every influence of literature, of poetry, and of art" is bringing society into accord with Christian principles. Law, however, is not humanizing; it is part of the structure holding the slave system together. Nevertheless, Stowe denies any "invidious feelings" toward people involved with "the legal relations of slavery."[58]

Stowe developed her critique of law in the first chapter of the novel by showing that even a kind slave owner is unable to preserve a slave family. The novel begins in the household of Master Shelby, where the saintly slave Uncle Tom lives with his wife, Aunt Chloe, along with Eliza and her son Harry. Master Shelby, though "good natured and kindly," is forced because of his debts to sell Harry and Tom to the slave trader Haley. It is debt, as well as the legal system's treatment of slaves as property, that turns the dream of the "oft-fabled poetic legend of a patriarchal institution" into a Gothic nightmare:

> [O]ver and above the scene there broods a portentous shadow,—the shadow of law. So long as the law considers all these human beings, with beating hearts and living affections, only as so many things belonging to a master,—so long as the failure, or misfortune, or imprudence, or death of the kindest owner may cause them any day to exchange a life of kind protection and indulgence for one of hopeless misery and toil,— so long it is impossible to make anything beautiful or desirable in the best-regulated administration of slavery.[59]

One of the first pictures Stowe presents the reader is the interrelationship of law and slavery, and the way that law wipes out humanity in the institution.

The direct advocacy of violation of existing law appears in stark form after Eliza and little Harry run away. They arrive on the doorstep of Ohio State Senator Byrd,[60] who has recently voted for a state statute outlawing the harboring of fugitive slaves. Just as Eliza appears at the door, the Senator and his wife are "twittering in an argumentative duet concerning the matter of lending 'aid and comfort' to runaway negroes."[61] The Senator, who wants to "reason" with his wife, acknowledges that "it would be a very painful duty" to cooperate with the law.[62] Mrs. Byrd's first response is that "I hate reasoning John,—especially reasoning on such subjects. That's a way you political folks have of coming round and round such a plain right thing; and you don't believe in it yourselves, when it comes to practice."[63] Mrs. Byrd draws a line between duty, which bound lawyers and politicians,[64] and feelings of humanity. She then counters that even if aiding runaway slaves leads to great public evil, the Bible commands it, and that "it's always safest, all round, to *do as He* bids."[65] She vows to break the abominable law.[66] The dialog between Senator Byrd and his wife is a clash between cold law and heated, religiously inspired passion. The lesson is that when the Byrds directly meet the immorality of slavery, their moral passion inspires a just action.

The whole family ends up breaking the law. The Byrds harbor Eliza and her child, and the Senator personally drives them to a Quaker settlement. Mrs. Byrd had correctly predicted that Senator Byrd would behave as a "man" and not as a senator; as he leaves to transport Eliza and Harry, she tells him, "Your heart is better than your head."[67] Stowe optimistically believed that when presented with a personal appeal for help, a person's humanity would emerge.

Yet, the harshest lessons on the capricious impact of the law on the slave are yet to come. After his sale, Tom works for several years in New Orleans with a kind owner, Augustine St. Clare, and develops a relationship as guardian of St. Clare's abolitionist daughter, Eva. In recognition of Tom's loyal service and to fulfill Eva's deathbed request, St. Clare promises Tom his freedom and begins the "legal steps necessary to [effect his] emancipation."[68]

Later that same day, St. Clare's abolitionist cousin Ophelia convinces him to transfer ownership of a young slave, Topsy, to her so that she can "take her to the free states and give her liberty." Ophelia insists that he transfer ownership immediately, because he might "die or fail, and then Topsy [would] be hustled off to auction, spite of all I can do." St. Clare draws a "deed of gift," signs it and (once again, thanks to Ophelia's watchfulness) has it witnessed, so that Topsy is Ophelia's property, at least, "by fiction of the law."[69]

Stowe has a strong reason for establishing that slavery could not be humane under any circumstances: to contest the common belief, nurtured by pro-slavery novelists, that slavery was, or at least could be, a benign patriarchal institution.

Hence she showed that the law prevents kind treatment by masters and the law provided essentially no protection to slaves burdened by unkind owners.

After one of St. Clare's slaves, Prue, is killed by a harsh overseer, Ophelia asks St. Clare why he does not take action to punish Prue's killers. He responds, "It's commonly supposed that the *property* interest is a sufficient guard in these cases. If people choose to ruin their own possessions, I don't know what's to be done."[70] St. Clare links the law with his impotence to punish Prue's killers: "If low-minded, brutal people will act like themselves, what am I to do? They have absolute control; they are irresponsible despots. There would be no use in interfering; there is no law that amounts to anything practically, for such a case."[71] Near the conclusion of the conversation, St. Clare tells Ophelia that slavery is a system based on power. He elaborates on the almost limitless power that the law confers to masters over their slaves: "[W]e would *scorn* to use the full power, which our savage laws put into our hands. And he who goes furthest, and does the worst, only uses within limits the power that the law gives him."[72]

St. Clare and Ophelia discuss the need to do "positive good." He resolves to free his slaves, in keeping with his belief that Christianity is inconsistent with "this monstrous system of injustice which lies at the foundation of our society." Before he effects Tom's emancipation, however, St. Clare is mortally wounded at a café. On the day that he promises Tom freedom and resolves to free his slaves and crusade against slavery—but before he accomplishes those tasks—St. Clare dies.[73]

On this stage, Stowe can then play out the saga of the "Unprotected." The slaves, whom the law regards "in every respect, as devoid of rights as a bale of merchandise," had no protection. Augustine's wife, Marie, contemptuously refuses to free Tom despite Ophelia's special plea that Marie abide Augustine's promise to free Tom. Even if Marie had wanted to free him, which she certainly did not, financial constraints prohibited it: "Tom is one of the most valuable servants on the place—it couldn't be afforded anyway."[74]

As part of the liquidation of St. Clare's estate, Tom was brought to the slave market in New Orleans and sold to Simon Legree, a short, bullet-headed man.[75] Simon Legree is the prime example of the way that law releases owners from moral responsibility for their actions. Stowe's most memorable advocacy of disobedience to unjust authority occurs when Tom refuses to beat Cassy, and later he refuses to tell Legree where the fugitives Cassy and Emmeline are hiding. Here Stowe explores the boundary between resistance and obedience. Despite encouragement from the other slaves, Tom refuses to answer Legree's questions.[76] Tom does not yield, and he is murdered by Legree.

Legree internalizes the calculus that an owner's property interest in a slave is the slave's only protection against abuse. He tells Tom, "I've made up my mind and counted the cost. I'll conquer you yet or kill ye." Stowe asks the reader, "Ye say the interest of the master is a sufficient safeguard for the slave. In the fury of man's mad will, he will wittingly, and with open eye, sell his own soul to the devil to gain his ends; and will he be more careful of his neighbor's body?" The answer is evident because Legree proceeds to murder Tom, "done under the shadow of thy laws!"[77]

Even Legree's conscience wrestles with the question whether he should kill Tom when Tom expresses his complete devotion to work for and even to die for Legree, so long as Tom is not required to harm others. But Legree's evil side wins and he kills Tom, as he planned when he asked himself the night before, "is n't he MINE? Can't I do what I like with him? Who's to hinder, I wonder?"[78]

The year after *Uncle Tom's Cabin* appeared, Stowe published a nonfiction companion to the novel called *A Key to Uncle Tom's Cabin*. It drew upon newspaper accounts of slavery, religious tracts, and even case reports to show that the novel often relied on actual cases and that it accurately represented southern thought. *A Key* highlighted several themes from *Uncle Tom's Cabin*—that the law was responsible for harm, partly by making it difficult or impossible for owners to treat slaves kindly and also by releasing owners from liability for their actions. Stowe encouraged observers of southern slavery to redirect their attention (and scorn) from the individual actors, from the "*person* of the slave-holder" toward "the horrors of the legal system."[79] It was the laws that released individuals from moral responsibility:

> [T]he law is a direct permission, letting loose upon the defenseless slave that class of men who exist in every community, who have no conscience, no honor, no shame; who are too far below public opinion to be restrained by that, and from whom accordingly this provision of the law takes away the only available restraint of their fiendish nature.[80]

Uncle Tom's Cabin and *A Key to Uncle Tom's Cabin* critiqued the established slave jurisprudence. The books cataloged the way that the legal system supported, indeed imposed, slavery. *Uncle Tom's Cabin* began the critique with the lesson that the legal enforcement of debt forced Tom's sale. As Stowe observed, "over and above" the scene of Tom's sale, "there broods a portentous shadow,—the shadow of *law*." The Fugitive Slave Law allowed the pursuit of Eliza and Harry, and even turned sympathetic whites into instruments of their recapture (or into lawbreakers). Later, Louisiana law prevented Tom's emancipation at St. Claire's death, converted him into Marie's property, permitted his torture and murder, and freed Legree from criminal liability. Much of what Stowe and abolitionists found wanting about the legal system was its omission of liability rather than its imposition of liability. Many rose to respond. Novelists, politicians, and college professors published their defenses of slavery, including that slaves were treated well, that the law was, on balance, positive rather than negative, and that the lives of many free workers were worse than that of slaves.

The Pro-slavery Reaction to the Critique of Law in *Uncle Tom's Cabin*

> In our author's eye, the slave-code is evidently a raw-head and bloody-bones—a monster of injustice—and she can hardly say enough against it.
> —Reverend Edward Josiah Stearns, St. John's College[81]

> [*Uncle Tom's Cabin*] strikes at the very essence and existence of all community among men, it lays bare and roots up all the foundations of law, order, and government.... Pandemonium itself would be a paradise compared with what all society would become, if ... action were accordingly regulated by it.
> —University of Virginia Professor George Frederick Holmes[82]

Stowe's contemporaries realized that she attacked law and slavery. Southern readers were acutely aware of her condemnation of slave law. They feared her attack on law could destroy their society, and they reacted forcefully against her contribution to the debate over the law of slavery. The responders interpreted Stowe's lessons for their audience. In place of the jurisprudence of love that she sought, they urged order.

In contrast to Stowe's appeal to sentiment, pro-slavery writers frequently appealed to reason and practical arguments. The problems with the heart were identified by University of Virginia professor George Frederick Holmes when he wrote that "all the heresies and distempers of the day, religious, social, political, and intellectual have their roots in unsound philosophy and inadequate logic."[83] Responders to Stowe appealed to the head to overcome sympathy for slaves. For example, James Waddell asked whether "the *feeling of humanity* towards the sufferer himself, ought to have been obeyed, without regard to those great 'interests of the state' which Mrs. Stowe seems to think unworthy to be taken into account, when the question refers to fugitive slaves."[84] Waddell, like other pro-slavery writers, justified slavery based on its utility—ensuring the greatest good for society, a calculus that required application of reason.[85] In their opinion, it was logical, dispassionate thought that ensured the best results for society.

Abolitionists' appeal to feelings of humanity over respect for the Constitution served as a rallying point for pro-slavery writers. There, Nehemiah Adams, writing in the *South-Side View of Slavery* in 1854, cautioned against placing sympathy

for the slave above respect for the Constitution. If that happened, the government would end. Adams censured abolitionist lawyers in particular:

> Until we divide the Union, or procure a change in the Constitution, if
> we resist one of its provisions from repugnance to it, and so nullify it,
> we make a breach in a dam which has behind it a desolating river. That
> lawyers should do or counsel this, not from professional necessity, but
> moved by their sensibilities, fills even some clergymen with surprise . . .
> a lawyer is supposed to discriminate between what is specially benevo-
> lent and the obligations which we owe to the social compact: from him
> we expect to learn that an unlawful way of seeking a supposed good is
> fraught with a destructive principle, before which every thing may be
> laid waste. That compassion for a fugitive slave which leads one to ab-
> rogate the constitution of society is not benevolent, nor does it secure
> respect for any but radicals—a class of men, in all ages of the world, who
> have uniformly failed to secure the confidence of mankind.[86]

Adams, like other pro-slavery writers, urged adherence to a dispassionate, calculating evaluation of the merits of slavery in place of abolitionists' sympathetic
perspective. Stowe might believe that *"feelings* of humanity are to be universally
obeyed, whenever they come into conflict with the exception of laws of which
we disapprove,"[87] but such feelings were inappropriate in the eyes of southern
responders to *Uncle Tom's Cabin.* In their rush to embrace the heart, abolitionists failed to understand the consequences of their doctrines, pro-slavery writers
charged.[88]

   One of the greatest virtues of slavery in the minds of Southerners who
responded to *Uncle Tom's Cabin* was its consistency with nature and its ability
to preserve order in southern society. "Why was it, that the abolition excitement in the North, produced such a panic in the South," asked Connecticut
physician Ashbel Woodward in his book *A Review of Uncle Tom's Cabin.* "It
was the revolting and shocking doctrines, which they openly promulgated. It
was their notorious disregard of the laws of God and man, and all those ties
which bind us together as one great nation; their denial of the right of the
South to hold slave property, notwithstanding that right had been guaranteed
to them by the Federal Constitution; their advocacy of the right of the slave
to arise in the night and cut his master's throat; or, else, burn his house over
his head."[89]

   Order, law, and government were particularly valued qualities in the antebellum
South. Southerners applied their belief that stability was a paramount goal of society to the lives of slaves as well. In his book, *Notes on Uncle Tom's Cabin,* Edward

Illustration 6.1 McDowell Hall, St. John's College, Annapolis, Maryland,
(Library of Congress, Prints & Photographs Division, HABS, Reproduction number HABS
MD,2-ANNA,40A—2.)

Josiah Stearns, a professor at St. John's College in Annapolis, Maryland (Illustration
6.1), argued that the life of slaves in the United States was superior to life in Africa:

> Hobbes in his Leviathan . . . thus describes the condition of Europe
> in the Middle Ages:—"No arts, no letters, no society,—and which is
> worst of all, continual fear and danger of violent death, and the life of
> man solitary, poor, nasty, brutish and short." And it must be owned that
> there is too much truth in the description. Yet Europe in the Middle
> Ages was paradise compared with Western Africa in *all* ages that we
> have any knowledge of her, the present included. She is the darkest of
> those "dark places of the earth" which, the Psalmist tells us, "are full of
> the habitations of cruelty."[90]

Because Southern thinkers valued law—as well as slavery—as a way of
achieving order, they argued that Stowe's attack on the subordination of the
slave to the master was misplaced. "This power that slavery gives to one man
over another is met with everywhere in society. Caleb Williams! Alton Locke!
Mary Barton! Parliamentary Blue Books! Mining Districts! Manufacturing
Districts! Combinations of Workmen! Combinations of Masters!—to which

shall we point especially?" asked one Southerner.[91] He argued that individuals might abolish distinctions, but the laws had not done so. Laws did not help labor against capital, nor did they "make the hard man lay down the power that he feels over his neighbor."[92] Some reformers sought to "unhinge these 'false relations'" but "Plato's model lives only in the brains of dreamers."[93]

It was against this background of regard for order and control that George Frederick Holmes published his review of *Uncle Tom's Cabin*. Holmes recognized the impact that Stowe would likely have on the order that he and other Southerners so desperately sought. He believed that Stowe's main thesis was that "any social institution which can possibly . . . generate such examples of individual cruelty as are exhibited in this fiction, must be criminal in itself, a violation of all the laws of Nature and of God."[94] That proposition, Holmes thought, "strikes at the very essence and existence of all community among men, it lays bare and roots up all the foundations of law, order and government."[95] The primary evil of *Uncle Tom's Cabin*, in Holmes' mind, was its attack on laws and, consequently, southern institutions. Other reviewers expressed similar concerns. James Waddell's *Review of Uncle Tom's Cabin* described the entire novel as "a tirade against American law."[96]

Even if the slave laws produced inequality, Holmes did not want them changed because they provided security to society. "It is no distinctive feature of the servile condition that individual members of the class should suffer most poignantly in consequence of the crimes, the sins, the follies, or the thoughtlessness of others. . . . The same results, with concomitant infamy, are daily produced by the operation of all penal laws, and the same anguish and distress are thereby inflicted upon the helpless and innocent, yet such laws remain and must remain upon our statute books for the security and conservation of any social organization at all."[97] Louisa McCord, an important pro-slavery political theorist and wife of a wealthy South Carolina planter, exemplified the sentiments of many southern commentators on *Uncle Tom's Cabin* when she predicted dire consequences from the changes in the law that Stowe advocated:

> Make your laws to interfere with the God-established system of slavery, which our Southern States are beautifully developing to perfection, daily improving the condition of the slave, daily waking more and more the master to his high and responsible position; make your laws, we say, to pervert this God-directed course, and the world has yet to see the horrors which might ensue from it. The natural order of things perverted, ill must follow. The magnitude of that ill, may heaven protect us from witnessing! . . . As the ocean to the wave—as the rill to the torrent—as the zephyr to the whirlwind—would any such scenes, if possible among us, be to those of Hayti, fearful as they were; and as ocean's gulf to rain puddle, would be the ensuing barbarism.[98]

Stowe's responders agreed that slavery served the needs of southern society by maintaining order. But besides expressing their fear that Stowe's ideas would destroy their society, Stowe's responders claimed that the law was not responsible for the hardships of slavery, that the law adequately protected slaves, and that free workers were treated no better than slaves; in essence, it was not the fault of law.

In response to the abolitionist critique that "the great objection against slavery is that the power of one man over another is so irresponsible, so little restrained by law or nature,"[99] pro-slavery writers argued that hierarchy was inherent in nature. Such natural distinctions could not and should not be abolished. Edward Pringle, writing under the pseudonym A Carolinian, in the 1852 pamphlet *Slavery in the Southern States*, a widely circulated response to Stowe, argued that no legislation "provide[s] altogether against those abuses which grow out of the evil passions of men."[100] Human nature mitigated the harshness of slavery, Pringle thought. "Theirs is the hard letter of the law,—nothing that is not 'in the bond'! With us the moral code becomes positive law where legal rights end."[101] Such was a common response to Stowe. The laws, reviewers asserted, did not represent the way that slaves were actually treated.

Pringle also counseled against indicting slavery simply because of the occasional abuses depicted by Stowe. "[T]he laws of property are respected still, though the oppression of the rich has wrung from the poor the bitter cry that 'property is robbery.' "[102] In response to the related charge that "the power of one man over another is so irresponsible, so little restrained by law or nature," Pringle believed that dependence was inherent. Are not northern workers more dependent than slaves? Pringle asked.[103] Slaves, he argued, had masters to protect them, but freemen, "weighted down by the inevitable ills that society is subject to, [have] no tyrant but the hard laws of demand and supply, stern and unchangeable."[104] Given the harsh results of northern laws, Pringle hoped that his readers would recognize that the laws were not responsible for the hardships of slavery. Some laws, however, he believed helped mitigate the harshness of slavery.

Many southern reviewers of *Uncle Tom's Cabin* responded to Stowe's challenge that it was slave law that accounted for the harsh treatment of slaves by arguing that law adequately protected slaves. Stowe's representation that Legree could murder Tom with impunity was probably the most frequently contested scene in the novel. In his review of the book, Holmes disputed Stowe's claim that Legree could not be convicted of Tom's murder. Holmes stated that Tom's death was "an outrage which every Southern man would reprobate with indignant scorn—and punish by the summary application of Lynch law, which may be sometimes profitably applied."[105] Others also believed that Legree could be punished. In opposition to Stowe's charge in *A Key* that "in the free states Legree

is chained and restrained by law; in the slave States, the law makes him an absolute irresponsible despot,"[106] Stearns wrote that Legree could be convicted of
murder. Legree's statement to George Shelby that "I gaved him the crudest flog-
ging I ever gave the nigger yet" could be used in court, Stearns argued, because it
was said to a white person.[107]

The Emergence of the Jurisprudence of Sentiment and the Empirical Response to Pro-slavery Law

While Southerners were responding to abolitionists by reference to established
law and by appeals to reason and considerations of utility, antislavery thinkers
were advancing an alternative vision of law: a jurisprudence based on sentiment.
Uncle Tom's Cabin was Stowe's first sustained critique of law and slavery; she followed it up with the nonfiction *A Key to Uncle Tom's Cabin*, which engaged explicitly with the problems with legal thought that was based on considerations
of utility. She tried to make people feel the evil of slavery and hoped that would
lead them to change their behavior. She completed the antislavery trilogy with
Dred: A Tale of the Great Dismal Swamp in 1856, by asking why people who opposed slavery still engaged in it. The next chapter takes up Stowe's final install-
ment in her antislavery trilogy and her powerful, if pessimistic, answer to why
there was not more antislavery action.

Others also recognized and extended Stowe's critique and advanced an alternative jurisprudence of sentiment. Solomon Northup's powerful and haunting
narrative *Twelve Years a Slave* presented the nonfiction story of a freeman who was
kidnapped in Washington, DC, and sold into slavery. He ended up laboring for
a dozen years in Louisiana along the Red River (the location of Simon Legree's
fictional plantation in *Uncle Tom's Cabin*). Northup's narrative offered a picture of
the brutality of slavery at odds with the dry pro-slavery literature that portrayed
slaves' lives in rosy terms and dealt in abstract terms with issues of economics,
theology, and morality. In a direct challenge to the abstractions of pro-slavery
writers, which put sentiment against reason, Northup wrote that "Men may . . .
discourse flippantly from arm chairs of the pleasures of slave life; but let them
toil with him in the field . . . let them behold him scourged, hunted, trampled on,
and they will come back with another story in their mouths."[108] Northup's searing
narrative presented a powerful challenge to the arguments made by pro-slavery
writers about the benefits of slavery, especially to the enslaved.

Abolitionist lawyer William Goodell's book *The American Slave Code in
Theory and Practice* articulated a sustained critique of slavery through an empirical investigation of the brutality of slave laws. Published in 1853, the book
drew on appellate cases and newspaper accounts of court cases to detail the real

meaning of what pro-slavery advocates tried to disguise as the "legal relation of master and slave."[109] That seemingly benign "legal relation," which received protection from lawyers and judges, perverted jurisprudence and equity. Goodell tested the morality of slavery by reference to law in practice. He found that such practices should not receive the name "law," for there were many evils permitted, indeed licensed, by the slave code. Slaves were subject to the despotic dominion of masters and were left in that status forever, as were their children. And when the slave code left people in that position, when it stole from them their personal right to protect themselves, it could not be law. Goodell asked at the conclusion of the volume how this could possibly be law:

> By what authority, by what rule, on what principle, with what consistency, and with what ultimate success, will the law, or the administrators and expounders of law, attempt to maintain, by the sanctions of penal infliction, the rights of White men, while they refuse thus to maintain the rights of Black, or Yellow, or Swarthy, or Brown men? Upon what maxims of civil law or of the science of jurisprudence will they proceed in doing this? Or will they proclaim to the world that there is no such thing as " Legal Science;" that the pretense of it is a cheat; that the belief in it is a delusion; that jurisprudence is a game of chance; that law rests upon caprice, and interposes no obstacle to aggression, no protection from brute force, no guaranties against despotic power? If this be the decision of grave jurists, who will care to have jurists? . . . Who will respect the magistracy? Who will venerate Law?[110]

There was a long antislavery lineage to Goodell's identification of the mistreatment of slaves as "unlawful" even though it was authorized by statute. David Walker's *Appeal* had drawn that distinction; he charged that slave owners had violated the law. And a generation before Walker, Thomas Jefferson's Declaration of Independence made a similar distinction. For that reason the First Annual Meeting of People of Colour in Philadelphia in 1831 concluded their minutes with extensive quotations from the Declaration.[111] This was far from the last time in American history that those who challenged the status quo charged the people in power with breaking the law.

The remedy in Goodell's mind was simple: cease doing evil through slavery and break the yoke of slavery. This was a conclusion based on sentiment and based on an empirical investigation of slave law. Like Emerson a few years before, Goodell referenced works of the common law from Fortesque to Coke to Blackstone and more recent commentators to conclude that such inhumanity could not be law.[112] The solution was to declare what had been seen as law as no longer law.

The sources of Goodell's argument are important. He drew evidence from statutes and from cases applying the statutes. Like the pro-slavery writers who frequently wrote about the world as it was and asked that slavery be judged by how it worked and how it compared to the reasonable alternatives, Goodell drew upon empirical evidence. He looked to statutes rather than norms of behavior (so often characterized as benign by pro-slavery writers). Thus, it is law, not norms of behavior, that are critiqued. And then, after showing the harshness of the law, he argued that legal relations determine the actual practice of master-slave interactions. His vision of slave law was that it influenced treatment of slaves and that harsh treatment of slaves in turn influenced statutes. So harsh treatment went from norms to law. As Goodell said, the slave code is a vigilant guardian of the legal relation of master and slave—even as the role of law ought to restrain power.[113] The role of law was to protect the weak, but it failed to do so.[114] One piece of this story that is important to jurisprudence before the Civil War is to see the turn to empiricism on all sides. While pro-slavery legal thinkers retreated to considerations of utility, antislavery lawyers, like Goodell, said that the utility of slavery is outweighed by the harm. At the same time, more radical people, such as Stowe, Emerson, and Thoreau, advanced a separate critique: Why look to considerations of utility at all? Judge, instead, on the basis of humane considerations for the enslaved people. They wanted a jurisprudence of sentiment in place of the jurisprudence of utility, legal logic, and precedent that was dominant in American legal thought at the time.

In 1851, Frederick Douglass made a shift from accepting that the Constitution was pro-slavery to thinking that there were other modes of constitutional interpretation that suggested it was antislavery. That shift represented a sense of aspiration—not what the cold legal logic had taught but what might be. It was a jurisprudence that loosened the bonds to the past and asked what the spirit of the Constitution was and in what direction it was headed. Many were interpreting the Bible as a progressive document, which helped raise humanity to a new level. Douglass took that approach toward constitutional interpretation. He answered his question, "Is the United States Constitution for or against slavery?" with the statement that the Constitution is against slavery because it contained limitations on slavery—for example, allowing the slave trade to be ended by Congress. That the Constitution was not more clearly pro-slavery meant it was antislavery.[115] Douglass was joined in this sense by some other leading legal scholars. For instance William Goodell's 1844 book *Views of American Constitutional Law: In Its Bearing upon American Slavery* argued that the spirit of the Constitution did not support slavery.[116] But the weight of authority was against the view that the Constitution was antislavery.

Yet, Douglass persisted in articulating a different way of thinking about the Constitution, just as Stowe had and as the more moderate Goodell was doing as well. In 1860, speaking on the question of whether the Constitution was pro-slavery or antislavery, Douglass advanced an astonishingly bold antislavery interpretation of the Constitution. Astonishing because it considered flexibility in the Constitution that few at the time subscribed to—and astonishing because of the sources used to construct that flexibility. He had a sense that the Constitution appealed to our better nature, that it looked toward the abolition of the slave trade, that by refusing to put the word "slave" in the Constitution the framers expressed their horror of the institution, and that subsequent events led to the belief that the Constitution might reflect changing values. All are remarkably modern interpretations. And then Douglass concludes with the abolitionists' wishes. Those wishes linked law and sentiment. He wanted the "intelligence, the humanity, the Christian principle . . . which they feel in their hearts" to appear in the ballot box, so that "Congress shall crystalize those sentiments into law, and that law shall be in favor of freedom."[117]

Still, the antislavery forces realized they faced ideas and people and institutions that were incredibly powerful and who were not ready to yield power. The third volume in Stowe's trilogy, *Dred: A Tale of the Great Dismal Swamp*, helped explain why that was and just how cold legal thought worked in opposition to the jurisprudence of sentiment. It is to that volume and Stowe's engagement with one very important North Carolina decision, *State v. Mann*, that we turn to next.

The Novelist and the Jurist

Harriet Beecher Stowe's Jurisprudence of Sentiment

In 1856 Harriet Beecher Stowe published *Dred: A Tale of the Great Dismal Swamp*. Appearing four years after her stunningly successful *Uncle Tom's Cabin*, the novel provides a "sympathizing heart" for "all those who now struggle for all that is noble in our laws and institutions."[1] Like *Uncle Tom's Cabin* and *A Key to Uncle Tom's Cabin*,[2] *Dred* dwelt on the harshness of slavery, focusing on the ways that southern laws released the passions of slave owners from control and thus licensed the horrors of slavery. An important part of the novel involves a young abolitionist lawyer who files suit against a man who abused a slave. The legal decision to free the abuser from liability is issued by the lawyer's father, a judge on the North Carolina Supreme Court. Stowe explores important issues at the intersection of humanity and law, including the role of a judge in mediating between law and "justice," the role of antislavery lawyers in the southern legal system, and the role of utilitarian thinking in supporting the law of slavery.

Stowe addressed the same issues (though from a different vantage point) as the other subjects of this study. She provides an outsider's perspective on how southern lawyers reasoned and on the importance of considerations of expediency and precedent. As a contemporary and opponent of the southern legal thinkers who populate the rest of this study, Stowe is able to interpret their actions and motives. Her trilogy of slave law—*Uncle Tom's Cabin, A Key to Uncle Tom's Cabin,* and *Dred*—shows the centrality of legal thought to the institution of slavery and the connections between law, slavery, and property.

Stowe's novel uncovers the conflict between humane treatment of slaves and the law that enveloped southern judges and lawyers. Stowe recognized how constrained judges thought themselves to be by their judicial role—and how unlikely it was that one could expect them to remove their judicial masks while on the bench. At the same time, other actors in the slave system, such as legislators, judges, and lawyers, had little interest—because of their own utilitarian calculations—in restricting slavery. *Dred* thus represents an abolitionist's answer to the question: How did judges and lawyers act within the slave system?

Dred: The Story

Where Stowe's first antislavery novel, *Uncle Tom's Cabin*, focuses on the "horrors suffered by the slave," *Dred* focuses on "the moral degradation, the bad feeling, the state of calm and of civil conflict, the poverty and misery of the master."[3] *Dred* centers on inhabitants of two North Carolina plantations, Canema and Magnolia Grove. The major characters are Nina Gordon, a beautiful though whimsical young woman, heiress of Canema; her brother, Tom Gordon, the harsh, demagogic pro-slavery politician; their half-brother, Harry, who is the son of their father, Colonel Gordon, and one of the slaves on Canema; Nina's lover, the young lawyer Edward Clayton, owner of Magnolia Grove; and Edward's father, the chief justice of North Carolina, Judge Clayton. Surprisingly, the figure for which the novel is named, Dred, occupies only a peripheral role during much of the novel. Dred, a fugitive slave, lives in the Dismal Swamp, where he aids runaway slaves.

Two court cases provide vehicles for exploration of the issues of law and humanity. The first arises when Nina hires out Milly, a slave, to a neighbor, Mr. Baker, for desperately needed cash. When Baker, in a drunken rage, tries to punish a slave boy for a small offense, Milly intervenes. Baker hits Milly, then shoots her when she tries to escape the punishment. When Nina hears of the atrocity, she asks Edward to sue Baker. Edward gladly takes the case and succeeds at trial, winning a jury verdict. He loses on appeal, in an opinion delivered by his father, Judge Clayton, which is modeled on North Carolina Supreme Court Justice Thomas Ruffin's 1830 opinion in *State v. Mann*.[4] Edward then resigns from the practice of law, and Nina dies of cholera.

Harry's sister, Cora, also falls victim to the law. Cora was taken to Louisiana by Colonel Gordon's sister, Mrs. Stewart; there Cora married Mrs. Stewart's son, George, who emancipated her. When George died, Cora inherited his plantation. But Mr. Jekyl, a lawyer from New Orleans, sues to oust Cora from her inheritance and return her to slavery.[5]

Edward and his sister, Anne, try to establish a school on Magnolia Grove to educate their slaves. Their neighbors attempt to dissuade them, however; a mob attacks and partially burns the plantation. Only the intervention of Edward's friend, the pragmatic lawyer-politician Frank Russell, who opposes slavery in private but supports it in public, stops the destruction. Edward and Anne Clayton soon leave North Carolina for Canada.

The Conflicts of the Antebellum Judge

This is one of those cases which a Court will always regret being brought into judgment—One in which principles of policy urge the Judge to a decision in discord with the feelings of the man.
—Thomas Ruffin, draft of opinion in *State v. Mann*, 1830[6]

There is but one sole regret; and that is that such a man, with such a mind, should have been merely an *expositor* and not a *reformer* of the law.
—Harriet Beecher Stowe, *A Key to Uncle Tom's Cabin* (1853)

My father, why could you not have been a reformer of the system?
—Edward Clayton, in *Dred: A Tale of the Great Dismal Swamp*, (1856)

Stowe first raised the conflict between humanity and law that motivated her examination of Judge Clayton in *A Key to Uncle Tom's Cabin* when she used Justice Thomas Ruffin's opinion in *State v. Mann* as a central part of her discussion of the law of slavery.[7] The case arose from the prosecution of John Mann for assaulting Lydia, a slave whose services he had hired for one year. Mann hit Lydia when she committed a small offense, and she ran away. Mann "called upon her to stop"; when she did not, he shot her. A jury convicted him of battery, but Ruffin overturned the conviction.[8]

Justice Ruffin captured the attention of abolitionists with his extraordinary opinion in *Mann* because he released the possessor of a slave from all legal consequences for harming a slave, despite his recognition of the inhumanity of his decision. Ruffin began by lamenting "the struggle . . . in the Judge's own breast between the feelings of the man, and the duty of the magistrate."[9] The opinion presents a mixture of rationales that together release Mann from liability for abusing a slave who was under his control. The issue, just as in Milly's case, was whether the hirer and possessor of a slave could be indicted for abuse.

The opinion employed utilitarian and instrumentalist rationales, as well as ones based on community standards. Ruffin began by observing that no owner had ever been held liable for abuse of a slave. Immediately, Ruffin places responsibility for the decision on others. Ruffin had to follow the community's rule of nonliability, for even if he thought differently, "we could not set our notions in array against the judgment of everybody else, and say that this or that authority, may safely be lopped off."[10] He then distinguished the restrictions placed on parents in correcting children and on masters correcting apprentices. In those cases, the children and apprentices were being taught how to act, but there needed to be limits on the corrections. In cases involving slaves, however, "the end is the profit of the master, his security and public safety; the subject, one doomed in his own person, and his posterity, to live without knowledge, and without the capacity to make any thing his own, and to toil that another may reap the fruits."[11] Such language demonstrates a keen awareness of the harshness of slavery. Ruffin follows a larger goal than his own feelings of morality, however.

Slaves, he knew, will almost certainly perceive their situation as unjust. "What moral considerations," Ruffin asked rhetorically, "would be addressed to such a being, to convince him what, it is impossible but that the most stupid must feel and know can never be true"?[12] To expect a slave "thus to labour upon a principle of natural duty, or for the sake of his own personal happiness" was unrealistic. Here Ruffin adopted a rule because he recognized that slaves would not accept their position in southern society unless they were compelled to by force. "[S]uch services can only be expected from one who has no will of his own; who surrenders his will in implicit obedience to that of another."[13] Such obedience only arises when the master has "uncontrolled authority over the body."[14] Ruffin's candid statement was extraordinary for its honesty and for its understanding that slaves would not abide by Southerners' moral philosophy, which taught that slaves should be content with their low place in southern society. While Southerners told themselves that liberty is denied only when people ask for more freedom than they are entitled to,[15] Ruffin understood that slaves would disagree. His understanding led him to articulate rules that subjected slaves to extraordinary control, for the good of southern society. The opinion fits with the picture of an antebellum judiciary that took the best interests of society into account when framing judicial decisions, as do many other slave cases from North Carolina. For example, *State v. Hale*, the only case cited in *Mann*, imposed liability on a stranger who assaulted a slave in part because Justice Taylor wanted to "kee[p] pace with the march of benignant policy and provident humanity . . . and which Christianity, by the mild diffusion of its light and influence, has contributed to promote."[16]

Ruffin's question also indicates that he recognized the artificial nature of slavery: that however necessary it might be to society, slavery needed the support of elaborate human institutions, such as law. Even as Southerners increasingly defended slavery as a natural outgrowth of—and necessary to—human society, they also emphasized the need for humans to construct their intellectual and social environment. Ruffin's position that he must construct a law to teach slaves their proper position in southern society, which they would otherwise reject, appears as part of the dominant southern philosophy that emphasized the control of nature through law.

Ruffin followed a rule laid down by the community—which gained further strength because it was dictated by the needs of the community. That led to Ruffin's confession of his "sense of harshness of the proposition."[17] Even though he felt the harshness "as deeply as any man can," and even though he believed "as a principle of moral right, every person in his retirement must repudiate it," Ruffin upheld the master's "uncontrolled authority over the body."[18] For no other rule could "operate to produce" submission of slaves to masters.[19] Ruffin's action was part of the separation between moral and legal duties, which moral philosophers frequently discussed at the time. He echoed an important strain of thought that sought to divide requirements imposed by law from those imposed by morals. The opinion was, moreover, part of the belief that antebellum judges were constrained by duty to uphold the society that surrounded them. It was also the fruit of the utilitarian calculus that governed some American judges.

Ruffin shifted the responsibility for the opinion to political necessity, for the discipline over slaves that Ruffin found so personally revolting "belongs to the state of slavery." That discipline and slavery could not "be disunited, without abrogating at one the rights of the master, and absolving the slave from his subjection. It constitutes the curse of slavery to both the bond and free portions of our population. But it is inherent in the relation of master and slave."[20] Such a justification was a useful strategy for judges who rested authority for their decisions in the sentiment of the larger community.[21]

He then further contrasted the instrumental approach, which justified legal rules based on the necessity to the community, with reasoning based on conscience. "That there may be particular instances of cruelty and brutality where the laws might properly interfere, is most probable." But Ruffin would not even begin such reasoning. In an abstract sense, one could ask about the master's right to discipline the slave. But "we cannot look at the matter in that light."[22] Ruffin rejected such abstract reasoning. He cast himself as a realist, who views the situation as it is, not in abstract terms. Grand notions of justice could not be permitted to interfere with deciding cases. Ruffin decided based on what was possible; he was driven by a consequentalist understanding of the implications of his decision. The strength of the rule that Ruffin announced—its binding force—came from the need to preserve slave society. That need—the imperative duty the law imposed on Justice Ruffin—forced him to release an abuser from any possibility of liability.

The centrality of the utilitarian and instrumentalist impulses appeared again in the conclusion. Ruffin felt that as long as slavery exists it is the "imperative duty of the judges to recognize the full dominion of the owner over the slave," unless absolved of that duty by statute. "This we do upon the ground that this dominion is essential to the value of slaves as property, to the security of the master, and the public tranquility." In short, the rule is commanded because it "most effectually secur[es] the general protection and comfort of the slaves themselves."[23]

As was characteristic of many judges of his generation, Ruffin had a veneration for precedent. In *Mann*, however, Ruffin felt unconstrained by precedent—there were no North Carolina cases that had decided the issue *Mann* presented;

although, there was a recent Virginia case, which released a man from liability for abuse of a slave in his custody and thus may have served as a model for Ruffin.[24] There was, however, a close adherence to "logical" inferences from established facts. The opinion, thus, represents the triumph of a pro-slavery instrumentalism, a cold calculation of the benefits from the rule Ruffin adopted and the costs involved in choosing another path.

Harriet Beecher Stowe's Critique of *State v. Mann*

Stowe took Ruffin up on his invitation to see the "struggle, too, in the judge's own breast, between the feelings of the man and the duty of the magistrate."[25] She detected "the conflict between the feelings of the humane judge and the logical necessity of a strict interpreter of slave-law."[26] Such separation between the judge's sentiment and his legal opinion puzzled Stowe, for she had written *Uncle Tom's Cabin* with the optimistic belief that she could harness sentimentality to make her readers feel passion and, therefore, undertake radical reform of the law.[27] Stowe, like many other sentimental writers of her period, hoped to harness sympathies to effect radical change.[28] But in 1853, when Stowe was writing *A Key to Uncle Tom's Cabin*, it seemed to her that the changes she sought were not to be and that puzzled her. She asked the question, why?

It was an inhumane coolness, represented by the legal mentality, that led Americans to accept slavery. Stowe contrasted the cold, logical, and strictly legal approach of judges and lawyers with the "white heat of enthusiasm" that ministers, such as her father Lyman Beecher, generated.[29] George Sand recognized the conflict between religious beliefs and law. A master would protest "against slavery during the innocent part of life when his soul belongs to God alone." But later, "when society takes him, the law chases away God, and interest deposes conscience."[30] The battle between cold law and hot evangelical religion continued in *Dred*. Stowe wrote, "Even in the soil of the cool Saxon heart the Bible has thrown out its roots with an all-pervading energy, so that the whole framework of society may be said to rest on soil held together by its fibers."[31] To maintain slavery, harshness was necessary.

Even when slaveholders felt passion, however, they failed to act on those feelings. Stowe saw men like Ruffin who were aware of the inhumanity of slave law, but "if they are going to preserve the THING, they have no recourse but to make the laws, and to execute them faithfully after they are made."[32] They recognized that if slavery were to survive, the laws must be severely enforced:

> Like Judge Ruffin, men of honor, men of humanity, men of kindest and
> gentlest feelings, are *obliged* to interpret these severe laws with inflexible

severity. In the perpetual reaction of that awful force of human passion and human will, which necessarily meets the compressive power of slavery,—in that seething, boiling tide, never wholly repressed, which rolls its volcanic stream underneath the whole frame-work of society so constituted, ready to find vent at the least rent or fissure or unguarded aperture,—there is a constant necessity which urges to severity of law and inflexibility of execution.[33]

Stowe came to admire Ruffin's legal reasoning; she thought that "one cannot but admire the unflinching calmness with which a man, evidently possessed of honorable feelings, walks through the most extreme and terrible results and conclusions, in obedience to the laws of legal truth."[34] She believed that none could "read this decision, so firm and so clear in expression, so dignified and solemn in its earnestness, and so dreadful in its results, without feeling at once respect for the man and horror for the system. The man, judging him from the short specimen . . . has one of that high order of mind which looks straight through all verbosity and sophistry to the heart of every subject which it encounters."[35]

There was some hope that Ruffin, once he recognized the humanity of the slaves, might modify the law. "So abhorrent is the slave-code to every feeling of humanity that just as soon as there is any hesitancy in the community about perpetuating the institution of slavery, judges begin to listen to the voice of their honorable nature, and by favorable interpretations to soften its necessary severities."[36] But Ruffin did not listen to that voice in drafting his opinion; instead, he applied cold logic to the issue. It was the cold logic that led to so many perverse conclusions:

> Every act of humanity of every individual owner is an illogical result from the legal definition; and the reason why the slave-code of America is more atrocious than any ever before exhibited under the sun, is that the Anglo-Saxon race are a more coldly and strictly logical race, and have an unflinching courage to meet the consequences of every premise which they lay down, and to work out an accursed principle, with mathematical accuracy, to its most accursed result. The decisions of American law-books show nothing so much as this severe, unflinching accuracy of logic.[37]

Stowe concluded her discussion of the law of slavery with a statement that illuminates her fascination with Ruffin's ability to separate his legal mind from his feelings: "There is but one sole regret; and that is that such a man, with such a mind, should have been merely an *expositor* and not a *reformer* of the law."[38]

Judge Clayton: The Judicial Mask Removed

Judge Clayton, constructed "according to artistic fit," reveals why Ruffin was merely an expositor and not a reformer of the law.[39] Ruffin appears in a light not possible while he was communicating solely through judicial opinions—through the eyes of an abolitionist explaining to her readers her understanding of Ruffin. Stowe created a character who shows abolitionists' beliefs about how jurists in slave states behaved and how they wrestled with the tensions between the feelings of humanity and the commands of law.

Judge Clayton, in appearance as well as action, represents the abolitionists' image of a cold, calculating judge. The first hint of his character comes when Stowe introduces the Clayton family. The Judge's appearance bespoke "a logical severity of thought." There was much to fear in him; there was "little to hope from any outburst of his emotional nature."[40] His stern, rigidly logical attitudes were apparent in his strictly impartial approach toward domestic life. He never hesitated "to speak the truth nor to acknowledge an error."[41] In Stowe's view, emotion drove one to do justice; coldness suggested a dangerous level of abstraction that did not allow for individual justice. Yet, there might be room for hope; deep beneath Judge Clayton's external coldness was "a severely repressed nature, of the most fiery and passionate vehemence."[42]

Stowe peers behind Judge Clayton's mask and listens to a conversation he has with his wife. He observes that it is "extremely painful" to have to deliver the decision to overturn the jury verdict in favor of his son's client. It is "the doctrine that I feel myself forced to announce" that disturbs him.[43] In response to questioning by his wife whether he must make that decision, the Judge responds: "Yes, I must . . . A Judge can only perceive and declare. What I see, I must speak, though it go against all my feelings and all my sense of right."[44] Judge Clayton agrees with his wife's statement that the decision will cause "the most monstrous injustice." But he tells her that "I sit in my seat, not to make laws, nor to alter them, but simply to declare what they are. However bad the principle declared, it is not so bad as the proclamation of a falsehood would be. I have sworn truly to declare the laws, and I must keep my oath."[45] Then Harry, Nina Gordon, and Edward Clayton assemble in the courtroom to hear the Chief Justice stand and announce in "a clear, deliberate voice" the opinion of the court. He delivers the opinion, which he privately acknowledges causes him considerable pain, with his usual coolness. The opinion was taken directly from *State v. Mann*. Stowe converted the case from one involving criminal law to one about tort law, omitting only the statement of facts and a paragraph that announced that treatment of slaves was improving, citing changes in statutes and community sentiments. That omission further suggests the hopelessness of reform of slavery. Shortly after, Edward resigns from the practice of law.

Within Judge Clayton, judicial duty prevailed over the "feelings of the man."[46] Two days after the decision and Edward's dramatic resignation from the practice of law, Judge Clayton spoke with his son. Judge Clayton accepted Edward's explanation for resigning from the practice of law. "Every man must act up to his sense of duty," the Judge acknowledged.[47] Judge Clayton explained that he undertook the acts he believed necessary from his station. He expressed his reason for supporting the law: it provides security to North Carolina society. "I have often myself pondered the question with reference to my own duties. My course is a sufficient evidence that I have not come to the same result. Human law is, at best, but an approximation, a reflection of many of the ills of our nature. Imperfect as it is, it is, on the whole, a blessing. The worst system is better than anarchy."[48] Stowe identified Judge Clayton with the antebellum moral philosophers who emphasized the need for order in society and the superiority of order over anarchy, as well as the legal thinkers who emphasized duty to the law.

Edward then asks the same question that Stowe asked about Judge Ruffin in *A Key to Uncle Tom's Cabin*: "[M]y father, why could you not have been a reformer of the system?"[49] The answer makes Clayton appear as a realist. He argued that until there is a conviction in society that slavery is a moral evil, there can be no reform. The lack of moral condemnation of slavery, Judge Clayton thought, was the fault of the church. "The decisions and testimonies of the great religious assemblies in the land, in my youth, were frequent. They have grown every year less and less decided; and now the morality of the thing is openly defended in our pulpits, to my great disgust. I see no way but that the institution will be left to work itself out to its final result, which will, in the end, be ruinous to our country."[50]

Stowe maps in wonderful detail why the judges could not break out of their utilitarian, legal reasoning. Judge Clayton could not because of his abstract duty to the law, symbolized by his oath to protect the Constitution, and because of his belief that society was actually better off with the decision he rendered than by doing individual justice to individual slaves, and, as Judge Clayton explains later, because no piecemeal reforms would work.[51] Moreover, Judge Clayton believed he was not "gifted with the talents of a reformer."[52] He was not gifted with those talents because he thought in legal terms, which recognized only analytical reasoning, not humanity.

The fictional Clayton tracks closely the historical Ruffin in statements made from the bench, although one can never know how Ruffin felt in private. Stowe rendered a relatively accurate portrait, one guesses, of how at least some southern judges thought, as she provides perceptive comments on legal thought.[53]

Judge Clayton's discussion with Edward regarding his decision to leave the practice of law reveals the limited options available to a southern abolitionist lawyer. When told by Edward that he resigned based on "the deepest and most deliberate convictions of my conscience," the Judge approved because Edward "could not do otherwise." The Judge then asked whether Edward could continue to be a slaveholder, and Edward told him that he was retaining ownership only "as a means of protecting my slaves from the cruelties of the law and of securing the opportunity to educate and elevate them."[54] Even this might bring Edward into conflict with the law, however. "If there is any reasonable prospect of having the law altered, I must endeavor to do that," Edward responded. The Judge probed further by asking what if there were no way to repeal the law without uprooting the institution. Here the Judge may be seeking an answer to his own doubts about how to respond to slavery, as much as questioning his son. Edward's answer is unsatisfactory to the Judge, however. Edward seeks individual justice for the slave, whatever the consequences to southern society: "I say repeal the law if it do uproot the institution."[55] That approach, so characteristic of abolitionists, found disfavor among pro-slavery politicians, who often emphasized a utilitarian balancing of benefits and harm in deciding political issues.[56]

Edward's discussion with his friend Frank Russell further contrasts Edward's abolitionist ideas with those of more moderate antislavery lawyers. Russell agreed with Edward that slavery was wrong, but thought there was little he could do to end it. "You see," Frank explained, "our party can't take up that kind of thing. It would be just setting up a fort from which our enemies could fire on us at their leisure." Frank, nevertheless, hoped that someday he might do something to reform slavery.[57]

The Utilitarian Calculus of Pro-slavery Politicians, Judges, and Lawyers

The antislavery Edward Clayton and Frank Russell have complements in *Dred*. Opposing them are the pro-slavery Judge Oliver, Representative Knapp, and lawyer Mr. Jekyl. Stowe uses those complements to show how pro-slavery politicians, judges, and lawyers reasoned.

Stowe examines the utilitarian views of pro-slavery lawyers through Mr. Jekyl. Jekyl is a lawyer from New Orleans who comes to announce to Tom and Nina Gordon that they have inherited an estate from their aunt. Mr. Jekyl, who had performed legal work for Colonel Gordon, tells a complicated story to Tom and Nina. Colonel Gordon's sister, Mrs. Stewart, inherited an estate from her husband. Their son, George, in turn, inherited from her. George married a "handsome Quadroon girl," Cora, who was Harry's sister, and took her to Ohio, where he executed a deed of emancipation.[58] When George died, Cora inherited the plantation.[59] Then an overseer who had been dismissed by Cora for his abusive treatment of the slaves told her story to Mr. Jekyl. He found that the emancipation deed was ineffective in Mississippi and, therefore, that Tom and Nina were the heirs to the estate. The havoc wreaked by Jekyl's interference was great. Cora took the children and ran away to Cincinnati, but they were recaptured. She then murdered her children, so that they might escape slavery.[60] Without Jekyl's meddling, it is likely that no one would ever have discovered that Cora and her children were slaves.[61]

Jekyl's callousness illustrated the pro-slavery legal mentality. Stowe allowed him to speak on more general issues of law and theology and to show the connection of law to theology and the centrality of utilitarian calculus to both. Jekyl spent his leisure time reading theology, particularly doctrine that focused on the nature of true virtue. "This, he had fixed in his mind, consisted in a love of the greatest good." He believed that "right consisted in creating the greatest amount of happiness; and every creature has rights to be happy in proportion to his capacity of enjoyment or being." Jekyl demonstrated that one who was immersed in formal law and theology long enough could no longer see humanity; the cold, rigid reasoning of law and Presbyterian doctrine overcame his feelings. His mind had been "petrified into such a steady stream of the consideration of the greatest general good, that he was wholly inaccessible to any emotion of particular humanity."[62]

Edward tries to stay on at Magnolia Grove even after resigning from practice, but his decision to leave is hastened by two visits to his plantation. The first comes from several distinguished pro-slavery neighbors, including Judge Oliver and Mr. Knapp, a North Carolina representative to Congress.

Judge Oliver explains that Edward is violating the law by teaching slaves how to read. When Edward protests that he thought the laws were "a relic of barbarous ages, which the practical Christianity of our times will treat as a dead letter," both the politician and the judge provide a utilitarian rationale to support the slave law.[63] Representative Knapp explains that Edward is mistaken to believe the laws will not be enforced. "Sir, they are founded in the very nature of our institutions. They are indispensable to the preservation of our property and the safety of our families."[64] Judge Oliver reminds Clayton that "there must be some individual rights which we resign for the public good."[65] Clayton acknowledges his duty under state law but finds "equally binding" his "responsibilities for the moral and religious improvement of those under my care."[66]

The visit to Edward's plantation sets up an instructive contrast between pro-slavery politicians and judges, as represented by Knapp and Oliver, and antislavery lawyers, as represented by Edward Clayton. The Claytons, father and son, are alike in one respect. Neither one cares about the consequences of his act; instead they follow, formalistically, another goal. Judge Clayton seeks legal formalism; his son, religious formalism. The pro-slavery politicians and judges, however, care *only* about consequences. They balance their perception of the good of society against fairness to individual slaves. Representative Knapp, a man who has the power to change the law and who is not bound by the formalism that binds jurists, refuses to change the law because that would destroy his society. Judge Oliver, who is acting in a private capacity when he visits Edward and who is not then bound by judicial formalism, likewise employs balancing the interests of southern society against those of Edward's slaves.

Dred posits a hierarchy of rationales. It is a hierarchy of how much one is bound by formalism. At the low end are three pro-slavery Southerners speaking in private: Jekyl the lawyer and Knapp the politician, neither of whom is bound by formalism, then Oliver the judge, who is bound by formalism only on the bench. All three advance utilitarian reasons for supporting slavery. Next in the hierarchy is Judge Clayton, who is bound by formalism and uses it to support slavery from the bench, while secretly opposing slavery. Together they expose the difficulty of reforming slavery through the legislature or the courts.

Stowe's parade of legal thinkers, from Jekyl, through Knapp and Oliver, to Judge Clayton details the unbreakable chords holding slavery to law. Neither formalism nor utilitarianism offers a solution. There are problems inherent in legal formalism: Judge Clayton's harsh decision is the result. There are also problems with Representative Knapp's utilitarian calculus: holding slaves in bondage for the preservation of southern society is the result.

Dred offers insights from the vantage of an abolitionist, not a southern jurist. Therefore, its most direct testimony is about Stowe's ideas regarding reform. Her three antislavery books, *Uncle Tom's Cabin, A Key to Uncle Tom's Cabin,* and *Dred: A Tale of the Great Dismal Swamp,* together constituted an abolitionist interpretation of southern legal institutions. The trilogy presents Stowe's vision of her jurisprudence of sentiment, which she came to realize was an unpersuasive view for a majority of Americans. Occasionally judges broke from their legal tradition. "Like a spring outgushing in the desert, some noble man . . . from the fullness of his own better nature, throws out a legal decision, generously inconsistent with every principle and precedent of slave jurisprudence, and we bless God for it."[67] But such judges were few. "All we wish is that there were more of them, for then should we hope that the day of redemption was drawing nigh."[68] Those decisions, the product of the judges' "voice of their more honorable nature," did "not comment themselves to the professional admiration of legal gentlemen."[69] Those humane judges were not, Stowe recognized, following legal tradition. With the abolitionist lawyer Edward, we see how the abolitionist legal mind might operate—how he focused on law as an instrument for justice and how that vision clashed with the cold judicial response. We also see Stowe's despair regarding the legal system; it is the same despair that abolitionist lawyers felt.

Judges, according to *Dred*, were constrained by a trio of related principles: their own sense of duty to law, their need to support the society against anarchy, and their perceived inability to make piecemeal reform. The judges' rhetorical response to the inhumanity of slave law was, according to abolitionists, part of a much larger legal ethos that impeded reform. A sense of duty, so common and powerful in the antebellum legal culture of which the judges were a part, exerted greater force on judges than did their antislavery feelings. Clayton coldly followed cases to their logical conclusions to choose the path that was "law" and then he upheld that law, no matter what the consequences to individual slaves.

PART III

THE CORE OF SOUTHERN
LEGAL THOUGHT

We turn now from the ideas of professors of moral philosophy and law, pro-slavery essayists, politicians, and antislavery lawyers and novelists. That world emphasized certain values that were important to many: ideas of utility, as judged by history and contemporary economics, of religious duties, and of secular ones. That world was inhabited by people of the mind—professors, novelists, and pamphleteers. Yet, people of action, like politicians, judges, and lawyers, thought in similar terms. The final five chapters of *University, Court, and Slave* turn to the decisions and the occasional articles and addresses by such people of action, to see how they fit considerations of hierarchy, history, the market, evangelical religion, and moral philosophy together to create a world of pro-slavery jurisprudence, and how that powerful body of thought responded to antislavery ideas. This reveals that many in the pre–Civil War era, from professors to voters, politicians, and jurists, spoke a common language and engaged in similar reasoning styles. The academics' world of well-developed pro-slavery theory helps us understand the language and the thought of the lawyer and the jurist.

Chapter 8 discusses one judge in depth whom we have already met, Thomas Ruffin of the North Carolina Supreme Court. It moves from the close read of Ruffin's *State v. Mann* opinion in Chapter 7 to look across the spectrum of his opinions and in comparison with William Gaston, another member of the North Carolina Supreme Court, who sometimes spoke and acted against slavery. The next chapter turns to another jurist,

Justice Joseph Henry Lumpkin of the Georgia Supreme Court and some of his colleagues, who were a generation younger than Ruffin. It reveals the increasingly strident pro-slavery ideas and actions of jurists in the years leading to the Civil War. Chapter 10 looks intensively at another Georgian, Thomas Cobb. Cobb was a lawyer, law professor, and later in life a Confederate general. His legal treatise, *An Inquiry into the Law of Negro Slavery*, pulled together both the historical and economic arguments in favor of slavery and used them to support a robust pro-slavery law. Cobb's treatise is the capstone of southern pro-slavery legal thought. We see in Cobb's treatise important parts of the origins of American jurisprudence, such as a focus on considerations of utility and the analysis of legal rules in the context of history, economics, and society. Chapter 11 turns to cases interpreting wills that attempted to free slaves and also the doctrine that slaves who were taken to free soil were freed, even if they returned to a slave state. Shifts in those areas of the law reflect the increasing dominance of pro-slavery thought in the southern judiciary. The final chapter pulls together the strands of pro-slavery thought that appeared in the secession debates, where Southerners repeated the stories of the centrality of slavery to their society and the U.S. Constitution. Those beliefs were used to support action against Union. They reveal the centrality of pro-slavery ideas and the role of considerations of history, economy, and property rights as our nation moved toward war.

8

Beyond *State v. Mann*
Thomas Ruffin's Jurisprudence

State v. Mann was one of Thomas Ruffin's first opinions as a justice on the North Carolina Supreme Court. Perhaps that helps account for its honesty.[1] After *State v. Mann* Ruffin wrote of slavery in more than 425 cases involving issues such as criminal prosecutions of slaves, emancipation, rights among owners and renters, and sales and gifts of slaves.[2] Those opinions rarely offer as penetrating a look inside the mind of Justice Ruffin as *State v. Mann* did, but they collectively portray him as a representative of the antebellum era—a judge who separated law from morality, who revered precedent and feared departure from precedent, and who reasoned based on considerations of utility with an eye toward sustaining the world as it was.

Ruffin's Slavery Jurisprudence

Ruffin's *State v. Mann* opinion is his best known, but he wrote hundreds of others that dealt with enslaved people. They helped keep the enslaved in their subordinate status and protected owners from liability for abuse and from liability for the actions of their slaves. They also limited the rights of owners to free their slaves. In some cases Ruffin continued with the approach he took in *State v. Mann* to set law in distinction to humanity. Yet, in a criminal case in 1839, Ruffin again confronted the criminal prosecution of a white person for abusing a slave. The result retrenched somewhat from *Mann*, however, for the decision in *State v. Hoover* upheld the conviction of a slave owner for the murder of a pregnant slave, Mira. *Hoover* acknowledges that *State v. Mann* generally left decisions about the severity of punishment to owners "own judgment and humanity." "In the nature of things" owners have a degree of latitude that nonowners do not. But it is "self-evident" that such circumstances would not relieve the owner of all legal culpability here. It was the court's "duty" to explain the circumstances why this owner was liable for homicide. "The acts imputed to this unhappy man do not belong to a state of civilization," wrote Ruffin. "They are barbarities which could only be prompted by a heart in which every feeling had long been stifled; and indeed there can scarcely be a savage of the wilderness so ferocious as to not shudder at the recital of them."[3]

In other cases, Ruffin turned to his understanding of slaves' behavior to decide the appropriate legal response. In, *State v. Caesar*,[4] he confronted the question of what constituted provocation in the context of homicide. Essentially, the question was how much abuse would slaves have to endure at the hands of white men before they could fight back and claim they had been so provoked that a homicide was reduced from murder to manslaughter. Where the majority of the court found that mitigation was possible, Ruffin dissented. He urged attention to precedent and explained why precedent is important:

> The dissimilarity in the condition of slaves from any thing known at the common law cannot be denied; and, therefore, as it appears to me, the rules upon this, and upon all other kinds of intercourse between white men and slaves, must vary from those applied by the common law.... Judges cannot, indeed, be too sensible of the difficulty and delicacy of the task of adjusting the rules of law to new subjects; and therefore they should be and are proportionally cautious against rash expositions, not suited to the actual state of things, and not calculated to promote the security of persons, the stability of national institutions, and the common welfare.

Ruffin spoke of previous courts' employment of "practical reason" of the common law and their application of general rules as well as their "guarded . . . respect to the rules themselves in detail." For precedent "as far as it goes . . . affords a sole footing upon firm ground gained in a morass." And then Ruffin reasoned from his observance about the behavior of slaves and from this particular case that there should be no mitigation. He reasoned from what he believed to be the state of things: Every individual in the community feels and understands that the homicide of a slave may be extenuated by acts, which would not constitute a legal provocation "if done by a white person."[5] So, it follows, as certainly as day follows night, that many things, which drove a white man to madness, will not have the like effect, if done by a white man to a slave.[6] Ruffin was trying to make what he wished—a world of subservience—a reality.

In other slave cases, Ruffin turned again to his understanding of human nature. He decided an evidentiary question in *State v. Charity* on "general principles" when he could find no precedent. *Charity* involved the trial of a slave for a capital crime, the murder of her child, and dealt with the question whether

her owner could be compelled to testify against her. Ruffin would not permit a master to testify in favor of a slave because the master's pecuniary interest was too great. Consequently, in a form of equal treatment, Ruffin would not compel a master to testify *against* a slave. Chief Justice Henderson's concurrence shed different light on the matter, however. Henderson thought that masters' testimony about slaves' confessions should not be admitted, for "the master has an almost absolute control over both the body and mind of his slave. The master's will is his slave's will."[7] Moreover, Henderson thought masters should be protectors of their slaves and, thus, should not be compelled to testify against them. Ruffin and Henderson arrived at the same result though from very different angles.

Justice Ruffin relied on his understanding of slave personality in civil cases as well. In *Heathcock v. Pennington*, Ruffin wrote of the ordinary duty of care required of people who rented slaves: "a slave, being a moral and intelligent being, is usually as capable of self preservation as other persons. Hence, the same constant oversight and control are not requisite for his preservation, as for that of a lifeless thing, or of an irrational animal." Ruffin, then, absolved an operator of a mine shaft of liability to his owner for the death of a young slave who was employed there and had, late at night, fallen into the shaft and died. *Heathcock* was part of the emergence of a modern tort law, which left the owner of a slave with a limited remedy and facilitated the operation of the mine at a low cost. The mine had to keep operating twenty-four hours a day and "some one had necessarily to perform at those times":

> No one could suppose that the boy, knowing the place and its dangers, would incur the risk of stumbling into the shaft by not keeping wide awake. It was his misfortune to resemble the soldier sleeping at his post, who pays the penalty by being surprised and put to death. The event is to be attributed to one of those mischances, to which all are more or less exposed, and not, in particular, to want of care by the defendant.[8]

Similarly, in *Parham v. Blackwelder*, Ruffin further explored the nature of slaves' personality and the law's need to decouple an owners' liability from torts committed by his or her slaves. *Parham* arose when a slave owned by Amelia Parham cut wood and carried it away from Elizabeth Blackwelder's property. There was no precedent supporting an owner's liability for the intentional torts of their slaves. Ruffin found that there was no liability given the nature and extent of slavery:

> We believe the law does not hold one person answerable for the wrongs of another person. It would be most dangerous and unreasonable, if it did, as it is impossible for society to subsist without some persons

being in the service of others, and it would put employers entirely in the power of those who have often, no good will to them, to ruin them.[9]

Ruffin took the realities and needs of the slave system into account.

Emancipation Cases

One way of gauging Ruffin's views is through an examination of his opinions on emancipation by will. Emancipation by will took several primary forms— immediate emancipation by will; establishment of a trust for emancipation; and establishment of a trust to hold the slaves in quasi-slavery. Ruffin interpreted these doctrines over several decades and nearly two dozen cases.

Southern states varied in their approaches to emancipation via will and by trust. An 1830 act of the North Carolina legislature largely prohibited eman- cipation via wills; emancipation was largely limited to cases where the county court found there had been meritorious service.[10] Likewise, in Alabama and Mississippi, for instance, emancipation was prohibited via will. However, south- ern courts were surprisingly willing to accept trusts for emancipation. Even Mississippi, which statutorily prohibited emancipation by will, gave effect to a trust that resulted in freedom for the testator's slaves.[11] An owner could use a testamentary trust to take the slaves outside the state and emancipate them.

Ruffin's first opinion on emancipation via will, *Sorrey v. Bright*, decided in 1835, struck down what became known as a trust for quasi-freedom, in essence giving slaves their freedom while still holding them as property. A testator be- queathed several slaves to John Simmons with the restriction that the "negroes to have the result of their own labor, but ever to be under [Simmons] care and protection."[12] Ruffin refused to give effect to this, for "every trust for emancipa- tion, and every direction in a will to that end, where the emancipation is to be absolute or qualified, is illegal and void."

Ruffin construed powers of emancipation fairly broadly and upheld a claim of a person that he had been freed against a claim of a creditor of the slave's former owner's estate.[13] The North Carolina legislature had reversed the common law preference for inferring intent for emancipation. Still, Ruffin found that the owner had completed the acts for emancipation and, thus, the slave was free. And in *White v. Green*, Ruffin found that two slaves who were to have been freed via will and provided with a small plot of land and a few animals, were—instead of becoming free—part of the general estate and thus subject to be used to sat- isfy the estate's debts. *White* relied heavily upon English precedent in interpret- ing how to characterize the two slaves who were to be freed but were not: as property of the surviving spouse or as residual (called surplus) property of the estate. Ruffin characterized them as property of the estate rather than the surviving spouse and then made them liable to pay the debts of the estate.[14]

Ruffin's series of opinions regarding Sarah Freeman's estate beginning in 1844 and running through 1851,[15] distinguished between trusts to take people outside the state and free them and those that held slaves in a state of qualified slavery (or quasi-freedom) in the state. The former were acceptable; the later prohibited. The first appearance of Freeman's will before the North Carolina Supreme Court, in *Thompson v. Newlin*, dealt with whether an executor must investigate allegations that there was a secret trust to hold slaves in quasi-freedom. The intestate heirs of a Quaker, Sarah Freeman, alleged that she had created a secret trust with Quaker John Newlin, who would transport her nearly thirty slaves to a free state and emancipate them. (The idea behind a secret trust is that a donor gives a donee property. It looks like the gift is outright, but there is a secret agreement between the donor and the donee, about what the donee will do with the property.) Ruffin ordered an investigation of whether there was a secret agreement in this case. He demanded an answer to the question of what the purpose of the secret trust was—to transport and emancipate them or hold them in quasi-freedom in North Carolina, for "the law will not allow itself to be baffled, and its policy evaded by secret agreements, the very objects of which are the evasion of the law itself." Ruffin's prior opinion in the case refused to give effect to a secret trust that would have essentially emancipated slaves (he referred to it as a state of quasi-slavery) and kept them in North Carolina.[16]

By 1850, the case was again before the North Carolina Supreme Court and the donee, John Newlin, had sent Sarah Freeman's thirty-five to forty slaves to Ohio and emancipated them there. Ruffin upheld that emancipation—perhaps he could do nothing else at that point, although he might have held Newlin civilly liable, one supposes. And on a petition for rehearing in 1851, he similarly upheld the secret trust. Ruffin cited other cases, like *Cameron v. Commissioners of Raleigh*,[17] that permitted transportation outside the state for emancipation. He characterized *Cox v. Williams*[18] as holding that "the policy of our law, as collected from the only legitimate source—our legislature—was said to be opposed to the residence of freed negroes in this state." But it did nothing to prevent emancipation outside the state. He thought it a duty to turn to other states "similarly situated with ourselves for aid in sustaining our judgments."

So while North Carolina restricted emancipation of slaves via will, they could be put in trust to someone who would free them in another state. *Cox v. Williams*, coming in the midst of the *Newlin* saga, clarified the rights of the master to emancipate, as long as the slaves left the state.[19] The right was based on the natural right of property owners to dispose of property. "In the nature of things, the owner of a slave may renounce his ownership, and the slave will thereby be manumitted, and that natural right continues, until restrained by positive statutes." Ruffin attributed the legislative policy against emancipation to the finding that freed slaves were "a charge on the community" and a "common nuisance" because of their "idleness and dishonesty." That police power regulation that prohibited emancipation by any means other than by leave of a court on showing of meritorious service "was not intended to impose any restriction on the natural right of an owner to free his slaves." If the slaves were removed from the state before being freed, that was perfectly acceptable. Ruffin attributed the legislative preference against emancipation to a concern over the burden that emancipation imposed on the community. "That was surely a regulation of police, and for the promotion of the security and quiet of the people of this state. . . . Emancipation was not prohibited merely for the sake of keeping persons in servitude in the State, and increasing the number of slaves, for the law never restrained their exportation."[20] Of course, the slaves could not be freed unless there was money in the estate, for "justice stands," Ruffin wrote, "before generosity."[21]

Green v. Lane, coming at the end of the *Newlin* saga, illustrates the distinction between a trust to remove slaves and free them and to hold them in semi-freedom (or quasi-slavery). The testator, William Morris, executed a will in 1831 (written by William Gaston, before he became a justice of the North Carolina Supreme Court) directing his executors to take his slaves out of the state and free them (he had already apparently taken them to Pennsylvania and freed them, then returned to North Carolina in 1828 and, thus, likely held them in quasi-freedom during his life). A subsequent codicil directed that executors keep the slaves and hold them in quasi-freedom in North Carolina. That attempted emancipation was void.[22] Ruffin saw the obvious parallels to the infamous case of *Hinds v. Brazealle*, one of the few cases that rivaled *State v. Mann* in the abolitionist repertoire, for he cited *Hinds* in his decision in *Green*.

It took relatively little, however, to trigger a finding that the trust was for the slaves. In some cases the bequest was quite patently for the benefit of the slaves. Thus, the donee was instructed in *Stevens v. Ely* "to permit the negroes to live together on [the donee's] land and to be industriously employed and continue to exercise a controlling power over their moral condition, and furnish them with the necessaries and comforts of life."[23] Yet, in other instances, the restraints on the donee were slight. Thus, in *Huckaby v. Jones*, the four donees were given the slaves "to be their lawful property, for them to keep and dispose of, as they shall judge most for the glory of God, and the good of the said slaves."[24] In those instances, the gifts for quasi-freedom were open and obvious and, obviously, invalid.

Lemmond v. Peoples likewise prohibited a secret trust to hold slaves for the benefit of the slaves rather than the donee. "The donee of the legal title cannot, in conscience, hold the negroes as property for himself, but must execute it for someone, and, as there is no one else who can claim, it must be for the donor."[25]

Lemmond addressed the meaning of slavery, for the donees in *Lemmond* claimed that the gift of slaves was to them and that the donor gave the slaves to them because they would treat the slaves kindly. The slaves were to be held as property; they were not to be freed. But Ruffin used that as evidence of what distinguished slavery and freedom. Such holding of slaves "would not come up to the claim of the property, absolute and unconditional." If the slaves were to receive the kindness of the donees, "How and why were the defendants to have this absolute property?" The donees were " 'to provide for the protection, comfort, and happiness of the woman and her children,' and that was to be effected, not by exacting moderate labour from them as humane masters, but by the [donees'] placing them, upon a colorable contract 'for a small consideration,' . . . [with] no control being exercised over them by the [donees], but such as might be necessary for their proper conduct and maintenance." This was a plain case of quasi-freedom, for—in language reminiscent of *State v. Mann*—Ruffin found "the family is only required to maintain themselves and the authority to be exercised over the children is that, not of owners, but of parents."

One of his last decisions reaffirmed the right to remove slaves for emancipation. And he even upheld the right to place the choice of slavery or freedom in the slaves' hands. Anne L. Woods placed three slaves in trust for her (Woods') life, with Osmond F. Long as trustee. Upon Anne Woods' death, the slaves had the choice of going to Liberia or remaining in slavery in North Carolina. It was by 1858 well-established that a donor could free slaves after transporting them outside the state. However, Ruffin confronted the question whether the slaves could be given the choice of freedom. Here he recognized—as he did in tort and criminal law cases—their humanity, even if considerations of humanity would not motivate him to take action to protect them:

> From the nature of slavery, they are denied a legal capacity to make contracts or acquire property while remaining in that state; but they are responsible human beings, having intelligence to know right from wrong, and perceptions of pleasure and pain, and of the difference between bondage and freedom, and thus, by nature, they are competent to give or withhold their assent to things that concern their state.[26]

Again, he employed a natural law sense to decide the case. For he believed that there was no need to have a "municipal law" to have the right to manumission or to accept emancipation. "They pre-exist, and are founded in nature, just as other capacities for dealings between man and man."[27]

To some extent, Ruffin was pragmatic when interpreting owners' attempts to free slaves via will (or trust created through a will). He was willing to interpret, at least somewhat broadly, the owners' power to free via will. At some times, when Ruffin issued a decision that resulted in continued slavery he revealed something like sympathy. For instance, his 1842 decision in *Mayho v. Sears* bears striking resemblance to the self-reflection that made *Mann* famous. In *Mayho* Ruffin confronted a claim to freedom by the grandson of a freed slave, Polly. Polly's owner, John Munroe, had executed a deed of manumission in 1805 that would give Polly her freedom in April 1814. Around 1810, Polly had a daughter. Both Polly and her daughter lived as freed people after 1814. That daughter in turn had a son about 1830. And then in 1838, Munroe sold Polly's grandson. So Ruffin confronted a question of whether Polly's daughter (and grandson) were the property of Munroe, because the daughter had been born before Polly was free. Ruffin spoke in terms reminiscent of his moral quandary in *State v. Mann*:

> There is a natural inclination in the bosom of every judge who favors the side of freedom and a strong sympathy with the plaintiff, and the other persons stated as he is, who have been allowed to think themselves free and act for so long as if they were. [28]

But Ruffin would not act on his "feelings." He concluded "the court is governed by a different rule, the impartial and unyielding rule of law . . . in law the condition of the plaintiff is that of slavery." He ended the opinion: "it becomes our duty to affirm the judgment; consoling ourselves that the sentence is not ours but that of the law, whose ministers we are." Ruffin largely abandoned talk of the disjunction between his feelings and his duty as a magistrate after *Mayho*; in fact, he largely abandoned the talk after *Mann*.[29]

In 1833 in *Redmond v. Coffin*, Ruffin emphatically denied the power of a testator who died in 1816 to leave his slaves to the New Garden Quaker Meeting, so that they might be freed. But *Redmond*—like *Mann* and *Mayho*—recognized that emancipation was a sentiment that pulled at the heart and was viewed as just. "However praiseworthy the motive for accepting such a trust, or however benevolent the will of the donors may be, it cannot be supported in a court of justice. A stern necessity arising out of the safety of the commonwealth forbids it. . . . That is not an odious, but it is a dangerous and unlawful species of mortmain; and a trust results to the next of kin, where there is no residuary clause."[30] At the margins, then, sympathy might affect legal doctrine. *Common v. Jenkins* allowed an executor to sell slaves in family groups rather than singly (where they would return greater value), because "the Court would not punish [the executor] for acting on the common sympathies of our nature, unless in so doing he hath plainly injured those, with whose interests he stands charged."[31] Sympathy usually did not enter Ruffin's opinions, however.[32]

Ruffin's ability to "see through" led him to understand and acknowledge slaves' powers of reasoning as humans, though not their humanity. In upholding a trust for emancipation established by will that freed a testator's slave if—and only if—they agreed to leave the state, Ruffin addressed the argument that slaves should not have the legal capacity to choose between staying in slavery in North Carolina and becoming free by leaving the state. "It is not true in point of fact or law, that slaves have not a mental or a moral capacity to make the election to be free."[33] Ruffin understood the difference between legal capacity and mental ability. "From the nature of slavery, they are denied a legal capacity to make contracts or acquire property . . . but they are responsible human beings, having intelligence to know right from wrong, and perceptions of pleasure and pain, and of the difference between bondage and freedom, and thus, by nature, they are competent to give or withhold their assent to things that concern their state."[34] Ruffin was more willing to accept freedom of choice than were courts in other states.[35]

One of Ruffin's most revealing discussions of slavery came in the obscure 1845 *Waddill v. Martin*, which excluded slaves' property from an estate's claim. *Waddill* posed the problem of whether an executor had to collect the property owned by slaves to satisfy debts against an estate; the executor had not collected the property and a co-executor charged that he should have. Ruffin thought that appropriate, for several reasons. First, no one had previously collected "the little crops of cotton, corn, potatoes, ground peas and the like, made by slaves by permission of their deceased owners."[36] Second, it was desirable to allow the slaves to keep such little property.

> An executor is not bound to strip a poor negro of the things his master gave him, nor to take away his petty profits from a patch, with the proceeds of which the slave, with the ordinary precaution of a prudent and humane master, may be induced, and in a measure compelled, to buy those needful comforts of food and raiment, over and above the allowances of the owner, which promote his health, cheerfulness, and contentment, and enhance his value. . . . [T]he slight indulgences are repaid by the attachment of the slave to the master and his family, by exerting his industry and honesty and a spirit to make and save for the master as well as for himself.

There was a combination of universal community sentiment and economy that evoked the rule Ruffin applied.[37]

And then there was one case in which Ruffin upheld—for procedural reasons—a trust for quasi-freedom. His 1833 opinion in *White v. White* refused to undo a trust of slaves given to a Quaker meeting that was to keep slaves in quasi-freedom, because the settlor's heirs who would take the slaves if the trust were struck down failed to sue within the statute of limitations.[38]

Justice William Gaston and Other Paths

Even in his Ruffin's place and time, there were alternative visions of slavery. A soon-to-be colleague of Ruffin's on the North Carolina Supreme Court, William A. Gaston, spoke against slavery in a graduation speech at the University of North Carolina in 1832. Gaston was a former member of Congress and also a well-known Whig lawyer. He told the students:

> Disguise truth as we may, and throw blame where we will, it is slavery which more than any other cause, keeps us back in the career of improvement. It stifles industry and represses enterprise—it is fatal to economy and providence—it discourages skill—impairs our strength as a community, and poisons morals at the fountainhead. How this evil is he encountered, how subdued, is indeed a difficult and delicate enquiry.[39]

The Nat Turner rebellion cast a shadow over Gaston's speech because he gave it less than a year after the rebellion.[40] Gaston was not the first graduation speaker at the University of North Carolina to criticize slavery. Three years before, in June 1829, Professor William Hooper more sharply criticized the institution. Hopper worried about a slave rebellion but also about the effects of slavery on the slave-holding community. "That slavery is a baneful parent of the vilest morals, every virtuous family in this southern country knows full well, and deplores that it holds within its own walls a fountain of moral poison, which, in spite of the most watchful care, is continually diffusing around its baleful influence and infecting the health of all the household." Hooper longed for the day when "the collective wisdom and resources of the nation shall be put into action for the extirpation of the bitter root from our soil."[41] Gaston's was not the first UNC graduation address to criticize slavery, but it was the last.

Perhaps because of the success of his 1832 speech, Gaston was invited to address a joint meeting of the Whig and Cliosophic literary societies at his alma mater, Princeton, in September 1835. The Princeton address was similar to Gaston's North Carolina address; it dealt with the duties of individuals. Then he transitioned to focus on law and the need for order. This topic was generated by the then-recent mob attacks on the Charleston convent and on African Americans, as well as other episodes of vigilante justice and mobbing.[42]

Gaston warned about the need for order and law. "Order is heaven's first law, and there can be no order without subordination. A deliberate breach of law shows profligacy and folly, the ferocity of an untamed, or the ignorance of an un-informed nature; but a cheerful submission to wise rule is the highest evidence of that reasoning energy and decision of purpose which are among the noblest attributes of an intellectual being."[43] Gaston solemnly concluded, "Law is the guardian of freedom."[44] Gaston echoed a common theme in the nineteenth century: law promoted freedom by restraining the passions of individuals, tyrants, and mobs. He gave a robust defense of law and the need to obey it because law channeled disputes and made a union out of diverse interests:

> The law here demands our obedience, because we have pledged ourselves to obey it, and a breach of this engagement is perfidy. Rebellion against the law, against the expressed voice of the commonwealth, of the regularly declared will of the embodied people, the only recognized sovereign, is *"crimen laesae majestatis,"* is in the nature of treason. The law deserves our obedience, for that alone can reconcile the jarring interests of all, secure each against the rashness or malignity of others, and blend into one harmonious union the discordant materials of which society is composed.[45]

Law also promised protection for everyone and thus safeguarded expectations and stabilized society:

> The law throws its broad shield over the rights and the interests of the humblest, the proudest, the poorest, and the wealthiest in the land. It fences around what every individual has already gained, and it ensures to him the enjoyment of whatever his industry may acquire. It saves the merchant against ruinous hazards, provides security for the wages of the mechanic and the labourer, and enables the husbandman to reap his harvests without fear of plunder. . . . It makes every man's hosue his castle, and keeps watch and ward over his life, his name, his family, and his property. It travels with him by land and by sea; watches while he sleeps; and arrays in the defense of him and of his, the physical strength of the entire state. Surely, then, it is worthy of our reverence, our gratitude, and our love. Surely obedience to its mandates is among the highest of our duties. Surely its existence is not incompatible with perfect freedom.[46]

Yet, Gaston saw around him the breakdown of law, from the mobbing of the Charleston convent to attacks on African Americans to vigilante justice. And probably in the minds of his audience was the Whig critique of the Democratic Party, which was seen as particularly casual in its attitude toward the rule of law. From Andrew Jackson's flouting of the Marshall Court's *Worcester v. Georgia* opinion (restricting Indian removal) to the Kentucky legislature's attack on vested rights, to the declining significance of property holding for the franchise, Whigs worried about what they saw as the Democrats' attack on law and property. Gaston invoked images of lawless mobs, then predicted that would be how despotism might emerge in the United States. "From such evils, despotism itself is a refuge. The unlimited rule of one master is more tolerable than the unsparing domination of many and ever-changing sovereigns." Indeed, one needed only to look around to find examples in the human experience. "The history of the world can scarcely be opened without meeting the annals of the decline and fall of freedom. The summary is short. Liberty becomes licentiousness, and bursts the bounds of law. Factions rage and war against each other. The war of factions is succeeded by a confiscating and sanguinary anarchy. Anarchy is superseded by tyranny."[47] Thus would end freedom. Yet, Gaston was an optimist. He placed hope in educated Americans to stop such scenes.

Those speeches give us some sense of Gaston's mind. Like other addresses of the era, they give us a sense of how an orator fit his world—or pieces of his world, anyway—together in the compass of about twenty pages. Gaston was, indeed, different from the usual justice of his era. He was Catholic, educated at Princeton, class of 1798, and a former Federalist. Born in 1778, he was a representative of an earlier era—of Federalism, where concepts of virtue, republicanism, and order were central. And also a representative of the era when slavery was not so robustly embraced as it was after 1800. While practicing law, Gaston represented a number of Quakers in their efforts to establish trusts for the emancipation of their enslaved humans.[48] He went on the Supreme Court in 1832 and served until his death in 1844, at age sixty-eight.

Gaston's opinions correlate with and complement the values he expressed in opinions. He wrote elegant opinions, rich with the language of moral philosophy, duty, and trust. Gaston was perhaps best known in his time for an opinion that limited the power of slave owners over their enslaved human property, the 1834 case *State v. Negro Will*.[49] It involved the prosecution of a slave who killed his overseer following a brief dispute with him. No one questioned that the slave had argued with the overseer and in the process of running away, the overseer shot and wounded him. But the question was whether Will was guilty of murder or the less serious charge of manslaughter. For the overseer had clearly been very aggressive in pursuing Will and had attacked him in a moment of irrational rage. The overseer was, the evidence suggested, going to kill Will. And so Will responded by cutting the overseer on the thigh and then the arm, which caused him to bleed to death. Whether Will was guilty of first-degree murder or only manslaughter turned on whether the law recognized that Will was legitimately (or maybe understandably is a better word) resisting the overseer or whether— as some might suspect—the overseer could expect absolute and uncontrolled obedience from Will at all times, even in the midst of a dispute.

Will's lawyer, famed North Carolina lawyer B. F. Moore—subsequently attorney general of North Carolina[50]—argued that the overseer had no authority to threaten Will's life. From there Moore developed Will's right to resist the attack. In an odd echo of Thomas Ruffin's statement in *State v. Mann*, Moore stated he felt the need "as strongly as any man can, the inexorable necessity of keeping our slaves in a state of dependence and subservience to their masters."[51] But Moore believed that if shooting was "necessary to prevent insolence and disobedience, it only serves to show the want of proper domestic rules, but it will never supply it; and never can a punishment like this effect any other purpose, but to produce open conflicts or secret assassinations."[52] Moore was arguing for the subordination of slaves and for everyone else to obey the law.

North Carolina Attorney General John R. J. Daniel, who argued the case for the state, turned to *State v. Mann* to show slaves' obligation to obey. Although he acknowledged that *Mann* had stated the master's power too broadly (for instance, an owner could not kill a slave),[53] Daniel maintained that Will had no legal right to resist the overseer. Moreover, the law could not recognize Will's reaction to the attack by the overseer by reducing the severity of Will's crime. Such indulgence, Daniel argued, "would beget desires for another, until nothing short of absolute emancipation would satisfy. It must then be had, or an alternative the most shocking to humanity would then be resorted to."[54] There was a large threat to changing the law and protecting slaves more—or perhaps it is better phrased as subjecting overseers to more court oversight.[55] And in fact Daniel—who later served in the U.S. House of Representatives as a Democrat—invoked the common argument about the ubiquity of slavery[56] and the dangers of failing to vigilantly control the enslaved population.[57] It seems likely that Daniel had read Thomas Dew's *Debate in the Virginia Legislature* because he used a quotation that appeared there in his argument in favor of the prosecution of Will for first-degree murder. Daniel quoted (without attribution) Robert Wallace's *Dissertation on the Numbers of Mankind* to the effect that "the world when best peopled, was not a world of freemen, but of slaves." The likely source of this quotation is Thomas Dew's pamphlet review of the Virginia debate on slavery in the wake of the Nat Turner rebellion, which is further evidence of the interaction between academic pro-slavery thought and the legal system.[58]

Gaston resisted the inclination to find Will guilty of first-degree murder. He recognized the process of change and harmonization of precedent involved in the common law.[59] Two important values mixed in Gaston's *Will* opinion. First, the desire to limit violence, particularly violence over slaves. While he recognized that "unconditional submission" was the "general duty of the slave," he thought that did not "authorize the master to kill his slave." From that principle, he found some authority for Will fleeing the overseer, and he found no authority for the overseer shooting Will. Second, Gaston recognized Will's humanity and the natural, human response he had to overseer's attack. Gaston explained the "strong impulses to action" that Will must have felt:

> Suffering under the torture of a wound likely to terminate in death, and inflicted by a person, having indeed authority over him, but wielding power with the extravagance and madness of fury; chased in hot pursuit; baited and hemmed in like a crippled beast of prey that cannot run far; it became instinct, almost uncontrollable instinct to fly; it was human infirmity to struggle; it was terror or resentment, the strongest of human passions, or both combined, which gave to the struggle its fatal result; and this terror, this resentment, could not but have been excited in any one who had the ordinary feelings and frailties of human nature.[60]

Will reflected Gaston's recognition of the humanity of enslaved people; it also had the effect of subjecting the overseer's behavior to scrutiny as well, for the court reviewed his behavior and considered it unlawful and giving rise to the slave's resistance. One might note that the battery in Mann—shooting a fleeing slave—might also have caused death. Thus, the behavior of Mann and the overseer in Will seemed remarkably similar. In this light, Will seems to have moved further from Mann than one might at first think. Moreover, Will represented an attempt to put everyone under the control of law—to recognize that an overseer could overstep his authority and to recognize that when that happened the law would also recognize that a slave might be understandably provoked. This would then mitigate the slave's liability and lead to a punishment in line with his culpability.

Gaston concluded with rather remarkable terms that there were insufficient precedents to hold a slave guilty of homicide in all cases where he kills a person who has dominion over him. Gaston refused to construe the precedents in that way:

> Unless I see my way clear as a sunbeam, I cannot believe that this is the law of a civilized people and of a Christian land. I will not presume an arbitrary and inflexible rule so sanguinary in its character, and so repugnant to the spirit of those holy statutes which "rejoice the heart, enlighten the eyes, and are true and righteous altogether." . . . The prisoner is a human being, degraded indeed by slavery, but yet having "organs, dimensions, senses, affections, passions," like our own. The unfortunate man slain was for the time, indeed, his master, yet this dominion was not like that of a sovereign who can do no wrong.[61]

Will, written between the UNC and Princeton literary addresses, reveals Gaston's concern with the subordination of everyone—master and slave—to the restraints of law. It also reveals his particular attention to human emotions. One might assess, then, Gaston's opinions as careful works, which protect the commercial interests and expectations of his society. However, he could see a middle path, different from Thomas Ruffin's extreme pro-slavery views. More than fifteen years later in the U.S. Senate, North Carolina Senator George Badger turned to Gaston's opinion in *Negro Will*. During debate over the Compromise of 1850, Badger spoke of North Carolina common law's protection of slaves. He was responding to an invocation of Justice Thomas Ruffin's 1830 opinion in *State v. Mann* that the master of a slave had uncontrolled authority over the body of the slave. Senator Isaac Pigeon Walker of Wisconsin had quoted from Ruffin's opinion to show how southern law failed to protect slaves.[62] In response, Badger discussed several opinions, including *Negro Will*, to demonstrate that slaves did have the right to resist their owners.[63] Badger confessed that dicta in *State v. Mann* had gone too far. Although many abolitionists turned to Ruffin's opinion for a particularly stark statement of the brutal reality of slavery, Badger thought such use inappropriate. He concluded with a quotation from Gaston's 1832 University of North Carolina graduation address on the dangers of disunion.[64]

Gaston acted and spoke against (or at least to limit) slavery—as an advocate while drafting trusts for Quakers to free enslaved people, while on the North Carolina Supreme Court in *State v. Negro Will*, and in both of his literary addresses. We can see how the ideas of order and law combined with Gaston's antislavery ideas to make a jurisprudence of slavery that was more flexible and less ardently pro-slavery than Ruffin's. And we can see via Gaston's literary addresses and his opinions how ideas were put in action. *Will* is a prime example of how Gaston's antislavery attitudes and his desire for order combined to limit the authority of a white person over an enslaved person.

9

JOSEPH HENRY LUMPKIN

Industrialism and Slavery in the Old South

Joseph Henry Lumpkin started off, he tells us in a judicial opinion, as an advocate of gradual emancipation. He became a zealous defender of the institution of slavery. Lumpkin was an evangelical Protestant and an advocate of property rights and economic development. He advocated the acceptable progressive movements—temperance, law reform, the extension of Christianity—as he embraced the market.[1] All the pieces of the antebellum South's aspirations for a modern, market economy based on slavery fit together in him.

Lumpkin was born in December 1799, studied for a while at the University of Georgia and graduated from Princeton in 1819, then studied law with Thomas W. Cobb (the father of Thomas R. R. Cobb, the subject of the next chapter). He began the practice of law in Lexington, Georgia, in 1820 and served briefly in the Georgia legislature in 1824 and 1825. Lumpkin was a successful practitioner and trainer of attorneys, and he was also a frequent advocate of moral reform, as well as trustee of the University of Georgia in the 1840s. As late as 1837, Lumpkin was working to raise money for the American Colonization Society in Georgia.[2] He also served on the board of the American Bible Society and the American Board of Commissioners for Foreign Missions—along with leading antislavery northern ministers.[3] In 1833 Lumpkin visited Boston; in a letter he wrote following the visit, he claimed he did not believe that Northerners intended to interfere with slavery, but he reserved the right to self-protection.[4]

Lumpkin, whose magnificent house still stands in Athens, Georgia, joined the Georgia Supreme Court when it was organized in 1845 and served on it until his death in 1867. (Illustration 9.1) In 1859, he cofounded the Lumpkin Law School (along with his son-in-law Thomas R. R. Cobb), which operated through the Civil War and later became the University of Georgia's law school. Justice Lumpkin, then, serves a critical role in our story: he spanned the antebellum years. He began as a lawyer in the year of the Missouri Compromise, 1820, and he continued through the years of sectional breakdown.

Illustration 9.1 Georgia Supreme Court Justice Joseph Lumpkin's house, Athens, Georgia. (Library of Congress, Prints & Photographs Division, HABS, Reproduction number LC-DIG-csas-00548.)

We can see in Lumpkin the trajectory of the South and also key themes in southern thought, from the desire for economic development and educational improvement to the shift from colonization to strong support for slavery. Some sense of Lumpkin's ideas appear in his extrajudicial writings and addresses. In an 1836 address laden with biblical imagery, Lumpkin spoke to the college literary societies at Mercer College. That was given at a time when he was already deeply concerned with religion, but before he opposed gradual emancipation.[5]

Important keys to Lumpkin's thinking appear in his lengthy address to the South Carolina Institute's Annual Fair in November 1850.[6] Delivered only four years after joining the Georgia Supreme Court, it presents an integrated picture of Lumpkin's thinking about economic and legal matters and about slavery as well. He marveled at the technological progress of the era, such as photography and railroad tunnels, and looked forward to plans, some fanciful, from the transcontinental railroad, to a suspension bridge connecting England and France, to "a balloon railway over the Sahara."[7] "Science and the arts will accomplish wonders of which it hath not entered the heart of man to conceive," Lumpkin boasted, correctly, obviously. The printing press and inexpensive paper ensured that the wonders of science would be spread widely. This was part of "republicanizing knowledge."[8]

In a case decided that year, *Merritt v. Scott*, Lumpkin prefaced the opinion with a statement that he hoped laypeople would read opinions and learn the law. *Merritt* dealt with a prenuptial agreement, and Lumpkin wished that property law could be easily understood by laypeople.

> Science, so long locked up in cloisters and colleges, has been brought, through the medium of popular tracts and lectures, to the hearth and home even of the cottager, and has thus been made eminently useful to the ordinary business of life. Shall botany, chemistry and philosophy in all its branches, be thus republicanized, and the law alone, in this age of inquiry and progress, remain a secret system, which the initiated only can pry into? The Americans, above all others, are a plain, practical people, and they will have justice dispensed to them in a plain and intelligible manner. . . . The sooner [law] is emancipated from the cumbersome appendages of the scholastic and feudal ages, the better.[9]

It was economic and physical progress that Lumpkin respected—he celebrated those who "cultivate, adorn, and improve the earth." For he found that to clear "the forests—drain the swamps—remove the stones and convert them into fences, walls, and fixtures—set the orchards—open the rivers—tunnel the mountains—fill up the valleys—make the crooked places straight, the rough places smooth, and web the land with highways for travels and transportation— erect schoolhouses, churches, private residences and public edifices," would be the highest attainment of perfection. And these achievements would be attained through industrialization and slavery.[10]

In the Institute speech he tried out arguments about the importance of slavery that appeared again and in greater amplitude in a series of decisions. "Under the influence of a mistaken philanthropy, we were inclined to go much too fast and too far upon" emancipation, Lumpkin said. But because of abolitionist "agitation," Southerners had reexamined the slavery and settled their minds about its importance:

> We believe that it had its origin in the same Divine wisdom and goodness which sent confusion among the impious builders of Babel, that every remote region of the earth might be replenished with inhabitants, each speaking its own tongue, and moulded into that form of society and government which should best subserve the benevolent designs of Providence.[11]

Such rethinking in the South led to a cut back on talk of emancipation. Moreover, the rethinking led to the belief that slavery was a positive benefit to the slaves. "The universal opinion of the South now is, that the spectacle of three hundred thousand barbarians, emerging, under the mild and humane treatment of their owners, into near four millions of civilized Christians, is not only without a parallel in the history of the African race, but of the whole world."[12]

Lumpkin frequently blamed (or perhaps credited is the proper term) the abolitionists for causing Southerners to rethink their attitudes toward emancipation for some time. In an 1848 letter to Senator Howell Cobb, Lumpkin made a similar statement attributing the South's shift toward the defense of slavery to a response to abolitionist advocacy:

> Had the Abolitionists let us alone we should have been guilty, I verily believe, of political and social suicide by emancipating the African race, a measure fatal to them, to ourselves, and to the best interest of this Confederacy and of the whole world. The violent assaults of these fiends have compelled us in self defense to investigate this momentous subject in all of its bearings, and the result has been a firm and settled conviction that duty to the slave as well as the master forbids that the relation should be disturbed; and notwithstanding Mr. Webster's false declaration as the result of his personal observations among us, there is but one mind among the whole of our people upon this subject. And we never will submit for one moment to the smallest aggression upon our constitutional rights.[13]

Lumpkin advocated in his agricultural society address economic and industrial self-help for the South, as a way of protecting against the "anti-slavery fever of the North."[14] The key to that self-help was to "breed, raise, and manufacture" as much as possible within the southern states.[15] Lumpkin has several specific suggestions. The first was to develop a law that promoted commerce. That included making it easier to mortgage property and thus secure credit, promoting corporations and limiting monopolies. "Associated wealth," Lumpkin believed, "is, in small degree the cause of modern civilization." Another suggestion was to have widespread education.[16]

These kinds of considerations of promotion of the market appeared in other cases as well. In 1854, with little reasoning but ample citations to cases in other jurisdictions, Lumpkin addressed the rights of a worker who suffered injury through the fault of a coworker. Like almost all other U.S. jurisdictions, Lumpkin held that the employer had no liability to the worker. This case arose when a railroad worker's son, who was riding on the train with him, died in a train wreck that was caused by another worker's negligence.[17] This raised an issue of what was known as "the fellow servant rule," first introduced in the late 1830s in the United Kingdom and quickly adopted throughout almost all the United States. The idea was that employees did not have a right to sue their employers for injuries caused by fellow workers. The rationales behind this were that workers were in as good a position to protect against those injuries as employers,[18] that employers should only be liable for their actions,[19] not those of others, and that employees who did not like this could leave.[20] The "fellow servant rule" absolved corporations of much of their liability in hazardous industrial settings; it also left workers with little protection. This was the world of free contract that Southerners so frequently criticized in their pro-slavery literature—the cruelties of the market left little protection from employers, corporations, and industrialization.

Yet, slaves occupied a very different position from free workers. In the 1851 case of *Scudder v. Woodbridge*, Lumpkin turned to an economic analysis to decide that the fellow servant rule did not apply to slaves.[21] Lumpkin turned to a basic economic analysis, that liability had to be imposed on the employer of the slave in order to give an incentive to protect the slaves from danger. If the employer were not liable, there would be no incentive to protect slaves from harm. If there were no liability, Lumpkin feared, "I hesitate not to affirm, that the life of no hired slave would be safe."[22]

Lumpkin maneuvered between a state statute protecting slaves from excessive cruelty and the economically grounded policy of maintaining control over slaves when a slave who had been rented for a year ran away from the hirer. The hirer tracked him down using dogs. It was alleged that the slave ran into a creek and drowned. What exactly happened was never made clear; perhaps the dogs chased him into the creek or maybe something more sinister happened, like the slave was drowned by his pursers. But as the case was presented to the Georgia Supreme Court, the question was whether someone pursing a runaway slave could track him using dogs. Lumpkin came to the conclusion that it was alright in two ways. First, the Georgia code protected slaves only from excessive abuse; second, it was necessary to give broad latitude in the reclamation of slaves, for many, perhaps 60,000 from across the South, had run away, which was causing losses to slave owners. Lumpkin closed the brief opinion with a dramatic paragraph drawn from Revelations. At judgment day, as the sun turned black and the moon blood red, as the stars fall from the heavens like figs from a tree blown by a storm, slaves would still be there. From this Lumpkin concluded that slavery would continue to the end of time. This was in 1855.[23]

This is the certainty with which pro-slavery lawyers, judges, and politicians approached slavery in the last few years before the Civil War. They believed it divinely created and approved, and something that would last forever—it should not be ended even if it could be. But it could not be—colonization was laughable; they could not envision a world without slavery, nor would they want to. They believed slavery was good for the enslaved and good for the owners. They built a law to preserve slavery. It was their world. And when the time came in 1861 to decide Georgia's fate, Lumpkin, Benning, and Starnes all participated in the Georgia secession convention. The ideas of hierarchy, order, slavery, and economy helped support their state's move toward war.

Regulating Emancipation of the Enslaved

Lumpkin's general interest in the promotion of economic development and in issues of efficiency appear in particularly stark terms in cases involving owners who attempted to free enslaved people. In those decisions we can see the interplay between legislation, common law precedent, and the influence of public policy. For the Georgia legislature established the broad framework for owners who wanted to emancipate enslaved human property in 1818. That statute prohibited the freeing of people inside the state, but left open the right of owners to take enslaved people outside the state and free them. A series of decisions then had to interpret how that legislation affected the common law right of owners to dispose of their human property, as well as the state's general policy that was in favor of restricting emancipation, restricting the number of free black people, and maintaining control over Georgia's population of both free and enslaved African Americans.

Lumpkin's first major opinion on this came in 1848 in *Vance v. Crawford*. He upheld a will that provided for three slaves to go, if they chose, to Liberia and be free there. Lumpkin found that permitted by statute and also consistent with Georgia's policy. But he went on to observe that it was not state policy to free slaves within the state. For state policy "forbids and rebukes, in the sternest terms, all attempts at domestic manumission, whether open or covert."[24] That policy is "founded in the most manifest wisdom and propriety" because freed slaves posed a danger to the white community. "They are incapable of taking part with ourselves, in the exercise of self-government."[25] Lumpkin invoked the divine sanction for the Georgia government and again wrote about the virtues of slavery to the enslaved:

> To set up a model empire for the world, God in His wisdom planted on this virgin soil, the best blood of the human family. To allow it to be contaminated, is to be recreant to the weighty and solemn trust committed to our hands. Republican institutions cannot exist in Mexico, or the commingled races of South America. And while we concede that the condition of our slaves is humble, still it is infinitely better than it

would have been, but for this very system of bondage, better than the lower orders in Europe, and better far than it would be, if they were emancipated here, "destroying others, by themselves destroyed."[26]

The key elements, limiting emancipation in the state, promoting slavery, and be-lieving that slavery was part of God's design were all there in *Vance*. Over the next dozen years, Lumpkin worked through a series of cases dealing with at-tempts at emancipation.

Like Thomas Ruffin and the judges discussed extensively in Chapter 11, Lumpkin wrote several of the leading opinions interpreting the power of testa-tors to place slaves in trust, to be transported out of the state and emancipated in a free state or in Africa. In 1854 in *Cleland v. Waters*, a case interpreting a will that attempted to free slaves, for instance, Lumpkin surveyed the his-tory of Georgia's attitudes toward emancipation. He began the story in 1816, when many in the state approved transporting slaves to Liberia. In 1820, the Governor ordered that slaves illegally imported into the state be turned over to the American Colonization Society. In the early 1820s, Georgians–still, in Lumpkin's mind unaware of "the true character" of slavery—supported coloni-zation and emancipation. When in 1825 Georgia's Governor warned about the need to protect against abolitionists, the legislature did nothing. But because of the "blind zealots of the North," there was a "settled conviction that it was wisely ordained by a forecast high as heaven above man's, for the good of both races, and a calm and fixed determination to preserve and defend [slavery], at any and all hazards."[27] Despite continuing evidence of the legislature's concern about colonization, judicial decisions had steadily supported the transporta-tion of slaves outside the state for emancipation. Lumpkin did not want to in-terfere with that precedent.

Lumpkin faced the issue another time when *Cleland v. Waters* was again before the court a year later in 1855.[28] This time the question was not whether the testator's intent was to free all his slaves, but rather whether his intent could be carried out. If the court interpreted the ambiguous will as an attempt to grant the slaves freedom in Georgia, then the plan would have been void. Lumpkin upheld the devise, however, on the rationale that the testator's desire for the ex-ecutors to petition for the slaves to be freed in Georgia, then if rejected, to free them in a nonslave state or country was enforceable under Georgia law.[29]

The second *Cleland* opinion, however, drew a dissent from Justice Henry Lewis Benning. Justice Benning, who was born in 1814 and graduated from Franklin College (now the University of Georgia) in 1834, joined the court in 1853 and served until 1860. Later he served as a Confederate general. Benning, the most strident pro-slavery and pro-states-rights jurist on the court, dissented from *Cleland* because he took a narrower view of the two statutes relied on by

Lumpkin and referred to his opinion in a case decided earlier that year, *Adams v. Bass*.[30] It was in this dissent that Benning provided a lengthier discussion of the growing pro-slavery sentiment.

In *Bass*, Lumpkin interpreted a will that provided for the transportation of the testator's slaves to either Indiana or Illinois, where they would be freed. By the time of the testator's death, however, both Indiana and Illinois prohibited free blacks from settling there, so the provisions of the will could not be enforced. Rather than allowing the slaves to be taken somewhere else, Lumpkin held those provisions of the will invalid but otherwise upheld the will.[31] Benning, by contrast, thought the entire will was an invalid attempt to get around Georgia's law limiting emancipation. Benning wanted no more emancipations outside the state. He feared that emancipation outside the state would lead to the same result as emancipation inside the state—"insubordination, massacre of free citizens, insurrection, and on the part of free citizens, by a war of repression, with its sequel of punishments." It was the "generic fact of freedom" that inspired slaves to rebellion and whites to oppression.[32]

Lumpkin faced these questions later, as anti-emancipation sentiment continued to grow. In 1858 in *Sanders v. Ward* he upheld again a testamentary trust in which a testator placed slaves into trust and then instructed the trustees to transport the slaves to a free jurisdiction and emancipate them. *Sanders* is particularly illuminating because Lumpkin upheld such a trust over a vigorous dissent.[33] It gives us a window into the nature of legal reasoning. Lumpkin is clear that he opposes emancipation. He said he had "no partiality for foreign any more than domestic manumission. I believe that policy, as well as humanity for the negro, forbid both. Especially do I object to the colonization of our negroes upon our northwestern frontier. They facilitate the escape of our fugitive slaves. In case of civil war, they would become an element of strength to the enemy, as well as of annoyance to ourselves." Lumpkin even opposed emancipation after an owner's death by taking the slaves outside the state. He noted that in the last session of the legislature, a bill to prohibit foreign emancipation was introduced but failed to pass. While he would have voted for the bill, he wondered: "Is it for the Courts, then, to inaugurate this new policy, or to be forever importuned and harassed with this subject, at each change of incumbents upon this Bench? I trust the question will be considered as settled, until the Legislature see fit to intervene. Let that body speak, and no one will take more pleasure than myself in obeying their behest. Sworn as I am, not to make but to administer the law, I never can torture the law, as it now stands, to a purpose for which I *know* it never was intended."[34]

But Lumpkin also believed that the legislation prohibited only domestic emancipation, not emancipation outside the state of Georgia. Given that interpretation, he was unwilling to insert his own interpretation. Lumpkin retreated, as did many at the time, to the argument that he would be making law were he to read the legislation differently:

> All writers on law, national and municipal, hold the same language, that the great aim should be to discover what the law-maker meant; never to lose sight of that object, and to give it effect, whatever may be our opinion of its wisdom or policy. "Whatever doubts I may have in my own breast," said Lord Mansfield, ... "with respect to the policy and expediency of this law, yet, as long as it continues in force, I am bound to see it executed according to its meaning."[35]

Lumpkin wondered what to make of his personal opposition to emancipation: "Shall I therefore undertake, by my individual opinion, to dictate to more than a half a million of my fellow-citizens, what shall be the law, by wresting these ancient statutes from what I believe to be their true and only meaning? A construction adhered to without variableness or a shadow of turning for a quarter of a century? Such is not my understanding of my duty or privilege."[36] Moreover, those who were outside the state and thus beyond the reach of the court at the time of the probate of the will were routinely freed. Lumpkin understood the folly of trying to come to a different result when he asked of the 1801 Georgia statute: "Did the Legislature of 1801 design to render themselves ridiculous, by the promulgation of a *brutum fulmen*, that slaves set free by their removal to a free State, should still be in a state of slavery?"[37]

In dissent, Justice Henry Lewis Benning thought that the best way to follow the legislature's spirit was to follow the letter of the law. He believed that the freed slaves would either never leave the state or that they would return. He referred to the slaves freed by George Waters' will, which had ordered them transported to Liberia. It is testimony to the transatlantic nature of the late antebellum period that Benning believed at least one of those slaves returned from Liberia to Georgia. So Benning offers a realistic portrait of the nature of emancipation and how the legal system ought to respond. He distinguished the precedent that Lumpkin relied upon by noting that it was from an era of antislavery feelings and that it should not be followed now:

> [T]hey are decisions of which the first was made before the anti-slavery sentiment had quite left us; and that the others are decisions which, as I persuade myself, merely followed the first, being made on the notion, that a precedent is to be followed, not questioned; and I say, that decisions made on that principle, cannot have as much authoritative force, as decisions made on the principle, that law is to be followed, even although a precedent has to be questioned. An echo is not entitled to rank with an original sound.[38]

Benning argued that courts should only follow erroneous decisions that have become common errors (*communis error*), that is "an error which must have been living and growing for a long time, so that it has its roots running and spreading every where in the community, and to tear it up, would be, to tear the community up with it." Changing the law in this case involved no such reliance interests:

> Its beginning was within less than thirty years ago; its few repetitions were quite recent—within the last dozen years; it has not a root running out into the community, for the beneficiaries of it, having gone abroad to the emancipation there prepared for them, have ceased to be a part of the community. Correcting the error, therefore, would not touch anything held by the community. True it may be, that correcting it would be disappointing expectation in the case in which the correction was made, and possibly, in some few others, those coming into existence at about the same time with that case; but this would happen, if the decision were not a decision correcting an error, but were an original decision.[39]

There is a classic confrontation between precedent, legislation, and judicial sentiments and a robust defense of alteration of the law to bring it into alignment with emerging pro-slavery sentiments. And there is a sense in Justice Benning's opinion that law evolves in keeping with changing political and social ideas, an idea that had some currency in antebellum legal thought. Here, then, is one place where that evolution of thought might have an impact. And as the nation moved closer to Civil War, the evolution became starker.[40]

Cases like *Ward* give us a look at the issue of judges whose private sentiments were at odds with the law. Often historians talk about this in cases where the judges were antislavery in private but faced a pro-slavery law. That was the problem of Stowe's fictional Judge Clayton in *Dred: A Tale of the Great Dismal Swamp* discussed in Chapter 7. But Lumpkin presented a mirror image of that judge. Here was someone who was pro-slavery in private but upheld a (very mild) antislavery law. The menu of responses that Lumpkin could choose from was small—attribute responsibility to the legislature or prior judges and follow "the law," or change (some might say break) the law through his opinion. Lumpkin's judicial conservatism led him to uphold the law, then campaign in the pages of his opinion for the legislature to act—which it did—to make it more difficult to free slaves.

Yet, Lumpkin was also willing to shade the law toward pro-slavery results. In 1857 in *American Colonization Society v. Gartrell*, Lumpkin construed narrowly the American Colonization Society's charter to limit its power to colonizing people who were already free. Thus, slaves left in a testamentary trust to the American Colonization Society to be freed and transported to Liberia was ineffective. Lumpkin's narrow construction of the will, narrow construction of the American Colonization Society's charter, and his refusal to allow the modification of the will under the equitable doctrine of "cy pres," frustrated the devise. Even there, Lumpkin introduced his pro-slavery sentiments into the opinion. He closed with an appeal to stop further emancipation.

> I was once, in common with the great body of my fellow citizens of the South, the friend and patron of this enterprise. I now regard it as a failure, if not something worse; as I do every effort that has been made, for the abolition of negro slavery, at home or abroad. Liberia was formed of emancipated slaves, many of them partially trained and prepared for the change, and sent thousands of miles from all contract with the superior race; and given a home in a country where their ancestors were natives, and supposed to be suited to their physical condition. Arrived there, they have been for a number of years in a state of pupilage to the Colonization Society, in order that they might learn "to walk alone and by themselves." And at the end of a half a century what do we see? A few thousand thriftless, lazy semi-savages, dying of famine because they will not work! . . . Under the superior race and no where else, do they attain to the highest degree of civilization; and any experiment, whether made in the British West Indian Island, the coast of Africa, or elsewhere, will demonstrate that it is a vain thing for fanaticism, a false philanthropy, or anything else to fight against the Almighty.[41]

Lumpkin thought such efforts at emancipation would "disinherit" future generations. He urged opposition to emancipation via will. He concluded with an appeal to "disabuse" slave-owners of the older antislavery idea that they should free slaves via will. He urged slave-owners to abandon "the false and unfounded notion that slavery is sinful and that they will peril their souls if they do not disinherit their offspring by emancipating their slaves!"[42]

Somewhere between Justice Benning's outlandish views and Lumpkin was Ebenezer Starnes, who joined the Georgia Supreme Court in 1853 and served until 1855. Starnes was born in 1810 in Augusta, Georgia, and graduated with a master's degree from the University of Georgia in 1832. He was admitted to the bar shortly thereafter and served as attorney general of Georgia from 1834 to 1840. Starnes was connected to the academy as well; he served as president of the Board of Trustees of the Medical College of Georgia. Though on the court for only a short period of time, Starnes filed several concurrences in slave emancipation cases in which he aligned with Lumpkin.

In Starnes' 1854 decision of *Jim v. State*, he faced issues similar to those that Justice Ruffin faced in *State v. Mann* back in 1830. But in *Jim*, the issue was the extent of criminal liability for a slave who attacked and killed an overseer. The enslaved person Jim was being beaten by a "slender youth" and, during that punishment, Jim fought back, chased his assailant, and killed him with a blow of an axe. The question then became was Jim liable for first-degree murder or some lesser charge because he had been provoked.

This led to several revealing statements by Starnes. The first was that non-Southerners could not understand the decisions in these types of cases. Starnes wrote, just as Ruffin had in *State v. Mann*, that the decision would be incomprehensible to those outside the South. And also like Ruffin, Starnes wrote that it was his duty to issue this decision:

> The legal principles which we shall deem it necessary to assert, and some of the sentiments which we may think it expedient to utter, in this connection, may shock those who are prejudiced against the institution of slavery—who are unmindful of the causes and the means which influenced, and the men who established that institution in our country—who are blind to the difficulties in dealing with the subject, on the part of those whose interests are involved in it, and their right to deal with it for themselves, according to their consciences, and in view of the solemn responsibilities under which they rest to their Maker. But we will not shrink from our duty, nevertheless, sincerely convinced, as we are, that it is of more importance to the best interests of the master and slave, where this relation exists, that justice should be administered on the principles we lay down, than that a diseased sensibility should be propitiated.[43]

Starnes could then turn to the specific issue, which was the amount of obedience that slaves owed to their owners and overseers. "Policy and humanity, both, demand this law of submission in the slave. Where the relation of master and slave exists, obedience in the latter to the former, is absolutely necessary to the maintenance of that subordination, on which depends, not only the comfort of both master and slave, but on which rests the very existence of the institution itself, as part and parcel of the body-politic."[44] As with many of Lumpkin's opinions, Starnes turned toward the divine approval of slavery and the subordination that was an inherent part of it.

> We find it, as a part of that system of laws, in the order of God's Providence, established by our fore-fathers, which it is our duty to administer; and we are convinced, that every reasonable man must see, with us, that whilst it does exist, due subordination, on the part of the slave, is a primary necessity, to both bond and free—more of a necessity, than is subordination, in the family circle, to the head of the household.

Starnes recognized that slaves could resist punishment only if they were going to be killed. "Such subordination," he wrote, "can only be maintained by the right to give moderate correction—a right similar to that which exists in the father over his children."[45]

Starnes also brought the imagery of masters treating their slaves kindly into an opinion that upheld a will that left instructions to an heir to give three slaves "as many privileges and liberties as the laws of the State will permit negro slaves to possess or enjoy."[46] The will was challenged as an attempt to basically free three people, though Starnes did not see it that way. There was substantial evidence that the testator in fact wanted to emancipate the slaves. The will introduced that clause with the observation that Georgia prohibited emancipation and then noted parenthetically that he wished the law were different. Yet, Starnes thought the clause might simply be instructions to treat the slaves well, which fit with the common idea that owners generally treated slaves well. Starnes put this devise into a framework of kind masters treating their slaves well:

> To give the construction insisted on by the plaintiff in error to such a will as this, would be, in effect, to hold that the owner of slaves, aged and infirm it might be, to whom he was attached by the pleasant memories of childhood, by the holy emotions of gratitude for long and faithful services to himself and his family, by the ties of a life-time association, in contemplation of his dying hour, could not make, without violation of law, some provision for the purpose of saving them being subjected to the chances of coming into the hands of strangers or of hard task-masters, by bequeathing them to some friend, of such means and character as would serve to give assurance of their future kind treatment, and by requesting that such friend, whilst controlling and holding them as slaves, would extend to them such privileges and indulgence as were compatible with law. We repudiate such a doctrine.[47]

In other opinions, Starnes drew upon medieval English history to interpret a will,[48] and he also turned to moral sensibility to gauge when it was proper to overturn a jury verdict.[49] He joined in the efforts to abandon confusing and outdated precedent, to stop "wandering up and down the labyrinth of uncertainty which has been created by the English Courts," and instead to "advance into the clear light and atmosphere of our own laws and policy."[50] Starnes drew upon history and his understandings of contemporary economics and moral philosophy to justify his decisions.

One important and overlooked part of Starnes' work is an epistolary novel, *The Slaveholder Abroad, Or Billy Buck's Adventure*, which he wrote in response to *Uncle Tom's Cabin*.[51] The novel was set in the United Kingdom, where a slave owner and his slave, Billy Buck, had gone on vacation. The novel, published in 1860 by the leading Philadelphia publishing house of Lippincott, was little more than a series of stories of crimes and poverty in England, which Starnes took from English newspapers. The stories were told in the form of letters from a slaveowner home to Georgia, and they recounted the experiences the slaveowner and his slave, Billy Buck, had while traveling in England. Abolitionists tried to entice Buck away. Elsewhere, Buck saw poverty, gambling, crime, and immorality of all kinds.

Starnes dedicated the book to "Colonel Joseph Bond, who, being one of the largest slaveholders in Georgia, and among her most worthy and successful planters, yet hazarded and lost his life in the protection of his slave, by one who was to him personally a stranger." The dedication presents a turn on the "faithful slave" narrative, that is, slaves who sacrificed and died to protect their owners. This was a story of an owner who died to protect his slave. Though the story is not quite as Starnes relates in the dedication. Bond— one of the wealthiest men in America at the time—apparently argued with an overseer about an injury the overseer inflicted on one of Bond's slaves. That led to Bond striking the overseer, who responded by shooting and killing Bond.[52]

Three things stand out about *The Slaveholder Abroad*. First, it focuses on how bad life is in the United Kingdom; second, like *Uncle Tom's Cabin*, it is based largely on newspaper accounts—everything from infanticide to domestic abuse of wives and children, to harsh working conditions. An implicit message may be that newspaper accounts are unrepresentative indicators of life in the United Kingdom—or in the South. Third, the appendix reprints several of Starnes' empirical studies of the conditions of slaves in the middle judicial district of Georgia. He compared the incidence of crimes prosecuted against slaves and white people and also surveyed prominent slaveowners in Georgia about the living conditions on their plantations. Starnes surveyed governors from northern states about the amount of crime and poverty among the free black population.[53] He sought to rebut in two ways the antislavery indictment of southern society by showing that slaves were treated well while also suggesting that they needed to be controlled. The sources were biased, of course; but those were the places that pro-slavery writers sought their evidence. The appendix concluded with a quotation from Thomas Cobb's *An Inquiry* about the happy life of slaves on the Cobb plantation. This was his attempt to demonstrate empirically what Lumpkin and many others were saying: for some, slavery was superior to freedom. Starnes contributed to the empirical nature of jurisprudence, which sought to have rights and laws calibrated to the station of the people they governed.

The novel suggested that the lives of free workers were no better than the lives of slaves. In seeking to understand pro-slavery jurisprudence, Starnes' *Slaveholder Abroad* is an important statement about the ideas that motivated it and how pro-slavery jurisprudence responded to the antislavery juggernaut.

10

Pro-slavery Jurisprudence

Thomas Reade Roots Cobb's An Inquiry into
the Law of Negro Slavery

"Philosophy is the handmaid, and frequently the most successful expounder of the law. History is the groundwork and only sure basis of philosophy. To understand aright, therefore, the law of Slavery, we must not be ignorant of its history," Thomas R.R. Cobb told his readers in the first paragraph of his *An Inquiry into the Law of Negro Slavery in the United States*.[1] Cobb's 1858 book brought together data and arguments from a generation of pro-slavery thinkers. *An Inquiry* stretches to nearly 600 pages, and it opens up important insights into the world of pro-slavery thinkers, academics, and lawyers. It tells us about the understanding of history, of philosophy, and of jurisprudence at the most sophisticated levels of southern thought. It allows us to understand how the southern world view fit together, how southern views of history and contemporary society supported a pro-slavery jurisprudence. *An Inquiry* links a sophisticated understanding of culture together with law and transatlantic jurisprudence. This chapter recovers Cobb's world and the connections of university faculty to the collection and dissemination of pro-slavery thought and to jurisprudence more generally.

Cobb's world was one of wide horizons. His vantage scanned from the beginnings of recorded human history—from ancient Egypt, Greece, and Rome—through the revolution in Haiti in the late eighteenth century and the United Kingdom's recent emancipation in the West Indies, to the contemporary sufferings in industrial cities in the North, in the United Kingdom, and among the colony of emancipated slaves in Liberia. Cobb also looked to legal cases and to statutes to judge the nature of slave jurisprudence. He mixed those pieces of history and contemporary society together to depict a world of hierarchy. He applied cold legal reasoning in place of abolitionists' passionate (and thus reason-bending) sympathy for slaves. Cobb inhabited a world of legal logic. It entailed reliance on precedent and considerations of utility. The factors plugged into those considerations of utility were based on a pro-slavery understanding of history, society, and economy.

Thomas Read Roots Cobb spent the early years of his life as a devout and pious student of the religion and the rights of the South. He was born in 1823 on Cherry Hill plantation in Jefferson County, Georgia, and educated at the University of Georgia. He was admitted to the Georgia bar in 1842, then married Marion Lumpkin, the daughter of Georgia Supreme Court Justice Joseph Henry Lumpkin. Cobb used his legal training and family connections to reform law through a codification of Georgia's statutes published in 1851,[2] through service as a trustee to the University of Georgia,[3] through *An Inquiry into the Law of Negro Slavery*, by starting a female seminary, and by cofounding the Lumpkin law school in 1859, which became the University of Georgia's law school.[4] Following the election of Abraham Lincoln in 1860, Cobb was a leading voice in the November and December 1860 debate in Georgia over secession.[5] He had used the educational system and the power of print and oratory to propagate his ideas of order and slavery, along with a world view of evangelical Christianity. He then joined the Confederate states' war effort. Cobb's life ended at age thirty-nine on the battlefield at Fredericksburg in 1862, fighting for the causes he had worked to preserve and create. Because Cobb was a law reformer, law professor, treatise author, participant in the secession movement, and, at the end of his short life, a general in the Confederate army, he offers an important opportunity for seeing the world of pro-slavery legal thought, especially its emphasis on reason, expediency, and history, and how those ideas moved from the minds of lawyers and judges into public discourse and action in the form of secession and war.

The Structure of *An Inquiry*

Cobb's *An Inquiry* represents the culmination of decades of scholarship on pro-slavery thought. It pulls together religious and academic thought with legal writing and shows how the entire world of pro-slavery thought fits together. It synthesizes works of ancient and modern history and contemporary politics; it also draws heavily upon antislavery writings. It is divided into two main sections: an introduction that presents "the history of negro slavery," which runs to more than 225 pages; then the legal treatise, which runs to more than 350 pages.

Cobb outlined what he thought important about the subject in an address on the "Educational Wants of Georgia" to the alumni of Franklin College (the University of Georgia) in August 1857. At that point *An Inquiry* must have been nearly if not fully completed. Cobb worried that college moral philosophy texts declared slavery inconsistent with natural law, and thus college students were left with the sense that "but one course is left to a God-fearing and God-loving nation": "immediate, unconditional abolition."[6] Cobb outlined the appropriate response, beginning with an "appeal to history" "as to the negro race—at home—abroad–in bondage—in freedom."[7] That history would reveal the "voice of God," which tells the Anglo Saxon race "that they are the keepers of this inferior race." Cobb was characteristically bold in his conclusion about the benefits and the morality of slavery. "That the negro is advancing physically, intellectually and morally under the comparatively mild restraint of southern slavery, is an undoubted fact. Whether that advancement will ever reach the point where he may or can govern himself, is a question of the future."[8]

An Inquiry draws on several elements of American jurisprudence. It relied on history, empirical studies of the economic benefits of slavery, political theory, and the common law to describe what the law was and what it ought to be. But this proved contentious as pro-slavery thinkers were advancing their arguments about history, economics, religion, political theory, and the common law, antislavery writers advanced very different views on history, economics, religion, and political theory.[9]

Cobb was part of the tradition of scholarship, stretching back to the late eighteenth century, of understanding law in its social context.[10] Joseph Priestley's four-volume history of Western civilization understood how law interacted with its surroundings.[11] But Priestley's volumes were different from many other historical studies of its time because Priestly found in history some evidence for the progression of society and for lessons that might destabilize the present legal system. Commonly, history served as a justification of the present. William Blackstone's *Commentaries* sometimes referred to history to make the present system look normal and provide a justification for the present.[12] Jeremy Bentham, writing in 1776, believed that Blackstone found in the present "everything as it should be."[13] For many, history taught the lessons that Alexander Pope taught in the middle of the eighteenth century: "everything that is, is right." Henry Hallam's early nineteenth-century *View of the State of Europe During the Middle Ages* built upon similar evidence as Priestley but for different purposes. Hallam demonstrated the place of property in the emergence from feudalism; his vision was that the security of property rights made freedom from government possible.[14] William and Mary Professor Thomas R. Dew presented a similar interpretation of the role of property in the development of Western civilization, which drew upon Hallam, in his posthumously published lectures.[15] Cobb swept across all human history, drawing on secondary sources to create a picture of a world of hierarchy, where property rights were central to the extension of freedom.

230 THE CORE OF SOUTHERN LEGAL THOUGHT

An Inquiry, thus, owes far more to Edmund Burke's history of the French Revolution than to Priestley.[16] It owes a lot to the pro-slavery literature—often pro-slavery legal literature—that grew in the years following Nat Turner's rebellion in 1831. There was a steadily growing sense that slavery's defense rested on a series of assumptions and understandings that were not immediately obvious to non-slaveholders. And the attacks of antislavery forces were gaining momentum. While the conservative United States might not be as susceptible to abolition sentiments as the United Kingdom, Southerners witnessed many examples of emancipation in their lifetimes—from Haiti at the end of the eighteenth century to the West Indies in the 1830s. So there were growing intellectual traditions in the United States that provided the intellectual building blocks that Cobb employed. He drew together arguments employed by Thomas R. Dew's 1832 *Review of the Debates in the Virginia Legislature*, Henry Drayton's 1836 book *The South Vindicated from the Treason and Fanaticism of Abolitionists*, and James Kirke Paulding's 1836 *Slavery in the United States*, as well as more recent periodical literature like Supreme Court Justice John Campbell's essays on Roman slavery and the West Indies,[17] and the book *Negromania*, by a different John Campbell, which reprinted articles focused on "scientific" "evidence" about Africans' supposed inferiority.[18]

The structure, in which extensive discussion of history preceded law, follows several models that linked historical studies with moral philosophy with legal analysis. There was an emerging jurisprudential style of writing that linked history and empirical studies with legal doctrine. Some of this drew upon Enlightenment literature like Baron de Montesquieu's *The Spirit of the Laws*. One might even link Cobb and Thomas Paine's *Rights of Man*, though each would have recoiled at the association with the other, for those treatises draw on history in making prescriptions about law.

In the 1850s, there emerged a particularly vibrant literature on both the antislavery and pro-slavery side that linked a close study of the law with social facts. Such works of Cobb's contemporaries included antislavery books like William Goodell's *American Slave Code in Theory and Practice,* Harriet Beecher Stowe's *A Key to Uncle Tom's Cabin,* and John Cobden's *White Slaves of England.* Those works are grounded in empirical evidence, too; but they ask for changes in the law.[19] Cobb's method is empirical, but it strives to halt rather than propel reform.

The Pro-slavery Historical and Empirical Arguments in *An Inquiry*

An Inquiry allows us to peer inside a well-developed pro-slavery theory. It serves several purposes in disclosing first, the structure of the thought; second, the sources of thought; and third, how historical and empirical ideas fit together with legal ideas. In short, we can see how all these arguments fit together. Because the treatise was published in 1858, after decades of theorizing about the virtues of slavery and the lack of alternatives to it, it represents more a gauge and culmination of these ideas than the generation of them. As such, its primary virtue may be in helping us understand these ideas.

Slavery from the 1830s to the Civil War was increasingly defended by cold calculations of utility that derived from a perception of hierarchy. That hierarchy was spoken about as ordained by nature. The architecture of conservative thought ran from the modest defense of the present to the fear of the future:

- the present system is provided by nature (or God);
- free labor is not better;
- no more than modest improvements are possible; and
- change may actually make things worse.

It was a conflict between the real and the ideal.

Part of Cobb's engagement with the virtues of slavery and the evils attendant to emancipation came from the architecture of conservatism; partly, though, it was dictated by Cobb's response to the antislavery argument, which itself had turned to context-specific empirical investigations of the lives of slaves and sympathy for individual slaves.[20] In several places Cobb engaged with abolitionists. Sometimes he cited their evidence to suggest that abolition had hurt the economy in the West Indies and left everyone, including the formerly enslaved people, in a worse condition. At several other points, he responded to the antislavery legal literature, such as William Goodell's *American Slave Code in Theory and Practice*. The abolitionist legal literature itself was increasingly contextual. In the eighteenth century, the antislavery argument rested on universal truths, such as "all men are created equal." In the 1830s and 1840s, abolitionist legal literature looked to statutes supporting slavery, as Theodore Weld's *American Slavery as It Is*, which was largely based on statutes, to gauge the nature of slavery. In the 1850s, the abolitionist literature looked past statutes to the treatment of slaves as revealed in court opinions. Cobb responded to those contextualized antislavery accounts by suggesting that slaves were better off in slavery than in freedom and by saying that they were (on average) well treated and had superior lives to free workers in northern and European cities. The nature of the debate had shifted by the late 1850s to a careful focus on the context of slavery. In addition to the traditional arguments about hierarchy and about the inferiority of slaves, there was much about how slavery improved the conditions of the enslaved and how emancipation worsened those conditions.

Those are precisely the ideas Cobb employed. History provided a way of understanding the possibilities of the human race. It also made slavery look natural and even necessary. For as Cobb told readers in the introduction, slavery "has been more universal than marriage, and more permanent than liberty."[21] Slavery was more universal than marriage, because nature requires that some people labor for others, and often those laborers are so dependent that they become slaves. Right from the start, Cobb made slavery out to be a familial, patriarchal system that benefited slaves more than their owners.

The first 228 pages (styled a "Historical Sketch of Slavery") contained a history of slave societies from the ancient world, stretching from the Old Testament, Egypt, India, Mesopotamia, Greece, and Rome, to the Middle Ages and slavery in Great Britain, then to the modern world with the African slave trade, the slave trade in the British-speaking Americas, the United States, abolitionist movements in the United States, abolition in Haiti and the British West Indies, the effects of abolition in the West Indies and the United States, and concluding with colonization. The second part was a discussion of contemporary slave law, which built in some ways on that history. Much of the legal treatise was not, however, connected to the historical sketch.

The treatise also helps us understand the mindset of a leader of the secession movement—a man who argued vigorously in favor of the legality and morality, indeed necessity, of secession. He links cultural ideas about slavery with legal thought and with practical action. So we can see how Cobb put his world together: if the bonds of slavery were loosened, violence and the destruction of his world would follow. Here is the marrow of intellectual history. This treatise allows us to peer into the crevices of a mind that was at the forefront of the movement for secession. While we have been hearing for decades about the "crisis of fear" that led to the South's decision to secede upon Lincoln's election, it remains something of a mystery why given the extraordinary economic and political power of pro-slavery interests there was a movement to secede. Abolitionists referred at the time to the "slave power." That term conjured up the power of pro-slavery interests and caused abolitionists to despair of their prospects for success.[22]

Thomas Cobb's treatise begins with the Old Testament's endorsement of slavery. He turns to Egypt, where the monuments left by the ancient Egyptians testified thousands of years later to the "fact" that the slaves were black. A comparison with slavery in India suggested that other forms of slavery were worse than slavery in the United States. For one of Cobb's key themes was that slavery in the United States was consistent with biblical requirements. It was, therefore, more humane than many other slave systems. And slavery in the United States was more appropriate than other systems because the people who were in slavery were best suited for that system.

Cobb saw slavery as an appropriate way of ordering society.[23] The treatise was a demonstration of why human nature and the facts of social organization demonstrated the need for slavery. Here Cobb drew on the latest scholarship, including John Fletcher's 1852 *Studies on Slavery*[24] and Josiah Priest's *Bible Defense of Slavery*.[25] In fact, he identified a whole class of pro-slavery contemporaries, including Thomas Dew, Chancellor Harper, John Archibald Campbell, John C. Calhoun, William Gilmore Simms, and James Henry Hammond.[26] In discussion of slavery in Egypt, Cobb confronted one of the great questions of antiquity—a question that continues in the twenty-first century debates on multiculturalism: how much was Egyptian society one of black Africans? Cobb had an obvious need, as did many in the nineteenth century, to minimize the contributions of blacks to Egyptian culture. He drew on ethnographic studies, like Francis Pulszky's chapter "Iconographic Researches on Human Races and Their Art," in *Indigenous Races of the Earth,* and *Types of Mankind,* a volume edited by physician Josiah Nott and Egyptologist George Roberts Gliddon. Those studies drew upon evidence of all sorts, from tomb inscriptions in Egypt to studies of skulls to fortify their arguments about the differences between the races and to advance the case that across the millennia Africans had been enslaved. They sometimes argued that black people and white people had separate racial origins.

Cobb referred to a plate in Nott and Gliddon's *Types of Mankind,* a drawing from an Egyptian monument, which purported to show enslaved Numbians being driven before the chariot of Ramses II.[27] That page from Nott and Gliddon is reproduced in Illustration 10.1. Another monument illustration from Nott and Gliddon, which purports to be a group of enslaved African women bound together, is reproduced as Illustration 10.2.

Cobb also relied on histories of Egypt such as Francis Hawks' *Egypt and Its Monuments* and Abraham Rees' *Cyclopedia*'s entry on Egypt to create a picture of slavery that was more oppressive than the Christian slavery of the antebellum South. Some of the tomb illustrations further illustrated the harshness of slavery (though other illustrations suggested a familial, friendly slavery).[28] A second point was that both black and white were enslaved. Yet, most of the time the slave-owners had lighter complexion than the slaves, which illustrated for Cobb the naturalness of enslaving Africans. The point was that slavery had existed since the dawn of recorded time.

Short chapters on slavery in India and elsewhere in Asia further established the theme of slavery's ubiquity and cruelty. The chapter on India in particular rested heavily on legal treatises to demonstrate the extraordinary harshness of the Indian caste system, which Cobb classified as a form of slavery. The caste system also illustrated alternatives to Western slavery, which involved fewer costs to the owners. In the caste system, there was a permanent class of workers, but the costs of supporting that class were not born so directly by the master class, as in the American South. This was yet another way in which the American South's slavery was made to appear superior to that of other countries. Works by British

with the fact that the same type, during some eight or ten generations of sojourn in the United States, is still preserved, despite of
transplantation.

The following representation (Fig. 167) is traced upon a spirited
reduction by Cherubini.[309] It is a double file of Negroes and *Baràbra*
(Nubians), bound, and driven before his chariot by Ramses II., at
Aboosimbel. This picture answers well as a complement to the two

FIG. 167.

preceding; for we here have the brown *Nubian* — a dark one, and a
light-colored family—admirably contrasted with the jet-black Negro;
thus proving that the same divisions of African races existed then as
now, above the first cataract of the Nile at Syene.

FIG. 168.

One of the same series (Fig. 168), on a larger
scale, taken from Rosellini.[310] It should be observed that he is shaded *browner* than the next
head (Fig. 169); thereby showing the two com-
monest colors and physiognomical lineaments
prevalent among Nubian *Baràbra* of the present
day; who, whether owing to amalgamation, or
from original *type*, approach closer to the Negro
than do the adjacent tribes — *Ababdeh, Bisha-
riba,* &c.

The same group supplies a lighter (cinnamon) shaded sample of a
Nubian *Berberri* (Fig. 169); whose name in the Arabic plural is *Baràbra*. The identical designation, BaRaBaRa, is applied to the same
people in the sculptures of several Pharaohs of the XVIIth and
XVIIIth dynasties, 1500 years B. C.[311]

Illustration 10.1 Nott and Gliddon, *Types of Mankind*, page 250. Thomas Cobb referred
to Josiah Nott's and George Gliddon's *Types of Mankind: Or, Ethnological Researches,
Based Upon the Ancient Monuments, Paintings, Sculptures, and Crania of Races, and Upon
Their Natural, Geographical, Philological and Biblical History* (Philadelphia, Lippincott,
Grambo & Company 1854) for evidence of slavery in ancient Egypt. This illustration,
which purports to show enslaved Nubians driven before the chariot of Ramses II, is from
page 250.

NEGRO TYPES.

Fig. 172.[314]

Karmac. The Negro's features are true to the life, if we deduct the ancient defective drawing of the eye; as must be done in all copies of Egyptian art.

We next present (Fig. 173) one of the many proofs that Negro *slavery* existed in Egypt 1500 years B. C. An Egyptian scribe, colored

Fig. 173.[315]

red, registers the black slaves; of which males, females, and their children are represented; the latter even with the little tufts of wool erect upon their heads: while the leopard-skin around the first Negro's loins is grotesquely twisted so as to make the animal's tail belong to its human wearer.

In connection with this scene, which is taken from a monument at Thebes, Wilkinson remarks: —

"It is evident that both white and black slaves were employed as servants; they attended on the guests when invited to the house of their master; and from their being in the families of priests as well as of the military chiefs, we may infer that they were purchased with money, and that the right of possessing slaves was not confined to those who had taken them in war. The traffic in slaves was tolerated by the Egyptians; and it is reasonable to suppose, that many persons were engaged, as at present, in bringing them to Egypt

Illustration 10.2 Josiah Nott and George Gliddon, *Types of Mankind*, page 252, has more illustrations that purport to show enslaved Africans in Egyptian monuments.

authors on the Indian legal system were of particular use to Cobb because they testified to Cobb's attention to the legal system as a gauge of the social system. The primary work was William Adams' *The Law and Custom of Slavery in British India.* Those works reminded the reader that slavery was established in the wake of war as an alternative to killing captives taken in war. The only people who were enslaved, then, were infidel captives and their descendants.[29] Again, slavery was made to look like a humane alternative; this made slavery less objectionable, for its origins were in humanity rather than barbarism.

The chapters on slavery in Greece and Rome were longer. Greece served as a particularly apt precedent, for it demonstrated that slavery fostered republics. Aristotle and Plato both testified to the presence of hierarchy and to the virtues of slavery in creating equality among free people. Thus, Cobb invoked Plutarch's aphorism that "at Sparta the freeman is the freest of all men, and the slave the greatest of slaves."[30] Slavery was interwoven with Greek culture; it even appeared in mythology. The lengthy chapter dealt with the origin of slavery in war and piracy, as well as the lives and work of slaves in Greece; the extensive number of slaves (perhaps there were three or four times as many slaves as free people) and their close relations to their masters' families. Still, at times masters so brutalized slaves that their souls became slavish, as Plato said. There are important parallels between Plato's observation and North Carolina Justice Thomas Ruffin in *State v. Mann* that slavery had to be brutal to convince the slaves of their subordinate position.[31]

The chapter on Roman slavery interpreted slavery as a fruit of Rome's empire. Rome's spirit of conquest, its orientation toward family (particularly the power of the father), and its concern about power more generally all pointed toward the development of slavery. The head of the family could sell his children into slavery; individuals could be enslaved to pay off their debt or as punishment for a crime. Other slaves were captured during war. The social and political culture of Rome promoted slavery; so did the legal system. There was a well-developed commercial culture around slave sales; slaves came with warranties, and purchasers often had a right to rescind sales contracts if the slaves were not as promised.[32]

While slavery had existed in Great Britain under Roman domination and in the early Middle Ages, there had been a gradual transition from slavery to serfdom and then an emancipation from vassalage. The transition from slavery to serfdom came about largely because of the adoption of Christianity in Great Britain. Then followed a gradual lessening of the controls of lords over serfs. The liberation from serfdom came because of the benevolence and negligence of lords. The benevolence part involved the voluntary lessening of control, in particular by allowing vassals to specify the duties they owed their lords; the negligence part involved lords failing to enforce obligations owed them. After a certain period of time, the obligations could no longer be enforced. Other historians in the antebellum South provided the story in substantially more detail. In essence, their narrative was that serfdom ended as the system of markets and private property allowed individuals to become more independent. That picture of the role of the market in remaking hierarchy may not have fit Cobb's larger agenda, or it may have been too detailed to warrant exploration in his treatise.

More important to Cobb's argument than how slavery and feudalism ended in Great Britain was his argument—common among pro-slavery thinkers—that the current condition of the working class was no better than that of slaves. His conclusion was that "necessity and hunger are more relentless masters than the old Saxon lords."[33] Cobb relied upon a series of contemporary accounts, including John Cobden's 1853 book *White Slaves of England* (Illustration 10.3) and Charles Dickens' *Household Words*. He grimly concluded the chapter with the observation that it was not clear how the evils might be remedied. That question is "today taxing the thoughts and burdening the hearts of the wise and good of the land."[34] He thereby raised the question where true philanthropy lay.

The following chapters brought the story to the Americas and then up to the present. They dealt with "negro slavery and the slave-trade," the abolition of slavery in the northern United States, the revolution in Haiti, the emancipation in the West Indies, the contemporary abolition movement in the United States, and the colonization movement.

The New World, Cobb recognized, was central to the revitalization of the slave trade. He credited, if that is the right word, the New World with creating huge changes in slavery and acknowledged that the demand for slaves increased war in Africa, as the natives sought humans to sell to European slave traders:

> The discovery of America in 1492 was an event, the effect of which upon the civilized world can never be calculated, and perhaps is seldom fully appreciated. . . . It stimulated enterprise and discovery. It furnished a receptacle for the innumerable slaves which the African petty kings offered in exchange for the manufacture and gaudy trinkets of Europe. The demand necessarily increased the supply, and of course gave stimulus to the petty wars and marauding expeditions by which that supply was effected; and thus we might travel from cause to effect almost *ad infinitum*.[35]

Native Americans proved ill-suited to slavery. They had been accustomed to freedom and "though morally heathen and intellectually the inferior race," Cobb observed, "still the Indian was not by nature qualified and capacitated for bondage." And so first Spanish and then other European colonists settled on the idea of using African slaves as the native population plummeted in the Americas. "Like oranges, they found their proper soil in Hispaniola," Cobb quoted Antonio de

Illustration 10.3 John C. Cobden's *Whites Slaves of England*, frontispiece (Auburn, NY, Derby and Miller 1853).

Herrera y Tordesillas, "and it seemed even more natural to them than their native Guinea."[36]

Cobb emphasized the role of English merchants in the slave trade, beginning in the middle of the sixteenth century. Merchants sold some slaves in England. Many more were brought to the Americas. In the seventeenth century, slave traders received a monopoly from the Crown, which continued in various forms until near the end of the century.[37] It served Cobb's purpose to emphasize both the profit that the British made from the slave trade and their embrace of slavery more generally. He invoked abolitionist accounts of slaves in England in the seventeenth and eighteenth centuries to remind readers that antislavery sentiments were of recent vintage.

One of the phrases commonly heard in antislavery circles was that the air of Great Britain was so free that as soon as slaves set foot on it, their shackles would fall from them. Cobb at several points mocked this phrase, which was taken from Lord Mansfield's statement in the 1772 case of *Somerset v. Stewart*.[38] Cobb pointed out that Mansfield was announcing a new doctrine. During the seventeenth century, "the negro page was indispensable to the English lady on her daily walks through the city thoroughfares; and for fear 'the pure air of Britain' might engender beneath his thick skull some idea of liberty, the collar . . . was fastened round his neck, with the name and residence of his mistress neatly engraved thereon."[39]

The story then shifted to the English-speaking Americas. Here Cobb replaced the image of the orange with the image of cotton. In North America, "the negro and the cotton plant seem to be natural allies." The story was of the growth of slavery in the American South where demand for cotton and tobacco "impressed upon Virginia and Maryland the position of slaveholding States." It was the New England merchants who first embraced and profited from the trade, and it was New England where the earliest code embraced the slave trade.[40]

The most direct and fullest lessons came from more recent history. More than half of the history section was devoted to slavery since the onset of the African slave trade. There were chapters on the slave trade, which was instituted at the end of the fourteenth century, though the vast majority Cobb's discussion related to events post-Columbus. Then Cobb turned to chapters on the efforts to abolish the slave trade, the abolition of slavery in the North, in Haiti, in the British West Indies, recent abolitionist efforts in the United States, and colonization in Africa.

Cobb tried in those chapters to establish a race-based form of slavery, to distinguish it from feudalism, blame the institution of slavery on northern merchants, and to point out that Africans were suited to slavery and not freedom. When Georgia adopted slavery, it was out of necessity. "Her climate and her soil demanded negro laborers, and her resources began to be developed when this demand was supplied."[41] Slavery was a blessing to the enslaved, Cobb concluded. "The negroes thus introduced into America, were gross and stupid, lazy and superstitious. With an occasional exception of a captive warrior, they were only transferred from the slavery of a savage to that of a civilized and Christian master."[42] Some of the colonies, for example, Virginia, Maryland, and Carolina, attempted to restrict importation of slaves, but the British government profited from slave trade. Georgia prohibited importation of slaves in 1789—nearly twenty years before the British government prohibited importation.[43]

Cobb depicted English and American abolition as the result of economic interests, not moral ones. And the infamous middle passage was depicted as better than commonly reported, in part because of the economic interest that slave traders had in making sure that their human cargo survived the trip. "Experience soon taught that the consequent pestilence and decimation of his cargo, more than overbalanced his gains. Self-interest co-operated with humanity in demanding a proper regard to the health and comfort of the victims. . . . Wholesome and bountiful food was provided, as a matter of calculation for the improvement of their appearance."[44] Then once the slaves reached America, they were (supposedly) happy and treated well. Despite abolitionists' depictions of the brutality of slavery, Cobb thought the slaves' lives easy and pleasant and in keeping with God's design for them:

> The negroes thus imported were generally contented and happy. The lamentations placed in their mouths by sentimental poets, were for the most part without foundation in fact. In truth their situation when properly treated was improved by the change. Careless and mirthful by nature, they were eager to find a master when they reached the shore, and the cruel separations to which they were sometimes exposed, and which for the moment gave them excruciating agony, were forgotten at the sound of their rude musical instruments and in the midst of their noisy dances. The great Architect had framed them both physically and mentally to fill the sphere in which they were thrown, and His wisdom and mercy combined in constituting them thus suited to the degraded position they were destined to occupy. Hence, their submissiveness, their obedience, and their contentment.

When Cobb turned to the abolition of the international slave trade, particularly Great Britain's actions in 1807 that outlawed the slave trade, he focused again on the economic basis. Where Great Britain (and New England merchants) had once supported the slave trade because it was so profitable, by the early nineteenth century, the interests of merchants pointed in another direction. If the price of sugar produced in the West Indies rose, that would make sugar from the East Indies more competitive. Those economic interests, not British philanthropy, was the prime motivator behind Great Britain's abolition of the international slave trade.[45] To add to the complexity, Cobb argued that the abolition of the slave trade made the conditions on slave ships, which were operating illegally by that point, even worse.

This picture of contented and well-cared-for slaves built to a crescendo of fear when Cobb turned to the emancipations that took place in the Americas. First, there was the revolution in Haiti from 1791 to 1804. Cobb's history of the Haitian revolution describes a vicious struggle and atrocities on all sides. Haiti's history, in which many white people were slaughtered in the process of revolution, illustrates what Southerners feared. The distribution of abolitionist literature and halfway measures in Haiti provided the impetus to revolution. In fact, one speech in France in 1791 laid responsibility on the abolitionist literature distributed from Paris.[46] Haiti provided an object lesson in the course of emancipation through revolution.

Emancipation came in 1834 to the British West Indies. Instead of revolution, the change was brought about by legislation, which first converted slaves to long-term apprenticeships. Those apprenticeships were, in turn, abolished in 1838 by legislation. But the results proved little more satisfactory to Cobb. Like Thomas Carlyle, he found emancipation, whether by revolution or by legislation, a failure. He quoted from Robert Baird's *Experiences of the West Indies* about Haiti's decline into chaos following emancipation: "From 1804 downwards, the history of this unfortunate island has been little or nothing else than the history of rapine—one black rising up to contest the sovereignty with another, and filling the island with scenes of confusion and misery, which go far to prove the theory of those who maintain that the negro race is by natural incapacity unfitted for self-government."[47] The picture was grim. Haiti was "the subject of ridicule and regret, . . . a transfer of an African despotism from Ethiopia to the West Indies."[48] And the peaceful emancipation "experiment" of the British West Indies offered a picture little better.

Again, Cobb linked the legislation to local conditions—to the character of the people subject to the legislation. And, as elsewhere, he interpreted the legislation through the lens of race. "The whole secret of their failure was their utter ignorance of the negro character. The same legislation for a body of oppressed Saxons or Celts, would have been productive of blessings commensurate with the sacrifices made."[49] He placed the blame on the character of the formerly enslaved people. "Not alone in material wealth has been the decline of these once flourishing colonies. The condition of the negroes physically, intellectually, and morally, keeps pace with this downward tendency."[50] His conclusion about emancipation in the United States was little better. It was based on a survey of governors of northern states. He concluded, "the negroes are less addicted to

crime, and are more healthy and long lived, in a state of slavery than of freedom."
The citation for this proposition was "numberless authorities, combined with
personal observations."[51]

These issues came together in a chapter on contemporary slavery in the
United States, the most important of the chapters in the history section of
An Inquiry. There were increasing dangers of abolitionist fanatics who sough
to inflame public passions and dethrone reason. The results were a series of
events that seriously threatened the U.S. government, even though the *Dred
Scott* decision had declared that there was no right to prohibit slavery in the
territories.[52] Here Cobb brought together his vision of slavery in the United
States. Slaves were treated well and were improving mentally and morally
under Christian slavery. His conclusion was that slavery was, on balance,
good for the slaves and likely good for the owners. "Both politically and so-
cially negro slavery has its benefits and its evils," Cobb stated. "To the negro
himself the former greatly predominate. To the owners, the masters, the
question is a great problem, and there is more room for honest differences
of opinion."[53]

A key advantage was that slavery put all white people in an "elevated class."
Even those who owned no one were above slaves, so "the poorest meets the rich-
est as an equal; sits at his table with him; salutes him as a neighbor." This avoided
the "war of classes" seen in free labor societies, like the North, where conflicts
between "labor and capital" were frequent. The institution of slavery gave slaveowners the opportunity for leisure to study politics. The effect of slavery made
the slaveowners statesmen: "Born to command, and habituated to rule, they
frequently commend themselves to the nation by their firmness, their independence, and their fearlessness."[54] Slavery was necessary for the South; free labor,
which might strike or otherwise refuse to work, would not suffice. And even
freed slaves would not work, as was evident from the experience in the West
Indies. Quite simply, slave labor was the only kind of labor that would suffice for
the South. Whites could not and would not perform the agricultural work. In a
revealing moment, Cobb asserted that slave labor was cheaper than free labor in
the South.

Slavery also had both benefits and detriments as a social system. The benefits,
in Cobb's mind, included the familial feelings that slavery generated. It made
slaves part of the owners' family and caused owners to want to take care of slaves.
He acknowledged some disadvantages of slavery, such as it tended to make masters overbearing. Yet, there was also "a spirit of independence, which brooks no
opposition." Cobb was not sure that was evil.[55] Thus, it appeared that slavery was
on balance a blessing. Or at least emancipation would be on balance a disadvantage. Cobb's conclusion was that emancipation in the United States was impossible. Colonization in Africa, which would be extraordinarily expensive, was the

only possibility. Yet, the minimal efforts at colonization that had already been made further demonstrated the futility of emancipation. Cobb concluded with skepticism about the prospects of colonization:

> The danger is, that as the generation of emigrants becomes extinct, their descendants will relapse gradually into the heathenism and barbarism which surround them. So long as annual exportations from the United States, of the most energetic and intelligent of our free colored population continue, an appearance of activity and life will be exhibited. But to prove the capacity of the negro for a self-evolving civilization, he must be left to himself for a few generations.[56]

The final sentence of the history section captured Cobb's cynicism: "Good men and wise men differ as to the final result. I must confess my own incredulity."[57]

Cobb's Vision of Slavery as Patriarchal

An important part of Cobb's argument is that slavery is good for the enslaved. This is in contrast to many of his predecessors who defended slavery on the basis of the benefits of political freedom to white people. Many pro-slavery theorists argued, as we have seen, that slavery gave white people a uniformity of interest. That gave all white people, slaveowners and nonslaveowners alike, a common interest. That gave all white people a certain level of equality, which freed them from certain manual labor. Such a theme appeared in Cobb's treatise, but only on a few pages out of hundreds.[58] Cobb focused instead on the social rather than the political advantages of slavery. The economic advantages, as well as the political advantages, of slavery were submerged in a text that emphasized the stability of the state. So there is some important divergence from other pro-slavery writers who emphasized more the economic advantages of slavery and the emergence of liberalism. There is also—and I think this particularly important—a divergence from southern judicial opinions, which emphasized the role of slavery in promotion of economic growth.

Instead, he focused on the supposed ways that southern slavery was familial and that the enslaved were not left to the mercy of the market, as were free workers, which was a great benefit. As we have seen, many pro-slavery writers of the 1850s made a similar comparison—slaves were treated better than the free workers of northern industrial cities and the United Kingdom. For instance, one response to *Uncle Tom's Cabin* was entitled *Uncle Robin in His Cabin in Virginia and Uncle Tom Without One in Boston.*[59] However, Cobb emphasized such arguments more than other pro-slavery lawyers and pro-slavery treatises. Cobb's

predecessors such as Thomas R. Dew and Beverley Tucker—as well as South
Carolina Chancellor William Harper—emphasized different aspects.

Where Cobb's predecessors wrote of the benefits to the white community,
he wrote of the patriarchal nature of slavery and the benefits to the enslaved, as
well as the difficulties attending emancipation. One passage, reminiscent of the
plantation mythology so common in postwar literature, depicted the plantation
as a moral place, where slaves were part of the owner's family. In this way, Cobb
tried to counter the common abolitionist attack on slavery as a brutal system:

> The slave bought from the slave-ship wielded his axe side by side with his
> master in felling the forest around his rude home. He was his compan-
> ion in wild hunts through the pathless woods. A common danger made
> them defend a common home from the wild beast and the more cruel
> savage. The field cultivated by their common labor furnished to each his
> daily bread, of which they frequently partook at a common board. The
> more wealthy master lived generally in the midst of his farm. No tempt-
> ing market enticed him to forget humanity in his search for gain. The
> return of the labor of his slaves was generally in grain, consumed mostly
> in reproducing more. Even tobacco was exported but in small quanti-
> ties. Cotton was reared almost exclusively to furnish employment for
> the females in extricating the seed, and then by the flax-wheel and the
> hand-loom, in providing clothing for the slaves themselves. The culture
> of rice required but moderate labor, except at harvest. . . . With all, the
> labor was light. The master was not therefore tempted to overwork his
> slave. Even upon the score of interest it was with him more profitable to
> breed than to buy.[60]

Part of the picture was due to the familial, as opposed to the commercial, nature
that Cobb depicted on the plantations in the United States. While no one now
takes seriously the idea of the plantation family, that was a common trope among
Cobb's pro-slavery contemporaries. The image of slaves as part of the plantation
family was a common response to counter the antislavery image of the brutality
of slavery. Harriet Beecher Stowe's work, and that of other abolitionists, caused
a shift among slavery's defenders. They shifted from talk of slavery's benefits to
whites to the ways that slaves were treated better than their free counterparts.[61]
Slavery's defenders emphasized slavery's contribution to stability in the midst of
a commercial society.

This theme appears multiple times in Cobb's work, although it seems to have
had little place in his interpretation of slave law. One effect of Cobb's patriarchal
interpretation, however, was the recognition that slavery was not just a labor
system, it was also "*a social institution*."[62] That recognition led to a very important

conclusion, to which the vast majority of white Southerners subscribed, that slavery was "a part of the social system, a social necessity." That necessity explains the South's response to attacks on slavery. It was so necessary and central to society that Alexander Stephens (soon to be vice president of the Confederacy) called it in 1861 a "cornerstone" of southern society, and it needed support.[63] When it appeared under attack, the unraveling of the United States was easily predictable. A significant part of Cobb's treatise is about the ancient and recent history of slavery and how that history supports a view that slavery is necessary and natural. This is consistent with a moral philosophy that taps an organic world view of natural hierarchy; it is also consistent with a moral philosophy that supports slavery for the benefits it brings to American society. Moreover, pro-slavery law supported a sophisticated commercial law, as was discussed in the two previous chapters on Thomas Ruffin and Joseph Henry Lumpkin.

The Jurisprudence of Cobb's Treatise

What has remained hidden in Cobb's treatise is how much he—in fact, how much antebellum southern jurisprudence—owes to a set of concepts: an understanding of history and empiricism, which supports a doctrine based on utility and precedent. Cobb's jurisprudence, then, combined formalism with instrumentalism, especially with a reading of the context of slavery in society. He looked to history and philosophy to explain contemporary law of comity, then he followed it with (what is at some points rather cursory) legal analysis.

So why would someone devote so much energy to write this book? Cobb consulted dozens of sources, some written in foreign languages, others in distant libraries, others through notes taken for him by academics in northern cities. A lot of labor went into this—as in the production of any scholarship in the antebellum period. It represents an important triumph of sorts of the pro-slavery intellect, for it collects the writings and arguments and presents them with a particular advocacy framework: to understand the law of slavery.

Cobb's introduction to the treatise ("Philosophy is the handmaid, and frequently the most successful expounder of the law. History is the groundwork and only sure basis of philosophy.") alludes to the historical method of Thomas Carlyle, whose essay "On History" provides the framework for what Cobb was attempting. Cobb phrased his purpose as understanding law, for which he needed to turn first to philosophy and then to history. Carlyle began with a parallel premise, that to understand philosophy, one needed to understand history. The essay served to expand the functions and practice of history, from something that he termed the "gazetteer," to people who understand (or sought to understand, at any rate) the beliefs that motivated people.

"On History" contains a clue to Cobb's linking of history and philosophy to understand law. Carlyle was author of an important history of the French Revolution, which emphasized the breakdown of order. He also wrote *Past and Present*, which lamented the shift from beliefs and social organization to law in the shift from medieval Europe to the modern state. (*Past and Present* is generally believed to depict a shift from belief to obedience as the guiding principle of social organization). Carlyle saw history and philosophy giving a sense of what law was—though he saw law as providing only a framework around which we live our lives. The rest—what he called "the essential furniture,

> He wrote, as William and Mary professor Henry Augustine Washington had noted, that "Laws themselves, political constitutions, are not our life, but only the *house wherein our life is led*; nay, they are but the bare walls of the house." Carlyle credited the furniture of the house—what he called "; all whose essential furniture, the inventions, and traditions and daily habits that regulate and support our existence," to the "Phoenician mariners, of Italian masons, and Saxon metallurgists, of philosophers, alchemists, prophets and all the long train of artists and artisans; who, from the first, have been jointly teaching us how to think and how to act, how to rule our spiritual and our physical nature."[64]

Legal historians have been echoing that admonition ever since, with varying degrees of success. Novelist Ralph Ellison, author of *Invisible Man*, echoed it, for instance, in the wake of the civil rights revolution of the 1950s and 1960s. In looking back on American history in 1976, he recalled that "the law ensures the conditions, the stage upon which we act. The rest of it is up to the individual."[65] Cobb's *An Inquiry* makes a similar interpretation: its most interesting part is the study of history and contemporary society, which explains why the law is as it is. It is an understanding grounded in experience; reason flows from that experience and is closely tied to it.

Carlyle was an appropriate model for Cobb for another reason as well. Carlyle was a prominent opponent of emancipation. In 1850 he published a semi-satirical account of the effects of emancipation in the British West Indies (which took place in 1838). Carlyle's account, which purported to be the report of a philanthropic society for the elimination of pain, depicted a failed economy, in which lazy freed slaves worked only enough to raise a few pumpkins to eat, extorted extraordinary wages from white sugar cane farmers, and then sat by while sugar cane rotted in the fields, unharvested.[66] It was to "fact and nature" that Carlyle claimed to turn for evidence about the wisdom of emancipation. "It was not Black Quashee, or those he represents, that made those West India islands what they are." It was the white European who reclaimed the land from the jungle. The riches of "cinnamon, sugar, coffee, pepper, black and gray" were lying asleep, waiting for the "white Enchanter" to awaken them and bring forth the riches of the Indies.[67] His claim was that it was the Europeans who made the islands what they were (to which John Stuart Mill had an apt retort: the slaves gave more to the whites who enslaved them than the whites who enslaved them gave to the slaves).

He pointed out that efforts were being made to compel white workers to labor in Europe and believed that the freed slaves had to be compelled to work. The mission was to find some kind of practical law that would fit the conditions in the West Indies. It was, as Carlyle recognized, a difficult problem, which required attention to surrounding circumstances of human nature. Such a law needed to take account of "relations the Eternal Maker *has* established between these two creatures [black and white] of His: what he has written down, with intricate but ineffaceable record, legible to candid human insight, in the respective qualities, strengths, necessities and capabilities of each of the two."[68] Carlyle thought the sources of a solution to the problem lay in human nature and in the continual remaking of law in light of new experience. One solution might be in the state's right to compel labor. There was even a name for the right to compel labor, "*adscripti glebae*." The freed slaves would become serfs who were bound to the land. Carlyle's idea was that they would labor for a fixed period of time for the state.[69]

John Stuart Mill wrote "The Negro Question" in response to Carlyle's "Occasional Discourse on the Negro Question." He labeled Carlyle's argument the "work of the devil."[70] Mill asked why it was so important to have the state compel labor. The exchange was a classic contrast between those like Carlyle who took account of the interests of the empire, the state, and the property owners and those like Mill who took account of the workers.

Many came down on Carlyle's side. His account captured the essence of conservative thought about emancipation and echoed what many others were writing. In 1849 Parliament issued a report about economic conditions in the West Indies critical of emancipation, and pro-slavery Americans turned to that pessimistic picture to argue against emancipation. Those Americans included Alabama lawyer (and later U.S. Supreme Court Justice) John Archibald Campbell. Later Cobb explored in detail this thesis, drawing in part upon Campbell's work. Cobb does not cite Carlyle's essay "On the Negro Question," though its insight was in wide circulation by the time *An Inquiry* was published. He does cite two of Carlyle's book, *Past and Present* and *Chartism*, in discussion of the burden of poverty in the United Kingdom.[71]

Cobb's Legal Theory

Cobb's book also contributed to jurisprudence by emphasizing historical analysis, empiricism, and legal reasoning over sentiment. Cobb, like Carlyle, is in dialog with abolitionists, and he looks at the great sweep of human history. Cobb then links this historically grounded, pragmatic picture to specific legal doctrine. Once we get beyond the cultural functions of slavery—how it preserves stability, a modern and premodern concept, of course—Cobb links his history and philosophy with legal doctrine. In the treatise portion, Cobb reveals a legal theory that is based very heavily on precedent. In many instances, he cites no reason for the rules he announces, only cases favoring the result. Precedent is its own answer. In other cases, he provides precedent with some supplemental reasons. For instance, state courts differed over whether slaves who had been freed by a court were entitled to compensation for their time as slaves. One suspects that Cobb was not in favor of such suits. Indeed, he offers some justification for not allowing suits for back wages: the nature of the benefits provided to slaves may have been sufficient compensation.[72] We can see his concern for precedent and for the pillars of slavery as established fact in three settings: in his extended discussion of slavery in natural law, in his treatment of evidence given by slaves, and in his treatment of the exclusion of slave testimony.

Slavery's Foundation in Natural Law

The first chapter of the legal section of *An Inquiry*, entitled "What Is Slavery, and Its Foundation in Natural Law," transitions from the historical sketch of slavery to the doctrine discussed in the remaining legal section. That transition chapter builds on the historical sketch by dealing in depth with the ways that slavery appears in history and how philosophers have treated slavery; it also prefaces much of the legal discussion because it explores how slavery is consistent with natural law.

Cobb needed to take on the common argument that slavery is inconsistent with natural law. From the eighteenth century onward, in Great Britain and the United States, many had seen slavery as inconsistent with natural law. Hence, courts demanded some evidence of positive law to support slavery. They often found that positive law, but the argument put pro-slavery forces at a disadvantage. So Cobb, like other pro-slavery writers of the late 1850s, maintained that slavery was, in fact, consistent with natural law.[73] He made that argument in several ways. He showed the difficultly of determining a fixed meaning of natural law by showing the conflicting beliefs about what was natural. (Hobbes thought war the natural condition of humans, whereas Montesquieu thought peace was.) This led him to adopt a definition that was contingent on historical circumstances. Natural law included some sense of what was natural to humans, and those natural conditions seemed to vary according to race, climate, and history.[74] Natural law, then, was concerned with utility under the circumstances as they existed in a particular location. It imposed an obligation "to attain the greatest happiness and arrive at the greatest perfection" possible given human nature.[75] Thus, there was not one answer regarding slavery's status under natural law: "slavery may be utterly inconsistent with the law of nature when applied to one race of men, and yet be perfectly consistent with the nature of others."[76] For Cobb, then, it made sense for the ancient Greeks (who he thought superior to their neighbors and thus entitled to impose slavery), whereas for the ancient Britons, slavery was a mere accident of birth. For those ancient Britons, slavery was inconsistent with natural law. Given the examination in the historical sketch, Cobb was poised to justify slavery because it best promoted the interests of the enslaved.

> [I]f the physical, intellectual, and moral development of the African race are promoted by a state of slavery, and their happiness secured to a greater extent than if left at liberty, then their enslavement is consistent with the law of nature, and violative of none of its provisions. Is the negro's own happiness thereby best promoted? Is he therein most useful to his fellow-man? Is he thereby more surely led to the discharge of his duty to God? These, as we have seen, are the great objects of the law of nature, "God, our neighbor, and ourselves."[77]

It was a pretty simple calculus, really. It rested on historical and scientific "knowledge" to argue for the inferiority of slaves. That part of the calculus did not look at the value of slavery to southern whites; however, other parts of the treatise recognized that slavery was indispensable to southern society.[78]

Somerset v. Stewart and Comity

The essence of Cobb's theory is that "the law deals with men and things as they are."[79] Cobb's argument that African slavery is consistent with natural law has an important concrete application in his treatise, in his attack on Lord Mansfield's 1772 opinion in *Somerset v. Stewart*. That case involved a slave who was owned by a British merchant, who traveled to Great Britain with the merchant. The slave then sued and won his freedom.

Since the time of *Somerset*, the issue of slaves' status while temporarily on free soil engaged significant attention among judges and the public. Cobb aimed to show that Lord Mansfield's decision was limited, that it did not represent the law at the time; that it was an emotional, rather than a legal opinion; and that is had subsequently been rejected ... or misinterpreted. International law required comity to other nations (or to other states), and rejection of comity invoked the specter of much worse harm—the destruction of the United States.

Following the critique of *Somerset*, a significant part of the legal treatise dealt with slaves who are in interstate (or international) transit and spend at least some time in a free state. Those opinions often relied upon *Somerset*. It was natural to both try to undermine that decision and to undermine other bases for those decisions. Cobb reasoned to a result from major premises regarding international law. In addition to showing that slavery was consistent with natural law (and therefore there should be no preference for freedom under *Somerset*), Cobb also argued from the centrality of slavery that there should be substantial comity for the laws of places where slavery was legal.[80] Cobb further extended the doctrine of comity from the U.S. Constitution. He grounded the doctrine in the need for peace and the conclusion that whatever injures one state injures the Union.[81]

Cobb saw the common law as something that should be emotionless, and it should be freed in particular from the abolitionists' passions for slaves. He praised, for instance, the dissenting opinion of Justice Clark Bissell of the Connecticut Supreme Court (and later a professor at Yale) in the 1838 case of *Jackson v. Bulloch*, which sought to apply comity to keep a slave in transit through the state in slavery.[82] Cobb praised Justice Bissell, who professed his opposition to slavery, for "boldly" arriving at the conclusions "to which principle and law guided him." That is, Bissell wrote that he had to follow the law rather than his internal moral compass.[83]

Cobb engaged explicitly with leading anti-slavery advocates, including William Goodell and Granville Sharp. His point was to make out of the storehouse of antislavery writing the case for slavery. Part of that involved demonstrating that New England merchants were, like many others, partly to blame for slavery in the Americas. "The enterprise of New England was not tardy in availing itself of the prospect for gain, held out in the cheap labor of negro slaves, and the rich returns of the slave-trade."[84]

Where Goodell and Stowe and other abolitionists turn to the facts of cases, Cobb looks to institutions, to statutes, and to the social facts surrounding slavery. He explains slavery as a social fact and as necessary. The minute details mattered not so much as meta-history, which looked to the large-scale causes of slavery and its effects. "The labor of the slave is only valuable where that labor can be applied to a routine of business which requires no reflection or judgment upon the part of the laborer, and which continues throughout the year."[85] Cobb offered occasional first-person testimony about the familial and benign nature of slavery. For instance, he noted that on his father's plantation there lived "an aged negro woman" who had more than 100 lineal descendants. "She did no labor for my father for more than forty years before her death."[86]

Slave Testimony

Cobb's vision of a patriarchal and familial system of slavery is in some tension with the market. While he points out certain places where the market furthered the development of slavery (for instance it fostered the transatlantic slave trade), he justifies slavery in large part on the basis of the good it does for the slaves by putting them in the care of Christian masters.[87] Even within his consideration of slaves' personal aspects—like the prohibition on their testimony—Cobb considers ways to maintain control over the slaves. The patriarchal image leads to further control and limitation. That control and limitation lead to the extraction of labor at the lowest cost and to a stable labor supply, which were key to the sugar market. So far from seeing Cobb as at odds with the market, his treatise often worked in conjunction with the market.

He defended the exclusion of slave testimony on several grounds. First, slave testimony was universally excluded by slave societies; second, slaves were notorious liars. Finally, slave testimony would work many injustices by putting the slaves in control of the administration of law. Cobb acknowledged that abolitionists had robustly criticized southern courts for excluding slave testimony and also acknowledged that the exclusion was, in some cases, an injustice. But he believed there would be more injustice by allowing slave testimony. Perhaps, he conceded, testimony could be taken in cases of mistreatment if there were ample safeguards regarding its veracity.[88]

Cobb, thus, brought together a lot of pro-slavery arguments, from the historical and religious arguments, to the focus on the supposed benefits for the enslaved, to the focus on the economic centrality of slavery and the attack on the sentimental affection for enslaved people. He amplified and brought into the legal sphere the arguments that Dew made about the ubiquity of slavery in history; he brought empiricism about the effects of emancipation on slave owners to a more sophisticated level; he applied additional focus on the supposed benefits of slavery for the enslaved. As he presented slavery as better for the enslaved than freedom, Cobb advocated hard-nosed reasoning based on the economic value of slave labor. He opposed the sentimental reasoning that had led judges to declare that slavery was inconsistent with natural law and to free slaves traveling in free states. This was a prime example of the cold legal logic and considerations of utility that Harriet Beecher Stowe and other antislavery writers had critiqued.

Cobb was not merely a compiler of pro-slavery arguments, however. *An Inquiry* also marked a shift in American jurisprudence, which joined the empirical and historical arguments to inform and sometimes change legal doctrine. These new treatises were emerging in both pro-slavery and antislavery circles. Some antislavery treatises drew upon empirical evidence to support an antislavery law, such as William Goodell's *American Slave Code in Theory and Practice* and Harriet Beecher Stowe's *A Key to Uncle Tom's Cabin*. There were also pro-slavery books like George Sawyer's *Southern Institutes*, which appeared the same year as Cobb's *An Inquiry* and made many of the same kinds of historical and empirical arguments as Cobb, though it was not nearly so comprehensive.[89] The treatises both pro-slavery and antislavery signaled the shift of jurisprudence toward historical and empirical analysis.[90]

Reading Cobb

Cobb was not just a signal of the changes in how Southerners defended slavery or in jurisprudence, however. People were reading and using his treatise. For instance, Mercer University President John L. Dagg relied on *An Inquiry* for his discussion of slavery in his 1860 textbook *The Elements of Moral Science*.[91] Judges, too, used *An Inquiry*. Between the publication of *An Inquiry* and the end of Civil War, "Cobb on Slavery," as judges referred to it, was cited more than twenty times by courts.

The most common citation was for the proposition that marriages between slaves were not legally binding, which continued to have importance even after the war.[92] In other instances, it was used to deny enforcement of contracts that slaves entered.[93] In one Alabama case during the war, Cobb was cited for the proposition that a person who appeared white was presumed free and someone who appeared black was presumed a slave. The case dealt with a claim that a riverboat had given passage to a slave and helped him escape. The riverboat's owner claimed the man appeared to be white and, thus, free.[94] The court concluded the riverboat's owner was not liable.[95]

At other times, courts used Cobb for fine points, such as criminal legislation must specifically refer to slaves to be applicable to them. In one case the Florida Supreme Court refused to apply a statute criminalizing gambling against a slave. After invoking Cobb, the court gave a succinct statement about the importance of keeping prosecutions of slaves out of common law courts and keeping the punishments in the local justice of the peace courts or in private before their owners.[96] On that same issue, the Mississippi Court of Errors and Appeals cited Cobb repeatedly in a short opinion that reversed a conviction of a slave for sexually assaulting another slave. Mississippi's general statute against sexual assault did not encompass slaves who assaulted other slaves.[97] Cobb noted that some courts found that the power of the master over the slave was absolute, but he concluded that homicide—a master killing a slave—was criminal, though lesser punishments might not be.[98]

In several cases, courts relied upon Cobb to address the limitations on the power of owners to emancipate their slaves[99] Justice Carruthers of the Tennessee Supreme Court (and a former professor of law at Cumberland law school) distinguished Cobb and allowed a slave to sue over rights granted in a will.[100] In one case at the beginning of the Civil War, *Creswell's Executor v. Walker*, Justice Walker of the Alabama Supreme Court took issue with Cobb's statement that Alabama precedent made it too difficult to emancipate slaves. Cobb thought that Alabama's 1852 case *Carroll v. Brumby* restricted emancipation too much when the Alabama Supreme Court ruled that slaves could not choose whether to stay in slavery or be transported to Africa. Their owner had given them that choice in his will.[101] Yet, in spite of that criticism, the Alabama Supreme Court continued to follow *Carroll* in *Creswell's Executor*. Where Tennessee found Cobb too proslavery, Alabama found Cobb too moderate.[102]

Cobb had planned on producing another volume, which he promised would consider the property aspects of slavery. He never produced that second volume. It is unclear if he even started on it, for there are no remnants of it in his surviving papers. That missing volume is unfortunate, for we do not know the extent of Cobb's market orientation. Perhaps he did not produce the second volume because those aspects did not interest him so much; he was more interested in historical and philosophical issues than fine doctrinal issues. Moreover, his patriarchal vision was better suited to talk of slaves' character than their role as property. But this we do know: Cobb was a smart man, who read his opponents and his intellectual companions. The interpretation he produced, biased though we now see it to be, was persuasive with his peers in the South. His treatise stands as both the capstone of southern thinking and a condensation of it. Cobb's ideas were powerful and were echoes of the ideas of Georgia justices in the 1850s. His treatise and his ideas of history, racial inferiority, and slavery appeared at the center of *Mitchell v. Wells*, a Mississippi case that adopted an extreme vision of the breadth of slavery, its support in natural law, and the deprivation of rights of slaves to receive freedom or property. *Wells* is part of the story of southern judicial ideas about slavery in the 1850s, so it appears in the next chapter. Cobb himself appeared again on the stage of action in 1861 and 1862, and so he will appear again at the end of this volume in the discussion of secession.

11

"The dictate of a wise policy"

Judicial Opposition to Freedom

Like other intellectuals in the old South, including academics and politicians, judges drew on common ideas of history, economics, and moral philosophy as they decided cases. They weighed considerations of precedent, utility, duty, sentiment, even sometimes humanity. The last three chapters depicted how a few judges and one academic combined economic and moral thought in their jurisprudence. The trajectory of judicial and social thought in the South from the beginning of the nineteenth century to the Civil War was from grand Enlightenment generalities about freedom to pro-slavery ideas. It was propelled by a series of events, including the Haitian revolution in the late eighteenth and early nineteenth centuries, the Missouri Compromise over slavery in the territories in 1820, Denmark Vesey's supposed conspiracy in Charleston in 1822, Nat Turner's rebellion in 1831, and the 1835 campaign by abolitionists to use the U.S. mail to distribute what Southerners identified as incendiary literature. The reality of the economics of slavery mixed with other ideas, borne of the era of Romanticism, which looked to historical context and contemporary social facts, rather than grand Enlightenment truths. White Southerners moved, for reasons big and small, from the belief that all people are created equal to a sense there was a sliding scale of freedom. That sliding scale gave racial groups and nations only the freedom that they were entitled to, calibrated to their history. The southern moral philosophy was backward looking. It made rights turn on a pessimistic reading of what had happened in the past, not on what was possible. It looked to history and to contemporary economics to define rights. Africans were less capable of handling freedom, and therefore less entitled to it, so the common thinking among Southerners went. This political theory was perfectly suited to the needs of the South since the labor of slaves was desperately needed.

That reasoning based on historical contextual and economic reality swept the field in the South in the years leading to the Civil War. Politicians and judges drew on a common well of ideas about utility and slavery. Yet, judges were often rather sparse in their discussions about the utilitarian framework that they employed, so we have turned to the writings of academics who were expansive in describing the contours of southern thought. Professors Thomas Dew of William and Mary and Albert Taylor Bledsoe of the University of Virginia, and lawyer and law professor Thomas R. R. Cobb of Georgia wrote treatises regarding the idea that enslaved people were not fit to govern themselves. They drew upon accounts of the history of slavery and of the results of the Haitian revolution and the emancipation in the British West Indies to argue that enslaved people should be kept in slavery for economic reasons. They employed utilitarian arguments to advance the cause of slavery. Those stories supported a pro-slavery law as well.

Two of the most famous utilitarian philosophers, Jeremy Bentham and John Stuart Mill, were both staunch opponents of slavery. So it is natural to associate utilitarian thinking with antislavery. But the calculation of whether slavery created more harm than good turned on who was making up the equation and what factors they included. Southern academics and judges frequently wrote that slavery was, on balance, a blessing to them and to the slaves. South Carolina Chancellor William Harper, one of the most important authors in the defense of slavery in the 1830s, acknowledged the differences between utility as he and other Southerners employed it and the idea of utilitarianism as commonly employed:

> If we should refer to the common moral sense of mankind, as determined by their conduct in all ages and countries, for a standard of morality, it would seem to be in favor of Slavery. The will of God, as determined by utility, would be an infallible standard, if we had an unerring measure of utility. The utilitarian philosophy, as it is commonly understood, referring only to the animal wants and employments, and physical condition of man is utterly false and degrading. If a sufficiently extended definition be given to utility, so as to include every thing that may be a source of enjoyment or suffering, it is for the most part useless.[1]

Yet the move to a pro-slavery law was not immediate and there were considerations other than pure utility, for law has a structure that judges are expected to follow. That structure included following the precedents established by previous judges. Often the pro-slavery nature of law limited the options of judges who wanted to act against the law. That was the problem confronting the fictional Judge Clayton in Stowe's *Dred: A Tale of the Great Dismal Swamp*.[2] But it was not limited to fiction. Many antislavery judges confronted the problem of the constraints of law on their conscience. For the central tendency of southern law was toward promotion of slavery.

This chapter turns to two areas of law, the rules governing emancipation of slaves via wills and the rules governing the slaves who traveled in free states to illustrate how precedent worked in conjunction with considerations of utility. In both these areas there was evolution in doctrine, which tended to entrench slavery from the 1820s to the Civil War. Thus, it became harder for owners to emancipate slaves from the 1820s to the 1860s, and it became harder for slaves who had been brought temporarily from a slave state to a free state to claim freedom. In both cases the evolution of doctrine occurred in conjunction with the growing literature on the importance of slavery. Because both Justices Thomas Ruffin and Joseph Henry Lumpkin dealt with cases on emancipation via will, we have already talked some about the growing restrictions on owners emancipating their slaves. This chapter looks more broadly at the contours of the law of emancipation across the South. The steady restrictions on the rights of owners to emancipate their slaves—and thus the restraint on how owners used their property—reveals the increasingly strenuous defense of slavery in the South. It thus links the public and academic talk of slavery with the judiciary. The chapter then turns to the problem of slaves who for some reason were brought to a free state temporarily. Often they accompanied their owners on visits to a free state. While in the 1820s such slaves were usually considered free, by the 1850s the result was usually different.[3] The most famous slavery case in U.S. history, *Dred Scott v. Sandford*, arose when Dred Scott and his family claimed their freedom based on the time they had spent in what they thought was free territory.[4] The opinion represents the culmination of pro-slavery thought and reflects the ideas of history, white supremacy, economics, and the law's support for slavery that Southerners had been developing for decades.

The Shifting Law of Emancipation via Will

In the early Republic, freedom was on the march. Northern states were abolishing slavery, and, in the South, legislatures were loosening the restrictions on emancipation, too. In 1782 the Virginia legislature passed a general emancipation statute that allowed owners to free their slaves.[5] The Virginia courts embraced the statute and the sentiment behind it and construed it broadly. In 1799 the Virginia Court of Appeals upheld the 1777 will of Quaker slave owner John Pleasants. His will ordered that his slaves be given the option of freedom when they reached age thirty if it was legal at that point—or later if it became legal afterward.[6] In the meantime the slaves would be given to Pleasants' heirs while the slaves waited for the legislature to act. Though slaves could not be given freedom via will when Pleasants wrote his will, he looked forward to the time when the legislature would allow it. That is precisely what happened in

1782. At that point, Robert Pleasants, who was the executor of John Pleasants' estate, sought to free the slaves.

John's heirs, who would continue to hold the slaves if they were not freed, objected to Robert's efforts to free them. One objection was that the provision for freedom created an invalid perpetuity. Because it was unclear at the time Pleasants died when, if ever, the condition for freedom would be satisfied, the heirs maintained that the contingency to free the slaves was invalid. Their argument relied on an obscure and confusing part of property law that invalidates "perpetuities." The rule—now known as the rule against perpetuities—invalidates grants of property that are subject to some uncertainty for a very long period. The idea is that it should be clear what will happen to property. The Pleasants heirs claimed that the freedom provision in the will violated the rule because it was unclear if the Virginia legislature would ever permit emancipation. Thus, the heirs would have, perhaps for even centuries, an uncertainty of whether they would lose the slaves they inherited from John Pleasants. However, the Virginia Court of Appeals concluded the contingency in John Pleasants' will did not violate the rule. The court interpreted the will as offering contingent freedom only to slaves who were alive at the time of will. Thus, either the slaves who were alive and known to Pleasants would get their freedom or they would die without freedom. The Virginia Court of Appeals' creative reading of the will upheld the gift and set a course for further emancipations.[7] Justice Spencer Roane, who wrote one of three opinions in the case, thus, did not need to address whether the state's policy in favor of liberty trumped the rule against perpetuities. But Roane hinted that the legislature's policy might trump the rule when he observed that since the era of the Revolution the legislature had a preference for freedom and that such sentiments were dear "to every friend of liberty and the human race."[8] Sixty years later the rhetoric among judges and other leaders of Virginia society was dramatically different.

By 1806 perhaps 10,000 people had been freed pursuant to the 1782 Act.[9] The prevalence of freed people in the state led the Virginia legislature to contemplate further restrictions on emancipation.[10] In 1806 it required that freed people leave the state within twelve months of their emancipation.[11] After this, emancipations were much more limited.[12] This was the story in the rest of the South, too. The legislatures could not abide people occupying a middle ground between slavery and freedom; there had to be free white people and enslaved black people. When the enslaved became free, they threatened the continued stability of the South's slave society. For the enslaved might look around and ask why they, too, could not be free?[13]

After the 1806 Act emancipations decreased dramatically, but sometimes testators still wanted to free slaves. They met the terms of the statute by providing for the slaves to be taken out of the state and freed. Sometimes owners also gave their enslaved property the choice to stay in the state in slavery or leave and be free. By the 1850s even giving a choice to slaves had become controversial; that gave too much autonomy to the slaves to direct their own future, according to some courts. The Virginia Court of Appeals, for instance, constricted the rights of owners to give choices to slaves whether to live in freedom outside the state or in slavery inside it. In 1858 in *Bailey v. Poindexter's Executor*,[14] the court refused to give effect to a provision in John L. Poindexter's 1835 will that allowed slaves to choose freedom outside the state or to be sold in the state. The court effectively adopted the position of counsel for the heirs who argued that "the slave has no civil rights and no legal capacity whatever."[15] *Bailey* represents a dramatically different approach to the law of freedom and slavery from *Pleasants*. Where *Pleasants* found a legislative preference for freedom, *Bailey* marked the idea that slaves had no rights and could not be given any by the state or their owners.

In the early nineteenth century as judges and legislatures were moving away from the idea of freedom, sometimes pro-slavery judges confronted fragments of the Enlightenment's legacy of antislavery law. One important example comes from the common law rules that permitted slave owners to free their slaves. By following such rules some judges were who pro-slavery issued antislavery opinions. One such jurist was Justice John Catron of the Tennessee Supreme Court.[16] No one thinks that John Catron was antislavery; he wrote a zealously pro-slavery concurrence in *Dred Scott* in 1857.[17] But before Catron was on the U.S. Supreme Court, he was a judge in Tennessee. He wrote in *Fisher's Negroes v. Dabbs*, a case of a master who died in 1827 leaving a will that emancipated some of his slaves, that the slave is "a degraded outcast, and his fancied freedom a delusion."[18] The legislature had passed an act in 1831, after Fisher died, to take jurisdiction away from the Tennessee courts in these kinds of cases by prohibiting slaves from suing for their freedom. Yet, in that same case where Catron wrote disparagingly of the folly of emancipation, he upheld the claim that Fisher's slaves should be freed. Why would Catron uphold the emancipation? And what does that say about the nature of law in the 1830s? He did that because he was charged with following the law, which at the time Fisher died allowed an owner to emancipate his slaves. Moreover, the subsequent attempt by the Tennessee legislature to close the courts to slaves was a violation of the Tennessee constitution. The decision represented little threat to slavery in Tennessee, but it is a sign of the ways that even pro-slavery judges might issue decisions that might benefit slaves.[19] Fisher had wanted them to remain in Tennessee, but Catron imposed an additional requirement—that they migrate to Liberia.[20]

Other judges who were antislavery took advantage of the opportunity to bend the law at the margins. We have already dealt some with North Carolina Justice William Gaston's efforts in *State v. Will* to subject masters to the constraints of law when they attacked slaves.[21]

Even before he went on the bench, Gaston had advised Quaker clients how to avoid the North Carolina restrictions on freeing slaves As far back as 1818 he set up a trust for a Quaker meeting to hold slaves in quasi-slavery. The slaves would have an owner, as required by North Carolina law, but the Quakers would allow the enslaved people substantial autonomy. This arrangement was challenged by heirs of William Dickenson, the man who gave the slaves to the Quaker meeting. Dickenson's heirs wanted to invalidate the gift and thus retain the slaves as part of his estate. Dickenson's son got possession of the slaves and refused to return them to the Quaker Society. When the Quakers asked for the slaves back, the local court refused to order them returned to the Quaker meeting. The challenge went to the North Carolina Supreme Court in 1827. There Gaston argued that the fact that the Quakers were not requiring slaves to work as slaves was irrelevant. "No man is obliged to make a profit of his slaves; if they roam about they may be hired out, and the owner is liable for them civiliy, but his is not obliged to make a profit out of them," he told the court.[22]

Actually, the North Carolina Supreme Court concluded that owners *are* obliged to make money out of slaves or at least not hold them in essential freedom. The court wrote, "If that law could be eluded by transferring slaves to this Society, there is no foreseeing to what extent the mischief might be carried."[23] The court feared such arrangements would lead slaves to dissatisfaction and perhaps rebellion. "Numerous collections of slaves, having nothing but the name, and working for their own benefit, in the view and under the continual observation of others who are compelled to labour for their owners, would naturally excite in the latter, discontent with their condition, encourage idleness and disobedience, and lead possibly in the course of human events to the most calamitous of all contests, a bellum servile."[24]

With increasing frequency, pro-slavery judges applied and constructed a law that limited the rights of owners to free their slaves. As we saw in Chapter 9, Georgia, under Justice Joseph Henry Lumpkin, moved toward restrictions on emancipation.[25] And then Lumpkin pointed out that loosening slavery's bond through emancipation by individual owners tended to undermine it everywhere. Justice Lumpkin thought that slaves should not be free because this led to insubordination by slaves in the state. This was a case where a judge's pro-slavery sentiments worked to create a pro-slavery law:

> I am fully persuaded that the best interests of the slave, as well as a stern public policy, resulting from the whole frame-work of our social system, imperatively demand that all post mortem manumission of slaves should be absolutely and entirely prohibited. Slavery is a cherished institution in Georgia—founded in the Constitution and laws

of the United States; in her own Constitution and laws, and guarded, protected and defended by the whole spirit of her legislation; approved by her people; intimately interwoven with her present and permanent prosperity.[26]

Lumpkin wanted to restrict the owner's rights to dispose of property via will. He acknowledged that it was impossible to restrain an owner from freeing slaves during his or her lifetime if they took their slaves to a free state; however, Lumpkin did not want to allow emancipations via will. Ideas that emancipation would benefit slaves were "false and fatal views of humanity." For emancipation led to further mischief. "Is not every exode of slaves from the interior to the seaboard, thence to be transported to a land of freedom, productive of evil," he asked. "Are there not now in our midst large gangs of slaves who expected emancipation by the will of their owners, and who believe they have been unjustly deprived of the boon? Are such likely to be good servants? On the contrary, are they not likely to sow the seeds of insubordination, perhaps of revolt, amongst the slaves in their neighborhood?"[27] The increasingly pro-slavery doctrine reflects the ideas of legislators and jurists toward protection of slavery and the idea that even gradual emancipation is dangerous. Such evidence of increasing pro-slavery action in courts confirms the picture that there was an increasingly strident pro-slavery doctrine.[28]

Much of this changed because state legislatures acted to prohibit emancipation via will and then judges in states like Alabama and Mississippi opted to interpret their states' legislation in pro-slavery ways. In 1842, for instance, in *Trotter v. Blocker*, the Alabama Supreme Court prohibited emancipation by will when it applied a recent statute limiting emancipation. Chief Justice Henry W. Collier also concluded that restraints on emancipation by will were "the dictate of a wise policy." He thought the policy wise because the state policy protected the institution of slavery:

As a measure of expediency, the State owes it to its citizens at large, to protect their interest, by throwing suitable guards around the institution of slavery. If emancipation were allowed, at the mere volition of the master, consequences, disastrous to the quiet of the country would likely result,—the public would be burthened with the charge of more paupers than it would be convenient to support, and slaves, themselves, would be turned loose upon society, who either from age, or the want of it, could not provide the comforts, or even the necessaries of life. And last, though not least, the demoralizing tendency of such a policy would be such as should induce every christian and philanthropist to deprecate its toleration.[29]

A decade later, in 1852 in *Atwood's Heirs v. Beck*, the Alabama Supreme Court faced a more difficult question: whether a will requiring the executor to take slaves out of the state and free them was valid. Frederick Beck, who had addressed the University of Alabama's Erosophic Society as a student in 1835, was the executor of the estate and he wanted to send the slaves to Ohio and emancipate them. Here the court faced the seemingly contrary precedent of *Trotter*, but it parsed the facts differently. Chief Justice Chilton surveyed much precedent. He noted the special attention the legislature had given slaves. "This general power which the master has over the slave, both in respect to his treatment and manumission, has been controlled and guarded by legislative checks, prompted alike by humanity for the slave and security for the State." After commenting on the right of lords to emancipate their villains in medieval England and parsing a series of conflicting precedents in other southern states, the court upheld the will. For it reasoned that an owner might take the slaves out of the state himself. Hence, an order in a will to an executor to take the slaves from the state and then free them was merely an exercise of the owner's preexisting right.

Atwood's Heirs was followed in *Abercrombie v. Abercrombie*, in which a testator instructed a trustee to "trea[t] them with humanity according to the position they occupy in society, and see that they are not imposed upon by others" until the youngest of the children reached age twenty-one, then to emancipate them in Alabama if it were legal or to take them outside the state for emancipation.[30]

Abercrombie is of particular interest because in that case Justice George Goldthwaite upheld what might very well have been a trust for quasi-freedom, that is, a trust to hold slaves for their own benefit rather than as slaves. He did so by acknowledging that the trust might be for a prohibited purpose but found insufficient evidence for that. Moreover, he acknowledged the moral duty to treat slaves humanely. Hence, the law took its direction in some ways from ideas of morality, in that it approved a suspicious trust on the ground that the patent terms of the trust were consistent with the dictates of morality. However, Justice Goldthwaite cited no source for his statement that "[i]t is the moral, if not the legal duty, of every master or owner, to observe towards his slaves the same general course of conduct, which the testator in these directions prescribed; and this being the case, we cannot say that there is anything illegal in them."[31] In fact, Goldthwaite cited only one case—the North Carolina opinion in *Washington v. Blunt*, which nominally rejected a trust for quasi-freedom, but upheld a provision of a trust the allowed enslaved people to choose to live in continued slavery or freedom. Perhaps Goldthwaite is yet another justice who subtly worked to shape an antislavery law, even in that zealously pro-slavery jurisdiction.[32]

On the eve of the Civil War, the Alabama Supreme Court similarly rejected efforts of testators to emancipate slaves.[33] In a short opinion in *Carroll v. Brumby*,

Justice Dargan narrowly construed a will in which the testator had offered slaves a choice of freedom and transportation outside the state or continued servitude for his daughter. The testator in *Carroll* offered the slaves a choice of being transported to Liberia where they would be freed or staying in slavery in Alabama; the Alabama Supreme Court found that the slaves did not have the legal capacity to make that choice. The testators' intestate heirs claimed that the slaves were not entitled to make such a choice and that, therefore, the entire provision failed and that the slaves should be part of the testator's intestate estate. The court rejected that extreme position and also the possibility of emancipation and left the slaves to the devisee, the testator's daughter.[34]

At its January 1861 term, the Alabama Supreme Court again rejected an attempt to give slaves the option of obtaining freedom by leaving the state. The court once again upheld *Carroll*, even as it realized that the majority of precedent from slaveholding states permitted slaves to choose whether to be freed and transported to another state or remain in slavery in their home state.[35] The Alabama court acknowledged that Thomas R. R. Cobb's treatise on slavery criticized *Carroll*.[36] Yet, the court reaffirmed the distinction it had previously drawn between holding slaves liable for criminal acts and permitting them authority to decide their fate. The issue was "can a master, by his will, clothe his slaves with the irrevocable power of determining and changing, by an uncontrollable act of their will, their own civil *status*?"[37] The court held no. It distinguished between civil acts (for which slaves were not considered persons—or as we might phrase it now, citizens) and criminal acts, for which slaves had liability. The court also distinguished cases where slaves were responsible as the agents of their masters.[38] It starkly concluded, "[b]ecause they are *slaves*, they are not necessarily, and, so long as they remain slaves, incurably, incapable of performing civil acts; and, in reference to too all such, they are *things*, not persons."[39] Or, in words reminiscent of Harriet Beecher Stowe's original subtitle for *Uncle Tom's Cabin*, "the man that was a thing," the court said, "in respect of civil rights and legal capacity to perform acts of a civil nature, the slave is not a person, but a thing."[40] Because the slaves could not be consulted to determine what should happen under the trust, the trust could not be completed and the trust failed.[41]

Probably the fullest advance of pro-slavery legal principles appeared in 1859 in the Mississippi Court of Errors and Appeals' expansive decision in *Mitchell v. Wells*.[42] The court faced a question about whether a Mississippi resident who took a slave to Ohio and freed her (she was also his daughter) could leave her property in his will. The Mississippi courts and legislature had for decades struggled to reach an understanding of just how restrictive the state should be when owners tried to free their slaves. In 1838 in *Hinds v. Brazealle* the Mississippi High Court of Errors and Appeals struck down Hinds' attempted emancipation of his child and the child's mother. Hinds had taken the pair to Ohio and executed a deed of emancipation there; his mistake was then bringing them back with him to Mississippi, where they lived until Hinds died. Although his will left the child his entire estate, Hinds' other relatives protested that the child was not free, but property of the estate, that Hinds could not leave property to him in his will, and that therefore the white relatives—not the child—were the rightful heirs of the property.[43] The Mississippi court agreed with this. It was an inauspicious precedent for those who wanted owners to be able to free their property via will in Mississippi. For it put the Hinds' family in slavery to his intestate heirs, his blood relatives.

But in a series of cases in the 1840s the Mississippi courts generally upheld emancipations as long as the will provided that the slaves were taken out of the state. In 1840 *Ross v. Vertner* upheld a will ordering that slaves be taken out of the state and freed.[44] Shortly afterward, in 1842, the legislature passed a statute prohibiting owners from freeing slaves in their wills, even if the slaves were taken outside the state.[45] That statute was interpreted narrowly in *Wade v. American Colonization Society*. The court upheld the will of a testator who died before the 1842 statute that prohibited testators from ordering that their slaves be taken out of state and freed.[46] Even for wills drafted after the Act, the Mississippi High Court of Errors and Appeals still construed the law narrowly. When the court invalidated a bequest of slaves to the American Colonization Society, it allowed another heir named in the will to take the slaves who were supposed to be free even though there were suspicions that the other heir might free the slaves. The court did not look into such allegations further.[47] "The design of the Act ... was not to interfere unnecessarily with the great and sacred right of testamentary disposition."[48] But attitudes were changing in the pro-slavery direction in Mississippi and they came to a focal point in *Mitchell v. Wells*.

That case dealt with similar issues to *Hinds v. Brezealle*. In October 1846 Edward Wells took a slave, Nancy (who also happened to be his daughter), to Cincinnati and liberated her according to Ohio law. Nancy Wells stayed for nearly two years in Ohio then returned to Mississippi in 1848, shortly before her father died. She stayed in Mississippi a few more years but in 1851 moved back to Ohio, and subsequently she sought the money her father had left her in his will. Edward Wells' executor refused to recognize Nancy as a free person. This set up the question whether a person who was once a slave in Mississippi could ever inherit property from a Mississippi resident. There was no question of putting Nancy Wells back in slavery, for at the time of the lawsuit she lived in Ohio; the only question was whether she could inherit from her father's estate.

Mitchell's question of whether a former slave, who no longer lived in Mississippi, could inherit property in Mississippi might seem like an inconsequential matter. Few people would be taken outside the state and freed and even fewer would be devised property by the will of a Mississippi resident. However, for Justice William L. Harris this became a vehicle for a lengthy opinion that brought together policy arguments about "the security of our institutions and the safety of our people."[49] Harris saw the case as promoting emancipation and as potentially recognizing the Ohio emancipation that he saw as inconsistent with Mississippi law. Harris framed the case as a test of comity, the respect that one state (or nation) gives to the laws (or judicial decisions) of another. This became a conflict between Ohio's act of emancipation and Mississippi law. The issue was whether Mississippi should recognize Ohio's act and allow one of its former slaves to receive property. Harris believed Nancy Wells should not inherit.

Harris constructed *Mitchell* around the idea that Mississippi would not allow slaves to be taken outside the state and freed. Once a slave in Mississippi, always a slave. Harris' lengthy and zealously pro-slavery opinion is remarkable for the breadth of pro-slavery judicial arguments just before secession. It is also revealing for how much Thomas Cobb's *An Inquiry into the Law of Negro Slavery*, which was published the year before *Mitchell v. Wells*, helped promote pro-slavery arguments. Harris seems to have drawn upon Cobb in many ways. For instance, Harris asked rhetorically, how courts might determine what is in the public's interest. "[A]re we to be guided by the nature and character of our institutions; our Constitution and form of government; their nature, character, and whole history; the manners, customs, and habits of our people; our climate, soil, and productions; the resolutions and public acts of her conventions and general assemblies, as sources of evidence indicating public policy?"[50] The answer, as with Cobb, was that history, manners, customs, and habits were all important. They all pointed toward slavery and against recognizing Ohio's actions.

Harris reasoned based on his reading of history, and on Mississippi's constitutional history and its statutes that the policy of the state was to restrict emancipation. He looked back to the framing of the federal constitution to support his belief the African race was in an "inferior, subordinate, subjugated condition. . . . They were so regarded then by all the States united, and because thus incapable of freedom or of self-government, and unfit by their nature and constitution to become citizens and equal associates with the white race in this family of States, they were rejected, and treated and acknowledged in the Constitution as slaves."[51] Mississippi entered the United States on the principle of white supremacy. It was "to be associated on terms of political equality, comity, or courtesy with the white race, who alone by that compact had a right to be thus associated." Slavery was recognized by Mississippi at the time it entered the United States. Mississippi "came into the Union with this institution, not only sanctioned, provided for, and protected by her own Constitution, by the direct act and recognition of the other States of the Union, and by the express provisions of that same Constitution which had originally excluded the African race from the privileges of citizenship, but with a right to full protection, under that instrument, both for the enjoyment of her property in slaves, and against the degradation of political companionship, association, and equality with them in the future." Slavery was a matter of economics and society. It was, indeed, the foundation of the state. For Mississippi's "climate, soil, and productions, and the pursuits of her people, their habits, manners, and opinions, all . . . require slave labor."[52] Many legislators in Mississippi in the 1830s were concerned with prohibiting importation of slaves into the state because they feared—so Harris wrote—that border states would sell their slaves to Mississippi and then, once they had lowered their slave population, would turn against slavery.[53]

In addition to the federal Constitution and the Mississippi constitution and statutes that together established the policy in favor of slavery in Mississippi, Harris turned to Thomas Cobb's *An Inquiry into the Law of Negro Slavery* for the argument that slavery was consistent with natural law, so that wherever the slave went a law of slavery went with him.[54] Despite some suggestions that slavery ended when a slave traveled to a jurisdiction where there was no positive law of slavery, the comity owed toward the slave's home state dictated that slavery continue. That is, while a slave visited a place where there was no law of slavery, the municipal law of the slave's home continued in force in the new state. This was one of Cobb's most creative and controversial arguments.

Harris also cited Cobb's *Inquiry* to show that comity did not require Mississippi to give effect to an attempted emancipation in Ohio.[55] For comity required mutual respect and mutual interest and there was little of either between Mississippi and Ohio at that point:

> The State of Ohio, forgetful of her constitutional obligations to the whole race, and afflicted with a negro-mania, which inclines her to descend, rather than elevate herself in the scale of humanity, chooses to take to her embrace, as citizens, the neglected race, who by common consent of the States united, were regarded, at the formation of our government, as an inferior caste, incapable of the blessings of free government, and occupying, in the order of nature, an intermediate state between the irrational animal and the white man.

It was not a question that Mississippi failed to grant comity to Ohio's emancipation action, but that Ohio was trying to undermine Mississippi in Harris' mind. Ohio's actions threatened the stability of slavery in Mississippi.

The most outlandish part of the opinion was a query at the end whether Mississippi would be expected to grant comity to Ohio if it granted citizenship rights to orangutans. "[A]re we to be told that 'comity' will require of the States not thus demented, to forget their own policy and self-respect, and lower their own citizens and institutions in the scale of being, to meet the necessities of the mongrel race thus attempted to be introduced into the family of sisters in this confederacy?"[56] Harris revealed a robust defense of slavery in Mississippi and disdain for the ideas of freedom in Ohio. Certainly Harris had those views independent of Cobb's *An Inquiry into the Law of Negro Slavery*, but Cobb helped give shape and legitimacy to the resistance to Ohio's emancipation. The ideas developed by southern academics worked in conjunction with those of southern politicians and jurists. Harris *Mitchell v. Wells* opinion reflects the anger and the entitlement felt by southern jurists and the slave-owning class. There were other paths that one might have taken. There was a dissent in *Mitchell v. Wells* by Justice Alexander H. Handy and the next year Justice John Belton O'Neall of South Carolina concluded that a former slave of South Carolina could inherit through the will of a South Carolinian.[57] But Justice Harris opinion illustrates well the centrality of constitutional rights to slavery and property and the ideas of white supremacy that helped steer the South toward secession.

Although, there were a number of cases in which judges who proclaimed pro-slavery sentiment issued opinions that freed people. In addition to the series of *Cleland v. Waters* opinions and *Sanders v. Ward*, consider two opinions from 1860. First, there is *Willis v. Jolliffee*, decided by South Carolina Justice John Belton O'Neall, which upheld a devise to take the testator's family (who were also his property) to Ohio and free them. O'Neall upheld the devise, even over a vigorous dissent, which likened him to an abolitionist.[58] The dissent invoked Irish abolitionist John Philpot Curran's oration about slavery and put it into the mouth of O'Neall. The dissent closed with Curran's statement about universal emancipation:

> The first moment a slaves touches the sacred soil of Britain [or Ohio] the alter and the god sink together in the dust; his soul walks abroad in her own majesty; his body swells beyond the measure of his chains that burst from around him; and he stands redeemed, regenerated, and disenthralled by the irresistible genius of universal emancipation.[59]

Second, there is *Phebe v. Quillen*, where Justice Hulbert F. Fairchild of the Arkansas Supreme Court interpreted an 1859 statute that prohibited emancipation as a prospective statute only. Thus, the court upheld a will executed before the statute that provided for the transportation of the testator's slaves to a free state seven years after the testator's death.[60] Fairchild understood that some wanted an interpretation in favor of freedom and others in favor of slavery, and he suspected there was reason to fear that pro-slavery sentiment might bend the law, even against poor white people. "[T]he great reaction in public sentiment in the southern States, relative to the emancipation of slaves, may produce a habit of construction so stringent as to endanger the even balance which should ever be extended to the rich and the poor, the white and the black, the free and the slave." Unfortunately, that provocative statement contained little explanation, although Justice Fairchild expressed the common pro-slavery idea that slaves were better off in a state of slavery than freedom.[61]

The Shifting Law of Emancipation by Travel in a Free State

The most famous case to endorse pro-slavery thought was the U.S. Supreme Court's 1857 decision in *Dred Scott v. Sandford*. It dealt with the question whether enslaved human beings became free if their owners took them to free jurisdictions. Once that was the law in many jurisdictions. It had been so in Missouri from time out of mind, so it came as something of a surprise when the Missouri Supreme Court ruled in 1852 that a slave, Dred Scott, who sued for his freedom with the claim that his owner had taken him to a free territory was still a slave.[62]

That set in motion an appeal to the U.S. Supreme Court, which gave the court the opportunity to make formal constitutional law what had for many years been only the constitutional theorizing of southern politicians like South Carolina Senator John C. Calhoun. Chief Justice Roger B. Taney's majority opinion in *Dred Scott* did at least two important things. First, it took away the right of citizenship, effectively silencing slaves in federal court. It did that by ruling that slaves were not entitled to citizenship.[63] Taney constitutionalized ideas that had been circulating in pro-slavery thought for decades when he ruled that people of African descent were inferior and that they were not entitled to U.S. citizenship. That limited their ability to sue in federal court. Taney wrote that Africans had been seen for decades "as beings of an inferior order, and altogether unfit to associate with the white race either in social or political relations, and so far inferior that they had no rights which the white man was bound to respect." The result of such thinking was, according to Taney, "that the negro might justly and lawfully be reduced to slavery for his benefit."[64] (Justice John Catron of Tennessee turned this doctrine into the broad statement that "[w]hereever a master may go within the United States, his slave is entitled to accompany him."[65])

Second, Taney's opinion also addressed the power of Congress to legislate for the territories. One part of the Missouri Compromise in 1820 prohibited slavery in the United States' territories north of Missouri's southern border.[66] If slavery was indeed illegal there, then presumably the Scott family's time in the territory of Upper Louisiana (what is now Minnesota) would make them free. But here Taney drew upon the idea popularized by Senator John C. Calhoun beginning in the 1830s: the Constitution protected slavery and Congress could do nothing that discriminated against slavery. Thus, Congress could not exclude slavery from the territories.[67] In Taney's phrasing, the United States has "the duty of promoting the interests of the whole people of the Union." Congress could not discriminate against slavery as a form of property. "No word can be found in the Constitution which gives Congress a greater power over slavery property" that any other kind of property. Thus Congress could not prohibit slavery in the territories.This took away the argument that Dred Scott had been freed by residence in a free territory. In fact, slavery had been legal in all the United States' territories despite the Missouri Compromise. Both of Taney's key points—that people of African descent could not be citizens and that Congress could not take action against property in slavery—were key elements of southern constitutional thinking. Slaves were incapable of exercising political rights and so should not have them. And the denial of citizenship silenced enslaved people. It wrote the southern belief that enslaved people were inferior and did not deserve rights into law. Moreover, it also wrote into formal constitutional law the southern belief that the Constitution recognized slavery and that the federal government could not act against it. These were the constitutional principles that went along with the understanding of history and moral philosophy that Southerners had been building for decades. The opinion incorporated the substance of southern thinking about slavery and federalism. It was a high watermark of southern constitutional thought in the Supreme Court. The process by which those ideas were made popular and introduced to the state courts and then brought to the Supreme Court is an important one, which has been told by many different people.[68] The opinion legitimized such thinking. It was cited numerous times before the Civil War, from Thomas Cobb's *Inquiry into the Law of Negro Slavery* to cases like *Mitchell v. Wells* in Mississippi to justify the deprivation of rights to enslaved people and to shore up support for the idea that slavery is constitutionally protected.[69]

One piece of this story that has not been told is how Associate Justice John Archibald Campbell employed a southern version of the history of slavery in his concurring opinion. That small story serves as a capstone to this volume, for Campbell was both a historian of slavery and slave law and a jurist. He wrote at least five articles on slave law before ascending to the U.S. Supreme Court in 1853. Thus, Campbell presents a direct link between southern understandings of history and slave law.

John Archibald Campbell was born in Georgia in 1804 and educated at Franklin College (now the University of Georgia), beginning at age eleven; he graduated at about age fifteen, then attended the United States Military Academy. He returned home in 1829, a year before he was to graduate, and read law. He was admitted to the bar in 1830, following study with Georgia's former governor, John Clarke.[70] Campbell moved to Montgomery, Alabama, and married

Anna Ester Goldthwaite, whose brothers George and Henry were prominent lawyers. Both brothers later served on the Alabama Supreme Court; their roots in New England (the family was from New Hampshire, though several of the Goldthwaites were born in Boston) may account for their somewhat more moderate approach to slavery than many judges in Alabama.[71] Campbell served in the legislature from 1836 to 1839. He moved to Mobile in 1839, then returned to the legislature in 1843. By the early 1850s, Campbell was a prominent Supreme Court advocate, had written articles on slavery and its constitutional protection in the United States, and had served at the Nashville Convention in 1850. Campbell also gave a number of speeches, including a funeral oration for his friend John C. Calhoun and addresses to the literary societies at both the University of Georgia and the University of Alabama.[72]

The first of Campbell's articles, "Slavery in the United States," appeared in July 1847 in the *Southern Literary Quarterly*. It was a lengthy, general synopsis of pro-slavery ideas that he would later explore in more depth in various pieces. There were the common arguments about the ubiquity of slavery in human history, that then turned to the history of the antislavery movement. It also established a theme that appeared in much of Campbell's later writings, the importance of slavery in the constitutional convention. He discussed the Haitian revolution and the decline in productivity in both Haiti and the British West Indies in the aftermath of emancipation in those places. His conclusion, so similar to that of other southern politicians, was that the South's protection would come—if at all—through a robust defense of the Constitution.[73]

That 1847 article invited more detailed attention to a number of issues, which Campbell provided, beginning the next year with an article "Slavery among the Romans."[74] It rebutted the abolitionist proposition that the slavery of the Bible was more humane than American slavery. Campbell emphasized the property aspect of Roman slavery and suggested that slavery always involved suffering. This is perhaps an odd argument. Instead of suggesting that American slavery was familial and benign, here Campbell made ancient slavery look harsh, though he still thought slavery more benign than the alternative, which was death following a war of conquest. Slavery, which had been recognized from the days of Plato to Christ, could not be ended until there was a replacement for the labor.[75] Later Roman history likewise showed that emancipation was a failure.[76] Such lessons had direct applicability to the United States.[77]

The next article in the series, on the emancipation in the "British West India Islands," appeared in 1850. It returned to a topic discussed in the first article in 1847, that is, about the problems with the labor supply in the wake of emancipation in 1833. The focus was on the decrease in supply of labor and its accompanying dramatic increase in cost of labor. The misguided philanthropy of abolition had been a financial disaster for British interests.[78] The former slaves' only appearance in this story was as people who would not work; Campbell took no account of the value of freedom, other than as something that allowed them to stop working. "The substantial benefit to the savage," Campbell thought about slavery, "consists in securing providence, care and protection of the white man over his person and interests." Freedom robbed the slaves of that benefit.[79] His grim conclusion was a warning to the South of what lay ahead. He had traced the effects of emancipation so "that our people might see in advance the end of which we now see the beginning."[80]

The final piece of Campbell's survey of the history of slavery was "Slavery Throughout the World," published in April 1851. It took up the theme of slavery's role in the evolution of society. Campbell theorized that every society starts in barbarism and then progresses, partly through the market, to a state where it can end slavery. When societies at a more advanced level clashed with those at a less advanced level, the more advanced enslaved the less advanced and then helped those enslaved people to rise, sometimes to the point where slavery could be ended. It was a theory tailor-made to support southern slavery. And while it suggested that African slavery might end at some point, Campbell held out no hope for that occurring anytime soon. In his mind, emancipation had been a failure in the West Indies, and it would be a failure in the United States. Slavery ended in Europe, but only after a millennium of progress. The lesson for Southerners was that they could not let northern abolitionists have a say in slavery. Southerners needed "absolute control over the whole subject."[81]

The most direct application of Campbell's historical ideas to the Constitution came in an article published in January 1851 and written in response to Campbell's participation in the Nashville Convention 1850, where southern states had sent representatives to help plan their next steps in the defense of slavery and debate their continued adherence to the United States. His essay, "The Rights of Slave States," returned to the framing era to demonstrate the pro-slavery nature of the Constitution. In fact, the protection given to states to regulate slavery was a cornerstone of the Constitution.[82] Campbell was building on several decades of constitutional theorizing by southern politicians, most notably John C. Calhoun, which rested on a belief in the equality of the states under the Constitution. The idea was that Congress could not act in a way that discriminated against states; in the context of slavery, this meant that it could not exclude slavery from the territories, nor from the District of Columbia. Perhaps it could not even regulate slavery through the Interstate Commerce Clause, though not all the boundaries of the equality of the states doctrine were tested before the Supreme Court. Campbell traced the widening gulf between North and South on issues of federalism, particularly in the wake of the South Carolina effort to nullify the federal tariff on the products of slave labor in the early 1830s.[83] That gulf widened further in the wake of the Nat Turner rebellion as northern antislavery societies, inspired by the Virginia legislature in Campbell's opinion, increased their agitation. Leaders like former president John Quincy Adams attacked slavery in the 1830s; by the late 1840s, abolitionists were pushing the Wilmot Proviso, which would foreclose slavery from the territory acquired in the Mexican-American War.[84] Campbell worried about the provision of the Compromise of 1850 that relinquished Texas' claim to New Mexico and then made slavery there dependent on what the settlers in New Mexico wanted. This "place[d] slavery at the mercy of its enemies, by the abdication of the government of its duties to the slaveholder. His property would then become a prey to rapacity or fanaticism."[85] In fact, the abolitionists were fanatics in Campbell's mind. They were "cut loose . . . from civil and ecclesiastical societies—denouncing governments and churches, without restraint."[86] Such refusal to compromise was a sign of their fanaticism and also an indictment of the practical in morals. Though Campbell, too, was opposed to compromise. He wanted to retreat to constitutional defenses, like the doctrine of the equality of the states, which had been a mainstay of the Nashville Convention of 1850. What the South needed was simple but bold: "The recognition of slavery, as an institution of property, in the States, entitled to the same rank, privilege and protection as every other institution of property."[87] The South was in danger, for the commercial and social interactions, coupled with the "revolutionary and innovating spirit of the times," led to the fanaticism Campbell saw everywhere.[88] The attacks struck deep; "they go to the foundation of our institutions," Campbell wrote, "and involve the existence of our social fabric."[89]

Campbell believed the situation quite dire. He used an odd analogy of the abolitionists to the American Revolution. One might not have thought that a pro-slavery advocate would compare the American Revolutionaries in any way to the abolitionists, but he hazarded one comparison. The Revolutionaries brought down the throne, "rooted for eight centuries," through efforts "hardly more concentrated and powerful than are employed against" the institution of slavery.[90] With what was perhaps an oblique allusion to Hobbes, Campbell noted that "fanaticism is short, direct, and thorough in its methods." The end of slavery seemed imminent in Campbell's mind. His solution was coordinated action by the slaveholding states.[91]

Soon, as a member of the Supreme Court, which he joined in March 1853, Campbell had a chance to take concerted action to establish the southern constitutional vision of equality of the states.[92] While on the Supreme Court, Campbell filed ninety opinions, including a concurrence in *Dred Scott*. Campbell concurred with Chief Justice Taney's lengthy opinion that denied Dred Scott was a citizen—and thus effectively silenced him in federal court—and also held that the equality of the states prevented Congress from legislating for the territories. Campbell's opinion has received relatively little attention despite all the scholarly attention on *Dred Scott*.[93] In part that is because it is something of a scholarly opinion, which goes back to early modern French law, among many other places, to explore the status of enslaved people who moved through free territory. The opinion wanders, in ways that do not seem entirely coherent, across centuries of precedent, including the *Somerset v. Stewart* case before settling on the principle of Lord Stovall's opinion in the *Slave Grace*. It held that a slave who returned from a free jurisdiction to the slave jurisdiction of Antigua became a slave once again.[94] Such a doctrine fit well with the idea that law, like other pieces of culture, should be adapted to its surroundings. In fact, Campbell articulated this in the opinion. "That there is a difference in the systems of States which recognize and which do not recognize the institution of slavery, cannot be disguised. Constitutional law, punitive law, police, domestic economy, industrial pursuits, and amusements, the modes of thinking and of belief of the population of the respective communities all show the profound influence exerted upon society by this single arrangement."[95]

Campbell returned to history for two purposes. First, to show that slavery was an important part of England's history, and second to argue that during the Revolution and the framing of the Constitution states had not ceded all of their power to the federal government. Campbell drew on the Americans' Revolutionary era arguments that there were limitations on the British Parliament's rights to legislate for the American colonies. That reservoir of power that was retained in the colonies and then the states was further confirmed by the Ninth and Tenth Amendments to the Constitution.

In 1859, two years after *Dred Scott*, Campbell spoke again at a university. This time he delivered an address, "The Institutions, Duties, and Relations of Alabama" to the University of Alabama. Campbell discussed the moral and political philosophy reflected in the Constitution. He surveyed centuries of history leading to the Constitution and found in that history "a statement of the causes and conditions which have aroused and invigorated the human conscience and intellect for five centuries."[96] The history of the Reformation demonstrated, to Campbell's reading, that "there exists an order of truths which are immutable, not subject to the control of government or society, but to which the State in its corporate capacity, as well as its members, owe obedience."[97] The problem became, how could a state preserve those truths (of which personal liberty was a critical part)? Here Campbell turned the lessons of history into a defense of the present. He praised England for its steady traditions. The English have "none of that presumption and pride that is displayed in rejecting the lessons of experience, the counsels and acts of ancestors, and they steadily refused to divide the life of their country by abandoning their old and seeking at large for new laws, institutions, and habits." It was the Revolution that established the principles that Campbell most supported: "that political power exists of right in the entire society, and that government derives its sanction from the consent of the governed."[98] Those principles appeared in the American Revolution, which was a sober return to original principles, rather than a radical break from England, and in the subsequent Constitution. The Constitution and the Northwest Ordinance, followed by local acts such as the Alabama constitution, established the principles of a government based in Christianity; subjection of the individual to the good of the whole; education and such other values as

> [e]nlarged commerce, intelligent industry, facilities of communication, wealth to promote the progress of science and liberal arts and to relieve indigence and penury, liberal and just legislation and efficient and vigorous execution of the laws, under the influence of a wise and regulated opinion of a religious, moral, and educated people. . . . In such a well-educated and well-regulated society, legislation would be benign.[99]

Campbell's legal theory was that in a well-functioning society, legislation merely confirms and gently pushes morality in the right direction. Thus, legislation springs from and must be in line with the prevailing sentiments of the community:

> Authority is then scarcely felt, so naturally and spontaneously do the members of society perform their appropriate functions; and when employed, it is to bring the members of society into closer union, by the gentle stimulants of law, literature, industry, and intercourse. Legislation then only consecrates as law the duties that have their sanction in the public conscience; . . . and justice, as pronounced by citizens selected temporarily to distribute it without aid from the insignia or array of power, is executed through the reverent sentiment for the sovereignty and majesty of law, in a self-governed, virtuous community.

In order to preserve the state, there must be "old customs, familiar household sympathies, the habits of subordination and obedience, the community of thought and opinion, the centres of worship" that hold the country together. Campbell supported the Union because he thought that it supported those connections. He found in the Constitution a further support for Union. The lecture allows us to see how a Supreme Court justice saw law as supporting and working in conjunction with the community's sentiments and for the support of order against change.

Campbell and other judges drew their ideas from the surrounding culture and contributed to it. They had done what they could to put into formal law many of the principles of jurisprudence that had been expanded by southern intellectuals. These principles were utility; and looking to history, religion, economy, and precedent to find a law that fit with the needs and station of southern states. Gone were the grand and universal principles of the Enlightenment. In its place were principles of empiricism that molded the law to local circumstances, which looked pessimistically to the ways that law needed to control other human beings and looked to the limitations of humans, which proclaimed their inability to handle freedom. This new jurisprudence developed a law based on the needs of the slave-owning class. The world of the slaveholding intellectuals was complex in some ways, transparently simple in others. One common principle was that the law was a piece of culture, partly a product of it, partly a creator of it. "Law" meant many things, including statutes, customs, and decisions of judges. Law fit together in harmony with other parts of culture, including the manners of the people and their institutions. As Southerners struggled to maintain control of their world, as they realized that the day of reckoning was coming, law was a central instrument in the attempt to maintain control.

Yet, an alternative world was gaining strength. It appealed to the sentiments on behalf of slaves; it sought to measure law in some terms other than utility. And soon it would be triumphant. Abraham Lincoln's first inaugural address in 1861 appealed to sentiments—like "the better angels of our nature"—on behalf of the Union. Sentiment was, indeed, a powerful motivating force—as moral philosophers like Brown University President Francis Wayland, legislators like Daniel Webster, and novelists like Harriet Beecher Stowe all realized. Lincoln's first inaugural appealed to the "national fabric, with all its benefits, its memories, and its hopes" and the "mystic chords of memory, stretching from every battle-field and patriot grave to every living heart and hearthstone."[100] Lincoln was, like his contemporaries, attuned to the power of sentiment; he sought to harness it for the purpose of maintaining the Union. The jurisprudence of sentiment and ideas of free labor were on the march, and southern slave owners were feeling increasingly isolated. They sensed that the days of slavery were drawing to a close. Yet, they told themselves that the Constitution protected slavery and that slavery was the basis for southern society. They could not imagine a world without slavery, and they were prepared to take action to protect it. The constellation of ideas of utility, history, religion, and economy that had been so carefully marshaled by southern intellectuals provided the framework for their thinking as they debated secession. In fact, the days of slavery *were* drawing to a close—because its adherents were so sure they were right that they advocated secession and then war.

Slavery, Property, and Constitutionalism in the Secession Debates

In March 1861 forty-year-old James Holcombe, then a law professor at the University of Virginia, urged the Virginia legislature to secede immediately. Holcombe was an activist-scholar. In addition to his academic duties, he was a member of the legislature, and he sought to put into practice his ideas about the Constitution's protection for slavery. He knew that Lincoln's election posed grave dangers to southern slavery. He opened his speech with the image of a ship in the North Atlantic threatened by icebergs:

> Who can recall the feelings of a landsman, unfamiliar with the terrors of the sea, overtaken by a night of storm and danger in the midst of the Atlantic, the ship pitching upon the waves, the fog too dense to be pierced by any human eye, the shrill tones of the alarm pipe sounding every moment in his ears, and more fearful by far, than wave, or mist, or blast, the rapid fall of the barometer indicating the close proximity of that most appalling because most irresistible enemy of the sailor, the tremendous iceberg, by whose fatal contact the most powerful vessel may be dashed to pieces in an instant.... We, sir, are tossing upon the surges of revolution; clouds and darkness cover our future track; an unerring moral instinct warns us of approaching collision between repulsive masses, in whose awful shock all that we love and value may perish.[1]

Holcombe was, of course, correct about the dangers; the war spelled the end of his world and a new birth of freedom for our nation, as four million human beings who had entered the war as slaves left it as free people. Our nation's journey toward freedom was shamefully long and was by no means complete at the end of the Civil War. But we had triumphed over the ideas that Holcombe wanted to protect.

Why, though, would Holcombe, who recognized those dangers to his society, opt for war? The South had so much of what it wanted. It controlled the Supreme Court. The *Dred Scott* decision just four years before established the constitutional principle that slavery would be protected robustly. Its implications were many. Congress could do nothing to hinder slavery in the territories or in the states or probably Washington, DC. There was more wealth in human beings than in any other kind of property than land. The South had disproportionate voting power because of the Constitution's three-fifth's compromise. Even if, as many people believed, slavery would not flourish in the territories, it was solidly protected in the Constitution and by voters in southern states. In some places in the West, slavery continued to do well. The California Supreme Court had protected property rights in slaves in 1852 in an opinion that presaged the reasoning of the *Dred Scott* decision.[2] Why go to war? The short answer was slavery was central to southern society and needed to be protected.

> The institution of slavery is so indissolubly interwoven with the whole framework of society in a large portion of our State, and constitutes so immense an element of material wealth and political power to the whole Commonwealth that its subversion through the operation of any unfriendly policy on the part of the Federal Government, whether that operation is extended over a long or short period of time, would, of necessity, dry up the very fountains of the public strength, change the whole frame of our civilization and inflict a mortal wound upon our liberties.[3]

That is, there was a threat to slavery because of Lincoln's election and, therefore, to southern society. Holcombe framed the case for secession in constitutional terms during his address to the legislature. He had spoken in similar terms in an address to voters in his home near Charlottesville in January 1860. Holcombe explained that the South was preparing for war—was "in arms"— "because recent events have convinced the most unbelieving amongst us that there is danger to our constitutional rights in the Union, and because, to a man, people are resolved to maintain those rights." In fact, the Constitution was central to his thinking; it structured his understanding of the crisis. He worried that the Constitution was the last protection for the South and that the Supreme Court would be converted to antislavery principles. The new Supreme Court justices might end up as people who "studied in the schools of the higher law." The result would be the abolition of slavery in the District of Columbia and the invalidation of the Fugitive Slave Act.[4] Holcombe predicted the changes to constitutional law would come through appointments to the executive and judicial branches.

> Will you resist, when the public printing is given to Greeley, and your own money appropriated to sustain a press which makes relentless war upon your rights and honor? Or when Beecher is appointed chaplain of the Senate, and preaches insurrection in ear-shot of your slaves? When Chase is nominated to the Supreme Court, would you . . . think it prudent to wait for unconstitutional decisions?[5]

> So long as Northern sentiment upon African slavery remains unaltered, the Constitution, as it stands, furnishes us no permanent security against Northern injustice. Upon the election of a Black Republican President, the Supreme Court will be the only remaining outwork of our constitutional independence; and that, if not stormed by legislation, must crumble as rapidly as human life.[6]

Moreover, the ideas circulated in the southern academy before the war were central to secession debates. Members of the academy, judges, and politicians spoke the same language. In many cases the very people who made those arguments in the academy also made them in public debates over secession. People like James Holcombe of the University of Virginia; Thomas R. R. Cobb, the legal educator and treatise writer from Athens, Georgia; and James Henley Thornwell, a professor of theology from Columbia, South Carolina. Even when they were not directly involved in secession advocacy, southern academics helped foster the pro-slavery thought that proved so powerful in southern minds. Sometimes the academics were dependent variables who repeated ideas developed first in politics. At other times, such as with Holcombe and Cobb, they were independent variables who brought together the strands of pro-slavery arguments from history, political theory, economics, and law. Each idea and motive reinforced the others.

Southern intellectuals' writings on slavery link their arguments about the Constitution's protection for slavery to their arguments about why the North had violated the Constitution and how that justified secession. This links economic and demographic reality to constitutional interpretation. By looking at secession in this way, we expand constitutional law from the decisions of the U.S. Supreme Court outward to members of Congress, religious leaders, academics, and ultimately the voters whose ballots set the South on the path toward nationhood and war.[7] Southerners often framed their dispute with the North in constitutional terms. When Southerners spoke about secession, they spoke about it not just as a dispute over the protection, expansion, and morality of slavery but also specifically as a dispute over the rights of states to protect slavery and to protect themselves against attacks on slave property. (We are hearing much about public constitutionalism and popular constitutionalism these days, though often that is about how the public provides a check on government power.[8]) The South's arguments about slavery and secession reveal widespread talk of constitutionalism during the secession crisis, for constitutional thought linked economic and social arguments as our nation moved toward Civil War.[9]

The Constitution contributed not just disproportionate political power through the three-fifths compromise and through representation of slave states in the Senate,[10] it also gave white Southerners political legitimacy through its pro-slavery parts, such as the Fugitive Slave Clause and the recognition that Congress could not end the international slave trade until 1808. Those parts were used to construct a pro-slavery interpretation of the Constitution, which received support from Supreme Court decisions.[11] It made abolition of slavery substantially more difficult because of the argument that the government could not purchase slaves to free them.[12] Constitutional arguments helped provide shape to Southern claims, and they also helped explain how Southerners believed slavery was at the center of their world.

This final chapter turns to how the Constitution's supposed protection of slavery was used to mobilize and to frame the case for secession. Southerners believed that the Constitution protected their property and slavery, and it primed them to take violent action to protect those rights. Southern politicians, lawyers, and judges—even federal judges—interpreted the Constitution in a pro-slavery fashion. This set of ideas propelled secession, and it also helped impede other options. It branded those who opposed the enforcement of the Fugitive Slave Act of 1850 as outlaws; it delegitimized opposition to slavery. It provided an argument that slavery was protected in the territories and thus limited the options to end slavery there and in the District of Columbia. It contributed to the tabling of abolitionist petitions; it made abolition substantially more difficult. The Supreme Court and the Constitution legitimized pro-slavery politics, much as *Brown v. Board of Education* legitimized the civil rights movement a century later.[13] When Southerners contemplated secession they referred to *Dred Scott's* implication that "the Constitution was formed by and for white men, and not negroes." Moreover, they criticized those like Princeton theologian Charles Hodge who did not recognize *Dred Scott's* conclusion about white supremacy as an accepted fact.[14] Then again the pro-slavery interpretation of the Constitution may have—in fact, probably did—bring about the abolition of slavery sooner than otherwise because it legitimized secession and the war that brought down slavery. While some, like Frederick Douglass, eventually arrived at the proposition that the Constitution is properly interpreted as antislavery, that was surely contrary to the majority opinion.[15]

How did the South arrive at this state of affairs where the Constitution was seen as protecting their radical pro-slavery vision? How could they think that the election of Lincoln in 1860 justified their secession? The roots of this lie deep in southern, indeed in American, culture. In the wake of Nat Turner's August 1831 rebellion, Virginians seriously considered plans to gradually end slavery. Those plans, like so many made by people who dream of a better world, were long on hope. They were short on feasibility. Slave labor was too valuable and the costs of emancipation too high wrote Professor Thomas R. Dew of William and Mary in an extended attack on the practicality and desirability of emancipation.[16] Southerners were increasingly defending slavery as an institution good for both the owners and the enslaved. Certainly, there had been pro-slavery ideas in the eighteenth century, but the idea that slavery was a vehicle for civilizing the enslaved and for uplifting the owners was gaining momentum.[17] The amplitude of the pro-slavery rhetoric increased over time. By the late 1830s, southern politicians had crafted an extensive pro-slavery constitutional theory, based on the idea that states were equal and that the federal government could do nothing to interfere with slavery in the states—even that nonslave states could do nothing to interfere with the rights of slave states.[18] The market and transportation revolutions that were gaining strength in the 1830s increased commerce between states and thus conflicts between slave and free states. Moreover, territorial expansion created the possibility that slavery would expand (or, conversely, that the free states would expand and greatly outnumber the slave states).

Meanwhile, the defense of slavery grew louder and more strident. The common arguments about slavery's virtues—it brought civilization and Christianity to the enslaved, the wealth it created for the slaver owners made intellectual advancement possible, and it ensured republican government for white people—appeared with increasing amplitude. These arguments appeared in the press, the pulpit, the academy, the courts, and the statehouses, as Southerners increasingly told each other that slavery was the foundation of their society, that they had a natural right to slavery, and that their property could not be taken away. Their intellectual arguments matched economic and demographic reality, particularly in the deep southern states.

At colleges, students learned the arguments supporting slavery—the economic necessity; the ubiquity of slavery in human history; the demographic and social catastrophe for the slave-owning class that followed emancipation; the political theory supporting racial hierarchy; and the pseudo-science behind racial hierarchy. In short, they were taught about the benefits that slavery conferred on the slave owners and the supposed benefits it gave to the enslaved, too.

In the 1850s, southern colleges increasingly taught pro-slavery doctrine. Randolph Macon President William Smith published his *Lectures on Slavery* and Georgia Law Professor Thomas Cobb published his *An Inquiry into the Law of Negro Slavery*. Those books taught the morality, indeed necessity, of slavery. James P. Holcombe of the University of Virginia Law School published a lecture on how slavery was consistent with natural law. The academy was a key point for the generation and dissemination of pro-slavery thought. Those pro-slavery ideas undergirded and amplified constitutional ideas about the centrality of slavery to the Constitution. And the South over time turned from talking about the importance of slavery to considering it axiomatic that slavery was a blessing and constitutionally protected. For instance, Charleston lawyer Richard Yeadon wrote an extreme defense of slavery and attack on abolitionists in 1835 when abolition literature was widely distributed through the U.S. mail. He called it *The Amenability of Northern Incendiaries as Well to Southern as to Northern Laws*. It was an extended brief in favor of slavery and in favor of prosecuting Northerners who tried to use the U.S. mail to distribute abolitionist literature.[19] Twenty-two years later, in 1857, when Yeadon addressed the Erskine College literary societies, he no longer felt the need to defend slavery. Instead, he focused on the constitutional rights of the South and the steps necessary to protect those rights. "In view of the aggressive spirit and faithless conduct of the North," Yeadon said, "which yet cloud the political heavens with portents, and jar the land with volcanic throes, we should continue to exercise that jealous and eternal vigilance, which is the price of liberty, and the only assurance of Southern rights and Southern safety."[20] Yeadon echoed the sentiments of South Carolina Senator John C. Calhoun when he said that "[w]e of the Southern States holding the institution of domestic slavery, to be interwoven with the fabric of our social existence, and to be our destiny, must keep the vantage ground we have gained, and, standing on the Constitution, insist on and maintain . . . our full measure of right."[21]

Yeadon's address illustrates the ideas about slavery, property, and constitutionalism in circulation in the South. And it is an important gauge of the mind of Southerners and their discussions of law and constitutionalism that preceded secession. We interpret the Civil War as a conflict over slavery, economics, and morality, which of course it was.[22] In contrast to the American Revolution, where we can see that political ideology and constitutional ideas had some independent influence on the Revolutionaries,[23] when it comes to the Civil War, historians often ignore constitutional arguments.[24] Yet, the secession debates reveal the role constitutional arguments played in shaping secession. For the debates frequently invoked the Constitution and the scope of protection it gave to their supposed right to slavery and property in human beings. Southerners believed the world of slavery was protected by the Constitution. They thought slavery was ubiquitous in history and that demographic disaster followed its termination, for example, in the British West Indies. Emancipation in the United States would lead, they believed, to the kind of carnage that followed emancipation in Haiti.[25]

As Yeadon's address shows, support for a southern nation had been growing on college campuses, as in the South generally, for a decade.[26] In 1850 students at the University of Virginia formed a Southern Rights Association and published a short pamphlet. Like so many polemics, it was brief and to the point: "everywhere the spirit of abolitionism reigns supreme," laws were being violated, and southern constitutional rights trampled.[27] It was drawn in part from the work of recent University of Virginia graduate Muscoe Garnett's *Union, Past and Future*,[28] which asserted Southerners had made too many concessions of territory and rights of property in slaves already. The North, not the South, needed to make future concessions, and already the students were dreaming of a southern nation that would "speedily become one of the first nations of the world."[29] The Association passed a series of resolutions that concluded with instructions to their secretary to forward their plea to newspapers and to other southern schools to seek other adherents.[30]

Students at the South Carolina College (now the University of South Carolina) followed with their own southern rights association. Their list of grievances was similar to that of the University of Virginia students: the federal government was increasingly hostile to slavery in the territories, the South was losing political power, and at some point slavery itself would be outlawed. Congressional action from the Northwest Ordinance to the Missouri Compromise, to the prohibition of slavery in the Oregon territory demonstrated that slavery was being constricted. Property in slaves was not secure, even though the securing of property is the purpose for government. "A Government which does not protect property is entitled to no support," the students wrote. That was a one sentence distillation of what had come before for decades and what would be the point of contention in 1861.[31] Students elsewhere were sometimes as bold as those at the University of Virginia and South Carolina College. At Emory and Henry College, G.W.W.M. Simms wrote about the threats to slavery in a remarkably aggressive article titled simply "The South," in the student literary journal in 1854. Simms invoked the typical arguments that the enslaved were incapable of self-government and that they were happier in slavery than they would be in freedom, that the 1850 Census supposedly demonstrated that free people were worse off than southern slaves, that the emancipations in Haiti and the West Indies were failures, and that "freedom is the black man's foe."[32] The South would not give up their rights to the enslaved. "We will cling to our institutions as the mariner clings to the floating wreck when the storm-spirit shrieks in the blast and the shades of despair settle upon the waste of waters!"[33]

Simms depicted the threats to the Union if antislavery agitation continued. Simms' brief depiction of the death that would follow civil war proved remarkably prescient. He concluded with an appeal to Northerners to prevent intervention in southern slavery. "As the demon of Fanaticism comes sweeping over the land, fresh breathing fire from the portals of hell, with murder in his eye and death in his hand," Simms implored Northerners, "strike one mighty blow for liberty and the Union, hurl the monster back to his home of darkness, and save our country from the impending destiny!"[34] Simms was threatening civil war if Northerners did not stop interfering in slavery. Simms stated simply, and in terms that were becoming commonplace, that the perpetuity of the Union depended on "the security of southern rights."[35]

Even as Southerners increasingly took uncompromising positions on slavery and asserted their belief that the Constitution protected their right to property in humans, voices supporting Union were still heard on college campuses. But often the voices in favor of Union said—as had Simms—that Northerners had to offer more support for the southern rights to slavery and property. Sometimes those voices appeared in student literary magazines. In October 1857 the lead article of the *Virginia University Magazine* was entitled "A Plea for the Union."[36] The author worried that if the Union unraveled there would be scenes of war that would destroy northern cities, farms, and civilization stretching from New York and Pennsylvania to Ohio and Indiana. And he predicted disastrous consequences for the world's economy and democracy, too. The solution required that both sections stand by the Constitution and the protection it offered, that the North abide its duties toward the South, and also that the North and South both forget their sectional grievances.[37] Such pleas for Union were growing quieter as the South increasingly stood on its interpretation of a radically pro-slavery Constitution. Yet, at Erskine College as late as 1859 an article written by someone with the pseudonym Marshall pled for the Union. Using language reminiscent of Abraham Lincoln, Marshall wrote: "Our government is merely experimental, and it has been said that if we fail the last iota of self Government will have departed from among men."[38] About a year later that magazine observed that the impending crisis of Union was the topic of conversation for everyone. In place of appeals to Union or to Stephen Douglas' policy of nonintervention in the South, secession was imminent. "The Illinois rail-splitter has invaded the boundaries, demolished the sacred principles to which they clung with death-like tenacity, and only awaits his inauguration as president."[39] In January 1860 the *Virginia University Magazine* responded to the December 1859 issue of the *Yale Literary Magazine*, which had written about the execution of John Brown the previous month. The *Yale Literary Magazine* article had derisively charged that the University of Virginia students who went to witness Brown's execution had gone home to Charlottesville when they heard that Yale students were coming to rescue Brown. That bit of college "humor" met with an angry response. The *Virginia University Magazine* warned that if the Virginia students were to run, it would "be with their faces towards the enemy." That was not all, however. "Should the necessity arise—which may heaven forbid!—we'll march in a body to the defense of our border."[40] With such threats, the students showed they were primed for war.

The addresses given to college literary societies and at graduations were moving from support for Union, to questioning its value, to sometimes support-ing a southern nation. This was the trajectory of addresses over the course of the 1850s at the Virginia Military Institute, discussed in Chapter 3. At the University of North Carolina, graduation speakers in from 1852 to 1856 all spoke in favor of Union. In 1856 Matt W. Ransom, a twenty-nine-year-old Whig lawyer who had already served a term as attorney general of North Carolina, asked his audience to "[t]ell me, if you can, what the Union is worth."[41] He believed the value incal-culable. For Ransom, the Union was bound together by a series of factors, begin-ning with the telegraph and mail. Other more diffuse but perhaps even more powerful interests running from commercial self-interest to sympathies based in our shared history helped hold our country together. But he concluded—in a phrase that follows Harriet Beecher Stowe's phrase of how the shadow of the law broods over the scenes of slavery—that "over and above" all those tendencies to Union, "more powerful than commercial exigencies, or the currents of rivers or massive mountains, is the overruling and absorbing sentiment of patriotism."[42] In response to the forces pushing us apart, Ransom urged his audience to seek to preserve the Constitution and "perpetuat[e] American liberty to all posterity." He saw a particular virtue in patriotism among scholars, for "what an influence is United America destined to exert on the mind of the human race."[43]

The next year, 1857, Henry Watkins Miller had a different message about Union. Miller was an 1834 graduate of the University of North Carolina. Miller had been an ardent critic of abolitionists.[44] Miller's was the most radical of the speeches given at UNC before the war. It surveyed the growth of the United States from the time of the Revolution and Constitution until his time—the growth in population, in agricultural production, in the number of schools, in territory. Miller gave credit for this growth to the Constitution. He also believed that the Constitution could protect the Union. "If that constitution be properly administered by the several departments of the federal government, it is im-possible that any State, or portion of the people, can suffer wrong or oppres-sion from those sources. Such evils cannot arise and work out their disastrous consequences, *under the sanction of the Constitution!*" Miller than invoked John C. Calhoun's praise of the Constitution. This was the only reference to Calhoun, the South Carolina expositor of extreme states' rights under the Constitution, in any of the UNC addresses.[45]

Miller did not think that the South could rely merely on the forms of the Constitution. The form was not enough; it would provide only a shadow of protection. There had to be a substantive commitment to the ideas behind the Constitution, and there had to be a vigilance on the part of Southerners to protect their rights under the Constitution.[46] The northern press was the vehicle for sectional discord. "Judging from the tone and spirit of many of these productions—the avidity with which they are circulated,—one would readily conclude, that there are no consequences to which they may lead, however disastrous to *our* peace and security, that would not be hailed by their authors and propagators with rapture." The discrimination against the South appeared even in school books produced in the North.[47] Miller feared sectional conflict and that the Constitution's protections of sections would end.[48] He predicted glumly that patriotism is the cornerstone of the Constitution. "When that great principle," patriotism, "is lost sight of—discarded—repudiated—and the lust of sectional domination, the laws of force, is substituted in its stead, and made the main-spring, the motive power of social and political action, the fate of our national constitution is sealed, and the downfall of the republic is inevitable!"[49]

Miller feared that the individual states would be overwhelmed by the central government, that their constitutional place would be lost. His prediction was dire, and his sense of oppression from the North severe. He saw the world around him arrayed against the South. "The press, the hustings, the halls of Congress, even the pulpit–*all* have been converted into so many batteries of fiery assault!"[50]

The shifting attitudes of students at the University of North Carolina in the last years before war appear in three addresses given to the literary societies in Chapel Hill.[51] In March 1857, the same month as the *Dred Scott* decision, one student from Eufaula, Alabama, delivered a speech to the Dialectic Literary Society that asked whether the Union would be preserved.[52] The conclusion was that preservation was possible, though preservation would require the North to be more conciliatory toward slavery. The next year a graduating student from Columbus, Mississippi, delivered a senior oration, "Two Sections of the Union," which emphasized the violation of southern constitutional rights. "Look to the infringements of rights, repeated depredation made on our property, and the arrow of death hurled at our elective franchise," the student said, "and put the question to yourselves what shall we do?"[53] Secession was his proposed remedy. Then, in November 1858, student Elijah B. Withers delivered a speech entitled "The American Union, a Failure," which again emphasized the ways that the North violated the Constitution.[54]

Many white Southerners believed that the Constitution protected their world and that the world was threatened by Lincoln's election in November 1860. Southerners employed their cultural and economic ideas about slavery during debates over secession in 1860 and 1861. These ideas teach us how they understood their actions—and perhaps even shaped some of their actions. Southerners drew upon the ideas of history, utility, and law that they had developed in the previous thirty years. The secession debates reveal the salience of the ideas that were generated and disseminated in the southern universities and courts.

The ideas employed by academics, politicians, lawyers, and judges in the South so widely in the three decades before Abraham Lincoln's election were central to the secession crisis. Ideas about slavery and the Constitution were employed to explain and mobilize support for secession. Thus, one is tempted to ask, what is the meaning of such references to the Constitution? Many Southerners realized that economics, ideology, and support for the Constitution all went together and all were dependent on public opinion.[55] Yet, Southerners appealed to the Constitution rather successfully until they realized that the old constitutional views would stand no longer against the challenges of people like Lincoln, Stowe, and Douglass. The Constitution, though, was understood as closely connected to culture—it was dependent on the culture and custom of the community. Southerners understood that the Constitution was part of a system that functioned together—the Constitution, values of Union, and religion that made a nation. This tells us about how constitutional law is formed and how it extends to the pages of the U.S. Supreme Court's *Reports*, then out from those pages to form values that shape political options and principles. The Constitution by itself is dependent on culture—and the interpretation of the Constitution is subject to those cultural values.

Southerners had this global sense of the Constitution for decades. When artist Charles Fraser spoke in 1828 at the placement of a cornerstone of a building on the College of Charleston's campus, he explained the effect education could have on supporting the Constitution and breathing life into the values of the Constitution.[56]

> The Constitution is an admirable effort of the human intellect. Foreigners passing through our country, and observing the result of the giant invisible agent in the uniform, peaceful, and harmonious operations of society, emphatically ask, where is your government? We might as emphatically reply, that it exists in the hearts and minds of its citizens—that its energies are derived from public opinion—that a rational respect for the laws and institutions of our country, impart to them that vital principle which pervades and regulates every part of the republican system. . . . If we would preserve the ark of our covenant in its original sagacity, let "Wisdom, judgment, and Understanding," be the lamps that burn before it.[57]

Fraser spoke of the public nature of the Constitution. It was not something that existed only as interpreted by the U.S. Supreme Court and state courts, but as something that existed in the minds of American citizens. This Constitution was an idea, something created in the hearts and minds of Americans. It was supported by our national action and by our culture. Such principles operated in the minds of Southerners especially as they interpreted the Constitution in light of the economic and demographic realities of slavery.

But there was a paradox, for the South needed to show why the Constitution—to which they clung so closely—did not bind them to the Union. Constitutional argument was a central trope of the South—this is a common element of conservatism—and they needed to show, also, that the Constitution supported what they wanted. In a conservative revolution it is best to point out that the revolution is itself in line with law—the focus on the Constitution is a classic conservative move. Constitutional arguments reassured advocates and convinced others that they were right—they developed their own modes of interpretation, they developed their own histories, and they then left when their interpretation was clearly not going to be followed.

This tells us about constitutional culture as a shaper of formal constitutional law and as dependent on formal constitutional law. Constitutional culture is part of political culture. We should learn about constitutional culture to understand the close relationship between formal law and its surrounding culture—to demystify the idol of the Supreme Court opinions, to see how formal constitutional law draws upon and contributes to public constitutional arguments. It is a lesson in how a sophisticated set of constitutional ideas are formed, how they are intimately related to culture, and how they shape culture. It gives constitutionalism a central role in understanding a central American experience. It shows how much the Civil War and constitutionalism were intertwined—how our nation's struggle to end slavery was hindered by the Constitution and law—and also helped by it.

In March 1860, Reverend John L. Girardeau spoke at the graduation of the College of Charleston.[58] Girardeau addressed the concern over the dark cloud, "black and threatening" hanging over the Union. He feared that the "Constitution and law of the land have lost their force and commanding authority," and he proposed to explain why they had and hoped this might be remedied.[59] Girardeau discussed the ways that government was calibrated to the needs of the people. At the end he confronted the Free Soil' support of a higher law over the Constitution.[60] Southern thinkers—and many northern ones as well—opposed the idea that the Bible commanded or even authorized antislavery action in contradiction of the Constitution. Girardeau, thus, turned to the ways that the Constitution was related to divine authority. He found no contradiction, for "the institution which [the Constitution] upholds is sanctioned by that law." Girardeau invoked eight southern writers (William Smith, Albert Taylor Bledsoe, Chancellor James Harper, James Henry Hammond, William Gilmore Simms, Thomas R.

Dew, William J. Grayson, and James Henley Thornwell) to remind his audience that the southern position on the lawfulness of slavery was well established and that it was consistent with the Bible. Girardeau's conclusion was that if slavery "be not condemned by the Word of God, the fact that it is sanctioned by the Constitution can furnish no ground of conscientious resistance of the provisions of that instrument. Resistance may be offered, but it is not a righteous resistance."[61] It was Northerners, then, who violated the Constitution when they opposed the return of fugitive slaves or resisted the *Dred Scott* decision.[62] It was Northerners who risked "rebellion against the authority of the Supreme Rule, faithlessness to the stipulations of solemn treaties, and treachery to the dearest interests of man."[63] With such rhetoric at a college graduation, one can understand how the movement for secession, based on the idea that the North had already violated the Constitution, unfolded over the next year.

In the wake of Abraham Lincoln's election on November 6, 1860, the response was almost immediate about the threat to the South. Slavery was in danger and the South was ready to respond. The South Carolina legislature called a constitutional convention for the next month. It was immediately clear that they would secede.[64] In Georgia, events were running behind their neighbor. The Georgia legislature first needed to decide whether to call a special election for a constitutional convention that would debate secession; some thought that the legislature should proceed by statute authorizing secession; others were simply against secession. The first step for Georgia, then, was debating the merits of a special election. Over the course of about a week, beginning on November 12, 1860, distinguished orators addressed the public in the Georgia legislature's Milledgeville building, in the evening hours after the legislature had finished its business for the day. (Illustration 12.1) Thomas Cobb was one of the key speakers;[65] another was Justice Henry L. Benning of the Georgia Supreme Court, an ardent secessionist.[66]

On November 12, 1860, Cobb urged the states to take further action. Cobb's speech was both legal and political. It proceeded from a legal question: Was Lincoln's election unconstitutional? And it worked its way up to legal, moral, historical, and political arguments for secession. Cobb had a hard argument here, for by its terms, Lincoln's election met the requirements of the Constitution. Yet, the election was unconstitutional because it violated the spirit (if not the letter) of the Constitution. Here Cobb invoked the language of Paul's letter to the Corinthians—"the letter killeth, but the Spirit giveth life." The election was brought about in part by African Americans, people who were not qualified to be citizens of the United States; it imposed the antislavery majority of the North on the pro-slavery minority of the South. Cobb portrayed the horrors of abolitionists—the attack upon slavery in the churches and in Congress; the distribution of abolitionist literature through the U.S. mail; the underground

Illustration 12.1 Old State Capitol, Milledgeville, Georgia.
(Library of Congress, Prints & Photographs Division, HABS, Reproduction number HABS GA,5-MILG,6—2.)

railroad assisted slaves to escape; John Brown tried to start a slave insurrection. As yet, Cobb saw no end to the abolitionists' efforts.

In fact, history taught him there would be no end. Here, again, Cobb drew on historical understanding to predict that abolitionists would never voluntarily go away. He turned to examples from ancient history to modern times and from India to Great Britain to show the power of fanaticism. Fanaticism had caused Rome to destroy Jerusalem and Mary Queen of Scots to kill hundreds of Protestants. In India, some threw themselves under the Idol of the Juggernaut, hoping to die and go to heaven. In a distinct echo of the first page of his treatise, Cobb concluded that fanatics frequently draw blood under the delusion that they were doing what God commands. "Such is the teaching of philosophy, and history, her handmaid, confirms its truth."[67] Cobb concluded with an appeal to take action now and for Georgia to take the lead in secession, at a time when it was powerful and wealthy enough to make the move. Later, in early April 1861, a week before the war began, Cobb addressed the citizens of Athens. He saw "a people with the most liberal political institutions, the most patriarchal and perfect social polity and the most pure unadulterated simple Christian faith that the world now contains."[68]

On November 21, Georgia's Governor Joseph Brown signed legislation calling for a special election for delegates for a constitutional convention to be held on January 4, 1861. As part of the campaigning on the question of secession, some of the most zealously pro-slavery states, such as Mississippi and South Carolina, sent delegates to their fellow southern states to make the case for secession. Mississippi, for instance, sent Justice William L. Harris—author of the opinion in *Mitchell v. Wells* discussed in the last chapter (you may recall it as the opinion that used an analogy of Ohio granting citizenship to orangutans in its discussion of African American citizenship)—to make the case to the Georgia legislature. On December 19, 1860, he delivered a brief but searing speech. It centered on the South's constitutional right to slavery and to citizenship for white men. Harris repeated in short compass the constitutional vision of *Mitchell v. Wells*, that people of African descent were inferior to white people, and that the Constitution protected the rule of white men and the right to property in enslaved humans. He added that the election of Lincoln signaled a shift to a vision of racial equality and that this was a violation of the constitutional rights of the South.[69] Harris, like Cobb and Holcombe, provides a direct link between the ideas of slavery, property, and constitutionalism that were nurtured and disseminated in the academy and the judiciary to the secession movement. When Georgia voted in January, the secession candidates appeared to prevail. Subsequent investigations have called into question just how successful the secession candidates really were; it appears that the secessionist governor manipulated the return totals. But at the time, people believed that the secessionists had won a narrow victory. Cobb's advocacy was one small factor in the multiple regression equation that explained Georgia's secession decision—a decision that was critical for the road to civil war. Georgia was a fulcrum for our country's move toward war. Here it will be helpful to turn to a quantitative analysis to add context to the qualitative arguments regarding the centrality of slavery to southern society. Michael Johnson's research showed a positive correlation (.239) between a Georgia county's vote for secession candidates in the January 1861 special election and the percentage of enslaved people in that county.[70]

The centrality of slavery correlated with prosecession attitudes in 1861, just as nearly thirty years before the percentage of slaves in Virginia legislators' home counties correlated with pro-slavery positions in their votes in the wake of the Nat Turner rebellion.[71] There was also a professional component to the secession movement. Many of the leading secessionists had legal training. Cobb traveled in the circle of the Georgia legal community that was closely tied to pro-slavery law. In addition to his father-in-law, Justice Joseph Henry Lumpkin, the Georgia Supreme Court had several staunch defenders of slavery, Henry Benning, Eugenius Nesbit, and Ebenezer Starnes. Cobb and Benning both spoke at the November 1860 debate. Thirty-two of the 164 representatives who initially supported secession in Georgia had worked as lawyers or judges. The only occupational group with greater representation was planters (72 of 164).[72]

The appeals to the Constitution operated often at a high level of generality and collected a constellation of ideas—about individuals, the community, slavery, art, nature, Christianity, and charitable organizations—that worked together to form constitutional culture. Constitutional thought was more than a written Constitution; it was a set of ideas, of patriotic impulses, of sentiments in favor of Union, and about states rights, too. The vision of constitutionalism in the secession debates is of virtue, community, public rights as well as collective private action, and morality, bolstered in many cases by references to Supreme Court cases. The debates reveal how well-educated people in the nineteenth century spoke about their relationship to the nation, of their states to the nation, and to each other; about the bonds that held us together as a nation, about the rights that states and individual property owners retained, and how we tried to reconcile principles as the United States expanded.

As people at the time understood, the Constitution was more than a document interpreted by the Supreme Court that defined and limited federal and state power. The Constitution provided a framework for public debate about a series of abstract but important ideas of law, individualism, the state, and how to hold together a Christian republic. In a series of addresses in the 1820s and 1830s, Daniel Webster helped establish the boundaries of constitutional culture, which drew on appeals to patriotic sentiment with backward glances toward the heroism of the Revolutionary generation, to the common culture of the United States, to Protestant religious doctrine that emphasized individual choice and responsibility, to the importance of individual freedom generally, and to the commercial benefits of the United States.[73] And John C. Calhoun articulated a competing set of principles made up of state equality, property in slaves, and autonomy from federal control.[74]

The Constitution helped structure the beliefs of individuals throughout the country on issues regarding the market, the role of the state in promoting the economy and morality, and the likely future course of the country. Though there were often areas of agreement across political parties, there were frequently issues of disagreement on the proper lessons to draw from the Constitution about federal intervention in the economy, about the power and desirability of the market, and about the relationship of individuals to the community. The leading activist-intellectuals of the slave-owning South, the judges, lawyers, academics, theologians, and politicians, advanced a vision of the Constitution that protected property in humans. It was a conservative social and intellectual movement that molded their interpretation of the Constitution and the "truth" of considerations of economy and society into a belief that slavery could not be ended and should not be ended. Thus, whatever threatened slavery was unconstitutional and must be opposed through force. Ideas, reinforced by economic necessity and social beliefs, supported aggressive action.

One of the most important pamphlets urging secession in the spring of 1861 came from James Henley Thornwell,[75] who had served as professor at South Carolina College and then as president from 1852 to 1855. In 1861, Thornwell was teaching at the Columbia, South Carolina, Presbyterian Theological Seminary.[76] His pamphlet, *The State of Our Country*, was widely read—including, apparently, by George Junkin, who referred to how Thornwell focused on Lincoln's election and the exclusion of slavery from the territories as the justification for secession.[77]

Thornwell demonstrates how central constitutionalism was to southern thinking at the time of secession. For he wrote that the "real cause of the intense excitement of the South . . . is the profound conviction that the Constitution, in its relations to slavery, has been virtually repealed."[78] Northerners had violated the spirit of the Constitution and revoked the promises of the Constitution to protect slavery. "The election of Lincoln," Thornwell wrote, "when properly interpreted, is nothing more or less than a proposition to the South to consent to a Government, fundamentally different upon the question of slavery, from that which our fathers established."[79] Thornwell believed that the Constitution's attitude toward slavery was equality among the states, in which the slaveholding states were treated the same as the nonslaveholding states (he did not say "free states"). Here he drew on decades of southern constitutional theorizing which demanded that slave owners be able to take their human property to all the territories of the United States and also that Congress could not act to limit or discriminate against slavery.[80] Slavery, which Thornwell asserted was the "universal custom of mankind," was justified by the Constitution and the world.[81]

Secession was a constitutional crisis produced by the violation of the Constitution, Thornwell believed. He interpreted the Constitution using its text, such as the Fugitive Slave Clause; the Supreme Court precedent of *Prigg v. Pennsylvania*, which struck down a Pennsylvania statute that added additional burdens to the return of fugitive slaves; and his sense of the ubiquity of slavery. He believed that the "Constitution covers the whole territory of the Union, and throughout that territory, has taken slavery, under the protection of the law."[82] The Constitution legitimated secession in many ways, as Thornwell's analysis of *Prigg* and then *Dred Scott* demonstrated. To show how much *Dred Scott* added legitimacy to the southern position, recall that William J. Grayson wrote in anger that "[t]he decision of the Supreme Court, that the Constitution was formed by and for white men counts nothing with Mr. Hodge."[83]

And there was a sense that the people could decide for themselves the meaning of the Constitution. For instance, Thornwell declared that the Constitution, which should have been supportive of the southern cause, had been perverted.[84]

Lincoln's election was "the death-knell of slavery." Thornwell believed that Northerners had evaded the spirit of the Constitution and that they would remake it further given the chance. The Constitution's form had stayed the same, but the substance had changed. "The very moment [Lincoln] goes into office, the Constitution of the United States, as touching the great question between North and South, is dead. The oath which makes him President, makes a new Union." The South, quite simply, was being "reduced to zero," as Southerners struggled for "their very being." Thornwell, thus, showed himself an agile interpreter of the Constitution. He cultivated, as did many Southerners, a reading of the Constitution that was firmly pro-slavery and drew on common southern beliefs about slavery as natural, rather than unusual. Such ideas, so widely discussed on college campuses, help us understand the secession movement. Those ideas go off the page of the written Constitution to address the sentiments of Union (or disunion) and the ways that social and economic imperatives relate to those constitutional decisions. In short, Thornwell lets us see in the compass of one pamphlet how Southerners understood their constitutional rights and acted on them.

But in the secession winter, the issue was framed as a violation of the Constitution. In the pulpit of the First Presbyterian Church in New Orleans, Benjamin Morgan Palmer delivered a sermon at the end of November titled "The South: Her Peril, and Her Duty."[85] Palmer spoke of the duties of Southerners, to themselves to protect slavery, to the slaves whom he thought they were civilizing, and even "to the entire civilized world"—for slavery was central to the world economy.[86] These were big-picture themes, but Palmer then turned to the Constitution and how the North had already violated it. "What does [the election of Lincoln] declare—what can it declare, but that from henceforth this is to be a government of section over section; a government using constitutional forms only to embarrass and divide the section ruled, and as fortresses through whose embrasures the cannon of legislation is to be employed in demolishing the guaranteed institutions of the South?"[87]

Palmer thought that "no despotism is more absolute than that of an unprincipled democracy, and no tyrant more galling than that exercised through constitutional formulas? But that plea is idle, when the very question we debate is the perpetuation of that constitution now converted into an engine of oppression, and the continuance of that union which is henceforth to be our condition of vassalage. . . . The Constitution [is] now converted into an engine of oppression, and the continuance of that union which is henceforth to be our condition of vassalage."[88]

Palmer had three important points here. First, that the Constitution—properly interpreted and applied—was pro-slavery. Second, that the Constitution had been perverted, and instead of ensuring the South's freedom it would be its undoing. Third, the South had the right to create a new nation. In a short compass Palmer captured the centrality of the South' s constitutional culture, what had gone wrong with it in their minds, and how it would be corrected: by secession.

The poet William J. Grayson's reply to Princeton Theology Professor William Hodge provided another brief for secession grounded in the Constitution: the Union was not perpetual and individual sovereign states could decide on their allegiance to the Union in light of the North's violations—such as the personal liberty laws that northern states had enacted to hinder the return of fugitive slaves.[89] Grayson used an analogy to the new technology of photography to support the innovation of secession. "We talk now of photographing an impression on the mind, as of painting it formerly. The new term indicates a new act. The terms secede, secession, are evidences of new modes of government, and of corresponding new remedies for mis-government."[90]

In words oddly presaging W. E. B. DuBois' observation that race would be the problem of the twentieth century, a *Virginia University Magazine* article said in 1856 that slavery "is the great problem of the nineteenth century." The article concluded that discussion of slavery "has done much; it will do far more to pull down the folly of man, and to build up the wisdom of God."[91] That was exactly what happened, just not in the way that the author believed. As the ideas of freedom and free labor were discussed, they took hold and then triumphed. The end of slavery was hastened, of course, by the war. And the war was brought on by the ideas of slavery and property that southern lawyers and judges—and so many others, too—believed in. The war designed to protect slavery had the completely unintended—though perhaps easily predicable—consequence that it brought about the destruction of slavery. Among the many unexpected storylines of the southern academics, politicians, and jurists who developed arguments to support their pro-slavery world and then followed those ideas to the point of war, this one is perhaps most important. Those who went to war to preserve slavery hastened the demise of slavery and the freedom of millions who in January 1861 had been enslaved and who had little cause for hope of liberation.

Academics such as Albert Taylor Bledsoe, Thomas R. R. Cobb, and James Holcombe advanced a political theory that reversed the Enlightenment idea that all people are created equal. Their theory was that people are inherently unequal and that some are better fit for slavery than freedom and that the state had a role in the enforcement of that order. They joined that theory with (and in part built it upon) economic and historical arguments about the importance of slave labor, to argue that natural law also supported slavery. Their jurisprudence focused on considerations of utility and historical context, which denied universal truths of equality in favor of calibration of rights according to station in society. In the

South in the years between 1832 and 1861, there emerged a widespread belief that political philosophy, natural law, economics, and history all pointed to the need for action to protect slavery. Each line of thought amplified the other and together with the demographic reality of slavery formed the foundation for a widespread belief that the Constitution was staunchly pro-slavery.

Thus, at the time of the inauguration of President Lincoln there was a robust legal defense of slavery and also a sense that the spirit if not the letter of the Constitution had been violated by the election. As Southerners debated secession, they frequently invoked arguments about natural law, history, economics, and the Constitution together. Such ideas constituted a comprehensive world view of hierarchy and slavery, which had been nurtured and disseminated in universities throughout the South.

As happened so frequently in American history, ideas mixed with economic reality and then led to violence. It did not take long to move from secession speeches and talk of property in slaves and constitutionalism to the mobilization for war and then to extraordinary efforts and soon extraordinary suffering on both sides. On the battlefield at Fredericksburg on December 12, 1862, General Thomas R. R. Cobb, one of the leading intellectuals of the old South, died. He was one of the few casualties on the Confederate side that day. For Cobb, the war ended sooner than for many others.

Cobb died in Fredericksburg, but his cause struggled on for a few more years. The corollary to Victor Hugo's apt observation that nothing is so powerful as an idea whose time has come is that there is nothing so powerless as an idea whose time has past. By 1862 it was becoming apparent that the era of slavery was drawing to a rapid conclusion. The ideas of hierarchy and economy that had been so powerful just three decades before—even less than a decade before—were proving remarkably ineffective as the idea of freedom swept the nation. It did not take long for Cobb's contemporaries to look back and wonder why they had thought rebellion would be so easy. They had ignored Cobb's advice to look to history, reason, and philosophy, even as they were led by Cobb to a false sense of what history, reason, and philosophy taught. The United States emerged from the war with a new law because the times demanded it. By the end of the war in 1865, it was time for a new order.

One of the last echoes of Cobb's work appeared in a most unusual place in 1901. Oliver Wendell Holmes, who had fought on the other side of Cobb and had been wounded in the war,[92] went on to expand the use of historical and empirical methods in law. First he did this in his 1881 book *The Common Law* and then as a jurist on the Massachusetts Supreme Judicial Court and finally on the U.S. Supreme Court from 1902 to 1932. In an extraordinary twist of fate, Oliver Wendell Holmes cited Cobb's treatise in one of his final opinions while on the Massachusetts Supreme Judicial Court. The case dealt with a claim over inheritance by the children of a formerly enslaved man. The man had been married during his time as a slave in Virginia and afterward escaped to Massachusetts where he remarried. The question was whether a child, born while the man was in slavery in Virginia, was the only legitimate heir or whether the children of the man who were born after he escaped and fled to Massachusetts were also legitimate children and thus entitled to inherit a share of his estate. Holmes distinguished Cobb's conclusion that slaves taken from a free state to a slave state continued as slaves (and thus could not remarry). Holmes concluded that certainly slaves who remained in Massachusetts were free and thus could remarry and, therefore, the second marriage was legitimate. Cobb, though he had been dead for more than thirty years, was part of the outcome of the case, even though Holmes departed from his textbook.[93] The methods of people like Cobb, Ruffin, Lumpkin, Ebenezer Starnes, the Georgia jurist who wrote a pro-slavery novel comparing the lives of slaves and free workers in England, and Campbell had looked to historical and empirical evidence to understand what the law was. Their law restrained change. Reformers in the antebellum era like Ralph Waldo Emerson often argued that we should not believe the past, while those who turned to history often had conservative motives. The turn to history and to context was part of the Romantic era's focus on the specific rather than grand Enlightenment era universal truths. As southern jurists turned toward history, they argued that people are not all entitled to or fit for freedom. That was a powerful argument restraining the move toward emancipation.[94]

Yet, in pragmatic fashion, other Americans looked to the world around them to understand law. That world was changing, and the law and the culture it supported with it. After the war people like Holmes looked to empirical evidence for a sense of what people had done and to help see what the law ought to be, based on the will of the people—not the limitations of the people. Before the war southern jurists thought history taught conservative lessons about how difficult it was to depart from slavery. After the war, in the hands of reformers like Holmes, history was used to show how law had become out of touch with present society. The methods before and after the war were often similar—a turn to history and to empirical investigation of the world around them—though the lessons drawn from such investigations were quite different.

NOTES

Introduction

1. Ludwell H. Johnson, *Between the Wars, 1782–1862*, in THE COLLEGE OF WILLIAM AND MARY: A HISTORY 163, 195 (Susan H. Godson, ed. 1994); 2 MICHAEL O'BRIEN, CONJECTURES OF ORDER: INTELLECTUAL LIFE AND THE AMERICAN SOUTH, 1810–1860 865–72 (2004); ROBERT BRUGGER, NATHANIEL BEVERY TUCKER: HEART OVER HEAD IN THE OLD SOUTH (1978); ERIC WALTHER, THE FIRE EATERS 8–47 (1992).

2. *See generally* KEVIN J. HAYES, THE ROAD TO MONTICELLO: THE LIFE AND MIND OF THOMAS JEFFERSON 43–72 (2008) (discussing William and Mary and Williamsburg); Terry Meyers, *Talking About Slavery at the College of William and Mary*, 21 WM. & MARY BILL RIGHTS J. 1215–57 (2013).

3. *See* Wythe Holt, *George Wythe: Early Modern Judge*, 58 ALA. L. REV. 1009, 1010 (2007); Julian Boyd, *The Murder of George Wythe*, 12 WM. & MARY Q. 514–42 (1955); W. Edwin Hemphill, *Examinations of George Wythe Swinney for Forgery and Murder: A Documentary Essay*, 12 WM & MARY Q. 543–74 (1955).

4. 11 Va. (1 Henn. & Munf.) 133, 134 (1806).

5. *See A Memoir of the Author, in* DECISIONS OF CASES IN VIRGINIA, . . . BY THE HIGH COURT OF CHANCERY BY GEORGE WYTHE xxxvii–xxxix (Richmond, J.W. Randolph 1852) (reprinting Wythe's will of April 1803 and codicils of February 1806 and June 1806); JOHN T. NOONAN, PERSONS AND MASKS OF THE LAW: CARDOZO, HOLMES, JEFFERSON, AND WYTHE AS MAKERS OF THE MASKS 29–35, 61–62 (1975); BRUCE CHADWICK, I AM MURDERED: GEORGE WYTHE, THOMAS JEFFERSON, AND THE KILLING THAT SHOCKED A NEW NATION (2009).

6. 11 Va. (1 Hen. & M.) 133, 141 (1806). *See also* Paul Carrington, *The Revolutionary Idea of a University Legal Education*, 31 WM. & MARY L. REV. 527 (1990).

7. 2 ST. GEORGE TUCKER, BLACKSTONE'S COMMENTARIES: WITH NOTES OF REFERENCE TO THE CONSTITUTION AND LAWS OF THE FEDERAL GOVERNMENT . . . AND THE COMMONWEALTH OF VIRGINIA appendix, Note H ("On the State of Slavery in Virginia"), at 43–44 (Philadelphia, 1803). For a more skeptical account of Tucker's plan, see Paul Finkelman, *The Dragon St. George Could Not Slay: Tucker's Plan to End Slavery*, 47 WILLIAM & MARY L. REV. 1213 (2006).

8. 2 TUCKER, *supra* note 7, at 43.

9. *Id.* at 63.

10. *Id.* at 71.

11. *Id.*

12. *Id.* at 77–78; 72–74.

13. Judge William Nelson took over in 1804; he was followed at his death in 1813, by his nephew Judge Robert Nelson, who served until 1819. Judge James Semple, a brother-in-law of future President John Tyler, served from 1819 until 1833. *See* Johnson, *supra* note 1, at 175, 204, 210, 235.

14. James L. Huston, Calculating the Value of the Union: Slavery, Property Rights, and the Economic Origins of the Civil War 26–27 (2002).
15. *Professor Dew on Slavery*, in The Pro-slavery Argument, as Maintained by the Most Distinguished Writers of the Southern States ... Containing the Several Essays on the Subject of Chancellor Harper, Governor Hammond, Dr. Simms, and Professor Dew 287, 293 (Charleston, Walker, Richards & Co., 1852) (1832).
16. *But see* discussion of Washington College President Henry Ruffner in Chapter 2.
17. 1 St. George Tucker, Blackstone's Commentaries, *supra* note 7, at 423–24.
18. *A Lecture on the Study of the Law: Being an Introduction to a Course of Lectures on that Subject in the College of William and Mary*, 1 S. Lit. Messenger 145–54 (Dec. 1834).
19. Nathaniel Beverley Tucker, *The Primary Form of Incipient Government*, in A Series of Lectures on the Science of Government Intended to Prepare the Student for the Study of the Constitution of the United States 52, 62 (Philadelphia, Carey and Hart 1845).
20. *Id.* at 64. *See* Adam Tate, Conservatism and Southern Intellectuals, 1789–1861: Liberty, Tradition, and the Good Society 152–57 (2005); Erik S. Root, All Honor to Jefferson? The Virginia Debate Over Slavery and the Development of the Positive Good Thesis 218–19 (2008).
21. Lectures, *supra* note 19, at 284.
22. *Id.* at 284–85.
23. For instance, Tucker concluded from his observation of Native Americans that government was established to protect people from the chaos that existed in nature. *Id.* at 144–45:

> The equal rights of all men and their equal right at first to equal things, form the foundation of the eventual inequalities of property, and their equal rights to things unequal. The rights of personal freedom of action, and of personal security, are inappreciable. But beyond these, liberty itself is only valuable as it permits the pursuit and secures the enjoyment of property. Property thus becomes the measure of the value of liberty, so far as it can be estimated by any standard; and few would value it at a higher price than the immense wealth often accumulated in a single lifetime by men who have but been left to pursue their fortunes, each in his own way.

24. *Id.* at 125 (concluding that "Eight-hundred years ago, the government of that which is now the freest country in Europe, was decidedly the most despotic; and the change has been effected by the peaceful operation of the acknowledged sanctity of the right of property, which purchased the emancipation of every other right."). *See also id.* at 149–50.
25. Nathaniel Beverley Tucker, *A Note to Blackstone's Commentaries*, 1 S. Lit. Messenger 227 (Jan. 1835).
26. *Id.*
27. *Id.* at 228.
28. This point is expanded by Dew in his "Review of the Debates in the Legislature," in The Pro-Slavery Argument 287, 461 (Charleston, Walker & Richards 1852) (1832) and then expanded in Thomas R. Dew, *On the Influence of the Federative Republican System of Government upon the Literature and Development of Character*, 2 S. Lit. Messenger 261–82 (1836).
    This was a common and important theme. In 1839, Virginia Judge Abel Upshur quoted Burke's speech on conciliation in an address at William and Mary. He concluded that both philosophy and history pointed toward the importance of slavery in supporting freedom:

> [T]he testimony of the historian attests the soundness of the reasoning of the speculative philosopher; and both concur in proving, that negro slavery tended to inspire in the white man a strong love of freedom, to give him a high estimate of its value, and to inspire him with those feelings of independence, self respect and proper pride, which fit him for the enjoyment of free institutions, and teach him how to preserve them. The government receives its form from the people, and give to them, in turn, a character corresponding with its own; and this happy adaptation affords the best possible security for the preservation of liberty.

> [Abel Upshur], *Domestic Slavery*, 5 S. Lit. Messenger 677, 679 (Oct. 1839). *See also* [William J. Grayson], *Slavery in the Southern States*, 8 Southern Q. Rev. 317–60 (Oct 1845).

29. Edmund Burke, *Speech on Conciliation with the American Colonies*, ¶ 42, reprinted in EDMUND BURKE'S SPEECH ON CONCILIATION WITH THE AMERICAN COLONIES DELIVERED IN THE HOUSE OF COMMONS MARCH 22, 1775, at 75–76 (William Crane ed. 1908). Tucker, *supra* note 25, at 230.

30. *Id.* at 230.

31. *Id.* at 230 ("Let them desecrate and demolish the tombs of their fathers, to build up a monument to their own praise. But what spell is upon us, that we should follow their example, and signalize our ingratitude to the men to whose teachings we owe all that is valuable in our institutions, by joining in a crusade against our own rights . . .?").

32. The editor's introduction to the issue of the *Southern Literary Messenger* where Tucker's address to students appeared dissented from Tucker's view that there are moral and political benefits to slavery. *Editorial Remarks*, 1 S. LIT. MESSENGER 254 (Jan. 1835) ("We regard [slavery] on the contrary, as a great evil, which society will sooner or later find it not only its interest to remove or mitigate, but will seek its gradual abolition or amelioration, under the influence of those high obligations imposed by an enlightened Christian morality.").

33. [A Virginian,] *Remarks on a Note to Blackstone's Commentaries, Vol. 1, Page 423*, 1 S. LIT. MESSENGER 266, 269 (February 1835). Elizabeth Fox-Genovese and Eugene Genovese attribute (I believe mistakenly) the essay to Nathaniel Beverley Tucker and thus credit Tucker with a shift in attitudes toward slavery between 1835 and 1844, when he published a two-part proslavery essay, *An Essay on the Moral and Political Effect of the Relation Between the Caucasian Master and the African Slave*, 10 S. LIT. MESSENGER 329–39 (June 1844) and 10 S. LIT. MESSENGER 470–80 (Aug. 1844). *See* ELIZABETH FOX-GENOVESE AND EUGENE GENOVESE, THE MIND OF THE MASTER CLASS: HISTORY AND FAITH IN THE SOUTHERN SLAVEHOLDERS' WORLD VIEW 110 (2005). Genovese and Fox-Genovese had Tucker's January 1835 lecture in mind, not the February 1835 response. The author of the response is unknown.

34. [N. Beverley Tucker], *Slavery*, 2 S. LIT. MESSENGER 336, 339 (April 1836) (reviewing JAMES KIRKE PAULDING, SLAVERY IN THE UNITED STATES (New York, Harper & Brothers 1836) and [WILLIAM H. DRAYTON,] THE SOUTH VINDICATED FROM THE TREASON AND FANATICISM OF THE NORTHERN ABOLITIONISTS (Philadelphia, H. Manly 1836)):

   > Nothing is wanting but manly discussion to convince our own people at least, that in continuing to command the services of their slaves, they violate no law divine or human, and that in the faithful discharge of their reciprocal obligations lie their true duty. Let these be performed and we believe (with our esteemed correspondent Professor Dew) that society in the South will derive much more of good than of evil from this much abused and partially-considered institution.

35. [Tucker,] *Slavery, supra* note 34, at 337.

36. *See* Tucker, *An Essay on the Moral and Political Effect of the Relation Between the Caucasian Master and the African Slave, supra* note 33.

37. Tucker, *An Essay* (June 1844), *supra* note 33, at 330.

38. *Id.* at 330.

39. *Id.* at 332.

40. *Id.* at 334.

41. *Id.* at 335.

42. Tucker, *An Essay* (August 1844), *supra* note 33, at 471.

43. In the twentieth century, historians again returned to such constructs to understand the South's role in the American Revolution. Yale University historian Edmund Morgan's 1975 book *American Slavery—American Freedom* returned to the question why Virginians so vigorously sought freedom while embracing slavery. EDMUND S. MORGAN, AMERICAN SLAVERY–AMERICAN FREEDOM (1975); DAVID ELTIS, THE RISE OF AFRICAN SLAVERY IN THE AMERICAS (2000). Morgan found that slavery joined the interests of all white people— slaveholder and nonslaveholder alike—against the interests of the slaves. And once those interests were linked, they could talk about the value of freedom. Morgan's interpretation, though subjected to scrutiny, is now widely accepted, by a range of historians, including African American historians who emphasize the role of slavery in uniting whites against blacks. *See, e.g.,* DERRICK BELL, AND WE ARE NOT SAVED: THE ELUSIVE QUEST FOR RACIAL

JUSTICE 40–42 (1987) (citing Edmund S. Morgan, *Slavery and Freedom: The American Paradox*, 59 J. AM. HIST. 1, 6 (1972) and MORGAN, AMERICAN SLAVERY, *supra*, at 381); Cheryl Harris, *Whiteness as Property*, 106 HARV. L. REV. 1707, 1717 (1993) (citing MORGAN, *supra*, at 376); Kimberle Williams Crenshaw, *Race, Reform, and Retrenchment: Transformation and Legitimation in Antidiscrimination Law*, 101 HARV. L. REV. 1331, 1374 (1988) (citing MORGAN, *supra*, for evidence of linking of slavery with freedom for whites, and invoking Morgan's statement, *id.* at 386, that slavery and racism was "an essential if unacknowledged, ingredient of the republican ideology that enabled Virginians to lead the nation").

Morgan's thesis occupies a central place in recent synthetic treatments of slaveholder ideology. *See, e.g.*, DAVID BRION DAVIS, INHUMAN BONDAGE: THE RISE AND FALL OF SLAVERY IN THE NEW WORLD 135, 145 (2006) (identifying Morgan's "brilliant thesis that in colonial Virginia slavery and racism became the social and ideological *basis* for America's dedication to freedom and equality for all whites").

44. During that time, Tucker also published *The Partisan Leader*, a strange, sort of fantasy about a future Civil War, in which the South seceded from the United States. That book, reprinted again in the 1850s, looked shockingly prescient by the time of Civil War in 1861. In 1850 Tucker published an essay on James Henry Hammond's proslavery address at South Carolina College. *Review of an Oration, Delivered Before the Two Societies of the South-Carolina College*, 17 SOUTHERN QUARTERLY REVIEW 37–48 (1850).

Tucker was followed as law professor by Judge George P. Scarburgh (1852–55), Lucian Minor (1855–58), and finally Charles Morris (1860–61). Of those faculty, we know the most about Minor. Minor's publications included *Discourse on the Life and Character of the late John A. G. Davis. . . June 29th, 1847* (Richmond, Shepherd and Colin 1847); *An Address on Education, as Connected with the Permanence of our Republican Institutions: Delivered before. . . Hampden Sidney College, . . . September 24, 1835* (Richmond, T. W. White 1835), excerpted in 2 S. LIT. MESSENGER 17 (Jan. 1835); *Reasons for Abolishing the Liquor Traffic. Addressed to the People of Virginia . . .* (Richmond, H. K. Ellyson 1853). He spoke against abolition at a court day meeting in Louisa in 1835. *See Louisa Meeting*, RICHMOND ENQUIRER (Sept. 25, 1835), at 3 (reporting that Minor delivered a brief speech before a meeting on Court day, which passed anti-abolition resolutions). *See also Study of the Latin and Greek Classics*, 1 S. LIT. MESSENGER 213–16 (Jan. 1835); Lucian Minor, *Review of Hallam*, 4 S. LIT. MESSENGER 111–13 (1838); Lucian Minor, *Cato the Elder*, 18 S. LIT. MESSENGER 732 (1852); Lucian Minor, *The Model Lawyer*, 20 S. LIT. MESSENGER 635–36 (Oct. 1854); Lucian Minor, *Liberian Literature*, 2 S. LIT. MESSENGER 158 (Feb. 1836); *Letters from New England*, 1 S. LIT. MESSENGER 84–88 (Nov. 1834). A brief biographical sketch appears in *The Late Lucian Minor*, S. LIT. MESSENGER 225–27 (Sept. 1858).

45. *See* JOSEPH WRIGHT TAYLOR, THE SOUTHERN UNIVERSITY: ITS ORIGIN, PRESENT CONDITION, WANTS, AND CLAIMS: AN ADDRESS DELIVERED BEFORE THE BELLES LETTRES AND CLARIOSOPHIC SOCIETIES OF THE SOUTHERN UNIVERSITY, ON THEIR ANNIVERSARY OCCASION, JULY 2, 1861 18 (Nashville, Southern Methodist Pub. House, 1861).

46. JOSEPH TAYLOR, A PLEA FOR THE UNIVERSITY OF ALABAMA: AN ADDRESS DELIVERED BEFORE THE EROSOPHIC AND PHILOMATHIC SOCIETIES OF THE UNIVERSITY OF ALABAMA ON THEIR ANNIVERSARY OCCASION, AUGUST 9, 1847 25 (Tuskaloosa, M.D.J. Slade, 1847).

47. Ralph Waldo Emerson, *The Fugitive Slave Law: Address to the Citizens of Concord, 3 May, 1851*, in 11 THE COMPLETE WORKS OF RALPH WALDO EMERSON 177 (1904).

48. James Henry Hammond, *Speech to the U.S. Senate, March 4, 1858*, CONG. GLOBE, 35th Cong., 1st Sess., Appendix 68, 70–71.

49. I am deeply indebted to Jeannine DeLombard for this point. *See* JEANNINE DELOMBARD, SLAVERY ON TRIAL: LAW, ABOLITIONISM, AND PRINT CULTURE 177–81 (2007).

50. *See, e.g.*, Stephen Davis & Alfred L. Brophy, *"The Most Solemn Act of My Life": Family, Property, Will, and Trrst in the Antebellum South*, 62 ALA. L. REV. 757, 786 (2011) (discussing will of Absolom Morton of Greene County, Alabama, who ordered his property sold and invested in enslaved people; the profits from their rental were to provide support and education for his relatives).

51. 2 HARRIET BEECHER STOWE, DRED: A TALE OF THE GREAT DISMAL SWAMP 76 (1856) (1896 ed.).

52. HARRIET BEECHER STOWE, A KEY TO UNCLE TOMS' CABIN 77 (Boston, John P. Jewett 1853).

53. *See, e.g.,* Alfred L. Brophy, *When History Mattered,* 91 Tex. Law. Rev. 601–14 (2013) (reviewing David Rabban, *Law's History: American Legal Thought and the Transatlantic Turn to History* (2013)).

54. *See* Antony Dugdale, J. J. Fueser, and J. Celso de Castro Alves, Yale, Slavery and Abolition (2001) available at http://www.yaleslavery.org/YSA.pdf.

    Slavery and Justice: Report of the Brown University Steering Committee on Slavery and Justice (2006), available at http://brown.edu/Research/Slavery_Justice/documents/SlaveryAndJustice.pdf.

    Sven Beckert, Katherine Stevens, et al., Harvard and Slavery: Seeking a Forgotten History (2012), available at: http://www.harvardandslavery.com/wp-content/uploads/2011/11/Harvard-Slavery-Book-111110.pdf.

    Craig Steven Wilder, Ebony and Ivy: Race, Slavery, and the Troubled History of America's Universities (2013). *See also* Jennifer Bridges Oast, Institutional Slavery: Slaveholding Churches, Schools and Colleges in Virginia, 1680–1860 (2016) (discussing slavery at William and Mary and Hampden-Sydney College).

55. Peter Carmichael, The Last Generation: Young Virginians in Peace, War, and Reunion (2005); Michael Sugrue, South Carolina College: The Education of an Antebellum Elite (Ph.D. dissertation, Columbia University, 1992); Jennifer R. Green, Military Education and the Emerging Middle Class in the Old South (2008); Mark Auslander, The Accidental Slaveowner: Revisiting a Myth of Race and Finding an American Family (2011).

56. *See, e.g,* Robert Bonner; Mastering America: Southern Slaveholders and the Crisis of American Nationhood (2009); O'Brien, *supra* note 1; Genovese and Fox-Genovese, *supra* note 33. And for the period just after my study ends, see Michael T. Bernath, Confederate Minds: The Struggle for Intellectual Independence in the Civil War South (2010) and Stephanie McCurry, Confederate Reckoning: Power and Politics in the Civil War South (2012).

57. Sarah N. Roth, Gender and Race in Antebellum Popular Culture (2014); Drew Faust, A Sacred Circle: The Dilemma of the Intellectual in the Old South, 1840–1860 (1977). The beginning of my story fits with the end of Lacy Ford's story on the development of paternalism in southern proslavery thought in the 1830s. *See* Lacy K. Ford, Deliver Us from Evil: The Slavery Question in the Old South (2009).

58. *See* The Antislavery Debate: Capitalism and Abolitionism as a Problem in Historical Interpretation (Thomas Bender ed. 1992) (presenting various theories about the reasons that antislavery sentiments grew in correlation with the development of capitalism).

59. Ralph Waldo Emerson, *Lecture on the Times,* in Ralph Waldo Emerson: Essays and Lectures 211, 221 (Joel Porte ed. 1983).

60. *Contrast* Fox-Genovese & Genovese, The Mind of the Master Class, *supra* note 33 with James Oakes, Slavery and Freedom: An Interpretation of the Old South (1990).

61. Sven Beckert and Seth Rockman, Slavery and Capitalism (forthcoming 2016); The Old South's Modern Worlds: Slavery, Region, and Nation in the Age of Progress (L. Diana Barnes, Brian Schoen, and Frank Towers, eds., 2011); John Majewski, Modernizing a Slave Economy: The Economic Vision of the Confederate Nation (2009); Edward Baptist, The Half Has Never Been Told: Slavery and the Making of American Capitalism (2014); Sven Beckert, Empire of Cotton: A Global History (2014).

62. Morton J. Horwitz, The Transformation of American Law, 1780–1860 (1977); Jenny Bourne Walh, The Bondsman's Burden: An Economic Analysis of the Common Law of Southern Slavery (2002); Ariela Gross, Double Character: Slavery and Mastery in the Antebellum Southern Courtroom (2000).

63. Robert S. Cover, Justice Accused: Anti-Slavery and the Judicial Process (1975); William Fisher, *Ideology and Imagery in the Law of Slavery,* 68 Chicago-Kent L. Rev.1051 (1993); Christopher Tomlins, Freedom Bound: Law, Labor, and Civic Identity in Colonizing English America, 1580–1865 (2010) (viewing law as an instrument of brutalization and colonization).

Chapter 1

1. SUPPLEMENT TO THE REVISED CODE OF THE LAWS OF VIRGINIA at 244–45 (Richmond, Samuel Shepherd & Co. 1833) chapter 186 (April 13, 1831). There was a previous attempt to pass a statute limiting the rights to teach slaves to read. *See* JOURNAL OF THE HOUSE OF DELEGATES 1829–30 at 172 (Richmond, Thomas Ritchie 1830); *The Pamphlet*, RICHMOND ENQUIRER, January 28, 1830; CLEMENT EATON, FREEDOM OF THOUGHT IN THE OLD SOUTH 123 (revised ed. 1960) (reporting on the stir caused by David Walker's *Appeal to the Coloured Citizens of the World* (1829) (Boston, David Walker revised ed. 1830)); ALISON GOODYEAR FREEHLING, DRIFT TOWARDS DISSOLUTION: THE VIRGINIA SLAVERY DEBATE OF 1831–1832, at 82–83 (1982).
2. http://www.virginiaplaces.org/population/pop1830numbers.html.
3. *See* CHARLES F. IRONS, THE ORIGINS OF PROSLAVERY CHRISTIANITY chap. 4 (2008) (discussing Turner as a preacher).
4. Thomas Parramore, *A Covenant in Jerusalem*, *in* NAT TURNER: A SLAVE REBELLION IN HISTORY AND MEMORY 58 (Kenneth S. Greenberg, ed. 2003); DAVID ALLMENDINGER, NAT TURNER AND THE RISING IN SOUTHAMPTON COUNTY (2014); PATRICK H. BREEN, THE LAND SHALL BE DELUGED IN BLOOD: A NEW HISTORY OF THE NAT TURNER REVOLT (2015).
5. Parramore, *supra* note 4, at 60.
6. *Id.* at 62–64.
7. *Id.* at 66.
8. *See* HENRY I. TRAGLE, THE SOUTHAMPTON SLAVE REVOLT xv–xvii (1971) (summarizing the course of the rebellion); Peter Wood, *Nat Turner: The Unknown Slave as Visionary Leader*, in BLACK LEADERS OF THE NINETEENTH CENTURY 21 (Leon Litwack and August Meier eds. 1988).
9. Parramore, *supra* note 4, at 67.
10. *Id.* at 67.
11. *Id.* at 67–68.
12. LOUIS F. MASUR, 1831: YEAR OF ECLIPSE 9–62 (2002); SCOT FRENCH, THE REBELLIOUS SLAVE: NAT TURNER IN AMERICAN MEMORY (2003).
13. Alfred L. Brophy, *The Nat Turner Trials*, 91 N.C. L. REV. 1817, 1858, 1863 (2013).
14. TRAGLE, *supra* note 8, at 177–245 (reprinting minute books of the trials); Brophy, *supra* note 13, at 1863.
15. THOMAS R. GRAY, CONFESSIONS OF NAT TURNER (Baltimore, Lucas & Deaver 1831), reprinted in THE CONFESSIONS OF NAT TURNER AND OTHER DOCUMENTS 39–58 (Kenneth S. Greenberg ed., 1996); SCOT FRENCH, THE REBELLIOUS SLAVE: NAT TURNER IN AMERICAN MEMORY 45–51 (2004). *See also* SAMUEL WARNER, AUTHENTIC AND IMPARTIAL NARRATIVE OF THE TRAGICAL SCENE WHICH WAS WITNESSED IN SOUTHAMPTON COUNTY (VIRGINIA) ON MONDAY THE 22D OF AUGUST LAST . . . (New York, Warner & West 1831).
16. We have recently learned of the important and previously neglected story from Eva Shepard Wolf. *See* EVA SHEPPARD WOLF, RACE AND LIBERTY IN THE NEW NATION: EMANCIPATION IN VIRGINIA FROM REVOLUTION TO NAT TURNER'S REBELLION at 231–33 (2006).

    In fact, the story of the debates has been told very well and in more detail than here by a series of historians from Joseph Clarke Robert's *The Road From Monticello: A Study of the Virginia Slavery Debate of 1832* (1941) to Freehling, *supra* note 1, William Shade, *Democratizing the Old Dominion: Virginia and the Second Party System, 1824–1861* 191–224 (1996), Wolf, *supra*, at 196–234, and Lacy K. Ford, *Deliver Us from Evil: The Slavery Question in the Old South* 379–94 (2009). My discussion highlights the importance of slavery in politicians' home counties as a correlate of their support for (or opposition to) discussion of slavery and even limited action against slavery; the importance of talk of property rights in the debate, and the way Thomas Dew used the debates as a basis for his work.
17. RICHMOND ENQUIRER, Feb. 4, 1832, at 2. Erik Root has edited the complete debates. *See* SONS OF THE FATHERS: THE VIRGINIA SLAVERY DEBATES OF 1831–1832 (Erik S. Root, ed. 2010); *see also* ERIK S. ROOT, ALL HONOR TO JEFFERSON?: THE VIRGINIA SLAVERY DEBATES AND THE POSITIVE GOOD THESIS (2008).
18. RICHMOND ENQUIRER, Dec. 15, 1831 (discussing debate over Roane's petitions). *See also* WOLF, *supra* note 16, at 209; FREEHLING, *supra* note 1, at 126; DICKSON D. BRUCE, JR.,

The Rhetoric of Conservatism: The Virginia Convention of 1829–30 and the Conservative Tradition in the South (1982).

19. Journal of the House of Delegates, Begun and Held at the Capitol in the City of Richmond, on Monday the Fifth Day of December, One Thousand Eight Hundred and Thirty-One 29 (Richmond, Thomas Ritchie 1832) (subsequently *JHD*).

20. Shade identifies five groups in the House of Delegates distributed among those four regions in his extended analysis of Virginia politics. *See* Shade, *supra* note 16, at 202, 297–98.

21. *See* chapter 2 (discussing Washington College and slavery).

22. Richmond Enquirer January 19, 1832, at 2, first column (" 'That all men are by nature free and equal' is a truth held sacred by every American, and by every Republican, throughout the world. The right to the enjoyment of liberty, is one of those perfect, inherent and inalienable rights, which pertain to the whole human race, and of which they can never be divested, except by an act of gross injustice."). *Id.* at 2, third column ("Does [the negro mind] not move, and feel, and think? Has it not existence? The hour of eradication of the evil is advancing—it must come—Whether it is effected by the energy of our own minds, or by the bloody scenes of Southampton and St. Domingo, is a tale for future history.").

23. Annette Gordon-Reed, The Hemmingses of Monticello: An American Family (2008).

24. Gary B. Nash & Graham Russell Hodges Friends of Liberty: Thomas Jefferson, Tadeusz Kosciuszko, and Agrippa Hull (2008).

25. David B. Davis, Problem of Slavery in the Age of Revolution 173 (1975).

26. Wolf, *supra* note 16, at 210–11; Joseph Clarke Robert, The Road from Monticello: A Study of the Virginia Slavery Debate of 1832 18–19 (1941); Speech of Thomas J. Randolph, in the House of Delegates of Virginia, on the Abolition of Slavery (Richmond, Samuel Shepherd & Co. 1832).

27. *House of Delegates*, Richmond Enquirer January 21, 1832, at 2 (reprinting speech of James Gholson).

28. *Id.* at 2, column 3.

29. Richmond Enquirer January 21, 1832, at 2, column 1.

30. Richmond Enquirer, January 24, 1832, at 2, second column.

31. Richmond Enquirer, January 24, 1832, at 2, second column:

> I have endeavored to show, that private property is sacred.—That slaves and their increase are property–and no high and overruling necessity exists for taking them from their owners. If I have succeeded, Sir, I have done enough. . . . It is here that the powers of Government over this subject end. "Thus far may ye go, but no farther." "We stand on our chartered right."

32. Richmond Enquirer, Jan. 21, 1832, at 2, column 3.

33. Richmond Enquirer, January 24, 1832, at 2. *See also* Freehling, *supra* note 1, at 137–39 (discussing Gholson's argument); A Virginian, *Communications*, Richmond Enquirer, January 21, 1832, at 1 (arguing that we should not allow concern for posterity to take imprudent emancipation action now).

34. Richmond Enquirer, January 24, 1832, at 2, final column.

35. Jesse Harrison commented on Marshall's moderation in [Jesse Burton Harrison,] *The Slavery Question in Virginia*, 12 Am. Q. Rev. 379, 382 (Dec. 1832) (reviewing The Speech of Thomas Marshall in the House of Delegates of Virginia, on the Abolition of Slavery, Friday January 20, 1832 (Richmond, Thomas White, 1832)). The speech is erroneously reported as delivered on January 20 in the title of the pamphlet. A second edition of the pamphlet corrected the date in the title. *See* The Speech of Thomas Marshall . . . in Relation to Her Colored Population, Delivered . . . January 14, 1832 (2nd ed., Richmond, Thomas White, 1832).

36. Marshall, *supra* note 36, at 4.

37. Randolph, *supra* note 26, at 22 (quoting *Thomas Jefferson to Edward Coles*, 5 Writings of Thomas Jefferson 416–20 (1906) (August 25, 1814)).

38. Richmond Enquirer, January 26, 1832, at 2, columns 3–4 (Bruce's discussion of January 19).

39. RICHMOND ENQUIRER February 2, 1832 at 1, column 5 ("As long as a "property was not dangerous to the good order of society, it . . . would be tolerated.").

40. Votes on Witcher Resolution

Region	For	Against
Tidewater	25	10
Piedmont	31	9
Trans-Allegheny	0	31
Valley	4	20

41. JHD, *supra* note 19, at 110.

42. FREEHLING, *supra* note 1, at 165.

43. 1 WILLIAM FREEHLING, THE ROAD TO DISUNION, SECESSIONISTS AT BAY, 1776–1854 at 165 (1990) (quoting letter from Thomas Jefferson Randolph to his wife, Jane Randolph, January 29, 1832).

44. RICHMOND ENQUIRER February 14, 1832, at 3 column 1 (Brodnax's speech of February 6); CHRISTOPHER PHILLIPS, FREEDOM'S PORT: THE AFRICAN AMERICAN COMMUNITY OF BALTIMORE, 1790–1860 223 (1997) (discussing mass meeting of free black people in Baltimore to oppose colonization).

45. RICHMOND ENQUIRER, February 14, 1832, at 4. John C. Campbell of Brooke also spoke against compulsory emigration on February 6. See *Richmond Enquirer*, February 14, 1832, at 4, column 4.

46. JHD, *supra* note 19, at 134 (reporting 28 yes votes, but the roll call only has 27 names, so this analysis has changed that number to 27 yes votes). The initial bill, "A Bill Providing for the removal of free persons of colour from this commonwealth," appears as an appendix to the *Journal of the House of Delegates, supra* note 19, appendix bill 7.

47. JHD, *supra* note 19, 136–37. Campbell's resolution read "that all persons of colour within this commonwealth who are now free, shall with their own consent, . . . be removed from this state to Liberia." *Id.* at 136; RICHMOND ENQUIRER, February 21, 1832, at 4 (reprinting debate of February 7).

   Id. at 29, 109, 110, 134–35, 158. See also *Richmond Enquirer*, January 26, 1832, at 3 (listing roll call); FREEHLING, *supra* note 1, at 182–83, 185; SHADE, *supra* note 16, at 298 (Appendix 2). The year 1806 was an important date in Virginia's history with slavery, because that was the year that the legislature required that newly freed people to leave the state within one year. Hence, all those freed since 1806 were in the state illegally already. See *An Act to Amend the Several Laws Concerning Slaves, in* 3 THE STATUTES AT LARGE OF VIRGINIA, FROM OCTOBER SESSION 1792, TO DECEMBER SESSION 1806, at 251, 252 (Samuel Shepherd ed., Richmond, 1836); KIRT VON DAACKE, FREEDOM HAS A FACE: RACE, IDENTITY, AND COMMUNITY IN JEFFERSON'S VIRGINIA 77 (2012).

48. JHD, *supra* note 19, at 187–88.

49. *An Act Concerning the County of Northampton*, JHD, *supra* note 19, 248–49 (Chapter 188, passed March 5, 1832); *id.* at 189, 208. This passed the Senate on March 5, 1832. *Id.* at 208.

50. The letters first appeared in the *Richmond Enquirer*, Appomattox, *The Two Communications*, RICHMOND ENQUIRER, February 4, 1832 at 2–3 and February 28, 1832, at 3. One antislavery correspondent of the *Richmond Enquirer* pointed out that Appomattox was a William and Mary graduate. See York, *Communication for the Enquirer to Appomattox*, RICHMOND ENQUIRER, March 3, 1832, at 1–2.

51. See also *From a Correspondent*, RICHMOND ENQUIRER, February 7, 1832, at 2 (arguing against government's ability to take away right of owners to after-born children).

52. SPEECH OF MR. LEIGH ON THE QUESTION OF CERTAIN MEMORIALS FROM CITIZENS OF OHIO: PRAYING CONGRESS TO ABOLISH SLAVERY WITHIN THE DISTRICT OF COLUMBIA. DELIVERED IN THE SENATE OF THE UNITED STATES ON THE 19TH OF JANUARY, 1836. See *also* [Benjamin Watkins Leigh], THE LETTERS OF ALGERNON SYDNEY IN DEFENCE OF CIVIL LIBERTY AGAINST A MILITARY DESPOTISM (Richmond, T.W. White 1830).

53. The essays under the pseudonym "Locke," appeared in March 15, 20, and 27 and April 3 and 17 in the *Richmond Enquirer. But see* Letter of "Caution" in the *Richmond Enquirer*, January 21, 1832, at 1.

54. Of those who voted for the Preston amendment, only 37 percent returned to the House of Delegates for the 1832–33 session, whereas 55 percent of those who voted against it returned. Breaking those numbers down a little more by region, of the 25 from the Piedmont who voted on the Preston amendment, six voted in favor of Preston; only two (33 percent) were returned, whereas twenty-three of the thirty-two (72 percent) voting against the Preston amendment were returned. Two moderates (that is, people who voted against Preston but in favor of Bryce) were also not returned. In the Tidewater, two of the three who voted in favor of Preston were returned; thirteen of the twenty-five who voted against it were returned; and three of the seven moderates were returned. All thirty of the Trans-Allegheny delegates voted in favor of Preston; ten returned. (Moderates are here defined as people who voted no on Preston's amendment and yes on Bryce's amendment). For a discussion of elections in the wake of the antislavery debate, see Aylett Alexander to William Alexander, Anderson Family Papers, Washington and Lee University Special Collections, Box 6, Folder 53.

55. The essay appeared as a pamphlet, *Review of the Debate in the Virginia Legislature of 1831 and 1832* (Richmond, T. W. White 1832) and later was printed as *An Essay on Slavery* (Richmond, J. W. Randolph 1849); *Professor Dew's Essays on Slavery*, 10 DE BOW'S REV. 658–65 (1851), 11 *id.* 23–30 (1851); 11 *id.* 220–26 (1851); 11 *id.* 340–48 (1851); *Professor Dew on Slavery*, in THE PRO-SLAVERY ARGUMENT . . . . 287–490 (Charleston, Walker, Richards & Co. 1852). An earlier version appeared in *Abolition of Negro Slavery*, 12 AM. Q. REV. 189–265 (1832) and was summarized in the *Richmond Enquirer*, March 12, 1833, at 2. Subsequent references in this chapter are to the 1852 edition in *The Pro-Slavery Argument*, which is conveniently available on books.google.com.

56. The College's official history discusses Dew's *Review* in detail. 1 SUSAN GODSON ET AL., COLLEGE OF WILLIAM AND MARY: A HISTORY 247–54 (1993).

57. Dew, like many other Virginians, read Turner's *Confessions*; he found evidence in it of "beyond a doubt, mental aberration." DEW, *supra* note 55, at 289.

58. THOMAS RODERICK DEW, A DIGEST OF THE LAWS, CUSTOMS, MANNERS, AND INSTITUTIONS OF THE ANCIENT AND MODERN NATIONS (New York, Appleton 1853); Thomas R. Dew, *The French Revolution*, 5 S.Q. REV. 1–102 (1844).

59. *See, e.g.,* ELIZABETH FOX-GENOVESE AND EUGENE GENOVESE, THE MIND OF THE MASTER CLASS: HISTORY AND FAITH IN THE SOUTHERN SLAVEHOLDERS' WORLDVIEW 201–204 (2005); EUGENE GENOVESE AND ELIZABETH FOX-GENOVESE, SLAVERY IN WHITE AND BLACK: CLASS AND RACE IN THE SOUTHERN SLAVEHOLDERS' NEW WORLD ORDER 17–18 (2009) (identifying Dew as an originator of the view that slavery in the abstract is good). The responses to the 1832 debate remind us how controversial Dew's view was within Virginia and how much there were alternative, though not triumphant, visions. *See, e.g.,* Jefferson, *To the People of Eastern Virginia*, RICHMOND ENQUIRER, February 16, 1832, at 2–3 (responding to Appomattox); York, *supra* note (same); Jefferson, *To the People of Eastern Virginia*, RICHMOND ENQUIRER, March 10, 1832, at 2–3 (same).

60. NATHANIEL BEVERLEY TUCKER, A SERIES OF LECTURES ON THE SCIENCE OF GOVERNMENT INTENDED TO PREPARE THE STUDENT FOR THE STUDY OF THE CONSTITUTION OF THE UNITED STATES 416 (Philadelphia, Carey and Hart 1845).

61. *See, e.g.,* JOHN R. THOMPSON, EDUCATION AND LITERATURE IN VIRGINIA: AN ADDRESS DELIVERED BEFORE THE LITERARY SOCIETIES OF WASHINGTON COLLEGE, LEXINGTON, VIRGINIA, 18 JUNE, 1850 (Richmond, H. K. Ellyson 1850).

62. DEW, *supra* note 55, at 279.

63. *Id.* at 304.

64. *Id.* at 295.

65. *Id.* at 288.

66. *Id.* at 290.

67. *Id.* at 291, 292.

68. *Id.* at 293.

69. *Id.* at 293.

70. *Id.* at 294; *id.* at 355, 392; *id.* at 451.

71. *Id.* at 325.

72. *Id.* at 326.
73. DEW, *supra* note 55, at 355.
74. *Id.* at 356.
75. *Id.* at 365–66.
76. *Id.* at 384.
77. *Id.* at 384.
78. Dew referred to James McDowell's statement that

> when [property] loses its utility, when it no longer contributes to the personal benefits and wants of its holders in any equal degree with the expense or risk or the danger of keeping it, much more when it jeopardizes the security of the public;—when this is the case, then the original purpose for which it is authorized is lost, its character of property in the just and beneficial sense of it is gone, and it may be regulated without private injustice, in any manner which the general good of the community, by whose laws it was licensed, may require.

See DEW, *supra* note 55, at 386 (quoting SPEECH OF JAMES M'DOWELL . . . JANUARY 21, 1832 15 (Richmond, Thomas Whyte 1832)).
79. *See generally* WILLIAM NOVAK, THE PEOPLE'S WELFARE: LAW AND REGULATION IN NINETEENTH CENTURY AMERICA (1996).
80. DEW, *supra* note 55, at 387.
81. *Id.*
82. *Id.*
83. *Id.*
84. *Id.* at 385–86.
85. *Id.* at 391. *See also id.* at 290.
86. *Id.* at 422. *See also* DOROTHY ROSS, ORIGINS OF AMERICAN SOCIAL SCIENCE 3–33 (1991) (discussing Dew's economic thought).
87. Dew, *supra* note 55, at 443–44.
88. *Id.* at 444.
89. *Id.* at 424–25.
90. *Id.* at 426.
91. EUGENE GENOVESE, SLAVEHOLDERS' DILEMMA: FREEDOM AND PROGRESS IN SOUTHERN CONSERVATIVE THOUGHT, 1820-1860 11–20 (1992) (discussing Dew).
92. DEW, *supra* note 55, at 440.
93. *Id.* at 459.
94. WALKER, *supra* note 1, at 46.
95. *See* chapters 6 and 7 discussing Ruffin's endorsement of brutality toward slaves as part of maintaining slavery.
96. DEW, *supra* note 55, at 459–60.
97. *Id.* at 467.
98. *Id.* at 489.
99. *Id.* at 490.
100. *See* [Harper], *Colonization Society*, 1 S.REV. 219–33 (1828); 2 MICHAEL O'BRIEN, CONJECTURES OF ORDER: INTELLECTUAL LIFE IN THE ANTEBELLUM SOUTH, 1810–1860 946 n. 19 (2004) (suggesting Dew's reliance on Harper).
101. *See also* A HOUSE DIVIDED: THE ANTEBELLUM SLAVERY DEBATES IN AMERICA, 1776–1865 (Mason I. Lowance ed. 2003); JEFFREY ROBERT YOUNG DOMESTICATING SLAVERY: THE MASTER CLASS IN GEORGIA AND SOUTH CAROLINA, 1670–1837 (1999).
102. WILLIAM SUMNER JENKINS, THE PRO-SLAVERY ARGUMENT (1935); LARRY TISE, PROSLAVERY: A HISTORY OF THE DEFENSE OF SLAVERY IN AMERICA, 1701–1840 (1987).
103. For citations to these works in Dew, see Alfred L. Brophy, *Considering William and Mary's History with Slavery: The Case of President Thomas Roderick Dew*, 16 WM & MARY BILL RIGHTS J. 1091, 1130–31 n. 263 (2008).
104. THOMAS COOPER AN INTRODUCTORY LECTURE ON LAW (Columbia, SC, 1834) 7 (fitting slavery into utilitarian calculus); Thomas Cooper, *Slavery*, 1 S. LIT. J. 185 (1837). Daniel Kilbride, *Slavery and Utilitarianism: Thomas Cooper and the Mind of the Old South*,

59 J. SOUTHERN HIST. 469–86 (1993); Hugh Swinton Legare, *Jeremy Bentham and the Utilitarians*, 26 S. Rev. 1–96 (1831).

105. There was already a very competent (though somewhat antislavery) entry on slavery in Francis Lieber's *Encyclopaedia Americana*. *Slavery*, ENCYCLOPAEDIA AMERICANA 429–38 (Francis Lieber ed., Philadelphia, Desliver, Thomas & Co. 1835). The entry on slavery begins—aptly—"The history of mankind shows that the empire of force gives way but slowly to the empire of reason. It is one of the most interesting and useful labors of the historian, though not the most flattering to human pride, to trace the steps by which this change takes place." The entry is generally suspicious of slavery and notes among other things that Muslim slave laws were more lenient than those of the Christian nations regarding emancipation and that some states in the United States prohibited teaching slaves to read. Nevertheless, it maintains that slaves were better treated in the United States than elsewhere. *Id.* at 432 (citing Robert Walsh, *Appeal from the Judgments of Great Britain* perhaps at 237 (Philadelphia, Mitchell, Ames, and White 1819)).

106. Although Dew plays a small part in Drew Faust's study of antebellum southern intellectuals, A SACRED CIRCLE: THE DILEMMA OF THE INTELLECTUAL IN THE OLD SOUTH, 1840–1860 125, 129 (1977), he fits with her picture of intellectuals employing the proslavery argument to make themselves more relevant. Yet, it is not so clear that Dew turned to proslavery because he wanted to make himself relevant. Perhaps Dew was relevant because he was a spokesman for slavery.

107. Dew, *supra* note 55, at 422.

108. *Id.* at 451.

109. Dew's *Review* serves as something of a Rorschach inkblot test; some see him as the transition to the argument that slavery is a positive good; others link him more to an earlier strain of reasoning, justifying slavery as necessary. Several recent commentators emphasize Dew's (relative) moderation. William Freehling began his discussion of Dew by noting that he "reiterated what had passed for 'proslavery' in the debate itself, which was never defense of perpetual slavery." *See* 1 FREEHLING, *supra* note 43, at 191. Freehling later states, "The trouble with seeing Dew as a transitional figure is that no transition took place. The professor did not lead a school of his Virginia contemporaries halfway towards the 1850s. In his state, he worked largely alone." *Id.* at 193. Lacy Ford sees Dew as a relative moderate who proposed industrial development as a gradual solution to slavery. *See* FORD, *supra* note 16, at 381. Others see a bigger break. *See, e.g.,* GENOVESE AND GENOVESE, SLAVERY IN WHITE AND BLACK, *supra* note 59, at 17–18; 2 O'Brien, *supra* note 100, at 942. That Dew did not extend to a defense of perpetual slavery is not robustly tested by the debate, for what was on the table was—at most—a plan for gradual abolition. Anything that tended to defeat the plan was useful to Dew and much of the review, thus, needed only to show that even gradual abolition was "totally impracticable." DEW, *supra* note 55, at 292. That Dew did not defend perpetual slavery still offered no promise that slavery might ever be terminated.

110. [Jesse Harrison], *The Slavery Question in Virginia*, *supra* note 35. Harrison's essay was reprinted in 9 THE AFRICAN REPOSITORY 1–51 (1833).

111. Harrison, *supra* note 35, at 387.

112. PROCEEDINGS AND DEBATES OF THE VIRGINIA STATE CONVENTION OF 1829–30 at 411 (Samuel Shepard, Richmond, 1830) (Nov. 21, 1829).

113. *Id.* at 427.

114. *Id.* at 413–14.

115. Harrison, *supra* note 35, at 379. *See also id.* at 400 ("We are fully persuaded ourselves that the emancipation of the slaves, and their transportation out of the limits of the State, will be the only mode of action on the subject, which will be beneficial to either the blacks or the whites.").

116. *Id.* at 403.

117. *Id.* at 404 (quoting without attribution Dew, *supra* note 55, at 359).

118. 9 MEMOIRS OF JOHN QUINCY ADAMS, COMPRISING PORTIONS OF HIS DIARY FROM 1795 TO 1848 (Charles Francis Adams ed. 1876). *See also* William Jerry MacLean, *Othello Scorned: The Racial Thought of John Quincy Adams*, 4 J. EARLY REPUBLIC 143–60 (1984). Adams wrote about Dew publically in 1839. *Mr. Adams's Letter: Letter II, To the Citizens of*

the United States, *Whose Petitions, Memorials, and Remonstrances Have Been Entrusted to Me, to Be Presented to the House of Representatives of the United States, of the Third Session of the 25th Congress,* VERMONT PHOENIX, June 28, 1839 (the first letter was originally published in NATIONAL INTELLIGENCER, April 23, 1839 and the second on May 21, 1839).

119. [WILLIAM DRAYTON,] SOUTH VINDICATED FROM THE TREASON AND FANATICISM OF ABOLITIONISTS 55 (Philadelphia, H. Manly 1836).

120. *Id.* at 61.

121. *Id.* at 100.

122. *Id.* at 109, 107–10.

123. *Id.* at 67–68.

124. *Id.* at 69–70.

125. *Id.* at 120.

126. See JEANNINE DELOMBARD, SLAVERY ON TRIAL: LAW, ABOLITIONISM, AND PRINT CULTURE 49 (2007).

127. 1 DOCUMENTS OF THE SENATE OF THE STATE OF NEW-YORK, FIFTY-NINTH SESSION 2 (Albany, 1836); Thomas M. Owen, *An Alabama Protest Against Emancipation,* 2 GULF STATES HIST. MAG. 26 (July 1903). *See also Wilcox Meeting* [Tuscaloosa,] ALABAMA INTELLIGENCER AND STATE RIGHTS EXPOSITOR 3 (September 19, 1835) (reporting resolutions of group in Wilcox County, opposing antislavery activists who appeared sometimes in the garb of peddlers and other times as Christians).

128. Drayon was skeptical of the ability of individuals to improve. DRAYTON, *supra* note 121, at 228.

129. *Id.* at 246–47. Drayton explained many of the evils of abolitionists with reference to the horrors of the Haitian revolution. (By contrast, as slaves became more "civilized" they became less likely to take part in a rebellion. *Id.* at 302–303.)

130. *Id.* at 75 (quoting DEW, *supra* note 55, at 460). *See also* DRAYTON, *supra* note 121, at vi, vii, 74, 80, 102, 110, 137–46, 245, 298 (quoting Dew's *Review, supra* note).

131. DRAYTON, *supra* note 121, at 116–17.

132. For instance, a Presbyterian minister in North Carolina wrote to the president of Washington College in the Shenandoah Valley in 1837 about the hardening of attitudes toward emancipation: "On the slavery question a few years ago we thought slavery an evil or at least a source of much evil and were anxious to be rid of it. But now we set about to defend it against the very charges which we all once brought against [it]." J. S. McCutchan to Henry Ruffner, January 3, 1837, Trustee Papers, Folder 117, Washington and Lee Special Collections

133. James Harper, *Harper on Slavery,* in THE PRO-SLAVERY ARGUMENT, *supra* note 55, at 1, 17–18, at 82.

134. *Id.* at 3. *See also* A SOUTHERN FARMER, BONDAGE A MORAL INSTITUTION SANCTIONED BY THE SCRIPTURES OF THE OLD AND NEW TESTAMENT 55 (Macon, Griffin & Purse 1837); *White and Black Slavery,* S. LIT. MESSENGER 193, 194 (1840) ("It is not our purpose to argue the cause of slavery—a subject already discussed with signal ability by Mr. Paulding the present Secretary of the Navy, Professor Dew, Chancellor Harper, and the last though not the least Judge Upshur."); *Slavery in the Southern States,* 6 S.Q. REV. 317, 320 (1845) ("The South is indebted, we believe, to Professor Dew, for the first clear and comprehensive argument on the subject of slavery."); *Slavery and the Abolitionists,* 15 S.Q. REV. 165, 215 (1849) (referring to Dew for comparisons of slavery and free white workers in the United Kingdom).

135. *Judge Tucker's Address,* 13 S.LIT. MESSENGER 570 (1847).

136. The vote totals but not a roll call appear in the *Richmond Enquirer,* February 9, 1832, at 3, column 5. The *JHD* records only the outcome. An attempt to have the costs of removal paid by a tax on slaves and free black people was rejected. *Richmond Enquirer,* February 9, 1832, at 3, column 5. Record of the debates in the House on February 7 appears in the *Richmond Enquirer,* February 21, 1832, at 4, column 3.

A vote on the compensation of a person whose slave was killed while defending a white family during the rebellion was rejected on February 7, by a vote of 21 to 76. RICHMOND ENQUIRER, February 14, 1832 at 5. In fact the legislature rejected all petitions for slaves killed during the rebellion (as opposed to those sentenced to death by a court afterward). *See* Brophy, *supra* note 13, at 1835.

137. The vote totals but not a roll call appear in the *Richmond Enquirer*, February 16, 1832, at 3, column 6. The *JHD* does not mention Brown's amendment, only that the substitute bill was "amended by the house, on motions severally made."

Chapter 2

1. John Robinson Will, April 26, 1825 (probated 1826), Rockbridge County Will Book 6, Virginia State Library, at 78–82, preamble (noting that he had "migrated to America just in time to participate in its Revolutionary struggle").
2. John Robinson Will, *supra* note 1.

> 9th It is also my will and desire that all the negroes of which I may die possessed together with their increase shall be retained for the purposes of labor upon the above lands for the space of fifty years after my decease, always saving the rights of hiring out, within that time, such and as many of them as the aforesaid shall consider so far necessary on the [terms?] and of selling such others as may render themselves by their crimes or by crimes or by mutinous habits, unsafe or injurious in their connections with their fellows. This right is to be exercised upon a sound discretion and in such manner as to give the negroes who are allotted for hire the alternative of being sold to masters of their own choice. In any disposition which may be made of these slaves and also in their treatment it is my earnest desire that the strictest regard be paid to their comfort and happiness as well as the interest of the Estate. At the expiration of these fifty years, the Trustees aforesaid are released from all restraint as to the disposal of the negroes and may sell or retain them as the results of their labor shall demonstrate to be best.

3. *See* NEELY YOUNG, RIPE FOR EMANCIPATION: ROCKBRIDGE AND SOUTHERN ANTISLAVERY FROM REVOLUTION TO CIVIL WAR 176 (2011) (listing several wills from the 1850s where testators imposed restraint on sale of human beings).*See, e.g.,* Mary Cashaden's Will, Greene County, Alabama Wills Book B (1835), at 295, 297 (providing that one enslaved person, Besty, "shall not be sold at any time but that she shall be kept in the family of my daughter"). *See also* Alfred L. Brophy and Douglas Thie, *Land, Slaves, and Bonds: Trust and Probate in the Pre-Civil War Shenandaoh Valley*, forthcoming W.VA. L. REV. (2016), available at http://papers.ssrn.com/sol3/papers.cfm?abstract_id=2113084.
4. Samuel McD. Reid to Phillip Lindsey, June 18, 1829, Reid Family Papers, 027A-1, Washington and Lee University Special Collections [hereinafter WLU SC].
5. Memorandum of Agreement, Trustees of Washington College and John Wallace, August 22, 1826, Reid Papers, 027A-3, Folder 52, WLU SC.
6. "Negroes for Hire," December 19, 1826, Reid Papers, 027-11, Folder 153 WLU SC. Emma Burris suggests that the college rented substantially fewer people (such as nine in 1835), based it appears on a list of rentals for which payments were in arrears. *See* Emma Lynn Burris, The Tale of "Jockey" John Robinson, His Slaves, and Washington College 33 (Honors Thesis, Washington and Lee University History Department, 2007). The "List of Negro Hires Due to Washington College," Trustee Miscellaneous Papers, Box 1, Folder 4, however, seems to be a list of unsettled accounts, not a complete list of hires. It appears that the college rented out substantially more people than Burris estimated. In the year of his death, Robinson's estate had rented nearly thirty of his slaves. *See* "A List of Negroes Belonging to the Estate of John Robinson," n.d., circa 1826, Reid Papers, 027A-3, Folder 52, WLU SC (listing approximately 28 "negroes" as "hired").
7. Rental Form, January 18th, 1835, Trustee Papers, Folder 93, WLU SC.
8. Chapman Johnson, September 12, 1829, Trustee Papers, Folder 85, WLU SC.
9. *See* Statement of Sale of Negroes, Trustee Papers, Folder 112 (reporting that Garland paid $20,671.94) and Trustee Papers (1844), Folder 115, WLU SC (listing accounts of sales of slaves and property from Robinson's estate). There was also an offer from William Abraham of Morganton to purchase the slaves for $23,500. *See* William Abraham, September 25, 1835 and August 22, 1835, Reid Family Papers, 027-3, Folder 32, WLU SC.
10. Jacob Ruff to William Read, January 4, 1842, Trustee Papers, Misc. Papers, Box 1, Folder 6, WLU SC (contract for $300 for Washington College to Read to maintain six "elderly and

infirm" slaves, "Susan, Sally, Creesy, Landon, Nero, and Dick"). According to the 1826 list of the slaves owned by Robinson's estate, Creasy was sixty-eight years old in 1826 and worth nothing; Landon was forty-one, nearly blind, and worth $20; Nero was fifty, with a club foot, and worth nothing; and Dick was fifty-five, lame, and worth $125. Susan and Sally do not appear in the list of Robinson's slaves. The college's ownership of people had declined to sixty-seven people by July 1834. *See* "A List of Slaves Belonging To Washington College, July 30, 1834." Reid Family Papers, 027A-3, Folder 56, WLU SC. At that point, nine of their enslaved human people were listed as charges, rather than as assets. *See also* Trustee Papers, Folder 109.

11. *See* John E. Stealey, The Antebellum Kanawha Salt Business and Western Markets 11 (1993).

12. An 1837 letter from a friend, Presbyterian minister John S. McCutchan, lamented the hardening of attitudes toward slavery and increasing opposition to emancipation in a way that suggests that McCutchan and Ruffner shared views. J. S. McCutchan to Henry Ruffner, January 3, 1837, Trustee Papers, Folder 117, WLU SC. The letter is quoted in Chapter 1 at note 176.

13. Henry Ruffner, *Jack Neal*, 4 W.Va. Hist. Mag. 308-21 (1904). The story is also discussed, with a few more details, in Carrie Eldridge, Cabell County's Empire for Freedom: The Manumission of Sampson Sanders' Slaves 14–16, 34 (1999).

14. Ruffner, *Jack Neal, supra* note 13, at 309.

15. Ellen Eslinger, *The Brief Career of Rufus W. Bailey, American Colonization Society Agent in Virginia*, 61 J. South. Hist. 39, 46 (2005) (discussing Ruffner's work on behalf of Rockbridge Colonization Society).

16. *See* Marie Tyler-McGraw, An African Republic: Black & White Virginians in the Making of Liberia 90 (2007) (discussing Dabney's emancipation of the Harris family); *id.* at 84–85 (discussing the Rockbridge Colonization Society); Young, *supra* note 3, at 174.

17. *Lexington Gazette*, June 7–8, 1843 (reprinting Ruffner address); *see also* 19 African Repository 220–21 (1843) (mentioning address).

18. A Slaveholder of West Virginia [Henry Ruffner], Address to the People of West Virginia: Shewing that Slavery is Injurious to the Public Welfare, and that it may be Gradually Abolished without Detriment to the Rights and Interests of Slaveholders (Lexington, R.C. Noel 1847). An abbreviated version appeared in the Lexington *Gazette*, October 28, 1847, at 1–2. *See also Valley Whig*, Lexington Gazette, November 18, 1847, at 2 (responding to *Valley Whig* editorial criticizing Ruffner proposal and saying that "now is the time" to take up issue of gradual emancipation).

19. Ruffner, *supra* note 18, at 23 (quoting Bruce). Bruce was at best a mild critic of slavery, though he was a long-time supporter of the Virginia Colonization Society. *See* Alfred L. Brophy, *The Republics of Liberty and Letters: Progress, Union, and Constitutionalism in Graduation Addresses at the Antebellum University of North Carolina*, 89 N.C. L. Rev. 1879, 1938 n. 287 (2011).

20. Ruffner, *supra* note 18, at 30.

21. *Id.* at 38.

22. *See* [Jesse Burton Harrison,] *The Slavery Question in Virginia*, 12 Am. Q. Rev. 379, 382 (Dec. 1832) (reviewing The Speech of Thomas Marshall in the House of Delegates of Virginia, on the Abolition of Slavery, Friday January 20, 1832 (Richmond, Thomas White, 1832)).

23. *See* Robert Fogel & Stanley Engerman, Time on the Cross: The Economics of American Negro Slavery 59–67 (1972) (summarizing historians' interpretation of the unprofitability of slavery from the early twentieth century); James Oakes, *The Politics of Economic Development in the Antebellum South*, 15 J. Interdisciplinary Hist. 305–16 (1984). Though there may have been a modernization crisis in Virginia in these years, the central tendency of debate seems to have more to do with the celebration of modernization. In the addresses, there is dispute about just how much "the utilitarian spirit of our age," as Presbyterian minister Benjamin Mosely Smith phrased it in 1847, would crowd out all competing values. *See* B. L. Smith, An Address on the Importance and Advantage of Classical Study ... Washington College, June 1849 18 (Lexington, Patton & Burgess n.d.).

24. William Gleason Bean, *The Ruffner Pamphlet of 1847: An Antislavery Aspect of Virginia Sectionalism*, 61 Va. Hist. Mag. 260, 270 (1953) (mentioning Franklin Society secretary's

notes of March 6, 1847, indicating that Brockenbrough's proslavery speech "was as able as could be made on that side").

25. *Professor Dew on Slavery*, in THE PRO-SLAVERY ARGUMENT ... 287, 405–18 (Charleston, Walker, Richards & Co. 1852). Dew's *Essay on Slavery*, as his essay was often known, was taught at VMI in the 1850s by F. H. Smith. *See* REPORT OF THE BOARD OF VISITORS AND SUPERINTENDENT OF THE VIRGINIA MILITARY INSTITUTE at 20 (n.p., July 1857) (stating that F. H. Smith taught Dew's *Essay on Slavery* to some of his mathematics students). A year earlier, VMI had reported to the state legislature that it included proslavery thought as a part of its curriculum:

> Believing that every citizen of Virginia should be instructed at least to some extent in the science of government, and made acquainted with the theory and nature of the constitutional union of the United States ... and especially believing it essential that he should understand and believe the foundation of that divine institution of slavery which is the basis of the happiness, prosperity and independence of our southern people, and thoroughly fortified to advocate and defend it, the board has been enabled, by extending the term of the course, to introduce into the curriculum of instruction these most important subjects. They have also, for a like reason, had an opportunity to add to the course the subject of general history, as taught in the able manual of President Dew.

REPORT OF THE BOARD OF VISITORS AND SUPERINTENDENT OF THE VIRGINIA MILITARY INSTITUTE, JULY 1856 4 (1856).

26. VMI REPORT, *supra* note 25, at 24.
27. *See* GEORGE ARMSTRONG, THE CHRISTIAN DOCTRINE OF SLAVERY 127–29 (New York, Charles Scribner 1857).
28. DUTIES OF MASTERS TO SERVANTS: THREE PREMIUM ESSAYS (Charleston, Southern Baptist Publication Society 1851).
29. Bean, *supra* note 24, at 277 n.39 (attributing Ruffner's resignation to a combination of factors, including local church politics, conflict within Washington College, and the pamphlet); WILLIAM HENRY RUFFNER, WASHINGTON AND LEE HISTORICAL PAPERS, no. 6, 77–79 (1904) (discussing factors leading to Ruffner's resignation).
30. Henry Ruffner to Board of Trustees, June 1848, Folder 125, WLU SC.
31. Board of Trustees, draft letter, June 1848, Folder 125, WLU SC
32. *See* Letter from P. Calhoun, George E. Dabney, George D. Armstrong, and Benjamin S. Ewall to Board of Trustees, June 22, 1848, in Board of Trustees Papers, Folder 125, WLU SC (citing editorial in *Valley Star*); undated and unsigned letter, James McDowell Papers, University of North Carolina, Folder 111, Washington College File (alluding to complaints about president and faculty, which included lack of discipline and also lack of respect for the president). After Ruffner's resignation, the board clarified that the faculty served at their pleasure. Board of Trustees, Draft of College Regulations, June 1848, Trustee Papers, Folder 125, WLU SC.
33. ELLWOOD FISHER, LECTURE ON THE NORTH AND THE SOUTH, ... BEFORE THE YOUNG MEN'S MERCANTILE LIBRARY ASSOCIATION ... JANUARY 16, 1849 (Cincinnati, 1849).
34. Some have attributed this, erroneously I believe, to Centre College president John Clarke Young. Duke University's copy of the *Review of Ellwood Fisher's Lecture* has a handwritten attribution to Young on the title page. Young had written about gradual emancipation, though the "Justice" essay seems a more robust defense of emancipation than he was engaging in by the late 1840s. *See* JOHN CLARKE YOUNG, AN ADDRESS TO THE PRESBYTERIANS OF KENTUCKY PROPOSING A PLAN FOR THE INSTRUCTION AND EMANCIPATION OF THEIR SLAVES (Newburryport, Charles Whipple, 1836); JOHN CLARKE YOUNG, SCRIPTURAL DUTIES OF MASTERS: A SERMON PREACHED DANVILLE, KENTUCKY ... (Danville, Presbyterian Church American Tract Society 1846).
35. JUSTICE, REVIEW OF ELLWOOD FISHER'S LECTURE ON THE NORTH AND THE SOUTH (Louisville, 1849). Oliver Crenshaw, *General Lee's College* at 59 (1969) and Neely Young attribute the pamphlet to Ruffner. *See* YOUNG, *supra* note 3, at 142.
36. Henry Ruffner to George Dabney, May 29, 1849, in William Henry Ruffner Papers, Box 1, Folder 8, Columbia Theological Seminary, Decatur, GA.

37. YOUNG, *supra* note 3, at 137–38.
38. GEORGE JUNKIN, THE INTEREST OF OUR NATIONAL UNION VERSUS ABOLITIONISM (Cincinnati, R. Donogh 1843). *See also To the Rev. George Junkin*, 23 JOHN C. CALHOUN PAPERS 450 (Sept. 17, 1846) (William Edwin Hemphill ed., 1996).
39. JONATHAN BLANCHARD & NATHAN LEWIS RICE, A DEBATE ON SLAVERY . . . UPON THE QUESTION: IS SLAVE-HOLDING IN ITSELF SINFUL, AND THE RELATION BETWEEN MASTER AND SLAVE, A SINFUL RELATION? 228 (Cincinnati, William H. Moore 1845) (noting that Junkin's lecture had "*Junkinized* the minds of the people for two whole days; and when he had done, I do not believe that the heads of his auditors contained two substantial ideas on the topics which he handled.").
40. JUNKIN, *supra* note 38, at 71.
41. *Id.* at 72.
42. *Id.* at 75.
43. *Id.* at 77.
44. *Id.* at 77–78.
45. *Id.* at 79.
46. *Id.*
47. *Id.* at 4.
48. *Speech of Mr. Webster*, CONG. GLOBE, 31st Cong., 1st Sess. 269 (March 7, 1850).
49. A brief summary of Junkin's constitutional thought, which follows the conservative Whig approach to constitutionalism, appears in D. X. Junkin's *The Reverend George Junkin* . . . 510–11 (Philadelphia, Lippincott 1871).
50. *See* ROBERT COVER, JUSTICE ACCUSED: ANTI-SLAVERY AND THE JUDICIAL PROCESS (1975). Junkin's argument makes clear that the value of Union was often the basis for arguments about tolerating slavery and even refusing to take action against it. This was an instance in which the religious and constitutional arguments multiplied together to form a strong bulwark against abolitionists. Even if, as Jeffrey Schmitt has recently suggested, the Fugitive Slave Act *was* unconstitutional, judges and professors supported the Act and slavery as a way to preserve Union. This suggests yet another way that the interests of enslaved people—and the conscience of abolitionists—were subordinated to considerations of Union, independent of the Constitution. *See* Jeffrey M. Schmitt, *The Antislavery Judge Reconsidered*, 29 L. & HIST. REV. 797 (2011).
51. JOHN MCCARDELL, THE IDEA OF A SOUTHERN NATION: SOUTHERN NATIONALISTS AND SOUTHERN NATIONALISM, 1830–1860 (1981); MITCHELL SNAY, GOSPEL OF DISUNION: RELIGION AND SEPARATISM IN THE ANTEBELLUM SOUTH (1994).
52. CRENSHAW, *supra* note 35, at 111.
53. GEORGE JUNKIN, AN ADDRESS DELIVERED BEFORE THE LITERARY SOCIETIES OF RUTGERS COLLEGE (New York, Pruden and Martin 1856).
54. *Id.* at 5–6, 8 (discussing materialism and Guizot's *History of European Civlization* (3rd Am. Ed., New York, D. Appleton 1843).
55. *Id.* at 13.
56. *Id.* at 21.
57. *Id.* at 30.
58. *Id.* at 31.
59. *See Dew on Slavery*, supra note 25, at 405–18 (Charleston, Walker, Richards & Co. 1852) (suggesting impracticability of paying for emancipation and transportation of Virginia's enslaved population outside of the United States).
60. JUNKIN, *supra* note 53, at 32.
61. *Id.* at 34.
62. HENRY RUFFNER, UNION SPEECH; DELIVERED AT KANAWHA SALINES, VA., ON THE FOURTH OF JULY, 1856 (Cincinnati, Applegate & Co. 1856). In January 1861, Ruffner reported to his son that West Virginia would not secede from the United States. Henry Ruffner to William Henry Ruffner, January 9, 1861, Ruffner Papers, Columbia Theological Seminary, Decatur, GA.
63. RUFFNER, *supra* note 62, at 7.
64. *Id.* at 9.

65. *Id.* at 11.
66. *Id.* at 14–15.
67. *Id.* at 16.
68. D. H. HILL, ELEMENTS OF ALGEBRA 124, 150, 153 (Philadelphia, Lippincott 1857). Another problem paints the slave system in a somewhat less favorable light: "A planter, who knows that his negro-man can do a piece of work in 5 days, when the days are 12 hours long, asks how long it will take him when the days are 15 hours long." *Id.* at 106.
69. HAROLD D. TALLANT, EVIL NECESSITY: SLAVERY AND POLITICAL CULTURE IN ANTEBELLUM KENTUCKY 38–39, 59–60 (2003); JOHN C. YOUNG, AN ADDRESS TO THE PRESBYTERIANS OF KENTUCKY: PROPOSING A PLAN FOR THE INSTRUCTION AND EMANCIPATION OF THEIR SLAVES (Newburyport, Charles Whipple 1836); *President Young on Slavery*, 11 AFRICAN REPOSITORY 119–23 (1835); JOHN WRIGHT, TRANSYLVANIA UNIVERSITY: TUTOR TO THE WEST 165 (1980).
70. See JOHN CLARKE YOUNG, AN ADDRESS DELIVERED BEFORE THE UNION LITERARY SOCIETY OF MIAMI UNIVERSITY ... AUGUST 8TH, 1838 12–13, 21–22, 24–26 (Oxford, W.W. Bishop 1838) (urging a policy of "national rectitude," including restriction of slavery and respect for Native American land claims).
71. RICHARD HOFSTADTER & WALTER P. METZGER, ACADEMIC FREEDOM IN THE AGE OF THE COLLEGE 255 (1955).
72. George Robertson, *Address on behalf of the Deinologian Society, of Centre College, Delivered at Danville on the 4th of July, 1834*, in GEORGE ROBERTSON, SCRAP BOOK ON LAW AND POLITICS, MEN AND TIMES 159, 162 (Lexington, Ky., 1855). *See also id.* at 162–63 ("The mariner's compass, the printing press, the discovery of America, the 'Reformation,' and other subsidiary agencies have opened light on the black cloud of ignorance and superstition which hung over Europe for ages ... [;] man, long subjugated and degraded, began to understand and to assert his imprescribable rights.").
73. *Deinologian Society, supra* note 72, at 164.
74. *Deinologian Society, supra* note 72, at 164.
75. *Introductory Lecture Delivered in the Chapel of Morrison College, on the 7th of November, 1835,* in SCRAP BOOK, *supra* note 72, at 170, 173.
76. *See Mr. Robertson's Speech ... on the bill to Modify the Law of 1833, Prohibiting the Importation of Slaves,* in SCRAP BOOK, *supra* note 72, at 318, 323. *Contrast Slavery Letters Addressed to the Editor of the Frankfort Commonwealth,* SPEECHES AND WRITINGS OF HON. THOMAS F. MARSHALL 84–101 (Cincinnati, Applegate and Co. 1858). *See also* LACY FORD, DELIVER US FROM EVIL: THE SLAVERY QUESTION IN THE OLD SOUTH 312, 386 (2009) (discussing colonization sentiments in Kentucky).
77. *Address Delivered by Mr. Robertson in the Chapel of Morrison College, on the 22nd of February, 1852 ...,* in SCRAP BOOK, *supra* note 72, at 352–62 (emphasizing the value of Union and also the importance of supporting the federal government); WRIGHT, *supra* note 69, at 93 (discussing Jefferson Davis' education at Tranylsvania).
78. See LEWIS W. GREEN, ADDRESSES DELIVERED AT THE INAUGURATION OF REV. LEWIS W. GREEN, D.D., AS A PRESIDENT OF TRANSYLVANIA UNIVERSITY AND STATE NORMAL SCHOOL, NOVEMBER 18, 1856, 26–28 (Frankfort, A.G. Hodges, 1856).
79. *Id.* at 27–28.
80. 2 WILLIAM W. FREEHLING, THE ROAD TO DISUNION: SECESSIONISTS TRIUMPHANT 508–10 (2007).
81. JAMES P. HOLCOMBE, AN ADDRESS DELIVERED BEFORE THE SOCIETY OF ALUMNI, OF THE UNIVERSITY OF VIRGINIA, AT ITS ANNUAL MEETING, HELD IN THE PUBLIC HALL 40 (Richmond, Macfarlane and Ferguson 1853).
82. *Id.* at 41.
83. *Id.* at 37.
84. *Id.* at 40.
85. *Id.* at 42.
86. Albert Taylor Bledsoe, *Liberty and Slavery: Or, Slavery in the Light of Moral and Political Philosophy,* in COTTON IS KING, AND PRO-SLAVERY ARGUMENTS 269 (Augusta, GA, Pritchard, Abbott & Loomis, E.N. Elliott ed. 1860). Commentary appears in *Professor*

Bledsoe's Book; Liberty and Slavery.–Professor Bledsoe, 16 SOUTHERN PLANTER 148 (May 1856) and *Liberty and Slavery.–Professor Bledsoe,* 22 S. LIT. *Messenger* 382 (May 1856). Bledsoe has received less attention among recent historians than one might expect. *See* 1 MICHAEL O'BRIEN, CONJECTURES OF ORDER: THE INTELLECTUAL AND THE AMERICAN SOUTH, 1810–1860 578 (2005) (mentioning *Liberty and Slavery*).

87. TERRY A. BARNHART, ALBERT TAYLOR BLEDSOE: DEFENDER OF THE OLD SOUTH AND ARCHITECT OF THE LOST CAUSE (2011).

88. Bledsoe, *supra* note 86, at 274.

89. *Id.*

90. *Id.* at 278.

91. *Id.* at 280.

92. *Id.* at 283–84. This is similar to the argument made by Beverley Tucker at William and Mary in the 1830s, discussed in the introduction.

93. Bledsoe, *supra* note 86, at 285.

94. *Id.* at 289. *See also id.* at 288 ("The very law which institutes public order is that which introduces private liberty, since no secure enjoyment of one's rights can exist where public order is not maintained.").

95. Bledsoe, *supra* note 86, at 287.

96. Bledsoe also responded to one of Massachusetts Senator Charles Sumner's addresses. *See Address at Chicago's Metropolitan Theatre, May 9, 1855,* in CHARLES SUMNER, RECENT ADDRESSES AND SPEECHES 475 (Boston, Higgins & Bradley 1856).

97. Bledsoe, *supra* note 86, at 382 (discussing WILLIAM E. CHANNING, SELF CULTURE. AN ADDRESS INTRODUCTORY TO THE FRANKLIN LECTURES, DELIVERED AT BOSTON, UNITED STATES, SEPTEMBER, 1838 57 (London: John Mardon, 1839)).

98. *Id.* at 388 (discussing HENRY CHARLES CAREY, THE SLAVE TRADE: DOMESTIC AND FOREIGN: WHY IT EXISTS AND HOW IT MAY BE EXTINGUISHED (Philadelphia, 1853) (1872)).

99. *Id. at* 382.

100. *Id.* at 386.

101. *Id.* at 336.

102. *Id.* at 299.

103. *Id.* at 409 (invoking Burke and asking for liberty through law).

104. [CHARLES B. SHAW,] IS SLAVERY A BLESSING? PROF. BLEDSOE'S ESSAY ON LIBERTY AND SLAVERY: WITH REMARKS ON SLAVERY AS IT IS (Boston, Jewett 1857); 3 PHILIP ALEXANDER BRUCE, HISTORY OF THE UNIVERSITY OF VIRGINIA; THE LENGTHENED SHADOW OF ONE MAN 49 (1908). Whether Shaw was the author or not may be in doubt, but the text was authored by someone with at least some knowledge of the University. *See, e.g.,* SHAW, *supra,* at 90 (mentioning University of Virginia's graduation requirements); *id.* at 94 (lavishing praise on University of Virginia as "the best of the Southern schools of learning"); *id.* at 96 (discussing University of Virginia's law faculty).

105. *Id.* at 4, 10.

106. *Id.* at 51 ("[W]e contest the humanity of any legislation by which the mental capacities of slaves are refused the opportunity of development; or the justice of any opinion, formed under their present circumstances, that they cannot be rendered capable of intelligent self government.").

107. *Id.* at 34.

108. *Id.* at 25.

109. *Id.* at 77.

110. *Id.* at 119–20.

111. GEORGE F. HOLMES, INAUGURAL ADDRESS DELIVERED ON THE OCCASION OF THE OPENING OF THE UNIVERSITY OF THE STATE OF MISSISSIPPI, NOVEMBER 6, 1848 19 (Memphis, Franklin Book and Job Office 1849).

112. *Id.*

113. *Id.*

114. *Observations on a Passage in the Politics of Aristotle Relevant to Slavery,* 16 S. LIT. MESSENGER 193 (April 1850).

115. [George Frederick Holmes], *Uncle Tom's Cabin,* 18 S LIT. MESS. 721, 727 (Dec. 1852).

116. James P. Holcombe, *Is Slavery Consistent With Natural Law?*, 27 S. LIT. MESSENGER 401 (Dec. 1858) (reprinting address to Union Agricultural Society). The meetings of state agricultural societies, like the Union Agricultural Society (as in Union of North Carolina and Virginia), which began an annual fair in 1854 to exhibit and discuss the latest ideas in agriculture, frequently reaffirmed the centrality of slavery. Thomas Gholson, who had first come to fame during the debate in the Virginia legislature after Nat Turner, spoke about the importance of slavery at the Union Agricultural Society's first meeting in 1854, as did North Carolina politician A.W. Venable. THOMAS S. GHOLSON, ESQ., VALEDICTORY ADDRESS . . . DELIVERED BEFORE THE UNION AGRICULTURAL SOCIETY OF VIRGINIA AND NORTH CAROLINA, OCTOBER 27, 1854 (Richmond, Office of the Southern Farmer 1854); A.W. VENABLE, ADDRESS . . . DELIVERED BEFORE THE UNION AGRICULTURAL SOCIETY OF VIRGINIA AND NORTH CAROLINA, OCT. 25, 1854 (Richmond, Office of the Southern Farmer 1854). *See also* THOMAS S. FLOURNOY, ADDRESS . . . DELIVERED AT THE SECOND ANNUAL EXHIBITION OF THE UNION AGRICULTURAL SOCIETY OF VIRGINIA AND NORTH CAROLINA, ON THE 25TH OCTOBER, 1855 (Petersburg, Lewellen and Marks, 1855).

117. Holcombe, *supra* note 116, at 402. *See also* MARK BRANDON, STATES OF UNION: FAMILY AND CHANGE IN THE AMERICAN CONSTITUTIONAL ORDER 87 (2013).

118. JAMES P. HOLCOMBE, SKETCHES OF THE POLITICAL ISSUES AND CONTROVERSIES OF THE REVOLUTION 4 (Richmond, William H. Clemmitt 1856).

119. Holcombe, *supra* note 116, at 405 ("The State was made for man, and not man for the State, but the cooperation of the State is yet so necessary to the perfection of his nature, that his interests require the renunciation of any claim inconsistent with its existence, or its value as an agency of civilization.").

120. *Id.*

121. Holcombe, *supra* note 116, at 404.

122. *Id.* at 402.

123. *Id.* at 404.

124. *Id.* at 418 ("Civilization is a complex result, demanding a multitude of special offices and functions, for whose performance men are fitted, and even reconciled by gradations in intelligence and culture. However exalting or ennobling might be the knowledge of Newton or Herschell, God in his Providence has denied to the larger part of the human family, the opportunity of obtaining it.").

125. *Id.* at 401.

126. *Id.* at 405.

127. *Id.* at 405–406.

128. *Id.* at 406.

129. *Id.* at 406 (a slight mis-quotation of Thomas Campbell's *The Pleasures of Hope* 81 (London, Longman, Hurst, Rees, Orme, Brown, and Green 1825)).

130. *Id.* at 420.

131. During the crisis over the coming of secession, Holcombe published a pamphlet whose title describes its thesis well: *The Election of a Black Republican President as an Overt Act of Aggression on the Right of Property in Slaves: The South Urged to Adopt Concerted Action for Future Safety: A Speech before the People of Albemarle, on the 2d day of January, 1860* (Richmond, C.H. Wynne 1860). Similarly, Holcombe's colleague Henry St. George Tucker, who taught law at the University of Virginia from 1841 to 1845, wrote two books of particular interest here, *Lectures on Constitutional Law: For the Use of the Law Class at the University of Virginia* (Richmond, Shepherd and Colin 1843) and *A Few Lectures on Natural Law* (Charlottesville, James Alexander 1844). The former supported a compact theory of the Constitution, which would allow states to judge the constitutionality of federal action for themselves and take action if they judged federal action as unconstitutional. The later supported the common idea that people had different abilities and, therefore, were entitled to varying levels of rights based on their capacity. It was at odds with the antislavery argument that all people have rights, such as self-determination. The latter also adopted Bledsoe's argument that humans exist in a state of society and that the state must place restrictions on individuals in order to maintain order and prevent some from infringing the rights of others. *Id.* at 44.

132. *An Inaugural Address, Delivered on the 5th of March, 1834, on the Occasion of His Induction into Office as President of Randolph-Macon College,* 2 THE WORKS OF STEPHEN OLIN, . . . LATE PRESIDENT OF THE WESLEYAN UNIVERSITY 271 (New York, Harper & Brothers 1854).

133. WILLIAM A. SMITH, LECTURES ON THE PHILOSOPHY AND PRACTICE OF SLAVERY: AS EXHIBITED IN THE INSTITUTION OF DOMESTIC SLAVERY IN THE UNITED STATES, WITH THE DUTIES OF MASTERS TO SLAVES 14 (Nashville, Stevenson and Owen 1857).

134. *Id. See also* CHARITY R. CARNEY, MINISTERS AND MASTERS: METHODISM, MANHOOD, AND HONOR IN THE OLD SOUTH 124–28 (2011).

135. SMITH, *supra* note 133, at 20.

136. *Id.* at 19.

137. ALEXANDER HAMILTON SANDS' RECREATIONS OF A SOUTHERN BARRISTER 153 (Philadelphia, J.B. Lippincott 1859).

138. W.R. A., *The Duty of Southern Authors,* 23 S. LIT. MESSENGER 241 (Oct. 1856) (praising Smith and calling for a comprehensive literature of southern slavery).

139. 6 *American Publishers' Circular and Literary Gazette* 8 (1860).

140. *Politics, Law, and General Morals,* 9 METHODIST Q. REV. 497, 498 (July 1857). There was also a very critical review in 10 *National Magazine* 567–68 (1857).

141. JOHN H. POWER, REVIEW OF LECTURES OF WM. A. SMITH, D. D, ON THE PHILOSOPHY AND PRACTICE OF SLAVERY . . . IN A SERIES OF LETTERS ADDRESSED TO THE AUTHOR (Cincinnati, Swormstedt & Poe 1859).

142. Moncure D. Conway, *Fredericksburg First and Last,* 17 MAG. AM. HIST. 449, 451–52 (1887).

143. MEMOIRS OF SAMUEL M. JANNEY: LATE OF LINCOLN, LOUDOUN COUNTY, VA.: A MINISTER IN THE RELIGIOUS SOCIETY OF FRIENDS 97 (Philadelphia, Friends' Book Association 1881); *Slavery Discussion in Virginia,* 3 NATIONAL ERA, Aug 30, 1849, 138; S. M. Janney, *M. Janney's Review of Rev. William A. Smith's Address on Slavery,* 3 NATIONAL ERA Oct 18, 1849, 168. *See also* DAVID B. CHESEBROUGH, CLERGY DISSENT IN THE OLD SOUTH, 1830–1865, 59 (1996).

144. *See* Smith v. Swormstedt, 57 U.S. (16 How.) 288 (1853); Smith v. Swormstedt, Fed. Cases No. 13,112 (D. Ohio, Oct. Term 1852).

145. SMITH, *supra* note 133, at 27.

146. *Id.* at 18.

147. *Id.* at 28.

148. *Id.* at 49.

149. *Id.* at 50.

150. *Id.* at 56–57.

151. *Id.* at 222.

152. *Id.* at 69.

153. *Id.* at 79, 62.

154. *Id.* at 250. The observation made often by Southerners that men were born and not made—however trite it sounded—held the key to understanding much of their world view. It was children who were born and their state of dependence suggested how much society owed to them to guide them in their development, as well as how completely incapable they were of governing themselves, to say nothing of rules governing others. The analogy of the state to natural organisms, such as humans (or often plants) has become known as organic philosophy. Many political philosophers employed organic metaphors, but the philosophy in the South has been most commonly associated with Jospeh LeConte, a professor at South Carolina's Charleston College. *See* Joseph LeConte, *The Relationship of Organic Science to Society,* 13 S. PRESBYTERIAN REV. 40 (1860); Theodore D. Bozeman, *Joseph LeConte: Organic Science and a "Sociology for the South,"* 39 J. SOUTHERN HIST. 565–82 (1973); JAMES OSCAR FARMER, THE METAPHYSICAL CONFEDERACY: JAMES HENLEY THORNEWELL AND THE SYNTHESIS OF SOUTHERN VALUES 105–107 (1986).

155. SMITH, *supra* note 133, at 69. *Id* at 55 (ship of state); *id.* at 58 (and using a somewhat different meaning of state, may have left their home state, presumably Virginia, because of opposition to slavery).

156. *Id.* at 116.

157. *Id.* at 128.

158. *Id.* at 187.

159. ALBERT BARNES, AN INQUIRY INTO THE SCRIPTURAL VIEWS OF SLAVERY 27 (1846).
That quotation was picked up by William Goodell *Slavery and Anti-Slavery* 147 (1855).
Little is know about Sims. He studied in Germany for a while and may be the author of
Translation from Professor Tholuck, 1 METHODIST QUARTERLY REVIEW 354 (July 1841).
His brother, Alexander Dromgoole Sims, was a South Carolina representative to Congress
and author of the proslavery pamphlet *View of Slavery, Morals and Politics* (Charleston,
A.E. Miller 1834) and a novel published under the pseudonym of Crayon Rigmarole, *Bevil
Faulcon: A Tradition of the Old Cherhaw* (Charleston, I. C. Morgan 1842).

160. *See, e.g.,* MICHAEL THOMAS SMITH, A TRAITOR AND A SCOUNDREL: BENJAMIN HEDRICK
AND THE COST OF DISSENT 68–85 (2003) (discussing the events leading to dismissal
of Hedrick by the University of North Carolina in 1856 for supporting Liberty Party);
Letter from Benjamin S. Hedrick to H. R. Helper, October 27, 1856, Southern Historical
Collection, University of North Carolina (discussing his removal and the case for Fremont).

161. 1 O'BRIEN, *supra* note 86, at 316.

162. HENRY AUGUSTINE WASHINGTON, THE VIRGINIA CONSTITUTION OF 1776: A DISCOURSE
DELIVERED BEFORE THE VIRGINIA HISTORICAL SOCIETY ... JANUARY 17TH, 1852
(Richmond, Macfarlane & Fergguson, 1852), reprinted in *The Virginia Constitution of 1776*,
18 S. LIT. MESSENGER 664 (November 1852). Washington said:

> [T]hose liberties which we enjoy and prize so highly, have sprung from no abstract
> theory of human rights and human equality; but are an entailed inheritance, transmitted
> to this democratic age and country, from the bosom of a haughty and exclusive aristoc-
> racy, and that this its true, not only of those liberties themselves, but also of the forms,
> the very machinery as it were, by which they have been preserved and perpetuated. The
> principle of *equality*, is indeed new; but *liberty* is old and aristocratic, and the great work
> assigned to modern society, is to reconcile ancient liberty with modern equality.

Id. at 19–20.

163. Henry Augustine Washington, *The Social System of Virginia*, 14 S. LIT. MESSENGER 65, 68
(February 1848).

164. *Id.* at 68 (quoting Thomas Carlyle, *On History*, in 2 THOMAS CARLYLE: CRITICAL AND
MISCELLANEOUS ESSAYS 83, 86 (1899) (1830)).

165. *Id.* at 68.

166. *Id.* at 69.

167. Quoting Guizot:

> The world will no longer agitate for the sake of some abstract principle, some fanciful
> theory, some Utopian government, which can only exist in the imagination of an en-
> thusiast; nor will it put up with practical abuses and oppressions, however formed by
> prescription and expediency, when they are opposed to just principles and the legiti-
> mate end of government. To ensure respect, to obtain confidence, governing powers
> must now unite theory and practice; they must know and acknowledge the influence
> of both. They must regard principles as facts; must respect both truth and necessity—
> must shun, on the one hand, the blind pride of the fanatic theorist, and, on the other,
> the no less blind pride of the libertine practician.

Id. at 67 (quoting GUIZOIT, GENERAL HISTORY OF CIVILIZATION IN EUROPE 89 (New
York, Appleton 1838)).

168. One example that Bancroft used of the aristocracy of Virginia was William Berkeley's statement in 1671 that "I thank God, there are no free schools, nor printing; and I hope we shall
not have these [for a] hundred years; for learning has brought disobedience, and heresy,
and sects into the world, and printing has divulged them, and libels against the best governments." *Id.* at 71 (quoting 2 BANCROFT HISTORY 192).

169. *Id.* at 73.

170. *Id.* at 77.

> The masses of mankind are not *amateurs* in labor. To induce them to labor, *motives*
> must be addressed to them, and, as a general rule, the amount of exertion which they

will make will be in exact proportion to the weight of the motives to which they are subjected.

Id. at 78 (concluding that the master-slave relationship not suited to economic development).

171. *Id.* at 79.

172. *Id.* at 79.

173. T. C. Thornton, An Inquiry into the History of Slavery: Its Introduction into the United States; Causes of its Continuance; and Remarks upon the Abolition Tracts of William E. Channing (Washington, William M. Morrison 1841).

174. *See* Edward Mayes, History of Education in Mississippi 116–17 (1899).

175. T. C. Thornton, Inaugural Address Delivered on the First Commencement Occasion of Centenary College, July 28, 1842 … (Jackson, Southron 1842). Tommy Rogers, *T.C. Thornton: A Methodist Educator of Antebellum Mississippi*, 44 J. Miss. Hist. 136–46 (1982); Ray Holder, *Centenary: Roots of a Pioneer College (1838–1844)*, 42 J. Miss. Hist. 77–98 (1980). That the title page identified Centenary College as at Clinton, Mississippi—the site first selected for it–suggests that it appeared even before the school opened. In the fall of 1841, when the school opened, it was in Brandon Springs.

176. Thornton, *supra* note 176, at 46.

177. *Id.* at 73–87, 98, 100.

178. *Id.* at 62–63, 66, 68.

179. *Id.* at 128, 139.

180. *Id.* at 140, 158–60.

181. 40 U.S. (15 Pet.) 449 (1841).

182. A. B. Longstreet, Letters on the Epistle of Paul to Philemon, or, The Connection of Apostolical Christianity with Slavery (Charleston, B. Jenkins, 1845). *See also* Mark Auslander, The Accidental Slaveowner: Revisiting a Myth of Race and Finding an American Family (2011).

183. John Donald Wade, Augustus Baldwin Longstreet: A Study of the Development of Culture in the South (1924).

184. Longstreet, *supra* note 182, at 11.

185. *Id.* at 8.

186. Augustus B. Longstreet, A Voice from the South: Letters from Georgia to Massachusetts 20–21 (Baltimore, Western Continent Press 1847).

187. *Id* at 22.

188. *Id.* at 24.

189. *Id.* at 53.

190. *Id.* at 32, 48–41.

191. *Baccalaureate Address Delivered at the University of South Carolina to the Graduating Class of 1859*, in Oscar Penn Fitzgerald, Judge Longstreet: A Life Sketch 97–106 (1891).

192. Elliott, *Slavery in the Light of International Law*, in Cotton is King, *supra* note 86, at 731–37.

193. *Id.* at 736.

194. *Id.* at 737.

195. *See* Christie Farnham, The Education of the Southern Belle: Higher Education and Student Socialization in the Antebellum South (1994). *See also* Jon L. Wakelyn, *Antebellum College Life and the Relations Between Fathers and Sons*, in The Web of Southern Social Relations: Women, Family, Education 107–26 (Walter J. Fraser, et al. eds. 1985); Steven Stowe, *The Not-So-Cloistered Academy: Elite Women's Education and the Family Feeling in the Old South*, in *id.* at 90–106; Elbert W.G. Boogher, Secondary Education in Georgia, 1732–1858 161–69 (Ph.D. dissertation, University of Pennsylvania, 1933) (listing courses offered to males and females in secondary schools in the antebellum era); Edgar Knight, The Academy Movement in the South (1920); Florence Davis, The Education of Southern Girls from 1750 to 1860 (Ph.D. dissertation, University of Chicago, 1951).

196. Syllabus of the Course of Study Recommended to the Students of South Carolina Female College Institute (1836). The syllabus is conveniently reprinted in 5 Edgar Wallace Knight, *Documentary History of Education in the South Before 1860* 404–17 (1953).

197. WILLIAM GILMORE SIMMS, INAUGURATION OF THE SPARTANBURG FEMALE COLLEGE, ON THE 22ND AUGUST, 1855 27–28 (Spartanburg, Trustees, 1855).

198. G. WARD HUBBS, GUARDING GREENSBORO: A CONFEDERATE COMPANY IN THE MAKING OF A SOUTHERN COMMUNITY at 65–66 (2003) (discussing Cocke's operation of his Greene County plantation in a state of quasi-freedom); ALISON GOODYEAR FREEHLING, DRIFT TOWARDS DISSOLUTION: THE VIRGINIA SLAVERY DEBATE OF 1831–32 222–28 (1982) (discussing Cocke's plans for training enslaved people in Virginia for transportation, then their lives in Liberia).

199. 2 LOREN SCHWENINGER, THE SOUTHERN DEBATE OVER SLAVERY: PETITIONS TO SOUTHERN COUNTY COURTS, 1775–1867 1–2 (2008) (describing case of estate of George Hays).

200. See HUBBS, *supra* note 198, at 71 (discussing distribution of Matthew Estes' *A Defence of Negro Slavery as It Exists in the United States* (Montgomery, Alabama Journal 1846) in Greene County); Johanna Nicol Shields, *Writers in the Old Southwest and the Commercialization of American Letters*, 27 J. Early REPUBLIC 471 (2007) (discussing challenges facing publishers in antebellum Alabama and noting in particular the problems with selling Estes). Estes also published a novel, *Tit for Tat* (1856), which emphasized English "white slavery."

201. CATALOGUE AND CIRCULAR OF THE GREENSBORO FEMALE ACADEMY 1855, Henry Watson papers, Duke University. *See, e.g., Washington and LaFayette Academy,* 7 ALABAMA INTELLIGENCER AND STATE RIGHTS EXPOSITOR (Oct. 3, 1835), at 4 (listing courses in mental and moral philosophy and also semimonthly lectures on science and literature and noting that University of Alabama faculty were on the board of visitors).

202. DUTIES OF MASTERS TO SERVANTS, *supra* note 29. Sturgis was the son-in-law of Samuel K. Talmage, an 1820 graduate of Princeton University, and the president of Oglethorpe University in Georgia. These arguments had been in circulation for several decades. *See, e.g.,* GEORGE W. FREEMAN, THE RIGHTS AND DUTIES OF SLAVEHOLDERS: TWO DISCOURSES DELIVERED ON SUNDAY, NOVEMBER 27, 1836, IN CHRIST CHURCH, RALEIGH, NORTH-CAROLINA (Charleston: A.E. Miller 1837); Estes, *supra* note 200, at 253–60 (discussing "duties towards slaves," although the discussion was primarily aimed at demonstrating that slaves were treated well). William T. Hamilton's *The Duties of Masters and Slaves Respectively, or, Domestic Servitude as Sanctioned by the Bible: A Discourse Delivered in the Government Street Church* . . . (Mobile, F. H. Brooks 1845) was more proslavery and had less on duties toward slaves than some similar works. Earlier, Hamilton had been an advocate of the American Colonization Society. *See* WILLIAM T. HAMILTON, A WORD FOR THE AFRICAN: A SERMON, FOR THE BENEFIT OF THE AMERICAN COLONIZATION SOCIETY . . . JULY 24, 1825 (Newark, W. Tuttle & Co. 1825).

203. DUTIES, *supra* note 28, at 55–56.

204. CAROLINA LEE HENTZ, LOVELL'S FOLLY (Cincinnati, Hubbard and Edmands 1833).

205. BENJAMIN BUFORD WILLIAMS, A LITERARY HISTORY OF ALABAMA: THE NINETEENTH CENTURY (1979); Lindsay Russell Whichard, Caroline Lee Hentz, Pro-Slavery Propagandist (Ph.D. dissertation, UNC, 1951); Jamie Stanesa, Slavery and the Politics of Domestic Identities: Ideology, Theology, and Region in American Women Writers, 1850–1860 (Ph.D. dissertation, Emory University, 1993).

206. See *Wild Jack, or The Stolen Child,* in CAROLINE HENTZ, THE BANISHED CHILD 47, 64 (Philadelphia, 1856). Among Hentz's improperly ignored work is the short story, "The Black Mask," which is about a woman who marries a man who always wears a black mask in her presence. The setting in Louisiana, well-known for its ambiguous racial boundaries, invites much speculation about the story's meaning. *See The Black Mask,* in THE BANISHED CHILD, *supra,* at 165. Alas, that and the meaning of Hentz's college stories must wait for another time.

207. See CAROLINE LEE HENTZ, THE PLANTER'S NORTHERN BRIDE (Philadelphia, T. B. Peterson 1853); CAROLINE LEE HENTZ, HUMAN AND DIVINE PHILOSOPHY: A POEM, WRITTEN FOR THE EROSOPHIC SOCIETY OF THE UNIVERSITY OF ALABAMA . . . AND RECITED BY A.W. RICHARDSON, DECEMBER 12TH, 1843 (Tuscaloosa, Journal and Flag Office 1844).

208. See Michael Sugrue, South Carolina College: The Education of an Antebellum Elite (Ph.D. dissertation, Columbia University, 1992); Michael Surgue, *"We Desire Our Future*

Rulers to Be Educated Men": South Carolina College, the Defense of Slavery, and the Development of Secessionist Politics, in THE AMERICAN COLLEGE IN THE NINETEENTH CENTURY 91–114 (Roger L. Geiger ed. 2000).

209. THOMAS COOPER, TWO ESSAYS 1. ON THE FOUNDATION OF CIVIL GOVERNMENT AND 2. ON THE CONSTITUTION OF THE UNITED STATES 45 (Columbia, D.J. & M. Faust 1826). *See also* LARRY E. TISE, PROSLAVERY: A HISTORY OF THE DEFENSE OF SLAVERY IN AMERICA, 1701–1840 372 (1987) (discussing Cooper).

210. JAMES OSCAR FARMER, THE METAPHYSICAL CONFEDERACY: JAMES HENLEY THORNWELL AND THE SYNTHESIS OF SOUTHERN VALUES (2nd ed. 1999).

211. *See, e.g.,* JAMES HENLEY THORNWELL, THE STATE OF THE COUNTRY (Columbia, SC, Southern Guardian 1861); JAMES HENLEY THORNWELL, LETTER TO HIS EXCELLENCY GOVERNOR MANNING ON PUBLIC INSTRUCTION IN SOUTH CAROLINA (1853); REPORT ON THE SUBJECT OF SLAVERY, PRESENTED TO THE SYNOD OF SOUTH CAROLINA, AT THEIR SESSIONS IN WINNSBOROUGH, NOVEMBER 6, 1851 ... (1851). One theme in his work was the obligations of Christian masters toward their slaves. JAMES HENLEY THORNWELL, THE RIGHTS AND DUTIES OF MASTERS: A SERMON PREACHED AT THE DEDICATION OF A CHURCH ERECTED IN CHARLESTON, SC, FOR THE BENEFIT AND INSTRUCTION OF THE COLOURED POPULATION (Charleston, Walker and James 1850).

212. JAMES HENLEY THORNWELL, LETTER TO HIS EXCELLENCY GOVERNOR MANNING ON PUBLIC INSTRUCTION IN SOUTH CAROLINA (Columbia, R.W. Gibbes 1853).

213. *See, e.g.,* Sugrue, *supra* note 208, at 302–306.

214. R. H. RIVERS, MORAL PHILOSOPHY 128–32 (1859) (Thomas O. Summers ed., 2d ed. 1861). *See also* Gerald F. Vaughn, *Teaching Moral Philosophy in the South During Slavery and Reconstruction: Edward Wadsworth of LaGrange College and Southern University,* 46 METHODIST HISTORY 179 (2008); ANSON WEST, A HISTORY OF METHODISM IN ALABAMA 632–33 (1893); WILLIS G. CLARK, HISTORY OF EDUCATION IN ALABAMA, 1702–1889 166–67 (1880); RICHARD HENDERSON RIVERS, THE LIFE OF ROBERT PAINE, D.D.: BISHOP OF THE METHODIST EPISCOPAL CHURCH, SOUTH (1884) (discussing life of LaGrange's first president).

215. ANSON WEST, A HISTORY OF METHODISM IN ALABAMA 611–21 (1893) (discussing Centenary Institute); MARION ELIAS LAZENBY HISTORY OF METHODISM IN ALABAMA AND WEST FLORIDA 1035 (1960); ANNUAL CATALOG AND CIRCULAR OF CENTENARY INSTITUTE (Summerfield, Southern Enterprise 1852). William Lipscomb's 1853 graduation address is in Dorman family papers, 1838–1897, UNC.

216. RIVERS, *supra* note 214, at 351.

217. *Id.* at 349–51.

218. *See, e.g.,* EDWARD GOODWIN, LILY WHITE 20–21(Philadelphia, Lippincott 1858); JOHN ALLEN WYETH, HISTORY OF LA GRANGE MILITARY ACADEMY AND THE CADET CORPS, 1857–1862, LA GRANGE COLLEGE 1830–1857 47 (1907) (commenting about *Lily White,* "the moral teaching is excellent, the language is chaste").

219. JOHN LEADLEY DAGG, THE ELEMENTS OF MORAL SCIENCE (New York, Sheldon & Co. 1860) (1st. ed. 1859). *See also* JOHN LEADLEY DAGG, AUTOBIOGRAPHY ... (1886); GEORGE PAUL SCHMIDT, THE OLD TIME COLLEGE PRESIDENT 129 (1930).

220. DAGG, *supra* note 219, at 362.

221. *Id.* at 345.

222. *Id.* at 349–50.

223. *Id.* at 369.

224. *Id.* at 372.

225. *Id.* at 373–74.

226. *Murder of Dr. Chamberlain,* NEW YORK TIMES (Oct. 17, 1851); SOUTHERN EDUCATION: ADDRESSES DELIVERED IN THE CHAPEL AT OAKLAND COLLEGE, ON THE DAY OF ANNUAL COMMENCEMENT, JUNE 29TH, 1854 (New Orleans, The Picayune 1854) (farewell address of moderately antislavery President Robert L. Stanton, who served 1851 to 1854, which emphasized need for funding for education). CHARLES H LIPPY BIBLIOGRAPHY OF RELIGION IN THE SOUTH 94 (discussing Stanton). Henry Hughes, author *Treatise on Sociology,* which sought to create a more perfect slavery (warranteeism)

through state-imposed regulations that might in some ways limit the rights of slave owners. See DOUGLAS AMBROSE, HENRY HUGHES AND PROSLAVERY THOUGHT IN THE OLD SOUTH (1996); Douglas Ambrose, *Statism in the Old South*, SLAVERY, SECESSION, AND SOUTHERN HISTORY 101, 105 (Robert L. Paquette & Lou Ferleger eds., 2000) (discussing role of state-imposed regulations around slavery in Hughes' work).

In a series of addresses to the literary socieites at Oakland, speakers developed proslavery arguments. See JOHN PERKINS, AN ADDRESS DELIVERED BEFORE THE ADELPHIC AND BELLE-LETTRES SOCIETIES, OF OAKLAND COLLEGE, APRIL 6, 1853: ON THE DUTY OF DRAWING FROM THE HISTORY AND THE THEORY OF OUR GOVERNMENT, JUST VIEWS OF INDIVIDUAL AND NATIONAL LIFE (Reveille Office, 1853) at Emory; John Murdoch, *Home Education and the Claims of Oakland College*, in SOUTHERN EDUCATION ADDRESSES DELIVERED . . . AT OAKLAND COLLEGE, . . . JUNE 29TH, 1854 (New Orleans, The Picayune, 1854). However, as with many other southern schools, as late as the 1840s, sometimes the addresses hinted at antislavery sentiments. See HENRY D. MANDEVILLE, JR., ADDRESS ON SOME OF THE DUTIES OF THE AMERICAN CITIZEN. DELIVERED BEFORE THE ADELPHIC INSTITUTE OF OAKLAND COLLEGE, TUESDAY, APRIL 5, 1842 at 7 (Vidalia, La., Concordia Intelligencer Office, 1842) (discussing rights of man); ADDRESSES, DELIVERED ON THURSDAY, DECEMBER 18, 1851 ON THE OCCASION OF THE INAUGURATION OF REV. ROBERT L. STANTON, AS PRESIDENT OF OAKLAND COLLEGE, MISS. (New Orleans, T. Rea, 1852).

227. On antebellum university library catalogs more generally see GUY HUBBS, DISSIPATING THE CLOUDS OF IGNORANCE: THE FIRST UNIVERSITY OF ALABAMA LIBRARY, 1831–1865, 27 LIBRARIES & CULTURE 20–35 (1992) (reconstructing intellectual life based on library catalog). Hubbs employs two catalogs from the antebellum University of Alabama, Richard Furman, *Catalogue of the Library of the University of Alabama* (Tuskaloosa, M. J. Slade 1837); Wilson G. Richardson, *Catalogue of the Library of the University of Alabama* . . . (Tuscaloosa, M. D. J. Slade 1848).

228. See, e.g., O'BRIEN, *supra* note 86; ELIZABETH FOX-GENOVESE & EUGENE GENOVESE, THE MIND OF THE MASTER CLASS: HISTORY AND FAITH IN THE SOUTHERN SLAVEHOLDERS' WORLDVIEW 505–27 (2005); MITCHEL SNAY, GOSPEL OF DISUNION: RELIGION AND SEPARATISM IN THE ANTEBELLUM SOUTH (1997); CHARLES F. IRONS, ORIGINS OF PROSLAVERY CHRISTIANITY: WHITE AND BLACK EVANGELICALS IN COLONIAL AND ANTEBELLUM VIRGINIA (2008).

229. Throughout this period, but particularly in the 1850s there was talk of the "virtues" of slavery for the enslaved, yet much of this was about how to make slaves more productive. See, e.g., DUTIES OF MASTERS TO SERVANTS: THREE PREMIUM ESSAYS, *supra* note 28. Very little if any of the talk of paternalism in the 1850s seriously addressed ways to significantly improve the lives of the enslaved. It was about making the system of slavery function well. This is different from those who held slaves in quasi-freedom as a midway point to emancipation, which is discussed in Chapters 10 and 11. When courts identified such cases they largely prohibited that practice. See, e.g., Trustees of Quaker Society of Contentnea v. Dickenson, 12 N.C. (1 Dev.) 189 (1827). This helps clarify the distinctions between kinds of paternalism that are in circulation. In *Deliver Us from This Evil: The Slavery Question in the Old South* 8–9 (2009), Lacy Ford describes similar varieties of paternalism from the early nineteenth century to the 1830s and beyond.

Chapter 3

1. KENNETH SACKS, UNDERSTANDING EMERSON: THE AMERICAN SCHOLAR AND HIS STRUGGLE FOR SELF-RELIANCE (2002).
2. Ralph Waldo Emerson, *American Scholar* in RALPH WALDO EMERSON: ESSAYS AND LECTURES 53, 64 (Joel Porte ed., 1983).
3. Ralph Waldo Emerson, *Nature* in ESSAYS AND LECTURES, *supra* note 2, at 7.
4. WILLIAM B. RODMAN, AN ADDRESS DELIVERED BEFORE THE TWO LITERARY SOCIETIES OF WAKE FOREST COLLEGE ON THE 9TH JUNE, 1846: AT THE SOLICITATION OF THE PHILOMATHESIAN SOCIETY 19 (Raleigh, W. W. Holden 1846).
5. JOHN QUIST, RESTLESS VISIONARIES: THE SOCIAL ROOTS OF ANTEBELLUM REFORM IN ALABAMA AND MICHIGAN 317 (1998).

322 Notes to Pages 98–102

6. Judson E. Crump and Alfred L. Brophy, *Cornelius Sinclair's Odyssey*, forthcoming, MISS. L.J. (2016), available at http://papers.ssrn.com/sol3/papers.cfm?abstract_id=2469529&download=yes.
7. *See* WILLIAM GASTON, ADDRESS DELIVERED BEFORE THE PHILANTHROPIC AND DIALECTIC SOCIETIES AT CHAPEL HILL, N.C., JUNE 20TH, 1832 19 (Richmond, Thomas W. White, 2nd ed. 1832); WILLIAM HOOPER, AN ORATION DELIVERED AT CHAPEL HILL ON WEDNESDAY, JUNE 24, 1829 . . . 14–15 (Hillsborough, Dennis Heartt 1829).
8. HENRY TUTWILER, ADDRESS DELIVERED BEFORE THE EROSOPHIC SOCIETY 12 (Tuscaloosa, Robinson and Davenport 1834).
9. HENRY TUTWILER, ADDRESS DELIVERED BEFORE THE EROSOPHIC SOCIETY AT THE UNIVERSITY OF ALABAMA, AUGUST 9, 1834 8 (Tuscaloosa, Robinson & Davenport 1834). *See also* KENNETH SACKS, UNDERSTANDING EMERSON: THE AMERICAN SCHOLAR AND HIS STRUGGLE FOR SELF-RELIANCE (2003).
10. TUTWILER, *supra* note 9, at 11–12.
11. For a fuller development of intellectual culture in Tuscaloosa, see A. JAMES FULLER, CHAPLAIN TO THE CONFEDERACY: BASIL MANLY AND BAPTIST LIFE IN THE OLD SOUTH (2000).
12. *Id.* at 222. Manly explained that statement in detail, which reveals his complex relationship with the institution of slavery. *See* Manly to Ide, August 27, 1844, in Manly Diary, 321–25 Hoole Special Collection Library, University of Alabama.
13. *A Poetical Oration*, 29 S. LIT. MESS. 318 (Oct 1859) (summarizing a number of literary orations).
14. [William Gilmore Simms,] *Popular Discourses and Orations*, 4 S.Q. REV. 317, 319 (Oct. 1851).
15. *See* [Beverley Tucker,] *An Oration, Delivered Before the Two Societies of the South-Carolina College. . .*, 17 S.Q. REV. 37 (1850).
16. *Editors Table*, 20 S.Q. REV. 59–60 (January 1854).
17. JAMES MCDOWELL, ADDRESS DELIVERED BEFORE THE ALUMNI ASSOCIATION OF THE COLLEGE OF NEW JERSEY, SEPTEMBER 26, 1838 34–36 (Princeton, John Bogart 1838).
18. *Id.* at 33.
19. *Id.* at 35.
20. *Id.* at 37.
21. *Id.* at 43.
22. *See Speech of James McDowell, of Virginia, on the Wilmot Proviso, Delivered in the House of Representatives, Tuesday, September 3, 1850*, CONG. GLOBE, 31st Cong., 1st Sess., 1678, 1684. McDowell's shift from the 1832 Virginia legislative debates, where he opposed slavery because of its harmful effects, through to the debate on the Wilmot Proviso in the early 1850s, suggests something about how attitudes in the South in general shifted over that time. Though McDowell was more antislavery than many at the start of his career—and less proslavery at the end of it—we can see how in one person the shift toward proslavery took place. McDowell's moderate proslavery position of the Princeton address was in opposition to abolitionists, and his thought that their radicalism was injuring the prospects of gradual termination. At the Wilmot Proviso debate in 1850, McDowell emphasized the ways that exclusion of slavery from the territories would subordinate the South and lead to disunion. Even there he acknowledged what seems to have been some questioning of slavery when he said that "whatever the opinions I . . . entertain upon the institution of slavery in the abstract, I have never doubted for a moment that as the white and the black races now live together in the southern States, it is an indispensable institution for them both." *Id.* at 1678.
23. MCDOWELL, *supra* note 22, at 45.
24. *Id.* at 48–49.
25. JOHN REUBEN THOMPSON, EDUCATION AND LITERATURE IN VIRGINIA: AN ADDRESS DELIVERED BEFORE THE LITERARY SOCIETIES OF WASHINGTON COLLEGE, LEXINGTON, VIRGINIA, 18 JUNE, 1850 11 (Richmond, H.K. Ellyson 1850).
26. *Id.* at 16.
27. *Id.* at 32, 35.
28. *Id.* at 32.
29. *Id.* at 33.
30. ROBERT TOOMBS, AN ORATION, DELIVERED BEFORE THE FEW AND PHI GAMMA SOCIETIES, OF EMORY COLLEGE, AT OXFORD, GA., JULY 1853 8 (Augusta, Chronicle & Sentinel 1853).

31. *Id.*
32. *Id.* at 10–11.
33. *Id.* at 26.
34. WILLIAM PORCHER MILES, REPUBLICAN GOVERNMENT NOT EVERYWHERE AND ALWAYS THE BEST; AND LIBERTY NOT THE BIRTHRIGHT OF MANKIND: AN ADDRESS DELIV ERED BEFORE THE ALUMNI SOCIETY OF THE COLLEGE OF CHARLESTON . . . MARCH 30TH, 1852 24, 26 (Charleston, Walker & James 1852).
35. ERIC. H. WALTHER, THE FIRE-EATERS 270–95 (1992). Miles had moved over time toward a more openly proslavery position. *See* WILLIAM PORCHER MILES, THE ANNUAL ADDRESS DELIVERED BEFORE THE CLIOSOPHIC SOCIETY, MARCH 29, 1847 (Charleston, 1847); WILLIAM PORCHER MILES, ADDRESS DELIVERED BEFORE THE CLIOSOPHIC SOCIETY OF THE CHARLESTON COLLEGE, ON THE OCCASION OF THEIR ANNIVERSARY, DECEMBER THIRD, 1841 (Charleston, T.W. Haynes 1847).
36. *See, e.g.,* WILLIAM H. STILES, CONNECTION BETWEEN LIBERTY AND ELOQUENCE: AN ADDRESS DELIVERED BEFORE THE PHI KAPPA AND DEMOSTHENIAN SOCIETIES OF FRANKLIN COLLEGE . . . 26 (Augusta, Georgia Home Gazette Office, 1852) ("eloquence has been a powerful aid in the preservation of liberty"); WILLIAM H. STILES, STUDY, THE ONLY SURE MEANS OF ULTIMATE SUCCESS. AN ADDRESS DELIVERED BEFORE THE THALIAN AND PHI DELTA SOCIETIES OF OGLETHORPE . . . (Milledgeville, Southern Recorder Office, 1854).
37. WILLIAM H. STILES, SOUTHERN EDUCATION FOR SOUTHERN YOUTH: AN ADDRESS BEFORE THE ALPHA PI DELTA SOCIETY OF THE CHEROKEE BAPTIST COLLEGE . . . 14TH JULY, 1858 5 (Savannah, George H. Nichols 1858).
38. *Id.* at 9.
39. *Id.*
40. *Id.* at 9–10.
41. *See* Carla Bosco, *Harvard University and the Fugitive Slave Act,* 79 NEW ENGLAND Q. 227, 242–45 (1996). *See also* SVEN BECKERT, KATHERINE STEVENS, ET AL., HARVARD AND SLAVERY: SEEKING A FORGOTTEN HISTORY 16 (2012) (discussing antislavery at Harvard in the 1850s).
42. STILES, *supra* note 37, at 10.
43. *Id.,* at 10–11.
44. *Id.* at 15 ("Slavery, as history informs us, is coeval with the origin of Society.").
45. *Id.* at 27, 24.
46. *Id.* at 28.
47. JOHN RANDOLPH TUCKER, ADDRESS . . . DELIVERED BEFORE THE PHOENIX AND PHILOMATHEAN SOCIETIES, OF WILLIAM AND MARY COLLEGE, ON THE 3D OF JULY, 1854 (Richmond, Chas. H. Wynn 1854).
48. *Id.* at 9.
49. *Id.* at 10.
50. *Id.*
51. *Id.* at 11.
52. *Id.* at 15.
53. *Id.*
54. ALEXANDER R. GATES, AN ORATION ON THE ANNIVERSARY OF AMERICAN INDEPENDENCE; DELIVERED BEFORE THE TWO LITERARY SOCIETIES OF THE UNIVERSITY OF ALABAMA 12 (Tuscaloosa, Erosophic Society 1841). *See also* JOHANNA NICHOL SHIELDS, FREEDOM IN A SLAVE SOCIETY: STORIES FROM THE ANTEBELLUM SOUTH 34–38 (2012) (discussing visit of William Gilmore Simms to University of Alabama).
55. GATES, *supra* note 54, at 8–9.
56. *Id.* at 16.
57. In that regard, they track the trajectory of thought in antebellum universities. *See* Eugene Genovese, *Higher Education in Defense of Slave Society,* in EUGENE GENOVESE, THE SOUTHERN FRONT: HISTORY AND POLITICS IN THE CULTURAL WAR 92–106 (1995).
58. JOSEPH TAYLOR, A PLEA FOR THE UNIVERSITY OF ALABAMA: AN ADDRESS DELIVERED BEFORE THE EROSOPHIC AND PHILOMATHIC SOCIETIES OF THE UNIVERSITY OF ALABAMA ON THEIR ANNIVERSARY OCCASION, AUGUST 9, 1847 (Tuskaloosa, M.D.J. Slade 1847).

59. *See* 4 THOMAS MCADORY OWEN, DICTIONARY OF ALABAMA BIOGRAPHY 1651 (1921).
60. TAYLOR, *supra* note 58, at 15.
61. *Id.* at 20.
62. *Id.* at 22.
63. *Id.* at 23.
64. *Id.* at 23–24.
65. *Id.* at 24.
66. *Id.* at 25.
67. *Id.* at 30.
68. *Id.*
69. *Id.*
70. *Summer Travel in the South*, 2 S. Q. Rev. 246, 247 (Sept. 1850). I am indebted to Rebecca McIntyre for this data.
71. 4 OWEN, *supra* note 59, at 1555.
72. GEORGE D. SHORTRIDGE, AN ADDRESS FROM THE ALUMNI OF THE UNIVERSITY OF ALABAMA, TO THE PEOPLE OF ALABAMA 7 [1850] (typescript copy in Hoole Library, University of Alabama).
73. *Id.* at 8.
74. MUSCOE R.H. GARNETT, AN ADDRESS DELIVERED BEFORE THE SOCIETY OF ALUMNI OF THE UNIVERSITY OF VIRGINIA, AT ITS ANNUAL MEETING . . . 29TH OF JUNE, 1850 6 (Charlottesville, O.S. Allen & Co. 1850). *See also* JOHN ALBERT BROADUS, AN ADDRESS DELIVERED BEFORE THE SOCIETY OF ALUMNI OF THE UNIVERSITY OF VIRGINIA . . . JUNE 26, 1856 (Charlottesville, O.S. Allen 1856).
75. GARNETT, *supra* note 74, at 10.
76. *Id.* at 27 ("[A]t last we began to believe what was so often dinned in our eras, that slavery was the moral, social and political evil they pretended.").
77. *Id.* at 29.
78. *Id.* at 30.
79. A CITIZEN OF VIRGINIA [MUSCOE R.H. GARNETT], THE UNION, PAST AND FUTURE: HOW IT WORKS, AND HOW TO SAVE IT (4th ed. Charleston, Walker & James 1850). *See also Is Southern Civilization Worth Preserving?*, 19 S.Q. REV. 190 (Jan. 1851) (reviewing [Garnett], *Union, supra*).
80. *See* THE ADDRESS OF THE SOUTHERN RIGHTS' ASSOCIATION, OF THE UNIVERSITY OF VIRGINIA, TO THE YOUNG MEN OF THE SOUTH (Charlottesville, J. Alexander 1851); ADDRESS OF THE SOUTHERN RIGHTS ASSOCIATION OF THE SOUTH CAROLINA COLLEGE, TO THE STUDENTS IN THE COLLEGES AND UNIVERSITIES, AND TO THE YOUNG MEN, THROUGHOUT THE SOUTHERN STATES . . . (n.p., 1851?).
81. JOHN RANDOLPH TUCKER, AN ADDRESS DELIVERED BEFORE THE SOCIETY OF ALUMNI OF THE UNIVERSITY OF VIRGINIA . . . 28TH JUNE 1851 62–64 (Richmond, H.K. Ellyson 1851).
82. JOSEPH HODGSON, AN ADDRESS DELIVERED BEFORE THE JEFFERSON SOCIETY OF THE UNIVERSITY OF VIRGINIA . . . APRIL 13, 1857 (Richmond, J.D. Hammersley & Co. 1857).
83. *Id.* at 15.
84. *Id.* at 16.
85. *The American Citizen*, in 1 FORTY YEARS OF ORATORY—DANIEL WOOLSEY VOORHEES 13 (Indianapolis, Bobbs Merrill 1896).
86. *Id.* at 38, 41.
87. *Id.* at 45.
88. *Id.* at 47.
89. *Id.* at 54. One of the most moderate southern schools during the antebellum era was the University of North Carolina. Several addresses in the 1820s and early 1830s questioned slavery. *See* Alfred L. Brophy, *The Republics of Liberty and Letters: Progress, Union, and Constitutionalism in Graduation Addresses at the Antebellum University of North Carolina*, 89 N.C. L. REV. 1879, 1882–83 (2011) (discussing addresses by William Gaston and William Hooper). In 1836, South Carolina politician Henry L. Pinckney used the invitation to give a graduation address at UNC to oppose nullification. (He would soon lose his seat in Congress

because of the perception that he was insufficiently strong in his support of slavery and opposition to federal power.) *Id.* at 1916–17. But even at UNC in 1857 a graduation address by North Carolina politician Henry Watkins Miller questioned the value of the Union and demanded that North Carolinians insist on their Constitutional rights to self-determination. *Id.* at 1953–55.

90. CNN Wire Staff, *Former State Trooper, 77, Pleads Guilty in Civil Rights Case*, available at http://www.cnn.com/2010/CRIME/11/15/alabama.civilrights.case/.

91. J. MILLS THORNTON, DIVIDING LINES: MUNICIPAL POLITICS AND THE STRUGGLE FOR CIVIL RIGHTS IN MONTGOMERY, BIRMINGHAM, AND SELMA 486–87 (2002); *see also* Mary L. Dudziak, *"The Case of "Death for a Dollar Ninety-Five": Miscarriages of Justice and Constructions of American Identity*, in WHEN LAW FAILS: MAKING SENSE OF MISCARRIAGES OF JUSTICE 25 (Austin Sarat & Charles Ogletree eds., 2009).

92. T. G. KEEN, AN ADDRESS DELIVERED BEFORE THE FRANKLIN & ADELPHI SOCIETIES OF HOWARD COLLEGE, . . . 14 (Tuskaloosa, Slade 1850). A picture of Judson Female Institute appears at 2 *Our Whole Country; Or, the Past and Present of the United States, Historical* 817 (1861).

93. *Monument to a Slave*, THE AFRICAN REPOSITORY 212 (July 1857) (reprinting article from the *Marion American*). The Alabama Department of Archives and History website has a photograph of Harry's monument taken around the 1930s. http://digital.archives.alabama.gov/cdm/singleitem/collection/photo/id/1898/rec/13.

A more recent photograph of Harry's monument in the Marion Cemetery is here http://www.thefacultylounge.org/2011/02/faithful-slave-monument.html.

Samford University's Library has an 1858 photograph of cadets in front of Howard College's main building. It is available here http://library.samford.edu/about/historypictorial.html.

94. *Monument to a Slave*, supra note 93.

95. THE CHARTER AND STATUTES OF JEFFERSON COLLEGE . . . 89 (Natchez, Book and Job Office 1840), which includes the library catalog at 21–29. CHARLES L. DUBUISSON, INAUGURAL ADDRESS (Natchez, Courier & Journal Office, 1835) (is not concerned with slavery). Shortly afterward, because of the declining student enrollment brought on by tough economic times, the college program was dropped and the school continued its secondary school.

96. GEORGE F. HOLMES, INAUGURAL ADDRESS DELIVERED ON THE OCCASION OF THE OPENING OF THE UNIVERSITY OF THE STATE OF MISSISSIPPI, NOVEMBER 6, 1848 19 (Memphis, Franklin Book and Job Office 1849).

97. See Chapter 2, at 67.

98. ADDRESS DELIVERED BY HON. JEFFERSON DAVIS, BEFORE THE PHI SIGMA & HERMEAN SOCIETIES . . . UNIVERSITY OF MISSISSIPPI . . . JULY 15, 1852 (Memphis, Appeal Book and Job Office 1852); JOHN FLETCHER, STUDIES ON SLAVERY: IN EASY LESSONS (Natchez, Jackson Warner 1852). *See also* GEORGE S. SAWYER, SOUTHERN INSTITUTES: OR, AN INQUIRY INTO THE ORIGIN AND EARLY PREVALENCE OF SLAVERY AND THE SLAVE TRADE (Philadelphia, J. Lippincott 1859).

99. ALBERT GALLATIN BROWN, AN ADDRESS ON SOUTHERN EDUCATION DELIVERED JULY 18, 1859, BEFORE . . . "MADISON COLLEGE," SHARON, MISSISSIPPI 8 (Washington, 1859). *Id.* at 6 (noting that the errors of abolitionists "are sufficiently apparent to a Southern audience without exposition from any quarter").

100. *Id.* at 4.

101. *Id.* at 5.

102. *Id.* at 6.

103. *Id.*

104. REPORT OF THE BOARD OF VISITORS AND SUPERINTENDENT OF THE VIRGINIA MILITARY INSTITUTE 24 (n.p., July 1857).

105. FRANCIS H. SMITH, COLLEGE REFORM (Philadelphia, Thomas, Cowperthwait & Co. 1851).

106. Bradford Alexander Wineman, Francis H. Smith: Architect of Antebellum Southern Military Schools and Educational Reform 199–200 (Ph.D. dissertation, Texas A&M, 2006).

107. JOHN WHITE BROCKENBROUGH, ADDRESS DELIVERED ON LAYING THE CORNER STONE OF THE NEW BARRACKS OF THE VIRGINIA MILITARY INSTITUTE. JULY 4, 1850 (New York, John Wiley 1850).

108. *Id.* at 18.
109. *Id.* ("In that dark hour, if come it must, she will turn with assured hope to the hundreds of alumni of this school, and can any doubt that they will be the first to rush to the rescue of their beloved Virginia, and repulse the invaders from her soil?").
110. B. J. BARBOUR, AN ADDRESS TO THE LITERARY SOCIETIES OF VIRGINIA MILITARY INSTITUTE ON THE 4TH OF JULY, 1854 (Richmond, Macfarlane & Ferguson 1854). The address also appeared in the *Southern Literary Messenger's* September 1854 issue at 513–28.
111. THOMAS WENTWORTH HIGGINSON, MASSACHUSETTS IN MOURNING. A SERMON ... JUNE 4, 1854 (Boston, James Munoe and Company 1854).
112. JAMES W. MASSIE, AN ADDRESS DELIVERED BEFORE THE SOCIETY OF ALUMNI OF THE VIRGINIA MILITARY INSTITUTE, JULY 3D, 1857 (Richmond, McFarlane & Fergusson 1857).
113. *Id.* at 37.
114. *Id.* at 34.
115. *Id.* at 39.
116. WILLOUGHBY NEWTON, VIRGINIA AND THE UNION: AN ADDRESS, DELIVERED BEFORE THE LITERARY SOCIETIES OF THE VIRGINIA MILITARY INSTITUTE 9 (Richmond, Macfarlane & Fergusson 1858).
117. *Id.* at 10.
118. *Id.* at 11. Newton continued with the economic benefits that slavery brought, including the production of cotton, which in turn "in the North has given wings to enterprise, built up cities—created, as if by magic, beautiful villages, and covered the whole face of the country with evidences of busy and prosperous industry." *Id.* at 12. *See also Address of Hon. Willoughby Newton, Before the Virginia State Agricultural Society,* ... *Feb. 19th, 1852,* 7 AMERICAN FARMER 413 (June 1852); *Address of the Hon. Willoughby Newton, Delivered Before the Maryland State Agricultural Society, at its Third Annual Exhibition, in the City of Baltimore, October 25th, 1850,* 6 AMERICAN FARMER 189 (December 1850).
119. NEWTON, *supra* note 116, at 26.
120. *Id.* at 27 ("[T]he safety and interests of the South may require positive legislation, as in the admission of new States or the acquisition of territory, as well as a negative on the power of the majority.").
121. *Id.* at 22.
122. *Id.* at 29–30.
123. *Id.* at 29.
124. *See, e.g.,* Royal C. Dumas, *My Son and My Money Go to the University of Alabama? The Students at the University of Alabama in 1845 and the Families That Sent Them,* 1 ALA. C.R. & C.L. L. REV. 67 (2011); Michael Sugrue, South Carolina College: The Education of an Antebellum Elite (Ph.D. dissertation, Columbia University, 1992) (finding that most of the nearly 3,000 students at the antebellum South Carolina College were children of the planter elite).
125. An important and growing body of scholarship addresses the literary society debates. *See* DANIEL J. SHARFSTEIN, THE INVISIBLE LINE 57–59 (2011) (discussing literary society debates at Yale); JOHN LUSTER BRINKLEY, ON THIS HILL: A NARRATIVE HISTORY OF HAMPDEN-SYDNEY COLLEGE 131–36 (1994); Mark J. Swails, Literary Societies as Institutions of Honor at Evangelical Colleges in Antebellum Georgia (M.A. thesis, Emory University, 2007); TIMOTHY J. WILLIAMS, INTELLECTUAL MANHOOD: UNIVERSITY, SELF, AND SOCIETY IN THE ANTEBELLUM SOUTH (2015); Heidi Rickes, Jurisprudence at Davidson College, 1838–1861 (seminar paper, 2013); Benjamin Kleinman, UNC Literary Society Debates, 1858–1859 (seminar paper, 2013).
126. EDWARD S. JOYNES, ADDRESS BEFORE THE PHOENIX LITERARY SOCIETY OF THE COLLEGE OF WILLIAM AND MARY ... 8TH OF DECEMBER 1859 32–33 (Richmond, Macfarlane & Ferguson 1860).
127. *See, e.g.,* Licivyronean Literary Society Records, 1839–1847, Swem Library, College of William and Mary, November 27, 1841.
128. *Id.,* February 26, 1842.
129. *Id.,* November 1, 1841.
130. *Id.,* November 11, 1843.

131. Graham Society Minute Books, Washington and Lee University Special Collections, January 10, 1852.

132. *See, e.g.,* Licivyronean Literary Society Records, *supra* note 127, May 9, 1840 (internal improvements); January 23, 1841 (capital punishment); November 21, 1840 (immigration); November 21, 1840 (Texas).

133. Swails, *supra* note 125, Appendix 2.D, Emory Phi Gamma Society Minutes, October 10, 1846 (concluding in the affirmative).

134. Swails, *supra* note 125, Appendix 2.D, Emory Phi Gamma Society Minutes, May 18, 1850 (negative).

135. Swails, *supra* note 125, Appendix 2.B, Mercer Phi Delta Society Minutes, August 24, 1844.

136. Swails, *supra* note 125, Appendix 2.D, Emory Phi Gamma Society Minutes, August 24, 1844 (asking "Is slavery a moral evil?" and concluding in the negative). A few years before, Emory's Phi Gamma Literary Society debated "Is it right for us to bring Africans over to America to become slaves?" They answered in the affirmative. *Id.,* September 15, 1838.

137. Euzelian Society Minutes, March 4, 1843, Z. Smith Reynolds Library, Wake Forest University (decided in the negative 5 to 6). But when the same topic was debated again in August of the same year, they came to the opposite conclusion. *Id.* August 28, 1843 (decided in the affirmative 7 to 3).

138. Euzelian Society Minutes, November 26, 1859 (decided in the negative 7 to 3).

139. Euzelian Society Minutes, November 6, 1847; *id.* July 28, 1849; *id.* October 4, 1850.

140. Graham Society Minute Books, Washington and Lee University Special Collections, June 23, 1855 (rejected, 3 to 6). This was also debated on June 24, 1846, by the Graham Society. The outcome is unknown.

141. Graham Society Minute Books, Washington and Lee University Special Collections, September 15, 1855 (affirmed 14 to 5).

142. Washington Society Minute Books, Washington and Lee University Special Collections, September 10, 1859 (set for debate on September 24, 1859).

143. Wake Forest Euzelian Society Minutes, April 16, 1858 (decided in the affirmative 16 to 4); Euzelian Society Minutes, August 20, 1859 ("Has the institution of African slavery been beneficial to the U.S.?") (decided in the affirmative 11 to 8).

144. Swails, *supra* note 125, Appendix 2.C, Mercer Ciceronian Society Minutes, September 25, 1858. *See also* Euzelian Society Minutes, May 19, 1844, Wake Forest University (concluding in the negative by a vote of 6 to 9 the question "Is it probable slavery will ever be abolished in the US?"); *id.* October 6, 1855 (concluding in the affirmative by a vote of 31 ro 13 that "Will African slavery be perpetrated in the United States?); *id.* November 2, 1860 (concluding the same question in the affirmative by a vote of 9 to 4).

145. Washington Society Minute Books, Washington and Lee University Special Collections, October 27, 1859, (affirmed 9 to 4).

146. Swails, *supra* note 125, Appendix 2.B, Mercer Phi Delta Society Minutes, February 15, 1845 (decided in the affirmative).

147. Washington Society Minute Books, Washington and Lee University Special Collections, February 7, 1857 ("Is the law of the United States prohibiting citizens from teaching their slaves to read a proper one?") (set for debate on February 25, and affirmed 16 to 11).

148. Graham Society Minute Book, 1848–51, Washington and Lee University Special Collections, at 95 (decided in the affirmative, 16 to 8).

149. Washington Society Minute Books, Washington and Lee University Special Collections, May 28, 1859. This was also debated on April 19, 1845.

150. Licivyronean Society Records, *supra* note 127, June 2, 1845.

151. Reginald Horsman, Josiah Nott of Mobile: Southerner, Physician, and Racial Theorist 81–103 (1987) (discussing Nott's ideas about polygensis).

152. Swails, *supra* note 125, Appendix 2.B, Mercer Phi Delta Society Minutes, May 12, 1838 (decided in the affirmative).

153. Benjamin K. Kleinman, The Road to Radicalism: UNC Students and the Jurisprudence of Disunion (seminar paper, 2013) (discussing growing support for secession in UNC student speeches, 1857–1860).

154. Dialectic Society Minutes, Southern Historical Collection, UNC, October 9, 1830.

155. Dialectic Society Minutes, Southern Historical Collection, UNC, August 22, 1848, April 6, 1849.

156. Dialectic Society Minutes, Southern Historical Collection, UNC, November 9, 1849.

157. Dialectic Society Minutes, Southern Historical Collection, UNC, August 17, 1849.

158. Dialectic Society Minutes, Southern Historical Collection, UNC, March 1, 1850.

159. *See, e.g.,* A. Sandie Pendleton, Cincinnati Oration, 1857, Washington and Lee Special Collections.

160. *See, e.g., Notice,* 1 HAMPDEN SYDNEY MAGAZINE 74 (1858) (mentioning Alexander B. Cralle's junior oration, "Our Country's Future"); *Senior Speaking,* 3 N.C. UNIVERSITY MAGAZINE 231 (1854) (Delano Whiting Husted's senior speech on "English Operatives and African Slaves"); *Editorial Table,* 4 N.C. UNIVERSITY MAG. 391, 394 (1855) (Boaz Whitfield's senior speech on "Hon. Preston S. Brooks"); *id.* (James Irving Groover's senior speech on "Avarice: The Incentive to English Philanthropy").

161. *The Feudal System,* 1 HAMPDEN SYDNEY MAG. 231–33 (1858).

162. 4 SOUTHERN REPERTORY AND COLLEGE REVIEW 239 (1855).

163. *See, e.g., The Effect of the Holy Wars Upon Civilization,* 1 VA. U. MAG. 260 (June 1857).

164. *See, e.g., The Study of History,* 4 ERSKINE COLLEGIATE RECORDER 12, 13 (June 1857) (referring to the "manners, customs and laws of different nations"); *The Historian—His Influence and Responsibility,* 4 ERSKINE COLLEGIATE RECORDER 136 (1857); *The Past and the Present,* 4 VA. U. MAG. 255–60 (February 1860); *The Voice of the Past,* 4 VA. U. MAG. 242–45 (1860); *The Advantages of Historical Study,* 4 VA. U. MAG. 57–66 (1860).

165. *Government a Divine Institution,* 4 VA. U. MAG. 326–29 (1860). *See also The Citizen and His Government,* 3 VA. U. MAG. 491, 491 (1859) (restraint of freedom is necessary, for it is the "only condition under which [a human] can become a member of that society whose wholesome, refining influences woo him to its embrace and teach him his true destiny").

166. *College Law and Order,* 3 VA. U. MAG. 311–17 (March 1860). *See also The Citizen and His Government,* 3 VA. U. MAG. 491–501 (1859).

167. 1 HAMPDEN SYDNEY MAGAZINE 81, 845 (March 1859). *See also Liberia,* 4 N.C. U. MAG. 228 (1855); *Wayland on Slavery,* 7 4 N.C. U. MAG. 128 (1857).

168. *The Utility of Slavery Discussion,* 1 VA. U. MAG. 26–30 (Dec. 1856).

169. *Cannibals All; Or, Slaves Without Masters,* 1 VA. U. MAG. 193–99 (May 1857).

170. *An Essay on International Law,* 5 ERSKINE COLLEGIATE RECORDER 3, 5–6 (June 1858).

171. *The Expulsion of the Indians,* 5 ERSKINE COLLEGIATE RECORDER 202–204 (February 1859) (justifying the expulsion of Native Americans).

172. *The Scalp Tree,* 1 VA. U. MAG. 232–37 (May 1857).

173. DOUGLAS AMBROSE, HENRY HUGHES AND PROSLAVERY THOUGHT IN THE OLD SOUTH (1996).

174. GEORGE S. SAWYER, SOUTHERN INSTITUTIONS: OR, AN INQUIRY INTO THE ORIGIN AND EARLY PREVALANCE OF SLAVERY 14 (Philadelphia, 1859) ("Laws and regulations relate to [slaves] only upon the true principle of self-government—the greatest amount of good to the greatest number.").

175. EMERSON IN HIS JOURNALS 348 (Joel Porte ed., 1982).

Chapter 4

1. *See* DANIEL LORD, ON THE EXTRA-PROFESSIONAL INFLUENCE OF LAWYERS AND MINISTERS: AN ORATION DELIVERED AT NEW HAVEN, BEFORE THE PHI BETA KAPPA SOCIETY OF YALE COLLEGE ... July 30, 1851 (New York, S.S. Chatterton 1851); TIMOTHY WALKER, THE REFORM SPIRIT OF THE DAY: AN ORATION BEFORE THE PHI BETA KAPPA SOCIETY OF HARVARD UNIVERSITY, JULY 15, 1850 (Boston, James Munroe & Company 1850); WILLIAM GREENE, SOME OF THE DIFFICULTIES IN THE ADMINISTRATION OF A FREE GOVERNMENT: A DISCOURSE, PRONOUNCED BEFORE THE RHODE ISLAND ALPHA OF THE PHI BETA KAPPA SOCIETY, JULY 8, 1851 (Providence, John F. Moore 1851).

2. WALKER, *supra* note 1, at 6.

3. DANIEL LORD, ON THE EXTRA-PROFESSIONAL INFLUENCE OF LAWYERS AND MINISTERS 15 (New York, S.S. Chatterton 1851).

4. DAVID S. KAUFMAN, ADDRESS ... BEFORE THE AMERICAN WHIG AND CLIOSOPHIC SOCIETIES OF THE COLLEGE OF NEW JERSEY, JUNE 25TH, 1850 17–18 (J.T. Robinson, 1850).

5. *Id.* at 28.

6. A. W. VENABLE, ADDRESS ... BEFORE THE AMERICAN WHIG AND CLIOSOPHIC SOCIETIES OF THE COLLEGE OF NEW JERSEY, JUNE 24TH, 1851 (1851). *See also* A.W. VENABLE, ADDRESS ... DELIVERED BEFORE THE UNION AGRICULTURAL SOCIETY ... OCT. 25, 1854 (1854).

7. VENABLE, WHIG AND CLIOSOPHIC SOCIETIES, *supra* note 6, at 33. Two years later, when Pennsylvania attorney Benjamin Harris Brewster spoke to the joint societies, the picture was different. Brewster later spoke out against slavery, though in 1853, he had nothing to say about it. ADDRESS DELIVERED THE TWENTY-EIGHTH JUNE, 1853, BEFORE THE AMERICAN WHIG AND CLIOSOPHIC SOCIETIES OF THE COLLEGE OF NEW JERSEY ... 8 (Philadelphia, McLaughlin Brothers 1853).

8. WILLIAM GREENE, SOME OF THE DIFFICULTIES IN THE ADMINISTRATION OF A FREE GOVERNMENT: A DISCOURSE PRONOUNCED BEFORE THE RHODE ISLAND ALPHA OF THE PHI BETA KAPPA SOCIETY, JULY 8, 1851 19 (Providence, John F. Moore 1851).

9. *Id.* at 16.

10. *Id.* at 18.

11. *Id.* at 18 ("Such minds rarely do much good for the whole of a thing.").

12. *Id.* at 18.

13. *See* SLAVERY AND JUSTICE: REPORT OF THE BROWN UNIVERSITY STEERING COMMITTEE ON SLAVERY AND JUSTICE 12–13 (2006) (discussing the building of University Hall), available at http://brown.edu/Research/Slavery_Justice/documents/SlaveryAndJustice.pdf.

14. FRANCIS WAYLAND, THE LIMITATIONS OF HUMAN RESPONSIBILITY (New York, D. Appleton 1838; and Boston, Gould, Kendall & Lincoln 1838).

15. For instance, Wayland's *Mental Science and Moral Science* both appear in the course catalog of Howard College for 1845–46. https://archive.org/stream/catalogueofoffic00howa#page/n21/mode/2up.
    And for 1848–49.
    https://archive.org/stream/catalogueofoffic1849howa#page/n17/mode/2up.
    And for 1860–61.
    https://archive.org/stream/catalogueofhowar1861howa#page/n17/mode/2up.
    Only Wayland's Political Economy appears in the 1852 catalog. https://archive.org/stream/catalogueofoffic1853howa#page/n15/mode/2up.
    Moral Science also appears in the Washington College catalog until the late 1850s. Wayland's *Elements of Political Economy* was part of the curriculum at the University of Alabama. *See* A. JAMES FULLER, CHAPLAIN TO THE CONFEDERACY: BASIL MANLY AND BAPTIST LIFE IN THE OLD SOUTH 255 (2000) (discussing President Manly's use of Wayland); *see also id.* at 216 (discussing President Manly's reaction to the Fuller-Wayland exchange).

16. FRANCIS WAYLAND, ELEMENTS OF MORAL SCIENCE 220 (New York, Cooke and Co. 1835).

17. *Id.* at 223–24.

18. *Id.* at 227.

19. *Id.* at 228.

20. *Id.* at 228.

21. *See* [Jesse Burton Harrison,] *The Slavery Question in Virginia*, 12 AM. Q. REV. 379, 382 (Dec. 1832) (reviewing THE SPEECH OF THOMAS MARSHALL IN THE HOUSE OF DELEGATES OF VIRGINIA, ON THE ABOLITION OF SLAVERY, FRIDAY JANUARY 20, 1832 (Richmond, Thomas White, 1832)).

22. Baxter at 8.

23. *Id.* at 7.

24. *Id.* at 23.

25. ELISHA MITCHELL, THE OTHER LEAF OF THE BOOK OF NATURE AND THE WORD OF GOD (n.p. 1848). The pamphlet also critiqued Theodore Parker and Theodore Weld.

26. *Id.* at 21–22.

27. Domestic Slavery Considered as a Scriptural Institution: In a Correspondence Between the Rev. Richard Fuller of Beaufort, S. C., and the Rev. Francis Wayland, of Providence, R. I. (New York, L. Colby; Boston, Gould, Kendall and Lincoln 1845). *See* Matthew S. Hill, God and Slavery in America: Francis Wayland and the Evangelical Conscience 118–64 (Ph.D. 2008, Georgia State University) (discussing Wayland-Fuller debate).

28. Domestic Slavery, *supra* note 27, at 28–29. *See also id.* at 31 ("And no law imposing slavery would not change the nature of the relations of the parties as people entitled to natural rights.").

29. Domestic Slavery, *supra* note 27, at 54–55. Wayland's recognition that Mosaic laws were not universal, *id.* at 55, correlates with antebellum legal thought on the evolution of the common law. *See, e.g.,* Alfred L. Brophy, *Reason and Sentiment: The Moral Worlds and Modes of Reasoning of Antebellum Jurists,* 89 Boston University Law Review 1361 (1999). That is, antebellum jurisprudence incorporated an understanding that law evolved and was contingent on its social surroundings. This appears in great detail in Thomas Cobb's *An Inquiry into the Law of Negro Slavery,* discussed in Chapter 9 of this book. The fulcrum between Wayland and Fuller is, as Catherine Smith of the UNC Law School class of 2017 has pointed out, over progressive revelation.

30. Domestic Slavery, *supra* note 27, at 74. Wayland, like many of his contemporaries, expressed concern over fanatics, who pay insufficient attention to results, including over immediate abolitionists. *Id.*

Fuller was, not surprisingly, even stronger in his condemnation of abolitionists:

[I]mmediate and unconditional abolition would be a revolution involving the entire South in ruin; breaking up all social order and peace and safety; and, in fact, inflicting on the slaves themselves irreparable mischief. It would suddenly give them a liberty for which they are wholly unprepared, and which would be only a license for indolence and crime. It would covert them, inevitably, from a contented and cheerful peasantry, into a horde of outlaws, a multitude of paupers with whom the white population could never amalgamate, who must forever feel themselves (witness their condition even at the North) degraded and outcast from the kindred and privileges of the superior caste; who, deprived of the master's protection, and no longer bound to their governors by the kindly and almost filial ties now existing, would endure perpetual humiliation and insult, and drag out a sullen life of envy and hatred and wretchedness; or, if instigated to revenge and insurrection, be certainly crushed, and either annihilated, or subjugated to an iron bondage, a military rule, from the rigors of which they would look back to their former state as one, not only of comparative, but real, substantial, contrasted liberty and happiness.

Id. at 136.

31. *Cf.* Eugene Genovese, The Slaveholders Dilemma: Freedom and Progress in Conservative Southern Thought, 1820–1860 (1993). Though other historians do not see the same conflict in southern minds between modernism and slavery. Others believe that Southerners accepted technological and economic progress, while still maintaining an overriding desire for stability and hierarchy. *See, e.g.,* James Oakes, Slavery and Freedom: An Interpretation of the Old South (1990).

32. Elisha Mitchell, The Other Leaf of the Book of Nature and the Word of God (n.p. 1848).

33. *See* Eugene Genovese, A Consuming Fire: The Fall of the Confederacy in the Mind of the White Christian South 8–9 (1998) (discussing Fuller and presenting him as a moderate and competent defender of slavery).

34. Domestic Slavery, *supra* note 27, at 211.

35. *Id.* at 211–12.

36. *Id.* at 222–23.

37. *Id.* at 145.

38. *Id.* at 148, 150 (discussing French Revolution and St. Domingue). Fuller painted a benign picture of slavery:

[Y]ou will find slaves tilling land for themselves; working as mechanics for themselves, and selling various articles of merchandise for themselves; and when you inquire of them some explanation, they will speak of their rights, and their property, with as clear a sense of what is due to them, and as much confidence, as they could if free.

    Id. at 151.

39. *Id.* at 12.
40. *Id.* at. 159.
41. *See* WILLIAM GOODELL, THE AMERICAN SLAVE CODE IN THEORY AND PRACTICE (New York, American and Foreign Anti-Slavery Society 1853).
42. DOMESTIC SLAVERY, *supra* note 27, at 112.
43. *Id.* at 99.
44. *Id.* at 41 ("I can never approve of those appeals which treat all men at the South as though they were in respect of slavery, under the same condemnation.").
45. *Id.* at 38–39.
46. Jia Lynn Yang, *Yale Slavery Report Questioned by Experts: Lack of Historical Context, Financial Support from Unions Cited,* YALE DAILY NEWS (December 12, 2001); EDMUND MORGAN, THE GENTLE PURITAN: A LIFE OF EZRA STILES, 1727–1795 36 (1983).
47. DOMESTIC SLAVERY, *supra* note 27, at 41 (guilt is continually changing).
48. *Id.* at 41.
49. FRANCIS WAYLAND, DISCOURSE ON THE LIFE AND CHARACTER OF NICHOLAS BROWN 8 (Providence, 1841).
50. *Id.* at 19–20. He continued, "A fountain has been placed, whose pure and fertile waters, are carried to every family." *Id.* at 20.
51. *Id.* at 28–29.
52. DOMESTIC SLAVERY, *supra* note 27, at 31 (Scriptural references suggest that an individual is liable for the immoral laws of society).
53. *Id.* at 46. There were, nevertheless, gradations of guiltiness. *Id.* at 40.
54. *Id.* at 43. Even if, as many feared, manumission would have led to bloodshed, there is a continuing duty to remove from culpability. *Id.* at 100. Yet, the law was used by slaveholders for their benefit. *Id.* at 44.
55. *Id.* at 107.
56. *Id.* at 107–108.
57. Wayland suggested that slaves deserved a greater portion of their labor than they had received:

It seems to me an elementary principle of justice, that when capital and labor combine in the creation of a product, the proceeds of such creation should be divided by some equitable law in which the rights of both parties shall be fairly represented. But what must be the condition of those who have no voice whatever in this distribution of their products, but are obliged to submit to just such a division as the caprice or pecuniary interest of the other party shall appoint?

    Id. at 113.

58. FRANCIS WAYLAND, THE DUTY OF OBEDIENCE TO CIVIL MAGISTRATES: THREE SERMONS 40 (Boston, Charles C. Little and James Brown 1847). *See also* HILL, *supra* note 27, at 182–84 (discussing Wayland's sermons as a part of his transition from critic to public activism).
59. *See* ANDREW P. PEABODY, THE IMMUTABLE RIGHT: AN ORATION DELIVERED BEFORE THE PHI BETA KAPPA SOCIETY OF BROWN UNIVERSITY, AUG. 31, 1858 (Boston, Crosby, Nichols, and Company, 1858).
60. *Id.* at 10.
61. *Id.* at 23. Wayland, too, objected to the Fugitive Slave Act and pledged to never aid in the arrest of a fugitive. HILL, *supra* note 27, at 193.

Chapter 5

1. [F. A. P. Barnard], THE HIGHER EDUCATION OF WOMEN ... (1882); F. A. P. BARNARD, SHOULD AMERICAN COLLEGES BE OPEN TO WOMEN AS WELL AS MEN (1884).

2. Charles B. Davenport, *Frederick Augustus Porter Barnard, 1809–1889*, in 20 NATIONAL ACADEMY OF SCIENCES . . . BIOGRAPHICAL MEMOIRS 259, 261 (1938).

3. FREDERICK A. P. BARNARD, LETTER TO THE PRESIDENT OF THE UNITED STATES: BY A REFUGEE (Philadelphia, J. B. Lippincott, 1863).

4. The letter is quoted in *Memoirs of Frederick A. P. Barnard, Tenth President of Columbia College* . . . 292 (John Fulton ed. 1896).

5. WILLIAM SMITH, REMINISCENCES OF A LONG LIFE: HISTORICAL, POLITICAL, PERSONAL AND LITERARY 245 (1889).

6. *Id.* at 235.

7. Frederick Barnard, *Art Culture: Its Relation to National Refinement and National Morality— An Oration Pronounced Before the Alabama Alpha of the Society of the Phi Beta Kappa, at Its Anniversary, July 11th, 1854*, in 2 REPRESENTATIVE PHI BETA KAPPA ORATIONS 111–39 (Clark S. Northup ed. 1927).

8. FREDERICK A. P. BARNARD, LETTERS ON COLLEGE GOVERNMENT, AND THE EVILS INSEPARABLE FROM THE AMERICAN COLLEGE SYSTEM IN ITS PRESENT FORM . . . (New York, D. Appleton, 1855).

9. JOHN W. QUIST, RESTLESS VISIONARIES: THE SOCIAL ROOTS OF ANTEBELLUM REFORM IN ALABAMA AND MICHIGAN 199–200 (1998).

10. The address is excerpted in *Memoirs of Frederick A. P. Barnard, supra* note 4, at 97.

11. *See* A. JAMES FULLER, CHAPLAIN TO THE CONFEDERACY: BASIL MANLY AND BAPTIST LIFE IN THE OLD SOUTH 173 (2000) (reporting suspicions of University of Alabama's president Basil Manly about Barnard's antislavery sentiments). The debate appeared in two books, Basil Manly, REPORT ON COLLEGIATE EDUCATION MADE TO THE TRUSTEES OF THE UNIVERSITY OF ALABAMA, JULY, 1852 (Tuskaloosa, M. D. J. Slade 1852) and F. A. P. Barnard, REPORT ON A PROPOSITION TO MODIFY THE PLAN OF INSTRUCTION AT THE UNIVERSITY OF ALABAMA (New York, Appleton 1855). Manly's proposal was discussed in "Report on Collegiate Education," 7 *Southern Presbyterian Review* 484–505 (July 1852).

12. F. A. P. BARNARD, NO JUST CAUSE FOR A DISSOLUTION OF THE UNION IN ANY THING WHICH HAS HITHERTO HAPPENED; BUT THE UNION THE ONLY SECURITY FOR SOUTHERN RIGHTS. AN ORATION DELIVERED BEFORE THE CITIZENS OF TUSCALOOSA, ALA., JULY 4TH, 1851 (J. W. & J. F. Warren, Tuscaloosa, 1851). *No Just Cause* is reprinted in *Memoirs of Frederick A. P. Barnard, supra* note 4, at 112–43. WILLIAM J. CHUTE, DAMN YANKEE! The First Career of Frederick A.P. Barnard 127–30 (1978) (discussing Barnard's oration and the interpretation of some that it was antisouthern).

13. *Memoirs, supra* note 4, at 117 ("At this very moment the entire energies of the Federal Government are put in action to secure the faithful execution of the law which has been re-garded as a test of its sincerity of purpose, and the local authorities, wherever called upon, as recently in Boston, have earnestly cooperated to the same end. Whatever bitterness of feel-ing individual or associated agitation or resistance at the North may have been calculated to awaken in the South, there is nothing to justify denunciations of the organic law of the land.").

14. *Id.* at 139.

15. Landon Cabel Garland, who would later be president of the University of Alabama, wrote a letter stating that in the 1830s Barnard attended one of his proslavery lectures and agreed with it. *See* L. C. Garland and J. J. Ormand, *in* RECORD OF THE TESTIMONY AND PROCEEDINGS IN THE MATTER OF THE INVESTIGATION OF THE TRUSTEES OF THE UNIVERSITY OF MISSISSIPPI, ON THE 1ST AND 2ND OF MARCH, 1860 OF THE CHARGES MADE BY H.R. BRANHAM, AGAINST THE CHANCELLOR OF THE UNIVERSITY 16 (Jackson, Mississippian Office, 1860). In 1860 Garland delivered three lectures on slavery at the Tuscaloosa YMCA. *See* JAMES BENSON SELLERS, SLAVERY IN ALABAMA 353–54 (1950) (1994 ed.). The ad-dresses were printed in the *Tuscaloosa Independent Monitor* March 10, 17, and 31, 1860.

16. 2 Basil Manly Diary, Hoole Special Collection, University of Alabama, at 299 (1843) (report-ing that students paid $75 to have a servant of Barnard's to "assis[t] the Professor."). For a brief mention of Sam and Barnard, see James Sellers, *History of the University of Alabama* 70 (1953).

17. 3 Basil Manly Diary, at 65; SOLDIERS OF CHRIST: SELECTIONS FOR THE WRITINGS OF BASIL MANLY, SR., & BASIL MANLY, JR. 105–107 (Michael A. G. Haykin, et al. eds. 2009) (reprint-ing Manly's diary entries regarding Sam).

18. *See, e.g.,* BY-LAWS OF THE UNIVERSITY OF ALABAMA, 1854 12 (Tuscaloosa, M. D. J. Shade 1854) ("A student shall not be permitted to inflict corporal punishment upon any servant employed by the University for any neglect of duty, or for any other actual or alleged offense. The student's remedy against a servant, in all cases, shall be to give information to the President or some other member of the Faculty."). For more on the context of this, see Sellers, *supra* note 16, at 38, 235 (describing origins of prohibition on students beating slaves in the aftermath of a student attack on the slave Moses). *See also* JENNIFER OAST, INSTITUTIONAL SLAVERY: SLAVEHOLDING CHURCHES, SCHOOLS, COLLEGES, AND BUSINESSES IN VIRGINIA, 1680–1860, 126–202 (2016) (discussing abuse of enslaved people on college campuses).

19. *See* SELLERS, *supra* note 16, at 38 (reporting on purchase of Ben in 1828 and reporting that Professor Geroge Benagh was sent to Virginia in 1860 with authority to spend $7,000 to buy slaves); Manly Diary, March 11, 1839 ("College Servant, Sam. This day a servant by the name of Sam came to me by order of the Governor, to be tried as a servant for the University. I set him to work immediately, and discharge Prof. Barnard's man, Johnson."). *See also* SELLERS, *supra* note 16, at 236 (discussing a woman owned by President Manly and citing Manly's Diary, 1848–55, at 85 (June 22)). For references to rentals to Professor Toumey, see Manly Diary 5 at 37 (rental of Ben to Toumey); at 184 (1851) (rental of "Little Mary" to Toumey). *See also* Manly Diary 346 (1854) ("The number of Students exceeding 100 the first term, the faculty thought it expedient to procure additional service for the Dormitories and the Laboratory, and after considering the probable rate of servant hire for the year 1854, they requested me to invest the proceeds of the sale of Sam in the purchase of another servant."). The faculty sometimes rented out their slaves. *See, e.g.,* SELLERS, *supra* note 16, at 38 (Professor H. S. Pratt hired three slaves to the University in 1837–1840).

20. University of Alabama Trustee Papers, Folder 90, Labor–Slaves, 1830–1860, Hoole Special Collections Library.

21. *See* University of Alabama Trustee Papers, Folder 90, Labor–Slaves, 1830–1860, Hoole Special Collections (September 29, 1831).

22. SELLERS, *supra* note 16, at 91 (the two slaves buried on campus are Jack in 1843 and Boysey, a seven year old, in 1844).

23. Basil Manly Diary, 1848-55, Hoole Special Collection, June 22, 1850, at 85; 236; SELLERS, *supra* note 16, at 236. *See also* FULLER, *supra* note 11, at 170–74 (discussing Manly's conflict with Barnard); CHUTE, *supra* note 12, at 122–26 (same).

24. For more on slavery at the University of Alabama, see ALFRED L. BROPHY, *The University and the Slaves: Apology and Its Meaning,* in THE AGE OF APOLOGY 109–19 (Mark Gibney et al. eds. 2008). It comes as no surprise that the students at the University of Alabama in this era were drawn from a slaveholding class. See Royal Dumas, *My Money and My Son Go to the University of Alabama: The Social Origins of Antebellum University of Alabama Students,* 1 ALA. CIV. RIGHTS & CIVIL LIBERTIES L. REV. 67, 80 (2011) (reporting that approximately 90% of University of Alabama in 1845 came from slave-owning families).

25. FULLER, *supra* note 11, at 265 (citing 1855 Alabama census). After the war, Manly signed a contract with his slaves and the Freedman's Bureau; they agreed to work under the usual conditions and to have some extra land set aside for them to work. 6 Manly Diary, Hoole Special Collection, at 75 (June 20, 1865).

26. See, e.g., University of Alabama Faculty Minutes, Hoole Special Collections Library (March 24, 1845) (student named Saffold stabbed slave with a fork); *id.* (June 4, 1845) (Saffold suspended); *id.* (February 16, 1846) (student named Robinson fined $1 for injuring Moses). *See also* SELLERS, *supra* note 16, at 236.

27. Ordinances and Resolutions of the Board of Trustees, Hoole Special Collection, at 22 (December 1845). The same resolution provided for the use of slaves by the University during recess: An ordinance, concerning the servants of the university. Be it ordered by the Trustees of the University of Alabama, that the servants, owned or employed by the University, shall, during vacations, attend to the reception of coal, and shall also perform in vacations the necessary cleaning, whitewashing, etc in, or about the Dormitories and Public Rooms, under the direction of the Faculty, and for their satisfaction, and the use which the Steward is permitted to make of their services, and compensation for their board shall not be construed so as to conflict with the provisions of this ordinance.

28. Basil Manly Diary, Hoole Special Collections, 157 (1850) ("Moses, beaten. Just now, Moses, college servant, came to me and says that Walthall and Robert Cochran, and others, had beaten him very much when he was over in Jefferson building—accusing him of having given me information of his being engaged in stealing those turkeys.").

29. Basil Manly Diary, Hoole Special Collections, (1851) at 112. The stories could be multiplied. For instance, according to one account, students asked a slave what he would do when the devil gets him—the perhaps apocryphal answer was, "wait on the students." SELLERS, *supra* note 16, at 41. There was a lot of waiting on students and faculty going on. Slaves were expected to wait on students and beaten when they did not. *See id.* at 236. In 1841 the trustees approved the hiring of slaves to serve the faculty. In 1832 the building committee of the Board of Trustees approved the sale of a slave named Ben for $450. Trustee Minutes, Hoole Special Collections, at 161. In 1838 the trustees approved the purchase of a slave. Trustee Minutes, Hoole Special Collections, at 261 (December 20, 1838). Almost yearly the trustees appropriated funds for the purchase or rental of slaves for the use of the University or faculty. *See* Trustee Minutes, December 20, 1838; December 12, 1839; December 19, 1839 (for hiring up to two slaves for University use, at price not exceeding $140 each); December 15, 1842 (authorizing purchase of slave and providing that steward has the services of two slaves during meals and vacations).

30. FREDERICK A. P. BARNARD, LETTER TO THE HONORABLE THE BOARD OF TRUSTEES UNIVERSITY OF MISSISSIPPI (Oxford, University of Mississippi, 1858).

31. *Id.* (discussing curriculum at the university).

32. Slave Schedule, Federal Census, Schedule 2, Lafayette County, Mississippi, page 92.

33. RECORD, *supra* note 15, at 18.

34. *Id.* at 23.

35. RECORD, *supra* note 15, at 13.

36. *Id.* at 18.

37. *Id.* at 9.

38. *Id.* at 15 (Carter's affidavit) (stating that the students "Furniss, Falconer and Shelby . . . proved an alibi with as much particularity as the indefinite character of the specifications would admit.").

39. *Id.* at 13.

40. *Id.* at 14. Then a third resolution was presented to permit the three who initially voted to convict Humphreys to explain their reasoning. That passed with only one dissenting vote, from Professor George W. Carter. *See also* HISTORICAL CATALOGUE OF THE UNIVERSITY OF MISSISSIPPI: 1849–1909 15 (1910).

41. *See Autobiographical Sketch of Dr. F.A.P. Barnard*, 12 PUBLICATIONS OF THE MISSISSIPPI HISTORICAL SOCIETY 107, 114 (1912) (discussing, in unflattering terms, Professor George W. Carter, focusing on his behavior during the Civil War and then on his term as a Republican in New Orleans after the war).

42. RECORD, *supra* note 15, at 6.

43. *Id.* at 3.

44. David G. Sansing, *The University of Mississippi: A Sesquicentennial History* 75 (1999) provides an excellent basic account of the "Branham affair," as does Craig Wilder's *Ebony and Ivy*: Race, Slavery, and the Trouble History of America's Universities 236–37 (2013).

45. Only a few people have ever cited, let alone discussed, Chancellor Barnard's trial. *See, e.g.,* Charles S. Sydnor, *The Southerner and the Laws,* 6 J. S. HIST. 3, 11–12 n. 19 (1940) (citing trial as evidence that academic courts "avoided the use of Negro testimony" and citing an ecclesiastical court as another example of a place where slave testimony was excluded); CHUTE, *supra* note 12, at 168–73. *Cf.* MARK AUSLANDER, THE ACCIDENTAL SLAVEHOLDER: REVISITING A MYTH OF RACE AND FINDING AN AMERICAN FAMILY 87–89 (2011) (discussing Emory President August Longstreet's supposed interview with a slave to decide whether to free her and send her out of the state or keep her in slavery).

46. RECORD, *supra* note 15, at 4.

47. *Id.*

48. ERIC FONER, FREE SOIL, FREE LABOR, FREE MEN: THE IDEOLOGY OF THE REPUBLICAN PARTY BEFORE THE CIVIL WAR (1970).

49. RECORD, *supra* note 15, at 7. One might recall here the frequent complaint among Southerners that their books and teachers were produced in the North. *See* JOHN MCCARDELL, THE IDEA OF A SOUTHERN NATION 203–15, esp. 206 (1978). Barnard himself attempted to refute some of those charges in his July 4, 1851 oration. Barnard, *No Just Cause for a Dissolution of the Union, supra* note 12.
50. *Id.* at 13.
51. *Id.* at 9, 15.
52. *Id.* at 24.
53. *Id.* at 11 (Richardson testimony).
54. *Id.* at 17.
55. Another of the great ironies of this story is that Richardson had served as a librarian at the University of Alabama before moving to the University of Mississippi. In that capacity, he edited the University of Alabama's library catalog. *See* WILSON GAINES RICHARDSON, CATALOGUE OF THE LIBRARY OF THE UNIVERSITY OF ALABAMA, WITH AN INDEX OF SUBJECTS (Tuscaloosa, M.D.J. Shade 1848).
56. Some of Stearns' ideas appear in a few surviving lectures. For instance, in one introductory lecture, Stearns explained the need to calibrate law to the surrounding culture, a common principle since at least Montesquieu:

> To the condition of a tribe of roving savages, that law may be best adapted which proceeds from the lips of a despotic chief, who decides each case, as it arises, according to his arbitrary will; but a people who are wealthy, and enlightened, and refined, must have a system of laws adapted to *their* condition. That system must be complicated in exact proportion to the degree of their civilization; and if the attempt be made to simplify it, in order to dispense with the agency of lawyers, precisely to the extent of the success of the attempt, will that people gravitate toward a state of barbarism.

WILLIAM F. STEARNS, A PRELIMINARY LECTURE, DELIVERED BEFORE THE LAW-STUDENTS OF THE UNIVERSITY OF MISSISSIPPI, ON THE 14TH OF SEPTEMBER, 1857 25–26 (Oxford, n.p. 1857). *See also Address Delivered by Br. William F. Stearns, at the Laying of the Corner Stone of the State University, at Oxford . . .*, 6 FREEMASON'S MONTHLY MAG. 17–21 (1847).
57. RECORD, *supra* note 15, at 14–15.
58. *Id.* at 23.
59. *Id.* at 25.
60. *Id.* at 27.
61. SANSING, *supra* note 44, at 99–100; JOHN N. WADDEL, MEMORIALS OF AN ACADEMIC LIFE 306 (1891). For contemporary accounts of the trial, see *Memphis Daily Appeal*, March 15, 21, April 13, 1860.
62. *Memoirs of Frederick A. P. Barnard, supra* note, at 251–52. Elsewhere the biography commented—in fashion typical of historians in the Jim Crow era that blamed northern abolitionist fanatics and hotheaded southern secessionists for the war—that Barnard blamed fanatics North and South for the Civil War:

> For the institution of slavery, in comparison with the permanence of the Union, he seems to have cared nothing either way; and hence he was equally indignant at the Northern agitators who were ready to imperil the Union for the sake of hastening emancipation, and at the Southern agitators whom he believed to be plotting the disruption of the Union under a pretext of resentment at Northern aggression. . . . [H]e could do nothing but recognize and accept facts which he deplored as national calamities. When the cotton States seceded, he did not seem to question that their secession, however needless or unwise, was an effectual act. . . . He continued, indeed, to "cherish a bright little secret hope" that the "delirium" might pass, and that the Southern States "might recover their position in the Union which had wrought so many blessings and so little of harm." A month after Mr. Lincoln's inauguration his hopes for a brighter future had grown daily more and more faint until he mournfully confessed himself "compelled to admit that the glory of the Union had departed forever."

Id. at 280–81.

Chapter 6

1. 9 STAT. AT LARGE 462 (September 18, 1850).
2. Henry David Thoreau, *Slavery in Massachusetts,* in 4 WRITINGS OF HENRY DAVID THOREAU 388, 388 (1906).
3. Henry David Thoreau, [*Resistance to Civil Government*] *Civil Disobedience,* in 4 WRITINGS OF HENRY DAVID THOREAU at 361 (1906). Thoreau credits Paley as "a common authority with many on moral questions." He went through a number of American editions. *See* DONALD H. MEYER, THE INSTRUCTED CONSCIENCE 8–9 *(1972)*; WILSON SMITH, PROFESSORS AND PUBLIC ETHICS (1956). On antebellum moral philosophy, see LOUIS GERTSIS, MORALITY AND UTILITY IN AMERICAN ANTISLAVERY REFORM (1987); RUSH WELTER, THE MIND OF AMERICA, 1820–1860 (1975); LOUIS PERRY, BOATS AGAINST THE CURRENT: AMERICAN CULTURE BETWEEN REVOLUTION AND MODERNITY, 1820–1860 (2003); Theodore Dwight Bozeman, *Inductive and Deductive Politics: Science and Society in Antebellum Presbyterian Thought,* 64 J. AM. HIST. 704 (1977); John M. McFaul, *Expedience vs. Morality: Jacksonian Politics and Slavery,* 65 J. AM. HIST. 25 (1975).
4. THOREAU, *Civil Disobedience, supra* note 3, at 387. Emphasis on slaves' suffering was the center of abolitionists' thought. *See* Elizabeth Clark, *"The Sacred Rights of the Weak": Pain, Sympathy, and the Culture of Individual Rights in Antebellum America,* 84 J. AM. HIST. 463 (1995).
5. On the Act's place in history, *see* DAVID POTTER, THE IMPENDING CRISIS, 112–14, 130–40 (1976); 1 WILLIAM FREEHLING, THE ROAD TO DISUNION: SECESSIONISTS AT BAY, 497–505 (1990); MARK GRABER, DRED SCOTT AND THE PROBLEM OF CONSTITUTIONAL EVIL (2006); Thomas J. Brown, *The Fugitive Slave Act in Emerson's Boston,* 2000 L. & SOC. INQ. 669 (reviewing Albert J. Von Frank, *The Trials of Anthony Burns* (1998)); Laura R. Mitchell, *Matters of Justice Between Man and Man': Northern Divines, The Bible, and The Fugitive Slave Act of 1850,* in RELIGION AND THE ANTEBELLUM DEBATE OVER SLAVERY 134–65 (John R. McGivigan and Mitchell Snay, eds., 1998). On the southern reaction to the Act, see JOHN HOPE FRANKLIN, THE MILITANT SOUTH, 1800–1861 223–26 (1961); WILLIAM J. COOPER, THE SOUTH AND THE POLITICS OF SLAVERY 301–21 (1978).
6. ROBERT COVER, JUSTICE ACCUSED: ANTI-SLAVERY AND THE JUDICIAL PROCESS (1975).
7. *See, e.g.,* Jeffrey Schmidt, *The Antislavery Judge Reconsidered,* 29 LAW & HIST. REV. 797 (2011).
8. Henry David Thoreau, *Civil Disobedience, supra* note 3.
9. Peter Karsten boldly argues that there was a strong jurisprudence of the heart in the nineteenth century, though that jurisprudence existed in areas other than slavery. *See* PETER KARSTEN, HEART VERSUS HEAD: JUDGE-MADE LAW IN NINETEENTH-CENTURY AMERICA (1997). Some have expressed skepticism of this interpretation. *See, e.g.,* Alfred L. Brophy, *The Moral Worlds and Modes of Reasoning of Antebellum Jurists* 79 B.U. L. REV. 1161 (1999).
10. *Speech of Mr. Webster,* CONG. GLOBE, 31st Cong., 1st Sess. 269 (March 7, 1850).
11. Thoreau, *Walden,* in 2 WRITINGS OF HENRY DAVID THOREAU, *supra* note 2, at 257.
12. *Speech of Mr. Webster,* CONG. GLOBE, 31st Cong., 1st Sess. at 270.
13. Ralph Waldo Emerson, *The Conservative,* in RALPH WALDO EMERSON: ESSAYS AND LECTURES 174–75 (Joel Porte, ed., 1983).
14. *Speech of Webster,* CONG. GLOBE, 31st Cong., 1st Sess. at 275.
15. *Id.*
16. *Id.*
17. *See, e.g.,* ALBERT TAYLOR BLEDSOE, AN ESSAY ON LIBERTY AND SLAVERY 69–70 (Philadelphia, J.B. Lippincott 1856); JASPER ADAMS, ELEMENTS OF MORAL PHILOSOPHY 15 (Cambridge, Folsom, Wells, and Thurston 1837) ("By this theory [of utility], the jurisdiction of conscience is abolished, her decisions are classed with those of the superannuated judge, and determination of moral causes is adjourned from the interior tribunal of the breast to the noisy forum of speculative debate. Nothing is yielded to the suggestions of conscience, nothing to the movements of the heart; every thing is dealt out with a sparing hand, under the stint and measure of calculation."); JOSEPH C. STILES, MODERN REFORM EXAMINED: OR, THE UNION OF NORTH AND SOUTH ON THE SUBJECT OF SLAVERY (Philadelphia, J.B. Lippincott 1857) (pointing out ways that abolitionists want change).
18. CONG. GLOBE, 31st Cong., 1st Sess., at 271.

19. *Id.*
20. Speech of Hon. T. G. Pratt, *id.* at 1238 (August 20-21, 1850) ("The American people are essentially a practical people, I never shall believe that they are willing to risk the destruction of this Government upon a mere abstraction.").
21. CONG. GLOBE, 31st Cong., 1st Sess., 1105 (July 6, 1850).
22. *Id.* at 1106.
23. *Id.* at 1102.
24. CONG. GLOBE, 31st Cong., 1st Sess., App. 311 (Feb. 21, 1850).
25. *Id.* at 531.
26. CONG. GLOBE, 31st Cong., 1st Sess., 1102 (July 6, 1850):

> But there is another class of enthusiasts which cannot be justly called fanatical, yet exercises a far more extensive and mischievous influences. Those are the subjects of a morbid sensibility, recluses–readers and authors of sentimental literature, who cannot bear the contemplation of the ordinary ills and hardships of real life, without a shock of their nervous system. They sigh for a state of society where wrong and injustice can never enter. Slavery at the south becomes the natural and favorite theme of the tongues and pens of these sentimentalists.

> Or, as Virginia's Senator R. M. T. Hunter said, "Some suffering . . . belongs to our condition; it is a part of the lot of humanity." Speech of R. M. T. Hunter, *id.* at 1632 (Sept. 3, 1850). *See also id.* at 1633.

27. *See* SARAH N. ROTH, GENDER AND RACE IN ANTEBELLUM POPULAR CULTURE (2014) (discussing sentimental literature pre-Stowe).
28. CONG. GLOBE, 31st Cong., 1st Sess., at 1105.
29. FRED A. ROSS, SLAVERY ORDAINED OF GOD 7 (Philadelphia, Lippincott 1857). Ross wrote that *"slavery is of God*, and to continue for the good of the slave, the good of the master, the good of the whole American family, until another and better destiny be unfolded." I am indebted to David Holland for reminding me of the importance of Providence in this debate.
30. CONG. GLOBE, 31st Cong., 1st Sess. at 1106.
31. *Id.* at 1105.
32. CONG. GLOBE, 31st Cong. 1st Sess. 530 (April 4, 1850).
33. *Id.* at 533.
34. *Id.*
35. CONG. GLOBE, 31st Cong., 1st Sess. 1593 (Aug. 20, 1850). Or, as Senator Robert Rhett of South Carolina said, "A law to have its practical effect must move in harmony with the opinions and feelings of the community where it is to operate." CONG. GLOBE, 31st Cong., 2nd Sess. 317 (1851).
36. *See, e.g.,* NATHANIEL COLVER, THE FUGITIVE SLAVE BILL: OR, GOD'S LAWS PARAMOUNT TO THE LAWS OF MEN. A SERMON, PREACHED ON SUNDAY, OCTOBER 20, 1850 (Boston, J.M. Hewes, 1850); GEORGE BARRELL CHEEVER, GOD AGAINST SLAVERY: AND THE FREEDOM AND DUTY OF THE PULPIT TO REBUKE IT . . . (Boston, Crosby & Nichols 1850); THEODORE PARKER, THE FUNCTION AND PLACE OF CONSCIENCE IN RELATION TO THE LAWS OF MEN: A SERMON FOR THE TIMES; . . . SUNDAY, SEPTEMBER 22, 1850 (Boston, Crosby & Nichols 1850); JOHN KREBBS, A DISCOURSE ON THE NATURE AND EXTENT OF OUR RELIGIOUS SUBJECTION TO THE GOVERNMENT UNDER WHICH WE LIVE . . . DELIVERED IN THE RUTGERS STREET PRESBYTERIAN CHURCH . . . DECEMBER 12, 1850 (New York, Charles Scribner, 1851) (responding to JOHN C. LORD, "THE HIGHER LAW," IN ITS APPLICATION TO THE FUGITIVE SLAVE BILL . . . (New York, Union Safety Committee 1851)); WILLIAM HOSMER, THE HIGHER LAW, IN ITS RELATIONS TO CIVIL GOVERNMENT . . . (Auburn [N.Y.], Derby & Miller 1852).
37. SAMUEL T. SPEAR, THE LAW-ABIDING CONSCIENCE, AND THE HIGHER LAW CONSCIENCE: WITH REMARKS ON THE FUGITIVE SLAVE QUESTION. A SERMON, PREACHED IN THE SOUTH PRESBYTERIAN CHURCH, BROOKLYN, DEC. 12, 1850 32 (New York, Lambert & Lane 1850). *See also* EDWARD PRINGLE, THE PROCEEDINGS OF THE UNION MEETING, HELD AT BREWSTER'S HALL, DECEMBER 24, 1850 . . . (New Haven Ct., W.H. Stanley 1851).
38. LORD, supra note 36. See *also* WILLIAM ADAMS, CHRISTIANITY AND CIVIL GOVERNMENT (New York, C. Scribner, 1851); ALBERT BARNES, THE CHURCH AND SLAVERY (Philadelphia,

Parry & McMillan 1857); MOSES STUART, CONSCIENCE AND THE CONSTITUTION: WITH REMARKS ON THE RECENT SPEECH OF THE HON. DANIEL WEBSTER IN THE SENATE OF THE UNITED STATES ON THE SUBJECT OF SLAVERY (Boston, Crocker & Brewster 1851).

39. LORD, *supra* note 36, at 4.
40. *Id.* at 6.
41. *Id.* at 7.
42. *Id.* at 10–11.
43. ICHABOD S. SPENCER, THE RELIGIOUS DUTY OF OBEDIENCE TO LAW: A SERMON, PREACHED . . . Nov. 24, 1850 (New York, M.W. Dodd 1850).
44. *Id.* at 13.
45. *Id.* at 15.
46. *Id.* at 16.
47. *Id.* at 20.
48. *See, e.g.,* CALVIN COLTON, A VOICE FROM ENGLAND TO AMERICA BY AN AMERICAN GENTLEMAN 38–60 (1839) (discussing increasing public concern with statutory law); Timothy Walker, *Advice to Law Students,* 1 WEST. L.J. 481, 482 (1844).
49. *The Fugitive Slave Law,* in 11 THE COMPLETE WORKS OF RALPH WALDO EMERSON 178, 190 (Edward Waldo Emerson ed., 1903).
50. *See, e.g.,* JAMES FREEMAN CLARKE, THE RENDITION OF ANTHONY BURNS: . . . A DISCOURSE ON CHRISTIAN POLITICS (Boston, Crosby & Nichols 1854).
51. *See, e.g.,* VON FRANK, *supra* note 5, at 203–19 (describing Burns' case from Loring's decision to Burns' departure from Boston).
52. *See* COVER, *supra* note 6; MARK TUSHNET, SLAVE LAW IN THE AMERICAN SOUTH: STATE V. MANN IN HISTORY AND LITERATURE (2004).
53. Henry David Thoreau, *Slavery in Massachusetts, supra* note 2, at 389.
54. CONG. GLOBE, 31st Cong., 1st Sess., at 1621.
55. Harriet Beecher Stowe to Calvin Stowe, February 1, 1851, quoted in JOAN HEDRICK, HARRIET BEECHER STOWE: A LIFE 205 (1995).
56. Harriet Beecher Stowe to Gamaliel Bailey, March 9, 1851, quoted in HEDRICK, *supra* note 55, at 206.
57. *See generally* COVER, *supra* note 6, at 149 n.* (discussing categories of abolitionist attacks on law).
58. *Harriet Beecher Stowe, Uncle Tom's Cabin,* in HARRIET BEECHER STOWE, THREE NOVELS 10 (Library of Am. Ed. 1982) (Boston, John P. Jewett 1852).
59. *Id.* at 19.
60. *See* [William Gilmore Simms?], *Review of Uncle Tom's Cabin,* 18 S. LIT. MESSENGER 630, 632 (1852).
61. *Id.*
62. STOWE, *supra* note 58, at 101.
63. *Id.* at 102.
64. *Id.* at 101.
65. *Id.* at 101.
66. *Id.* at 100.
67. *Id.* at 108.
68. *Id.* at 356.
69. *Id.* at 360–61.
70. *Id.* at 258.
71. *Id.* at 258.
72. *Id.* at 262.
73. *Id.* at 365, 368.
74. *Id.* at 377.
75. *Id.* at 391.
76. *Id.* at 414.
77. *Id.* at 479–80.
78. *Id.* at 476.
79. HARRIET BEECHER STOWE, A KEY TO UNCLE TOM'S CABIN 115 (Boston, John P. Jewett 1853).

80. *Id.* at 86.
81. EDWARD JOSIAH STEARNS, NOTES ON UNCLE TOM'S CABIN, BEING A LOGICAL ANSWER TO ITS ALLEGATIONS AND INFERENCES AGAINST SLAVERY AS AN INSTITUTION xx (Philadelphia, Lippincott, Grambo & Co. 1853).
82. [George Frederick Holmes], *Uncle Tom's Cabin*, 18 S LIT. MESS. 721, 727 (Dec. 1852).
83. George Frederick Holmes, quoted in DREW FAUST, A SACRED CIRCLE: THE DILEMMA OF THE INTELLECTUAL IN THE OLD SOUTH, 1840-1860 63 (1977).
84. JAMES WADDELLL, UNCLE TOM'S CABIN REVIEWED; OR AMERICAN SOCIETY VINDICATED FROM THE ASPERSIONS OF MRS. HARRIET BEECHER STOWE 43 (Raleigh, 1852).
85. *See, e.g., id.* at 45–46.
86. NEHEMIAH ADAMS, SOUTH-SIDE VIEW OF SLAVERY 136 (Boston, Ticknor & Fields, 4th ed.1860).
87. WADDELL, *supra* note 84, note 42.
88. *See, e.g., id.* at 45 ("We have no right to do a positive good to the few, when our act involves a positive injury to the many."); *id.* at 46 ("'The greatest good to the greatest number' is beyond the range of [philanthropy's] contemplation."); Louisa McCord, *Uncle Tom's Cabin*, 23 S.Q. REV. 81, 119 (1853) ("Utopias have been vainly dreamed. That system is the best which, not in theory, but in practice, brings the greatest sum of good to the greatest number.").
89. A. WOODWARD, A REVIEW OF UNCLE TOM'S CABIN, OR AN ESSAY ON SLAVERY 93 (Cincinnati, Applegate & Co. 1853).
90. STEARNS, *supra* note 81, at 70–71.
91. A CAROLINIAN [EDWARD J. PRINGLE], SLAVERY IN THE SOUTHERN STATES 20 (Cambridge, J. Bartlett 1852).
92. *Id.* at 21.
93. *Id.* at 21.
94. Holmes, *supra* note 82, at 727.
95. *Id.* at 728.
96. WADDELL, *supra* note 84, at 49.
97. Holmes, *supra* note 82, at 728. Holmes devotes substantial attention to slave law, to demonstrate its humanity. Such arguments appeared frequently in public discourse. In debate over the proposed repeal of the Fugitive Slave Law in 1852, Senator James of Connecticut wondered "how the cause of philanthropy and humanity is to be promoted by a process tending to produce anarchy, strife, and, perhaps civil war and bloodshed." CONG. GLOBE, 32nd Cong., 1st Sess., 1123 (August 23, 1852).
98. McCord, *supra* note 88, at 109.
99. PRINGLE, *supra* note 91, at 22 (characterizing abolitionist critique).
100. *Id.,* at 12. *Cf.* [DAVID BROWN], THE PLANTER; OR THIRTEEN YEARS IN THE SOUTH 37–40 (Philadelphia, H. Hooker 1853) (discussing Stowe's image of a "brooding shadow").
101. PRINGLE, *supra* note 91, at 46.
102. *Id.* at 9.
103. *See id.* at 22.
104. *Id.* at 25.
105. G.F.H. [George Frederick Holmes], *A Key to Uncle Tom's Cabin*, 18 S. LIT. MESSENGER 321, 328 (1853).
106. STEARNS, *supra* note 81, at 172 (quoting STOWE, KEY, supra note 79, at 40).
107. *Id.* at 54–55.
108. SOLOMON NORTHUP, TWELVE YEARS A SLAVE 206 (New York, Miller, Orton & Mulligan 1855) (1853).
109. WILLIAM GOODELL, AMERICAN SLAVE CODE IN THEORY AND PRACTICE 394 (New York, American and Foreign Anti-Slavery Society 1853).
110. *Id.* at 400.
111. MINUTES AND PROCEEDINGS OF THE FIRST ANNUAL CONVENTION OF THE PEOPLE OF COLOUR . . . IN THE CITY OF PHILADELPHIA, FROM THE SIXTH TO THE ELEVENTH OF JUNE . . . (Philadelphia, Committee of Arrangements 1831).
112. GOODELL, *supra* note 109, at 401–403.
113. *Id.* at 400, 337.

114. *Id.* at 157.
115. Frederick Douglass, *Is the Constitution For or Against Slavery,* FREDERICK DOUGLAS' PAPER, *in* 5 LIFE AND WRITINGS at 194–999 (Philip S. Foner ed. 1975). *See also* MARK BRANDON, FREE IN THE WORLD: AMERICAN SLAVERY AND CONSTITUTIONAL FAILURE 75–76 (1999) (explaining Douglass' shift and its meaning for constitutional interpretation). This was later developed in Douglass' July 5, 1852 address "What to the Slave is the Fourth of July?" *See* JAMES A. COLAIACO FREDERICK DOUGLASS AND THE FOURTH OF JULY (2006).
116. WILLIAM GOODELL, VIEW OF AMERICAN CONSTITUTIONAL LAW, IN ITS BEARING UPON AMERICAN SLAVERY (Utica, Jackson & Chaplin 1844). *See also* WILLIAM WIECEK, THE SOURCES OF ANTISLAVERY CONSTITUTIONALISM IN AMERICA, 1760–1848 240 (1977).
117. Douglas, *Slavery Unconstitutional, Lecture Delivered in Glasgow, Scotland 26 March 1860, in* 3 THE FREDERICK DOUGLASS PAPERS: 1855–63 340 (John W. Blassingame ed. 1979).

Chapter 7

1. 1 HARRIET BEECHER STOWE, DRED: A TALE OF THE GREAT DISMAL SWAMP xiv (Boston, 1856), reprinted (1896).
2. HARRIET BEECHER STOWE, A KEY TO UNCLE TOM'S CABIN (Boston, 1853).
3. Book Review, 101 QUARTERLY REVIEW 324, 324 (1857) (reviewing Dred).
4. 13 N.C. (2 Dev.) 263 (1830).
5. Hinds v. Brazealle, 3 Miss. (2 How.) 837 (1838).
6. 4 THE PAPERS OF THOMAS RUFFIN 249 (J.G. de Roulhac Hamilton, ed. 1918).
7. State v. Mann, 13 N.C. (2 Dev.) 263 (1830).
8. Id. at 266.
9. Id. at 264.
10. Id. at 265.
11. Id. at 266.
12. Id.
13. Id. at 266.
14. Id.
15. See, e.g., John C. Calhoun, *A Disquisition on Government, in* 1 WORKS OF JOHN C. CALHOUN 55 (R. Crallé, ed., 1851) ("It is a great and dangerous error to suppose that all people are equally entitled to liberty. It is a reward to be earned, not a blessing to be gratuitously lavished on all alike; . . . not a boon to be bestowed on a people too ignorant, degraded and vicious, to be capable either of appreciating or of enjoying it."); id. at 52 ("For to extend liberty beyond the limits assigned, would be to weaken government and to render it incompetent to fulfill its primary end—the protection of society against dangers, internal and external.").
16. 9 N.C. (2 Hawks) 582, 582 (1823).
17. Mann, 13 N.C. at 266.
18. Id.
19. Id.
20. Id. at 266–67.
21. See, e.g., Mitchell v. Wells, 37 Miss. 235 (1859) (interpreting Mississippi emancipation law in light of state policy).
22. Mann, 13 N.C. at 267.
23. Id. at 268.
24. Commonwealth v. Turner, 26 Va. (5 Rand.) 678 (1827), 1827 WL 1087 (opinion of William A.G. Dade).
25. Mann, 13 N.C. at 263.
26. STOWE, KEY, supra note 2, at 77.
27. See HARRIET BEECHER STOWE, UNCLE TOM'S CABIN 513, 515 (1852) (Library of America ed., 1983) (appealing to the "public sentiment" of southern readers and urging readers to "see to [their] sympathies in this matter").
28. See, e.g., STOWE, *supra* note 27, at 513 (attributing her motivation for writing the novel to the belief that "Christians cannot know what slavery is; if they did, such a question could never be open for discussion"). Elizabeth Clark has shown how the turn to sympathy in American

thought was harnessed by religious reformers to change peoples' attitudes. *See* Elizabeth Clark, *"The Sacred Rights of the Weak": Pain, Sympathy, and the Culture of Individual Rights in Antebellum America*, 82 J. AM. HIST. 463 (1995). Stowe's contemporaries recognized the radical potential of fiction. *See, e.g.,* Catherine Beecher, *Preface, in* HARRIET BEECHER STOWE, THE MAYFLOWER xii (Boston, 1844) ("Works of imagination *might be* made the most powerful of all human agencies in promoting virtue and religion."); George Frederick Holmes, *Review of Uncle Tom's Cabin,* 18 S. LITERARY MESSENGER 721, 724 (1852) ("The potency of literature, in this age of the world, when it embraces all manifestations of public or individual thought and feeling, and permeates, in streams, more or less diluted, all classes of society, can scarcely by misapprehended.").

29. *See* LIFE AND LETTERS OF HARRIET BEECHER STOWE 58 (Annie Fields ed., 1897).
30. Letter of George Sand, Nov. 15, 1852, *printed in* LIFE AND LETTERS, *supra* note 29, at 154.
31. 1 STOWE, DRED, *supra* note 1, at 264.
32. *Id.* at 71.
33. *Id.* at 71.
34. *Id.* at 77.
35. *Id.* at 78–79.
36. *Id.* at 71.
37. *Id.* at 82.
38. *Id.* at 79.
39. 1, STOWE, DRED, *supra* note 1, at xiv.
40. 1 *Id.* at 26.
41. *Id.*
42. *Id.*
43. 1 *Id.* at 439.
44. 1 *Id.* at 438.
45. 1 *Id.* at 440.
46. 1 *Id.* at 442.
47. 1 *Id.* at 450.
48. 1 *Id.* at 450.
49. *Id.*
50. 1 *Id.* at 450–51. Stowe's indictment of the church through Judge Clayton suggests that she believed in 1856 that reform of the law by itself was insufficient to root out the evils of slavery. For different reasons, proslavery writers likewise believed that slave law was a mere manifestation of the order inherent in nature, which could not be eliminated even with changes in law. The Mississippi lawyer George Sawyer, for example, wrote:

> Law, for the government and regulation of this institution is the creature of slavery. The real cause and ultimate necessity of human bondage in some form or other, have had, in all ages and nations, an anterior existence to all human law; their foundation is laid broad and deep in the philosophy of human nature.... Laws may, it is true, change the form and modify, for better or for worse, the system under which any state of servitude may exist; but they can no more abolish the substantial relation of master and slave, than they can do away with ... poverty.

GEORGE SAWYER, SOUTHERN INSTITUTES 309 (Philadelphia, Lippincott 1858).
51. 2 STOWE, DRED, *supra* note 1, at 16–17.
52. 1 *Id.* at 451.
53. Stowe's explanation is, of course, that of an abolitionist who had trouble believing that people would permit slavery if they knew "what slavery is." STOWE, UNCLE TOM'S CABIN, *supra* note 27, at 513. Therefore, Stowe's depiction of Judge Clayton may have been biased by her search for an explanation why people who understood what slavery was still failed to act against it. Stowe's perspective on Clayton may, thus, tell us more about Stowe's own incredulity about how people act than about the actual motives of southern judges.
54. 1 *Id.* at 449.
55. *Id.*
56. *See generally Remarks of Senator Charles Tillinghast James,* CONG. GLOBE 32nd Cong., 1st Sess., App. 1123 (Aug. 26, 1852) ("My own views of philanthropy and humanity lead me

to the conclusion that, of two evils, we should choose the least; and I certainly form no just estimate of the enormous difference between the evils resulting from the return of a few fugitive slaves to their owners, and those to result to the entire people of the United States, from a course likely to annihilate the glorious fabric of the American Union."); Remarks of Rep. R.M.T. Hunter, CONG. GLOBE, 31st Cong., 1st Sess., App. 1632 (Sept. 3, 1850) ("Some sufferings, sir, belong to our condition; it is a part of the lot of humanity, and although you may point me to cases which I admit to be cases of hardship, cases which shock the feelings of every humane and benevolent man, cases which I would gladly relieve if I had the power, yet if it be shown to me that in relieving them I shall inflict an injury upon a larger class of the community—upon a whole caste—I must refuse to do it."); GEORGE S. SAWYER, SOUTHERN INSTITUTES: OR, AN INQUIRY INTO THE ORIGIN AND EARLY PREVALENCE OF SLAVERY 14 (Philadelphia, Lippincott 1858) ("Laws and regulations relate to [slaves] only upon the true principle of self-government—the greatest amount of good to the greatest number.").

57. 2 STOWE, DRED, *supra* note, at 102.
58. 1 *Id.* at 72–73.
59. 2 *Id.* at 67.
60. 1 *Id.* at 426–27; 2 id. at 67.
61. Cora's story is based upon *Hinds v. Brazealle*, 3 Miss. (2 How.) 837 (1838).
62. 1 *Id.* at 210.
63. 2 *Id.* at 181.
64. 2 *Id.* at 181–82.
65. 2 *Id.* at 185.
66. 2 *Id.* at 187.
67. STOWE, KEY, *supra* note 2, at 72.
68. *Id.* at 72.
69. *Id.* at 71.

Chapter 8

1. At least some of Ruffin's defenders thought so. After defending Ruffin's opinion and pointing out the limitations law placed on owners, Edward Josiah Stearns commented, "In justice to the Judge, I should state that this opinion was delivered more than twenty-three years ago, and was among the first, perhaps the very first, delivered by him on the back of the Supreme Court." *See* Edward Josiah Stearns, *Notes on Uncle Tom's Cabin: Being a Logical Answer to Its Allegations and Inferences against Slavery as an Institution* 194 (1853).Before he went on the Supreme Court, Ruffin served as a trial judge, where he had ample opportunity to see the brutality of slavery and the North Carolina code. The sentence of death he imposed of a free black youth for breaking into a house occasioned an editorial opposing the severe sentence and encouraging construction of a penitentiary. *See Raleigh Register* April 27, 1827.

2. For biographical sketches of Ruffin, see MARK TUSHNET, SLAVE LAW IN THE AMERICAN SOUTH: STATE V. MANN IN HISTORY AND LITERATURE 74–96 (2003); TIMOTHY S. HUEBNER, THE SOUTHERN JUDICIAL TRADITION: STATE JUDGES AND SECTIONAL DISTINCTIVENESS, 1790–1890 130–59 (1998).

3. State v. Hoover, 20 N.C. (3&4 Dev. & Bat.) 500, 503 (1839).
4. 31 N.C. 391 (1849).
5. 31 N.C. at 422–23 (quoting State v. Tuckett, 8 N.C. 210, 217 (1820)).
6. *Id.* at 423.
7. 13 N.C. (2 Dev.) 543 (1830).
8. 33 N.C. (11 Ired.) 640 (1850). In dissent in *Wiswall v. Brinson*, 32 N.C. (10 Ired.) 554 (1849), Ruffin tried to limit the liability of a property owner for the damage caused by one of his employees to a neighbor's horse. The property owner, Wiswall, contracted to have a Gaskill move a house 200 yards, from one of his properties to another, and Gaskill dug a whole on a public road, as part of the moving. Later that evening, as Brinson was driving a coach over the road, one of his horses was injured by the hole. Over a vigorous and

lengthy dissent by Ruffin, the Supreme Court concluded that Wiswell was liable for Gaskill's negligence.

Limitation of liability of owners and employers was important to Ruffin. He dissented in 1846 in *Junter v. Jameson*, 28 N.C. (6 Ired.) 252 (1846) from the Supreme Court's imposition of a warranty of fitness. The seller's agent had warranted the goods without the seller's permission. Taken together these illustrate Ruffin's desire to limit liability, in contract, tort, and property cases; and especially when humans (free or slave) other than the person held liable were the agents of the damage.

9. 30 N.C. (8 Ired.) 446 (1848). Moreover, he drew upon the common proslavery argument that compared poor whites with slaves and argued that slaves were treated better. In this case, Ruffin thought that poor free workers would have little resources. "For, in general, the pecuniary responsibility of menials, though so by contract, is but nominal, and in cases of aggravated injuries, it is altogether inadequate."
10. 1 Rev. State. Chap. 111, sec. 57.
11. *See* Garrett v. Cowles, 39 Miss. (10 George) 60, 64 (1860); Read v. Manning, 30 Miss. (1 George) 308, 317–18 (1855).
12. Sorrey v. Bright, 21 N.C. (1 Dev. & Bat. Eq) 113 (1835).
13. Sampson v. Burgwin, 20 N.C. (3 & 4 Dev. & Bat.) 21, 30 (1838).
14. White v. Green, 36 N.C. (1 Ired. Eq.) 45 (1840).
15. Thompson v. Newlin, 38 N.C. (3 Ired. Eq.) 338 (Fall term 1844), 39 N.C. (4 Ired. Eq.) 312, 41 N.C. (6 Ired. Eq.) 380 (1849); 43 N.C. (8 Ired. Eq.) 32 (Dec. Term 1851). *See also* Lemmond v. Peoples, 41 N.C. (6 Ired. Eq.) 137 (1849) (invalidating secret trust for quasi-slavery).
16. *Contra* Redmond v. Coffin, 17 N.C. (2 Dev. Eq.) 437, 440–41 (1833). 3 Ire. Eq. 338 (1844).
17. 36 N.C. (1 Ired. Eq.) 436 (1841).
18. 39 N.C. (4 Ired. Eq.) 15 (1845).
19. 39 N.C. (4 Ired. Eq.) 15 (1845). Memory F. Mitchell, *Off to Africa with Judicial Blessing*, 53 N.C. HIST. REV. 265–87 (1976).
20. *Id.*
21. *Id.* (citing Haywood v. Craven, 2 N.C. L. Rep. 557; Cameron v. Commissioners of Raleigh, 1 Ired. Eq. 436; Thompson v. Newlin, 38 N.C. (3 Ired. Eq.) 338). *See also* Thompson v. Newlin, 43 N.C. (8 Ired. Eq.) 32 (1851) ("[T]he power of the owner to five, and the capacity of the slave to receive, freedom, exist in nature, and therefore may be used in every case and in every way, except those in which it is forbidden by law."). Or, as Ruffin phrased it in *Lemmond v. Peoples*, 41 N.C. (6 Ired. Eq.) 137 (1849), "every country has the right to protect itself from a population, dangerous to its mortality or peace; and hence the policy of the law of this State prevents the emancipation of slaves."
22. 43 N.C. (8 Ired. Eq.) 70 (1851).
23. 1 Dev. Eq. 493.
24. 2 Hawks 120.
25. Lemmond v. Peoples, 41 N.C. (6 Ired. Eq.) 137 (1849) (citing Stevens v. Ely, 1 Dev. Eq. 493; Thompson v. Newlin, 3 Ired. Eq. 338).
26. Redding v. Long, 57 N.C. (4 Jones Eq.) 216 (1858). Even though he affirmed the right to remove slaves, Ruffin maintained his proslavery position. In an address to the state agricultural society in 1855, Ruffin maintained the benefits of slavery to both slaves and society. *Address of Thomas Ruffin, Delivered Before The State Agricultural Society Of North Carolina, October 18th, 1855*, 4 PAPERS OF THOMAS RUFFIN 323, 330 (J.G. de Roulhac Hamilton ed. 1920). Moreover, as Eric Muller has demonstrated, he was a stern master of the people whom he owned. *Judging Thomas Ruffin and the Hindsight Defense*, 87 N.C. L. REV. 757–98 (2009).
27. 57 N.C. at 216.
28. 25 N.C. (3 Ired.) 224, 226 (1842).
29. Another opinion along these lines is State v. Williams, 39 N.C. (4 Ired. Eq.) 15 (1845).
30. Redmond v. Coffin, 17 N.C. (Dev. Eq.) 437 (1833). *Redmond* cited, among other precedent, Trustees of Quaker Society of Contentnea v. Dickinson, 12 N.C. (1 Dev.) 189 (1827), which had prohibited a trust of slaves. *Dickinson* derived in part from suspicion of religious trusts, as well as opposition to emancipation. *See also* White v. White, 18 N.C (1 Dev. & Bat.) 260

(1833) (refusing to give relief, based on statute of limitations, to residuary heir who claimed that Quakers held slaves in quasi-freedom and thus the slaves should be forfeited by the Quakers).

31. Common v. Jenkins, 1 Dev. Eq. 422 (1830). *See also* Tarkinton v. Guyther, 35 N.C. 100 (1851).

32. *See, e.g.,* Griffin v. Simpson, 33 N.C. (11 Ired.) 126 (1850).

33. Redding v. Long, 57 N.C. (4 Jones. Eq.) 216 (1858).

34. *Id.*

35. 15 Ark. 151 (1854) (citing *Parham v. Blackwelder,* [actually *Thompson v. Newlin*], 43 N.C. (8 Iredell) 44 (1852)).

36. 38 N.C. (3 Ired. Eq.) 562 (1845).

37. Ruffin looked to the consequences of his decision to gauge the appropriateness of the rule he was announcing in other cases as well. In *State v. Davis,* 52 N.C. (7 Jones) 425, 427–28 (1859), he dissented from the reduction of a slave's conviction for murder of a white to man-slaughter on the grounds that the slave was provoked. "It seems to me to be dangerous to the last degree to hold the doctrine, that negro slaves may assume to themselves the judgment as to the right or propriety of resistance. . . . It may be apprehended that they will end in denouncing the injustice of slavery itself, and, upon that pretext, band together to throw off their common bondage entirely." In *State v. Samuel,* 19 N.C. 170 (1836), Ruffin addressed the question whether a couple, who were slaves, were married. The issue arose because the wife sought immunity from testifying against her husband. He analyzed the consequences of con-struing the couple as married; although it would be beneficial to the wife in this case, it might subject others to prosecution for bigamy. He was not prepared "without a mandate from a higher authority than our own, to apply . . . a rule, which would in innumerable instances, either subject them to legal criminality of a high grade, or deprive them almost entirely of their greatest solace—having families of their own."

38. White v. White 18 N.C. (1 Dev. & Bat.) 260 (1833). *White* distinguished between legal title to a slave and moral right.

39. WILLIAM GASTON, ADDRESS DELIVERED BEFORE THE PHILANTHROPIC AND DIALECTIC SOCIETIES AT CHAPEL HILL, JUNE 20, 1832 14 (Raleigh, Jos. Gales & Son, 1832).

40. The invitation to speak at Carolina's graduation was made to Gaston the month after the Turner rebellion, while both Virginia and North Carolina were still dealing with the raw emo-tions, violence, and trials in the wake of the rebellion. See Letter from Philanthropic Soc'y to William Gaston, Sept. 15, 1831, Gaston Papers, Southern Historical Collection, University of North Carolina at Chapel Hill; Alfred L. Brophy, *The Nat Turner Trials,* 91 N.C. L. Rev. 1817, 1869 (2013) (discussing invitation to Gaston to speak at Carolina's graduation).

41. WILLIAM, HOOPER, AN ORATION DELIVERED AT CHAPEL HILL ON WEDNESDAY, JUNE 24, 1829 . . . 14–15 (Hillsborough, Dennis Heartt, 1829).

42. WILLIAM GASTON, AN ADDRESS DELIVERED BEFORE THE AMERICAN WHIG AND CLIOSOPHIC SOCIETIES OF THE COLLEGE OF NEW JERSEY, September, 29, 1835 27 (Princeton, John Bogart, 1835). Mob violence rose dramatically in the 1830s. *See* DANIEL WALKER HOWE, WHAT HATH GOD WROUGHT? THE TRANSFORMATION OF AMERICA, 1815–1848 431 (2007) (listing riots per year in 1830s).

43. *Id.* at 9.

44. *Id.* at 24.

45. *Id.* at 25.

46. *Id.* at 25–26.

47. *Id.* at 27–28.

48. *See* Jessica Lee Thompson, "'Toward Freedom for All': North Carolina Quaker Legal Theory on the Trust for Manumissions," available at http://papers.ssrn.com/sol3/papers.cfm?abstract_id=2477963.

49. State v. Negro Will, 18 N.C. (1 Dev. & Bat.) 121 (1834); State v. Jarrott, 23 N.C. (1 Ired.) 76, (1840).

50. *See Moore, Bartholomew Figures,* in 4 DICTIONARY OF NORTH CAROLINA BIOGRAPHY 294–95 (1991).

51. *State v. Will,* 18 N.C. at 145.

52. *Id.* at 145. In fact, contrary to those who argued for further control over slaves in the wake of the Turner rebellion, Moore believed that "the despair of individuals cannot last forever; neither will that of a numerous people inflicted with common wrongs and exchanging a common sympathy." *Id.*
53. 18 N.C. at 160–61.
54. 18 N.C. at 163.
55. *Id.* at 162–63.
56. *Id.* at 153–54.
57. *Id.* at 162–63.
58. Thomas R. Dew, *Professor Dew on Slavery,* in THE PRO-SLAVERY ARGUMENT ... 287, 447, 485 (Charleston, Walker, Richards & Co. 1852) (quoting Robert Wallace, A *Dissertation on the Numbers of Mankind* (Edinburgh, G. Hamilton and J. Balfour 1753)).
59. State v. Negro Will, 18 N.C. 121, 168 (1834).
60. *Id.* at 167.
61. *Id.* at 172 (quoting Psalm 19 and William Shakespeare *Merchant of Venice,* Act III, scene 1).
62. CONG. GLOBE, 31st Cong., 1st Sess. 284 (March 6, 1850) ("This judge depicts in terms so bitter the institution of slavery, that if any northern man were to use similar words here, he would be called *fanatical.*").
63. CONG. GLOBE, 31st Cong., 1st Sess. 285–86 (March 8, 1850).
64. *Speech of Mr. Badger,* CONG. GLOBE, 31st Cong., 1st Sess., 382, 383 (March 18/19, 1850); CONG. GLOBE, 31st Sess., 1st Sess. 286 (March 8, 1850). The difference in approach between Ruffin's 1830 *State v. Mann* opinion and Gaston's 1834 *State v. Negro Will* reveals the differing perspectives of Ruffin, a Democrat and a person who supported few if any constraints on the power of the master, and Gaston, who privately (and sometimes publicly) advocated antislavery measures. This may reveal the political-ideological divisions of the conflicts of humanity, law, and economy that historians have identified in southern approaches to slavery. *See, e.g.,* Reuel E. Schiller, *Conflicting Obligations: Slave Law and the Late Antebellum North Carolina Supreme Court,* 78 VA. L. REV. 1207–51 (1992). Perhaps it was not so much that sometimes considerations of humanity trumped considerations of law; Gaston and Ruffin articulated different visions of the law's scope and the point where law ended and the master's "authority over the body of the slave," as Ruffin phrased it, began.
Will, of course, arose in a different setting from *Mann.* In the former, the court dealt with the question of the slave's scope of resistance to an abusive overseer, and in *Mann* it was the scope of the criminal law to punish an abusive owner (or possessor). It is entirely possible that the law would recognize the authority of the owner to injure a slave while also recognizing that slaves might, as human beings, respond to an abusive overseer.

Chapter 9

1. See TIMOTHY HUEBNER, THE SOUTHERN JUDICIAL TRADITION (1999); J. P. Reid, *Lessons of Lumpkin: A Review of Recent Literature on Law, Comity, and the Impending Crisis,* 23 WM & MARY L. REV. 571–602 (1982); PAUL DEFOREST HICKS, JOSEPH HENRY LUMPKIN: GEORGIA'S FIRST CHIEF JUSTICE (2002); D. Grier Stephenson & Mason Stephenson, *"To Protect and Defend:" Joseph Henry Lumpkin, the Supreme Court of Georgia, and Slavery,* 25 EMORY L.J. 579–608 (1976).
2. *Secretary's Report,* AFRICAN REPOSITORY 302 (Oct. 1837) (reporting on Lumpkin's efforts at fund raising).
3. HICKS, *supra* note 1, at 99; THIRTY-NINTH ANNUAL REPORT OF THE AMERICAN BOARD OF COMMISSIONERS FOR FOREIGN MISSIONS at 6 (Boston, Board 1848); JOSEPH HENRY LUMPKIN, ADDRESS DELIVERED ... AT THE METHODIST CHURCH IN THE CITY OF MILLEDGEVILLE, AFTER THE CONCLUSION OF THE CEREMONY OF LAYING THE CORNER STONE OF OGLETHORPE UNIVERSITY (1837) (at Emory).
4. See HICKS, *supra* note 1, at 55 (discussing the media attention Lumpkin received following an 1833 speech in Boston and his letter in the *Niles Register* October 5, 1833).
5. JOSEPH HENRY LUMPKIN, AN ADDRESS ON NATURAL HISTORY, DELIVERED BEFORE THE PHI DELTA AND CICERONIAN SOCIETIES, ON THE 1ST DAY OF JULY, 1836 (Washington, Georgia, Office of the Christian Index 1836).

6. JOSEPH H. LUMPKIN, AN ADDRESS DELIVERED BEFORE THE SOUTH-CAROLINA INSTITUTE AT ITS SECOND ANNUAL FAIR ON THE 19TH NOVEMBER, 1850 (Charleston, Walker & James 1851).

7. *Id.* at 6–7.

8. *Id.* at 7.

9. 6 Ga. 563, 569 (1849)(1849) (interpreting a prenuptial agreement so that the decedent's next of kin, first cousins, did not fall within the marriage consideration).

10. LUMPKIN, *supra* note 6, at 9–10.

11. *Id.* at 13.

12. *Id.* at 16.

13. Lumpkin to Howell Cobb, on January 21, 1848, in THE CORRESPONDENCE OF ROBERT TOOMBS, ALEXANDER H. STEPHENS, AND HOWELL COBB 94–95 (Ulrich B. Phillips ed. 1913).

14. LUMPKIN, *supra* note 6, at 15.

15. *Id.* at 18.

16. *Debow's Review* published an excerpt from the speech the next year. [Joseph H. Lumpkin], *Industrial Regeneration of the South,* 2 DEBOW'S REVIEW 41 (Jan 1852). *See also* Young v. Harrison, 17 Ga. 30, 1855 WL 1644 (1855) (upholding eminent domain and commenting in regard to offset of gain to corporation by virtue of public works that "[n]o one can dispute the strong natural equity which dictates the propriety of considering the advantages, which the land holder has gained by reason of his land having been taken for some public work, as an offset to the injuries. And if this be naturally just, and the forms of law do not obstruct, why should not the award or verdict be rendered accordingly?"); Moultrie v. Smiley, 16 Ga. 289, 1854 WL 1584 (1854) (winding up bank corporation that goes into bankruptcy; majority, with concurrence by Starnes and dissent by Benning).

17. Shields v. Yonge, 15 Ga. 349, 357–58, 1854 WL 1606, at *6–7 (1854) (finding that because the decedent was an employee of the railroad, any claim filed by his father was barred by the fellow-servant rule).

18. *See, e.g.,* Farwell v. Boston & R.R. Corp., 45 Mass. 49, 57, 1842 WL 4002, at *7 (1842) ("[A]nd we are not aware of any principle which should except the perils arising from the carelessness and negligence of those who are in the same employment, these are the perils which the servant is as likely to know, and against which he can as effectually guard").

19. Honner v. Illinois C.R. Co., 15 Ill. 550, 552 (1854), 1854 WL 4734, at *1 (Ill. 1854) ("[T]he doctrine of respondeat superior does not extend to the case of an injury received by one servant through the carelessness of another servant . . . injuries to other servants arising from want of proper care and skill are deemed casualties, which the employer does not take to insure against").

20. Illinois C.R. Co. v. Cox, 21 Ill. 20, 26 (1858), 1858 WL 6152, at *5 (Ill. 1858) ("[O]ne servant should not recover against the common master for the carelessness of his fellow-servant . . . it must be understood that each servant, when he engages in a particular service, calculates the hazards incident to it, and contracts accordingly").

21. Scudder v. Woodbridge, 1 Ga. Rep. 195, 1846 WL 1156 (Ga. 1846). *See also* Gorman v. Campbell, 14 Ga. 137, 143 (1853), 1853 WL 1656, at *5 (Ga. 1853) (rejecting fellow servant rule in cases involving slaves, because "humanity to the slave, as well as proper regard for the interest of the owner" requires that slaves be given special protection). It is hard to know if this is humanity to the slave or for the economy of the slave owner, for there was a coincidence of them here.

22. *Scudder,* at 200, 1846 WL 1156, at *7. That decision later was the basis for limiting the fellow-servant rule for white workers in an industrial setting to places where the workers actually knew one another. *Cooper v. Mullins,* 30 Ga. 146, 150, 1860 WL 2109, at *4 (1860), read *Scudder* as resting on the assumption that "because slaves from their status were incapable of influencing their associate employees towards fidelity and care in the common business."

23. Moran v. Davis, 18 Ga. 722 (1855).

24. 4 Ga. 445, 1848 WL 1510 (1848).

25. *Id.* at 459, 1848 WL 1510, at *10.

26. *Id.*

27. 16 Ga. at *13. *See also* Henderson's Heirs v. Rost, 5 La.Ann. 441 (1850) (reprinting will that provided for limited emancipation, while criticizing abolitionists).
28. 19 Ga. 35 (1855), 1855 WL 1788 (Ga. 1855).
29. *Id.* at 37, 1855 WL 1788, at *3 (interpreting the Georgia statutes of 1801 and 1818 to allow for such a devise).
30. *Id.* at 65, 1855 WL 1788, at *20 (Benning, dissenting) (referring to his dissent in *Bass* for finding the provision void and "it is needless, therefore, to repeat the reasons here"). Benning's most famous opinion was in *Paddleford v. Savannah*, 14 Ga. 438 (1854), 1854 WL 492 (Ga. 1854), which advanced an extreme southern interpretation of the U.S. Constitution in that it allowed Georgia to ignore the Interstate Commerce Clause. I am indebted to Andrew Lincoln, UNC Law School class of 2009, whose seminar paper taught me much about Benning.
31. 18 Ga. 130 (1855), 1855 WL 1641 (Ga. 1855).
32. *Id.* at 165, 1855 WL 1641, at *23 (Benning, dissenting). Lumpkin had an easier time prohibiting emancipation by will in *Bryan v. Walton*, 14 Ga. 185 (1853), 1853 WL 1662 (Ga. 1853). There a free black man attempted to free slaves he had inherited, while a white man claimed that he had rightful ownership based on a "purchase" that took place after the purported act of emancipation. Lumpkin concluded that free black people were "in a state of perpetual pupilage or wardship." The legislature had not empowered them to free slaves that they owned, and so Lumpkin validated the white man's ownership. In a precursor to the Chief Justice Taney 1857 opinion in *Dred Scott*, Lumpkin remarked that free black people were not citizens:

> In no part of this country, whether North or South, East or West, does the free negro stand erect and on a platform of equality with the white man. . . . To him there is but little in prospect, but a life of poverty, of depression, of ignorance, and of decay. He lives amongst us without motive and without hope. . . . . Generally, society suffers, and the negro suffers by manumission. . . . The Courts of this country should never lean to that construction, which puts the thriftless African upon a footing of civil or political equality with a white population which are characterized by a degree of energy and skill, unknown to any other people or period. Such alone, can be *citizens* in this great and growing Republic, which extends already from the Atlantic to the Pacific, and from the St. Lawrence to the Rio Grande.

Walton, 14 Ga. at 206, 1853 WL 1662, at * 15.
33. 25 Ga. 109, 1858 WL 1914 (1858).
34. *Id.* at 120, 1858 WL 1914, at *7.
35. *Id.* (quoting *Pray v. Edie*, 1 T.R. 313).
36. *Id.* at 124, 1858 WL 1914, at *10.
37. *Id.* at 113, 1858 WL 1914, at *3.
38. Sanders v. Ward, 25 Ga.109, 131, 1858 WL 1914, at *14 (1858) (Benning, dissenting).
39. *Id.* at 131–32, 1858 WL 1914, at *14.
40. In *Mitchell v. Wells*, discussed extensively in Chapter 11, Mississippi Justice William L. Harris moved even more strongly in favor of restrictions on emancipation. Mitchell v. Wells, 37 Miss. (8 George) 235, 1859 WL 3634 (1859) (rejecting the contention that a female slave freed pursuant to Ohio law, who then returned to Mississippi, was entitled to receive an inheritance left to her by her father).
41. 23 Ga. 448, 464, 1857 WL 2072, at *11 (1857). Mississippi took a similar path in denying the American Colonization Society's power to take bequests of slaves. *See* Lusk v. Lewis, 32 Miss. (3 George) 297, 1856 WL 4022 (Miss. Er. App. 1856) (refusing to allow trustees to take bequest of slaves for the benefit of the American Colonization Society, because the Society's charter only allowed them to colonize, not own people). *See also* Lusk v. Lusk, 35 Miss. (6 George) 401, 1858 WL 4592 (Miss. Err. App. 1858) (refusing to allow American Colonization Society to take $3,500 bequest).
42. *Gartrell* at 465, 1857 WL 2072, at *11.
43. 15 Ga. 535, 541, 1854 WL 1652, at *5 (1854).
44. *Id.* at 542, 1854 WL 1652, at *6.
45. *Id.* at 542–43, 1854 WL 1652, at *6. Starnes continued the analogy to parents and children: "If the master exceed the bounds of reason and moderation, in his chastisement, the slave must

submit, as the child submits to the correction of its parent, and trust to the law for his vindi-
cation. He cannot, himself, undertake to redress his wrong, unless the attack upon him be
with an instrument, or in the use of means calculated to produce death." *Id.* at 543, 1854 WL
1652, at*6.

46. Harden v. Mangham, 18 Ga. 563, 565, 1855 WL 1736, at * 3 (1855).
47. *Id.* at 566–67, 1855 WL 1736, at *3.
48. Harris v. Smith, 16 Ga. 545, 549–50 (1855), 1855 WL 1617, at *4 (relying on old English law
to interpret the will as conveying a remainder subject to an executory interest in the testator's
grandson):

> To come at once to the point: Let us admit that our Act of 1821 holds us to the Statute
> of Westminster, commonly called De Donis, &c. as the touchstone of those terms
> which shall constitute or pass an estate tail. And the more advantageously to consider
> this subject, let us look to some features in the history of that Statute. That history
> bears fruitful evidence to the struggle which has so long been going on between what is
> rightly called "the true policy of the Common Law," and the baronial or feudal system.

49. Williamson v. Nabers, 14 Ga. 286, 310, 1853 WL 1677, at *15 (1853):

> We cannot sanction the position taken in the argument, that justice would be sub-
> served if the Court would in all cases set aside a verdict when manifestly against the
> weight of evidence. It may be true, as eloquently insisted by the Counsel, that it is
> the high province of the Judge to stand in the breach, and resist the passion and the
> prejudice which sometimes overcome the jury. But it is also true, that the jury may
> sometimes stand in the breach, and resist the assaults of oppression and tyranny to
> which the Judge succumbs. Lessons may be learned from chapters in the history of the
> Second James, and the Third George of England, full of the struggles and the triumphs
> of the trial by jury; and fraught with instruction for freemen.
>   Our Laws have wisely divided responsibility in this respect, by appointing for our
> judicial system separate spheres in which these two Constitutional bodies shall re-
> volve; and it is the duty of our Courts to avoid all shock from their improper collision.
> That such collision may be avoided, we have frequently held, and now again repeat,
> that the Court should not grant a new trial merely because the verdict is against the
> weight of evidence; and never because of this, unless the preponderance be so great as
> to shock the understanding, and moral sense.

50. Williams v. Allen, 17 Ga. 81, 84, 1855 WL 1691, at *4 (1855) (refuting an English interpretation of the testator's will and finding that the testator conveyed only a life estate to her
daughter).
51. Joseph Jones [Ebenezer Starnes], The Slaveholder Abroad: or, Billy Buck's
visit, with his master, to England. A series of letters from Dr. Pleasant Jones
to Major Joseph Jones, of Georgia (Philadelphia, J.B. Lippincott & Co., 1860). *See also*
H. Prentice Miller, *The Authorship of The Slaveholder Abroad*, 10 J. S. Hist. 92–94 (1944).
What one might also add to Miller's case is that the appendix is acknowledged to be by Judge
Starnes. Thus, it is unlikely that William Tappan Thompson is the author, as some people have
previously suggested.
52. Joseph P. Reidy From Slavery to Agrarian Capitalism in the Cotton Plantation
South: Central Georgia, 1800–1860 106 (1992).
53. Starnes, *supra* note 51, at 491–502. *See also* Alfred L. Brophy, *Antislavery Women and the
Origins of American Jurisprudence*, 94 Tex. L. Rev. 115, 124 (2015) (discussing Starnes).

Chapter 10

1. Thomas R. R. Cobb, An Inquiry into the Law of Negro Slavery in the United
States xxxv (Philadelphia, T. & W. Johnson 1858).
2. Thomas Read Rootes Cobb, A Digest of the Statute Laws of the State of
Georgia: In Force Prior to the Session of the General Assembly of 1851 (Athens,
Ga., Christy, Kelsea & Burke 1851).

3. WILLIAM B. McCASH, THOMAS R.R. COBB (1823–1862): THE MAKING OF A SOUTHERN NATIONALIST 118 (1983).
4. TIMOTHY HUEBNER, THE SOUTHERN JUDICIAL MIND: STATE JUDGES AND SECTIONAL DISTINCTIVENESS, 1790–1860 76 (1999).
5. SECESSION DEBATED: GEORGIA'S SHOWDOWN IN 1860 3–30 (William W. Freehling and Craig M. Simpson, eds., 1992).
6. THOMAS R. COBB, EDUCATIONAL WANTS OF GEORGIA; AN ADDRESS DELIVERED BEFORE THE SOCIETY OF THE ALUMNI OF FRANKLIN COLLEGE AT ITS ANNUAL MEETING, 4TH AUGUST, 1857 8 (Athens, Reynolds & Bro. 1857). *See also* McCASH, *supra* note 3, at 125 (citing Thomas Cobb, "Prospectus of University of Georgia Law School 1 June 1859".) Some other evidence of the Cobb family comes in the interview given by Susan Castle, who had been owned by Thomas Cobb's family. *See* 12 THE AMERICAN SLAVE, SUPPLEMENT SERIES 1, at 178–81 (George P. Rawick et al. eds., 1977). Castle's positive view of the Cobb family may say more about what the role that African Americans were expected to fill as supplicants during Jim Crow than about the actual experience of slavery.
7. COBB, *supra* note 1, at 8.
8. *Id.* at 8–9.
9. *See* Chapter 7 (discussing antislavery jurisprudence of Stowe, Goodell, Emerson, and Douglass and its grounding in history, economics, and common law); Chapter 5 (discussing antislavery religious thought of Francis Wayland).
10. *See* KUNAL PARKER, COMMON LAW, HISTORY, AND DEMOCRACY IN AMERICA, 1790–1900: LEGAL THOUGHT BEFORE MODERNISM (2011). Cobb occupies a place in Parker's analysis. *Id.* at 184. *Cf.* DAVID RABBAN, LAW'S HISTORY: AMERICAN LEGAL THOUGHT AND THE TRANSATLANTIC TURN TO HISTORY (2013) (locating turn to historicism in high-brow jurisprudence after the Civil War).
11. 2 JOSEPH PRIESTLEY, LECTURES ON HISTORY AND GENERAL POLICY 197 (Northumberland, Pa., 1803) ("Many things in the present state of the law are unintelligible without the knowledge of the history and progress of it.").
12. In Bentham's apt phrasing, Blackstone was "that sort of man who is ever on his knees before the footstool of Authority." JEREMY BENTHAM, A FRAGMENT ON GOVERNMENT 13 (1776) (1977 ed.).
13. BENTHAM, *supra* note 12, at 10.
14. HENRY HALLAM, THE VIEW OF THE STATE OF EUROPE DURING THE MIDDLE AGES (1818) (reprinted 1856).
15. THOMAS R. DEW, A DIGEST OF THE LAWS, CUSTOMS, MANNERS, AND INSTITUTIONS OF ANCIENT AND MODERN NATIONS (New York, Appleton 1853).
16. EDMUND BURKE, REFLECTIONS ON THE REVOLUTION IN FRANCE (London, 1790).
17. John Campbell, *Slavery Among the Romans*, 14 S. Q. REV. 414 (Oct. 1848); *British West India Islands*, 16 S. Q. REV. 342–77 (Jan. 1850). *See also* John Campbell, *Slavery in the U.S.*, 12 S. Q. REV. 91 (July 1847); *The Rights of the Slave States*, 19 S. Q. REV. 101–45 (Jan. 1851); *Slavery Throughout the World*, 19 S.Q. REV. 305–40 (Apr. 1851).
18. This encyclopedia of sorts invites close study to see the world in miniature. The tapestry of *An Inquiry* tells us much about the ideas that resonated with Cobb. Though Cobb consulted dozens of works, he relied heavily upon a relatively small number of them. So part of the story here is how a southern intellectual engaged with the larger world. The book was written in Athens, Georgia, using the texts available there, and supplemented with occasional works that he viewed while on trips and with excerpts sent by his colleagues elsewhere. Cobb wrote about the challenges of doing research with a limited library. "Residing in an interior village, I have felt the want of access to extended libraries. I have taken advantage of occasional sojourns in the cities of Washington, Philadelphia, and New York, to examine references previously noted, and such books as related to my subject. I have added also a number of works to my own library, which I could not otherwise examine." COBB, *supra* note 1, at ix–x. *See also id.* at cxxxix (noting in discussion of early Spanish settlement in the West Indies that Cobb did not have access to Antonio de Herrera's *Historia general de los hechos de los Castellanos en las islas y tierra firme del Mar Oceano* (Madrid 1730)).

19. *See* Cobb, *supra* note 1, at 36 (citing Harriet Beecher Stowe, *A Key to Uncle Tom's Cabin* (Boston, John P. Jewett 1853)); *id.* at cxxx (citing William Sampson, *Sampson's Discourse: And Correspondence with Various Learned Jurists, Upon the History of the Law* (Washington, Gales and Seaton 1826)); *id.* at cxxxi (citing John Cobden, *White Slaves of England* (Auburn, Derby and Miller 1853).

20. Here antislavery writers drew on two traditions. One sought empirical evidence about the harms of slavery on a large scale—which might provide a counter to proslavery calculations of utility of slavery; the second focused on sympathy for individual slaves, independent of whatever larger calculations of utility might suggest.

21. COBB, *supra* note 1, at xxxv.

22. Historians are increasingly focusing on the transatlantic context of slavery that led to the war. In fact, one of the most celebrated of many recent works on the coming of the Civil War emphasizes the role of emancipation in the West Indies in conditioning the South to fear abolition. *See* EDWARD BARTLETT RUGEMER, THE PROBLEM OF EMANCIPATION: THE CARIBBEAN ROOTS OF THE AMERICAN CIVIL WAR (2008). Cobb adds important weight to that interpretation. For the *Historical Sketch* presents a growing drum beat about the importance of slavery and the hazards of abolition.

23. COBB, *supra* note 1, at xxxv–xxxvi.

24. JOHN FLETCHER, STUDIES ON SLAVERY: IN EASY LESSONS (Natches, Jackson Warner 1852).

25. JOSIAH PRIEST, BIBLE DEFENSE OF SLAVERY (Glasgow, Ky, W.S. Brown 1852).

26. *See* COBB, *supra* note 1, at xxxiv.

27. *Id.* at xlv (citing Josiah Nott & George Gliddon, *Types of Mankind* 250 (Philadelphia, Lippincott, Grambo and Company 1855)).

28. *Id. at* xlvi–xlvii (quoting Francis Hawks, *Egypt and Its Monuments; Or, Egypt a Witness for the Bible* (New York, G.P. Putnam 1849)).

29. COBB, *supra* note 1, at lii.

30. *Id.* at lix.

31. *Id.* at lxix.

32. *Id.* at lxxix–lxxx (citing, among other works, William Smith's *Dictionary of Greek and Roman Antiquities* 868 (Boston, 1842) and Henri Alexandre Wallon, *Histoire de l'Esclavage* (1847)).

33. COBB, *supra* note 1, at cxxxi.

34. *Id.* at cxxxiii.

35. *Id.* at cxxxvi.

36. *Id.* at cxl (quoting *Historia de la conquista de la isla española de Santo Domingo* (1616–15)). *See* COBB, *supra* note 1, at cxxxix n.2 (noting that he did not have access to Herrera and citing Bancroft as the source of his quotation on another point). The quotation most likely came from Washington Irving's *History of the Life and Voyages of Christopher Columbus* (Philadelphia, 1841), for Bancroft did not include the quotation. Moreover, Cobb relies upon Irving at several points. *See* 1 GEORGE BANCROFT, HISTORY OF THE COLONIZATION OF THE UNITED STATES 15th ed. (Boston, Little, Brown, and Co. 1856).

37. COBB, *supra* note 1, at cxlii.

38. 98 Eng. Rep. 499 (K.B. 1772). *See also* William Wiecek, *Somerset: Lord Mansfield and the Legitimacy of Slavery in the Anglo-American World*, 42 U. CHI. L. REV. 86–146 (1974).

39. COBB, *supra* note 1, at cxlvi.

40. *Id.* at cxlvii.

41. *Id.* at cli.

42. *Id.* at cli–clii.

43. *Id.* at cliii.

44. *Id.* at clv.

45. *Id.* at clxv.

46. *Id.* at clxxvi (citing November 3, 1791, speech). *See* A PARTICULAR ACCOUNT OF ... INSURRECTION OF THE NEGROES IN ST. DOMINGO ... MADE TO THE NATIONAL ASSEMBLY, THE 3D OF NOVEMBER 1791 ... (London, J. Sewell 1792).

47. COBB, *supra* note 1, at cxcvi (quoting ROBERT BAIRD, EXPERIENCES OF THE WEST INDIES AND NORTH AMERICA IN 1849 82 (Philadelphia, Lea & Blanchard, 1850)).

48. COBB, *supra* note 1, at cxcvii.

49. *Id.* at cxcviii.
50. *Id.* at cxcix. Cobb predicted failure for the emancipated countries around the Caribbean basin. "The most ordinary marks of civilization are fast disappearing" and Guiana will again be in "the condition in which civilized men first found it." *Id.* at cc.
51. Among the authorities he cited were Frederick Law Olmstead, *Seaboard Slave States* and John Campbell's *Negromania*. *See* COBB, *supra* note 1, at ccv.
52. *Id.* at ccix–ccx.
53. *Id.* at ccxiii.
54. *Id.* at ccxiv.
55. *Id.* at ccxix.
56. *Id.* at ccxxviii.
57. *Id.* at ccxxviii.
58. *See, e.g., id.* at ccxiv.
59. JOHN W. PAGE, UNCLE ROBIN, IN HIS CABIN IN VIRGINIA, AND TOM WITHOUT ONE IN BOSTON (J. W. Randolph Richmond 1853).
60. COBB, *supra* note 1, at clix.
61. *See* SARAH N. ROTH, GENDER AND RACE IN ANTEBELLUM AMERICA (2014) (discussing the shifting images of enslaved people among both antislavery and proslavery writers).
62. COBB, *supra* note 1, at clx.
63. Alexander H. Stephens, *Cornerstone Address,* in SOUTHERN PAMPHLETS ON SECESSION, NOVEMBER 1860–APRIL 1861 402–12 (Jon L. Wakelyn ed. 1996).
64. *Id.* at 68 (quoting Thomas Carlyle, *On History,* in 2 THOMAS CARLYLE: CRITICAL AND MISCELLANEOUS ESSAYS 83, 86 (1899) (1830)).
65. Ralph Ellison, *The Perspective of Literature,* in GOING TO THE TERRITORY 321, 338 (1986).
66. [Thomas Carlyle,] *West India Emancipation,* 8 DE BOW'S REVIEW 527, 530 (June 1850) (reprinting *Occasional Discourse on the Negro Question,* 40 FRASER'S MAGAZINE (February 1849)).
67. *Id.* at 533.
68. *Id.* at 536.
69. *Id.* at 537.
70. Mill's response was "On the Negro Question," 24 LITTELL'S LIVING AGE 465–69 (1850) (reprinted from Fraser's Magazine (1850)).
71. *See* COBB, *supra* note 1, at cxxxii (quoting Carlyle's observation in *Past and Present* that "Liberty, I am told, is a divine thing. Liberty, when it becomes the liberty to die by starvation, is not so divine." *Past and Present,* book III, chapter xiii); *id.* at cxxxiii (citing Carlyle's *Chartism* in discussion of poverty in United Kingdom).
72. COBB, *supra* note 1, at 255–56 ("The question has been much discussed, whether, upon a verdict establishing freedom of the applicant, damages, or hire, should be given the plaintiffs. In some of the States, such damages are given by special statute. . . . Other courts insist, and with great force, that the peculiar condition of the slave, and relation that he bears to the white race, the difficulties surrounding the master, and the interest of the freedman himself, render it inexpedient to make his freedom relate back farther than the judgment pronouncing him free.") (citing against compensation, among others cases, Scott v. Williams, 12 N.C. (1 Dev.) 376 (1828); Woolfolk v. Sweeper, 21 Tenn. (2 Humph.) 88, 96 (1840); Phillis [Free woman of color] v. Gentin, 9 La. 208 (1836); Thompson v. Wilmot, 4 Ky. (1 Bibb) 422 (1809), all for compensation in limited circumstances, and Peter v. Hargrave, 46 Va. (5 Grat.) 12 (1848); Paul's Admr v. Mingo, 31 Va. (4 Leigh) 163 (1833); Henry v. Bollar, 34 Va. (7 Leigh) 19 (1836)).
73. *See, e.g.,* James Holcombe, *Is Slavery Consistent with Natural Law?,* 27 S. LIT. MESSENGER 401 (Dec. 1858). Holcombe's ideas are discussed in Chapter 2.
74. COBB, *supra* note 1, at 12.
75. *Id.* at 16.
76. *Id.* at 13.
77. *Id.* at 21–22.
78. *Id.* at 60 (contending that slavery was not a "necessary evil").
79. *Id.* at 27 (Carlyle essay, "Letter on the Rights of Man," cited at 30).

80. *Id.* at 179.
81. *Id.* at 185.
82. 12 Conn. 38, 1837 WL 60 (1838).
83. COBB, *supra* note 1, at 211.
84. *Id.* at cxlvii.
85. *Id.* at clxx.
86. *Id.* at ccxviii.
87. This is one place where Cobb sees slavery as antimarket. *Id.* at clix.
88. *Id.* at 233.
89. GEORGE SAWYER, AN INQUIRY INTO THE ORIGIN AND EARLY PREVALENCE SLAVERY AND THE SLAVE-TRADE WITH AN ANALYSIS OF THE LAWS, HISTORY, AND GOVERNMENT OF THE INSTITUTION IN THE PRINCIPAL NATIONS, ANCIENT AND MODERN, FROM THE EARLIEST AGES DOWN TO THE PRESENT TIME (Philadelphia, Lippincott 1858).
90. *See also* Alfred L. Brophy, *Did Formalism Never Exist?*, 92 TEXAS L. REV. 383, 403–405 (2013) (discussing Cobb's use of history); Alfred L. Brophy, *When History Mattered*, 91 TEXAS L. REV. 601, 604–607 (2013) (discussing the pre–Civil War turn to historical jurisprudence, including Dew, Cobb, and Goodell).
91. JOHN LEADLEY DAGG, THE ELEMENTS OF MORAL SCIENCE 338–59 (New York, Sheldon & Company 1860). Dagg is discussed in Chapter 2.
92. Roche v. Washington, 19 Ind. 53 (1862).
93. Martin v. Reed, 37 Ala. 198 (1861); Sterrett's Ex'r v. Kaster, 37 Ala. 366 (1861); *see also* Mose v. State, 36 Ala. 211 (1860) (argument of counsel).
94. Bell v. Chambers, 38 Ala. 660 (1863).
95. *An Inquiry* was also cited a few times afterward, mostly in cases involving the legal status of marriages among enslaved people during the era of slavery. Probably its most prominent use came in *Hall v. United States*, decided by the U.S. Supreme Court in 1875. 92 U.S. 27 (1875). There the Court quoted extensively from *An Inquiry* to show that slaves could not marry during the era of slavery. The Court then went on to deny the right of children of such a marriage to inherit from their parents, because the Court concluded such children were non-marital. One particularly prominent and odd invocation is discussed at the end of Chapter 12 of this book.
96. Murray v. State, 9 Fla. 246 (1860) ("It is much better for the master, the slave, and the community at large that provisions be made for the summary punishment of slaves for such offences before a Justice of the Peace, than that the slave be dignified and brought into court with the same importance with the white man, and the master in consequence thereof put to heavy expense in employing counsel and protecting his slave.").
97. George, A Slave v. State, 37 Miss. (8 George) 316 (1859).
98. Minor v. State, 36 Miss. (7 George) 630 (1859).
99. *See* Heirn v. Bridault, 8 George 209 (1859); Hunt v. White, 24 Tex. 643 (1860).
100. Stephenson v. Harrison 3 Head 728 (1859).
101. *See* COBB, *supra* note 1, at 302 (citing Carroll v. Brumby, 13 Ala. 102 (1848)). This is discussed further in Chapter 11.
102. 37 Ala. 229 (1861). Often *An Inquiry* was cited for a proposition that slaves and even slave owners were under disabilities. But the Texas Supreme Court used Cobb to acknowledge that a slave might act as agent for his owner. Sanders v. Devereux, 25 Tex.Supp. 1 (1860).

Chapter 11

1. William Harper, *Harper on Slavery*, in THE PRO-SLAVERY ARGUMENT . . . 1, 17 (Charleston, Walker, Richards & Co. 1852). *See, e.g.*, William J. Grayson, *Slavery in the Southern States*, 8 S.Q. REV. 317 (Oct. 1845) (discussing Chancellor Harper's *Memoir on Slavery*, James Hammond's *Letters to Mr. Clarkson* and Francis Wayland's and Richard Fuller's *Domestic Slavery Considered as a Scriptual Institution*).
2. *See* Chapter 7.
3. *See, e.g.*, ROBERT COVER, JUSTICE ACCUSED: ANTI-SLAVERY AND THE JUDICIAL PROCESS 95–98 (1975).
4. Dred Scott v. Sandford, 60 U.S. (19 How.) 393 (1857).

5. Eva Sheppard Wolf, Race and Liberty in the New Nation: Emancipation in Virginia from the Revolution to Nat Turner's Rebellion 34–35 (2006); *An Act to Authorize the Manumission of Slaves*, 11 The Statutes at Large . . . of All the Laws of Virginia, chap. 21, at 39–40 (William Waller Henning ed., Richmond, George Cochran 1823) (May 6, 1782).

6. 6 Va. (2 Call) 319, 319–21 (1799).

7. 6 Va. at 226–38.

8. *Id.* at 340.

9. Wolf, *supra* note 5, at 45.

10. *Id.* at 122–27.

11. *An Act to Amend the Several Laws Concerning Slaves*, 3 Statutes at Large of Virginia, from October Session 1792, to December Session 1806 sec. 10, 251, 252 (Samuel Shepherd, ed., Richmond, Samuel Shepherd 1836).

12. Wolf, *supra* note 5, at 131.

13. This chapter is necessarily selective. For more on the law of emancipation via will, see Andrew Fede, *Roadblocks to Freedom: Slavery and Manumission in the United States South* (2012); Bernie Jones, *Fathers of Conscience: Mixed-Race Inheritance in the Antebellum South* (2009); Thomas D. Morris, *Southern Slavery and the Law, 1619–1860* 371–423 (1996).

14. 55 Va. (14 Gratt.) 132, 1858 WL 3940 (1858).

15. *Id.* at 136.

16. *Fisher's Negroes v. Dabbs*, 14 Tenn. (6 Yerg.) 119–66 (1834). *See also Opinion of Justice Catron*, 13 African Repository 125–29 (April 1837) (reprinting Catron's opinion).

17. Dred Scott v. Sandford, 60 U.S. (19 How.) 393, at 493 (1857) (Catron, concurring).

18. 14 Tenn. at 132. The Chancellor's opinion below, which Catron adopted as part of his opinion, stated his personal opposition to emancipation. "I feel satisfied that I have no sympathies which would have misled me in this matter; for, when permitted to indulge my feelings and opinions as an individual, I find them in strong and direct hostility to all schemes for emancipating slaves, under existing circumstances, in the bosom of our community." 14 Tenn. at 139. Catron's concurrence in *Dred Scott* reflects those proslavery sentiments. 60 U.S. at 493.

19. *See also* State v. Foreman, 16 Tenn. (8 Yerg.) 256, 1835 WL 945 (1835) (Catron's extensive opinion discussing history and status of Native Americans); Tim Alan Garrison, The Legal Ideology of Removal: The Southern Judiciary and the Sovereignty of Native American Nations 198–221 (2010).

20. *Fisher's Negroes*, 14 Tenn. at 132.

21. *See* chapter 8. Judge Nathaniel Green of the Tennessee Supreme Court dealt with this in 1846 in his opinion in *Ford v. Ford*, 26 Tenn. (7 Humphreys) 92, 1846 WL 1497 (1846).

22. *Trustees of Quaker Society of Contentnea v. Dickenson*, 12 N.C. (1 Dev.) 189, 192, 1827 WL 292, *3 (1827). Earlier a gift to members of the Methodist Church to "to keep or dispose of as they shall judge most for the glory of God, and good of said slaves" was held to be an illegal trust for the slaves. Huckaby v. Jones, 9 N.C. (2 Hawks) 120 (1822).

23. *Dickenson*, 12 N.C. at 203.

24. *Id.* Yet a dissenting justice, Hall, saw it differently:

> Preachers, individually, have the capacity to purchase slaves, and when they become owners of them, are, like other citizens, subject to the laws made for their government, and when they form themselves into religious societies and the Legislature confers upon them the capacity to purchase, the transfer of power is general. The Legislature have made no exceptions on account of religious tenets, and it appears to me not to be the province of this Court to discriminate and make any. As to their liberation of them, for which purpose it is said they purchase them, it can be effected only in the way pointed out by law, and when it can be effected in that way they have a right in common with other citizens, to avail themselves of it. If they permit them to hire their own time or otherwise mismanage them, they are like other citizens, amenable to the law for such conduct. It is not for this Court, by legal anticipation, to apply a preventive remedy.

> *Id.* at 207.

25. *See* Chapter 9, text at notes 24- 42 (discussing Lumpkin's emancipation decisions).
26. Cleland v. Waters, 19 Ga. 35, 43 (1855), discussed in Chapter 9 at notes 27–30.
27. *Id.* at 43–44.
28. While works like Lacy Ford's *Deliver Us from This Evil The Slavery Question in the Old South* (2009) and Larry Tise's *Proslavery: A History of the Defense of Slavery in America, 1701-1840* (1987), have persuasively argued that key parts of proslavery doctrine were established before 1830, the trajectory of doctrine towards making emancipation more difficult suggests that proslavery attitudes were growing in amplitude over the course of the antebellum era. Ford's nuanced argument points up the varieties of proslavery thought in the South and those varieties—and their amplitude—appear in judicial decisions, too. But the central tendency in the judiciary was towards more restrictions on enforcement, which suggests yet again the ways that popular and legal culture reinforced each other.
29. 6 Porter 269, 1838 WL 1294 (Ala. June term 1837).
30. Abercrombie's Executor v. Abercrombie's Heirs, 27 Ala. 489, 1855 WL 465 (1855). *See also* *Hooper v. Hooper*, 32 Ala. 669 (1858) (citing *Atwood's Heirs*, as well as a North Carolina opinion that was generous in interpretation of a trustees' power to emancipate, *Thompson v. Newlin*, 8 Ired. Eq. 32).
31. 27 Ala. 489, 491 (1855).
32. 43 N.C. (8 Ired. Eq.) 253, 1852 WL 1198 (1852).
33. *Evans* explicitly overruled *Prater v. Darby*, 24 Ala. 496, 1854 WL 437 (1854) (though not *Atwood's Heirs*), which upheld a contract to emancipate.
34. 13 Ala. 102, 1848 WL 301 (1848) (with citation of only one case, *Trotter v. Blocker*, 6 Porter 269 (1838)).
35. *Creswell's Executor v. Walker*, 37Ala. 229, 1861 WL 362 (1861).
36. Thomas R.R. Cobb, An Inquiry into the Law of Negro Slavery in the United States (Philadelphia, T. & W. Johnson 1858). Cobb, though, thought *Carroll v. Brumby* was incorrect in its rigid refusal to allow emancipation. He wrote that "The theory of a complete annihilation of will in the slave, is utterly inconsistent with all recognition of him as a person, especially as responsible for criminally for his acts." *Id.* at 302.
37. 37 Ala. at 233.
38. 37 Ala. at 237, 1861 WL 362 at *6 (distinguishing *State v. Hart*, 26 N.C. (4 Ired.) 246 (1844)).
39. *Id.* at 236. *See also* id. at 235–36 ("Such a bequest is an effort on the part of the testator to impart to slaves rights which belong exclusively to freemen,–thus placing them in that middle state between absolute freedom and absolute slavery, which our law, upon grounds of paramount public policy, refuses to recognize as legally possible.").
40. *Id.* at 236. *See* The Illustrated Uncle Tom's Cabin xxxi (Henry Louis Gates & Hollis Robbins eds., 2007) (discussing original subtitle).
41. 37 Ala. at 237–38.
42. 37 Miss. 235, 238 (1859).
43. 3 Miss. (2 How.) 841 (1838).
44. 6 Miss. (5 How.) 323 (1840).
45. *An Act . . . In Relation to Free Negroes and Mulattoes,* Code of Mississippi 537, 539 sec. 11 (A. Hutchinson ed., Jackson, Miss., 1848) (date of act 1842) ("Hereafter it shall not be lawful for any person by last will or testament to make any devise or bequest of any slave or slaves for the purpose of emancipation; or to direct that any slave or slaves shall be removed from this State for the purpose of emancipation elsewhere").
46. Wade v. American Colonization Society, 15 Miss. (7 Smedes & M.) 663, 1846 WL 3004 (1846). *Wade* was implicitly overruled the next decade. *See Lusk v. Lewis*, 32 Miss. 297, 1856 WL 4022 (1856); Mahorner v. Hooe, 17 Miss. (9 Smedes & M.) 247, 1848 WL 1937 (1848) (upholding Mississippi legislation that restricts emancipation beyond the state).
47. *See* Garnett v. Cowles, 39 Miss. (10 George) 60, 61 (1860) (arguments of counsel, pointing to a letter in the *Liberia Advocate*, a paper of the American Colonization Society, where testator discussed his intentions in the will).
48. Garnett v. Cowles, 39 Miss. (10 George) 60 (1860).
49. 37 Miss. 235, 238 (1859). I learned a lot about Justice Harris from Christopher Dwight's fall 2013 seminar paper on him.

50. *Id.* at 251.
51. *Id.* at 252.
52. *Id.* at 252.
53. *Id.* at 253–54. *See also An Act in Relation to Free Negroes and Mullatoes*, REVISED CODE OF THE STATUTE LAWS OF THE STATE OF MISSISSIPPI Chap. 33, art. 9, at 234, 236 (Jackson, E. Barksdale 1857).
54. *Id.* at 258–59.
55. 37 Miss. 235 (1859).
56. *Id.* at 264. Alabama had earlier, in 1852, allowed a freed person in Ohio to receive a bequest. *See* Atwood's Heirs v. Beck, 21 Ala. 590, 1852 WL 212 (1852). Perhaps Justice Harris took the example of an orang-outang from a discussion of similarities between Africans and orang-outangs. *See* Cobb, *supra* note 36, at 25.
57. 37 Miss. at 265 (Hardy, dissenting); Willis v. Jolliffe, 32 S.C. Eq. 447 (1860).
58. 11 Rich. Eq. 447, 1860 WL 3897 (S.C App.Eq 1860).
59. *Id.* at *39 (Wardlaw, dissenting). Curran was quoted often, by both anti-slavery and proslavery writers. *See, e.g.,* Frederick Douglass, *The Cambria Riot, My Slave Experience, and My Irish Mission: An Address Delivered in Belfast, Ireland, on December 5, 1845, in* 1 THE FREDERICK DOUGLASS PAPERS: SERIES ONE—SPEECHES, DEBATES, AND INTERVIEWS 86 (John Blassingame et al., eds. 1979); HARRIET BEECHER STOWE, UNCLE TOM'S CABIN, chapter 37 (1852); MARY H. EASTMAN, AUNT PHYLLIS' CABIN: OR, SOUTHERN LIFE AS IT IS 95 (Philadelphia, Lippincott, Grambo & Co., 1852).
60. 21 Ark. 490 (1860), 1860 WL 770 (Ark. 1860).
61. *Id.* at 500, 1860 WL 770, at *5.
62. Scott v. Emerson, 15 Mo. 576 (1852); LEA VANDERVELDE, MRS. DRED SCOTT (2008); LEA VANDERVELDE, REDEMPTION SONGS: SUING FOR FREEDOM BEFORE DRED SCOTT (2014); Dred Scott v. Sandford, 60 U.S. (19 How.) 393, 431 (1857) (discussing the Scott family's travels in Illinois and in federal territory with their owner, Major Taliaferro, a physician with the United States Army).
63. *Dred Scott,* 60 U.S. at 427.
64. *Id.* at 407.
65. *Id.*at 493, 516 (Catron, concurring).
66. DON E. FEHRENBACHER, THE DRED SCOTT CASE IN LAW AND POLITICS 137–39 (1978).
67. *Id.*at 46–49, 122–23, 134–39 (discussing Calhoun's ideas brgininning in the 1830s about the federal government as agent of the states and the equality of the states and their implication for protection of slavery); 60 U.S. at 451–52.
68. *See, e.g.,* FEHRENBACHER, *supra* note 66; MARK A. GRABER, DRED SCOTT AND THE PROBLEM OF CONSTITUTIONAL EVIL (2006); CHRISTOPHER TOMLINS, FREEDOM BOUND: LAW, LABOR, AND CIVIC IDENTITY IN COLONIZING ENGLISH AMERICA, 1580-1865 509–69 (2010); AUSTIN ALLEN, ORIGINS OF THE DRED SCOTT CASE: JACKSONIAN JURISPRUDENCE AND THE SUPREME COURT, 1837-1857 (2006).
69. *See, e.g.,* COBB, *supra* note 36, at 205–209; *Mitchell v. Wells,* 37 Miss. 235, 259 (1859) (citing *Dred Scott*). *See also* Alfred L. Brophy, *Considering Reparations for Dred Scott, in* THE DRED SCOTT CASE 177, 182 (David Thomas Konig, Paul Finkelman, and Christopher Alan Bracey eds. 2010).
70. ROBERT SAUNDERS, JOHN ARCHIBALD CAMPBELL, SOUTHERN MODERATE, 1811-1889 (1997).
71. *See, e.g.,* Abercrombie's Executor v. Abercrombie's Heirs, 27 Alabama 489 (1855) (opinion by George Goldthwaite) and discussion of the *Abercrombie* at notes to above.
72. JOHN ARCHIBALD CAMPBELL, AN ADDRESS UPON THE LIFE AND PUBLIC SERVICES OF JOHN C. CALHOUN, DELIVERED AT MOBILE, ON THE 13TH OF DECEMBER, 1850 (Mobile, Dade, Thompson, 1851); JOHN ARCHIBALD CAMPBELL, SUBSTANCE OF THE REMARKS OF JOHN A. CAMPBELL AT THE ORGANIZATION OF THE SOUTHERN RIGHTS ASSOCIATION (Mobile, Dade, Thompson 1850); JOHN A. CAMPBELL, THE INSTITUTIONS, DUTIES AND RELATIONS OF ALABAMA. AN ORATION BEFORE THE EROSOPHIC AND PHILOMATHIC SOCIETIES OF THE UNIVERSITY OF ALABAMA. JULY 12TH, 1859 (Tuscaloosa, Jno. F. Warren 1859); JOHN A. CAMPBELL, ADDRESS DELIVERED BEFORE THE ALUMNI SOCIETY OF THE UNIVERSITY

OF GEORGIA ... AT THE ANNUAL COMMENCEMENT, IN AUGUST, 1853 (Athens, J.S. Peterson 1853).

73. See John Campbell, *Slavery in the U.S.*, 12 S. Q. REV. 91 (July 1847).
74. John Campbell, *Slavery Among the Romans*, 14 S. Q. REV. 414 (Oct. 1848).
75. *Id.* at 445.
76. *Id.* at 452.
77. For earlier explorations of similar topics, see Benjamin Ober, *Slavery: A Lecture Delivered before the Lyceum in Attleborough, Jan. 4th, 1838* (Pawtuckett, Mass, Robert Sherman 1838); William Blair, *State of Slavery Among the Romans* (Edinburgh, Thomas Clark 1833).
78. *Id.* at 361.
79. *British West India Islands*, 16 S. Q. REV. 342, 374–75 (January 1850).
80. *Id.* at 377.
81. *Slavery Throughout the World*, 19 S.Q. REV. 305, 339 (April 1851).
82. *The Rights of the Slave States*, 19 S. Q. REV. 101, 102 (Jan., 1851), also printed as A CITIZEN OF ALABAMA, THE RIGHTS OF THE SLAVE STATES ([Charleston?], Southern Rights Association, 1850). A similar, though somewhat less elegantly written pamphlet, *The Prospects Before Us: An Inquiry into the Nature and Results of the Anti-Slavery Agitation* (Mobile, Dade and Thompson, 1851) is bound in the University of North Carolina with *The Rights of Slave States* under the heading "Two Speeches by J.A. Campbell." Whether Campbell is its author is uncertain. Robert Saunders, *John Archibald Campbell, Southern Moderate, supra* note 70, is a useful biography, though its subtitle conflicts with the analysis of Campbell presented here.
83. Campbell, *Rights of Slave States, supra* note 82, at 112.
84. *Id.* at 124.
85. *Id.* at 132.
86. *Id.* at 134.
87. *Id.* at 139.
88. *Id.* at 134.
89. *Id.* at 138.
90. *Id.* at 142–43.
91. *Id.* at 143, 145.
92. One of his first duties was to deliver an address to the University of Georgia alumni society in August. It celebrated the Anglo-Saxon race's contributions to American liberty. This was another part of the picture of rights depending on a race's fitness for freedom. This was also part of defining the groups that were entitled to freedom and excluding other races, seen as inferior. CAMPBELL, ADDRESS DELIVERED BEFORE ... UNIVERSITY OF GEORGIA, *supra* note 72.
93. Fehrenbacher, *supra* note 66, at 396–401 (discussing Campbell).
94. Dred Scott v. Sandford, 60 U.S. (19 How.) 393, at 498 (1857) (Campbell, concurring, discussing *Somerset* and *Slave Grace*).
95. *Id.*
96. JOHN ARCHIBALD CAMPBELL, THE INSTITUTIONS, DUTIES AND RELATIONS OF ALABAMA: AN ORATION BEFORE THE EROSOPHIC AND PHILOMATHIC SOCIETIES OF THE UNIVERSITY OF ALABAMA, JULY 12TH, 1859 (TUSCALOOSA: JNO. F. WARREN, 1859).
97. *Id.* at 5.
98. *Id.* at 14–15.
99. *Id.* at 22.
100. *First Inaugural Address*, in LINCOLN: SPEECHES AND WRITINGS 1859-1865, at 215, 224 (Don E. Fehrenbacher ed. 1989).

Chapter 12

1. 2 PROCEEDINGS OF THE VIRGINIA STATE CONVENTION OF 1861 75 (George H. Reese 1961).
2. In re Perkins, 2 Cal 424, 450 (1852). *See also* Alfred L. Brophy, *Let Us Go Back and Stand Upon the Constitution: Federal-State Relations in Scott v. Sandford*, 90 COLUM. L. REV. 192, 213 (1990).

3. Holcombe, *supra* note 1, at 76.
4. JAMES P. HOLCOMBE, THE ELECTION OF A BLACK REPUBLICAN PRESIDENT AN OVERT ACT OF AGGRESSION ON THE RIGHT OF PROPERTY IN SLAVES 12 (Richmond, C.H. Wynne 1860).
5. *Id.* at 12.
6. *Id.* at 15.
7. Much recent literature on the old South links ideas about slavery to southern nationalism and secession. *See, e.g.*, DREW GILPIN FAUST, THE CREATION OF CONFEDERATE NATIONALISM: IDEOLOGY AND IDENTITY IN THE CIVIL WAR SOUTH (1989); JOHN MCCARDELL, THE IDEA OF A SOUTHERN NATION: SOUTHERN NATIONALISTS AND SOUTHERN NATIONALISM, 1830–1860 (1979); MITCHELL SNAY, THE GOSPEL OF DISUNION: RELIGION AND SEPARATISM IN ANTEBELLUM SOUTH (1997); MARK M. SMITH, DEBATING SLAVERY: ECONOMY AND SOCIETY IN THE ANTEBELLUM SOUTH (1998); ROBERT BONNER, MASTERING AMERICA: SOUTHERN SLAVEHOLDERS AND THE CRISIS OF AMERICAN NATIONHOOD (2009). These issues continued through the Confederacy as well, for obvious reasons. *See, e.g.*, MICHAEL T. BERNATH, CONFEDERATE MINDS: THE STRUGGLE FOR INDEPENDENCE IN THE CIVIL WAR SOUTH (2010).
8. LARRY D. KRAMER, THE PEOPLE THEMSELVES: POPULAR CONSTITUTIONALISM AND JUDICIAL REVIEW (2004); Lucas A. Powe, *Are "The People" Missing in Action (and Should Anyone Care)?*, 83 TEXAS LAW REVIEW 855 (2005) (reviewing Kramer).
9. One can see the linking of constitutional arguments to secession in several ways. In addition to the pamphlets and speeches given a close read in the remainder of this chapter, constitutional arguments appear in the editorials reprinted in Dwight Lowell Dumond's *Southern Editorials on Secession* (1931) and in the pamphlets in Jon L. Wakelyn's *Southern Pamphlets on Secession, November 1860–April 1861* (1996). *See also* MARK S. NEELY, LINCOLN AND THE TRIUMPH OF THE NATION 237–74 (2011) (discussing secession and constitutionalism).
10. *See, e.g.*, DON E. FEHRENBACHER, THE SLAVEHOLDING REPUBLIC: AN ACCOUNT OF THE UNITED STATES GOVERNMENT'S RELATIONS TO SLAVERY 34–36 (2001).
11. MICHAEL VORENBERG, FINAL FREEDOM: THE CIVIL WAR, THE ABOLITION OF SLAVERY, AND THE THIRTEENTH 9–12 (2001); WILLIAM WIECEK, THE SOURCES OF ANTISLAVERY CONSTITUTIONALISM IN AMERICA, 1760–1848 240 (1977) (quoting John Calhoun's statement about Wendell Phillips *The Constitution a Proslavery Compact* (New York, American Anti-Slavery Society 1856) that "we might circulate it to great advantage excluding a few paragraphs").
12. FEHRENBACHER, *supra* note 10, at 80, 280–82; DON E. FEHRENBACHER, THE DRED SCOTT CASE: ITS SIGNIFICANCE IN AMERICAN LAW AND POLITICS (1978).
13. *See, e.g.*, LUCAS A. POWER, THE WARREN COURT AND AMERICAN POLITICS (2002); JAMES T. PATTERSON, BROWN V. BOARD OF EDUCATION: A CIVIL RIGHTS MILESTONE AND ITS TROUBLED LEGACY (2002).
14. [WILLIAM J. GRAYSON], REPLY TO PROFESSOR HODGE ON THE "STATE OF THE COUNTRY" 16 (Charleston, Evans & Cogswell 1861).
15. *See also* MARK BRANDON, FREE IN THE WORLD: AMERICAN SLAVERY AND CONSTITUTIONAL FAILURE 75–76, 128–29 (1999) (discussing Frederick Douglass and Abraham Lincoln on the antislavery nature of the Constitution).
16. *See* Chapter 1.
17. *Cf.* 1 WLLIAM W. FREEHLING, THE ROAD TO DISUNION: SECESSIONISTS AT BAY, 1776–1854 (1990); LARRY TISE, PROSLAVERY: A HISTORY OF THE DEFENSE OF SLAVERY IN AMERICA, 1701–1840 (1987); LACY K. FORD, DELIVER US FROM EVIL: THE SLAVERY QUESTION IN THE OLD SOUTH (2009).
18. This was particularly true for John C. Calhoun, who from the late 1830s through the end of his life advanced a political and constitutional theory in support of slavery. *See, e.g.*, *Remarks Made During the Debate on His Resolutions, in Respect to the Rights of States and the Abolition of Slavery, January 12, 1838*, 3 WORKS OF JOHN C. CALHOUN 141 (Richard K. Cralle ed., New York, D. Appleton and Company 1854).
19. [.Richard Yeadon], THE AMENABILITY OF NORTHERN INCENDIARIES AS WELL TO SOUTHERN AS TO NORTHERN LAWS . . . (Charleston, T.A. Haden 1835).

20. Richard Yeadon, An Address ... Before the Euphenian & Philomathean Literary Societies of Erskine College ... August 12th, 1857 48 (Due West, S.C., Due West Telescope 1857).
21. *Id.* Yeadon's focus on constitutionalism was similar to Calhoun's Speech on the Territories February 19, 1847, for instance. *See* John C. Calhoun, *Remarks on Presenting His Resolutions on the Slave Question*, 4 The Works of John C. Calhoun 339, 347 (New York, Appleton 1888).
22. James L. Huston, Calculating the Value of the Union: Slavery, Property Rights, and the Economic Origins of the Civil War (2003); Gavin Wright, Slavery and American Economic Development (2006); David Potter, The Impending Crisis, 1848–1861 (1976); 1 & 2 William W. Freehling, The Road to Disunion (1990, 2008).
23. *See, e.g.,* Bernard Bailyn, The Ideological Origins of the American Revolution (1967).
24. *But see* Mark Neely, Lincoln and the Triumph of the Nation: Constitutional Conflict in the American Civil War 239–74 (2011); Donald E. Fehrenbacher, Constitutions and Constitutionalism in the Slaveholding South (1989).
25. *See, e.g., Professor Dew on Slavery*, in The Pro-slavery Argument ... 287, 440, 464 (Charleston, Walker, Richards & Co. 1852) (discussing Haiti); Thomas R. R. Cobb, An Inquiry into the Law of Negro Slavery in the United States cxcvi (Philadelphia, T. & W. Johnson 1858) (discussing emancipation in British West Indies). For further discussion of Dew and Cobb on emancipation, see Chapters 1 and 10.
26. *See generally* Paul Quigley, Nationalism and the American South, 1848–1861 (2011); Drew Gilpin Faust, The Creation of Confederate Nationalism: Ideology and Identity in the Civil War South (1988); John McCardell, The Idea of a Southern Nation: Southern Nationalists and Southern Nationalism, 1830–1860 (1979).
27. The Address of the Southern Rights' Association, of the University of Virginia, to the Young Men of the South 6 (Charlottesville, James Alexander 1851) available at http://search.lib.virginia.edu/catalog/uva-lib:2241100/view#openLayer/uva-lib:2248298/3461.5/2289.5/0/1/0.
28. *Id.* at 7 (citing A Citizen of Virginia [Muscoe R.H. Garnett], The Union, Past and Future: How It Works, and How to Save It (4th ed. Charleston, Walker & James 1850)).
29. *Id.* at 7.
30. *Id.* at 8.
31. Address of the Southern Rights Association of the South Carolina College, to the Students in the Colleges and Universities, and to the Young Men, Throughout the Southern States (Columbia, A.S. Johnson 1851).
32. G.W.W.M. Simms, *The South*, Southern Repertory and College Review 222, 224 (1854).
33. *Id.* at 225.
34. *Id.* at 226.
35. *Id.* at 225. *See generally* Peter Carmichael, The Last Generation: Young Virginians in Peace, War, and Reunion 89–120 (2005) (discussing prosecession ideas among the generation in college in the decade before Civil War).
36. *A Plea for Union*, 1 Va. U. Mag. 289–96 (1857).
37. *Id.* at 291–92.
38. Marshall, *Esto Perpetua*, 6 Erskine Collegiate Recorder 132 (1859).
39. *In a Dilemma*, 7 Erskine College Recorder 157 (1860). The unknown author still hoped for Union but proclaimed his willingness to "lay down our life" for the South. *Id.* at 158. *See also We Would, If We Could*, 7 Erskine Collegiate Recorder 158–59 (1860) (discussing secession rally in Due West, South Carolina, attended by many Erskine students).
40. *Editor's Table*, 4 Va. U. Mag. 204, 208 (January 1860) (responding to "Editor's Table," 25 *Yale Literary Magazine* 134–38 (December 1859)).
41. Matt W. Ransom, Address Delivered Before the Dialectic and Philanthropic Societies of the University of North Carolina, June 4, 1856 15 (Raleigh, Carolina Cultivator 1856).
42. *Id.* at 20.
43. *Id.* at 21.

44. Miller gave a number of public speeches, including *Speech of Henry W. Miller, Esq., Delivered at Oxford, North Carolina, November 5, 1850, in Reply to Hon. A.W. Venable on the Compromise of 1850* (n.p, 1850); Henry W. Miller, *The False or Pretended Philanthropy of the Age*, in NORTH-CAROLINA READER: CONTAINING A HISTORY AND DESCRIPTION OF NORTH CAROLINA, SELECTIONS IN PROSE AND VERSE 249 (C.H. Wiley ed., New York, A.S. Barnes 1855).

45. HENRY W. MILLER, ADDRESS DELIVERED BEFORE THE PHILANTHROPIC AND DIALECTIC SOCIETIES OF THE UNIVERSITY OF NORTH CAROLINA, JUNE 3, 1857 at 12–13 (Raleigh, Standard 1857).

46. *Id.* at 14.

47. *Id.* at 18.

48. *Id.* at 14–15.

49. *Id.* at 23.

50. *Id.* at 25.

51. I am indebted to Ben Kleinman's excellent work recovering these speeches. *See* Benjamin K. Kleinman, The Road to Radicalism: UNC Students and the Jurisprudence of Disunion (seminar paper, fall 2013).

52. *See* James G. McNab, Our Union, Will It be Preserved? (March 1857), Records of the Dialectic Society No. 40152, University Archives, University of North Carolina at Chapel Hill, Southern Historical Collection, Wilson Library, UNC, transcription available at http://docsouth.unc.edu/unc/unc08-02/unc08-02.html.

53. Edward T. Sykes, Two Sections of the Union (1858), at 13, Records of the Dialectic Society No. 40152, University Archives, University of North Carolina at Chapel Hill Southern Historical Collection, Wilson Library, UNC, transcription available at http://docsouth.unc.edu/unc/unc08-05/unc08-05.html.

54. *See* Elijah B. Withers, The American Union, a Failure (Nov. 7, 1858), Records of the Dialectic Society No. 40152, University Archives, University of North Carolina at Chapel Hill Southern Historical Collection, Wilson Library, UNC, transcription available at http://docsouth.unc.edu/unc/unc08-06/unc08-06.html.

55. JESSE CARPENTER, THE SOUTH AS A CONSCIOUS MINORITY 141 (1930) (discussing the swing to constitutionalism and quoting Abel Upshur and Henry St. George Tucker on dependence of Constitution on support of the population).

56. CHARLES FRASER, AN ADDRESS . . . AT THE LAYING OF THE CORNER STONE OF A NEW COLLEGE EDIFICE . . . 12TH JANUARY, 1828 1 (Charleston, J.S. Burges 1828).

57. *Id.* at 11–12.

58. JOHN L. GIRARDEAU, CONSCIENCE AND CIVIL GOVERNMENT: AN ORATION DELIVERED BEFORE THE SOCIETY OF ALUMNI OF THE COLLEGE OF CHARLESTON . . . MARCH 27TH, 1860 (Charleston, Evans & Cogswell 1860).

59. *Id.* at 4.

60. *Id.* at 16.

61. *Id.* at 17.

62. *Id.* at 18–19.

63. *Id.* at 19.

64. 2 WILLIAM W. FREEHLING, THE ROAD TO DISUNION: SECESSIONISTS TRIUMPHANT 258 (2007); STEVEN A. CHANNING, CRISIS OF FEAR: SECESSION IN SOUTH CAROLINA (1974).

65. *See* THOMAS READ ROOTES COBB, SUBSTANCE OF REMARKS MADE BY THOMAS R.R. COBB, ESQ.: IN THE HALL OF THE HOUSE OF REPRESENTATIVES, MONDAY EVENING, NOVEMBER 12, 1860 (Atlanta, John H. Seals 1860), reprinted in SECESSION DEBATED: GEORGIA'S SHOWDOWN IN 1860 at 5 (William W. Freehling and Craig M. Simpson, eds., 1992). *See also* THOMAS READ ROOTES COBB, SUBSTANCE OF AN ADDRESS OF T.R.R. COBB TO HIS CONSTITUENTS OF CLARK COUNTY, APRIL 6TH, 1861 (n.p., circa 1861).

66. HENRY L. BENNING, SPEECH ON FEDERAL RELATIONS (n.p., n.d.), reprinted in SECESSION DEBATED, *supra* note 65, at 115.

67. Cobb, HALL OF THE HOUSE OF REPRESENTATIVES, *supra* note 65, at 21.

68. *Speech of T.R.R. Cobb to Citizens of Athens, April 6*, SOUTHERN BANNER (April 10, 1861); *The Correspondence of Thomas Reed Rootes Cobb, 186 – 1861*, 7 PUBLICATIONS OF THE SOUTHERN HISTORICAL ASSOCIATION 142–85, 233–60, 312–28 (1907).

69. ADDRESS OF HON. W. L. Harris, COMMISSIONER FROM THE STATE OF MISSISSIPPI, DELIVERED BEFORE THE GENERAL ASSEMBLY OF THE STATE OF GEORGIA ON MONDAY, DEC. 17TH, 1860 (Milledgeville, Ga., 1860), reprinted in CHARLES B. DEW, APOSTLES OF DISUNION: SOUTHERN SECESSION COMMISSIONERS AND THE CAUSES OF THE CIVIL WAR 83–89 (2002).

70. MICHAEL P. JOHNSON, TOWARD A PATRIARCHAL REPUBLIC: THE SECESSION OF GEORGIA 195–97, tables 1 & 2 (1977). A factor analysis revealed three key variables related to secession votes: slaveholding, residence in a town, and political affiliation. The secession vote had a relatively low loading on each of those factors. *See also* Michael P. Johnson, *A New Look at the Popular Vote for the Delegates to the Georgia Secession Convention,* 56 GA. HIST. Q. 259–75 (1972).

71. *See* Chapter 1, Table 1.2.

72. Ralph Wooster, *The Georgia Secession Convention,* 40 GA. HIST. Q. 21, 27 (1956) (listing occupations of members of the Georgia secession convention). It remains for further research to investigate the educational backgrounds of those delegates. *See also* James C. Cobb, *The Making of a Secessionist: Henry L. Benning and the Coming of Civil War,* 60 GA. HIST. Q. 313–23 (1976).

73. In his 1825 address on the laying of the cornerstone for the Bunker Hill monument, Webster appealed to reason, imagination, and sentiment for the purpose of "national independence." *See* DANIEL WEBSTER, AN ADDRESS DELIVERED AT THE LAYING OF THE CORNER STONE OF THE BUNKER HILL 8 (4th ed. Boston, Cummings, Hilliard 1825). *See generally* PAUL NAGEL, ONE NATION INDIVISIBLE: THE UNION IN AMERICAN THOUGHT, 1776–1861 (1964).

74. *See, e.g.,* WILLIAM W. FREEHLING, PRELUDE TO CIVIL WAR: THE NULLIFICATION CRISIS IN SOUTH CAROLINA, 1816–1836 159–76 (1966); LOUIS HARTZ, THE LIBERAL TRADITION IN AMERICA 158–67 (1955).

75. JAMES HENLEY THORNWELL, THE STATE OF THE COUNTRY 20, 24–25 (Columbia, Southern Guardian 1861).

76. JAMES OSCAR FARMER, THE METAPHYSICAL CONFEDERACY: JAMES HENLEY THORNWELL AND THE SYNTHESIS OF SOUTHERN VALUES 58 (1999).

77. GEORGE JUNKIN, POLITICAL FALLACIES: AN EXAMINATION OF THE FALSE ASSUMPTIONS, AND REFUTATION OF THE SOPHISTICAL REASONINGS, WHICH HAVE BROUGHT ON THIS CIVIL WAR at 265–66 (New York, Charles Scribner 1863). Junkin was likely referring to Thornwell's pamphlet, which refers to Lincoln's election and to the future of slavery in the territories. *See* THORNWELL, *supra* note 75, at 20, 24–25.

78. THORNWELL, *supra* note 75, at 9.

79. *Id.* at 9.

80. *See, e.g.,* DON E. FEHRENBACHER, THE DRED SCOTT CASE IN LAW AND POLITICS (1978).

81. THORNWELL, *supra* note 75, at 14.

82. *Id.* at 16.

83. *Id.* at 16. *See also An Essay on International Law,* 5 ERSKINE COLLEGIATE RECORDER 3, 5–6 (June 1858) (quoting Chief Justice Marshall's opinion in *The Antelope* to justify and legitimize the international slave trade).

84. THORNWELL, *supra* note 75, at 21.

85. BENJAMIN MORGAN PALMER, THE SOUTH: HER PERIL, AND HER DUTY. A DISCOURSE DELIVERED IN THE FIRST PRESBYTERIAN CHURCH, NEW ORLEANS, ON THURSDAY, NOVEMBER 29, 1860 (New Orleans, True Witness and Sentinel 1860).

86. *Id.* at 9.

87. *Id.* at 12.

88. *Id.* at 12.

89. GRAYSON, *supra* note 14, at 15.

90. *Id.* at 26.

91. *The Utility of Slavery Discussion,* 1 VA. U. MAG. 26, 30 (Dec. 1856).

92. G. EDWARD WHITE, OLIVER WENDELL HOLMES, JR. 22 (2005).

93. Irving v. Ford, 179 Mass. 216, 221–22 (1901). Another prominent twentieth-century use came in *Estate of Campbell,* 108 P. 669, 673 (Cal. App. 1910). There the court quoted the U.S. Supreme Court's decision in *Hall v. United States,* 92 U.S. 27 (1875) which cited *An Inquiry,*

to show that slaves could not contract during the era of slavery. The California court went on to deny the right of children of such a marriage to inherit from their parents because such children were illegitimate. This is one example of post–Civil War reasoning, which effectively extended the disabilities of slavery for decades after slavery ended. Such reasoning, focusing on the nature of contract, looked narrowly at legal doctrine without looking at its social context or its likely consequences.

94. *See* Alfred L. Brophy, *When History Mattered*, 91 Texas Law Review 601–14 (2013) (reviewing David Rabban, *Law's History: American Legal Thought and the Transatlantic Turn to History* (2013)).

INDEX